Drawing Lots

Drawing Lots

From Egalitarianism to Democracy in Ancient Greece

IRAD MALKIN
JOSINE BLOK

OXFORD
UNIVERSITY PRESS

Oxford University Press is a department of the University of Oxford. It furthers
the University's objective of excellence in research, scholarship, and education
by publishing worldwide. Oxford is a registered trade mark of Oxford University
Press in the UK and certain other countries.

Published in the United States of America by Oxford University Press
198 Madison Avenue, New York, NY 10016, United States of America.

© Oxford University Press 2024

All rights reserved. No part of this publication may be reproduced, stored in
a retrieval system, or transmitted, in any form or by any means, without the
prior permission in writing of Oxford University Press, or as expressly permitted
by law, by license, or under terms agreed with the appropriate reproduction
rights organization. Inquiries concerning reproduction outside the scope of the
above should be sent to the Rights Department, Oxford University Press, at the
address above.

You must not circulate this work in any other form
and you must impose this same condition on any acquirer.

Library of Congress Cataloging-in-Publication Data
Names: Malkin, Irad, author. | Blok, Josine, author.
Title: Drawing lots : from egalitarianism to democracy in ancient Greece /
Irad Malkin, Josine Blok.
Description: New York, NY : Oxford University Press, 2024. |
Includes bibliographical references and index. |
Identifiers: LCCN 2023049319 (print) | LCCN 2023049320 (ebook) |
ISBN 9780197753477 (hardback) | ISBN 9780197753491 (epub) |
ISBN 9780197753507
Subjects: LCSH: Equality—Greece—History—To 1500. |
Social participation—Greece—History—To 1500. |
Political participation—Greece—History—To 1500. |
Democracy—Greece—History—To 1500. | Greece—Civilization—To 146 B.C.
Classification: LCC HN650.5.Z9 S65 2024 (print) | LCC HN650.5.Z9 (ebook) |
DDC 302/.1409495—dc23/eng/20240102
LC record available at https://lccn.loc.gov/2023049319
LC ebook record available at https://lccn.loc.gov/2023049320

DOI: 10.1093/oso/9780197753477.001.0001

Printed by Integrated Books International, United States of America

For my beloved parents, Felice and Yaakov Malkin
Irad Malkin

To Wessel, with love—again
Josine Blok

Contents

Preface Josine Blok, Irad Malkin   xiii
Acknowledgements Irad Malkin, Josine Blok   xix
Abbreviations   xxi

Introduction: **Irad Malkin** Greeks Drawing Lots: The Practice
and the Mindset of Egalitarianism   1
  1. An egalitarian mindset   1
  2. From egalitarianism to democracy   4
  3. What is new about this book? The previous discussion
     of the field of inquiry   5
  4. A mindset for drawing lots   10
  5. Vocabulary and mindset   11
  6. Portions and fairness   13
  7. Equality and the "middle"   15
  8. Mixture lotteries and the egalitarian mindset   17
  9. Mixture, equivalence, and interchangeability   20
 10. Did Greeks draw lots to divine the will of the gods?   21
 11. The lot and democracy, ancient and modern   26
 12. Contents and contours: Parts I and II   29

PART I IRAD MALKIN
THE LOTTERY MINDSET:
RELIGION AND SOCIETY

1. Lotteries Divine and Human: The World of the Homeric Epics   41
   Endnote 1: The debate about the distribution of spoils in the *Iliad*
              and the *Odyssey*   82
   Endnote 2: "Getting by lot" and the verb *lanchano*   91
   Lanchano as simply "to get"?   92
   Etymology   94
   Endnote 3: Group distribution and the verb *dateomai* in Homer,
              Hesiod, and the *Homeric Hymns*   95

2. When Does the Lot Reflect the Will of the Gods? Lots, Oracles,
   Divination, and the Notion of *Moira*   98
   2.1 Lot oracles and divination   106
   2.2 The god Hermes   108

2.3 The lot oracle at Delphi	113
2.4 Delphi: Themis, the Pythia, and the lot	114
2.5 Delphi: Beans used as lots	117
2.6 Delphi: Mythical history and oracular procedure	120
2.7 The oracle of Dodona	126
2.8 What is religious about lot oracles?	130
2.9 One's portion in life: *Moira* between the concrete and the abstract	132
3. Sacrifice and Feast: Social Values and the Distribution of Meat by Lot	138
3.1 The lot and the sacrifice: Frequency and ubiquity	138
3.2 Sacrifice, equality, and sharing in the city	139
3.3 Expressions of citizenship and belonging	141
3.4 Honorific shares	142
3.5 The lot, the victim destined for sacrifice, and the priests	144
3.6 The equal feast	146

PART II IRAD MALKIN
EQUAL AND FAIR:
INHERITANCE, COLONIZATION, AND MIXTURE

4. Partible Inheritance by Lot	151
4.1 Brothers sharing an inheritance	151
4.2 Equality versus primogeniture	153
4.3 The *oikos* and the *kleros*	155
4.4 Inheritance at home and abroad	157
4.5 Poetry and myth	161
5. Drawing Lots on the Athenian Stage	163
5.1 Inheritance, sortition, booty, captives, and military procedures	163
5.2 The lot and Aeschylus's *Seven against Thebes*	169
6. Founding Cities and Sharing in the *Polis*: Equality, Allotment, and Civic Mixture	176
6.1 Introduction	176
6.2 Section I: Things done	182
6.2.1 The setting: Greek colonization	182
6.2.2 Equal chances and equal outcomes: Kleros, inheritance, and colonization	188
6.2.3 The archaeology of *kleroi* in the archaic period	190
6.2.4 Egalitarianism and equality in a Greek colony	191
6.2.5 Territories and grids	192
6.2.6 Equal lots: Megara Hyblaia	195
6.2.7 Syracuse	204
6.2.8 Himera	205
6.2.9 Perimeters	207

	6.2.10 Classical colonization	208
	6.2.11 Athenian klerouchies	211
6.3	Section II: Things said: The lot, the "first plot," equality, and the unity of the *kleros*	214
	6.3.1 The First Lots articulated	219
	6.3.2 First Lots: Inclusion and exclusion	222
	6.3.3 First Lots and equality: Was there an aristocracy among Greek colonists?	223
	6.3.4 First Lots and equality: Social and economic differentiation	229
	6.3.5 Things said: The *kleros* and the *polis*	232
	6.3.6 Quasihistorical accounts: Sparta and its colony Thera	237
	6.3.7 Quasihistorical accounts: The great migrations	242
	6.3.8 Religion and the distribution of *kleroi*	243
	6.3.9 Equal and fair: *Isos kai homoios*	245
	6.3.10 How to found a colony? Late archaic and classical inscriptions	247
	6.3.11 Saving a *polis*: Lottery, mixture, and social engineering	256
	Endnote 1: The *cui bono* argument and the ancient sources	260
	Endnote 2: *Isomoiria*	261
	Endnote 3: Women and the *kleros*	264
	Endnote 4: Archaeology and "text-based information"	266

PART III JOSINE BLOK: DRAWING LOTS IN POLIS GOVERNANCE

7.	Setting the Stage	271
	7.1 Introduction	271
	7.1.1 The lot becomes political	271
	7.1.2 Agents, time frame, and sources	276
	7.2 What did *poleis* use the lot for?	282
	7.2.1 Divination	284
	7.2.2 Selection	284
	7.2.3 Distribution	286
	7.2.4 Procedure	291
	7.2.5 Military command: procedure and distribution	295
	7.3 The political background of office distribution in ancient Greece	300
	7.3.1 *Polis* offices and social value (*time*)	300
	7.3.2 Drawing lots for office: A special case	306
	7.3.3 Political inequality and equality in the Greek *poleis*	309
8.	Drawing Lots for *Polis* Office	316
	8.1 Introducing the lot for office	316
	8.1.1 The lot in Solon's *politeia*	316
	8.1.2 Solon's introduction of the lot: A first anchorage	322
	8.1.3 Solon's *politeia*: The council and the court	326

    8.2 Political divergence and patterns of allotment   328
        8.2.1 Allotment for *polis* office in oligarchies   334
        8.2.2 Democratic Athens   339
            8.2.2.1 Cleisthenes's constitution   339
            8.2.2.2 Did Cleisthenes reintroduce allotment for political office? 342
            8.2.2.3 Forerunners of Cleisthenes's innovations   350
            8.2.2.4 Reforms in the mid-fifth century: Toward full allotment   353
        8.2.3 Selection for office by lot elsewhere in ancient Greece   363
            8.2.3.1 Drawing lots for political office outside Athens   364
        8.2.4 Drawing lots for cultic offices, in Athens and beyond   373
    Endnote 1: The historicity of Solon and his laws   379
    Endnote 2: The *Ath.Pol.* and the *Politics* on Solon's constitution   381
    Endnote 3: *Ath.Pol.* 8.1 on the procedure in Solon's *klerosis ek prokriton*   384
    Endnote 4: The vocabulary of the lot in the Ancient Near East   384
    Endnote 5: Solon's council of four hundred   385
    Endnote 6: The *diagramma* for Cyrene   386
    Endnote 7: The new body politic in Cleisthenes's system   388
    Endnote 8: Allotment tokens from Athens   389

9. Drawing Lots for Governance: A Political Innovation   393
    9.1 Drawing lots for *polis* governance: An evaluation   393
        9.1.1 Ancient Greeks on selection for office by lot   393
        9.1.2 What does selection for office by lot mean for *polis* governance? Some modern views   400
    9.2 Conclusions: Drawing lots for *polis* governance in ancient Greece   404
    Endnote: James W. Headlam, *Election by Lot at Athens* (Prince Consort dissertation 1890; London 1891)   412

PART IV CONCLUSIONS AND ENVOI

Irad Malkin Conclusions and Implications   419
    1 The mindset: Antiquity, Ubiquity, and Religion   419
    2 Equality and fairness   423
    3 Group definition   424
    4 The will of the gods   424
    5 Lot oracles   425
    6 Frequency, ubiquity, and sacrifice   426
    7 Partible inheritance by lot   428
    8 New foundations   430
    9 Cleisthenes and the constitutive lottery   437
   10 Our modern democracies   438

Josine Blok Envoi: Drawing Lots Today: Fair Distribution and
a Stronger Democracy   441

Elena Iaffe *Appendix: A Lexicographical Survey of Lottery*
Practices in the Archaic and Classical Periods   447
Lexicographic overview of the key terms of lottery   448
  1. Instruments used in lottery practices   448
  2. Words indicating a participant in a lottery   449
  3. Words for the procedure of drawing lots   449
  4. Verbs of lottery practices   450
    (a) Verbs related to the participants of a lottery   450
    (b) Verbs indicating the type of lottery   451
    (c) Verbs related to the procedure itself, e.g., the action "of" or "upon"
       the instrument of drawing lots   452
  5. The semantic fields of the disputed key terms of lottery: *lanchano* and
    kleros   453
  6. List of references for key lottery terms in archaic and classical Greek
    literature and inscriptions   459
    Key lottery terms, excluding metaphoric usages   459
    Metaphoric and idiomatic usages of lottery terms   461
    Epigraphic evidence for lottery, excluding metaphorical usages
    (a selection up to the end of the fourth cent.)   461

Bibliography   463
Index of Names and Places   505

Preface

Across the ancient Greek world, drawing lots was a common practice for distributing goods and land, for the selection of individuals, and for setting the order of turns. Before lots became a political instrument, Greeks drew lots for distribution, selection, inheritance, determining procedures, initiating social and political mixture, and divination. Across the spectrum of Greek society, Greeks participated in lotteries on an equal basis, defining the contours of the community while expressing the values of equality and fairness in the process. Drawing lots was considered a fair method: the Greeks believed the equal chance of the lot for all who participated in the procedure to be just and right.

A systematic investigation of the uses of the lot reveals an egalitarian mindset that constituted a substantial dimension of Greek civilization. This mindset entailed perceiving the community as deriving authority from within itself by reciprocal and shared sovereignty. In Greek society, this "horizontal," egalitarian vector was counterpoised by a "vertical," hierarchical vector, and the tension between the two vectors deeply impacted Greek history. Drawing lots was the manifest expression of the horizontal forces.

Yet, drawing lots as a common denominator, or even an entire dimension, of ancient Greek civilization has yet to be observed, let alone studied, in its full spectrum. Elements of the practice have been elucidated in, for instance, the valuable work of Bořivoj Borecký on the vocabulary of distribution by lot (1963; 1965) and the pioneering study of James Headlam (1891) on the political meaning of allotment in democratic Athens. For modern observers, drawing lots for political office has generally been the most conspicuous application, especially as practiced in classical Athens. Some excellent studies of the past decades are devoted to aspects of this political use. Nevertheless, a complete understanding of drawing lots in ancient Greece has been conspicuously absent.

This book is the first comprehensive study on the subject, examining the practices of drawing lots in ancient Greece, their contexts, and the egalitarian mindset that enabled and expressed them. A novelty of this study is the very assessment of drawing lots as an institution, zooming in on an overlooked aspect of Greek civilization and studying it from a hitherto untried perspective. Although drawing lots and egalitarianism are closely linked, this book is not a history of Greek egalitarianism as such, but about the relation between the institution of drawing lots and certain significant aspects of egalitarianism, set off against the impact of the opposite vectors of hierarchy and inequalities in Greek society.

Can the lot be applied to modern societies? What may happen should we introduce random selection into a political system? Would it, for example, contribute to broader citizen involvement, fairer choices, and elimination of lobbies and corruption? Beyond academic scholarship, this book may have a broader impact. In recent years, allotment for office in classical Athens has enjoyed a renewed and enthusiastic interest outside the field of professional ancient history. Awareness of how drawing lots may enhance social and political equality and give true meaning to sharing in the *polis* has made sortition a hotly debated option among people who seek to enhance the democratic qualities of present-day representative elective systems. There is no point in regarding the drawing of lots as a mere efficient mechanism without understanding the world of values associated with it. The discussion would benefit from an accessible study that clarifies what drawing lots for office meant in the broader societal context of ancient Greece and especially how this particular application was connected to the other practices of drawing lots. "Equal portions" (*isomoiria*) would sometimes lead to *isonomia*, equality of assigned "portions of law" (comparable to our "equality before the law") that was the first term to denote "democracy" in ancient Greece. Since the drawing of lots in the political sphere appeared only after some three centuries of ubiquitous uses of drawing lots, their extension to governance cannot be fully understood without first identifying and observing the broad spectrum of drawing lots and its emphasis on individual, equal, or equitable "portions," and the interchangeability (hence equality) of participants.

This book aims to do precisely that. It brings together several significant spheres where drawing lots was the customary method, of which governance is chronologically the latest.[1] Although one sphere may derive from the others, our book does not merge them. The first two parts, written by Irad Malkin, offer a full exploration of the drawing of lots in the foundational applications for divination, the distribution of goods and land, inheritance, selection, procedure, and mixture, and the egalitarian mindset embodied in these practices. Malkin's chapters focus on the archaic era, with a few excursions to the classical and Hellenistic ages. He examines the actual practices, the cultural attitudes, and the social values underlying the drawing of lots from the Homeric epics and the Athenian stage, through the distribution of portions of sacrificial meat, divination by using lots, partible inheritance by lot, land plots in the numerous Greek colonies, to the procedural setting of turns by lot and the mixture of people into citizens in new *polis* units. With a light diachronic touch, these two parts offer primarily a synchronic-inspired account of what made the Greeks tick when drawing lots

---

[1] All relevant texts are translated; unless indicated otherwise, translations are our own. All dates are BCE, unless indicated otherwise. In Athens, the year named after the archon ran from July to July the following year in our present time reckoning, so dates in Athenian history are often indicated by a double number (for instance 508/7).

and why they did so exceptionally frequently. The third part, written by Josine Blok, offers an overview of how the lot was introduced into the domain of *polis* governance and particularly for the distribution of *polis* offices across Greece. More precisely, the chapters seek to clarify how drawing lots, with its inherent equality, could be anchored in the Greek *polis*, where public office was traditionally assigned according to a wide-ranging value system based on hierarchy and social difference. The chapters address the ups and downs engendered by negotiating egalitarianism with societal and material inequality. On the available evidence, the lengthy process of introducing the drawing of lots to politics began in the early sixth century. Blok traces the successful spread of the lot and the resistance against it among oligarchies and democracies until ca. 150 BCE. While building on the underlying attitudes described by Malkin, this part is overall diachronic in structure and geared toward political analysis. Finally, the fourth part contains a section of conclusions (Malkin), an *envoi* (Blok), and an appendix prepared by Elena Iaffe on the vocabulary of drawing lots.

With this structure, each part of the book has its style, methods, and focus. When, coincidentally, we discovered that we, long-standing friends and colleagues, were both working on the same topic, we decided to join forces because it was evident that our expertise and different approaches would complement each other perfectly. Nevertheless, we were equally confident that attempting to merge the parts into a single whole, written jointly, would not work for us as authors or for the topics we wanted to address. Instead, while creating our parts, we worked closely together on the entire book, reading each other's chapters, discussing all aspects in depth, finding common ground where initially our viewpoints diverged and correcting and enhancing our interpretations. For the entire picture of drawing lots in ancient Greece, Malkin's parts need Blok's part to be complete, and Blok's part needs Malkin's parts to explain why and how this application worked. Fittingly, there are some overlaps, for instance, where the social purpose of a mixture (Malkin) ties in with the political reconfiguration of the *polis* (Blok) or when the archaic selection for *polis* office in Athens (Blok) relied on the distribution of inheritance and heroic selection (Malkin). We deliberately left such moments in place to show how these factors cohere, adding cross-references to refer to a fuller discussion elsewhere in the book. And while Malkin's part has an overriding synchronic flavor and Blok's part is predominantly diachronic, the book as a whole tries to strike a balance between the structural features of the Greek mindset about the drawing of lots and the historical processes involved in the applications of the lot in the numerous, diverse Greek *poleis*.

The book is the first to present a comprehensive study of lots in ancient Greece and aims to reach a wider audience. While we try to establish our arguments as professional historians, we have opted for a broad, coherent, and accessible overview. Inevitably, this choice affected the space for detailed, technical discussions of problematic elements and debates with different academic viewpoints. Where we thought that, on our academic conscience, detailed discussions could not be left out, we have added succinct endnotes at the end of some chapters. In other places, specialists will notice that we decided to leave out certain contested or (too) uncertain aspects altogether. Furthermore, the drawing of lots took place in a wide range of historical domains that would deserve a more detailed exposition than we could or wanted to provide here. Since our book concentrates on historical questions, some specific fields, such as games of chance, have been left out of the discussion, except when we considered some pertinent points.[2] Excellent and extensive studies are available on colonization, kinship, inheritance, Homeric society, the political institutions of democratic Athens, and the impact of the Hellenistic empires on *polis* life, to which we refer in our footnotes but that we do not wish to duplicate here.

Although the evidence on drawing lots is extensive, rich, and colorful, it is also diverse and disparate. It compels us to leave some matters open, either because it is impossible to arrive at a firm conclusion or because there is simply a gap in what we know. One challenging but vital aspect is how the Greeks saw the gods' involvement in drawing lots. When lots were drawn for divination, discovering the will of the gods was the central event, but for other domains, the picture is not always clear. After intensive discussions, we conclude that the gods were evoked and considered as the guardians of the procedure, but they were not expected to predetermine the outcome. Most lotteries were not for divination. However, depending on circumstances and individual piety, Greeks could think the gods were more closely engaged in the procedure.

A note on terminology: there are various available terms in English, such as "drawing lots," "lotteries," "casting lots," and "sortition." Each term evokes a different mental image (e.g., "casting" conveys throwing, whereas "drawing" conveys pulling or lifting). Since our emphasis is not on the precise protocols of using lots (we discuss them in context) but on the institution, we opted, somewhat arbitrarily, for "drawing lots" and "lotteries" interchangeably.

And a note on gender: whenever we use "men" or "women," we refer to historical male and female persons either as members of their communities or as they were imagined by ancient poets and historians. We try to avoid "Man" in a generic sense and anachronisms in general. For example, when mentioning a citizen forwarding a proposal in the assembly, we always refer to the citizen as a "he," never "he or she," since the context is historical and women did not participate in the assemblies.

---

[2] See, e.g., *Des dieux, des jeux—et du hazard? Actes du XVIe colloque international du CIERGA. Kernos* 35 (2022).

For the transliteration of Greek names, easy understanding has been our guideline. Familiar names (Thucydides, Corinth) appear in their conventional, latinized form; less common names (Hekataios, Kameiros) in their Greek form. Full consistency in this matter is impossible, however, since for one reader a name is familiar, for another it is not. Bibliographical references appear in the footnotes in abbreviated form; the full references can be found in the Bibliography at the end of the book. References to sources are abbreviated in the footnotes according to standard systems, for which the reader can consult the Abbreviations. An appendix by Elena Iaffe provides a lexicographic survey. It aims to identify in the literary and epigraphic evidence the extant vocabulary for lottery practices in archaic and classical Greece in political, religious, legal, military, and civil contexts. One result is that some keywords with ambiguous translations are now securely anchored in the world of drawing lots. Based on Iaffe's research and preparation of the database, a dedicated internet site, *kleros.org.il*, supported mainly by the Gerda Henkel Foundation, is now hosted at Tel Aviv University. The Israel Science Foundation supported research for the six chapters by Irad Malkin.[3] The part by Josine Blok contributes to the Research Program "Anchoring Innovation" of the National Research School in Classical Studies in the Netherlands.[4]

---

[3] Israel Science Foundation grant no. 1033/17.
[4] "Anchoring Innovation" is the Gravitation Grant research agenda of the Dutch National Research School in Classical Studies, OIKOS. It is financially supported by the Dutch ministry of Education, Culture and Science (NWO project number 024.003.012). For more information about the research program and its results, see the website www.anchoringinnovation.nl.

Acknowledgements

Irad Malkin wishes to thank the Zvi Yavetz School of History at Tel Aviv University for its support. Special thanks are due to Oxford University and the Faculty of Classics, which have been hosting me as a Visiting Professor during the past years, and to the various Oxford Colleges, All Souls, Brasenose, Wolfson, Worcester (a Massada Fellow), and New College. I have lectured on specific issues in various contexts and had several significant discussions for which I wish to thank especially Andrew Cockburn, Simon Hornblower, Naomi Rokonitz, Yoshiyuki Suto, Véronique Dasen, Cecilia d'Ercole, Vinciane Pirenne-Delforge, Gabriella Pironti, Lou de Barbarin, Jean Christophe Sourisseau, Ariadne Konstantinou, Juval Portugali, Yael Tamir, Andrew Wallace-Hadrill, Nicholas Purcell, Robert Parker, Antonios Rengakos, Elizabeth Fentress, Nicholas Laubry, Michel Gras, Franco de Angelis, Lin Foxhall, Gabriel Zuchtriegel, Massimo Osanna, Naoíse MacSweeney, Frédéric Hurlet, Tsur Shezaf, Alon Idan, Liana Lomiento, Federica Cordano, and Josephine Crawley Quinn. I owe personal thanks to my friend Leslie Cockburn who first suggested I turn an article on democracy and drawing lots that I had once published in the daily newspaper *Haaretz* into a book. I am particularly grateful to Elena Iaffe, research assistant to the project who wrote the Appendix, prepared the index, and created the internet site *kleros.org.il*.

Josine Blok warmly thanks Saskia Peels-Matthey and Liam Klein for collecting evidence on uses of the lot for office in ancient Greece and Julia Krul for her help on the use of the lot in the Ancient Near East. My work on drawing lots for *polis* governance owes much to stimulating discussions with colleagues from various disciplines. I want to thank Henk te Velde for inviting me to a conference on and with Bernard Manin; Ingrid Robeyns, Bert van den Brink, and Margo Trappenburg for collaboration on a project for the Royal Dutch Academy of Sciences on the political philosophy and governance of using lots; and Ineke Sluiter and Saskia Peels-Matthey for preparing projects for the Dutch Foundation for Scientific Research. Invitations for lectures gave me the opportunity for valuable exchange about my work, for which I warmly thank the audiences and my hosts, especially Claudia Rapp, Susanna Elm, Robert Parker, Froma I. Zeitlin, Peter Funke, Johannes Hahn, Violaine Sebillotte Cuchet, Martin Jehne, Franziska Luppa, Frédéric Hurlet, Julie Bothorel, Akiko Moroo, Yazuro Hashiba, and Yoshiyuki Suto. I am very grateful to the institutions which hosted me to work on this project, especially the Fondation Hardt at Vandoeuvres, Exeter College at Oxford, Paris 1 Sorbonne, and to the colleagues who made these visits possible.

We both are very grateful to Margalit Finkelberg, Hans-Joachim Gehrke, and Kurt Raaflaub for reading parts of the book and giving us their valuable advice. We also express our gratitude to the two anonymous referees for Oxford University Press whose critical comments did much to improve the text. Last but not least, we express our warm gratitude to our colleagues in the Network for the Study of Ancient Greek History for their friendship and wisdom: Kostas Buraselis, Mirko Canevaro, Madalina Dana, Gunnel Ekroth, Lin Foxhall, Hans-Joachim Gehrke, Maurizio Giangiulio, André Lardinois, Nino Luraghi, Naoíse MacSweeney, Christian Mann, Oswyn Murray, Christel Müller, Thomas Heine Nielsen, Vinciane Pirenne-Delforge, François de Polignac, Robert Rollinger, Eftychia Stavrianopoulou, Rosalind Thomas, and Marek Węcowski, and in warm remembrance of our dear friend Kurt Raaflaub.

November 2023
Irad Malkin, Tel Aviv
Josine Blok, Utrecht

Abbreviations

Abbreviations of classical authors and texts follow those in the *Oxford Classical Dictionary* (4th edition; online: https://oxfordre.com/classics/page/3993), supplemented by those in LSJ; abbreviations of epigraphical corpora not included below follow those of the *Packard Humanities Institute* (https://inscriptions.packhum.org/); abbreviations of journals not included below follow *L'année philologique* (https://www.brepols.net/series/APH-O).

AIO	*Attic Inscriptions Online* (www.atticinscriptions.com)
BNP	*Brill's New Pauly: Encyclopedia of the Ancient World*. Cancik, Hubert, Schneider, Helmuth (eds.: Antiquity), Landfester, Manfred (ed.: Classical Tradition). Leiden: Brill; Brill Online
BTCGI	*Bibliografia topografica della colonizzazione greca in Italia e nelle isole tirreniche*. Nenci, G., Vallet, G. (eds). Rome: Centre Jean Bérard (1975–)
CGRN	*Collection of Greek Ritual Norms* (http://cgrn.ulg.ac.be)
FGrHist	Jacoby, Felix. *Die Fragmente der griechischen Historiker*. Berlin 1923–1930; Leiden 1940–1958; Leiden: Brill (1958–)
FHG	Müller, Karl Otfried (1841–1873). *Fragmenta Historicorum Graecorum*. Müller, Theodor, Langlois, Victor (eds.). Paris: Ambrosio Firmin Didot
GGM	Müller, Carl Friedrich Wilhelm (1855). *Geographi Graeci Minores*. Hildesheim: G. Olms
LAC	Gagarin, Michael, Perlman, Paula (2016). *The Laws of Ancient Crete, c. 650–400 BCE*. Oxford: Oxford University Press
LIMC	*Lexicon Iconographicum Mythologiae Classicae*. Zurich: Artemis (1981–)
LR	Leão, D. F., Rhodes, P. J. (2015). *The Laws of Solon: A New Edition with Introduction, Translation and Commentary*. London: I. B. Tauris
LSAM	*Lois sacrées de l'Asie Mineure*. F. Sokolowski (ed.). Paris: Ed. de Boccard (1955)
LSCG	*Lois sacrées des cités grecques*. F. Sokolowski (ed.) Paris: Ed. de Boccard (1969)
LSJ	Liddell, H. G., Scott, R., Jones, H. S., McKenzie, R. (9th ed. 1996) *A Greek-English Lexicon, with a Supplement*. Oxford: Oxford University Press
ML	Meiggs, Russell, Lewis, David M. (1989). *A Selection of Greek Historical Inscriptions to the End of the Fifth Century B.C.* Rev. ed. Oxford: Clarendon Press
Nomima	Van Effenterre, H., Ruzé, F. (1994–1995). *Nomima. Receuil d'inscriptions politiques et juridiques de l'archaisme grec*. 2 vols. Rome: École Française de Rome

OR	Osborne, Robin, Rhodes, P. J. (2017). *Greek Historical Inscriptions, 478–404 BC*. Oxford: OUP
Osborne I-IV	Osborne, M. J. (1981–1983). *Naturalization in Athens*. 4 vols. Brussels: Paleis der Academiën. Verhandelingen van de Koninklijke Academie voor Wetenschappen, Letteren en Schone Kunsten van België, klasse der Letteren, 45 no. 109
PCPhS	*Proceedings of the Cambridge Philological Society*
RE	Pauly, August, Wissowa, Georg, et al. (eds) (1894-1980). *Paulys Realencyclopädie der classischen Altertumswissenschaft*. Stuttgart: Metzler.
Rhodes, CAAP	Rhodes, P. J. (1993²). *A Commentary to the Aristotelian Athenaion Politeia*. Oxford: Oxford University Press
RO	Rhodes, P. J., Osborne, Robin (2003). *Greek Historical Inscriptions 404–323 BC*. Oxford: Oxford University Press
Schwenk	Schwenk, Cynthia J. (1985). *Athens in the Age of Alexander: The Dated Laws & Decrees of "the Lykourgan Era" 338–322 B.C*. Chicago: Ares Publishers
SGDI	*Sammlung der griechischen Dialekt-Inschriften*. H. Collitz and F. Bechtel (eds). Göttingen: Vandenhoek & Ruprecht (1884–1915).
TLG	*Thesaurus Linguae Graecae* (https://stephanus.tlg.uci.edu/)

Introduction: Greeks Drawing Lots: The Practice and the Mindset of Egalitarianism

1. An egalitarian mindset

Ancient Greeks drew lots within an astonishingly broad spectrum of practices and conventions. The drawing of lots reflected the values, practices, and egalitarian mindset that were prevalent for nearly three centuries before the most famous appearance of the lot as the salient feature of Athenian democracy. Greeks often turned to random choices by drawing lots to ensure equality and fairness and avoid undue influence and corruption. Without the wide-ranging use of lotteries in the archaic period, classical democracy would never have emerged as it did: reshuffling the entire citizenry by lot and gradually expanding its use for governing posts. We shall observe the drawing of lots in archaeology, myth, poetry, drama, ritual, historiography, and political thought and practice. The pre-democratic range is impressive and apparent in the earliest Greek literature.

Modern democracies have mostly abandoned the drawing of lots for citizens' social, economic, judicial, and political involvement—salient features, as I hope to show, of the ancient Greek world. Instead, when modern democratic regimes opted for elected representation, they probably did not foresee its attendant risks, familiar today, of distaste for politics, political ignorance, alienation, elitism, sectionalism, and the ever-present danger of undue influence. Moreover, representative government and political parties in modern democracies often stand for discrete sections of society (real or imagined), deepening internal divisions. By contrast, one salient feature of drawing lots in ancient Greece is a social *mixture*, when randomly chosen citizens find themselves doing something together. Today, such random selection by lot is rare, apparent in jury selection and experiments of citizen committees. Representation, even if limited in time and subject to rotation, implies some form of top-down governance. By contrast, when Greeks drew lots, their vision of society was horizontal rather than vertical, and participants were interchangeable and hence perceived as equal individuals.

The following categories of drawing lots are apparent during the archaic, classical, and early Hellenistic periods of Greek history (ca. 750–150):

Drawing Lots. Irad Malkin and Josine Blok, Oxford University Press. © Oxford University Press 2024.
DOI: 10.1093/oso/9780197753477.003.0001

- *Distributive* lotteries define the contours of the relevant group (or community), which is also sovereign to decide the action of drawing lots. They express a "horizontal" vision of society, the reverse of a vertical, top-down view of authority. Distributive lotteries were employed to distribute inheritance, sacrificial meat, colonial lands, booty, catch, and positions in the state; even the entire cosmos and the provinces of the gods were believed to have been distributed by lot by and among the Greek gods.
- *Selective* lotteries too imply the contours of some groups, when picking soldiers for military campaigns, colonists for new settlements, warriors for particular tasks, and at some point even sorting out who were to be worshiped as ancestral tribal heroes at Athens.
- *Procedural* lotteries were especially useful for rotation and turns, such as guard shifts, stations on a race course, allocation of court cases, and rotating days of the presidency of the Athenian Council (*boulê*). In the fifth century, even entire theatres of war were sometimes assigned to generals by lot.
- *Mixture lotteries* were used to "homogenize" the mother cities at the time of the foundation of new colonies and to do the same in the colonies, mixing the nucleus of settlers from a specific mother city with other Greek immigrants who joined a foundation. Sometimes they "mixed" the people to avoid discord and civil strife and, specifically in Athens, to reshuffle the deck of citizens to create the basis of Athenian democracy.
- *Divination by lot* (lot oracles) was a discrete category for divining the intention of the gods for *ad hoc* issues, prevalent at the oracles of Delphi and Dodona.

Drawing lots drew a line around the community: it defined communities and groups in terms of access (and exclusion), with each participant considered equal, equivalent, and interchangeable before the chance, and therefore as a recognized individual.[1] The lottery implied, sometimes expressly, an emphasis on equality and equity or "fairness." Before lots are drawn, the chance is equally fair, but Greeks often tried to have equal outcomes. A history of the lot is how people distribute things, how they regard and select individuals, how they take turns, how they inherit, and how they mix to form a more cohesive community or, sometimes, avoid civil strife. It is also a history of the ideas of equality and

---

[1] I do not enter the discussion about the individual as distinguished from a "person"; in terms of social and political life—which are the ones that concern us here—no one is "an island"; cf. Vernant (1989); note the implicit understanding of the role of distribution: de Polignac and Schmitt-Pantel (1998) "idios *en effet ne designe pas l'individu en tant que "personne" ... mais en tant que détenteur d'un statu social déterminé par sa position dans cet espace de distribution.*" Cf. Müller-Prost (2002).

fairness, or fairness as close as possible to equality. Drawing lots was a salient feature of the ancient Greek mindset or worldview, a perspective mostly lost today.

It is a story of the idea of a *horizontal community*: Like everybody else, Greeks knew elites and top-down rule, but unlike most societies throughout history, its opposite, a *horizontal* vision of society, was never out of their frame of reference. In my view, a constant vector was at play in archaic and classical Greek history, oscillating between the vertical/elite (top-down) and the horizontal/egalitarian. In Greek colonies (ch. 6), for example, egalitarianism was expressed in a distinct category of "equal First Lots" (*protoi kleroi*). Those were distributed by lot during the first generation of foundation (the "egalitarian vector"). However, the "elite vector" would prevail within one or two generations, and social and economic differentiation arose.

The history of drawing lots is one of a community that recognizes itself as a community (not necessarily a political one), making sovereign decisions about and for itself, with no recourse to external authority. Access to a distributive lottery defines, exclusively, the contours of the group of "sharers": who is in, who is out. Drawing lots implies "members only": the "group" might be tiny, for example, two brothers sharing partible inheritance by lot (ch. 4) or seven brothers who draw lots to send one of them to war (ch. 1). It can also be substantial, such as an entire home community drawing lots to select settlers for a new colony; or the community of colonists, with each getting by lot (*kleros*) an equal portion of land (*kleros*, again; ch. 6); or citizens—not outsiders—deserving equal "portions of law" in a democracy (ch. 7).

With distributive lotteries, whether among Olympian gods who allot the sea to Poseidon by lot or among humans, the source of authority is not external to the group of participants and draws its legitimacy from inside. For the most part, Greeks did not turn to the lot to "reveal the will of the gods," as I shall demonstrate (ch. 2). No oracle, to my knowledge, had ever commanded any Greek to hold a lottery; it was always a human decision to turn to random devices, including lot oracles, which, as a discrete category, were indeed a device of divination. We might need to take a moment to realize how remarkable it was to turn to the lot *not* for the sake of divination. Most lotteries had not been to reveal something divinely predetermined, nor do we hear of any ancient Greek claiming that. Athena did not select Athens's magistrats and judges; the Athenians did that, and by lot.[2]

---

[2] See ch. 8 (with the possible exception of priests chosen by lot from a *genos*). Cf. Hansen (1999) 74–76.

Before the lot became political, drawing lots and establishing a mindset of equal chances and portions were already ubiquitous during the centuries before Cleisthenes laid the foundations for democracy in 508. They touched upon a whole spectrum of life and death, both private and public. They expressed values of individuality, fairness, and equality. Moreover, the "archaeology of equality" (such as equal plots in new settlements, ch. 6) seems to support the notion of equal distribution by lot.

2. From egalitarianism to democracy

As a history of Greek values and practices associated with drawing lots, this book could stand alone without mentioning drawing lots in Athenian democracy or governance in general. On the other hand, teleology aside, the transition to the political sphere (ch. 7) is better understood with the earlier history of drawing lots. For example, mixtures by drawing lots (chs. 2, 4, 6) were politically first expressed in Cleisthenes's reforms. The selection of magistrates was preceded by centuries of selective lotteries (chs. 1–6); procedures in the Athenian democracy, such as the rotating Chair of the Council, are already evidenced in Homer. Distributing equal concrete portions by lot, "equally and fairly," seems to explain the transformation to the abstract level of "equal portions of law" (*isonomia*; the term "democracy," its equivalent, appeared somewhat later). The expression *metechein tes poleos*, "sharing in the state," is apt for the notion of citizenship (each citizen, as it were, having an equal portion of it). Aristotle, with good reason, defined the state as a "partnership" (*koinonia*).

Distributive lotteries, in particular, had been defining the contours of the group or community for centuries: The "whole" among which a distribution by lot is made is the exclusive group (e.g., a family, an army, a community); inside, the individual must be recognized and counted (outsiders may not share) and becomes a "sharer." The "unit," the individual (or the individual household, *oikos*), deserves a portion. That is no trivial matter: the stress on the one-to-one relations (one portion / one individual) will prove consistent from the eighth to the fourth centuries, expressed in a whole spectrum of "portions."

Sharing equally in the state overlapped with the idea that a state should consist of a precise correspondence between the number of households (*oikoi*) and the number of *kleroi* (*kleros*: lot; a plot of land). Revolutionary cries—for example, at Sparta, Leontinoi, Syracuse, and Herakleia Pontike (ch. 6)—were sometimes framed as a call for a reshuffling of the deck of citizens and redistribution of equal plots of lands (*ges anadasmos*), reverting to some ideal and primordial past when that supposedly had been the case.

3. What is new about this book? The previous discussion of the field of inquiry

This book claims to open a window on a new area of observation and analysis, which, in my view, is a key to understanding ancient Greek civilization, aside from the specific question of democracy and governance. Although classics is the oldest academic discipline, no one to date has written a comprehensive study of the drawing of lots in ancient Greece.[3] Faced with much fewer sources of knowledge than other historical disciplines and taking note of the continuous and exhaustive work to extricate the maximum from them, one would think that no new fields are left to explore. Our dialogue with the past is ever-changing, but here we have an entire field of inquiry that has never received sufficient attention or recognition. The last word on the subject in book form was *Election by Lot at Athens*, the first draft of which had been written before the discovery of the "Constitution of Athens" (*Athenaion politeia*, a fundamental text about the Athenian regime).[4] This excellent monograph by James Wycliffe Headlam was published in 1891 and was chronologically restricted to Athens in the fifth and fourth centuries. The studies that followed Headlam, such as those by Mogens H. Hansen and Bernard Manin, never attempted anything comprehensive. They, too, are restricted to politics while entirely missing out on centuries of the use of the lot before it became relevant to democracy. By contrast, in this book, the substantial section on democracy by Josine Blok, a true expert on ancient citizenship and Athenian democracy, comes at its end; it is also chronologically the latest. In short, the subject needed identification and research of an entire field that no one had ever treated comprehensively. One of my conclusions is that it ought to have been. Historians like to privilege their subject choices, and I am consciously doing the same, hoping to justify that endeavor. The result presented here is a history of a significant institution that permeated the lives of Greeks during the archaic period and impacted how they saw human society and structured their expectations and behaviors.

The political reawakening of interest in the use of the lot and sortition goes hand in hand with a renewed interest in the ancient Athenian democracy and the use of the lot in governance.[5] Yet the first constitutive act in the foundation

---

[3] Other studies either concentrate on Athens in the form of chapters or articles: de Coulanges (1891); Ehrenberg (1927); Hansen (1999); Manin (1997); or in general encyclopedia articles, Glotz (1907); Ehrenberg (1927). Cf. Demont (2010); Buchstein (2009); Blok (2017); Sintomer (2011); (2020). See ch. 9 and *Envoi*.

[4] See ch. 9, Endnote.

[5] The list is constantly growing, e.g., Goodwin, B. ([1992] 2005); Dowlen (2008); Stone (2011a); Sintomer (2007); Dowlen, Delannoi, (eds.) (2010); Sintomer and Lopez-Rabatel (2020); Demont (2010); Van Reybrouck (2016); Fishkin (2018); see also https://www.sortitionfoundation.org/.

of democracy in Athens by Cleisthenes was not to apply the lot to selecting magistrates; he implemented a mixture lottery on a vast scale, creating a new basis for the political citizenry. He replaced the "strong ties" of localism, patronage, and kinship, which often threatened to fragment the society, with a cohesive network of citizens.[6] On the other hand, regardless of the democracy that he founded in 508, it was already Solon (ca. 594) who introduced allotment to public offices (see ch. 7): the magistracies of the Nine Archons, and the *Tamiai* (treasurers) of the goddess Athena, who were to be drawn by lot from a preselected group. About a century later, the Athenian democracy adopted the practice, gradually extending it from preselected groups to "from everyone" (*ex hapanton*). The ancient Athenian democracy falsifies any claim of inefficiency: with a population nearing the size of modern Iceland, it was run efficiently by lot, fought and won wars, and managed its economy. Athenians did not need computers: a block of stone (a *kleroterion*) with drilled vertical shafts and white and black balls running through them was sufficient.[7]

Can the drawing of lots work in modern, contemporary democracies? People rarely believe facts, says the Nobel Prize laureate Daniel Kahneman.[8] They would rarely believe the straightforward answer: it can work today, and it did in antiquity. The experiment had been successfully conducted and proven in ancient Athens (and to a degree in some medieval Italian republics).[9] Yet, the typical reaction I encounter to introducing lotteries to contemporary politics is condescending, uninformed ridicule: it was all very well for them back then, but today? We seem to adhere to the notion that elections and representation are the salient democratic feature, but are they? We rarely consider that our system of representative democracy in France and the United States was the late-eighteenth-century reaction *against* democratic forces.[10]

A representative government retains the vertical *direction* of a top-down rule while drawing its authority from "the bottom." By contrast, the horizontal perspective expressed in drawing lots engages people, keeps them informed, and frees them from manipulation. The drawing of lots expressed respect for politics and suspicion of politicians. It succeeded in enhancing public involvement and eliminating sectarianism. There was no room for political lobbies because nobody knew whom to influence or bribe. Significantly, lotteries prevented resentment against a person chosen for a post and generally provided a sense of equality and fairness. They were efficient, fast, and very cheap. However, there is not much point in contemporary suggestions to reintroduce the lot into politics[11] merely as a mechanism *à la grecque*.

---

[6] Cf. Granovetter (1973) on strong and weak ties in a society; Ismard (2010)
[7] Kosmetatou (2013).
[8] Kahneman (2011).
[9] Sintomer (2011; 2020).
[10] Manin (1997); van Reybrouck (2016).
[11] Van Reybrouck (2016).

We need to understand the Greek world of values, the frame of reference, and the egalitarian mindset associated with the lot. These features made its wide-ranging use possible and desirable in antiquity, as it may be today.

In archaic Greek culture, a discrete "portion" and a discrete individual seem to overlap. A *moira* (portion) could be a portion of a cow in the form of sacrificial meat, which an individual gets by lot (ch. 3); on a metaphoric level, *moira* may also mean the "fate" of that individual. However, of what is it a portion? What is the "whole" to which it relates? Let us stay with cows for a moment, starting with a non-Greek contrast. In the book of Genesis, we meet the clever Joseph, who convinces Pharaoh to create grain stores for the forthcoming seven bad years, represented by the seven lean cows that devoured the seven fat cows that the pharaoh had seen in his dream. Once the lean years arrived, the pharaoh made a huge profit selling the grain Joseph had stored in central granaries (Genesis 41). The "whole" of those grain gifts were "portions" that belonged to the divine ruler. The portions came trickling vertically from above, top-down, whereas the "whole" had never belonged to those finally sharing in some of it.

Let us divert our gaze from an Egyptian cow to a Greek one. We now observe an opposed notion of "portion." When Greeks ate meat, it was usually in the context of a sacrifice. After an honorary portion (*geras*) had been set aside for the priest performing the sacrifice, on most occasions, the rest of the cow was divided into equal portions of roasted or cooked meat and apportioned by lot among a predefined group of sharers (see ch. 3). Unlike the pharaonic "whole," whence top-down portions would drop down, the Greek "whole" (in this case, the cow) belonged, *a priori*, to the entire, predefined group. The vision is not top-down but *horizontal*: not the pharaoh, but the group, or the community, conducts the sacrifice and the distribution of portions by lot.

Was the drawing of lots a value as such? Greeks stored much importance in the *collective distribution of equal portions*. Drawing lots was but a device to implement this. In distributive lotteries, sometimes one draws a lot because of the *difference* in the value of each portion. For example, the equally sized *kleroi* (plots of land) distributed by lot to new settlers were equal in size but not in the soil quality or distance from the center.

When Odysseus distributes a booty of captured goats, each ship gets nine. Yet he conducts a lottery "so that no one will be deprived of his equal share." Why draw lots if each crew would get its nine goats anyway? However, a simple arithmetical distribution would have been unfair to those resenting getting the old and skinny goats. The lot expresses justice because it is arbitrary, and being impersonal, it eliminates resentment toward anyone except one's "luck."

Drawing lots was not a value; the collective distribution of equal portions was. We can demonstrate this in cases of collective distributions when drawing lots became unnecessary. When an exact equivalence was possible, drawing lots became superfluous. The Greeks knew that. The Siphnians, for instance, distributed to each citizen the income from their gold mines, and the Athenians considered doing the same with their silver mine at Laurion. However, in contrast to equal units of gold and silver, most objects for collective distribution could not be split into units of precise equivalence, such as "ten drachmas for each Athenian." Thus, recourse to the drawing of lots became frequent and ubiquitous (see ch. 6). Such insistence on equality of both chance and result within the framework of distributive lotteries reveals an egalitarian mindset. Let there be no confusion: egalitarianism and equality are not synonyms. Homeric society provides a good illustration (ch. 1): in the *Iliad*, the leaders ("Kings") are unequal compared to the rest of the soldiers. A hero may enrich himself privately by grabbing *enara*—that is, personal captures, such as weapons, horses, or ransom. Publicly, however, a hero expects a *geras*, a special honorary gift, ostensibly from the army; otherwise, booty is brought "to the middle," to the "common store," whence it is redistributed by lot as individual portions. The "group" is comprehensive since leaders also participated in the general lotteries. Therefore, the distributive lottery is egalitarian, while the status of influential leaders and heroes is unequal. The "companions," *hetairoi*, of Odysseus appear equal among themselves yet inferior to the leader. In contrast to the "World of Odysseus," the historical, archaic Greeks hardly knew any kings, the *geras* was shifted to the priests, and when booty was concerned, the gods received a tithe (*dekate*), a practice unknown to Homer.

In short, instead of a top-down approach, the lottery and its vocabulary reflect a lateral or horizontal view of society more than any other institution in ancient Greece. It is the reverse of the vertical, hierarchical mode of authority. One might argue it is a question of degree, but the degree is significant. Greeks, too, knew top-down types of control (e.g., elites, tyrants, oligarchies). Still, the language, instruments, and power structure differed from the top-down Ancient Near East. With some exceptions around oracular institutions, ancient Greeks had no castes of priests, kings were exceptional, and tyrants were considered illegitimate. As some medieval Italian states illustrate, nothing inherent in a city-state should prevent authoritarian rule, and Greeks also knew tyrants. Greeks were also familiar with oligarchies, except that oligarchies too expressed an egalitarian mindset and were willing to share power equally, yet among a restricted group.

We should remember that the peculiar structure and cohesiveness of the Greek world discouraged centralism and encouraged horizontal perspectives. There never was (until 1821 CE) an actual country named "Greece." By the time Alexander the Great had died (323), there were over one thousand Greek city-states (*poleis*), often with no contiguous borders, sprinkled along the coasts of the Mediterranean and the Black Sea, from what are today Georgia and Ukraine in the east to Spain in the west. About a third were founded between the late eighth century and the sixth. They illustrate the "frontier aspect" of ancient Greek colonization: the option to leave an oppressive background.[12] Despite geographical distances and differences in dialects, and although most Greeks lived side by side with hinterland Barbarians, they recognized themselves and were so recognized by others as Greeks. It may seem a historical paradox, but the fact is that Hellenicity crystallized and spread during the archaic period, right at the time when Greeks were distancing themselves from each other as far as possible. It was a process of civilizational convergence through geographical divergence. I have argued elsewhere that Greek civilization emerged the way it did, not despite those differences and distances, but because of them.[13] The "self-organization of a complex system," or the network dynamics of the "small Greek world" ("small worlds" is a crucial term in network theory) that operated among the nodes of the "Greek web" enhanced Greek commonalities of practices and values, especially those associated with the drawing of lots. This "small world" (where distances are measured not geographically but by the number of links and the flows of content) also enhanced specific, common *attitude d'esprit* against a top-down approach. The instrument of the lottery came closest to actualizing it

Using the lot among Greeks was a norm rather than an exception. Remarkably, we may observe it throughout the Greek world, despite the heterogeneity of that world and its numerous, geographically disconnected city-states. Moreover, Greeks recognized sub-ethnic identities and spoke a variety of dialects. Under such conditions, commonalities of value and practice are all the more remarkable. The concepts and practices related to the lot are apparent throughout those vast spaces dotted with Greek *poleis*. They are often embedded in the ancient Greek vocabulary, with a primarily consistent set of verbs and nouns that reveal the associated concepts and perspectives (below).[14] The full spectrum of drawing lots is apparent already in the *Iliad* and the *Odyssey*, the earliest extant Greek literature. I aim to unravel a significant aspect of the life experience of ancient Greeks and perhaps add it to "the list of legacies" of classical Greece. In addition, if this reconstruction also helps to explain why both Herodotus and Aristotle regarded the drawing of lots as defining what democracy was all about, all the better.

I wish to explore, expose, and restore practical and mental uses of the lot. Whereas in the earlier archaic period, we may speak of a "mindset of the lot," in the later, classical Athenian democracy, the mindset had become something close to an "ideology."[15] That is not the ideology of modern political parties, but

---

[12] Hansen (2006) 84; Purcell (2005) 121–122 (following Ettore Lepore's discussion of Turner's thesis of the frontier in American history ([1921] 1962).
[13] Malkin (2011).
[14] See Iaffe, Appendix.
[15] On mentalities and ideologies, see Vovelle (1990).

the abstraction of the practices associated with the lot into an idea that, by the later fifth century, could become the very definition of democracy. But what was this mindset? How does one go about asking questions about it?

4. A mindset for drawing lots

A collective mindset is a common mental frame of reference that endures through time and is expressed when reacting to similar contexts and issues. It may be self-aware or not and can be articulated in language, values, myths, collective representations, and implementation in practice. A mindset is equivalent to "that is how we do things," based on values, customs, and traditions that form a worldview. For example, when distributing something such as booty, meat, land, and inheritance, "we" (= Greeks) think in terms of *equal or equitable portions* and turn to the lot to actualize the distribution. It is a mindset where the relational idea of "equal portions" of some "whole" implies a horizontal view of a group or society. That "whole" may be expressed concretely, such as portions in partible inheritance by lot (ch. 4); it may be abstract, such as "the state," where the entire community shares equal "portions," expressed in allotted, rotated political posts. As noted, that is probably how we should understand the semantic field of *isonomia*: an equal portion of "law" for every participating citizen, what we might call "equality before the law."

This book is not a general *histoire de mentalités*. It does not claim to reconstruct a general "Greek mentality," nor do I think it possible. I wish only to expose and articulate a Greek frame of reference that has been ubiquitous and consistent for several centuries. The framing of the question above is meant to avoid confusion with trends in historiography that have different aims, as can be observed when following the trajectory of *histoire de mentalités* through the works by, for example, Lévy-Bruhl, Mandrou, Vernant, Le Goff, Chartier, Burke, and (the critical) Lloyd.[16] Remarkably, there is significant overlap among key terms employed by those historians, such as those revolving around "thought": "systems of thought," "cognitive systems," "modes/styles of thought (*manières de penser*)," "mental habits," "collective representations," and *imaginaire collectif*. To the extent that those terms come close to the idea of a mindset defined earlier, I am happy to acknowledge an intellectual debt. Despite much valuable criticism, mainly by Geoffrey Lloyd, Peter Burke is right to claim, "Something is needed to occupy the conceptual space between the history of thought and social history."[17] Instead of

---

[16] Lévy-Bruhl (1910); Mandrou (1961); Vernant (1965b); Burke (1997a; 1997b); Lloyd (1999); Chartier (2015); Le Goff (1974). Cf. Hutton (1981).

[17] Burke (1997b) 165 wishes to "avoid having to choose between an intellectual history with the society left out and social history with the thought left out."

the "Greek worldview," I wish to observe a discrete yet common attitude of mind toward the same phenomena and problems that influenced emotions, thoughts, and understanding of a situation and its potential, and actual practices.

5. Vocabulary and mindset

One way to reveal the lottery mindset among ancient Greeks is to examine the relevant vocabulary as individual words in conjunction with each other and the context of their semantic fields. Certain words will prove more prominent than others, but all relate to notions of distributing and giving, equality and fairness, and the actual working of the lot. The ancient Greek vocabulary best illustrates the wide-ranging uses of the lot, the type of practices associated with it, and the associated values that guided it. By examining discrete uses and, more significantly, when lot-associated words appear together, a salient trait of a Greek worldview comes into relief. Unfortunately, for the history of scholarship and its moods, those keenly interested in the Greek vocabulary of sharing were Marxist historians writing at the height of the Cold War. Their work is mostly ignored or, because of some unconventional terminology (e.g., "primitive communism," "tribalism"), their ideas sometimes appear bizarre. That should not be the case, however; George Thomson (1972; 1978), and especially his student Bořivoj Borecký, understood this. In particular, the latter followed up the ancient Greek vocabulary of lotteries, distribution, sharing, and equality, as illustrated in his cumbersome yet informative title: *Survivals of Some Tribal Ideas in Classical Greek: The Use and the Meaning of Lanchanō, Dateomai, and the Origin of Ison Echein, Ison Nemein, and Related Idioms* (1965). His work needed updating and the inclusion of more epigraphical evidence, a project effected with Elena Iaffe, which we have tried to complete here (see the appendix and the dedicated internet site *kleros.org.il*. Borecký was the only one who did in-depth research on the distribution vocabulary with an eye to social implications. He saw one of the most important implications: the direct connection between equality, fairness, and the lot.

I have expanded and updated his research to include more terms and additional types of evidence, observing and analyzing semantic fields and metaphoric uses. One conclusion stands out immediately: the two more frequent and significant words—the noun *kleros* and the verb *lanchano*—are primarily associated with the lot, although both can have other meanings. For example, the *Greek English Lexicon* gives the sense of the verb *lanchano* as "to get by lot" as well as "to get," *tout court*. Our study confirms the lottery associations and demonstrates that about 73 percent of the uses of the verb *lanchano*, down to and including the first half of the fourth century, are directly associated with drawing lots.

Such findings imply that we may translate specific texts more accurately and pursue them as further evidence, especially when a context is missing. The appendix provides the research results, and the dedicated internet site now provides an accessible database of forty lemmas dating to the early Hellenistic age. The database collects all the literary and epigraphic evidence for political, legal, religious, military, and civic lottery practices.[18] At the risk of losing some ambiguous examples, we listed only the ones associated with lottery practices.[19] For example, especially in lyric poetry, the verb *lanchano* is mainly used in the metaphoric sense of "fate" or "one's lot in life," completely disconnected from an actual lottery practice (yet semantically linked with *moira*).

Another illustrative case concerns verbs of giving and distribution. In Homer and Hesiod, most allotments seem to be accompanied not by a verb of direct giving, *didomi*, but of distributing *dateomai* (cf. *dasmos*, the act of distribution). English does not have the middle voice in which we find most occurrences of such distributions, mainly in the plural. The participants are giving/distributing to themselves, expressing the opposite of a top-down approach.

The Athenians invented the lottery machine, apparently called a *kleroterion* (the evidence for the term is late). The word constitutes another critical term for understanding ancient practices and mindset: *kleros*, a piece of material used as a lot in a lottery. The verb *kleroö* signifies "to draw lots," while *klerosis* is the lottery itself. However, *kleros* can also mean a landed estate. The word illustrates the shift, back and forth, between the lot (*kleros*), the drawing of lots (*klerosis*), and its result (*kleros*, again). In inheritance laws (ch. 4), the land may be divided into equal parts and distributed by lot. The result, the landed estate, is also called a *kleros*. We also find such *kleroi* in colonies (ch. 6), where settlers got equal *kleroi* (plots of land) by lot (*kleros*). Chantraine defines its meaning as "an object representing a person participating in a lottery, hence sortition (. . .) "that which is allotted by the lot, hence "a section of land, property, etc." Originally, says Chantraine, the *kleros* signified an object (such as a stone or a piece of wood) used for the lottery. In short, *kleros* in the sense of "lot" is primary, whereas *kleros* in the sense of a portion of land is secondary[20] (see further discussion in ch. 6). Semantically,

---

[18] The database was researched and prepared by Elena Iaffe as part of a research project financed by the Israeli Science Foundation project no. 1033/17, the Gerda Henkel Foundation, and the School of History at Tel Aviv University. See the appendix to this volume.

[19] λαγχάνω group: λαγχάνω, ἀπολαγχάνω, διαλαγχάνω, ἐπιλαγχάνω, ἐκλαγχάνω, μεταλαγχάνω, προλαγχάνω, συλλαγχάνω, λάχος, λῆξις/λάξις, σύλληξις; κληρόω group: κληρόω, ἀποκληρόω, διακληρόω, ἐπικληρόω, συγκληρόω, κλῆρος, ἔγκληρος, ἀπόκληρος, σύγκληρος, προκληρόω, κλήρωσις, διακλήρωσις, κληρωτός, κληρωτήριον, κληροπαλής, ἀνεπικλήρωτος, ἄκληρος, κληροπαληδός; *κυαμεύω group*: κυαμεύω, κύαμος, κυαμόβολος, κυαμευτός, ἀποκυαμεύω (epigraphy); *καυνός group*: καυνός, διακαυνιάζω; *πάλλω group*: διαπάλλω, πάλος; *πίπτω group*: πίπτω, πότμος.

[20] Ménager (1987) 112, quoting Chantraine (1968-1980) who seems in agreement with both ancient and modern dictionaries. Hesychius, s.v. *kleros*: "a thing thrown in lottery, or a stone, or a property, or a portion." See Beekes (2010), s.v.: "lot, allotment, inheritance, piece of ground"

one may point out parallels in Latin (*sors*) and Biblical Hebrew (*goral*); both can mean the material "lot" (e.g., a marked pebble placed in a helmet), the lottery, and the result (e.g., a portion of inherited land). Such parallelism with *sors* and *goral* may need further study.[21] Our study of *kleros*, therefore, should demonstrate the overlapping, integrated meanings of the lottery and its outcome, with a clear primary sense of a lot.

6. Portions and fairness

As noted, what gets distributed by lot are "portions," often perceived as *equal*. A portion is *moira*, but it is not the same as a "portion of life" (again, *moira*) allotted by the "fate" *moirai*-goddesses, which is individual and hence variable. More often than not, *moira* relates to the length of one's life rather than its content ("destiny"). However, whereas "fate"-oriented *moira* varied individually, when it was the human decision to draw lots for portions (*moirai*), Greeks tried to level the field by applying their notions of equality and fairness: the concrete portions were to be equal or equitable. To illustrate: In some cultures, it is considered fair that the eldest son should inherit all or get the lion's share (primogeniture). He is "lucky" to be the firstborn, and because he is firstborn, he "deserves" that lion's share. However, with the Greek practice of partible inheritance by lot, all brothers are equal before the chance, all equally deserve, and all receive equal or equitable portions, agreed upon in advance, before the drawing of the lots.

In general, there are two competing notions of fairness: one relies on a status where fairness is *proportionate*, according to one's position or state: if we are to have a *fair* race, the turtle ought to have a different starting point from Achilles. However, as we will see, for many Greeks, fairness was not in what was "proper to one's station" but in equality. In other words, Greeks often saw equality as overlapping with equity, a recurring theme in this book. There must have been some mental implications for young men expecting equal portions assigned to each by lot (inheritance, colonization). Life decisions determined by lot were on

---

Etymology: "originally a shard of stone or a piece of wood that was used as a lot." Frisk (1960): "lot, portion, inheritance, portion of land"; Gaisford ([1848] 1994): "a piece of wood or a stone with engraved sign (name) used in lottery to designate the participants; or property, or a portion of land." In Biblical Hebrew, *goral* has a similar history: a material such as a piece of wood, then the "lot," and then the portion of land; see Bar-On (2020). Latin *sors* has also a similar pattern. Cordano and Grottanelli (2001). See also ch. 1, Endnote 2. See also López-Rabatel (2019).

[21] Cf. Bar On (2020). Etymologically the Latin *sors* is also parallel to the Gallic *clar* (lot). Bar-On (2020); Ménager (1987) 112; Chantraine (1968-1980) 542–543. On Accadian *isqu*, see ch. 8, Endnote 4.

their horizon of expectations, implying their awareness of the values of equality and fairness and their connection with drawing lots.

Is fairness proportionate or equal? The question is not new. In the Pirate Code of Henry Morgan (1678 CE) it is considered *fair* that the captain should get more portions of booty than the cook. However, Greeks saw it differently: in the *Iliad*, booty was instead distributed by lot (ch. 1). I do not claim unanimity of thought among the Greeks. Homer's Achilles protests: "Stay at home or fight your hardest—your share will be the same. Coward and hero are given equal honor."[22] However, the protest testifies to an accepted custom. When Odysseus, for example, returns to the men left behind while he was busy at the cave of the Cyclops, he distributes the captured flocks among all his men, both to those who witnessed the harrowing cannibalism at the cave and those who were happily sunbathing while waiting for him.

Fairness and justice are close concepts. Settlers for a new colony, for example, would sail on "equal and like" terms (*isai kai homoiai*), signifying "equal and equitable" or "fair," sometimes even "equal and just" (*dikaios*). It is remarkable how close Greek ideas of justice and fairness were, and how close the notion of fairness was to that of equality.[23] At Athens, in the classical period, the political values of liberty (*eleutheria*) were identified with *isos*-compounds, notably *isokratia* (equal powers), *isegoria* (the right of free speech for every *individual* citizen), and *isogonia*, the claim that all Athenian citizens were originally descendants of a common ancestor, hence equal.[24]

Archaic Greeks were well aware that being equal did not mean being identical. People are simply different in terms of age, wealth, weight, and so on. They found a solution in the formula "equal and like" (*isos kai homoios*), with the latter qualifying the former: equality, but only concerning specific issues, such as civic status. "They shall sail on equal and fair terms [*isai kai homoiai*]" is a formula found in a fourth-century copy of the foundation decree of Cyrene, a point paralleled by Herodotus's account of the episode (ch. 6). The "terms" seem to relate to the *kleros* each settler would receive. The first extant evidence for the collocation (pairing combination) of the two adjectives *isos* and *homoios* is in inscriptions from the classical period. However, its use as a formula seems to go back much earlier: by the time we encounter it, the adjectives have no specific subject (equal and like *what?*). In later periods, it was also the formula for admitting new citizens into a *polis*, followed by *epiklerosis*, a lottery to place them in civic units (see ch. 7). Homer already uses *isos* as an adjective or an adverb in

---

[22] *Il.* 9.318-20; cf. Arist. *Pol.* 2.1267a1-2 who cites Achilles's complaint and states that upper classes are unhappy that the *timai* are *isai*, and the masses complain inequality (*anison*) in distribution.

[23] For modern attitudes to fairness between deserts (equity) and equality, see Rawls (1985): the equality principle is the component of justice as fairness establishing distributive justice.

[24] *Isokratia* Hdt. 5.92.1; See Loraux ([1984] 1993); Hansen (1999) 81–85.

distribution contexts, especially in the formula "so that no-one is deprived of an equal share" (e.g., *Od.* 9.42). The earliest instance of *homoios* appears with the distributive formula *emmore times* that connect "portion/part" with *time* ("honor," "realm of power").[25] Therefore, *isos* and *homoios* appear in our earliest Greek texts as criteria for equal and fair distribution.[26]

7. Equality and the "middle"

Equality is linked in Greek thought with the notion of "the middle." J.-P. Vernant and Marcel Detienne perceive the idea of "the middle" (*to meson*) as a pattern of thought in early philosophy with some concrete expressions.[27] The middle, says Detienne, is equidistant by definition. It is where the "common store" is placed, whence it is distributed (*dasmos es to meson*), "radiating" from the center. The middle validates; it is transparent, public, and open. A public speaker stands there; prizes of competition and booty are "brought to the middle," in the public eye, witnessed by the assembly.

Drawing lots, equal distribution, and the idea of "the middle" seem to be joined in early Greek thought and practice. A collection of early poems (seventh–sixth centuries) attributed to Theognis connects the social order with allotment. It employs the metaphor of the "ship of state" and complains that

> they have deposed the noble helmsman who skilfully kept watch, They seize possessions by force, and discipline (or "order," *kosmos*) is lost; no longer is there an equal distribution in the common interest (literally: "when the sharing out, *dasmos*, is still brought to the middle, *es to meson*, to be shared out equally, *isos*). (trans. Douglas E. Gerber, Loeb-ed.)

The poetic persona of the snobbish Theognis laments the disappearance of the old social distinctions. Theognis is certainly not egalitarian, but he is precisely that concerning his own narrow circle within which equal distribution ought to be the standard. Theognis here is significant for the values implied in *es to meson* and the equal (*isos*) distribution (*dasmos*) within a defined group; an alternative adverbial reading (*isos* instead of the adjective *isos*), "distributing equally" among members of a defined group, signifies the same for our purpose.[28] The point about Theognis's equal *dasmos* is which circle deserves *equal* distribution. In the

---

[25] *Il.* 1.278 : ὁμοίης ἔμμορε τιμῆς. Finkelberg (1998).

[26] Compare the material evidence on the ground dating to the late eighth century for equal demarcation of plots of land (ch. 6).

[27] Vernant ([1963] 1983; 1965a); Detienne (1965).

[28] Theognis 678. Cf. Cerri (1969). Some mss. have *isos* ("equal"), not an adverb (equally" [*isos*]), but the general meaning is the same. Nagy (1985) nn. 8, 9. I thank William Mack for discussing this passage with me. Cf. Borecký (1965) 73; Figueira and Nagy (1985) 112–158. Note Edmond's

cited passage, Theognis complains about the disappearance of clear demarcating lines of inclusion and exclusion when those undeserving "take possessions by force" (*bia*) instead of the "equal distribution." In that sense, it may be comparable to the *symposion*, namely a narrow, elitist, exclusive, snobbish circle among whose members distribution should be equal. It is the very narrow circle's egalitarianism, but it is all the same.

The expression *es to meson* is literally "directed at the center," referring to the communalization of possessions that are marked for orderly distribution by the group/community (see more below).[29] Gerber metaphorically translates *es to meson* as "in the common interest." The expression indeed can work that way. However, within the more comprehensive metaphor used by Theognis for the "ship of state," *es to meson* forms a concrete image: it is that of a concrete convergence of the tangible stuff to be distributed "in the middle [of the ship]." Thus *es to meson* retains its concrete aspects (e.g., bringing gain "to the middle" whence it is distributed by lot; see ch. 1) that overlap with its social image and implications.

The idea of the middle can be politically significant. For example, when Cyrene underwent a reform by Demonax of Mantineia, he transferred power to the people: "to be held by the people in common (literally, "the middle")."[30] Herodotus says that at Samos, Mariandrios attempted to "return power to the people" (literally, "to bring it to the middle," *es to meson*). He did this, says Herodotus, because he thought "people should be *homoioi*," "equal" (i.e., "like" each other concerning their political status, as they had been before the tyranny).[31] The Spartan "equals" (*homoioi*, perhaps better translated as "peers") imagined the origins of their *polis* and its regime in terms of colonization ("a colony, *apoikia*, of the Dorians")[32] and a drawing of lots on a large scale: an initial redistribution by a lot of equal portions of land, *kleroi*, providing the basis for Spartan egalitarianism. When recounting the actions of the semilegendary Spartan lawgiver Lycurgus, Plutarch's words reflect the actual practices of the foundation of new cities. In the *Life of Lycurgus* he says, "He persuaded his fellow citizens to make one parcel of all their territory [the text says "to bring it to the middle, *es meson*"] and divide it up anew (*ex arches*)."[33]

The middle implies a definition of the exclusive contours of the predefined group. the middle, being "middle," is perceived as "equidistant" from all

---

translation (Loeb-ed.): "they seize the cargo perforce; order there is none, and fair division for all is no more." See also Figueira (1985).

[29] Cerri (1969).
[30] Hdt. 4.161.
[31] Hdt. 3.142.3. I thank the anonymous reader for clarification on this.
[32] Pind. *Isthm.* 7.12–15, with Malkin (1994a) ch. 1.
[33] Plut. *Lyc.* 8.1.

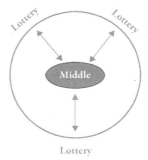

Figure I.1 The Middle. Radiating outward, the Middle "defines" the group from within; the drawing of lots, with a view "inward" toward the Middle, depends on the exclusive predefinition of the relevant group or community.

participants; when the lot is employed, it also implies the equality of chance for those participants. Since participants must be predefined before a distributive lottery, emphasizing equal access implies another aspect of exclusiveness and access. In other words, whereas the drawing of lots defines the community from the circumference, the middle indicates that same circumference. It "observes" the community from a point radiating outward, whereas the drawing of lots does the same in reverse. See figure I.1

8. Mixture lotteries and the egalitarian mindset

Mixture lotteries "reshuffle the deck" of a community. In 508 Cleisthenes refounded Athens by creating ten new tribes (*phylai*) and distributing the citizens by a lot over and among them (ch. 8). Cleisthenes submitted a list of one hundred heroes to the Pythia at Delphi, and she drew lots to select ten eponymous tribal heroes (chs. 2, 8). Such a mixture over and within "tribes" is also a salient feature of new foundations: either a *synoikismos* (a new settlement created through a political merger of existing components) or by founding a new colony *ex nihilo*, mixing Greek settlers of various origins and traditions to align with the organized nucleus of colonists. Mixture lotteries provide yet another horizontal perspective, counterbalancing top-down inclinations. In Cleisthenes's reforms, mere residents became citizens (a one-off application of *ius soli*, not repeated), and citizens from different locations in Attica were shuffled into the new tribes. It was a deliberately complicated and effective system of dissemination. Moreover, with that action, Cleisthenes, in one stroke, cut off many of the traditional, local ties of allegiance, dependency, and patronage.

Cleisthenes did not invent this. Incorporating settlers into "tribes" probably had been going on for two centuries previously (the pattern of three or four tribes is consistent in colonies).[34] Some forty years before his reform, the Delphic oracle directed the conflicting Cyrenaeans to invite Demonax of Mantineia as an arbitrator in their civil strife at Cyrene (ca. 550). He kept the framework of the three tribes (common in Greek-Dorian communities) and "reshuffled" the existing population into the reconfigured three tribes (Herodotus does not report their names).[35] Notably, Diodorus calls him an arbitrator, *diaitetes*, a word that belongs to the semantic field of distribution. We do not know how Demonax allotted citizens to tribes, but a mixture by drawing lots is highly probable.[36] When Aristotle speaks of Cyrene as if the association is self-evident, he proceeds to generalize about the need for mixture: "every device must be employed to make all the people as much as possible *intermingled* with one another, and to *break up* the previously existing groups of associates."[37]

The network theory of "weak and strong ties" further validates those words of Aristotle. Networks of various kinds exist in every society: family and kin-oriented or based on locality and region, cult, commerce, patronage, and so on. Sometimes, discrete networks might undermine, prevent, or even eliminate the cohesiveness of society. What holds a community (or a "nation") together is a much-discussed question I shall avoid;[38] what breaks it up structurally is often more apparent. When personal, sectarian, or local interests predominate, society might fragment into various components. Discrete, specific networks constitute what Mark Granovetter calls "strong ties."[39] Since circles of strong ties are often relatively small, reaching out to them is difficult. A society where mostly strong ties predominate is weak and fragmented. It is instead the "weak ties" (of the type: "someone who knows someone who knows someone") that hold it together. The weak ties exist in a "low-density network" and form a crucial link between the densely knit, discrete clusters of close kin, friends, or dependents. Social systems with strong ties and lacking weak ones, says Granovetter, will be fragmented and incoherent; new ideas will spread slowly, and scientific endeavors will be handicapped. In other words, the "strength of weak ties" may explain how large networks that extend beyond the realm of strong, fragmenting ties can have all-encompassing dynamic connectivity within a society. The mixture type of lot drawing enhances the overarching network of "weak ties."

---

[34] Generally speaking, the *phylai* were "born with the city"; Roussel (1976) 265, 365. Cf. Hölkeskamp (1993) 409–421. Tribal reshuffling did not necessarily imply equality, as the case of Cleisthenes of Sikyon who—privileged one tribe over the others—illustrates. Hdt. 5.68.
[35] Malkin (2023) and section 8.2.2.3 of this volume.
[36] Hdt 4.161; Diod. 8.30.2.
[37] Arist. *Pol.* 1319b, trans. H. Rackham (Loeb-ed.).
[38] See Tamir (2019).
[39] Granovetter (1973; 1983).

INTRODUCTION: GREEKS DRAWING LOTS   19

A mixture by drawing lots works on various levels, sometimes simultaneously: individual families are "internally mixed" when brothers share equitable portions of their inheritance by lot, with no regard for primogeniture. On a communal level, families are also internally mixed when a drawing of lots within each household (*oikos*) sorts out from among brothers, soldiers, or colonists. In all of the above, each son is interchangeable with another. Hence each son is considered equal. War and colonization are communal projects. When a household with more than one son was drawing lots, at the same time, other households were doing the same for a communal purpose that transcended the single *oikos*.

Knowing which household would have more than one son requires a comprehensive community vision, as we shall see with Thera (ch. 6). It follows that the contours of entire communities are defined by identifying the households within them, then distinguishing which households have more than one son. In short, it implies a kind of census. One might wonder how that was possible, but it seems probable that some form of "citizen registries" did exist early on. Moreover, we now know that archaic Greeks had a much higher literacy level than previously thought, based on erroneous Medieval *comparanda*. In the mid-sixth century even shepherds at the outlying reaches of Athens could read and write.[40]

Sectarianism, segmentation, and fragmentation pose a grave danger to any political community, whether ancient or modern. Every society has dividing lines and distinct identities, such as local interests, cults, classes, clans, patronage, and so on. If the dividing lines become too entrenched, priorities change, and "civil strife" might be imminent. The Greek countermeasure, that is, mixing up the entire community through drawing lots, reached beyond such dividing lines. Such lotteries create artificial ties (e.g., Cleisthenes's tribes) that transcend entrenched political and social clusters. A lottery that reshuffles the citizen body bypasses deeply rooted, preexisting lines of separation. It implies an overarching homogenization of society in contrast to deep-seated local positions of power and relations of patronage.

On the one hand, the strong local ties and local power bases have been working at Athens in the direction of fragmentation, as was the case before democracy; on the other hand, by mixing up the citizens, the drawing of lots worked toward homogenization and cohesiveness. Today, perhaps, it is a lesson to remember: identity politics threaten to split modern democracies into smaller and smaller components. At the same time, collective foci, such as "party," "class," or "nation," are being diluted or disappearing altogether. The mixture by lots broke

---

[40] Herders: Langdon (2015); van de Moortel and Langdon (2017). For an eminently convincing study of citizen-registries, see Faraguna (2015). For literacy at Thera ca. 600, see von Gaertringen (1899; 2014).

up or bypassed discrete "strong ties" to make the *polis* a stronger political community, a network with, ideally, no hubs, based on the randomization of the lot.

The mixture by lot was also a device for settling civil strife, as we shall observe in the cases of Herakleia on the Black Sea and Nakone, where external arbitrators forced two quarreling factions to mix up into a more cohesive community by drawing lots. Significantly, at Nakone, the successful mixture was concluded with a newly established cult of Harmony (Homonoia). Therefore, such lotteries function as impersonal arbitrators, with all sides to a conflict agreeing to accept their results in advance. It is a fact (hopefully borne out by this book) that a whole spectrum of lotteries arbitrating results kept appearing in various aspects of life, at least since Greeks were listening to the Homeric epics. Therefore, conducting lotteries and accepting their outcomes became conventions or norms in their own right. With accumulated practices, the authority of the lot was augmented, enhancing a mindset willing to accept randomness as an expression of values and desired (or at least acceptable), nonresentful outcomes.

9. Mixture, equivalence, and interchangeability

The mixture lotteries are yet another illustration of interchangeability, with the immediate implication of each one's equality and discrete individuality.[41] The idea is first apparent in the *Iliad*, where the lot chooses one son out of seven to go fight at Troy.[42] It would be hard to exaggerate the significance of interchangeability since participants are equal with respect to the specific purpose of the lottery, be it selective, distributive, or procedural. The assumption of interchangeability, expressed in the wide spectrum of drawing lots, is perhaps the most significant base for Greek egalitarianism.

One might object to the idea of interchangeability: the existence of property classes at Athens, for example, could argue against it. For instance, when archons (annual chief magistrates) began to be selected by lot (487), they were sorted out from a preselected group drawn only from the top economic class. Yet within that class, all were interchangeable concerning the lot, so the idea was waiting for its extension to other political community members, as it eventually did. Moreover, Solon introduced property as the criterion for "class," allowing for upward or downward economic mobility. Mobility assumes an equal (potential) value for each person without presumption of *inherent* inequality based on "blood."

---

[41] On Greek relational individuality, see Eidinow (2013) esp. at 21–29.
[42] *Il.* 24.399–400, trans. R. Lattimore (1949). The "soldier" is in fact a deity in disguise, but the lie attempts to resemble truth, which is what matters here.

As noted, the extension of egalitarianism also applies to a similar extension with the notion of *isonomia*. The term, which came to denote "democracy," appeared earlier yet was restricted to upper-level circles. Athenian elites celebrated the "tyrant slayers," Harmodios and Aristogeiton, for making "the Athenians" *isonomoi*, apparently referring to themselves.[43] An oligarchy could also be perceived as an *isonomos oligarchia*.[44] By contrast, Cleisthenes extended *isonomia* to incorporate the entire *demos*. In short, equality and interchangeability had been around for a while, arriving at the fullest extension of their political implications under classical democracy. As Josine Blok shows, the more democratic Athens became during the fifth and fourth centuries, the more the dividing lines between those classes blurred, with the ever-widening use of drawing lots and minimizing or abolishing criteria of property for the definition of the "group." Eventually, the entire citizen body would become the predefined group.

10. Did Greeks draw lots to divine the will of the gods?

We are not ancient Greeks and should not make assumptions that too easily bridge the gap between now and then. It is a mistake to have too much intellectual empathy: ancient Greeks did not necessarily think like we do, nor did they share our attitudes and worldviews.[45] However, whereas we may have enormous empathy with Greek "reason," "philosophy," and "theater," drawing lots—the origin of democracy—has been out of our field of vision. Lotteries might seem weird, perhaps distasteful, smacking of the ill repute of gambling. I find that drawing lots is often explained away as "religion," as if religion was an answer instead of a question. Paradoxically, some admirers of Greek rationality, perhaps uneasy with all those lotteries (especially at Athens, that "city of reason" of Jean-Pierre Vernant), try to save ancient Greek rationality by claiming that Greeks drew lots *irrationally* as a tool for divination in many areas of life. However, Greeks did not live like Luke Reinhard's *Dice Man* or Borges's *Babylonian Lottery*.[46] Let me be

---

[43] Ath. Deipn. 15.50 = *Carmina convivialia* (Page 1962 *Poetae Melici Graeci*) frs. 9–12.

[44] Thuc. 3.62.3. "Thucydides's oligarchic Thebans . . . emphasize their distance from tyranny and *dunasteia*, applying to their *oligarchia* a concept normally associated with democracy in the fifth century, *isonomia* or "equality under the law." Simonton (2017) 77; cf. Ostwald (2000) 25.

[45] Cornford (1991) 1–72; cf. Murray (1990); (1996); Detienne (2007).

[46] Luke Reinhart (George Cockroft) (1971). Jorge Louis Borges's *The Lottery at Babylon* ([1941] 2015) comes to mind, except that its framework is the sale of lottery tickets. Cf. "Plato (*Rep.* 10.604c) . . . compared life to a game of dice, in which we must try, not only to throw what suits us best, but also, when we have thrown, to make good use of whatever turns up." Cf. Plut. *On Tranquility of Mind* 467a; Terence *Adelphoi* 6.737–741.

clear: Those ancient, rational Greeks made a rational decision to apply a *random* device to so many aspects of their lives, and reasonably so.[47]

There is a difference, however: with the Dice Man, who lets the dice throw determine his choices, it is the blind chance that rules his life, and the view of the lot is more akin to certain late Hellenistic notions of blind Tyche or Roman Fortuna. On the other hand, divine will and intention are another matter, even if the relation between the Olympians and *moira* seems ambiguous (ch. 2.9) However, Greeks did not spend their lives following paths in the dark forest of determinism, even when they used lot oracles explicitly for divination. To anticipate my conclusion: depending on the specific context of the use of the lot, the gods were "present" on a *spectrum* from a mere invocation or prayer (in most cases) to expressing their direct will through the medium of the lot oracle. This is not a question of religion versus secularism since the gods were never absent for Greeks. Let me clarify my position: On one end of the spectrum, we find "lot oracles," the explicit purpose of which was precisely to divine the gods' will. On the other end of the spectrum, the gods remain in the background, and the drawing of lots could occur "under their auspices" without expecting divine intervention. The gods may preside over any public procedure, but they do not decide its outcome. The *decision* to draw lots never followed divination: no god ordered anyone to draw lots. The decision to do so depended on the *sovereign* "group." In myth, which is a human projection (see below), the Olympian gods distribute realms of power among them: clearly, the purpose of *their* lottery was *not* to divine the will of yet other gods. I return to this issue later.

It is curious how modern ancient Greeks become when we want them to be (they knew the earth was round) yet how alien when we prefer to gaze at those "dark shadows" behind the bright stage that so attracted Jane Ellen Harrison of the Cambridge School. One suspects that some of those attitudes stem from the legacy of Christian morality. Christian thinkers often considered all lotteries a type of divination;[48] since God directs everything, the lottery is a device for making God speak.[49] However, because of that, says Thomas Aquinas,[50] lots should be employed as a last resort, and Protestant thinkers objected to the casual summons of God. Today we may suspect lotteries of trivializing matters, but medieval thinking warned against the opposite: its use for trivial questions. That is also one of the reasons why chance games were regarded as blasphemous.

---

[47] Not all Greeks were happy with the idea of randomness. Leucippus claimed that "Nothing happens at random; everything happens out of reason and by necessity." Leucippus (fr. 67.B.2 Diels and Kranz (1956). In general, Greeks had no theory of probability; Bennett (1998) Kindle location 598.
[48] Duxbury (1999) 16–23; Demont (2020).
[49] David (1962) 13–20 (referring to the sentence above).
[50] *Summa Theologiae* II.ii.95.8; cf. Aquinas (1963) and see ch. 1.

However, in 1627 Thomas Gataker published his *On the Nature and the Use of Lots: A Treatise Historicall and Theologicall*, where he argues against the idea that the will of God is expressed by the lot and therefore denies it the aspect of divination.[51] Lots, after all, produce unexpected and contrary results every time and thus cannot be identified with God, he claims, unless we suspect God to be as capricious as the dice. The point is famously echoed in Einstein's dictum that "God does not play dice with the universe." Says Gataker, "Is it not frivolous, if not impious, therefore to say, that upon every second shaking or drawing God alters his sentence ... and so to charge him with contradiction or contrariety."[52]

Ancient Judaism had no problem with drawing lots. A fascinating study by Shraga Bar-On on the use of the lot in ancient and medieval Judaism traces its various usages in the Old Testament up to the medieval sages. The scope of its application was surprisingly broad, although negative attitudes became more explicit in later Judaism. For example, in the Old Testament, the Hebrew tribes were assigned their lands by lot; the lot was used to flush out both the criminal Achan (who took unsanctioned booty, Joshua 7) and the prophet Jonah (Jonah 1:7), Saul, Israel's first king, was also chosen by lot (1 Samuel 10). Note, too, that one of the twelve apostles, Matthew, was chosen by lot to replace Judas (Acts 1:17, 26). Other ancient societies, such as the Hittites, used the lot too, but nowhere was its application so wide-ranging and ubiquitous as it was among ancient Greeks.[53]

The best place to observe a mindset is myth, which also reveals the limits of the imagination. Greek myths about the powers of the gods demonstrate the horizontal aspect of drawing lots with not even a hint of employing lots to seek external, top-down authority. When the gods decide to hold a lottery and abide by its outcome, it is their own decision. It emanates from the participants who are, in that sense, sovereign, as would be the case among historical Greeks. Greeks did not have a transcendent God as a subject for whom the world was an object. The Olympians (third-generation divinities) did not create the world; they were born into it and won their supremacy by violent revolution. The *Iliad* tells us how Hades, Zeus, and Poseidon drew lots: Zeus got heaven; Hades, the underworld; and Poseidon, the sea. It is absurd to imagine that these three Olympian deities were conducting a lottery to "reveal the will of the gods" since they were the gods. As with most selective, distributive, and procedural lotteries—that is, human lotteries—the three brothers were the "sovereign group" to decide on the

---

[51] See the excellent and detailed discussion by Demont (2020).

[52] Quoted by Duxbury (1999) 21, from Gataker (1627) 159. For a thorough discussion of Gataker and its relevance to the ancient Greek context, see Demont (2020), quoting Gataker: "the casualty of an event does not simply of itself make it a work of God's special or immediate providence."

[53] Bar-On (2020); cf. Londblom (1962); Taggar-Cohen (2002); Champeaux (1990); Hurlet (2017). Roman sortition: Hurlet (2019) cf. Johnston (2003).

drawing of lots, conduct it, and abide by its decision, which became equivalent to their own.

Zeus was undoubtedly the king of the gods, a position to which the other Olympian gods chose him, says Hesiod; by contrast, he got his own specific realm, the sky, by lot. Hesiod and the Homeric Hymns mention more divine lotteries and sometimes not Zeus alone, but "the gods" become the agents of distribution: the group distributes to itself, while Zeus presides but does not determine the result. We shall note that the appropriate verb for such distribution, *dateomai*, usually appears in the middle voice plural, denoting a distribution by the group of participants to its members.

Despite the Greek world's geographical, ethnic, and linguistic fragmentation, the *Iliad* and the *Odyssey* were common to all Greeks. I feel safe to assume that the epics reflected attitudes and values (sometimes "distanced" on purpose to a heroic past) that were current or, at least, familiar in the eighth and seventh centuries. A common argument in Homeric scholarship is that the memory of "things" (e.g., a boar-tusk helmet) may have been floating down the river of oral poetry for centuries, whereas terminology, values, and attitudes needed to conform to contemporary audiences of the early archaic period (eighth and seventh centuries) to be understood. In short, in terms of an archaic Greek frame of reference, the Homeric epics provide significant evidence.[54] The epic poems alluded to well-known myths, shaping them into a common reference point.

Homer's myth of the Olympian distribution (*Il*. 15. 185-210) encapsulates the vocabulary, practice, purpose, and values of human lotteries. The entire set will prove consistent and frequent throughout archaic and classical Greek history. Remarkably, the Homeric myth also expresses the tension between egalitarianism and authority: Poseidon has an equal share (*isomoron*) but not equal power. We shall observe a common Homeric expression, *emmore times*, that combines the notion of "portion" (*meros*) and "honor" *time* in the sense of a realm of authority, domain, or "honor"). *Time* expresses a *distributive* value.[55]

So, when did the gods express their will via lots? In my view, a discrete category of divination through lot oracles (ch. 2) distinguishes it from distributive, selective, procedural, and mixture lotteries. However, views expressed around one century ago that still prevail saw all uses of the lot as the expression of the "will of the gods." This view was supported from different angles (with some circular presuppositions) by Numa-Denis Fustel de Coulanges (1864; 1891), followed by Gustav Glotz (1907) and Victor Ehrenberg (1927). Headlam (1891), on the other hand, was on the secularist side. The discourse, however, has been limited: since the nineteenth century, the discussion has been about Athenian

---

[54] Malkin (1998) 259–273 for my position on Homeric issues.
[55] Finkelberg (1998) 15 with n. 1. Distributive value: "he/she has been allotted a *time*."

politics, although the latter is a late addition to centuries of the previous, wide-ranging uses of the lot.[56] In short, we should not turn to the Greek gods to block our thinking.

In sum, we cannot be sure how precisely Greeks understood the gods' involvement in drawing lots, except to assess degrees on the spectrum. As Josine Blok demonstrates (ch. 8), the gods' involvement becomes somewhat more explicit in the choice of priests by lot. The distinction between drawing lots for divination and its "civic" uses is apparent, as we shall see, even at Delphi, Apollo's famous sanctuary and oracle: aside from drawing lots for divination, Delphians were drawing lots for turns for inquiry with the Pythia, Delphic personnel was selected by lot, and in myth (Aeschylus), the oracle kept changing hands among several gods by lot. Apollo is its most recent possessor.

In a Greek world "full of gods,"[57] there was no clear distinction between secular and religious spheres. Whereas at one end of the spectrum, the explicit purpose of divination-by-lot was to reveal the will of the gods, at the other end, the annual selection by lot of six thousand judges at Athens and the daily procedural lotteries for selecting *ad hoc* panels from among them, and then to assign them by lot to court cases, was on what *we* would call the "secular" end of the spectrum, with the gods merely "invoked." There is no point in introducing a dichotomy in the form of a secular category where it never existed. The gods were "present" in all public affairs that were always conducted under their auspices; however, such matters were not subject to constant, active divine intervention.

What about *moira*? One might argue that the notion of *moira* in the sense of fate or destiny points to a divine determination of the results of drawing lots. However, the only divinity perceived by ancient Greeks as directly involved with drawing lots, the goddess who also assures the commitment to follow the result, is the goddess Lachesis, one of the three *moirai*-goddesses. Her very name signifies a "goddess of casting lots" (the verb related to her name is *lanchano*, "to get by lot"). However, she neither determines nor intervenes in the results but witnesses the procedure. A discussion of *moira* follows in a separate section of chapter 2. I shall lay stress on the overlap between concrete and metaphoric "portions" (*moirai*), the related semantic fields of *aisa* (an equivalent concept), and the implications for social values of distribution, fairness (*kata moiran*), and equality. "Portion," I argue, is a critical term in archaic Greek thought and practice. Greeks concretely and metaphorically expressed it as *moira*, *aisa*, or *meros*. The distribution and allotment (*dateomai*, *nemein*) of equal portions by drawing

---

[56] Recently, Paul Demont (2020) has also expressed a general, vague notion of the role of the gods as being somehow in the background, which I find unhelpful, as noted earlier: the statement is always true, yet unless specifically qualified is of little significance.

[57] "Some think that the soul pervades the whole universe, whence perhaps came Thales's view that everything is full of gods." Arist. *De An.* 411a7–8 = DK 11 fr. A22.

lots overlap with notions of fairness and equality. The use of those terms across a comprehensive spectrum, from the family to the community, confirms the expression of the mindset of egalitarianism, which was often at odds with the competing vector of elitism.

11. The lot and democracy, ancient and modern

Today it would be hard to imagine that a state lottery could determine the order of your day. This happened in the flourishing Athenian democracy, characterized by Herodotus as a regime where "The rule of the people has in the first place the loveliest name of all, *isonomia* ['equality before the law'; the term 'democracy' came later].... *It determines offices by lot*, and holds power accountable, and conducts all deliberating publicly" (Hdt. 3.80.6). The inception of their democracy (508) was marked by extensive use of the lot to mix and reform the citizen body. In the next two centuries, the Athenians kept extending the use of the lot for governance and allotment for offices, as well as expanding the circle of participants until they eventually included the entire *demos*. By Aristotle's time, except for a limited number of elected positions, most governance was run by lot, from specific citizen boards responsible, for example, for the docks of the Piraeus, all the way to priests, the council (*boule*) members, and even the state ministers (archons). We need to remember, however, that the sovereign body to enact laws was not a citizen body drawn by lot but the citizen assembly, the membership of which was universal (ch. 7). Aside from the *mixture* and homogenization of the citizen body and *selective* lotteries and allotment for office, *procedural* lotteries determined order and rotation: for example, assigning fields of operation to generals by lot, or determining office rotation. For example, by the fourth century, the chair of the council would be replaced daily by lot.

In what sense was the drawing of lots democratic?[58] On the one hand, at least in the way the Athenians practiced it, its democratic aspects were enhanced because of the constant, rotating mixture of citizens that kept "arching" over sectionalism and particular interest while encouraging citizen engagement with equal chances for sharing in the community. Drawing lots was cheap, efficient, quick, and decisive. On the other hand, it was democratic because drawing lots would prevent resentment *ad hominem*. It was also an excellent device against undue influence, bribery, corruption, lobbying, sectarian or local interests, and even the emergence of political parties in the modern sense. Take lobbies, for example: Because of the large numbers involved and frequent rotation, it would have been close to impossible, as it is today, to invest in long-term influence.

[58] See also below, ch. 9 and *Envoi*.

There would have been no point in forming any lobby—that bane of modern democratic politics—in the first place.

Conversely, elections were a different matter, and influential and affluent Athenians vied for the few remaining elected posts, notably the *strategoi* (a body of ten generals). To illustrate, Claire Taylor has brilliantly shown that elected persons came from the wealthiest quarters of Athens (i.e., personal influence). In contrast, those selected for office by lot hailed from all over Attica (i.e., a more democratic cross-section of the entire political community).[59] The lottery, implying constant mixture and rotation in the allotment for offices, worked against the emergence of the entrenched elite of the rich and powerful exercising power, either officially or behind the scenes, through networks of dependents. By the later fourth century, the institution of drawing lots in governance at Athens and elsewhere reached its fullest, comprehensive application (ch. 8).

Today, some suggest reintroducing the lot to modern politics, often referring to the ancient Athenian example. However, it would be a mistake to consider drawing lots as only a *mechanism* that improves efficiency, enhances stability, prevents corruption and lobbying, and enlarges public participation. One purpose of this book is to understand better the practical and mental world involving the use of the lot and perhaps call for adopting not just the mechanism but also the Greek horizontal mindset and the implied values. Those include public engagement, equality, fairness, and the prevention of implied opposites: apathy, unfair advantage at the starting points of wealth and status, party-backing, and political deals.

What about elections, an institution many would regard as defining democracy? In elections, one elects "representatives" who would be the "best men" to do the job, as Thomas Jefferson thought. He believed in the natural existence of "best men" and wrote to John Adams about "a pure selection of these natural *aristoi* into the offices of government."[60] In ancient Greek, the "rule of the best" spells "aristocracy," *aristokratia*. So instead of a top-down rule of kings in the grace of God, we now have a top-down power by elected officials (for fixed terms), drawing their authority from "the people." However, the vertical direction, top-down, has remained the same since the time of the pharaohs. As Bernard Manin has shown, both the French and the American Revolutions preferred elections to the equality of democracy: "Representative government was instituted in full awareness that elected representatives should be distinguished citizens, socially different from the ones who elected them."[61] By contrast, Aristotle thought

---

[59] Taylor (2007).
[60] A letter to John Adams, Monticello, October 28, 1813, http://www.let.rug.nl/usa/presidents/thomas-jefferson/letters-of-thomas-jefferson/jefl223.php. It is remarkably similar to the speech of Magbyzos in Herodotus 3.81 that extols oligarchy: to "pick out a company [*homilie*] of the best [*aristoi*] men and hand over power [*kratos*] to them."
[61] Manin (1997). Quoted and translated by van Reybrouck (2016) 62. See also below, ch. 9.

there should be no distance: political freedom consisted of governing and being governed in turn. Instead of the top-down approach, using the lot in politics implies a horizontal view of society with constant rotations, governance truly by the people, and involving all citizens who are the source of power and sovereignty. The people's assembly, the sovereign body to enact laws, was neither elected nor selected by lot.[62] It was supposedly comprehensive. Nobody summed it up better than Aristotle: elections are the salient feature of oligarchies, he says, whereas democracies are based on drawing lots.[63]

Democratic Athens kept extending the use of the lot, administering the state efficiently in this way for about two centuries before outsiders curtailed the system. Should we follow its example and reintroduce the lot into politics? Drawing lots would undoubtedly be an excellent tool to increase "sharing in the *polis.*" Some current thinkers, mainly with a political science orientation, recommend precisely that, pointing out the obvious advantages of using the lot as a corrective mechanism of the system.[64] Suggestions range from revising the existing political mechanisms to introducing new buffering organs into politics. Citizen assemblies or committees chosen by lot, for example, could function as a buffer between politicians and the public.[65] Nobody has proven that large numbers of intelligent people are any less efficient than problem-solving by a few "best and brightest." The latter can hardly be charged with cognitive diversity, which is what groups of large numbers of citizens selected by lot may demonstrate, if only because they would be diversely composed.

The lot does not select according to merit or expertise, a sore point of criticism already in antiquity. Socrates objected to the use of the lot, saying he would prefer a professional captain of a ship rather than a captain chosen by lot.[66] Wrong, would reply most Athenians; governance (with some exceptions such as elected *strategoi*) must be in the hands of the nonprofessionals, who would be the ones in charge of the expert captain or navigator.

The criticism, often justified, against drawing lots for governance concerns inefficiency, lack of professionalism, and lack of long-term planning. We may need to consider combining the lot with elections, as the Athenians and several thinkers today have suggested. I am not a political scientist and would

---

[62] There were areas of overlap, e.g., the Athenian *boule*, the council selected by lot, which also prepared proposals for the assembly. Here I am drawing basic distinguishing lines. See Rhodes (1972).
[63] Arist. *Pol.* 4.1294b–e. But for nuance of this statement, see below, ch. 8.
[64] See, e.g., https://www.sortitionfoundation.org/; cf. Sintomer and Lopez-Rabatel (2020).
[65] See, e.g., van Reybrouck (2016); https://www.sortitionfoundation.org/. No such buffer had existed with the British Brexit (52 percent voted to leave the European Union, many admitting to ignorance), whereas the two Irish referenda of 2015 and 2018 that permitted same-sex marriages and abortions had been prepared by citizen-committees chosen by lot that informed and involved the public, with the astonishing result for Catholic Ireland of almost 70 percent in favor in both referenda.
[66] Xen. *Mem.* 1.29.

hesitate to provide specific recipes. Drawing lots is more than just a mechanism. Whatever our thoughts on the matter may be, we should take note of the egalitarian mindset and values that concern the "equal and like" portion of a citizen as articulated by the ancient Greeks. It would behoove us to remember those who created the first democracy, especially the mindset that led to its birth: The ancient Greek frame of reference with its egalitarian values and the idea of citizens as *sharers* that made the ancient democracy possible. The lack of such values today might disintegrate our own.

12. Contents and contours: Parts I and II

Chapter 1 discusses the drawing of lots in the Homeric epics and Hesiod's poetry, emphasizing distributive, selective, and procedural lotteries among gods and humans. The lot-related vocabulary reveals the salient features of drawing lots and implied egalitarian values. Homer and Hesiod represent the gods as a sovereign group that decides to draw lots, sometimes with Zeus presiding over the procedure, to distribute realms of power and "honors" (*timai*). No authority external to the "group" is ever imagined, thus expressing a horizontal mindset and values of equal chances.

The parallelism with the poetic representation of how human beings draw lots is striking. It is most evidenced in the distribution of booty by lot, often expressed with a plural form of the verb of distribution (*dateomai*) in the middle voice (i.e., a group distributing to itself). I argue against top-down distribution and stress the role of the community or army that gives a *geras* (honorary gift) to the leaders in the field or land (*temenos*) back home. Aside from the *geras* and private booty (classified as *enara*), booty is brought to the "middle" (*to meson*), whence it is distributed by lot to all, including the leaders. I place a particular emphasis on the meaning of the drawing of lots (*lanchano*) and values of equality (e.g., *ep'ises*).

Procedural lotteries appear self-evident, as they also function in current sports events,[67] such as drawing lots for positions in a chariot race or establishing turns by lot in an arrow-shooting context. Selective lotteries relate to both heroes, such as Aias (lots shaken in a helmet), and ordinary soldiers, such as companions of Odysseus selected by lot to spy on the land or blind the Cyclops. Selective lotteries also appear within individual families, such as a soldier (Hermes in disguise), chosen by lot from among his brothers to go to war, similar to how colonists (ch. 6) could be selected by lot from households with more than one son.

---

[67] See Ajootian (2007). Since the procedural use of the lot in sports is quite similar to its use today, I shall not be discussing it in depth. For the role of the lot in ancient sports, see Mann (2017).

Soldiers are more precisely "companions" (*hetairoi*) who seem to be equal among themselves and receive *equal portions* by lot. When capturing booty as pirates (*leisteres*), Odysseus's companions follow a code of equal sharing. Sharing and equal distribution, I argue, was a salient feature of archaic Greek society (sometimes directly confronting opposite claims for elite privileges). Ever since Homer, we may observe that any member of the group/community/army was counted individually and deserved a share or a "portion" of some "whole."

Chapter 2 discusses the role of the gods. As an institution, lotteries deserved their particular gods, notably the *moira* Lachesis (her name derives from *lanchano*, "to get by lot")[68] and the god Hermes, yet neither determined results. However, aside from those divinities, did Greeks draw lots to divine the will of the gods? Some studies, few as they are, take it as self-evident that they did. The issue further affects the horizontal mindset and Greek attitudes toward equal chances and equality. For example, in selective lotteries, all participants are presumed equivalent and interchangeable, but not if the gods intervene. Suppose the god selects according to some unequal merit that escapes the human eye; that would imply that drawing lots is a way to ask the gods who are *unequal*.[69]

I arrive at the opposite conclusion. However, caution is due: religious implications probably varied according to context (e.g., the selection of priests by lot, ch. 7), and various Greeks may have seen things differently.[70] However, I argue that although Greek gods were always present in the background, and although Greeks often *invoked* them, they did not decide the outcomes of lotteries.

Greeks did expect divine determination of outcomes within a discrete category of lot oracles. Even then, the decision to use the lot to address an inquiry to the god and formulate the question itself (expecting a yes/no reply) depended on the human inquirer. Both inspired prophecies (e.g., the Pythia at Delphi), and oracles by lot were considered as if coming from a god, as I note in the discussion of Apollo, Hermes, and Zeus. For example, the Pythia at Delphi is known for her inspired prophecies, but sometimes she seems to have "picked up the lot" (literally *anhairein*, also meaning "to prophesy"). Other forms of lot oracles existed, such as the "oracle by the two beans." The discussion then moves to Zeus's oracle at Dodona, where to date have been discovered some four thousand small tin tablets with individually inscribed private inquiries, ranging in questions such as, "Is that my son?" and "Should I join a colony?"

In contrast to fixed occasions and appointed times, a mindset's actual "test" is its practical application in *ad hoc*, frequent, or unexpected circumstances. How frequently did Greeks use the lot? Chapter 3 discusses the distribution by drawing

---

[68] Cf. *kleros.org.il* s.v.
[69] I thank Josine Blok for illuminating this issue.
[70] Cf. Cicero *de Div.* ii.85–87 with Grotanelli (2005) at 131.

lots of portions in a sacrifice. Many sacrifices were conducted on appointed days, but there were *ad hoc* occasions, such as feasts or funerals. Someone's death, for example, would necessitate the instant implementation of whole sets of rituals and customs, such as the distribution of inheritance by lot (chapter 4). Far from being exceptional, drawing lots was interlaced with practices and values that both shaped and expressed the archaic Greek mindset. Its frequency and ubiquity (the evidence for similar patterns of sacrifice ranges from the Black Sea to the western Mediterranean) reaffirm the mindset as "Greek." Dialects, subethnic identities, and the existence of over one thousand *poleis* spread over vast geographical horizons distinguished Greeks among themselves. It is all the more remarkable to find distinct commonalities of values (equality and fairness) and practice (drawing lots).[71]

The vocabulary of meat distribution is relational—that is, one's portion is equal to another's within the relevant circle. Whether at the banquet or the sacrifice, distribution, so I shall argue, follows the same guidelines that we observe in the distribution of booty or land (chs. 1, 4, and 6): striving to distribute the "whole" into equal portions to a predefined group. Sometimes Greeks reserved a choice portion (*geras*) to a king, such as the mythical Oedipus (or the historical kings of Sparta) or the officiating priests. Otherwise, meat was divided into equal portions and distributed (sometimes we hear about it explicitly) by lot.[72]

Equality, again, is apparent in various stages: we note it as equality of chance; we observe it when an animal is chosen by lot from a herd for sacrifice; we see it in the results of the distributive lottery, namely, the portion, roasted (weights were discovered in sanctuaries) or cooked, distributed in equally sized bowls. *Isomoiria*, the equality of "parts," or portions,[73] expresses both the equality of chance and the equally resulting portions. The distribution of portions is relational (one portion compared to another) and horizontal; it does not follow notions of hierarchical, "top-down" dissemination. It is, in other words, "fair."

In Greek antiquity, sharing in the community, or "citizenship," was articulated not in terms of political rights (e.g., the right to vote) but by access to and sharing in a cult. The gods may have been universal, but not the city cults, usually forbidden to foreigners. At the public sacrifices, sharing in the community was concretely expressed by the distribution of equal portions by lot (exceptions aside) while keeping up the covenant with the gods.

Not everyone gets to share in war booty, colonial lands, or a portion of meat at the "equal banquet" or the sacrifice. However, everyone dies. Death does not depend on appointed days; it is frequent and ubiquitous. Following death, an

---

[71] For networks of commonalities Malkin (2011).
[72] I shall mention cases where specific circles of participants (within which distribution was equal) were unequal to others.
[73] See ch. 6, Endnote 2 on *isomoiria*.

inheritance would often become "partible inheritance by lot" (ch. 4). In partible inheritance by lot, we may observe both equal, "blind" chances and the expression of personal choice. A simplistic scheme for distributing inheritance by lot would go as follows: The inheritance (the estate) is split into equal or equitable parts, either agreed upon in advance by the brothers or through arbitration. Drawing lots then takes place to determine which of the brothers can declare his preference. This procedure was not merely a legal issue but integral to the Greek mindset. For example, the tragic plot of Aeschylus's *Seven against Thebes* revolves around the refusal of a brother to respect the terms of the lot. In chapter 5, I discuss inheritance-by-lot and other types of drawing lots on the Athenian stage.

Equality and fairness stand in the foreground: since inheritance is not dependent on inherent seniority (no primogeniture), all legitimate brothers were equal and interchangeable before the lot. The practice is consistent with ideas of conscription by lot, either for war or colonization. At Athens (ch. 8), Josine Blok studies the drawing of lots within a *genos* to select priests. Partible inheritance seems to have encouraged colonization: instead of, say, two brothers splitting up a *kleros* (plot of land) at home, each brother would now get a whole *kleros*, one at home, the other in a colony. Moreover, partible inheritance by lot would also encourage "secondary colonization." When a colony became a mother city, the same dynamics of splitting the inheritance into smaller units probably drove young men to establish more and more new settlements.

The overlap of "land issues" between practices of inheritance and colonization is remarkable, especially in cases when drawing lots determines turns for declaring preferences. With no primogeniture, partible inheritance by lot is a "fractal" of the entire *polis*: the "group" is predefined; all of its members have "shares"; an arbitrator may help resolve a dispute about family inheritance or resolve civil strife; there is no innate hierarchy; all "group" members are interchangeable, and sovereignty and authority stem from within the group, not from the gods nor destiny. The heir (or the settler, ch. 6) got a *moira* (portion) of the inheritance, but it was not his *moira* (destiny) to choose it.

Greek drama provides excellent evidence for the place of the lot in the Greek mindset. The themes and conventions of drawing lots must have been familiar to tens of thousands of Athenians sitting in the theater, relying on a shared mental frame of reference, as we discuss in chapter 5. In Greek drama, the vocabulary of drawing lots is consistInt. It moves between the concrete and the metaphoric, playing with overlapping meanings of *lanchano, kleros, epiballo, palos, potmos,* and some *moira*-related words. The playwrights used drawing lots as a narrative device, an idiom, and a poetic metaphor. An entire spectrum of the use of the lot is present on the Athenian stage. Does the drawing of lots for selection empty the meaning of personal choice? For example, becoming aware that she is about to be sacrificed "for the sake of Hellas," Iphigeneia rejects the alternative suggested by the herald: to draw lots among the sisters. In Euripides's *Trojan Women*, each captive woman is assigned by lot to some hero (a kind of distributive lot-drawing).

Inheritance issues and *procedural* lot drawing, especially "*pairing lots*," play a prominent role in Stesichoros and Aeschylus's *Seven*, where the main problem is the violation of the inheritance agreement between the sons of Oedipus. Whereas the besiegers of Thebes draw lots to pair the seven heroes with the seven gates of Thebes, the autocratic ruler of Thebes assigns them. Here I follow Paul Demont's brilliant observation that the allocation of gates by lot is "democratic" in contrast to posting them by the ruler in Thebes as a mark of tyranny.[74] This distinction corresponds to the difference between top-down and horizontal authority that draws its legitimacy from the mutually recognized, relational context.

Chapter 6, a substantial section, discusses the foundation of new settlements. The practice, the values, and the vocabulary of drawing lots are consistent in areas that used to be studied discretely. However, they shed light on each other in a way that justifies the removal of certain *a priori* notions regarding specific fields. Equality of chance and equality of "portions" appear the same in various domains. In particular, land ownership has mainly been studied regarding law and property, especially regarding inheritance. However, unlike disagreements among historians and archaeologists about the distribution of equal plots of land in Greek colonies, the existence of "partible inheritance by lot" (with equal or equitable portions) is mostly uncontroversial. However, I shall point out that inheritance and colonization are connected with overlapping practices and values. Greek colonization was a significant historical phenomenon: I *poleis* founded between 750 and 500 constituted about a third of all known *poleis*.

In chapter 6, perhaps the most wide-ranging and complicated one in Parts I and II of this book, I discuss the distribution of equal portions of land to the new settlers by drawing lots. Many men who went to settle overseas were the brothers of those left behind. Both must have been aware of the practices and values attached to equal distribution of plots of land by lot. In both partible inheritance at home and allotment of *kleroi* overseas, we observe marking equal portions of land in advance and their distribution by lot.

By the late eighth century, a clear preference emerged for a single household over a single *kleros*, and colonization was a solution when there was more than one heir. With the vast number of new settlements, a Small-World phenomenon of sharing similar experiences and facing similar issues resulted in the emergence of commonalities of value and practice.[75] Moreover, since portions would also get halved in colonies, that probably stimulated colonies to become *metropoleis* and provide new *kleroi* in newer settlements. Sicilian tyrants often followed

---

[74] Demont (2000).
[75] Malkin (2011).

the same conventions in their refoundations of cities (with notable exceptions of abuse). Allotment of *kleroi* fit the general interests of the *polis*: possessors of *kleroi* were fighting men. Some ancient thinkers explicitly stated that the number of households (*oikoi*) and the number of *kleroi* ought to be the same.

There is yet another parallelism: Conquered land constituted "permanent booty," and its distribution, I argue, conformed to other modes of distributive lotteries. The pattern is consistent in all historical and imaginary sources: Greeks were settling an empty land (usually made vacant by expulsion, *eremos chora*) and allotting plots equally, by lot. Although variations, abuse, and even contradictions are apparent on the ground, that schematic blueprint seems to have existed in the heads of most Greek colonists, and we have some archaeological evidence to confirm it.

One purpose of analyzing what Greeks had to say about such matters is to observe the limits of the historical imagination: we never hear (tyrants excepted) of top-down distributions by founders, nor was there a special status for leaders and elites. The posterity of *oikistai* (founders) never enjoyed special status.[76] Such inequality was outside the frame of reference of Greek writers of myth, history, and political philosophy. Egalitarianism was expressed in equal portions distributed by lot, and no alternative distribution criteria are ever mentioned.

Ancient sources mention an initial distribution to all settlers consisting of equal "first lots" (*protoi kleroi*) that should be inalienable. "Plots by lots" were allotted (*nemein*); the privileged status of the *protoi/palaioi kleroi* ("the first" or "the old plots"), or *archaia moira*, (the ancient portions) were a discrete category of minimum holding for an individual (not the upper limit). They expressed an equal share in the community. Otherwise, settlers could be unequal, bringing unequal money and equipment (*chremata*). Within two generations, we often observe growing inequality and the emergence of economic elites.

I shall maintain that equality in Greek colonies was not an ideology but a convention, an expression of a mindset. It was a legacy of equal sharing of both booty and inheritance. When Odysseus distributes sheep by lot, he gets a *geras*, an extra ram (which he then sacrifices and shares with his *hetairoi*). In colonies, the *geras* disappears, and the "pirate code" of Odysseus's companions is transformed into a more formal and concrete equal division of land-booty to colonists (who were, at some cases, themselves chosen by lot in the mother city). Colonists initially expected to "sail on equal and like/fair terms," with each hoping to set up a household (*oikos*) on his equal *kleros*. However, there was a contradictory vector: economic and social differentiation was a common feature of inequality that went against the grain of the egalitarian mindset. Some scholars

---

[76] Contrast Rome, where we find unequal, status-based distribution of *iugera*. App. *Reg.* 123; Plut. *Publ.* 21.6 [6]; cf. Gras (2019/21) 14.

argue against the notion of absolute equality, a futile exercise. Greeks were not founding socialist kibbutzim: it was never their idea to have communities based on *absolute* equality.

Therefore, apparent archaeological contradictions that suggest material inequality are of little relevance, especially when they relate to long periods of land use (endnote 4). Egalitarianism and equality are not synonyms: aside from the "first lots," there was no cap on acquiring wealth and more land, and material inequality was already apparent, especially in the second and third generations. Perhaps the drive to found yet new "colonies of colonies" was the need of a younger generation to claim for itself the same horizon of expectation as their grandparents had.

Equal distribution of first lots by drawing lots was also a *mixture* lottery since "whoever wished" (*ho boulomenos*) could join an organized foundation and thus co-opt into, say, a "Chalkidian" colony.[77] For example, Thasos became "Thasos" when "all the misery of Greeks" joined the initial foundation, as Archilochos (seventh century) complains. Moreover, later evidence suggests that settlers were assigned to "tribes"—that is, joining the civic body, also by lot. Drawing lots, therefore, contributed to the cohesiveness of the new settlement.

In my view, we should not look for an "aristocracy" in most Greek foundations. Single-named founders, not "elite groups," founded Greek colonies. Homer, for example, sings of Nausithoos, who led a migration, founded (Scheria) Phaiakia, became its king, received a special landed estate, and established a royal dynasty. By contrast, while the *hetairoi* of a historical founder were equal, the founder's exceptional status ended with his death, and his posterity had no special distinction. After his death, the *oikistes* was elevated to heroic status with which no one could compare.[78] The emphasis shifting from the Homeric captains to the historical companions is yet another expression of the tension between egalitarianism and elitism, indicating the shifting pendulum between the vertical and horizontal vectors.[79]

In both archaic (the eighth through the sixth centuries) and classical colonization (fifth and fourth centuries), we can observe various types of grid planning with equal plots that seem to conform to the idea of "equal and fair terms." However, grid planning is not inherently "democratic," and I note several examples from other historical periods that illustrate that. However, I argue that in Greek colonies, such as Megara Hyblaia in Sicily, the grid does imply egalitarianism. Some have tried to go further and with the formula grid = democracy. And since "democracy" is easy to refute, the "democracy straw man" has

---

[77] Malkin (2009; 2017a).
[78] Malkin (1987a) part 2. Cf. Leschorn (1984); Lane (2009); (2012).
[79] Cf. Ma (2016) 417.

been set up merely for the sake of refutation and then to deny the existence of equal apportionment (*isomoiria*) in Greek colonies (Endnote 2). However, while "democracy" is a nonissue for the late eighth century, *isomoiria* is significant. Moreover, as others have argued, concrete equal portioning led to the more abstract equal portioning of "law": from *isomoiria* to *isonomia*.

I repeatedly argue against compartmentalization. The distribution of equal plots of land is not just a question of "land and property" (*problèmes de la terre*). Instead, it belongs to the larger canvas of the "distribution of goods" in Greek society, of which land is a subset. That is because the same mindset, vocabulary, and practice are consistent in other contemporary distribution areas. Declarative, prescriptive, and descriptive statements in Greek sources concerning land all point to a clear conclusion: the First Lots were a discrete category; they were equal in size, supposedly inalienable, were distributed by lot, and their purpose was to create a community of sharing members. When the vector shifted too much toward elitism (Sparta is a famous example), revolutionaries would call for a return to primordial equality, conforming to the guideline of "one *oikos* per one *kleros*." They would advocate *ges anadasmos*, an equal redistribution.[80]

"In early times ... in many states there was legislation prohibiting the sale of the *original allotments*," says Aristotle.[81] First Lots constituted a minimum, inalienable holding. They were usually small, as were the archaic colonies, which generally started as small, planned centers from which people could walk to their fields. In general, egalitarianism is more apparent in the early phases of a colony's life; over generations, with territorial expansion and the creation of private estates, social and economic gaps kept growing.

As with any distribution of goods, those sharing in the distribution of First Lots would constitute a pre-demarcated group that, by definition, would not let others, or local populations, participate.[82] Like pirates, for the most part, Greek colonists acquired a settlement site by force and treated the land as "empty," ready for distribution. Violence (*hybris*) was explicit, as Mimnermos of Kolophon (the later seventh century) illustrates.[83] The rarely quoted words of Archilochos (mid-seventh century) are significant: "they founded (*ektisen*) another house and another orchard they had evacuated so many acres of land (*gyai*) without arousing anyone's pity."[84] Thucydides (6.3) is straightforward: "Syracuse was founded ... by Archias, one of the Herakleidai from Corinth, who began by driving out the Sikels from the island upon which the inner city now stands."

---

[80] Solon fr. 34, 6–9 (West). Asheri (1966) chs. 2–4; Fuks (1968).
[81] Arist. *Pol.* 6.1319a.10–11.
[82] Cf. Hodos (2006); Bérard (2017). I discuss notable exceptions, such as L'Amastuola, Francavilla maritima, etc.
[83] Mimnermos, fr. 9 (West) [Strabo 14.1.4].
[84] See Archilochos fr. 1 (Gerber).

We have several foundation decrees for Greek colonies, inscribed or paraphrased, formulated at the home community. Sometimes their prescriptions do not match the archaeological evidence, and in one case, no one has ever found the colony in question (the Athenian foundation decree of Brea). The relationship between archaeology and texts is problematic. Whereas archaeology can reveal results, it is blind to unrealized intentions. Foundation decrees tell us what people intend to do; they do not describe but prescribe. Foundation decrees do not testify to what happened once settlers had arrived at a site.

Similarly, ancient theoretical discussions, such as Plato's *Laws* or Aristotle's *Politics*, are also prescriptive (although Aristotle's *Politics* also provides some historical examples). In short, there is no point in finding contradictions between the professed equality of a foundation decree and implementations on the ground. Happily, in some of the earliest colonies in Sicily, the notion of *isos kai homoios*, "equal and like/fair," seem to be expressed on the ground. Foundation decrees—especially those of Naupaktos, Black Corcyra, and Cyrene—are excellent sources for observing mindset, values, expectations, and general practices. They are prescriptive yet are well aware that people might not comply. That is why foundation decrees often include dire warnings against deviation or transgression.

Let me illustrate a case where we have both the account of an ancient historian and a late inscription that quotes Thera's original, seventh-century foundation decree, sending out a colony to Cyrene in Libya. The points of overlap between the two are sufficient to accept the role of drawing lots throughout the process when the Therans were about to sail "on equal and fair terms." Like Homeric soldiers, colonists from homes with more than one son, were chosen by drawing lots. The lottery was comprehensive: the Therans drew lots among all Theran households, a point attested by both sources. Two generations after Cyrene had been successfully founded, the Cyrenaeans wished for more settlers and turned to the Oracle of Delphi. Apollo issued a migration oracle addressed this time not to the mother city but *eis Hellenas pantas*, "to all the Greeks":

Whoever goes to beloved Libya after
The fields are divided
(*gas anadaiomenas*), I say, shall be sorry afterward.

Herodotus, who quotes the oracle, continues, "So a great multitude gathered at Cyrene, and cut out great tracts of land from the territory of the neighboring Libyans." Clearly, the conventions implied in the drawing of lots were relevant to "all Greeks."[85]

[85] Hdt. 4.153, 159.

Irad Malkin

PART I
THE LOTTERY MINDSET
Religion and Society

1
Lotteries Divine and Human: The World of the Homeric Epics

Imagine you are a Greek, living over two and a half millennia ago. When still a child, your nanny, simplifying a myth related by Homer and Hesiod, told you how it all came to be:[1] There had once been a war with cosmic proportions, the greatest ever, which ended with the victory of the Olympian gods over the Titans and the division of the cosmic spoils—the Sky, the Sea, and the Underworld—through a lottery. In Hesiod's "Birth of the Gods" (ca. 700), the poet addresses the Muse (vv. 108–113):[2]

> Tell how at the first gods and earth *came to be*, and rivers, and the boundless sea with its raging swell, and the gleaming stars, and the wide heaven above, and the gods who were born of them, givers of good things, and how they (the gods) divided (*dateomai*) their wealth among themselves, and how they shared their honors (*timai*) amongst them (*hos timas dielonto—diaireo*), and also how at the first they took many-folded Olympus. (trans. Evelyn-White 1914)

The poet asks how, at first, gods and earth "*came to be*," not "who created them." The name "creation myth," sometimes attributed to Hesiod's *Theogony*, is a Judeo-Christian misnomer, relying on the idea of a transcendent Creator, a supreme being. All authority emanates from him, much like an ancient Near Eastern king. Greek religion had no external god to pronounce, "Let there be light," and the gods "shared their honors amongst themselves." An external deity would be "transcendent" because it would exist before and "outside" the world it creates. For such a god, the world exists in the accusative case, as an *object*, and the source of authority in the world is external. Modern Western democracies arose precisely in opposition to the idea that power comes "from above" and not from society or people.

Drawing lots implies an equal chance for its result and the equal status of all participants with the same chance. When lotteries were used in ancient Greece for distribution (of booty, land, priesthoods, political offices, etc.), they defined,

---

[1] Plato *Rep.* 2.377c–e on children's version of known myths.
[2] See the discussion by Leclerc (1998).

Drawing Lots. Irad Malkin and Josine Blok, Oxford University Press. © Oxford University Press 2024.
DOI: 10.1093/oso/9780197753477.003.0002

exclusively, who was an eligible sharer or "citizen." The combination of lottery and equality, mainly when applied to politics, reveals an exceptional attitude that few complex societies have ever shared: a horizontal vision of the world. A top-down approach would have been natural for an ancient Egyptian pharaoh or an Assyrian king, but not the Greeks. As we shall see, among Greeks, the authority to distribute by lot is not transcendent, "from above," but primarily emanates laterally, from within. After a few centuries of practicing the drawing of lots and thinking in terms of "portions" and "shares" (mostly *equal* or *equitable* portions), the Athenians in the fifth century extended the lottery to the working of their democracy. More than any other aspect of ancient democracies, so Herodotus, Plato, and Aristotle tell us, the salient feature of democracy—indeed, its very definition—was not elections but the drawing of lots.

A rare glimpse of the early archaic Greek mindset, one that emphasizes a relational society, is afforded by the names of the Nereids, as Jeremy McInerney beautifully observes:[3] Eukrante, "Good ruler"; Protomedeia, "First counsel"; Leiagore, "Addressing the people"; Euagore, "Good speech"; Laomedeia, "Counsel the people"; Polynoe, "Thoughtful"; Autonoe, "Sensible"; Themisto, "Justice"; Pronoe, "Forethought"; Nemertes "Truth." These names reflect values that imply or explicitly speak of the *people* and what it seems to deserve: good counsel, justice, good (public) speech, and qualities of thoughtfulness, sensibility, and truth.[4]

Probably reflecting various traditions, Greek myths about the gods oscillate between emphasizing the supposedly supreme power of Zeus and seeing him as merely first among equals. All Greeks would have agreed that the Olympian gods did not create the world but were born into it. Kronos and the Titans had deposed Ouranos and Rhea, and Zeus and the Olympians won their revolution against the Titans. The source of authority (to divide the realms of the world) rested horizontally with the participants, of which Zeus was one. Specifically, the circle included only the three brothers: their right as victors overlapped with their position as three brothers, sharing a partible inheritance by lot, which was another common Greek practice.[5]

People create their gods in their own image, as Xenophanes had remarked in the sixth century: "Ethiopians say that their gods are snub-nosed and black, Thracians that theirs are blue-eyed and red-haired."[6] Human conventions were

---

[3] McInerney (2004) 33, his translation.

[4] McInerney (2004) 34 observes that "The catalogue of the Children of Night" (Hes. *Theog.* 211–232) is composed the same way and can be read as a counterpoint to the Nereids.

[5] Plato seems to think of the division of the world among the gods in terms of inheritance in *Gorgias* 523a: "By Homer's account, Zeus, Poseidon, and Hades divided the sovereignty amongst them when they took it over from their father." On partible inheritance, see ch. 4.

[6] Xenoph. frs. 13, 14 Diehl. He goes on to say that "13 ... if horses or oxen or lions had hands or could draw with their hands and accomplish such works as men, horses would draw the figures of the

mirrored on Olympus to a certain degree: the lateral image of the society of the gods, drawing authority by and from within the group of participants, was a reflection of attitudes and practices current in Greek society.

Homer reminds us of the story that seems to be the background of Hesiod's various descriptions of the distribution by drawing lots of honors and powers among the gods.[7] When the Trojans and Achaians (Greeks) were fighting over Troy, the gods were divided among themselves and kept intervening in battle on the opposing sides. At one point, Zeus had had enough and ordered his fellow gods and goddesses to step back. His brother Poseidon, more stubborn than the rest, needed special attention, so Zeus sent the goddess Iris to tell him to get away. Should he not obey, Zeus threatened to "come down" and fight Poseidon, his brother, claiming superiority of strength and reminding Poseidon that he, Zeus, was the "elder born."[8] Poseidon did not like the pretense of superiority and insisted (although not to Zeus, only to the messenger) that he was, in fact, an equal. He reminds his brother of their victory in the cosmic war, the greatest ever, which ended with the division of the spoils through a lottery among equals.

> "No, no. Great though he is, this that he has said is too much, if he will force me against my will, me, who am his *equal in rank*. Since we are three brothers born by Rhea to Kronos, Zeus, and I, and the third is Hades, lord of the dead men. All was divided among us (*dateomai*) three ways, each given his domain (*hekastos d'emmore times*). I when the lots were shaken (*pallo*) drew (*lanchano*) the grey sea to live in forever; Hades drew the lot of the mists and the darkness, and Zeus was allotted the wide sky, in the cloud and the bright air. But earth and high Olympos are common to all three (*ksune panton*). Therefore, I am no part of the mind of Zeus. Let him in tranquility and powerful as he is stay satisfied with his third share (*moira*).... But this thing comes as a bitter sorrow to my

gods as similar to horses, and the oxen as similar to oxen, and they would make the bodies of the sort which each of them had" (trans. Lesher [1992]).

---

[7] Note that Hesiod speaks of "the gods" doing the distribution among them. However, when it comes to specific honors, it is usually Zeus, whose position as supreme ruler Hesiod takes pains to emphasize, who does the allocating. Cf. Leclerc (1998). A lottery as such is not mentioned in Hesiod, although it seems to be implied or expressed in the *aisa* of Hekate, distinct in the degree of honor when juxtaposed with the portions of *time that* others have "won by lot," *lanchano* (or, simply, "got," as some would have it, but see Appendix). It seems extremely unlikely that Hesiod was unaware of the lottery myth in Homer. He never denies it and employs the terminology of lottery and distribution, as noted. On the other hand, he is never explicit and instead emphasizes Zeus's kingship. When specific honors are allocated, Zeus is presented as the one doing the actual giving, implementing the result. There may have existed various contemporary versions of what happened after the victory of the Olympians; the fact that the earliest and major one (Homer) recounts the story of the divine lottery and distribution of the cosmos is enough for our argument; Greeks followed no dogma. Yet on each occasion when Hesiod tells of Zeus's distribution, he could be understood as having presided over the lottery and its consequences, not deciding which *time* ought to go to which god or goddess.

[8] Greeks could be inconsistent on that point. He is the youngest in Hes. *Theog.* 137.

heart and my spirit, when Zeus tries in words of anger to reprimand one who is his equal in station (*isomoron*), and endowed with destiny (*aisa*)[9] like his." (*Il.* 15.185-210 trans. Lattimore)

Having protested vehemently, Poseidon then retreats and gives up.[10] As we shall see, the vocabulary of this distributive lottery is consistent for both gods and humans. A key term is *dasmos*, "distribution," and related words (used once by Hesiod in the quoted passage): "All was *divided* among us three ways," says Poseidon, and the poet Pindar (early fifth century) sings of the time "when Zeus and the immortals were *dividing/distributing* (*dateomai*) the earth among them."[11] Similarly, the *Homeric Hymn to Demeter* also mentions the primordial lottery. He encourages the goddess, lamenting the fate of her daughter Persephone whom Hades, Lord of the Dead, had kidnapped and is now forced to marry him:

But, goddess, cease your deep mourning—nor must you at all in vain keep hold of boundless rage. A not unsuitable match amongst the immortal gods for your daughter to marry is he, Aidoneus, Commander of Many, your very own brother by birth, sown from selfsame seed. And as regards honor (*time*), he gained his share by lot (*lanchano*) at the first, when the three-way division (*diatricha*) was made: He dwells amongst those whose sovereign it fell to his lot to be. (*Homeric Hymns* 2.82-87; Crudden 2001)

Sharing implies some distributed "whole" and the predefined group whose members deserve the shares. "All was divided (*dateomai*) among us": the verb is related to *dasmos*, a division, and distribution among a group by the group members (Endnote 3). When Hesiod similarly inquires how they (the gods) divided their wealth, he uses *dateomai*, a verb which "in Homer ... is only used of people sharing out *among themselves* [my emphasis], not allotting to someone else," as Martin West comments (see also Endnote 3 in this chapter).[12] As I see

---

[9] More literally, a "portion" of what the gods ought to have, namely divine power. On *aisa*, see below.

[10] Cf. Apoll. *Bibl.* 1.2; Callimachus (*Hymn 1*, 60-63) refers to the *equality* of that lottery (*ep' isaie ... pallo*) among the participants. Cf. Plato *Critias* 109b-d: "Once upon a time the gods were taking over by lot the whole earth according to its regions—not according to the results of strife.... So by just allotments they received each one his own, and they settled their countries" (trans. W. R. M. Lamb).

[11] Pind. *Ol.* 7.55.

[12] West (1966) *ad Theog.* 520. In the fifth century *dasmos* changed its meaning to "tribute," reversing the order of group distribution for the group. See, e.g., Hdt. 3.97.1; 5.106.6; 6.48.2; 6.95.1; 7.51.1; 7.108.1; Aesch. *Pers.* 586-590; Soph. *OT* 35-39; cf. Soph. *OC* 634-635. *Dasmos* is a rare word. In pre-Hellenistic literature there are approximately 47 occurrences (including Aristotle), and an overall count of 458 in the whole Greek corpus. A very small number are dated to the archaic period (except for the Epic, only one instance in Theognis). More than half of the occurrences relate to

it, Zeus presides over the process of lottery and distribution, not deciding what each divinity should get. The point is significant since it explains a few quoted words of the lyric poet Alkman (seventh century), who says, "He (Zeus) himself (*hoiethen*) shook the lots and distributed (*dateomai*) the *daimones* (presumably the portions of the gods, here called *daimones*)."[13] Yet the verb *dateomai* is usually used with a plural subject, meaning distribution by (or on behalf of) a group and for the group. It is another expression of a horizontal vision of society. In the poetry of Homer and Hesiod only four instances (in active voice) out of forty-two are in the singular."[14] The exceptions, where the verb is used in the singular, are cases where the community gives someone the right (or the duty) to share out something among them.[15]

This divine lottery indicates a notion of equality, or, more precisely, a "more or less equal" or "equitable" division. The English translation "each given his domain" glides over some key terms. The words convey the idea of getting a "part" or "portion" (*meros, moira*), a term that signifies a perception of some "whole" to be divided up among a predefined collective. *Emmore times* is an expression that combines the notion of "portion" (*meros*) and "honor" (*time* in the sense of a realm of authority, domain). It is a recurring expression in Homer, applied to the divine and the human spheres alike. *Time* expresses a distributive value.[16] Characteristically, the only Homeric formula in which the word *time* occurs is *emmore times*: "he/she has been allotted a *time*." Homeric poetry uses "*formulae*," set units of words (such as "swift-footed Achilles") that are repeated verbatim, often for metric reasons, and are characteristic of oral epic poetry in general. However, they testify to accepted conventions. There would be no point in having a *formula* only for a single occasion, a fact that implies that the poet considered the practice of fair distributions as habitual. In the *Homeric Hymn to Aphrodite*, for example, the power of the goddess of Love can divert even Zeus:

Even the heart of Zeus, who delights in thunder, is led astray by her [Aphrodite]; though he is greatest of all and has the lot (*emmore times*) of highest majesty. (5.36–37)

Cyrus, several (Plato and Aristotle) to the legendary King Minos. The search for the lemma *dasmos* has been executed via *TLG* (accessed June 29, 2020).

[13] Fr. 65 Page.
[14] The search for the lemma *dateomai* has been executed via *TLG* (accessed June 29, 2020). For example: Hes. *Theog.* 517–520: "And Atlas through hard constraint upholds the wide heaven with unwearyingly head and arms, standing at the borders of the earth before the clear-voiced Hesperides; for this lot (*moira*) wise Zeus distributed/assigned to him. ταύτην γάρ οἱ μοῖραν ἐδάσσατο μητίετα Ζεύς. Hesiod seems to allude to the general lottery.
[15] See Hes. *Theog.* 885; *Od.* 6.11. Cf. *Il.*9.333, where Agamemnon similarly hands out booty.
[16] Finkelberg (1998) 15 with n. 16. For a detailed study of Greek vocabulary of distribution and the conception of equality as "equality of shares," see Borecký (1963).

46   DRAWING LOTS

The framework of the cosmic lottery and the distribution of particular places and specific *timai* seem to have been a constant in the Greek *imaginaire*. Here is how Plato describes it some four centuries after the probable composition of the *Iliad* and the *Odyssey*. He employs a contemporary Athenian term (*klerouchoi*) for colonists occupying new *kleroi*: "As they received what was naturally theirs in the allotment of justice (*dikes klerois*), they began to settle their lands.... In the case of Hephaistos and Athena, ... they both received this land as their portion in a single lot (*mian* {one} *lexin* {allotted portion, a derivative of *lanchano*} *eilechaton* {*lanchano*})" (Plato, *Critias* 109b–d, trans. Diskin Clay).

The story about the divine lottery parallels a myth in the ancient "Near East," a vague and misleading term covering varied areas (from the Persian Gulf to Anatolia) during millennia and cultures as distinct from each other as Semitic-speaking Hebrews and Indo-European Hittites. It is likely (some would say highly probable) that the Greek theme of the divine lottery was adopted from elsewhere. However, it is not a question of "stolen wisdom,"[17] and we should not be obsessed with the question "who was the *first* to...." Rather, we need to see what Greeks did with such a story to make it "Greek": what particular emphasis or addition do we find here? By analogy, it is well known that archaic Greek statues of young men (*kouroi*) were quite similar to their inspiration: Egyptian temple sculpture.[18] However, Greeks placed them in different contexts and, most significantly, made those statues "free-standing" (not attached to a wall), thus providing a new direction and meaning to sculpture. Alternatively, take another, less-known example: the names of some Greek musical instruments and the tradition of professional musical "families/dynasties" have their origins in the Near East. However, Greek musicians, moving among hundreds of city-states, belonged to no central court, and what they did with their music was very different.[19] Thus, beyond the general implication that people had contact, pointing out Near Eastern parallels to the divine lottery carries little salience if we wish to understand what the Greeks did with it.

The framework of the story of a victory of the young gods and the subsequent division by lot among them appears in the ancient Near East.[20]

> They had taken the [clay jar?] by the neck, / Anu went up to heaven, / [Enlil too]k the earth for his subjects, / [The bolt], the trap of the sea, / [they had gi]ven to Enki the leader

---

[17] Cf. James (1992).
[18] It has been generally accepted since the late nineteenth century; cf. Richter ([1942] 1970).
[19] See Sachs (1943) 63; Franklin (2007) 27–32; (2006) 52–62; Ivanov (1999); Yerucham (2015).
[20] *Atrahasis* (*Enuma Elish*) Tablet 1, ll. 11–16 with Rollinger (2015) 20.

There are significant differences with the Homeric version: "While the *Iliad* describes the partition of the Heavens, the underworld and the seas, while the earth and Olympos *remain a common dominion*," says Robert Rollinger, "the Atrahasis myth instead mentions the partition of Heavens, Earth and the subterranean sweet water sea, which are *juxtaposed as separate cosmic realms*"[21] (my emphasis). Note, especially in the Greek version, the "common ground" (Olympos, Earth) belongs to the "community" of all the gods,[22] which is paralleled in common lands (public, agricultural, pastoral, and sacred) in Greek cities.[23]

The way Greeks perceived how the world came into being and the subsequent division of realms of power and responsibility among the gods reflects a general outlook and a mindset. The notions of "fairness and equality," perceived in terms of equal chances and approximate equal results, occupy a constitutive prism in this outlook. Some habits, norms, and conventions of human society were projected onto what they expected of the gods, albeit in meta-human terms of eternity and divine attributes that distinguish them from human beings. The "society of the gods" is not an exact reflection of human society, and we must

---

[21] Rollinger (2015) 20; cf. Burkert (1992) 89–91. See also West (1997) 110, who also refers to a Hittite ritual lottery determining the ritual positions of deities in a cult. Gysembergh (2013) also discusses Assyrian "eponymous" officials chosen by lot from a narrow aristocratic circle. A text from Ugarit, the area that became identified with Phoenicians, tells how the three sons of El, the father of the gods, divide the world among themselves through the casting lots: Baal, who is the equivalent of Zeus in several ways, receives the sky; Yam, the sea; and Mot, the underworld. Mondi (1990) 165; López-Ruiz (2010) 120. For the Hittites, see Taggar-Cohen (2002). For the possibility of using clay balls for drawing lots in second-millennium Cyprus, see Ferrara and Valério (2017). See also Bar On (2020).

[22] Macé (2014) 446 thinks differently: "He is not telling him that the original stockpile from which portions might be distributed no longer exists, but rather that they have not yet set aside stock from which to begin new allocations." 447: "The common is not that which precedes the act of distribution but rather that which is excluded from it." 450: "Commons are the things that are set aside from the distribution, not those set aside in order to be distributed." This is true, at least for the regular occurrence of the "commons." However, when Zeus, Hades, and Poseidon distributed their domains, not everything was divided three ways in an absolute sense, but only that which was divisible, not the rest. Gods will have specific places on earth to worship them, such as Helios at Rhodes, but that would be a *geras*, not a "part of the earth" given at the expense of already held portions, as Macé thinks. So precisely because no god is eligible for a plot of earth, Earth (indivisible mother) and Olympus are excluded; they are not "parts." That is right, but the fact that they cannot be divided is itself not an argument against Macé's understanding of "common"; the only difference is the reason why it is not divided. Although nowhere does it say that it was set aside *before* the distribution, Macé states that confidentially and builds his argument on that premise. It seems to be part of the deal; "all of us" could mean all the other gods too, since that was the case anyway in the Greek perception of the gods.

[23] See also Burkert (1992) 89–91; West (1997) 109–110, 385; Gysembergh (2013), who examines the plausible venues by which Mesopotamian motifs reached the Greek world. The point, again, is not whether Greeks "borrowed" (they probably did), but what special significance and what notable *differences* (such as the "common ground") integrated those motifs and made them "Greek." The author is aware of the issue: Gysembergh (2013) n.24. For further reservations, see Kelly (2008), who does not contextualize the question in the broader framework of the Greek practice of lotteries, among whom the use of lotteries became much more common than in the Near East; see also section 8.1.

assess any such mirroring in context. In the *Iliad* and the *Odyssey*, both gods and humans appear as demarcated collectives that not only share the fruits of victory by lot but also expressly hold assemblies: the gods in Olympus, the Greek and the Trojan armies in the field, the people of Ithaca, Odysseus's island, and also the fabulous Phaiakians.[24] In one sense, Poseidon had been right: once he had been an *equal*, but that was before the gods *elected* Zeus as king. That initial status of equality will prove of enormous significance.

Such an outlook of equal sharing expressed by drawing lots must have emerged during the centuries following the Mycenaean civilization's collapse (ca. 1200). The Olympian world of Homer seems very different from Mycenaean norms and conventions.[25] When the Mycenaean tablets written in Linear B were deciphered, scholars were surprised to discover that some of the names of the gods were the same as those in later periods, thus adding a few centuries to the history of the Greek gods, the earliest mention of whom had been Homer's *Iliad* and *Odyssey* (ca. eighth century).[26] However, Mycenaean society seems to have been palace-oriented, hierarchical, centralized, and interventionist. By contrast, the society of the Homeric Olympus is chaotic and loose; like their divine counterparts, Homer's human heroes are strong-willed and individualistic but nevertheless confined by collective conventions. The source of authority among humans was fragmented: the *wanax*, probably some supreme ruler in the Mycenaean world, vanished after the collapse. Instead, there were many *basileis* ("kings"; the term exists already in Linear B to denote a high-ranking person) but no *wanax* in the sense of a supreme ruler. Therefore, we have plenty of princes but not one single king. Agamemnon is no emperor; he is an elected supreme commander exercising his authority on the battlefield of Troy.[27]

The description of the cosmic lottery contains the basic terms of Greek lotteries: the lots (*kleroi*), "shaking" the lots (*pallo*), drawing a lot and obtaining its result (*lanchano*), "distributing and sharing among themselves" (*dateomai*, and cognates such as *dasmos*;), and "portion" (*aisa*; more often we shall find rather *moira*). As for the gods' realms of power, *timai*, the poet(s) of the *Homeric Hymns to the Gods*, a series of poems dedicated to specific gods that were probably written in the seventh and sixth centuries, resort to formulae that contain all the major terms we have just been observing. One such poem was a hymn for the young Hermes (it took Hermes one whole day to grow up once he was born, yet somehow he never matured enough for a beard). He is once called a *daimon* (our "demon" descends from it), usually understood as some form of divinity, but *daimon* too derives from *dateomai*, hence the meaning *daimon* as "divine

---

[24] Bonnet (2017).
[25] Finley (1978) 166.
[26] Chadwick (1967), 84–101.
[27] Finley (1978 59–60; Carlier (2006); Drews (1983); Lenz (1993).

dispenser."[28] Here we observe Hermes himself singing about the "portions" of the gods (*Homeric Hymn to Hermes* 4.423–430):

> Then the son of Maia (Hermes), harping sweetly upon his lyre, ... sang the story of the deathless gods and of the dark earth, how at the first they came to be, and how each one received (or rather "gained," i.e., by lot, *lanchano*) his portion (*moira*). (Trans. H. G. Evelyn-White)

I shall have more to say about *moira* (ch. 2.9), a word more familiar as "fate." It is "fate" in the sense of "one's lot upon this earth," namely the portion (*moira*) of life one gets to have. Often, *moira* relates to the measure, or the length of one's life, not necessarily to what will happen in it. However, this may also overlap with life's content (in the sense of "destiny"). However, the phrasing is often ambiguous: "and the immortals have given to mortals each his own due share (*moira*) all over the grain-giving corn land" (*Od.* 19.592; Lattimore). Here is not the place to open a discussion about determinism. Let us just note that Achilles, for example, at least in one major episode, was not *destined* to die in Troy; at least on one occasion in the *Iliad*, Achilles *chooses* not to listen to his mother's advice to return home and grow old, but to remain in the field, die young, and enhance his reputation (*Il.* 1.38–43). He had two "destinies" from which to choose. Words and their semantic range—here, the overlap between "destiny" and "portion"—open another window to a mental world shared by ancient Greeks where a lottery too could determine one's portion.

Let us return to Poseidon: The poet of the *Homeric Hymn to Poseidon* (22.4–5), probably following the *Iliad*, sings of some of Poseidon's specific powers (*timai*) as the result of a distributive lottery. The *Homeric Hymns* were composed later than the *Iliad* and the *Odyssey* (opinions about their date range between the late eighth and the mid-sixth centuries). However, this is not a difficulty: first, the subjects of the *Hymns* concern specific *timai*, not the "territorial" division of the world, which we see in the *Iliad*. Second, such hymns were not mere literary creations but were performed publicly. Thus, they addressed traditions about divine lotteries that were well known to their audience. This hymn describes a distribution conducted by the gods as a distinct group they all share. The verb *dateomai* implies the lot since some specific means of distribution must have been self-evident to the public, and no other manner of group distribution is mentioned in our sources (see also the Appendix).

---

[28] Vergados (2012) *ad* 550b–551.

A two-fold office (*time*) the gods allotted (*dateomai*) you, O Shaker of the Earth (Poseidon), to be a tamer of horses and a savior of ships! (*Homeric Hymn* 22.4–5, trans. Evelyn-White)

The division by lot of the world into three parts and the allotment after that of specific powers is a good illustration of the *distributive* kind of lottery. It should be distinguished from other types, as noted in the Introduction: divination via lot oracles; the "one/some out of many" type (*selective* lotteries), *procedural* lotteries (establishing turns, or positions, e.g., in a chariot race), or *mixture* lotteries.

Equality is a salient feature of such lotteries. When Poseidon mentions having an "equal station" (literally, an equal part, *isomoron*), he implies a claim to equal merit or *eligibility* to get a share, but not necessarily an equal share. That is when Poseidon elides the issue: "one (Poseidon himself) who is his equal in station (*isomoron*, literally "equal portion") and endowed with a "destiny (*aisa*; it too means a portion) like his" (*home pepromenon aise*). However, Poseidon gives up precisely because his *aisa*, the result of the lottery, is unequal: Zeus is the possessor of the heavens, because of the lot drawing; but he is also king, a position he got not by lot but by election. He was *chosen* (not by lot) to be king by the other gods:

By the prophecies of Gaia they urged far-seeing Zeus to become king and to rule over the immortals; and he divided (*diadateomai*) their honors well for them. (*Theog.* 881–885, trans. Glenn Most)[29]

Kingship, in this case, is a "political" position supported by a prophecy of Gaia. The position of king is discrete and has nothing to do with lotteries that divide the *timai*. Zeus *presides* over their division, but he does not decide them. "Divided" might sound too active in translation, as if Zeus also decided what each deity should get. In Pindar's ode, Zeus is remorseful since he cannot give anything to the Sun God Helios, who had missed the initial lottery among the gods. As the one conducting the distribution, "Zeus distributed (*diatasso*) fairly (*homos*) to the immortals their portions and declared their privileges (*timai*)" (*Theog.* 73–75). A key word is "fairly," *homos* (equitably), to which I shall return. Otherwise, Greek uses words such as "arrange" (*diatasso*, also in l. 885) and "point out, make known, indicate" (*epi-phrazo*);[30] these are compatible with presiding over a procedure, not deciding its content. Similarly, when Odysseus distributes booty (a

---

[29] Most (2006) *ad loc*. The *Homeric Hymn to Aphrodite* distinguishes between Zeus as the "greatest" and Zeus as having the "highest lot" (*emmore timês*): Zeus is "the greatest of all and has the lot of highest majesty" (ὅστε μέγιστός τ' ἐστὶ μεγίστης τ' ἔμμορε τιμῆς).
[30] Cf. Leclerc (1998) 92.

catch of wild goats), he conducts the lottery and then takes care to have the distribution conducted fairly (Od. 9.159-160).

Finally, when Hesiod gets to an actual description, Zeus is not mentioned. As quoted earlier, the poet asks the Muse to tell "how they (the gods) divided (*dateomai*) their wealth among themselves, and how they shared their honors (*timai*) amongst themselves (*hos timas dielonto—diaireo*)."

That Zeus presides over lotteries that end up in "apportioning" may seem sufficiently implied in what we have seen so far. However, there may be more: Alkman mentions "Zeus the Apportioner" (*Klarios*), and in his play *The Suppliant Maidens*, Aeschylus calls Zeus (of Argos) *Klarios*, "the righteous Zeus the Apportioner who hears suppliants."[31] The title may be clarified in another myth that tells a story of a primordial apportionment of land, Arkadia, not too far from Argos. We hear about Arkas, after whom Arkadia is named. When Pausanias visited the Arkadian city of Tegea, he saw

> The . . . 'Common Hearth of the Arkadians.' . . . The lofty place, on which are most of the altars of the Tegeans, is called the place of Zeus Klarios (of Lots), and it is plain that the god got his surname from the lots cast for the sons of Arkas. Here the Tegeans celebrate a feast every year" (8.53.9, trans. W. H. S. Jones and H. A. Ormerod, Loeb-ed.)

The story alludes to the primordial division/inheritance among Arkas's sons, somewhat parallel to the division of the Peloponnese by lot among the descendants of Herakles.[32] It needs to be emphasized that the title Klarios and the myth are anchored in social reality: the annual public festival implies communal involvement in ritual, not just myths told to an author of a travel guide, as was Pausanias. Therefore, we transcend the realm of "just myth" and observe an active, public cult.[33] A distributive lottery (here, dividing up the cosmos) is at once comprehensive (everyone gets a share) and exclusive (only those who "belong" can participate). A distributive lottery, therefore, implies a self-aware image of the predefined group of the eligible, those who have the right to participate. It also implies a precise sense of *fairness*: Every eligible group member gets a portion, and all have an equal chance to get the best portion. "They shall sail on equal and fair terms" is a formula applied to colonization that we will encounter

---

[31] Alkman frg. 65 (Page). *The Suppliant Maidens* (360) Zeus (of Argos) *Klarios*, the "righteous Zeus the Apportioner who hears suppliants." The meaning of Klarios may be open to other interpretations. Klarios is also a title of Apollo, sometimes also referring to the city of Klaros in Anatolia. We have not advanced much beyond the commentary on Pausanias by Sir James Fraser (1898: ad loc) and Farnell (1921) vol. 1, .56; cf. Cook (1903) vol. 2, 874. Cf. the unsubstantiated claim that Pausanias is merely "guessing": Bowen (2013) *ad* Aesch. *Suppl.* 360.

[32] Paus. 4.3.5.

[33] Cf. Apollodorus 3.9.

later. Equality and fairness are closely linked in early Greek thought and practice, which is not self-evident. In societies where a hierarchy among social classes is the norm, an aristocrat getting more than others may consider it fair. As I shall point out throughout this book, the horizontal mindset was never exclusive, and there was a constant tension between elitist (top-down) and horizontal forces pulling in opposite directions.

Already the *Iliad* contains indications of that tension. Homeric leaders are given a special prize from the general booty (*geras*) yet which is considered unique and outside the general distribution in which they too participate. Achilles neatly distinguishes between the two: when threatening to break away and return home, he says he would take with him the spoils (iron, gold, women, etc.)—"all that fell to me by lot (*lanchano*)";[34] on the other hand ("*de*"; the Greek has a way to stress the contrast), "the *geras* given (*didomi*) to me" was forcefully taken etc. (*Il.* 9.365). The distinction between what fell to Achilles by lot, in contrast to what was purposefully and specifically *given* to him, is clear.

Although some have ignored or denied the role of the lot in the distribution of booty (see Endnote 1), Achilles is clearly stating a contrast here: not between what "he got" and what "he took," but between "what he got" and . . . "what he got." He is making a distinction between two types of "getting," and in both, he is the object, not the subject. The difference must lie, therefore, in the mode of getting. The manner of getting a *geras* is explicit: it consists of a ritualized, public gift to him from "The Achaeans."[35] Nevertheless, we cannot leave open the question of how he "got" the rest: There must have been another mode of "getting," of being distributed a portion, and this mode must be implied in the verb *lanchano*, translated as, "I got by lot." In and of itself, *lanchano* may mean "to get," but that would still leave open the question of "how," and especially, what is Achilles contrasting here? The verb *lanchano* hardly means being the recipient of a top-down gift from a king (verbs such as *lambano, tunchano, katamao,* or *dechomai* would have been more appropriate). (See Endnote 2).

Moreover, Achilles was "given" (*didomi*) the *geras* but merely "getting" the rest. The one obvious answer, which many translators have indeed followed, is to understand *lanchano* as "I got by lot," a prevalent meaning of the verb. Moreover, studies of B. Borecký, supplemented in this book,[36] show that up to the end of the fifth century the verb *lanchano* retained its association with the lot in 73 percent of the extant cases, overlapping with (often religious) terminology of portions and *moirai*; one of the *moirai* was named Lachesis, goddess of casting lots. I return to such issues later.

---

[34] On the meaning of the verb *lanchanô* see ch. 1 Endnote 2 and Borecký (1965). Cf. *Odyssey* 14.229–233, where the same distinction is made by Odysseus.
[35] Cf. Scheid-Tissinier (1994) 234–244; 251–253.
[36] See Appendix.

Aside from the *geras,* the distribution of spoils was expected to be equal and fair. To illustrate the issue of the link between fairness and equality, we may observe by way of contrast to Homeric princes, pirates of a different era. For the Buccaneers, fairness consisted in what was proper to one's status. The Buccaneer Code of Captain John Phillips (1724) says, "I. Every Man Shall obey civil Command; the Captain shall have one full Share and a half of all Prizes; the Master, Boatswain, and Gunner shall have one Share and quarter." Similarly, the code of the Caribbean privateer Henry Morgan (item 4) is fair but unequal. "Shares of booty are provided as follows: "the Captain, or chief Commander, is allotted five or six portions to what the ordinary seamen have; the master's Mate only two; and Officers proportionate to their employment. After whom they draw equal parts from the highest even to the lowest mariner, the boys not being omitted."[37]

In contrast, aside from the special portion set aside for the Homeric king, fairness comes closer to the notion of equality since the distributive lottery consists of equal chances to get whatever portion. The outcome signifies nothing special about a specific recipient since participants are interchangeable when confronting the lot. What may not be equal in either size or value could be the units distributed, such as expensive and cheaper cups. However, when possible, Greeks strove for the results also to be equal. As we will see in more detail, equality was a major priority for Greeks at least since the last third of the eighth century. It is apparent in patterns of land distribution in Greek colonies (city blocks and fields), where we can observe almost obsessively marked equal-size plots of land. These were called *kleroi*—literally, "lots," or "that which is drawn up by lot." Such *kleroi*, too, could not have been of equal quality (soil) or value (location) yet equal in respect of size (chapter 6). The Greek contrast between the "special portion" marking status and the rest of the booty argues against the idea that fairness was perceived in the Buccaneer mode.

The special portion of a god—that is, her or his specific realm of divine authority—is usually called *time,* but sometimes *geras,* a term that overlaps with the unique, personal prize a Homeric king would receive aside from his general, allotted share of the booty. Let us observe Hestia, a goddess with no known myths, yet of major importance as the goddess of the hearth. Since the hearth was in every home, it became its symbol, down to our days. In French, for example, the idea of "home" is best expressed as *foyer,* "hearth," since *maison* can be confused with "house." The hearth was the place of fire and cooking. When a child was born, it was presented at the hearth (i.e., signifying integration into the

---

[37] Exquemelin (2000); Phillips: https://americainclass.org/wp-content/uploads/2013/09/9-Pirate-Articles.pdf; Morgan: https://sites.google.com/a/uconn.edu/pirate-articles-aka-pirate-codes/surviving-pirate-articles/articles-of-henry-morgan

house); a torch was lit there to accompany a bride to the hearth of her husband's home. Founders of colonies would take fire from the common hearth (*koine Hestia*) to light a fire in the common hearth of a colony.[38] Here is how a poet addresses her, using the same formula as for Demeter (*Homeric Hymn to Hestia* 29.1–6):

> Hestia, you who obtained as your lot (*lanchano*) in the lofty abodes / Of all the immortal gods and of humans who walk on the earth / A seat that forever endures as the honor (*time*) due to your age, / Possessing a beautiful portion (*geras*) and honor.[39]

The special quality of Hestia is her *geras*, in respect of which she is *not* equal to other gods. Similarly, what marks the Homeric hero as exceptional is not his share of booty but his personal *geras*, a gift apparently selected by him yet "given" to him by the army. In the *Iliad* and the *Odyssey*, the spoils of war were divided up by the army and for the army, or by the "companions" (*hetairoi*) and among them, "fairly and equally." As we shall see, the heroes, or the "kings" (*basileis*), would each get from the "people" (*laos* in Greek means both "people" and "army")[40] their special prize, *geras*, specifically chosen for (or by) the hero, such as the lovely young Chryseis whom Agamemnon picked for himself. Aside from this special prize, the hero would participate in the general distribution with everyone else, as we saw with Achilles. This relation between the special prize and the general lottery is also paralleled in other lottery-related myths about the gods.

Helios, the god of the Sun, happened to have missed the cosmic lottery that distributed "special places" to the gods and did not get his special prize. He was sorely disappointed, and Zeus, embarrassed, suggested a recall and a restart: a new lottery and redistribution.[41] However, since such redistribution was neither practical nor desired, new land was created to be Helios's *geras*: the island of Rhodes was made to rise from the sea floor.[42] It was to be Helios's special place, where his cult became prominent. That is how Pindar, writing at the beginning of the classical period (the fifth century), tells the story (*Olympian* 7.54–71):

> The ancient stories of men tell that when Zeus and the immortals were *dividing up* the earth among them, Rhodes was not yet visible in the expanse of the sea, but the island was hidden in the salty depths. Helios was absent, and no one

---

[38] Malkin (1987a) 114–134.
[39] Crudden (2001).
[40] A common observation. Montanari (2015,) s.v.; see recently Pepe (2015) 16.
[41] See Demont (2000) 310 n.30 for *ampalos* and the *hapax anapalos*.
[42] Hes. *Theog.* 303, where "the gods" (plural) gave out, *dassanto*, to Echidna a *dwelling*.

marked out (*endeiknumi*) an allotted share (*lachos*) for him; in fact, they left him without any *kleros* (*aklaroton*), although he was a holy god.

And when Helios mentioned it, Zeus was about to order a new casting of lots (*ampalon*),[43] but Helios did not allow him. For he said that he himself saw in the gray sea, growing from the bottom, a rich, productive land for men, and a kindly one for flocks. And he bid Lachesis (goddess of Lotteries) of the golden headband raise her hands right away, and speak, correctly and earnestly, the great oath of the gods . . . that that island, when it had risen into the shining air, should thereafter be his own prize of honor (*geras*). And the essence of his words was fulfilled and turned out to be true. There grew from the waters of the sea an island, which is held by the birth-giving father of piercing rays, the ruler of fire-breathing horses (Helios). (Trans. Diane Arnson Svarlien)

It is remarkable to find Lachesis raising her hands "and speak[ing], correctly and earnestly, the great oath of the gods." She was a *moira*, one of the three personified *moirai* that are usually rendered in English as "fates."[44] Her name, Lachesis, relates to *lanchano*, to gain by lot. It expressly refers to her function as a goddess responsible for casting lots, in direct connection to the drawing of lots and Helios. No lottery is to take place again, but Lachesis is needed to integrate and "legitimate" Helios's special gift with the entire lottery distribution of all the gods.

The *moirai* are ancient, said to be the daughters of Nyx, the primordial night (they can also be the daughters of Zeus and Themis, thus co-opting them into the new regime).[45] They stand apart from the younger gods, the current rulers of Olympus, and so may administer their oath for them. Lachesis's gesture, raising her right hand and administering the oath, perhaps points to some ritual with a human counterpart. Lachesis administers the oath on behalf of the "community" of the gods, which probably frames the participants and obliges them to accept, *a priori*, the eventual results of the distribution.

This is not a myth explaining why Helios is the god of the Sun (that would be his special province, his *time*) but of his special prize, his *geras*: a land especially devoted to his worship (Rhodes), just as Argos or Samos were primarily devoted to Hera. When Helios missed the drawing of lots, he became "*kleros*-less," *aklaroton*. In human terms, when founding a new city, for each citizen, a *kleros* became the entry ticket to the membership of the community. Being an *akleros*, "*kleros*-less," is the worst, lowliest social position.[46] Unlike the gods, who divided

---

[43] Cf. Demont (2000) 310 n.30. The use of a *pallo* compound *ampalon*—literally, "a throw-again"— makes it certain that this is a lottery. Cf. Eusthat. *ad Il.* 1.124.
[44] For the connection between Lachesis, *moirai*, and sortition: Guidorizzi (2001) 42–44.
[45] Hesiod, *Theog.* 901–906. On *moira*, *aisa*, and related terminology see ch. 2.9.
[46] *Od.* 11.489–491.

up the earth into sites of special worship but left out Helios, colonists had more foresight: they took care to leave "undivided land" for future settlers.

Rhodes was Helios's special prize, distinguished from his *time* as the god of the Sun, an honor predating the Olympian lottery; Helios was a Titan and, like the Titan-Goddess Hekate (below), he kept his *time* under the new regime. Pindar clarifies that Rhodes was a special compensation for not participating in the initial lottery. In that lottery, the gods were further allotted more specific domains. However, Helios missed the party, presumably because he had been busy elsewhere exercising his *time* as the god of the Sun. "Rhodes," not yet in existence, could not have been a part of the common store for which the gods drew their lots. Hence its special status, and no other god might claim it.

The notion of a divine *time* can be confusing since it indicates both a quality with which a god or a goddess is born; the value and honor attached to, or emanating from, the particular divinity; and a more precisely defined "province," either of action or place. The poet seems to make such a distinction when he sings of Aphrodite's specific *moira*:[47]

> She has that very *time* (*tauten timen*) from the beginning, and this is the portion (*moira*) allotted to her (*lanchano*) amongst men and undying gods, the whisperings of maidens and smiles and deceits with sweet delight and love and graciousness." (Hes. *Theog.* 203–206; Evelyn-White)

Successful revolutionary leaders often leave in place what had been there before. When the Olympians took over the cosmos, some of the formerly supreme Titan gods, such as the darkly threatening Hekate, stayed in place.[48] "She received honor also in starry heaven," sings the poet Hesiod around 700. "Receiving honor" is expressed, again, as *emmore times*, signifying a "portion" (*moira*) of *time*. Moreover, the poet goes on to employ the effective terms of lottery, division, and allocation (*lanchano*, *time*; *moira* and its equivalent *aisa*).[49] Hekate has her portion, her *aisa*, distinguished among what the other children of Earth and Ocean had received by lot (*timen lanchano*). The wording is formulaic, but taken literally, it implies that even the Titans—the second generation of

---

[47] Cf. *Hom. Hymn to Aphrodite* 5.36–37, speaking of her powers of love and seduction: "Even the heart of Zeus, who delights in thunder, is led astray by her; though he is greatest of all and has the lot (*emmore times*) of highest majesty" (trans. Evelyn-White).

[48] Hesiod, *Theog.* 73–75: "By force had reached a settlement with the Titans regarding honors." See Most's version—*Th.* 74: "and he distributed well all things alike to the immortals and devised their honors" (trans. Glenn Most Loeb-ed 2018). Cf. Boedeker (1983).

[49] Leclerc (1998) 94 draws our attention to the exceptional concentration of distribution-related terms in ll. ca. 400–450: *geras* (twice); *lanchano* (twice); *meiromai* (twice); *moira* (once); *time* (five Il. times); *timao* (three times); *tio* (twice). In the "Prayer to the Fates" (Simonides?), the three *moirai* are called Aisa, Klotho, and Lachêsis. See Bowra (1958).

gods, a generation preceding the Olympians—had once also made a distribution (*dasmos*), apparently by lot.⁵⁰

> For as many as were born of Earth and Ocean amongst all these she (Hekate) has her due *portion* (*aisa*). The son of Kronos (Zeus) did her no wrong nor took anything away of all that was her *portion* among the former Titan gods: but she holds, as the division (*dasmos*) was at the first from the beginning, privilege (*geras*) both in earth, and in heaven, and in sea. (Hes. *Theog.* 414–425; Evelyn-White)

The special prize, the *geras*, marks the uniqueness of the one who gets it. It depends on his or her particular quality; it is a reward that recognizes status and balances the lottery's randomness. In the real world of archaic Greece, the *geras* given to leaders would disappear; yet in the "earlier" heroic world, as reflected in the *Iliad* and the *Odyssey*, the *geras* was the equivalent of the hero's honor. Without it, he is left with "nothing," rendering him equal to any other participant in the lottery since ordinary soldiers get no special prizes. In what way was the particular portion of the king contrasted with the drawing of lots? The question is significant since the position arguing for a top-down distribution, mainly depending on the kings, does not recognize the drawing of lots as an instrument for fair distribution of booty among all.⁵¹ I disagree; the *geras* too was formally a gift *given* to a leader by the "people" or "army." The presence of the "community" is significant.

Homer's *Iliad* starts with an assembly that forces the king's hand: he must give back his *geras*, the girl Chryseis, to her father, the priest of the god Apollo.⁵² King Agamemnon is left with "nothing," although otherwise he is still the richest and the most powerful. This *geras* has nothing to do with what he might have received in addition by lot. To compensate himself, Agamemnon abuses his authority, or so he is expressly told when he forces Achilles to hand over Achilles's *geras*, the girl Briseis. Now Achilles is the one "left with nothing" since the *geras*, a singular and unique gift, had marked him as memorable in terms of honor and reputation. The "wrath of Achilles" follows, and the hero goes on strike, resulting in awful harm to the entire Achaian host.

---

⁵⁰ Cf. *Theog.* 390ff. Leclerc (1998) 91–92; for the general implications of *dateomai* and the lack of any other means for such group distribution in our sources see ch.1 Endnote 3. Macé (2014) 450 misses the point of the previous lottery. Moreover, he thinks that Zeus draws on his *own* portion to give to Hekate, that of his brother, and also the commons. This seems speculative and perceives the issue as a zero-sum division of "territory" in human, not cosmic, terms.

⁵¹ See Endnote 1 especially with reference to the work by Hans van Wees (1992).

⁵² Raaflaub (1993) 55 on the role of the assembly as controller and witness to the distribution of spoils.

Was it a petty, self-indulgent overreaction? Achilles is not alone. In a lost Greek epic poem, *Thebaïs*, that predates the mid-seventh century, the old and blind Oedipus curses his sons, prophesying they will die at each other's hand because they neglected to give him the choice cut of meat he deserved. This is not the behavior of a petty father. The "wrath of Achilles" that launches the whole sequence of the *Iliad* arises when the hero is robbed of his *geras*; similarly, the wrath of Oedipus arises not because he missed having his filet mignon for dinner. The loss of the choice cut represented being cheated of his *geras*. The *geras*, in this case, was the choice portion of sacrificial meat that mythological kings and historical priests expected to get. Being cheated (Oedipus) or robbed (Achilles) of the special portion goes beyond a mere insult: it is a strike at the very essence of honor and position.[53]

Therefore, Agamemnon also has a point since both heroes fear the same thing: to be left without their special *geras*. Unlike the gods, who could conjure up the island of Rhodes when Helios was left with nothing, among humans, this was a zero-sum game. Since the entire distribution of the booty had already been done, says Achilles in the *Iliad*, there is nothing in reserve, and it would be impossible to bring back all the booty to the "common store" and hold a redistribution.[54]

Like the angry Poseidon claiming initial equality with Zeus, Achilles complains that Agamemnon ought not to have treated him, an *equal*, in such a manner, as if he, Achilles, was a "migrant with no rights" (*Il.* 9.648, 16.59). The contrast with the "alien" emphasizes the exclusiveness of the group of "equals" who raid together and share booty together, fairly and equally. The conventions seem clear to the participants: when Odysseus raids Ismaros in Thrace, he takes care to oversee the distribution of the booty equally among his companions (*hetairoi*), so that "none might go cheated of his 'equal' or 'fair' (*ise*) portion" (*Od.* 9.39–42, trans. Lattimore).

Aside from the *geras*, heroes could also be distinguished by selective lotteries. In such lotteries, a person is singled out of the group of (equal) participants in the drawing of lots. The group consists of "equals," yet they are all heroes; only such equals may participate in a chariot race or an arrow-shooting contest.[55] Aias was selected by lot to fight Hektor from among several other heroes. In such selective lotteries, the entire "group" is distinguished from the army by their heroic status. The *order* of the chariots in the chariot race or the arrow-shooting context is also

---

[53] Cingano (2004) with Cingano (2000). Cf. Athenaeus 11.465e; Laurentinian Scholiast on Sophocles's *Oedipus at Colonus* 1375: "And when Oedipus noticed the haunch, he threw it on the ground and said: 'Oh! Oh! My sons have sent this mocking me.' So he prayed to Zeus the king and the other deathless gods that each might fall by his brother's hand and go down into the house of Hades."
[54] *Il.* 1.124–126, and see below.
[55] Finkelberg (1998) 14.

set by a ("procedural") lottery: "They chose their lots and shook them up in a brazen helmet" (Lattimore).[56] Here the lottery appears in its role of "establishing turns," which later, in the fifth century, will find a political expression and use in terms of the rotation of offices.

The following scene about the selection of Aias stresses the idea of the lottery for the selection of "one out of many": nine mighty heroes volunteer to fight a duel with the terrible Trojan warrior, Hector. Who will be the one? The nine warriors throw their personal markers into a helmet, old Nestor shakes it, and the marker of the mighty Aias is the first to pop out.[57] Thus, a choice has been made: no one will contest it, nobody's honor has been humiliated, and no resentment follows. Avoiding resentment and affording a new starting point is one of the significant advantages of decisions made by lot.

> Now before them again spoke the Gerenian horseman, Nestor: Let the lot be shaken (*pallo*) for all of you, to see who wins it. . . . So he spoke, and each of them marked a lot as his own one lot. They threw them in the helmet of Atreus's son, Agamemnon, and the people, holding up their hands to the gods, prayed to them. Then would murmur any man, gazing into the wide sky: Father Zeus, let Aias win the lot, or else Diomedes, Tydeus's son, or the king himself of golden Mykenai (Agamemnon). So they spoke, and Nestor the Gerenian horseman shook (*pallo*) the lots, and a lot leapt (*throsko*) from the helmet, that one that they all had wished for, the lot of Aias; . . . glorious Aias, he held forth his hand, and the herald stood by him, and put the lot in it, and he saw his mark on the lot, and knew it, and his heart was gladdened. (174–191, trans. Lattimore)

The lots (*kleroi*) may be pebbles or potsherds with an individual mark (*sema*). The language is traditional, and we find the same terms used in lotteries centuries later. The "shaking with the lot" (the verb is *pallo*) is a general expression for casting lots, and the other verb, *lanchano*, is for winning or getting something through the lottery. The combination (*lanchano, pallo, kleroi*) assures us that Homer understood *lanchano* in the sense of "to get one's share/place by lot."[58]

The scene had a long life in terms of public exposure and representation in drama and art.[59] In the first half of the fifth century, the sculptor Onatas made statues that the Achaians supposedly dedicated at Olympia, representing Nestor and the participating heroes casting lots, perhaps enhancing the significance of procedural lotteries for pan-Hellenic athletic competitions at Olympia.[60]

---

[56] *Il.* 23.862. Cf., for the practice in later periods, Soph.Elec. 698–711 (chariot race at Delphi).
[57] *Il.* 7.169–199; cf. *Il.* 3.314–325; *Od.* 10.203–207.
[58] See Appendix.
[59] Soph. *Ajax* 1283–1287; Paus. 5.25.8–10.
[60] As convincingly argued by Ajootian (2007) 121–122; Paus. 5.25.8–10.

There are also offerings dedicated by the whole Achaean *ethnos* in common; they represent those who, when Hector challenged any Greek to meet him in single combat, dared to cast lots to choose the champion. They stand, armed with spears and shields, near the great temple. Right opposite, on a second pedestal, is a figure of Nestor, who has thrown the lot of each into the helmet. (Trans. W. H. S. Jones—Loeb ed.)

Pausanias identifies the heroes, all present, except Odysseus (Nero had grabbed that statue for himself) and quotes the "signature" of Onatas.

In Homer, the language of prayer to Zeus (that the chosen lot may belong to either Aias or Diomedes or Agamemnon) does not convey the expectation that Zeus would determine the result of the lottery. It is rather an invocation for the lottery to take place under the auspices of Zeus. I shall return to this passage to discuss the extent to which gods were involved with lotteries and their results.

The choice of "one out of many" is paralleled by the selection of a group for a dangerous mission. It is not composed of volunteers but by lot. Odysseus, trapped in the cave of the Cyclops, says,

Next I told the rest of the men to cast lots, to find out which of them must endure with me to take up the great beam and spin it in Cyclops' eye when sweet sleep had come over him. The ones drew it that I myself have wanted chosen, four men, and I myself was the fifth, and numbered among them. (*Od.* 9.330ff., trans. Lattimore, adapted)

Note that Odysseus, as a leader, does not participate in the lottery. However, even as a leader, he does not always get to decide who does what. When arriving in the land of Circe, Odysseus divides his men into two groups. One was to stay behind by the ship, the other to explore the land, with the eventual dire consequences of Circe turning the group into pigs:

Promptly then we shook (*pallo*) the lots in a brazen helmet, and the lot (*kleros*) of great-hearted Eurylochus (chosen to go and explore) sprang out (*throsko*). (*Od.* 10.206–207, Lattimore)

An entire army can be made up of men chosen by lot from tiny groups. At least some of the soldiers who went to besiege Troy were thus chosen. For example, a family with seven sons was obliged to send one of them to fight in the Trojan War: "He has six sons beside, and I am the seventh, and I shook lots (*pallo*) with the others, and it was my lot (*kleros*) to come on this venture" (*Il.* 24.399–400, Lattimore). That was a common practice even in later periods: "When Perdikkas (king of Macedonia) heard of the revolt of the Greeks, he drew by lot from the

Macedonians three thousand infantry and eight hundred horsemen."[61] We shall return to the use of the lot in military affairs (chapter 5.1), but let us just note that even from a purely military point of view, a lottery is an effective means of conscription: if you keep putting the best soldiers in elite units, you end up with most other units weakened. The lottery provides a *mixture*, an essential characteristic of distributive lotteries. In the *Iliad* we find the allies stationed by lot: "By Thymbre are stationed by lot (*lanchano*) the Lykians and the proud Mysians with the Phrygians" (*Il.*10.430, Lattimore, adapted).

In the *Iliad* the chances for the seven brothers who had to send off one to war are equal, and there is no question of seniority: a brother is chosen regardless of the order of his birth. We observe the same principle early in the historical period: In the middle of the seventh century, when the community of the island of Thera (Santorini) sent a colony to Libya, one brother was chosen from each household through a state lottery. "The Therans determined to send out men from their seven regions, taking by lot one of every pair of brothers."[62] Choosing by lot a son to fight or colonize implies *a priori* equality of status. No brother is predestined to be senior in position or fulfill a specific future role (in contrast to the medieval notion of "the firstborn to war, the second to the clergy"). The egalitarianism within families is also expressed by rules of inheritance (no primogeniture): the drawing of lots determined the distribution of inheritance (ch. 4), a custom also attested in modern Greece.[63]

While being different in their purpose, lotteries that fix distribution, mixture, turns, and positions, or that single out a person or a specific group, share the assumption of the equality of both status and merit (eligibility). All are equal before the chance and interchangeable, thus expressing an egalitarian outlook. They differ, of course, in how they define the group of participants and their purpose. With distributive lotteries, the group of "sharers" is predefined and self-aware: all the Olympian gods got their portions of honors (*timai*), all Greek colonists got portions of land, and all soldiers received portions of booty.

A closer focus on the soldiers reveals that they are often treated as "companions," *hetairoi*, of the hero such as Achilles and his "Myrmidons" or Odysseus and his men. Those companions provide another angle for explaining why "equal and fair" sharing is so intimately integrated into Greek practice. Curiously, in the foundation decree of Cyrene (ch. 6), the settlers to be sent out with the founder Battos are defined as *hetairoi*.[64] However, those *hetairoi*, unlike

---

[61] Diod. 18.7.3; on Hellenistic Crete, *poleis* agreed in treaties to deal with military threats together by selecting soldiers by lot and joining forces, e.g., between Malla and Lyttos, *IC* I xix 1, ll. 4–8 (late third–early second centuries).
[62] Hdt. 4.153; the point is repeated in an inscription that quotes the foundation decree (Chapter 6)
[63] Levy (1956); Friedl (1963) 60–64; Herzfeld (1980).
[64] ML 5 l. 27. Cf. Donlan (1998).

Homeric *hetairoi*, stood for an entire community, as demonstrated by the fact that the Theran *hetairoi* were selected by lot, one from each household: they were not a personal retinue of the founder. Such a transition from "captain and personal *hetairoi*" to the entire political collective is implied in the story of Kolaios. About one generation before Cyrene's foundation, Kolaios of Samos struck it rich in Spain, followed by a dedication at the Samian Heraion not on his behalf but of "the Samians" (see ch. 6).[65] On the other hand, Homeric *hetairoi* were "godlike companions" (*Od.* 14.247), but they could also be *leisteres*, pirates (17.426–443), probably with their code of equal sharing of booty. That is how Herodotus, for example, envisages the distribution of booty following a battle. Specifically, following the battle between the Carthaginians and the Etruscans against the Phokaians, Herodotus says, "As for the crews of the disabled ships, the Carthaginians and Tyrrhenians drew lots for them (*dia-lanchano*)."[66] The entire Achaian army in the *Iliad* was roughly a pastiche of bands of companions and their leaders.

Theirs was basically an egalitarian pirate code of sharing the booty of raids with an extra share in the form of *geras* to the captains. It was thus very different from the Caribbean pirates mentioned earlier, whose code was proportional to rank. The Achaians, often led by Achilles, raided or conquered islands such as Lesbos and Tenedos, or places on the mainland belonging to allies of Troy. Achilles proudly announced that he had led successful raids against twenty-one cities, some quite distant from Troy: "But I say that I have stormed from my ships twelve cities of men and by land eleven more through the generous Troad" (*Il.* 9.328–329, Lattimore).

Agamemnon would conveniently avoid those raids and stay in the field, a fact that Achilles presents as evidence of his cowardice. Nevertheless, aside from the raids, there must have been plenty of distribution all the time, and a chief leader would be responsible for the whole army. We need to remember that only major raids brought exceptional booty. The conquest of the islands of Lemnos and Lesbos, for example, provided riches and slaves, and the island kept serving as a source of wine for the army stationed before Troy on the mainland (*Il.* 7.467–475). However, the need to distribute spoils was probably a matter of daily routine, especially with food distribution (often in the form of live animals), a point obscured by the poet's emphasis on gold, silver, and concubines. Odysseus, we shall see, divided up goats and the flock captured from the Cyclops. It is perhaps significant that in biblical Hebrew and Akkadian, one "eats" the booty: *'akhol šelal* (enjoy the use of [literally, eat/consume] the spoil), and in Akkadian, *šalallatum*

---

[65] Hdt. 4.151.2; cf. Humphreys (1978) 168 (the dedication at Delphi was made by the crew). Discussed in ch. 6.
[66] Hdt 1.167.1. Cf. Bagnasco (2001).

akalum.[67] Therefore, the accepted norms, conventions, and mechanisms for such distributions were probably familiar to all. It is no wonder the same arguments are hurled at Agamemnon both by Achilles and by Thersites, a common soldier, in the assembly of the soldiers (*Il.* 2.225–240).

Thucydides, the skeptical fifth-century Athenian historian, never doubted the historicity of the Trojan War. He explained why it took as long as ten years to capture the city: the besieging Greeks were too few, and half of them were busy getting food for the other half.[68] He probably had a point: in a world with no means of conservation (canned food did not appear until Napoleon),[69] getting provisions was a matter of almost daily effort, and perishable spoils (except captured live animals, which were the best way to preserve meat) needed to be distributed among companions of raiding parties. The account of the Athenian Xenophon about the "March of the Ten Thousand" (the *Anabasis*) tells the story of the Greek mercenaries who made their way, fighting, through Kurdistan to the Black Sea. Most soldiers were preoccupied with getting food: they were either negotiating to buy it or simply robbing it.

Xenophon does not tell us how soldiers divided up the "catch" or perishable booty; apparently, it was too self-evident to mention.[70] A few centuries earlier, Homer did. Having captured some goats, Odysseus and his companions divide them up by lot: "Now there were twelve ships that went with me, and for each one nine goats were portioned out (*lanchano*)" (*Od.* 9.159–160, trans. Lattimore).[71] It is reasonable to assume that division of goats and other foodstuffs were frequent and common, with constant rotation among the companions. Recourse to some distributive measures, with the lottery here explicitly attested, must have been a constant feature of life in the field.

As in the *Anabasis*, the soldiers fighting in Troy came from all over the Greek world, and the division and distribution of foodstuffs and booty was a problem relevant to all. The army besieging Troy was similarly pan-Hellenic, composed of groups from far-flung regions. Standard conventions for what was "equal and fair"—namely, equality of portions and the mode of their distribution—probably developed following an ethos of the "warrior band" when a leader got a special portion and the rest of the booty was distributed among the companions or *hetairoi*.[72]

We need to distinguish who is in charge of distributive lotteries and who has the authority to decide what to give. In the myth of Helios, Zeus conducts the

---

[67] Algavish (2002) 245.
[68] Thucydides 1.11.
[69] The first conserves were invented by Nicolas Appert in 1810 and were first used for Napoleon's army; cf. Appert (1810)..
[70] Cf. Dalby (1992); Garlan (1989).
[71] See Endnote 1 for a detailed discussion of equality in such contexts.
[72] Kitts (2002) surveys theories related to sacrifice and the notion of *Männerbund*.

drawing of lots; down on earth, the kings were apparently responsible for the procedure of distributing booty. However, they are not the givers; they do not decide who gets what. We have explicit statements made to the effect that it is not the king but the "community," either that of soldiers or the people back home, that has the authority to give. The army gives the *geras* to the kings and gives (distributes) to itself the rest of the booty through a mechanism of drawing lots, which the kings may oversee. However, the *geras*—the unique, privileged prize that seems to be chosen by the recipient—might seem to contradict such a notion, especially when we hear of complaints that Agamemnon took not one item but plenty and left the others with little to distribute. On the one hand, we hear that the king got his prize from the army/people; on the other, if Agamemnon could pick and choose for himself, then where was the community? The question is important if we are to understand the "horizontal" perception of Greek political communities (*poleis*) in the centuries to come, expressed too by the use of the lot.[73]

If control of the booty were entirely up to the king, that would imply a top-down situation, an arbitrary distribution, and an insignificant role of the "people." The implications of the lottery as expressing a definition of the community (who merits access?), signifying values of equality and fairness, and indicating that the source of authority rested with "the people" would be diminished.[74] Scholars seem to disagree on this point, and understandably so since the text implies some contradictions. On one hand, there are explicit statements that the "king" gets his prize as a gift *from* the people/army (*laos*). On the other hand, the king appears to dispense booty as he feels like, and some heroes are clearly in possession of personally gained riches that never went to any common store. I discuss these matters at Endnote 1, where I conclude that evidence for personal riches possessed by heroes is no contradiction but simply points to the (neglected) category of booty called *enara*. Otherwise, booty was first brought to the middle (*es ton meson*), whence a *geras* was given and the rest distributed and allotted to all.

The *enara* were mostly arms and armor stripped from the slain, their horses, or live captives who were captured either as concubines or for ransom.[75] In contrast to *enara*, the *geras* becomes the honorary gift in public, a ceremonious giving and distribution of spoils that provides the recipient of a *geras* with glory and reputation. *Enara* are property, not prize. Personal wealth merely makes the recipient rich, with no linked public recognition for his *kleos*. Briseis, the *geras* of Achilles forcefully taken away by Agamemnon, provides an excellent example for apparent contradictory statements that could be resolved simply by

---

[73] Raaflaub (1993).
[74] See Simonton (2017) 13–20 for a survey of the presence of the *demos* in archaic Greece.
[75] On ransom see Wilson (2002), with details and comparison to biblical types of booty in Endnote 1.

observing her change of status and transfer: the private capture of Achilles ("acquired by Achilles's spear"; *Il.* 9.343), chosen out and taken by Achilles (*Il.* 2.689–691), publicly given (= ceremoniously handed over) to Achilles by Agamemnon (9.367–368) after having been given by the Achaians to Achilles. Thus, apparent contradictions become a linear progression: stages from a private capture to a public *geras* (see analysis in Endnote 1).

A common soldier, Thersites, gets up in the assembly and protests to Agamemnon:

> "Son of Atreus, what things further do you want, or find fault with, / now? Your shelters are filled with bronze, there are plenty of the choicest / women for you within your shelter, whom *we Achaians / give to you* first of all whenever we capture some stronghold." (*Il.* 2.225–228, Lattimore)

Note that the speech of Thersites is the only speech on behalf of the body of Achaians and not of a leader. This is the only place where the verb "to give," *didomi*, and "Achaians" appear in the first-person plural. Thersites speaks on behalf of the Achaians as a whole (he is a common soldier).[76]

Homer cleverly provides us with contradictory attitudes that too often color our interpretation of this straightforward statement of fact: "We Achaians give to you."[77] Regarding attitude, Thersites is described as disgustingly ugly and of a lower class. When he finishes talking, Odysseus beats him up, followed by the mockery and jeering of the other soldiers, supposedly identifying with the punishment Odysseus metes out. However, do they? They say that his beating of Thersites, a lowly, defenseless soldier in the assembly, is a greater feat than all of Odysseus's other heroic exploits. This seems sarcastic, coming from the veterans. As for Thersites, what matters is not the framing of his words (ugly person, clownish soldier) but the content of his speech, which is cogent, to the point, and implies larger issues such as class, hierarchy, and military discipline.[78] Concerning the spoils, Odysseus beats him but does not contradict him: reacting to Thersites, he actually reiterates the role of the army as giving to the king, not vice versa (*Il.* 2.254–256): "Yet you sit here throwing abuse at Agamemnon, Atreus' son, the shepherd of the people, because the Danaän fighters give him much" (trans. Lattimore).

Therefore, "the Achaians" are the ones to give a portion of the booty to the king, not vice versa. The point is stated a few times, primarily by the peers of

---

[76] *Perseus under Philologic*, s.v. Thersites as a common soldier: contra Marks (2005).
[77] See Rihll (1992) 44.
[78] Note the response in 2.204–205: "Lordship for many is no good thing. Let there be one ruler, one king, to whom the son of devious-devising Kronos gives the scepter and right of judgement, to watch over his people." (Lattimore)

Odysseus, not by common soldiers. Specifically regarding Chryseis, for example, it is expressly said that the "sons of the Achaians" gave the daughter of the priest of Apollo to Agamemnon. There are quite a few such cases.[79] It is noteworthy that such "giving" is articulated with varying, nonformulaic expressions (revolving around the verb *didomi*, "to give"), so it is clear that the poet is attentive in describing the *action* that takes place. In social terms, a significant implication of the army/people giving to the king is the apparent sense of a *bounded group*, self-aware of itself as the source of authority and power.

At one point, the tough hero Achilles tearfully seeks solace with his mother, the goddess Thetis (manly Greek heroes weep quite freely). He reminds her that

> "We went against Thebe, the sacred city of Eëtion, and the city was sacked, and carried everything back to this place, and the sons of the Achaians made a fair distribution (*eu dassanto—dateomai*, 'distributed well among themselves') and for Atreus' son they chose out Chryseis of the fair cheeks." (*Il.* 1.365–369, Lattimore)

The convention seems consistent: a raid, a capture, some "personal booty," a special prize chosen and given by the army to the chief (a prize, one assumes, he sets his eyes on himself); the rest of the booty is divided up among all.

Let us take another example, but this time we need to trust the words of a liar. On several occasions, the hero Odysseus, suffering through ten years of wanderings, hides his true identity and invents one for himself, such as that of a Cretan marauder. From a literary angle, what Homer does is ingenious: the fantastic tales, such as encountering a one-eyed giant cannibal, are "the truth," whereas all the lying tales are realistic. This verisimilitude (resembling truth) is heaven-sent for a historian trying to tweak out snapshots of reality.[80]

Therefore, in the guise of a Cretan, here is Odysseus, boasting of his successful raids before the Trojan War. The passage expresses the relationship between the leader's special prize (*geras*) and the leader's participation in the lottery *together* with everyone else. In the passage, Odysseus distinguishes between what he "gets" in the general distribution by lot and what he personally chooses. The distinction indeed contradicts the view that it is all up to the king, as we have also seen with Odysseus, who says, "Of this I would choose what pleased my mind, and much I afterward obtained by lot (*Od.* 14.232)."

---

[79] *Achaians* to Agamemnon: *Il.* 1.123, 1.127–128, 1.135, 1.368–369, 2.227–228, 2.255–256; to Achilles: *Il.* 1.162, 1.276, 18.444; *Achaians* to Nestor: *Il.* 11.625–626; Phaiakians to Alkinoös: *Od.* 7.9–11.
[80] Malkin (1998) ch. 1.

In the "true" story, Odysseus and his companions stop at an island that faces the land of the cannibalistic Cyclops. Except for goats, the island is empty. As mentioned earlier, the distribution of the goats by lot (nine per ship) implies fairness and the avoidance of resentment: a sailor might feel unhappy if he got the old billy goat instead of the delectable kid, but he could blame no one. Moreover, the chief gets a special portion *from* his companions: "to each nine goats fell by lot (*lanchano*), but for me alone, they chose out (*exaireo*) ten."[81]

Odysseus and some of his men cross over to the rich land facing the island and arrive at the cave of Polyphemos, a giant cannibal who stuffs his stomach with a pair of companions for each meal. Now the two types of Homeric lottery combine: "one/some out of many" and the distributive lottery. First, Odysseus offers strong, undiluted wine to the Cyclops; Polyphemos then falls asleep in a drunken stupor, and Odysseus, together with some of his men, sinks a red-hot stake into his single eye. The men were not volunteers but selected by lot (*Od.* 9.331). The lottery is a procedure; it becomes equivalent to "good luck" when those whom Odysseus preferred were the ones chosen.

Having blinded the giant, Odysseus and his *hetairoi* were still stuck in the cave since Polyphemos, after he had let his herd of sheep enter the cave, blocked the entrance with a huge stone that no human could remove. Nevertheless, on the morning after, blind and furious as he was, he still had to let his flock out for grazing; each one of the companions hid under the fleece of a sheep and, hanging upside down, managed to escape from the cave while the blind Cyclops was groping in vain at the fleece above, searching for his tormentors.

Having escaped from the cave, Odysseus hurries to amass the Cyclops's flock and returns to the safety of the island opposite where the rest of his companions have been waiting for him. Now the lottery becomes distributive and includes everyone, both those who were at the cave and those who stayed behind. Apparently this was the convention despite Achilles's protest: "Stay at home or fight your hardest—your share will be the same. Coward and hero are given equal honor" (*Il.* 9.318–319).[82]

> Then we took from out the hollow ship the flocks of the Cyclops, and divided them among ourselves (*dateomai*), that so far as in me lay no man might go defrauded of an equal share (*epi ises*). But the ram my well-greaved comrades gave to me alone, when the flocks were divided, as a gift apart; and on the shore I sacrificed him to Zeus, son of Cronos, god of the dark clouds. (*Od.* 9.548–552; Murray, adapted)

---

[81] *Od.* 9.159–160.
[82] Cf. Finkelberg (1998) 15; 18 on *emmore times*. She rightly claims (15) that "*Time* is a 'distributive value.'"

Counting sheep, goats, pigs, horses, and even captives is possible so that the fairness and equality of the distribution become evident.[83] Again, the men choose for Odysseus once an extra goat and, on another occasion, a ram, while he conducts the procedure, insisting that "no man might go defrauded of an equal share."[84] Similarly, this is how Odysseus described his raid on the Kikones (*Od.* 9.40–42): "There I sacked the city and slew the men; and from the city, we took their wives and great store of treasure, and divided them among us, that so far as lay in me no man might go defrauded of an equal share" (trans. Murray). The leader is explicitly dependent on his companions, and the authority *to choose out and give* emanates from them. However, this repeated insistence on fairness hints at occasions when equality/fairness could be abused. Aside from that, during the distribution of booty at Ismaros, Odysseus enriched himself through personal capture (*enara*), as seems to be the case of Maro, Apollo's priest captured for ransom, who gave Odysseus the wine with which he intoxicated the Cyclops.[85] Odysseus mentions "gifts," pointing to guest-friendship as another source of personal wealth beyond that of mere companions. However, grabbing too much personal booty is considered abusive. Fairness, it seems, means not only that everyone gets an equal share by lot, but also that the leader refrains from abusing his power to get an exaggerated (unfair) portion, as Achilles complains about Agamemnon. Odysseus's companions were not stupidly greedy when they opened the "sack of winds." The plot aside, it is their *expectation* that needs to be taken into account. They react to the gifts given to Odysseus by Aiolos that he took for himself (as gifts of guest-friendship?) while they were apparently expecting a distribution. The companions, in short, felt abused (10.40–42):

> "See now, this man is loved by everybody and favored by all, whenever he visits anyone's land and city, and is bringing home with him handsome treasures taken from the plunder of Troy, while we, who have gone through everything he has on the same venture, come home with our hands empty. Now too Aiolos in favor of friendship has given him all these goods. Let us quickly look inside and see what is in there, and how much silver and gold this bag contains inside it." (*Od.* 10.39–45, trans. Lattimore)

Conventions of fairness of what a leader may keep for himself are better revealed in an open-ended episode, told by the old counselor Nestor about his

---

[83] Cf. Pritchett (1991) 375 on the same formula in *Od.* 9.42 (Ismaros): the scholion also says that the spoils (*laphura*) are distributed equally. Alternative translation (that also distances the leader from the results of distribution): "in such a way that no man went away deprived of his equal share through me."

[84] Cf. *Od.* 9.160 where each ship gets nine goats and Odysseus ten with the same insistence on equality.

[85] *Od.* 9.197–205.

days of youth (*Il.* 11.678ff.) and his first *razzia*. Because they were frequently raided and robbed by the Epeians (from the historical region of Elis in the northwestern Peloponnese), Nestor led his people, the Pylians (from Pylos, likewise in the northwestern Peloponnese), on a successful counterraid, and, like Odysseus stealing the flocks, Nestor drove back herds of all kinds. Since this was not a mere raid but one that was supposed to get back a "debt owed," the distribution of the booty takes the form of proportional payback: each person gets to compensate himself for the personal loss the Epeians had inflicted on him in the past. What is left is distributed fairly and equally. It seems unclear who, except for the leaders themselves, gets to decide what is owed, and the story has been misinterpreted as one of disproportionate grabbing by the elite, an illustration of the arbitrary power of the king and the diminished role of the community.[86]

Neleus (Nestor's father) was owed much. Nestor, his son, returned with a considerable amount of booty, with 50 herds of each category: cattle, sheep, swine, and goats, in addition to 150 "chestnut mares and many of them had foals at the teat."

> And next day as dawn showed the heralds lifted their clear cry for all to come who had anything owed them in shining Elis. In addition, the men who were chiefs among the Pylians assembling divided the spoil. There were many to whom the Epeians owed something since we in Pylos were few and we had been having the worst of it. (*Il.* 11.685–689, Lattimore)

The most prominent leader, Neleus (Nestor's father), took for himself more than anyone, a "vast amount." The large portion of booty may be confusing, implying abuse, unequal division, and elite grabbing. We note that the overall booty is defined as *rhusia*, "pledges against security for repayments, or simply booty seized in reprisal." It is a unique term in Homer, denoting that here we have exceptional circumstances of reprisal, not a simple raid.[87]

On a close count Neleus recompensed himself modestly, despite the hyperbole ("vast amount"). He got one herd of cattle and a flock of 300 sheep "with their herdsmen" (11.696) out of 200 herds (50 herds each of sheep, cows, pigs, and goats), and none of the 150 mares. As a leader, he was entitled to *enara*, which included personal capture: "the herdsmen" and four chariot-racing horses, a personal compensation because he had once sent a four-horse team to a chariot competition, but the greedy king Augeias confiscated them.

---

[86] Van Wees (1992) 299–311 and fuller discussion in Endnote 1.
[87] *Il* 11.674, with Hainsworth's commentary.

The numbers seem fantastic, but the proportional division is realistic. That is epic, and it glorifies the horse rustlers and sheep thieves. Nevertheless, the conventions for the division of booty and the proportions between leaders and "the people" seem consistent and clear: the "leaders" (not a single king) make decisions about what particular portions should be allocated as compensation.

> Now aged Neleus, angry over things said and things done, chose out (*exaireo*) a vast amount for himself (actually a small percentage, as just observed), and gave the rest to the people to divide (*daitreuo*) among them, so no man will be defrauded of his equal (or "fair," *ise*) share. (*Il.* 11.703–705, Lattimore, adapted)

These words—"so no man will be defrauded of his fair/equal share"—are precisely the same as those used by Odysseus earlier and constitute an epic "formula," reflecting a convention. Neleus works within a communal framework: it is the community, or rather "the leaders of the Pylians," who "gathered together and made division" (*Il.* 11.687).

In sum, even with poetic exaggeration and the focus on the hero rather than the people, we observe a mechanism of decision and established conventions of what is to be set aside for leaders and general distribution. In the episode just recounted, the "leaders" (not a single ruler) make decisions regarding special portions, and "the people" get to have the rest of the booty distributed, with each person getting an "equal share." Neleus, who may be suspected of abuse ("vast amount"), in fact takes a very reasonable percentage. He is the opposite of Agamemnon, who flaunts conventions and keeps far too much for himself. That is one reason why Nestor brings up the fair distribution of booty at Pylos, to contrast it with Agamemnon's abuse.

This practice seems consistent and is found elsewhere in the *Odyssey*. With his raft blown to pieces, the wretched Odysseus finds himself naked on the beach in Phaiakia. Soon the generous Phaiakians would be sending him home. We are at the moment when Princess Nausikaa takes the naked, shipwrecked Odysseus under her wings and escorts him home, where her elderly maiden slave is waiting. Now we turn our attention to her: how was she enslaved?

Somehow, the supposedly peace-loving Phaiakians, who are also fantastic sailors (yet live in total isolation), had once been raiding and kidnapping like everyone else:

> There an old woman of Apeire, Eurymedousa the chamber attendant, lighted a fire for her. Oarswept ships once carried her over from Apeire, and *the men chose her out from the spoil* as a prize (*geras exelon*) for Alkinoös because he ruled all the Phaiakians and the people listened, as to a god. (*Od.* 7.7–12, Lattimore, adapted)

It is "the Phaiakians" who "choose out" for their king his *geras,* just as Odysseus's companions "chose out" (*exaireo*); the same verb is used in both cases) an extra goat and, later, a ram. The Greek verb for this kind of choice and gift is "choose out," which also appears in the context of land set aside for the gods in colonies. For instance, a fifth-century Athenian decree to found a colony specifies that the "chosen-out lands" (*exaireo*), the sacred precincts, should remain as they are, aside from the general division of the plots of land to the colonists.[88]

Why choose out anything? Alkinoös received the female slave from the people because he was the king, and leadership was contractual. A set of values revolving around reciprocity seems to emerge: just as the woman Eurymedousa was given to the king of the Phaiakians by the people, old Nestor had a woman who was also "given to him," but now a reason is specified for what the people expected of him.

> And lovely-haired Hekamede made them a potion, she whom the old man won from Tenedos, when Achilleus stormed it. She was the daughter of great-hearted Arsinoös. The Achaians chose her out for Nestor, because he was best of them in counsel. (*Il.* 11.624, Lattimore)

Similar to the Phaiakians, we have here a more explicit *quid pro quo*: the Achaians give her to him because he is such a wise counselor. Similarly, as we shall see, the "Elders of the People" promise to give rich estates to a hero in return for killing a wild boar and fighting their enemies.

Yet some passages in the *Iliad* give a different impression, that of an arbitrary king who grabs as many spoils as he wants. When Achilles is sulking in his tent, refusing to participate in the fighting, he retorts angrily to those trying to convince him otherwise:

> From all these [Achilles's own raids] we took forth treasures, goodly and numerous, and we would bring them back, and give them to Agamemnon, Atreus' son; while he, waiting back beside the swift ships, would take them, and distribute them little by little, and keep many. (*Il.* 9.330–334, trans. Lattimore)

Achilles carries (*phero*) the booty to Agamemnon, who eventually distributes (*dasasketo, dateomai*) too little. The expression "Agamemnon distributed" does not signify that the king had arbitrary powers but that he acted arbitrarily. As noted, the verb *dateomai* is only used of people sharing out *among themselves*, not allotting to someone else (Endnote 1). The verb *dateomai* (δατέομαι) is

---

[88] Malkin (1984) 44–48.

mostly employed with a plural subject.[89] Agamemnon, therefore, *presides* over the distribution, as did Zeus when he presided over the distribution of *timai*. Agamemnon was acting precisely like Neleus:[90] deciding how much to keep and what to distribute. However, in contrast to Neleus who respected the correct proportion (perhaps taking slightly more than usual since had a "debt owed"), Agamemnon, who had nothing to do previously with the people sacked by Achilles (i.e., no "debt"), was simply abusing his powers, or so Achilles implies. Agamemnon kept disproportionate chunks of the booty without justification, not bringing it to the middle, to the common store.

Why does Homer make Nestor use the example of Neleus to convince Agamemnon to give up on Briseis? (Nestor is explicit about it.) His story implies, first, that Neleus had kept to the right proportion; second, that Nestor felt it necessary to justify his father taking extra booty (debt owed) as distinct from the current situation and Agamemnon's grabbing: it implies that this was a divergence from the expected norm, namely one unique *geras* to a leader and the rest for distribution. As we saw in the case of Oedipus, who cursed his sons because they abused his *geras*, *geras* was mostly about honor, not quantity.

Once the *geras* has been chosen and given by the army, the rest is assembled in a common store and distributed among all. We saw how Zeus offered Helios, who missed the initial divine lottery, to cancel the results and hold a new lottery, a suggestion Helios turned down. The idea of a second drawing of lots and distribution seems similarly inconceivable in the Greek camp:

> "How shall the great-hearted Achaians give you [Agamemnon] a prize now? There is no common store (*xuneia keimena*) of things lying about I know of. But what we took from the cities by storm has been distributed (*dateomai*); it is unbecoming for the people to call back things once given." (*Il.* 1.124–126, Lattimore, adapted)

The "common store" is public, seen by all, and its contents known to all. Marcel Detienne rightly emphasizes the role of "the middle" in Greek thought and pays special attention to "distribution *in* (or *toward*) the middle": *dasmos es to meson*.[91] Prizes of competition and booty are "brought to the middle," in the public eye, witnessed by the assembly. In short, booty is a "common treasure (*xyneioa*: *Il.* 1.124) that belongs to the *laoi*, so that only the *laoi* can replace it in the middle and distribute it again (*Il.* 1.124–126), normally in equal parts."[92]

---

[89] West (1966) *ad Theog.* 520. See especially *Theog.* 885; *Od.* 6.11; cf. Hes. *Theog.* 537, 544. See also Alkman fr. 65 Page.
[90] Hom. *Il.* 11.703–705.
[91] For the following points see Detienne ([1965] 1996) 91–105. Cf. Wallace (2015) 7–8.
[92] Pepe (2015) 19.

Speakers in the soldiers' assembly speak from the middle, and when Agamemnon abuses this public convention and speaks from where he sits, the poet makes a special note of that.[93] That was a common, persistent notion applied by historical Greeks. We saw a few examples in the introduction—for example, Theognis saying, "Who knows even when booty (literally 'when the sharing out,' *dasmos*) is still 'brought to the middle' (*es to meson*) to be shared out equally (*isos*)?"[94] At Samos, to "return power to the people" was expressed as placing power "in the middle."[95] We may enlarge on that. In Greek, deliberation on the course of action may be expressed as "to set the matter down in the middle." Herodotus also links the term *isonomia* (democracy) with "the middle."[96] That is how he also imagines the center in his famous dictum: "I know only one thing, and that is if all men were to bring their own ills *into the center* (*es meson*) so that they might be exchanged with those of others, in casting an eye on those of his fellows, each would be happy to take home with him those he had brought."[97] Furthermore, "the middle" and "equality" can be considered as an expression of what *just* men do: instead of holding on to supreme power, a man named Kadmos, because of his sense of justice (*dikaiosune*), "placed power in the middle," that is, returned it to the people as a whole.[98]

When Agamemnon finally capitulates and wishes to pay Achilles, Odysseus (Agamemnon's emissary) suggests bringing the promised gifts to the "middle of our assembly." That is what happens later (*Il*. 19.173, 242). Agamemnon has to bring it to the middle: had he personally given the gifts, Achilles would have been indebted to him directly instead of to the public.[99] So Odysseus "re-creates" the original situation of public distribution, witnessed by all. Setting things in the middle (apparently of the assembly) transforms them, making them public, and exposed to a common gaze.[100] Whereas the lottery defines the community (through access) from the circumference, the "middle" implies that circumference. It implies a view of the community from the center radiating outward, whereas the lottery does the same in reverse.[101]

---

[93] *Il*. 19.76–77.
[94] Theognis 678
[95] Hdt. 3.142; cf. 4.161.3 (the "middle" in Demonax's reforms at Cyrene); 7.164, the "middle," Kadmos at Kos.
[96] Hdt. 3.80.2; cf. 80.6; 3.142.3.
[97] Hdt. 7.152.2, emphasis added.
[98] Mariandrios: Hdt. 3.142.3; Kadmos: Hdt. 7.164.
[99] Redfield (1975) 16: "By the offered terms of settlement Agamemnon would convert Achilles into his dependent."
[100] Cf. Ready (2007).
[101] See figure 1.1 Detienne ([1965] 1996) 97: "A single spatial model dominates the interplay of all these institutions—deliberative assemblies, booty distribution, funeral games: a circular and centered space within which, ideally, each individual stands in reciprocal and reversible relationship to everyone else."

74 DRAWING LOTS

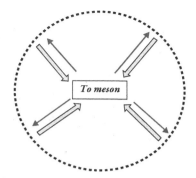

Figure 1.1 Distribution of booty *es to meson* and the circle of lottery participants: booty brought to the middle (the wider arrows) whence it is redistributed (the thinner arrows) to the predefined circle of participants. Cf. figure 1, Introduction.

His unique position facilitates the abuse of Agamemnon and therefore may not be used as testimony to expected conventions. We need to recognize that Agamemnon's situation was different and exceptional. Since he was a leader of leaders, it appears that he was the one responsible for dividing the common store into parts—but first taking a cut for himself. Each of the leaders would then oversee the distribution of the part he received to his companions. This exceptional position[102] may explain why he might have justified getting not one but several *geras*-units. The poet may have understood him as interpreting the *geras* owed him not as one item from the entire hoard but as one item from each of the portions given to individual leaders for them to distribute among their companions. This specific point of divergence from the convention may constitute the abuse. It is also possible that he forcefully asked "to be given" some of the personal *enara* from those who captured them, who, like underlings in the Mafia, felt it prudent to give to the boss.

The counselor Nestor, an old man, illustrates the confusing contradiction between the actual bullying power of Agamemnon and the accepted and often-articulated convention when he publicly addresses Agamemnon about the proper convention:

> You, great man that you are, yet do not take the girl away but let her be, a prize as the sons of the Achaians *gave* her first (to Achilles). (*Il.* 1.274–276, Lattimore)

---

[102] Havelock (1978) 129; see also Detienne ([1965] 1996) 91–101.

He then turns to the furious Achilles, with a different argument, about Agamemnon's special status:

> Nor, son of Peleus, think to match your strength with the king, since never equal with the rest is the portion of honor (*homoies emmore times*) of the sceptered King to whom Zeus gives magnificence (*kudos*). (*Il.* 1. 277-9 Lattimore)

The argument of "Don't dare, Achilles, Agamemnon is king and is much stronger" is similar to the threat of Zeus, the god whom the other gods chose to be their king. Agamemnon is stronger because of his overarching position as the king who was able to make other "kings" join him before the walls of Troy. Nestor's language distinguishes between the *kudos* that comes from Zeus and Agamemnon's *time* that is "allotted"; like Poseidon's *time* (using the same expression, *emmore times*), it is comparable to other *timai*, which are not equal to his.

The use of the two words, *emmore times*—namely, *time* combined with the verb *meiromai*, "receive as one's portion" (cf. *moira*)—is consistent. It emphasizes that *time* is partitive in relation to the group where all have some *time*.[103] Poseidon's *time* is compared with that of his brothers and peers (gods); Agamemnon's, with other human heroes. Poseidon's rule over his allotted portion is eternal (there is no question of a son inheriting), whereas Agamemnon rules with the inherited scepter that Zeus granted his ancestors. However, his position, mighty as it is, is spoken of in terms of *partial* allotment. Unlike an Egyptian pharaoh, Agamemnon does not have all the *time*. In any case, Nestor is explicit about who gave Briseis to Achilles: not Agamemnon, but the "sons of the Achaians" gave the *geras*.

Can such a *time* be expressed in an unequal distribution of booty? Agamemnon seems to indicate that this was feasible, but each time we hear of it, the implication is that of a breakup of convention. Both Thersites, as we saw earlier, and the mighty Achilles express public resentment at the disproportion: "Never, when the Achaians sack some well-founded citadel of the Trojans, do I have a prize that is equal to your prize" (*Il.* 1.163–164, Lattimore), says Achilles.

Paradoxically, the second time we hear of disproportionate booty, it is in the form of a promise of a future bribe. It is an offer similar to the one made by Achilles in Book One, and similarly rejected: Agamemnon should wait and be compensated when Troy is finally captured (*Il.* 1.127–129). Eventually, with Achilles on strike and the war going badly, Agamemnon realizes his mistake. He promises that once Troy has been taken (a future, not entirely trustworthy promise), a disproportional share of booty will fall to Achilles, much more than a single *geras*. We are observing a fluid world with some overlap between

---

[103] See Finkelberg (1998), and Introduction 7.

categories of *leïa* (spoils): on the one hand, *enara* that remain in the hero's hands and do not make it into the common store, and on the other, the *geras* (converted private booty, placed in the middle with *kleos* attached). Now even Agamemnon reverts to the convention that the "Achaians" are the ones who give, yet with a distortion:

> If hereafter the gods grant that we storm and sack the great city of Priam, let him go to his ship and load it deep as he pleases with gold and bronze, when *we Achaians divide the war spoils among ourselves* (*dateomai*), and let him choose (*haireo*) for himself twenty of the Trojan women who are the loveliest of all after Helen of Argos. (*Il.* 9.138, Lattimore, adapted)

Note that the now-obsequious Agamemnon has switched from "I" to "we Achaians." Contrast this with the "virtuous" Odysseus, who prides himself on conducting the division by lottery fairly and equally, relative to his own proportionate *geras*. Clearly, Agamemnon's wild promissory note, made under desperate circumstances (and dismissed by Achilles), cannot be used as evidence of the powers of the Homeric king.[104] Even when Agamemnon makes his promise, the poet still adheres to the convention "We Achaians divide the war spoils among ourselves." The convention is explicit: the *dasmos* is done by and for the army, with some clear sense of what is and is not fair.

Fairness is in contrast to the abuse of power among those who divide the spoils. Back home in Ithaka, the suitors are "fair" among themselves. While devouring Odysseus's wealth, they imagine a future distribution *kata moiran*, literally, "according to portion," but meaning "fairly":

> Then let us surprise him and kill him (Telemachos), in the fields away from the city, or in the road, and ourselves seize his goods and possessions, dividing them among ourselves (*dateomai*) fairly (*kata moiran*, portion for portion), but give his palace to his mother to keep and to the man who marries her. (trans. Lattimore)[105]

It is essential to recognize the "army" or "the people" as a community that has the authority to "give" and whose members are fairly equal to each other in respect to their chances through the mechanism of distribution, the lottery. Some interpret the evidence differently (see Endnote 1), hesitating to accept the repeated, explicit statements of "the people *giving to* the king" and distribution by lot. However, the question is not limited to issues of "war and society." The context

---

[104] Van Wees (2011) s.v. Kingship on Finkelberg (2011). Cf. Carlier (1984); (2006).
[105] *Od.* 16.383–386. Cf. *Od.* 20.213–216; 3.313–316; 15.10–13; 17.79–81.

is broader and relates to the community's role in granting the king an estate. The king's estate back home is a grant of the people, such as "the Lykians."

When founding new city-states, the leaders or "founders" (*oikistai, ktistai, archegetai*) would oversee the parceling of lands according to four categories: the sacred (*temenos*, or sacred precinct), the public (*demosion*, such as roads), the private *kleroi* ("plots-by-lots") of equal size, and undivided land held as a reserve for future settlers. As noted, those are comparable to the "common" in the Olympian lottery. With one or two exceptions, neither the leader nor his posterity received any special land grants. During the archaic period of colonization (ca. 750–500), the *temenos* became the sole reserve of gods and heroes. The only *temenos* a founder would receive was conditioned on his death: it would be a small precinct serving his communal hero cult around his grave. It was his only *geras*, as it were.[106]

In Homer, a *temenos* could be the site of the "fragrant altar," a cult place. On the other hand, *temenos* could mean simply revenue-bearing land for the use of the *basileis*,[107] a meaning it had lost later with the general disappearance of the *basileis*. In the *Iliad*, there is a detailed description of the magnificent shield that the bronze-smith god Hephaistos had made for Achilles, with various scenes of life in peace and war. One scene portrays a *temenos basileion*, showing harvesters reaping (*Il.* 18.550). Nothing religious seems implied; this is simply the particular estate of the king. The two functions, a site for sacrifice upon an altar (built temples were not necessary for the Greek cult), and specially demarcated lands for agricultural revenue, continued during the archaic and classical periods. However, the revenue-bearing lands would no longer belong to individuals but to the state and to the gods, to finance the state cult.

That, however, is not the case in the *Iliad*. So how does the *basileus* come to possess a royal *temenos*? Again, as with booty and *geras*, the community does the giving. Consider this myth, also found in Homer: There was a time when the goddess Artemis was furious with Meleager's father, Oineus, king of the Aitolians, who forgot (or deliberately neglected) to give her first fruits from his orchard. She then sent a monstrous wild boar to ravage the land; the boar was not too discriminating and brought havoc and death to many Aitolians aside from the culprit. However, the boar was not their only problem: enemies (the Kuretes) besieged their central place, Kalydon. Under such threats, the "elders of the Aitolians" turned to Meleagros for help.

---

[106] Malkin (1987a) Part II and see ch. 5.2.
[107] We cannot tell who they are exactly, but clearly, no one-man-rule is involved, and they somehow are, or represent, the "people." The origins of the "royal" *temenos* can be pointed out in tablets written in Linear B. One tablet mentions a quantity of grain from the *temenos* (*te-me-no*) of the *Wanax* and of the *Lawagetas*, both positions of political (and religious?) prominence in the Mycenaian world. PY Er 312.1 with Casevitz (1984) 85 and Donlan (1989). Cf. Hahn (1977); Link (1994b).

Sending their noblest priests of the immortals, . . . they offered him a great gift: wherever might lie the richest ground in lovely Kalydon, there they told him to choose out a piece of land, an entirely good one, of fifty acres, the half of it to be vineyard and the half of it unworked plough land of the plain to be furrowed." (*Il.* 9.575ff., Lattimore)

The episode indicates what a community expected from its warrior heroes in return for granting them land: hunting wild boars (a common theme in Greek myth) not for pleasure but for safety and to ward off human enemies.[108] After the enemies were warded off, the Aitolians reneged on their promise, indicating the community was perceived as strong enough to do so to a hero with impunity.[109]

The implications are fascinating. What seems to be implied is a comprehensive grasp of "land" or territory, which is for the community to parcel out and give, just as the "common store" of booty is the army's to dispense. Specifically, the "elders" have the right to dispose of as-yet-uncultivated land as well as attesting the "political" community that has the authority to do that.[110] That is a reverse image of the top-down Medieval "Crown," allocating lands to vassals.

There is an explicit difference between what a *basileus* may grant and what is within the authority of the community to give. In the Homeric version of the myth of Bellerophon, the king of Lykia wishes to reward him. He can give to Bellerophon his daughter and half of the royal honor, or *time*, but he cannot give him land. This power, by contrast, belongs to "the Lykians," who allot Bellerophon a prominent *temenos* (*Il.* 6.193–194). The verb signifying allotment (*temno*) marks the "cutting apart" aspect of the land that somehow had been in a state of reservation by the community, similar to the reserved land in Greek colonies. Similarly, the verb for holding (*nemo*) signifies not ownership as such but allocation:

There the Lykians cut out a piece of land, surpassing all other, fine plow-land and orchard for him to *hold as his portion* (*ofra nemoito—nemo*).

Therefore, what we have here is "possession" dependent on allocation by "the Lykians," an expression denoting a community (or political community) in ancient Greek.

---

[108] Raaflaub (1993) 54 compares Meleagros with Idomeneus: *Od.* 14.235: "But when Zeus, whose voice is borne afar, devised that hateful journey which loosened the knees of many a warrior, then they bade me and glorious Idomeneus to lead the ships to Ilios, nor was there any way to refuse, for the voice of the people pressed hard upon us" (trans. Murray).
[109] *Il.* 9.658-9.
[110] Donlan (1989). Cf. Scheid-Tissinier (1994) 230–231.

The same distinction between royal (personal) honor and community allocation is expressed in Achilles's encounter with the Trojan prince Aeneas. Achilles asks why he wants to fight with him: Will the king of Troy, Priam, place the *geras* (apparently the kingship) in his hands? Or did "*the Trojans* cut off a *temenos* [the same expression as above] of orchard and plow-land so you may [literally] hold it allocated to you (again, the same verb as above) if you kill me (*Il.* 20.184–185)?" Here the *temenos* is perceived as a reward for heroic action on behalf of the community. Homer is consistent in this respect. At one point, one of the Trojan allies, Sarpedon, elaborates on the relationship between status, possessions, and duty (*Il.* 12.309–328, esp. 313): men "gaze upon us," he says, "as on gods"; we are held in honor in the banquets, we "hold" (the verb is *nemo*), he says, "a *temenos* of plow-land and orchard by the river Xanthos," and therefore, concludes Sarpedon, we must fight in the forefront of the battle—an explicit *quid pro quo*.

Homer makes it quite clear that the perception of land as agricultural, divisible, and subject to the decision of an entire community ("Elders of the Aitolians," "the Trojans," and "the Lykians") is both familiar and traditional. That notion will prove significant also in chapter 6, which discusses equal land allocation by the community to its members. The role of the *basileus* in Homer as probably overseeing the distribution of booty should not mislead us as to the nature of his authority in such matters: the special prize that is taken from the "whole" booty, or the special tract of land taken from the "whole" land, is a gift from the people/army.

The *temenos* of a *basileus* is mentioned a few more times, with the *basileus* already possessing it. Like a colonial *kleros*, acquired initially through the lottery but which became simply a "plot of land," or simply "inheritance" (ch. 4) to its inheritors, so too was the Homeric "royal" *temenos*. It could be an inherited estate, as was the *temenos* of Iphiton (*temenos patroion*; *Il.* 20.391).[111] The *temenos* of Alkinoös, the king of the Phaiakians, is similarly the king's estate. One of the most touching scenes in the *Odyssey* occurs when Odysseus's pitiful old dog, Argos, recognizes his master-in-disguise; Odysseus averts his gaze, and the old dog dies of a broken heart. The dog is lying on a pile of dung, which is used to fertilize the prosaically "broad *temenos*" of Odysseus (*Od.* 17.299), clearly a "landed estate." In another scene, this time in the underworld (*Od.* 11.184–185), Odysseus meets his mother, thus finding out she had died during his long absence. She tells him that "the *geras* (position, honor) that was ours no one else possesses and your son still holds the *temenea* (plural form), and equally participates in banquets." "Still holds" implies he might not have done so.[112] Thus

---

[111] Cf. *Od.* 11.184; the *temenos basileion* on the shield of Achilles with workers reaping: *Il.* 18.550. Cf. Link (1994b).

[112] Something similar to Telemachos's position is implied in the words of Achilles to the dying Trojan Otrynteus: "You die here (far from) the *temenos* of your fathers" (*Il.* 20.391).

temenos is both an agricultural estate, providing for the aristocratic lifestyle of mutual banqueting, and is potentially inheritable but uncertainly so.

As noted, historical founders of colonies never got a personal *temenos* (in the sense of a landed estate) from their community, aside from a small sacred precinct for their posthumous hero cult. In contrast, Nausithoös, who was a leader of the exodus-type of migration of the Phaiakians (with no mother city remaining) to Scheria, did get a special prize: a personal land-*geras* in the form of a *temenos*, probably as a reward for his leadership. The *temenos* became hereditary since his son, King Alkinoös, who hosted Odysseus, had a personal *temenos*, most probably the same one (*Od.* 6.291). Apparently, this was also the case in the historical period when a community rewarded persons of unique contributions with a *temenos*: The people of Kroton in Italy allotted *temenea* to the family of the seer Kallias: "The people of Kroton ... point out the numerous allotments within their borders which were assigned to Kallias the Elean by their countrymen, and which to my day remained in the possession of the family" (Hdt. 4.45).

Rarely do we find kings among historical Greeks; indeed, one comparable historical case is that of the exceptional Greek city in Libya, Cyrene. It did have kings until the people were fed up and invited an external arbitrator who reformed their constitution. Among other things, "He *chose out* certain *temene* (*temenea exelon*) and priesthoods for their king Battos, but all the rest, which had belonged to the kings, were now to be held by the people in common (literally, 'the middle')."[113] The "rest which had belonged to the kings" was their particular portion. The parallelism between the *geras* and the *temenos* is well articulated by Walter Donlan: "The chiefly *temenos* is to the *kleros* (the individual plot of a settler) as the *geras* ... is to the equal *dasmos* (division and distribution)."[114]

So who gets to participate in a distribution? A primary condition for distribution through a lottery among members of a group necessitates having, *a priori*, a mutually accepted notion of who belongs to the group and who does not. This distinction between inclusion and exclusion, defining and marking the group as distinct from others (such as soldiers, worshipers, pirates, colonists, citizens, etc.), will prove valid for a broad spectrum of communal sharing: the distribution of equal portions of sacrificial meat in a ritual, or equal plots of land in colonization, or political, juridical, and religious positions among citizens in a democracy.

Most scholars would agree that the *Iliad* reflects some aspects of a social situation that existed much later than the Mycenaean period, probably that of the eighth or early seventh centuries (opinions vary), that is, the transition to the archaic period, with some poetic "distancing," reflecting older values. Therefore,

---

[113] Hdt. 4.161.
[114] Donlan (1999) 305; cf. Donlan (1975).

the claim made here that such a clear notion of a group identity of "equals" is explicit already in the *Iliad* may clarify other expressions of equal sharing very early in Greek history. For example, it may explain why, already at the last quarter of the eighth century, we have material evidence on the ground for how settlers of the newly founded Greek city-states ("colonies") perceived themselves as defined groups, insisting on equality and sharing equal plots of land among the settlers allocated by lot (see ch. 6).

Moreover, such values explain the background to the egalitarian ideology found most expressively already in seventh-century Sparta: ideally, Spartans were *homoioi*, "one like another" or "equal as peers." To be equal does not mean to be identical, but to be equal in certain respects. Spartan soldiers excelled in fighting in closed ranks as heavy foot soldiers (hoplites) bearing the same weapons. Ideally, they were equal also in respect of property. Each Spartan held an equal-size *kleros* that supposedly remained inalienable and unchanged since the time of the original conquest and the division of their territory.[115]

By the archaic period (750–500), the Homeric "special prize" to the king seems to have disappeared and been replaced by something else. By the end of the eighth century, we see Greek communities assuming the form of city-states, the political community of the *polis*, and most of the kingly powers (the *timai*) seem to have been expressed in several annual magistracies. At Athens, for example, the "kingly minister," or *archon basileus*, was responsible for some religious functions; the *archon polemarchos* had military responsibilities. The *geras*, that special portion, was no longer given to commanders and became the perquisite for priests. A special portion did appear, but in a form unknown to Homer: a tithe (*dekate*) to the gods, such as tithes on behalf of the *polis* to Apollo's sanctuary at Delphi.[116] Prominent individuals, such as founders of new city-states, received no special prizes in the archaic period. The exception proves the rule: in a unique state like Sparta that had a dual kingship, the kings got a double portion of the sacrificial meat (compare Oedipus, earlier).[117] In the *Iliad*, we saw the *laos*—the army or the people—giving the special prize to the king. Aside from

---

[115] For a fuller discussion of Sparta, the egalitarianism of the *homoioi*, and their supposedly equal plots of land (*kleroi*), see ch. 6 and Endnote 2.

[116] Achilles promising to dedicate the armor of a vanquished victim in a temple is rather a dedication, not a tithe (*Il.* 7.83). The earliest mention of *dekate* seems to be Eumelus fr. 11.1 (a Corinthian poet, dated to the late eighth–seventh centuries): Bernabé (1966) (Kinkel edition no. 12). Cf. Jim (2014). See also Pritchett (1991) 363–368: the Homeric system had been translated, more or less intact, he says, from the heroic individual to the *polis*. Dedications of precious-metal booty and captured arms and armor at Delphi celebrated glorious victories of specific *poleis*. The Persian Wars booty was apportioned to *polis* contingents based on their performance in battle. See, e.g., Hdt. 9.81.1 or a second-century inscription from Crete (*IC* vol. III.4. ll. 53–58), where it says that each side shall receive its share according to the number of men taking part . In the same way, they shall share the tithe.

[117] Hdt. 6.56-60.

Sparta, and with a significant mix of transformation and continuity, in the archaic world, the political community—the *polis*—gave the special prize not to a person but to the gods. The *dekate* expresses, on one hand, the communal sovereignty to decide on the tithe to the gods and, on the other, the equalizing of all members of the community.

Endnote 1: The debate about the distribution of spoils in the *Iliad* and the *Odyssey*

A diametrically different view of procedures for the distribution of booty is offered by Hans van Wees, suggesting a top-down procedure whereby leaders get *gera* ("prizes") and hand out "portions" to their followers.[118] He suggests five stages: (1) Bringing the spoils to a common store; the leader then picks a *geras*. (2) He gives *gera* to other princes. (3) Each prince picks a *geras* for him, and (4) assigns portions to subordinate leaders. (5) Each leader distributes part of his portion to his followers. There is no room for drawing lots in this reconstruction, which must also belittle the frequent, explicit statement that the people give the *geras* to the king, not the other way around. Van Wees relies on a few statements that seem to explicitly contradict the idea of a single *geras*, or others that state the opposite of the people's role. Most such contradictions, however, could be explained by the category of *enara*, which van Wees does not discuss.

Booty was also shared among the noncombatants, a point that van Wees uses to indicate the personal power of princes. Odysseus, as we saw, distributed the flock of the Cyclops among all his companions, including those who stayed on the beach waiting for him while he was busy at the cave of Polyphemos. Yet this comprehensive aspect rather underlines not arbitrary power but the coherent conception of the "community." In an army context, such distributions express a vision of war as a long-term affair (instead of an *ad hoc* raid) in which all are expected to participate.

Moreover, van Wees rapidly glosses over the drawing of lots by stating that *lanchano* means not "to get a share by lot" but simply "to get," which is indeed a possible meaning. Finally, he reinterprets *ise* as "fair," or proper to one's status (hence proportionate, not equal, distribution) instead of "equally."

My approach is closer to that of A. T. Murray and Jonathan L. Ready.[119] Passages pointing to Agamemnon's arbitrary powers, on which van Wees places significant emphasis, have been shown to exist in heated rhetorical contexts, in contrast to the "official" situation at the assembly. Time and again, Agamemnon's

---

[118] Van Wees (1992) 299–311. In general on booty: Nowag (1983).
[119] A. T. Murray (1917); Ready (2007).

behavior seem to flaunt convention, not represent it. It is the convention we need to care about, not its apparent abuse.

Some explicit examples contradict the framework of a (single-item) *geras* to the leader, given to him by the Achaians. For example, we hear that Agamemnon picked up not one but nine women from the spoils of Achilles's raid (*Il.* 9.128–130 = 270–272), or of spears personally taken to one's tent, armor being stripped off a corpse, and captives held for personal ransom.[120] Such cases may seem to strengthen van Wees's argument that it is basically up to the leader to make arbitrary decisions and that the distribution of booty is a top-down affair.

Aside from Agamemnon, the one other major case used to support this view is the "vast amount" taken by Neleus that seems highly disproportionate, leaving a small part of the spoils to be distributed by the Pylian leaders to the "people." However, as shown earlier, when one disregards the poetic hyperbole and stops to count the personal take of Neleus, one arrives at a very different and relatively modest count. Proportionally, apart from its characterization as "vast," Neleus takes very little from the spoils. Leaders could take more than one item for a specific reason, such as compensation for past losses. The difference between Neleus and Agamemnon is precisely the disproportionate grabbing by Agamemnon of which Thersites and Achilles accuse him.

Some examples indicate that not only Agamemnon but even Achilles and some other heroes took much more than a single item given to them by the people. For example, the personal spoils Achilles got from Thebe included the *phorminx* he played (at 9.188), his horse Pedasos (16.152), and an iron weight given as a prize (23.826). Achilles got ransom "beyond counting" for Andromache's mother (6.414–428); at Ismaros, Odysseus shared booty but "protected" the priest Maro (basically a shake-off ransom for sparing him), who showered Odysseus individually with "gifts," as did Aiolos, king of the winds. Thus, personal ransom and guest-friendship contacts explain the discrepancy between captains and their companions. Odysseus's companions complained, but since they all perished (note the excessive apology of the poet for their loss in the opening lines), the riches the Phaiakians had given Odysseus were his alone both by default and because they were "gifts," not booty.

In what contexts do heroes get such personal booty? Does this personal booty contradict the idea of sharing booty "equally" and by lot? We hear of heroes capturing and keeping for themselves women, horses, armor (which they strip off their enemies), and captives (men) kept for ransom.[121] Nevertheless, one may argue, Thersites complains that when he had captured someone in the field for

---

[120] E.g., *Il.* 11.104–106; 21.34–44; 6.421–424. Cf. Wilson (2002) 38.
[121] For example, *Il.* 17.155; 12.640–642; Il. 6.46–50; *Il.* 13.260–262; Il. 10.487–514; Il. 10.56–569; Il. 21.40–41. Cf. Ready (2007) 13; Wilson (2002) 38.

ransom, the captive now goes to Agamemnon (Il. 2.226–232). He does not protest the given social reality, nor is he an ideologue claiming what *ought* to be correct. Instead, Thersites protests against flaunting what *is* right, against deviation from convention, specifically, that the captive and his prospective ransom should belong to the one who captured him.

Does the acquisition of personal booty that goes neither to the king nor to the common store falsify the notion of communal distribution of spoils? Does it imply that leaders may take whatever strikes their fancy? Framing the question differently, Jonathan Ready calls attention to a process of "conversion," a transfer from a short-term acquisition (capturing during battle) to a long-term transaction (bringing the spoils to the middle for public redistribution). That is why Briseis is being "given" the second time, by the people, to Achilles. This public gift crowns him with *kleos*, not merely spoils that would make him privately rich (but with no *kleos* attached). However, these personal riches are surprisingly irrelevant since they belonged to another category of booty.

As mentioned earlier, such a discrete category is explicit among other ancient people, and the analogy may elucidate my point. In his study "The Division of the Spoils of War in the Bible and the Ancient Near East," David Elgavish analyzes the terminology of booty in the Old Testament.[122] He draws our attention primarily to two different terms: The noun *bizzah* and the verb derived from it (root: ב.ז.ז) that "generally denote personal taking by soldiers, a seizure that is not organized by the state authorities"—for example, "But in the ranks, everyone kept his booty for himself" (*Num.* 31:53). By contrast, *šelal* (שלל) is public booty to be brought before the leader to redistribute—for example, "The wealth of Damascus and the spoils *(šelal)* of Samaria . . . shall be carried off before the king of Assyria" (*Isa.* 8:4). In Akkadian, the parallel word *šelalu* also covers the capture of people, animals, and property. Unlike *bizzah*, *šelal* is often joined by the verb ח.ל.ק, "to divide up, distribute": "Benjamin is a ravenous wolf, in the morning devouring the prey and at evening dividing the spoil."[123]

Is there such a distinction in Homeric Greek? It seems there is. *Enara* (ἔναρα) are the "arms and trappings of a slain foe" (LSJ). The word occurs precisely in circumstances where the hero takes spoils for himself. Nestor urges the soldiers not to stop fighting in order to strip their dead enemies of their armor, but to do so only after the battle was over—see *Il.* 6.67–72: "Let no man now abide behind in eager desire for spoil *(enara)*, . . . nay, let us slay the men; thereafter in peace shall ye strip the armor from the corpses that lie dead over the plain." Compare *enara* in 6.479–481; 10.526–529; 15.346–347; 17.12–13; 17.540–542;

---

[122] Elgavish (2002). I thank Alexander Fantalkin for the reference.
[123] Gen. 49:27: בִּנְיָמִין זְאֵב יִטְרָף, בַּבֹּקֶר יֹאכַל עַד וְלָעֶרֶב, יְחַלֵּק שָׁלָל. (trans. English Standard Version).

22.243–246; at one point, Hector wonders about fighting Diomedes, "whether I shall slay him with the bronze and bear off his bloody spoils (*enara*)." Achilles's tent contains such spoil (*enara*) at 9.185–188 and 13.267–268. Common soldiers could trade slaves and other spoils for wine at Lemnos (*Il.* 7.467–475).[124] Such personally gained spoils are apt for dedication by Odysseus to Athena: "And on the stern of his ship did Odysseus place the bloody spoils (*enara*) of Dolon until they should make ready a sacred offering to Athene" (*Il.* 10.570–571).

The hero may capture booty directly, and he may (or be expected to?) transfer all or much of it to the common store (*Il.* 10.38). I think the explicit use of *enara* as a subcategory of *leia* (spoils) is sufficient to establish that Homeric Greek knew a distinction such as between the personal *bizzah* and state *šelal*.[125] It is from the stock of the former (*enara*) that a Homeric hero could lend a companion (Idomeneus) a spear (*Il.* 13.260–263; *Il.* 13.267–271). Women, armor, horses, and captives for ransom all seem to belong to that category. As noted, Briseis provides an excellent example of apparent contradictory statements that could be resolved simply by observing her transfer from the private capture of Achilles to the public gift and recognition as *geras* ceremoniously handed over ("given"). The former merely enriched the new proprietor; the latter made him glorious. Let us now observe in more detail. Briseis was

a. "Acquired by Achilles's spear" (*dourikteten*; 9.343). Achilles says that "we led (*ago*) all the things [i.e., spoils]" from Thebe (1.367) and "I led (*ago*)" captured women from Lyrnessos.
b. She was directly chosen out and taken by Achilles: "the fair-haired Briseis, whom he took out for himself (*exaireo*) from Lyrnessos after toiling greatly, sacking Lyrnessos and the walls of Thebe" (*Il.* 2.689–691; cf. 19.291–299).
c. She was given (= ceremoniously handed over, in my view) to Achilles by Agamemnon (9.367–368): "Agamemnon gave Briseis to me: but my prize, the very man who gave it, committing an act of hubris lordly Agamemnon took back again."
d. She was given (the people as the source) to Achilles *by the Achaians*, a point repeated several times.

---

[124] In his commentary Kirk is needlessly surprised: "The next term, ἀνδραπόδεσσι, is as remarkable for the term itself as for the idea of war-captives belonging to ordinary troops."

[125] At one point we also find the term *andragria* (ἀνδράγρια): Il. 14.508–510. *Laphura* is a somewhat later term for spoils. In tragedy it may denote spoils for dedication in a temple (Aesch. *Sept.* 276–278a/279; Soph. *Aj.* 91–93), at home (Aesch. *Sept.* 477–479), or just generally: "Hellas won those glorious spoils of the barbarian maid, and they are safe in Mycenae" (Eur. *Her.* 416–418; cf. Soph. *Trach.* 644–645). In Xenophon we meet the *laphuropoles*, a seller of booty in a world that knew coinage and mercenary service (verb: *laphuropoleo*). See Xen. *An.* 6.6.39; Xen. *Hell.* 4.1.26–27; Xen. *An.* 7.7.56–57.

86 DRAWING LOTS

Jonathan Ready's insistence on the category of personal capture is convincing. However, he does not discuss *enara*, and his purpose is to frame the acquisition of booty in illuminating terms of short- and long-term transactions.[126] This category of *enara*, which is parallel to the biblical *bizzah*, helps to turn the four contradictory statements about Briseis listed above into a linear story: The spoils acquired in the field at Lyrnessos, for example, belong to a category of immediate capture (horses, men, armor, women—[a] and [b] above). The booty (all or some—this is where abuse may be evident) is then transferred "to the middle" for public distribution, *presided* over by the king. In my view, this is how (c) should be understood: once the people have decided to give Briseis to Achilles (in fact, to ratify Achilles choosing her), Agamemnon *hands her over*. He neither chose her for Achilles from a crowd of captive women nor was it he who decided to give her to Achilles. He "gave" but did not decide to give. That was the people's decision (hence the perceived abuse when he takes her) (d), and he handed her over as supreme lord and responsible for the entire procedure. That, I think, is how we should understand the process. The four discrete categories (a, b, c, and d) are stages in turning Briseis into a public, "official" prize gift. By contrast, had Achilles merely captured and held her without bringing her "to the middle," she would have been his, for sure, but not considered a "prize," contributing nothing to his general *kleos*. We hear of other slaves similarly captured: for example, the women lamenting Patroklos were "female slaves whom Achilles and Patroklos took captive (*leïzomai*)" (*Il.* 18.28; cf. *Il.* 9.666), as were male slaves. Telemachos speaks of "slaves (*dmoön*), whom divine Odysseus took captive (*leïzomai*) for me" (*Od.* 1.398). However, none of these could be regarded as a publicly acknowledged prize. As we saw, when Agamemnon finally relents and wishes to give Briseis back, Achilles insists he will not hand her to him directly (which would imply a personal "debt" to Agamemnon) but publicly.

At some point, Agamemnon promises Achilles a considerable chunk of booty; clearly, it would be *his* gift.[127] Van Wees uses it to illustrate the arbitrary powers of Agamemnon. However, these are unrealized promises (rejected by Achilles, who suggests something very similar in Book 1: let Agamemnon be compensated by the Achaians (!) when Troy has been taken. Nobody takes this seriously.[128] In any case, they bear no direct relevance to what happened to spoils once they got "to the middle," and how much of what had been captured effectively got there. We are dealing with a loose and flexible world, yet expectations and conventions seem clear to its participants. Should the leader keep too much for himself, or

---

[126] For Lyrnessos, see Ready (2007) 35.
[127] There are also promises to Teukros (*Il.* 8.289).
[128] *Il.* 1.127–132; cf. 1.118.

worse, keep someone else's *enara* for himself (Thersites's captive?) It was in his effective power to do so, but it was not considered to be his right.

To sum up so far: the extraordinary amount of booty at the hands of a king or a prince is not a demonstration of "powers" but perhaps relates to *enara* and, specifically, to the *Iliad*'s theme of unaccepted arbitrariness and ensuing wrath. Abuse complaints relate not to the moment of final distribution but to the one before that: the abuse consists in keeping too much and in not bringing the spoils "to the middle," to the "common store," in order to effect public gifts of *geras* and the sharing of *moirai*. What matters, therefore, is the transition from private capture to the public domain. Neleus provides a nice example in which his right to choose what he is owed is self-evident. However, what he actually chooses is very modest proportionally and hence considered fair. Nestor is arguing for fairness: the army gave the *geras* to Achilles, he tells Agamemnon. Why else would he bring up the episode about his father if it did not demonstrate the point? When the personal take of Agamemnon or Odysseus seems disproportionate, we hear complaints by the likes of Thersites or the *hetairoi* of Odysseus (*Od.* 10.38). Van Wees (1992: 299) sees "The booty . . . put at the disposal of the highest-ranking prince." I agree with that statement, except that I take "at the disposal" to mean that once having placed the spoils "in the middle," in the public eye, to witness the procedure, the "prince" is then responsible for conducting rites of *geras*-giving (handing over the prize) and fair distribution through the lottery (*lanchano*).

In what way would the leader distribute spoils? In the framework of five stages that van Wees suggests, there is no place for an instrument of distribution of *moirai* "to the people," as Nestor says. Without such a mechanism, how exactly could one imagine the public process (no one denies that public aspect) to have taken place? The lottery would be such an instrument. Van Wees thinks that a leader decides at each point what moves further down the chain of hierarchy. Elsewhere van Wees claims notions of "reciprocity" between a leader and people, which are also top-down. He suggests a parallel: a Tahitian chief who donates all his income, including gifts, to his tribe, leaving for himself only the necessary minimum.[129] In such a scenario, the distribution of goods in terms of reciprocity plays a major role in the political power balance between the *basileus* and the people. Yet I fail to see the similarity; such reciprocity is evident, say, with the community giving land to a hero (e.g., Meleagros, Sarpedon, Bellerophon, Aeneas), that is, a one-off affair, and the direction is from the community to the leader, not vice versa. Moreover, there is hardly any attestation for van Wees's chain, whereas the explicit statements about "from/to the people" are well attested and comprehend everyone as eligible. Van Wees brushes aside the question of instruments or mechanism (lottery) with the noncommitted—and

---

[129] Van Wees (1998) 44.

not followed-up—statement that *lanchano* "need not" mean "to get one's share by lot."

The vocabulary of the lottery in the *Iliad* needs to be examined lexically: how does *lanchano* function in Homeric Greek? The verb *lanchano* is used, as we have seen, quite often. We present here in the Appendix a comprehensive study of that verb and other words related to the lottery. The conclusion is that in over 73 percent of pre-fourth-century Greek, the meaning is indeed associated with lottery practices.[130] Achilles and Odysseus both distinguish between the gift of a *geras* and whatever else fell to them by lot (*Il.* 9.365). Specifically, in each of the statements where *lanchano* stands alone, one might argue that it simply means "to get." However, when used in a distribution context, the "how"—and especially a wider context of the vocabulary in Homeric Greek of the lottery—would be missing. The passage where the gods divide up the universe uses identical terms to what humans do with victory spoils or with portions of land in inheritance and colonization. *Lanchano* undoubtedly appears there in conjunction with other lottery-specific words, such as *pallo* (to shake the lots) and *kleroi* (lots). Or, to take a scene from the human world, we observe the same typical conjunction of lottery-procedure and lottery-related terms: "Then took they the lots (*kleroi*) and shook (*pallon helontes*) them in a helmet of bronze, and Teucer drew by lot (*lanchano, kleros*) the first place (*Il.* 23.862, trans. Murray).[131]

It is true that the word *lanchano* in Greek may mean "to get," just as *kleros* could mean a "lot," a "plot of land gotten by lot," or a "plot of land" *tout court*. "The verb may equally mean simply 'to obtain as one's share (cf. LSJ),'" says van Wees, "and it need not have the connotation 'by lot,' here" (302). There is no further discussion of why this need not be so or of *lanchano* in general. However, aside from our appendix, the wide-ranging lexicographic studies by Bořivoj Borecký indicate the opposite of the limited sense of "to get" and show that, in and of itself, "to get" is the secondary meaning.[132] Borecký shows that down to the end of the fifth century, *lanchano* retains its associations with the lot. Its function "to get" appeared mostly from the fourth century onward. These studies, from the early 1960s, are overlooked in van Wees's reconstruction, yet they demonstrate the wide use of *lanchano* in lottery contexts (see Endnote 2). Our work, complementing Borecký's, gives strong support to his conclusions. The

---

[130] See Appendix and Endnote 2.

[131] Note, however, the position of Perpillou (1996), who acknowledges the meaning of sortition but claims it is not always the case (as such he is right) (165–204): "Le verbe *lanchano* ne dénote pas l'obtention par tirage au sort, mais plus généralement l'appropriation légitime, dont le tirage au sort n'est qu'une modalité parmi d'autres." However, the participle *pallomenon* denotes sortition. Cf. Demont (2000) n.31. See Endnote 2 in this chapter for further refutation and discussion.

[132] Borecký (1965); see also Borecký (1963). Neither is referenced in van Wees's discussion. See the Appendix for further updating. Borecký's conclusions appear justified.

straightforward meaning "to get" is derivative; its common use in that sense is relatively late.

Unless it were all up to a leader's whim, which by now I hope one is convinced otherwise, one would need to assume some mechanism of distribution from the common store (with an emphasis on "common"). Since time and again we observe the use of *lanchano* in such contexts, I see no reason to second-guess the text, to deny its meaning as "to get one's share by lot," and to assume that no mechanism had existed for the sake of distribution from the common store "to the people." That "the people" merited distribution is acknowledged by van Wees (e.g., Pylos), yet he does not clarify how this was done. In short, aside from personally acquired booty (*enara*) that might enrich a hero but with no publicly acknowledged glory, aside from the *geras* publicly given to the leader by the people—aside from these, there was a common store from which, by means of drawing lots, booty was distributed apparently to all, *including the leaders* themselves (e.g., *Il.* 9.365). The coherent presence of the "community" is evident.

"But provide me with a prize of honor forthwith, lest I alone of the Argives be without one, since that would not be proper. For you all see this that my prize goes elsewhere" (*Il.* 1.117). This is not Achilles but Agamemnon who is speaking to the assembly, thus acknowledging his position as the recipient and that of the assembly as the giver. Similarly, Achilles tells the assembly that it takes away what it has given him (*Il.* 1.299). The "assembly," therefore, is a significant factor. Both Walter Donlan and Kurt Raaflaub have emphasized the role of Homeric assemblies (and councils) in contrast to Moses Finley's view of them as primarily passive. There are assemblies on both the Trojan and Greek sides, illustrating a coherence of society as well as its conventional (not to say "official") status of the people. With no community of sharers, the lottery would make no sense. On the other hand, once we acknowledge first the need for a mechanism of distribution; second, the "community"; and third, the drawing of lots, we may observe how the latter could express the former.

The explicit vocabulary of equality and equitability (*ise, ep'ises, isos*) poses another "complication," says van Wees (in fact, a solid contradiction), for the top-down approach. If there were an insistence on fairness/equality in the sense I have demonstrated earlier, the entire top-down reconstruction would be shaken, if not crushed. To avoid the implications of equality, van Wees suggests that rather than meaning "equal, equally," we need to understand *ise* as "fair" or "proper," similar in its guiding principle (my comparison) of the buccaneers' codes where shares are proportionate to rank yet considered fair. However, the meaning of *ise* in the sense of *equal, equally* is rather clear; Achilles complains that a good man and a bad man ought not to get *equal* portions (*Il.* 11.316–319), which means that they actually do. At the inconclusive wrestling match between Diomedes and Aias (*Il.* 23.734–737; 823), "Achilles himself stood up and spoke to stop them: 'Wrestle no more now; do not wear yourselves out and get hurt. You have both won. Therefore take the prizes in equal division (*d' is' anelontes*) and retire, so the rest of the Achaians can have their contests.'" And, again (v. 823): "they called for them to stop and divide the prizes equally (*ise*)" (trans. Lattimore, adapted).[133] In a simile concerning the division of a land, *ise* means "equal": "as two men with measuring-rods in hand ... in a narrow space contend each for his *equal share (peri ises)*" (*Il.* 12.421-423, trans. Murray). In the *Odyssey* the suitors contemplate dividing up Odysseus's property *ise*, which could hardly mean "proportionally" in that crowd (*Od.* 2.203). Meat at the feast is expressly divided equally (*ise*), in *equal portions* (*Od.* 20.280, 294). Let us also remember the passage in Theognis: "Who knows even when the sharing out, *dasmos*, is still 'brought to the middle' (*es to meson*) to be shared out equally (*isos*)?"[134] Aside from noting this straightforward sense of equality, contradicting his line of argument, van Wees goes no further with its implications. In general, notions of equality permeate the text of the *Iliad*, especially when we find a protest against their abuse (*Il.* 16.53; 9.367-368).

Why assume inequality and proportionate distribution in the first place? Equality is apparent whenever possible, as when we get countable spoils in actual numbers. As we saw, nine goats, for example, are distributed *equally* per ship, and the action is characterized as *ise*. So it is "fair" that distribution is *equal*, not proportionate. Moreover, fairness consists also in holding a lottery, since better- and lesser-quality goats are distributed by lot.

The recurring complaint (I spill my blood, so why should you too get a share?) actually attests to the comprehensive nature of the distribution of spoils. Further, it refutes the replacement of "equality" with proportionate fairness. Achilles is unhappy with the fact (but a fact it is) that "an equal share awaits one who stays behind and one who goes to battle" (*Il.* 9.315-318). We find the same idea in the *Odyssey* (*Od.* 9.943-949): Odysseus's *entire* group of men share in the Cyclops's flocks, including those who did not go to Polyphemos's island.

Finally, aside from countable spoils such as captives or animals (which must have also varied in perceived quality), in a world without coin, no distribution of material spoils could have resulted in precisely equal shares (note the exception of the gold and silver mines at Siphnos and Laurion; see ch.6.1). Let us note that, in Greek, *isos* means both "equal" and "equitable"; perhaps this is why.[135] So, the

---

[133] Lattimore translates "evenly."

[134] Theognis 678. As noted, some mss. have *isos* ("equal"), not an adverb ("equally" [*isos*])—but for our purpose, to emphasize equality over proportionate fairness, both are supportive. Cf. Borecký (1965) 73.

[135] LSJ, s.v. ἴσος I.1, I.3, II.2, II.3. As Robert Wallace (2015) 14 rightly comments, "A quick glance to the *Lexikon des frühgriechischen Epos* shows that already in Homer the adjective *isos* does not cover only the semantic field of the word 'equal,' but also that of the terms 'equitable,' 'adequate/proportionate,' 'fair,' 'just.'" Cf. Raaflaub and Wallace (2007); See Snell and Meier-Brügger (1991), s.v. *isos*.

way to understand the frequent use of *ise* as "equitable" is in conjunction with the full meaning of *lanchano*, getting portions (*moirai*) by lot. Equality consists first in equal chances, right before the result, then in equitable, as equal as possible, and "fair," results.[136]

Endnote 2: "Getting by lot" and the verb *lanchano*

Among the Greek words that constitute the vocabulary of the lot (see Appendix), the verb *lanchano* is central. However, its meaning "to obtain by lot," accepted by both ancient lexicographers and modern dictionaries, has been challenged by Jean-Louis Perpillou, who suggests instead that its central meaning is "to get by right, *legitimately*" (*l'appropriation légitime*).[137] We claim that this is not a refutation. Perpillou is right, except that legitimacy is there not despite the lot but because of it. It is the lottery that renders a process legitimate. Moreover, the right to participate in the lottery, in and of itself, attests to the legitimacy of the participant. Perpillou's contribution to the meaning of *lanchano* (legitimacy) does not contradict the commonly accepted (and now demonstrated, see Appendix) view of "to get by lot," but, on the contrary, highlights the social importance of the use of lottery in ancient Greek society.

What seems to underlie Perpillou's objection to the association of *lanchano* with the lot is his perception (or distaste) of lotteries as inappropriate to important matters such as justice, inheritance, and the lawful acquisition of goods, *because* of their random character.[138] Perpillou's perception of the lottery is far too close to that of gambling: a chaotic, unregulated, and uncontrollable process.

The scope of Perpillou's study is limited, unrepresentative, and insufficient to deny lottery aspects to *lanchano*. He aims to reestablish the meaning of the verb by closely examining 58 instances in poetry, 8 instances in the Gortyn Code, and another 5 instances in four other inscriptions.[139] However, the verb

---

[136] The proportion is the measure of fairness when it comes to what is specifically due to a leader. There is in fact a Homeric word for *proportionate* portions: *epieikeia, epieikês* ("proportionate, appropriate, of the proper size") used for compensation (*Od.* 12.382) See ch. 6.3.9.

[137] Perpillou (1996) 165–204.

[138] This claim is repeated through the whole chapter. See subchapter 9.2.2 (p. 167): "*La juste attribution contribue à l'équilibre du monde ... sans qu'une faveur capricieuse ni un hasard quelconque interviennent dans son administration*"; 9.3.6 (p. 185): "*Il serait difficile de prétendre que ... l'archétype le plus solennel du marriage légitime, soit due à l'effet d'une quelconque distribution réglée par tirage au sort*"; 9.4.4 (p. 191): "*la notion d'une égalité de traitement ... exclut toute attribution par le sort.*"

[139] *SEG* 27.631, *IG* IX (1) 334, *LSCG* 10 and 113. For an alternative interpretation of *LSCG* 10 = *IG* I³ 244 = *CGRN* 19, see J.-M. Carbon and S. Peels (*CGRN* 19), who accept the use of lottery in this case: "The sacrifice at Skambonidai is undertaken by the demarch and the sacrificial agents appointed by the deme, and the animal is chosen by lot (λε̑χσις).... The verb used of this distribution (λαγχάνω) probably points to the idea that in this case these portions are assigned by lot, as indeed the animal sacrificed was also selected by this mechanism." Retrieved under CC license on February 20, 2020, at http://cgrn.ulg.ac.be, *CGRN 19*.

is attested 174 times in archaic and classical poetry and over 400 times in prose up until Aristotle. Historiography is overlooked (Thucydides, Herodotus, and Xenophon) where *lanchano* (see Appendix) is mostly used in explicit contexts of a lottery and means "to obtain by lot."[140]

Among literary texts, Perpillou's discussion is limited to poetry: Homer, Hesiod, and just two Lyric poets—Pindar and Bacchylides. Perpillou's corpus, therefore, cannot be taken as representative. Moreover, in poetry, the use of *lanchano* is often metaphoric: poetic language, rich in metaphors and allusions, may suggest but may not represent historical reality—for example, the verb *lanchano*, as applying to marriage, that is, with *gamos* or *eune*, is present only in poetry as a poetic figure.[141] The use of the verb here is evidently metaphoric, alluding to marriage as one's Fate, not to an actual practice of the lottery. J.-L. Perpillou uses an example from Pindar *Pythian* 2.27–28[142] to illustrate the impossibility of the lottery in this case. However, he makes no methodological distinction between the striking genre-related differences. Forensic language would differ a bit from the everyday; narrative historiography is closest to everyday language, while poetry, the art of words, uses them as art objects in figurative speech. Therefore, additional caution is required when reading the examples from (Lyric) poetry and interpreting them in terms of everyday prose language.[143]

Lanchano as simply "to get"?

Perpillou rightly points to the close relationship between *lanchano* and *lambano* that frequently appears in proximity. The semantic field of the two verbs overlaps since both have the meaning of "to get." However, *lanchano* has a more specific meaning, nicely pointed out by Perpillou, to get by *legal* right; the two meanings do not contradict each other, as one has to have a legal right to participate in a lottery, and the lottery itself lends legitimacy to a procedure. In forensic language, the meaning may be strikingly different. δίκας λαμβάνειν means to receive a punishment, but δίκας λαγχάνειν means to bring a suit in a court (historically,

---

[140] Thuc. 8.30, Hdt. 1.94.5, 3.83.2, 3.128.1, 4.94.2, 4.153; Xen. *Cyr.* 1.6.46; Xen. *Mem.* 3.9.10 et al.
[141] Soph. *Antig.* 917; Phocylides, fr. 2.7; Pindar. *Pyth.* 2.27 (cited by Perpillou).
[142] τὰν Διὸς εὐναὶ λάχον πολυγαθέες, "... who was allotted to the joyful bed of Zeus").
[143] Perpillou (1996) 168. Perpillou lists the numbers of instances of the verb in present, perfect, and aorist tenses in Epic, and in Pindar and Bacchylides. He points to the inequality of tenses represented and the differences in the use of the tenses in poetic examples examined and the Gortyn Code, yet those numbers contribute little to the meaning of the verb. The questions concerning the meaning of aorist and present tenses remain unanswered, while the perfect tense (which is not the prevalent one), according to Perpillou, signifies the just enjoyment of legitimate acquisition.

because the date and the place of a proceeding were appointed by lot).[144] In short, Perpillou is right about legitimacy; what he misses is that it is precisely the lottery that makes the outcome legitimate.

Our database citing all appearances of *lanchano* (see Appendix) is clear in its results. In the archaic and classical periods, 73 percent of verb occurrences are lottery-associated. *Lanchano* is a polysemous verb whose meaning alters depending on the literary genre and context. As noted earlier, Perpillou examines only two of the Lyric poets: Pindar and Bacchylides. However, the prevailing use of this verb in poetry in general, and in Lyric poetry in particular, is metaphoric and closely connected to the notion of fate. One must take into account that Lachesis was one of the three Moirai, as we've noted. The notion of fate is present in the semantic field of *lanchano*. However, it may not be considered as prevalent: the overall count of instances of metaphoric use comprises less than 15 percent, predominantly in poetry and funerary metrical inscriptions.[145] Both types of texts are centered on the individual fate of a human. Contrary to Perpillou's claim, funerary metrical inscriptions may not serve as a representative example of the use of the verb due to their specific funerary context and idiomatic language, and metaphoric figures used in poetry. Thus, the presence of this verb in poetry in a funerary context is not surprising and may be related specifically to the sense of destiny and not to a right that derives from social status, as Perpillou claims,[146] given that the burial is not only a right of the deceased, unrelated to his status but also a duty of the society.

Perpillou seems to provide a single meaning to the verb, irrespective of genre or context, although any verb behaves differently in various contexts and genres. In the cases where *lanchano* is related to marriage (poetry) and where *lanchano* appears in funerary (metrical) inscriptions, to ask about an actual lottery taking place is futile since the metaphoric use of "fate" in some sense is evident. Specifically, among forty-eight pre-Hellenistic inscriptions with *lanchano*, only seven are funerary, and only those are the instances of metaphoric use of the verb.

---

[144] For an allotment of a court see Dem. 25.27.4. For an allotment of the date for the proceeding see Dem. 43.15.4; Lys.17.5.9.

[145] For funeral inscriptions dated to the classical period, see Bernand, *Inscr. Métr.* 42 Egypt and Nubia, 10 (V), *SEG* 28.248 (Attica, IV), et al. For the sense of fate related to *lanchano* in other poets, see Sappho fr. 33.2; Theognis 1.934. For the distribution of the semantic field in poetry and prose see the Appendix. *Lanchano* is connected to the notion of "to get by fate/chance" in approximately 40 percent of instances in poetry, as opposed to approximately 5 percent of this sense in prose. In classical inscriptions, *lanchano* is used in the metaphoric sense of "to get as one's lot" only in a funerary context.

[146] Perpillou (1996) 178–179: "*Il s'agit de l'acquisition par le défunt d'un titre ou d'un statut définitif, ou de la célébration des mérites hérités ou conquis de son vivant, et qu'il serait difficile d'attribuer au seul hazard d'une distribution aveugle.*" The biased perception of lottery is repeated.

Etymology

The etymology of *lanchano* is relatively obscure, and no scholarly consensus exists on the word's origin. Perpillou discusses three possible theories of the etymology of the verb: (1) the connection of the present and aorist stem λαγχ-/-λαχ- to Old Prussian and Old Slavonic languages, following Fick and Boisacq,[147] where the verbs mean "to obtain," "to receive as one's part"; (2) a connection of *lachos* to a Sanskrit word for "game"—"*laksa;*" and (3) the connection of the perfect form λέλογχα to a Hittite root "*linganu*" meaning "to bring an oath." A connection to the Hittite verb is possible only with the *-leng-* variant of the stem, which is not present in any form of *lanchano*. However, Perpillou favors this theory, claiming a common origin of *lanchano* and *elencho*, thus tying the verb to the Hittite origin. Perpillou substantiates this connection only in the possibility of a conceptual similarity of the two verbs, claiming that both *lanchano* and *elencho* were originally used in a judicial context.[148]

In modern Greek *lacheía* means "lottery, gambling," but this, claims Perpillou, does not suggest credible evidence for reconstructing the original meaning of the ancient Greek verb.[149] We need to be cautious when applying modern forms and meanings influenced by centuries of monotheism and a biased view against the lottery and immoral games of chance. However, if the comparison to a modern Greek word is inappropriate for the study of the meaning of an ancient Greek verb that shares the same stem and is linked with the drawing of lots, we cannot accept that a doubtful comparison to a Hittite verb is any more helpful.[150]

In conclusion, J.-L. Perpillou has successfully illuminated a shade in the meaning of the verb in specific contexts: "*l'appropriation légitime.*" However, he is unconvincing when denying the meaning of "to get by lot." The two are not mutually exclusive but complementary. The work of Borecký, our database (*kleros.org.il*), ancient lexicographers, and the range of ancient sources not cited by Perpillou confirm the frequent meaning of *lanchano* as "to get by lot." Perhaps contrary to the express intentions of the author, the added meaning of *l'appropriation légitime* highlights the importance and legitimacy of drawing lots in ancient Greece.

---

[147] Perpillou (1996) 199 nn.30, 31. Fick (1890) 536, cited in Boisacq (1923) 549.
[148] Perpillou (1996) 202.
[149] Perpillou (1996) 165 n.1.
[150] Perpillou (1996) 200–204.

Endnote 3: Group distribution and the verb *dateomai* in Homer, Hesiod, and the *Homeric Hymns*

In his commentary on the *Theogony*, Martin L. West has pointed to the usual meaning of the verb *dateomai* in Homer as "distributing among themselves."[151] We follow his observation with a detailed analysis of all the instances of the verb, made possible thanks to the technological advancements of corpus search, unavailable to West in 1966.[152] The results confirm that the verb is usually employed in the plural form and West's claim that the meaning is "a distribution by a group." Further contextual analysis and close reading reveal that only four instances of the verb in singular form (in active voice) refer to distribution to the community by a person appointed *by the community*. In addition, four instances of the verb occur in the passive voice. As our inquiry is into the subject (the agency) and not the object of the distribution, the passive forms are less significant. Below we present the complete data of the verb's instances and a contextual analysis of the use and the meaning of the verb in Homer, Hesiod, and the *Homeric Hymns*.

Count of instances: Total forty-three, plural twenty-seven, infinitive eight, subjects:

Hes. *WD*.767—pl.; Hom. *Od*. 20.216—pl. Hes. *WD*. 447—impersonal σπέρματα δάσσασθαι; Hom. *Il*.18.511—pl.; Hom. *Il*.22.120—impersonal; Hom. *Il*.23.21—pl. Hom. *Il*.18.27—pl.; Hom. *Il*.22.476—pl.; **Singular (4):** (1) Hes. *Theog*. 520 Zeus: ταύτην γάρ οἱ μοῖραν ἐδάσσατο μητίετα Ζεύς.; (2) Hes. *Theog*. 537 Prometheus (meat): καὶ γὰρ ὅτ᾽ ἐκρίνοντο θεοὶ θνητοί τ᾽ ἄνθρωποι; Μηκώνῃ, τότ᾽ ἔπειτα μέγαν βοῦν πρόφρονι θυμῷ; δασσάμενος προέθηκε, Διὸς νόον ἐξαπαφίσκων; For when the gods and mortal men had a dispute at Mekone, even then Prometheus was forward to cut up a great ox and set portions before them, trying to deceive the mind of Zeus;[153] (3) Hom. *Od*. 6.11 Nausithous: ἀμφὶ δὲ τεῖχος ἔλασσε πόλει καὶ ἐδείματο οἴκους; καὶ νηοὺς ποίησε θεῶν καὶ ἐδάσσατ᾽ ἀρούρας. About the city he had drawn a wall, he had built houses and made temples for the gods, and divided the ploughlands; (4) Hom. *Il*. 9.334 Agamemnon: τάων ἐκ πασέων κειμήλια πολλὰ καὶ ἐσθλὰ (330); ἐξελόμην, καὶ πάντα φέρων Ἀγαμέμνονι δόσκον; Ἀτρεΐδη· ὃ δ᾽ ὄπισθε μένων παρὰ νηυσὶ θοῇσι δεξάμενος διὰ παῦρα δασάσκετο, πολλὰ δ᾽ ἔχεσκεν. "From out all these I took much spoil and goodly, and all would I ever bring and

---

[151] M. L. West (1966), *ad Theog*. 520: "... in Homer this verb is only used of people sharing out among themselves, not allotting to someone else."
[152] The search for the lemma *dateomai* has been executed via *TLG* (accessed February 9, 2019). The texts and translations were accessed via the Perseus Digital Library.
[153] Translation of the *Theogony* by Hugh G. Evelyn-White.

give to Agamemnon, this son of Atreus; but he staying behind, even beside his swift ships, would take and apportion some small part, but keep the most."[154]

The subject of the verb δατέομαι is, as a rule, in the plural, which suggests that the verb is mainly used for a group dividing and distributing among themselves and rarely for a single person making a distribution. However, the verb is sometimes used in impersonal expressions such as "the water is allotted to her" (Hes. *Theog.* 789; "no one younger is better in scattering the seeds" (*WD* 447). The exceptions, where the verb is used in the singular, are cases when the community gives someone the right (or the duty) to share something among its members. In Hes. *Theog.* 885, the gods urge Zeus to rule over them and he then divides the honors among them (Zeus presides over the procedure); or in Hom. *Od.* 6.11—Nausithous is (presumably) given the duty to divide the territory of a new founded colony as a founder; or Hom. *Il.* 9.331–333—Agamemnon divides (*diadateomai*) the spoils, keeping a large part to himself after Achilles has given it to him in order to distribute to people (see my views in ch. 1). Achilles criticizes Agamemnon's conduct of the distribution, further asking a rhetorical question: "What for then the Argives are fighting the Trojans?" (337–338). This criticism implies an expectation that the spoils should have been distributed in a more egalitarian manner. All four instances of the verb in active voice in singular depict the distribution of a communal property on behalf of the group.

We have also examined the verb *diadateomai*, with the prefix "dia-" emphasizing distribution. The verb has only two instances in Hesiod and none in Homer. Both instances are in singular form: in *Theogony* 544, Prometheus is dividing the sacrificial meat for the gods, and in *Theogony* 885, Zeus apportions the "honors," *timai*, to the Olympian gods and Titans. The example of Prometheus illustrates a division on behalf of a group. Notwithstanding his initiative in taking the duty of fair distribution,[155] rather than being appointed by the community as in other cases, he is not giving the meat to the gods but divides a sacrificial ox that belongs to the group already. It is characteristic for both verbs *dateomai* and *diadateomai* to refer to a distribution of communal property, not in a top-down manner, even when being executed by one person on behalf of the group. The verb reflects a Greek mindset of receiving one's *portion* of a communal property rather than being given a gift from a king or an army leader.

---

[154] Translations of the *Iliad* and the *Odyssey* by A. T. Murray.
[155] Zeus is reproaching Prometheus for unjust distribution in the same line. Th. 544: "How unfairly you have divided the portions!" (trans. Evelyn-White).

The close reading of the passages containing the verb *dateomai* in Homer, Hesiod, and the *Homeric Hymns* provides tangible evidence for a more precise definition of the verb *dateomai*. The prevalence of the plural forms confirms West's claim that the meaning of the verb "distribute among a group" further signifies a distribution *by* the group. The only cases where a singular form is employed describe situations where the group authorizes a leader to distribute among the group members.

2
When Does the Lot Reflect the Will of the Gods?

Lots, Oracles, Divination, and the Notion of *Moira*

Lotteries produce unpredictable results. That is their point: the use of lots assumes the neutrality achieved by the luck of the draw, hence their freedom from the danger of manipulation. Imagine throwing up a coin and betting heads or tails. You would think you could not possibly know on which face it will fall, but you would be wrong. With sufficient information (unavailable under normal circumstances), you could always tell. Therefore, what appears random for humans is not truly random, but one would need superhuman capabilities to get the result. Did Greeks view their gods in that way? Did they use random devices, believing the result would not be a mere chance but an expression of the will of the gods? Time and again, the question has been raised whether Greeks drew lots to get an answer from the gods. I claim they did, but mainly within the strict category of lot oracles.

A lot oracle is a type of divination where an inquirer, instead of expecting a verbal answer, asks the god to choose between already-known alternatives, either in the form of a "yes/no" choice or by selection from among several preset options. The inquiry is made with drawing lots, and the lot that is picked up "randomly" provides a definite answer. But if the god "knows" and decides the outcome, is there still an element of chance? Is a god of divination by lot equivalent to a physicist who can theoretically know how the coin will drop? According to current scientific theory, randomness is a human illusion, and true randomness exists only on the quantum dimension: in quantum physics, the moment of observation is always synonymous with the event/object observed, and no one can ever predict an event.[1] The quantum god plays dice with the universe all the time.

So, what does the throw of the coin tell us?[2] Why would two knowledgeable physics professors, while sitting in the cafeteria, still toss a coin to see who would pick up the check? Because both know that the relevant information is lacking without the aid of a sophisticated lab. Communicating with the gods

---

[1] Gordon (2014); cf. Bennett (1998); Aaronson, Scott (2014).
[2] Bennett (1998) chs. 5–6.

via lot-oracles is very similar: what appears random for humans is supposedly known and directed by the gods at the moment of choice.

When using divination by lots, one may ask Apollo to help choose between two alternatives either for knowledge ("Is the baby my son?" "Is there anyone wiser than Socrates?"), or for action ("Should I go on this voyage?" "Should we accept the truce?"). Sometimes we hear of a selective lottery, such as choosing a name from among several others; that is how the Thessalians operated when asking Delphi for the choice of a king. The means appear random: no one can predict or influence which lot will jump out or be picked by the Pythia. But Apollo can: he has information human beings lack, analogous to what is at the disposal of the physics professor in her lab. The latter *knows* why and how the penny drops, but that information ceases to be relevant in the cafeteria; Apollo, too, has nonhuman information and can determine the results. Divination by lot does not presume randomness.

Are *all* lotteries then simply a form of divination? Did other types of lotteries reveal to humans the will or the plan of the gods, or did they perhaps reveal "blind fate" or "chance" that may have nothing to do with the gods planning anything? In other words, can we distinguish between religious and secular/rational lotteries? For example: When the Athenians, every year, selected by lot five hundred members of the *boule* (supreme council) through a complicated procedure of drawing lots, was it self-evident to them that each individual choice represented a deliberate decision of the gods? Was each *boule* member perceived as divinely selected? With no Greek source saying that,[3] so perhaps we need to distinguish between distributive, selective, mixing, and "civic" lotteries on the one hand, and divination-related lot oracles on the other. However, if we draw the distinction too sharply, our point of view might become anachronistic, applying the modern religious/secular dichotomy to antiquity. European secularism has developed from the distinction between the two swords of the church and the state, a distinction that was irrelevant to the ancient, polytheistic Greek society. In contrast, in Greek antiquity, the "civic" and the "religious" existed on a single spectrum since the world was "full of gods," as Thales had said,[4] and some involvement of the gods in almost any aspect of public life is easily discernable. What is this "some," and how are we to understand it in relation to lotteries?

The question (mostly ours, not an ancient Greek one) is nevertheless significant. If all is preordained and the lottery is merely the means to divine that which is predetermined or pre-chosen, then the inference, when carried to its logical conclusion, would be that Greek civilization had a deterministic outlook or one that left decisions to apparent chance. Such is the case with Luke Reinhart's *The*

---

[3] For possible exceptions, see below.
[4] Thales fr. A22(b) (D–K); Arist. *de Anima* 411a7.

Dice Man (1971), where human agency becomes irrelevant (except for the choice of when to employ the dice). Yet determinism is not a salient feature of Greek civilization. Moreover, oracular use need not imply that *all* applications of the lottery mechanism imply a divine intervention (e.g., for deciding about inheritance, the choice of soldiers or colonists, and the distribution of lands and offices). "Drawing lots *as* divination" should be a fundamental issue if we wish to reconstruct a Greek mindset and the values the lottery implies—namely, equality, fairness, justice, lawfulness, and order. Where does the emphasis lie? With lotteries being so ubiquitous, can we still accept the rightly famous cliché that Greeks placed man at the center of their "cities of reason"?[5]

Headlam (1891) was the first to claim that most lotteries were secular.[6] J.-P. Vernant follows this line with the contrast between, on the one hand, divination, where knowledge is imparted from above, and the "city of reason," where deliberation and persuasion rule the day. Yet Vernant ignores drawing lots, that infrastructure of the Athenian democracy. So, his approach still begs the question, taking us a step behind his argument, unless lotteries are to be included within "reason": the Athenians, after all, "rationally" chose a device that produced random outcomes, based on chance, with no identifiable cause.

It is essential to remind ourselves that the lottery exists on a spectrum of associations, enhancing our understanding of the lots in their overlapping, broad applicability, revealing mental attitudes and attesting to practices and institutions. To adapt what Esther Eidinow says in connection with related concepts, the use of lots need not "be considered as indicating a single concept, but instead as having activated a mental pattern of connections, a network of associations, dependent on both the context of their use and the experiences of those using and apprehending the terms."[7] The overlap within the spectrum (divination/mundane) seems to exist over issues of choice, distribution, procedure (e.g., taking turns by drawing lots), and prophecy.

We see, then, that the effort of neatly distinguishing among the functions of lotteries may need to be revised since they share the same mindset and mental framework whereby, according to context, the lottery can be both divinatory and a rational mechanism producing random results. The religious significance of lotteries probably varied according to context, and even within the same context, the lot probably meant something different to various individuals.

---

[5] Vernant ([1974] 1991) 306; cf. Murray (1990).

[6] Headlam ([1891] 1933²); cf. Hansen (1990) 51, and Manin (1997) ch. 1, in contrast to Fustel de Coulanges (1891) and Victor Ehrenberg (1927), who basically regarded all categories of lotteries as somehow revealing the will of the gods. Also Glotz (1907; [1928] 1988) 219–224. See also Demont (2020).

[7] Eidinow (2011) 9.

Let us recall the scene in the *Iliad* about the lottery held among nine heroes to determine who will fight Hektor, now to observe the role of religion. They placed their markers in a helmet, old Nestor shook it, and the mighty Aias's marker jumped out.[8]

> [Nestor speaking] Let the lot be shaken for all of you, to see who wins it.... So he spoke, and each of them marked a lot as his own one lot. They threw them in the helmet of Atreus' son, Agamemnon, and the people, holding up their hands *to the gods, prayed to them*. Then would murmur any man, gazing into the wide sky: *"Father Zeus, let Aias win the lot, or else Diomedes, Tydeus' son, or the king himself of golden Mykenai* (Agamemnon)." So they spoke, and Nestor the Gerenian horseman shook the lots, and a lot leapt from the helmet, that one that they all had wished for, the lot of Aias. (trans. Lattimore; emphasis added)

In the *Iliad* the language of the prayer to all the gods and then specifically to Zeus does not prioritize Aias: they pray that the chosen lot belongs to *either* Aias *or* Diomedes *or* Agamemnon. After they conduct the lottery, they seem to have preferred Aias. Their prayer is not about expecting Zeus to influence the result. The language of the prayer does not convey the specific expectation that all the gods or just Zeus would determine the result of the lottery; all they say is, "Let X win." First, the gods (plural) are invoked; then, while turning to the sky (= Zeus), they seem to ask that he preside over the ritual. It does not read like divination.[9]

Upon their victory over the Titans, the three Olympian brothers, Zeus, Hades, and Poseidon, defined and distributed their realms by lot (see ch. 1). No Greek could have conceived of this lottery as "divination" since there was no other divinity to ask for the results. We also noted the distribution to other gods, often explicitly by lot, of powers, unique places, and "honors" (*timai*), mainly in Hesiod and the *Homeric Hymns*. Zeus, as I read the sources, is *presiding* over the drawing of lots and the distribution, not deciding what each divinity should specifically get. The point is strengthened by a few quoted words of the lyric poet Alkman (early seventh century), who says, "He [Zeus] himself [*hoiethen*] shook the lots and distributed [*dateomai*] the *daimones* [presumably the portions of the gods, here called *daimones*; the word *daimon* too is *related to dateomai*]."[10] Aeschylus also calls him expressly Zeus the Apportioner, *Klarios*.[11] Yet as noted, the verb *dateomai* is usually used with a plural subject, meaning distribution by (or on behalf of) a group and for the group. The exceptions, where the verb is used in the

---

[8] Hom. *Il.* 7 170-189; cf. *Il* 3.314-325; *Od.* 10.203-207.
[9] Cf. Aubriot-Sevin (1992) 386-387.
[10] Fr. 65 Page.
[11] *The Suppliant Maidens* (360) Zeus (of Argos) *Klarios*, "the righteous Zeus the Apportioner who hears suppliants."

singular, are cases where the community gives someone the right (or the duty) to share something among them.

Another moment in the *Iliad* is when the Greeks and Trojans agree to settle the war through a duel between Menelaos and Paris, who had stolen the former's wife, Helen. Odysseus and Hector oversee the process, and again they draw lots to see which of the warriors will first throw his spear.

> Hector now, the son of Priam, and brilliant Odysseus, measured out the distance first, and thereafter picked up two lots, and put them in a brazen helmet, and shook them, to see which one of the two should be first to cast with his bronze spear, and the people on each side *held up their hands to the gods, and prayed to them.* Thus would murmur any man, Achaian or Trojan: "Father Zeus, watching over us from Ida, most high, most honored, *whichever man has made what has happened happen to both side*s, grant that *he be killed* and go down to the house of Hades. Let the friendship and the sworn faith be true for the rest of us." So they spoke, and tall Hector of the shining helm shook the lots, looking backward, and at once Paris' lot was outshaken. (*Il.* 3.314–325; Lattimore)

Unlike the prayer during the lottery in which Aias's *kleros* jumped out from the bronze helmet, here the prayer asks that Zeus's *justice* be done, that the end of the war should come, that the one to blame for the war should die as a result of the duel. They do not pray that their respective hero gets the first shot, which is the immediate purpose of the lottery. It seems that those praying to Zeus do not stand before their god as ignorant humans seeking information, but to Zeus as the god under whose auspices the entire procedure would take place. The prayer assures legitimacy, ensuring that all participants accept the lottery as final arbitration among the participants, namely, those who hold the lottery and have access to it. On a more general level, the prayer is not for the specific outcome of the lottery but rather for the end of the war, which does depend on Zeus.[12]

So, whose authority does the lottery represent? Was it Zeus who made the *kleros* jump out for Aias? Were the heroes praying for Zeus to make a decision? I claim that the drawing of lots implies equal chances and interchangeability, while the source of its authority is the group of participants, a "lateral authority." However, if Zeus is the one to choose the "best one," the lottery would be equivalent to divination, "exposing" the best one. In terms of trying to reconstruct a Greek mindset, whether the lottery was perceived as vertical ("from above," the will of the gods) or horizontal (laterally, from and among human communities) is, therefore, a major question.

---

[12] I wish to thank Margalit Finkelberg for help on these issues.

I doubt that Greeks seriously thought that all lotteries expressed a divine choice in every single domain of their application. Indeed, the gods were always invoked, whether in the law courts, the assembly, the theater, or any other institution. *Theoi!* ("Gods!") is the opening word, a formula, for every public decree of the Athenians. But it is not the gods, but the people who are at the center, since the formula "Gods!" precedes what follows: "the People and the *Boule* [council] decide" or, more literally, "it pleases the People, etc.," words that place an even stronger emphasis on the nondivine part of the formula. So there is a difference between invoking a god and a direct call for divine involvement, as we shall now see with oracles. Had divine will been predominant in all lotteries, we would expect to find at least a hint of that, especially in the various lottery myths, and we have quite a few. Yet it is never spoken of in such terms.

Moreover, as noted, the lottery *among* the gods was not directed to divine their own will. Homer's words describe drawing lots in precisely the same terms as the human, "horizontal" lotteries. Lachesis was one of the more ancient gods involved in the procedure of at least one Olympian lottery, as we have seen with Helios. Still, she was the *Moira* of lot casting, whose name implies getting by lot (*lanchano*). But she was a witness and an administrator of an oath, not a transcendent decision-maker.[13]

Aside from the explicit use of drawing lots for divination, to which I shall turn soon, we can hardly find any statement in Greek texts of the archaic and classical periods claiming that the gods determine the results of drawing lots. Plato may come close, notably in the *Laws*, yet he contradicts himself in the *Republic*, where he imagines a prophet distributing lots to souls before reincarnation: "No divinity," he says, "shall cast lots for you, but you shall choose your own deity. Let him to whom falls the first lot first select a life. . . . The blame is his who chooses: god is blameless" (*Rep.* 617e, trans. Paul Shorey).

Plato indicates the *pairing* of lots with results (Plato *Rep.* 617c), combined with an element of personal choice (see also ch. 6.3.10). The scene is imaginary but builds on standard practice, evident in land allotments and partible inheritance by lot (see chs. 4 and 6). It concerns pairing "lots and patterns of lives" using the three *moirai* and assigning them to souls.[14]

> And there were another three who sat round about at equal intervals, each one on her throne, the *Moirai*, daughters of Necessity (*Ananke*), clad in white vestments with filleted heads, Lachesis, and Clotho, and Atropos, who sang in unison with the music of the Sirens. . . . Now when they (the souls) arrived

---

[13] On the connection between Lachesis, *moirai*, and sortition: Guidorizzi (2001) 42–44 Cf. Macé (2016).

[14] Cf. Plato *Phaedrus* 249b: "But in the thousandth year both come to draw lots and choose their second life, each choosing whatever it wishes." See also Demont (2014).

they were straight-way bidden to go before *Lachesis*, and then a certain prophet first marshalled them in orderly intervals, and thereupon *took from the lap of Lachesis lots and patterns of lives* (*kleroi, bion paradeigmata*) and went up to a lofty platform and spoke, 'This is the word of Lachesis, the maiden daughter of Necessity, Souls that live for a day, now is the beginning of another cycle of mortal generation where birth is the beacon of death. *No divinity shall cast lots for you, but you shall choose your own deity. Let him to whom falls the first lot* (*protos d'ho lachon*) *first select* (*haireo*) *a life*. . . . The blame is his who chooses: god is blameless.' So saying, the prophet flung the lots (*kleroi*) out among them all, and each took up (*anaireo*) the lot that fell by his side, except himself (the prophet); him they did not permit. And whoever took up (*anaireo*) a lot saw plainly what number he had drawn (*lanchano*).[15] (*Rep.* 617d–e, trans. Paul Shorey)

A few points stand out in this imaginary scene: first, as noted, Plato expressly removes the gods from any responsibility for the lottery or its results. In this passage, at least, the lottery procedure places the burden squarely on the one whose *turn* to make a choice was established by lot, as in procedural lotteries. Second, the three *moirai* create "patterns of life" but do not decide who gets them. Third, the material lots are described as concrete, picked up from the lap of Lachesis and thrown randomly to be "picked up" by each soul. Fourth, there are two actions of picking up (*anaireo*), implying not one, but two selections: picking up a lot with a numbered turn and then choosing a "pattern" from among those the priest had taken (at random, it seems) from Lachesis. Fifth, each would find out "what number he had drawn by lot (*lanchano*)": the meaning need not be concrete, as if each lot was inscribed with a number, although this would make sense. Sixth, "This is the word of Lachesis," says the prophet, and goes on with the procedure. As we have seen in the case of Helios, Lachesis presides over the lottery, and gods swear by her to abide by her results. Lachesis *is* the lottery and, as such, has no say about its results. Seventh, the prophet, like the Pythia or the personnel at Dodona, was conducting the lottery and overseeing the "pairing" of souls with patterns of lives using *kleroi*, lots. He is expressly not part of the lottery. That is a fantastic image concocted in Plato's head, yet it refers to acceptable notions and familiar procedures of drawing lots: random establishing of turns combined with a personal choice once the lot had been cast.

Things are a little different in Plato's *Laws*, the framework of which is the hypothetical foundation of a colony. In his discussion of the plots of land (*kleroi*) originally allotted during the colony's foundation, Plato refers to a common Greek

---

[15] "What number he had drawn": LSJ cites this passage for this meaning. Cf. "in what or which place in numerical order."

notion that such *kleroi* ought to be kept intact and inalienable.[16] The reason he gives is that the law sanctions this and because the "apportioning lot" (*neimas kleros*) is a god (*theos*)." I am not sure that even the exceptional Plato implies here that a god named *Kleros* determines human fate, nor that *as a god* does it serve as the expression of another god's will. Elsewhere, Plato does not mention the divine when envisioning an ideal parcellation of his colony into twelve parts and assigning them by lot.[17] It seems that, like most Greeks, he only means that the *institution* of the lottery itself is divine, as is any other institution in the *polis*. Moreover, the "first lots" in a colony had a special status, sanctioned by the first lottery upon the foundation, a sacred act (ch. 6). Specifically, as we shall see, a city's foundation was under the general sanction of the oracle of Delphi, hence the "divine" status of the first plots of land allotted to the settlers.

Similarly, even more obliquely, Plato speaks of the choice by lot and rotation of office holders under the auspices of the gods' favor, and he adds, "good luck" (*eu-tyche*) (*Laws* 3.690c).

> Dear to the gods (*theophile*) at any rate, and successful (literally: lucky, fortunate, *eutyche*), is what we call the seventh sort of rule—where we bring forward someone for a drawing of lots (*eis kleron tina*) and assert that it is just for the one who draws a winning lot (*lachonta*—a derivative of *lanchano*) to rule and for the one who draws a losing lot (*dysklerounta*—a derivative of *kleroö*) to give way and be ruled. (trans. R. G. Bury)

The expression "dear to the gods" does not imply that the gods make a choice. One could read the sentence in reverse: because a person is chosen by lot, that is a sign of good luck. In any case, *Tyche* here implies an open-ended result. In a passage about the selection of priests, Plato becomes more explicit while still linking his abstract "the god" (in the singular) to "good luck":[18]

> "In establishing all these offices, we must make the appointments partly by election and partly by lot, mingling democratic with non-democratic methods. . . . We shall entrust it to the god himself to ensure his own good pleasure, by committing their appointment to the divine chance (*theia tyche*) of the lot" (*Laws* 759b-c, trans. R. G. Bury)

One could make a case that Plato means a divine dispensation, but his addition of the "divine chance" would be superfluous. A ritual formula for invoking *both*

---

[16] Plato *Laws* 5.741b. See ch. 6.3
[17] Plato *Laws* 6.760b-c.
[18] Plato *Laws* 6.759b-c; cf. Arist. *Pol.* 4.1300a. See also section. 9.1.1 in this volume.

Tyche and Apollo indicates that "luck" and the god were discrete concepts as, in the formula "O Luck and Loxias, do you give an oracle to so and so?"[19] It is more likely that Plato is thinking in general terms: It is god's pleasure that men leave those decisions to divine chance, not to Him.[20] It is consistent with his statement in the *Republic* that "No divinity shall cast lots for you, . . . god is blameless" (quoted earlier). Gods do not choose magistrates; they provide divine auspices and sanction.[21]

Lot oracles are a discrete type of divination with formulaic questions that appear only in divinatory contexts. That means Greeks also distinguished between those and other procedural, distributive, selective, or mixing categories of drawing lots. They were not divorced from the religious spectrum (nothing was) but on the other end of it.[22]

2.1 Lot oracles and divination

A lot oracle is a type of divination in which an inquirer, instead of expecting a verbal answer, asks the god to choose between already-known alternatives. After casting the lots, the lot picked up "randomly" provides a definite answer. Inquirers at lot oracles surely expected a divine or heroic response, and most divination oracles offered the means to choose between alternatives that the

---

[19] Simp. in Ph. II, p. 75: ὦ Τύχη καὶ Λοξία.

[20] Speaking of equality achieved by the lot ought to be employed when "on account of the discontent of the masses, and in doing so to pray, calling upon god and Good Luck to guide for them the lot aright towards the highest justice . . . but that form, which needs good luck, we should employ as seldom as possible' (*Laws* 6.757e–758a), trans. R. G. Bury. Eidinow (2011) 45–52 discusses the slow rise of Tyche, Chance (*Fortuna*) from being unmentioned in Homer to Hellenistic prominence. "Quite paradoxically, as the cult of a rather ambiguously defined goddess Τύχη ('Fortune') was spreading, fate increasingly seemed to be deprived of any religious value" (Demont [2020] 314–315; cf. Kindle location 2295.)

[21] Cf. Eidinow (2011) 9. In contrast to the assumption of Fustel de Coulanges: the choice of a magistrate by lot is a sign of the "sacerdotal character belonging to the magistrate." The lot was "the revelation of the divine will" (Fustel de Coulanges [1878]; [1891] 242–243). Contra: Headlam ([1891] 1933[2] 51). Hansen (1991) 51: "There is not a single good source that straightforwardly testifies to the selection of magistrates by lot as having a religious character or origin." Cf. Manin (1997) ch. 1. Demont, relying on the same passages of Plato, returns to Fustel de Coulange's position: "It is impossible, in my opinion, to contest that we have here a genuine text from the end of the classical era attesting to the belief in divine intervention during the designation by lot of magistrates (the most explicit passage actually speaks of the selection of priests)." However, Demont, who starts out with that bold statement ("divine *intervention*"), eventually can only point to oblique implications from the associated religious terms, as I have already pointed out. He ends with a conclusion of attributing "religious importance" to lots, relying heavily on Plato. But "importance" is rather the question, not the answer: How important? In what way? To whom? etc. As I keep arguing, since the gods (not "religion") were "everywhere," they were invoked, not asked for their decisions in most types of drawing lots.

[22] See section 8.2.4 in this volume on the selection of priests by lot in the Athenian *genos*, hinting at a divine preference.

inquirer had formulated.[23] Any choice made by drawing lots that favorably singles out one alternative implies active *non*choosing of other alternatives. In that sense, there is a "technical" overlap between divinatory and selective lotteries. When Aias was chosen by drawing lots to fight Hector, it also meant that neither Diomedes, Agamemnon, nor anyone else was chosen, although the soldiers prayed for all participants equally. With lot oracles, often only a dual choice was proffered, expecting either a positive or a negative answer. Both private and public inquiries by lot concern such issues as, "Is it better and more advantageous/profitable that I do this / or refrain from doing this?" "Is it better and more profitable that I marry her / go on this trip / make the trade / dishonor a truce?" For the sake of evenly spreading out chances and outcomes, randomness is the purpose of selective, distributive, procedural, and mixture lotteries. By contrast, lot oracles seek one definite "truth."[24]

In Greek society, as in many others, "inspired prophecy" had a much higher reputation than cleromancy (divination by lot, a word deriving from the combination of *kleros* and *manteia*).[25] Inspired prophecy happens when the god speaks through a prophet directly and instantaneously, as Apollo did through the Pythia at Delphi. He may also reveal the words to a prophet who would then (but not at the moment of revelation) serve as his mouthpiece; such were most of the Biblical prophets. Inspired prophecy is generally considered a higher order: "Many are the dice-throwers (*thrioboloi*) but few are the prophets," was a popular maxim.[26]

The image of the Pythia, the prophetess of Apollo at Delphi, has captured Western imagination with her inspired prophecies. She was the mouthpiece of Apollo, literally in-spired (the "spirit" of Apollo enters her) and en-thusiastic (*enthousiasmos* implies the entering of the divine into the person). Did the lot choose the Pythia? In Euripides's *Ion*, she is addressed in such terms: "Prophet of Phoibos, preserving the ancient law of the tripod, selected from all Delphic women."[27] The relevant verb is *exaireo/exairesthai*, meaning to choose by lot or "to select." But at Delphi, as we shall see later, it has particular connotations with prophecy using lots, in addition to its role in the choice of personnel of Delphi.

---

[23] J.-P. Vernant considers Greek divination different from Ancient Near Eastern divination, which, unlike the Greek, constituted a true semiology, decoding the universe with the inherent assumption of omniscience. Vernant ([1974] 1991) 316.

[24] Klingshirn in Luijendijk and Klingshirn (2018) 1, on the use of lots: "in a game, this assures the participants of a fair result; in the division of land, it assures them of an equitable result; in lot divination it assures them of a true result." Lot oracles are a "vehicle for producing a definite outcome against every *appearance* of randomness." Id. (2018) 2 (emphasis in original).

[25] Burkert (1985) 111 is dismissive of lot oracles as a "decision-making mechanism." I disagree; cf. Greaves (2012) 201.

[26] Zenobius, *Cent.* v.75; Stephanus Byzantius, s.v. Θρία. Cf. Eur. *El.* 399–400; Plato *Phaedros* 244d. Beerden (2013) 37, 123. Dice oracles: Johnston (2008) 99–100.

[27] Eur. *Ion*, 1322–1323. *All* Delphian women form the pool for drawing lots. A choice of men from select families (ibid. 416) is not relevant to the Pythia; cf. Plut. *Mor.* 292d.

108　DRAWING LOTS

Inspired prophecies and divination by lot express a mental attitude and constitute a social institution coherently included in the entire body of social thought. Adopting an anthropological perspective, J.-P. Vernant says that "[Divination is] an official instance of legitimation that, at a time when choices are fraught with consequences for group equilibrium, offers decisions that are socially 'objective,' that is, independent of the desires of the parties at issue and benefitting from a general consensus of the social body that puts this type of response above dispute."[28] Oracular divination is tantamount to outsourcing the decision-making: the decision is deferred to divine "arbitration," and its legitimation is to be recognized by all. Legitimation is partly based on randomization: "Divination relies on randomization as its fundamental logical step: into a chain of human causality, introduces a gap where the hand and mind of the divinity can interfere: casting the dice is the randomizing opening in the process, as is drawing the lot."[29] So how were the gods involved? Regarding divination by lot, Apollo is not the first god to note, but Hermes.

2.2. The god Hermes

"Because you are Hermes you will proceed with the lot" (*kleros*).
Aristophanes *Peace* 364–365 (trans. Eugene O'Neill)

Aside from Lachesis, one of the three Moirai, whose name derives from *lanchano*, "to get by lot," Hermes was the Greek god of lotteries. A myth related by [Pseudo-]Apollodorus (first–second centuries CE) tells of a deal between Apollo and Hermes. Hermes had made a pipe, the music of which was so captivating that Apollo coveted it and agreed to barter, which resulted in Hermes getting "mantic pebbles" for divination:

Hermes wished . . . to acquire the art of divination. So he gave the pipe (to Apollo) and learned the art of *divining by pebbles.* (*ten dia ton psephon mantiken*). (Apoll. 3.10.2, trans. Frazer 1898)

The *Homeric Hymn to Hermes* that dates centuries earlier (sixth century) has a parallel but far more intricate story and a different type of divination.[30] Apollo refuses to share the true prophecy with Hermes because "the mind of Zeus"

---

[28] Vernant ([1974] 1991) 302–303.
[29] Graf (2005) 60–61.
[30] Vergados (2012) 130–148 for the date of the *Hymn*.

(*Dios noös*) decreed this. It is Apollo who then expounds the will of the gods.[31] Apollo's central prophetic role is being a mediator and expounder, an *exegetes*, a monopoly he would not share. He thus implies a distinction between inspired prophecies, precisely that which represents Zeus, and other types of divination, such as interpreting omens observed in the flight of birds, where *kleroi* may have been used as well.[32]

> [Apollo:] But as for soothsaying (*manteia*), noble, heaven-born child, of which you ask, it is not lawful for you to learn it, or for any other of the deathless gods: only the mind of Zeus knows that. I am pledged and have vowed and sworn a strong oath that no other of the eternal gods save I should know the wise-hearted counsel (*boule*) of Zeus. (*Homeric Hymn to Hermes* 534–537 trans. Hugh G. Evelyn-White)

Apollo goes on to tell of three bee-maidens of Mount Parnassos (Delphi) whose honey may serve inspired prophecy.

> And when they are inspired through eating yellow honey, they are willing to speak truth; but if they be deprived of the gods' sweet food, then they speak falsely, as they swarm in and out together. These, then, I give you; enquire of them strictly and delight your heart: and if you should teach any mortal so to do, often will he hear your response—if he has good fortune.
> (*Homeric Hymn to Hermes* 560–566, trans. Hugh G. Evelyn-White)

So where are the "divining pebbles" mentioned by Pseudo-Apollodorus? The manuscripts name the three bee-maidens *moirai* (portions, fates) or *semnai* (venerable ones). However, a philological conjecture is to blame for introducing the lots into the *Hymn*: Gottfried Hermann emended the text (line 552), replacing *moirai* with "Thriai," which, in later sources, were indeed understood as "lots." Philochoros says that "nymphs inhabited Parnassus, the nurses of Apollo, three,

---

[31] For "the mind of Zeus," see Warden (1971). What Apollo seems to mean is that it is his task to reveal, *ad hoc*, the "counsel" (*boule*) of the gods (*HH Apollo* 484). See also *HH Hermes* 538. Vergados (2012) *ad* 535: "For Zeus's mind knows (i.e., he has decreed) this (sc. that no one else know his will)."

[32] Eur. *Phoen.* 838–840; *Hipp.* 1057–1059 with Mastronarde (1994) *ad* 838. Mastronarde cites Barrett (1964) (on Eur. *Hipp.* 1057–1058): "evidently a note of some kind which the *mantis* makes after observing the flight of birds; from the name *kleros* I should suppose that he keeps a stock of them, recorded as occasion offers, and then when consulted takes one or more at random to use as the basis of his soothsaying." Cf. Pindar *Pyth.* 4.190. Mastronarde (with earlier references): "The props carried by the silent extra in this scene may have been small tablets of wood (with or without wax) or pieces of papyrus. . . . Three narrow, stiff lots (representing thin wooden ones?) are shown in the hand of Lachesis in two relief sculptures (in Madrid and Tegea) that go back to an original of the classical period: cf. *JÖAI* 6 (1903) 99 fig. 48 and Taf. 5–6; for the Madrid example, see Robertson (1975) 301–302.

called *Thriai*, after whom the mantic pebbles are called *thriai* and prophesying, *thriasthai*."³³ At some unknown point, it seems, the lot oracle at Delphi (or another nearby) came to be identified with the *Thriai*, Apollo's nurses from Mount Parnassus. Late sources mention that Apollo, jealous of the reputation of the *Thriai*, went to Zeus, who made divining by lot untrustworthy.³⁴

So far, there seems to be a clear distinction between true prophecy (Apollo, knowing the mind of Zeus) and divination/prophecy by lot.³⁵ However, we will soon observe a significant overlap between the seemingly discrete domains of Apollo and Hermes. The god Hermes covers the spectrum from games of chance to cleromancy (lot divination). Dice for gambling were no strangers to ancient Greeks.³⁶ Arnaud Macé astutely observes, "Game practices were embedded in the warrior culture of the Greeks."³⁷ There is a story, for example, about how an irritated group in Athens burst into the house where one Pittalakos was living. They smashed the implements of his trade and tossed them into the street— sundry dice, boxes, and gaming utensils.³⁸ But with regard to divination, the issue is not the dice as such but the context of their use: some oracles, such as that of Heracles at Boura in Achaea, delivered their responses through the medium of knuckle-bones (*astragaloi*), and others again with dice, the rolling of which referred to preestablished sentences in a list of predictions.³⁹

> On descending from Boura towards the sea, you come to a river called Buraikos, and to a small Heracles in a cave. He too is surnamed Buraikos, and here one can divine by means of a tablet and dice. He who inquires of the god offers up a prayer in front of the image, and after the prayer he takes four dice, a plentiful supply of which are placed by Heracles, and throws them upon the table. For

---

³³ Herman, discussed by Larson (1995). Philochorus *FGrHist* 328 FI95; Suidas, s.v. *Thriai*; Hesychius, s.v. *Thriai, thriazein* (please note *thriazein* = *enthousiazein*: θριαζειν φυλλολογεῖν, ενθουσιάν, ἐνθουσιάζειν). Etym. Magn. s.vv. Thriai; Bekker Anecd. I.265, 8.V. *thriason pedion*; Philochorus fr. 196 ap. Zen. Prov. cent. v. 75; Schol. in Callim. *Hymn Ap.* 45. Later sources add a few more details. Callimachus, for instance, lists *thriai kai manties* as part of the province of Apollo (*Homeric Hymn to Apollo* 45), and the scholiast informs us that " the *thriai* are mantic pebbles, said to have been found by three nymphs."

³⁴ Zenob. Cent. V.75; Steph. Byz,. s.v. *thria*. Other issues connected with the *Thriai*, including the role of Athena in one version, are not pertinent here. Cf. Berman (2007) 168 n.4; McInerney (1997).

³⁵ The distinction was not necessarily clear. Cf. Philo *Legatio* 99.

³⁶ Halliday (1913) 205–234; Bouché-Leclercq (1879–1880) 1:189–194; Ehrenberg (1927) 1451–1467.

³⁷ Macé (2020) 97; Kindle location 1945). He adds that "Plato suggests that we should think of the immanent justice at work in the universe through analogy with the game of *petteia* (*Laws* X 903c-e)."

³⁸ Aeschines 1.59 [ἀστραγάλους διασείστους *astragalous diaseistous*, "shaken astragali"].

³⁹ Paus. 7.25.10. Halliday (1913) 212; Bonnechaire (2007) 145–160; Brixhe and Hodot (1988) 134–164; Donnay (1984); Kurke (1999) 288–289. An ancient commentary on Pindar says that the ancients used to divine by lot: astragals laid on holy tables in temples. Halliday (1913) 207, scholiast on Pindar, *Pyth* 4.337. Cf. Kidd (2017). For various types of astragales, see Greaves (2012) 183–188. Apparently *astragaloi* were not used for divination before the classical period; see Dillon (2017) 271–274. Cf. Neils (1992).

every figure made by the dice there is an explanation expressly written on the tablet. (Paus. 7.25.10, trans. W. H. S. Jones, H. A. Ormerod)

The three Parnassian maidens, whether Thriai or not, may offer another clue to oracular associations. Jennifer Larson identifies them with cave nymphs, associated explicitly with the nymph sanctuary discovered at the Corycian Cave, a few kilometers from Delphi. Inside the cave were some twenty-five thousand astragals, which, she suggests, were used for divination by inquirers with lesser means, with many coming from the vicinity.[40] The cult activity began in the seventh century and became particularly intensive between 550 and 350.[41] Inquirers turned to the nymphs and Hermes, whose presence in the cave is not attested but may be implied by his otherwise close association with Nymphs, suggests Larson. Even without this attractive reconstruction, the evidence of both astragals and dice inside the cave probably points to a lot oracle, but the case remains uncertain (cf. Figure 2.1).[42]

Hermes's own "constitutive" myth, namely his birth, his growth into a young adult god in a single day,[43] and his domains, articulated through his primordial actions, place him squarely as a god of lots and distribution. We encountered Hermes when discussing equal portions distributed by lot to the twelve gods:

Homeric Hymn to Hermes 128–139

Next glad-hearted Hermes dragged the rich meats he had prepared and put them on a smooth, flat stone, and divided them into twelve portions (*moirai*) distributed by lot (*kleropaleis*). (trans. Evelyn-White)

Klero-paleis, signifying lottery, is explicit, combining *pallo* (shaking the lots) with *kleros* (the lot as such). The lottery Hermes conducts does not seem to have much to do with divination since its purpose is to reveal what a god knows or plans, which would be redundant with Hermes himself.[44] However, it is noteworthy that one of the first constitutive acts of the newly born god concerns a drawing of lots and the distribution of meat portions. Note that the *moirai* (portions) are probably equal since Hermes distributed them by lot, not according to position or seniority.[45] In other words, Zeus had the same chance as Hephaistos.

---

[40] Amandry (1984); Amandry and Jacquemin (1984) 153ff.; Parke (1985); Ustinova (2009) 165-8.
[41] Amandry and Jacquemin (1984) 154ff; 396ff.
[42] They might have signified other functions, such as dedications by young boys. See Larson (1995).
[43] Versnel (2011) ch. 4.
[44] Jaillard (2012) 99 thinks a mantic quality is implied in relation to Hermes's own position among the gods. The point is insufficiently developed.
[45] Cf. Plut. *Quaes. Conv.* 643c (table ii.10): unlike music, the distribution of meat and bread aims to be equal.

112 DRAWING LOTS

Figure 2.1 Astragal with an image of Omphale. 340–303. Metropolitan Museum of Arts. Gift of Egypt Exploration Fund Accession Number: O.C.428. CC0 license (creative commons—Public domain dedication).

Equal distribution forms a central motif within the range of associations and the frame of reference connected with the lottery. As Grottanelli notes, the fables of Aesop serve as a further illustration.[46] Once, "Zeus decided that Hermes should inscribe on *ostraka* the faults of men and deposit these *ostraka* in a little wooden box near him, so that he could do justice in each case (*ostraka* were shards of pottery used in public procedures, as we might use scrap paper). But the *ostraka* got mixed up, and some came up sooner, others later, to the hands of

---

[46] This is an excellent observation of Grotanelli (2001); cf. Versnel (2011) 329–332.

Zeus."[47] Here the mix-up of *ostraka* is parallel to the category of mixture lotteries and metaphorically alludes to the general human mix-up between merits and deserts. The mixture, a salient trait of lotteries, appears here as the reverse of a deterministic *moira*.

An early prose example is provided by Xanthos of Lydia (mid-fifth century; *FGrHist* 765 F 29) who combines a religious tale (or myth) with the normal, "secular" practice of jury courts. Once Hera brought Hermes to trial and charged him with slaying her pet monster, Argos. While the judges realized it was all Zeus's fault, and so exonerated Hermes, they still lapidated him with their ballots, or *psephoi* (note the overlap of the same word, *psephoi*, also used for cleromancy).[48] Xanthos uses the term *kibotia*, which refers to the container in which jury lots were mixed before their selection to their post.

The notion of equality comes up in three other fables (Chambry [1925] 111, 112, 120). In these, Hermes prepares *equal portions* for distribution to all humanity. The fables also show how equal distribution might result in inequality. For example, Hermes distributed equal portions of intelligence (*nous*) to all; however, whereas shorter men were filled up by their portions, there was not enough for the tall, burly folks. The general frame of reference is significant for our purpose: notions of equality, distribution, and images of containers that include a mixture of names are all there and all associated with Hermes. So Hermes was a god of drawing lots, as well as a god of divination, both cleromantic and inspired. He also had his own (very few) oracles where divination by lot was not practiced. Hermes was a god of luck, of the unexpected, of dice used in gambling and cleromancy. Yet he was not Zeus's spokesman: that province belonged to Apollo, the divine *exegetes* (expounder), and, of course, to Zeus himself. To understand better what divination by lot means, we need to turn to Apollo's oracle at Delphi and that of Zeus and his partner, the goddess Dione, at Dodona.

2.3 The lot oracle at Delphi

Associated with the sacred tripod at Apollo's oracle, some late sources tell us, was a container with "mantic pebbles" that rattled upon inquiry, either of their own accord or when deliberately shaken. These mantic pebbles were either in the bowl on the top of the tripod or in a *phiale*, a shallow container, held in the hands of the Pythia. Perhaps one waited for a lot to "jump" out. Only then was

---

[47] Chambry (1927) 57.
[48] On *pséphomantiké* cf. Bouché-Leclercq (1963 [1879]) 191. Cf. Philochorus, *FGrH* 328 fr. 195. Cf. Létoublon (2014).

the Pythia inspired to give Apollo's message.[49] In this version, the lots are the first phase before the inspired prophecy that follows them.

Delphi is famous for the Pythia, a prophet inspired (both literally and metaphorically) by Apollo. We have just seen that, in comparison, lot oracles were considered second-rate. However, contrary to the expectations in the *Homeric Hymn to Hermes*, we have several indications that lots were used at Delphi, with no regard for Hermes. Perhaps the link with inspired prophecy, which supposedly "covers" any prophecy coming from Delphi (Apollo speaks in various ways), blurred what at first seems a sharp distinction.

Lot oracles existed at Delphi, but their association with the Pythia is unclear. We can do no more than pose questions:[50] Were the lots used in a preliminary inquiry to allow the Pythia inspiration, as the passage mentioned earlier indicates? Were they used to see if the god should answer at all (in which case the lot oracle would simply constitute a phase leading up to inspired prophecy)?[51] Alternatively, were inspired prophecy and lot oracles two independent techniques used by the same (the Pythia) personnel or by a separate one and perhaps different clientele?

There are two types of evidence for lot oracles at Delphi. The one mentioned is the more explicit one and may be indirectly supported by the Greek verb signifying "to make an oracular prophecy." It is *anaireo*, which literally means "to pick up."[52] Sometimes we find the expression in the imperative, "Pick up the *kleros*!" Interestingly, the ancient Latin etymology of *sors* (lot) also implies "to come out" and *sortiri* (the present-day English word "sorcery" is a derivative).[53]

2.4 Delphi: Themis, the Pythia, and the lot

> Near the city (Delphi) was a temple of Apollo, called Pytho. In this, a brazen tripod was set up and above this was a basin which held the prophetic lots. Whenever those who were consulting the oracle

---

[49] See discussion and citations (mostly late sources, e.g., Suda, s.v. *Pytho*) in Amandry (1950) 29–30.
[50] Vernant (1974) 305.
[51] Halliday (1913) 211.
[52] Halliday (1913) 211. See below on Dodona and the discussion by Parker (2015). Cf. Carbon (2015) 80.
[53] Johnston (2008) 99–100. Note how Plato envisages a choice by lot: "And from the sons of citizens who happen to have more than one son over ten years old, ten shall be chosen by lot (*klerosai*) ... and the names thus chosen (the verb is *lanchano*) shall be sent to Delphi; and that man whom the oracle names (*aneilei*, 'picks up') shall be established as the allotment-holder in the house of those departed" (Plato *Laws* 856d–e, trans. R. G. Bury).

asked a question some were drawn out, and the Pythia, employing them, or becoming possessed, declared that which Apollo revealed.[54]

The Greek verb *anaireo*, to pick up, seems to support the use of lots.[55] One famous illustration of consultation with the Pythia (as the goddess Themis is seated in her stead)[56] shows her sitting on the tripod, holding an olive branch in one hand, and gazing into a *phiale* she is holding, which probably contains lots.[57] The lots were apparently rattled, either to make one "jump" or to be "picked up" and to shuffle them as we do with cards before picking one out.[58] We have no idea what the distinguishing marks were on such lots or what they signified.

We observe parallels for such *kleroi* in inscribed *astragali* of varying detail. These were knucklebones, usually of sheep, used as four-sided dice (Fig. 2.1). In a late period, we find, for example, a popular oracle with 216 citations of Homer referred to on lots, and the relevant verse would carry a meaningful prophecy.[59] Elsewhere, the oracle of Heracles at Boura in Achaea (see above) delivered responses using knucklebones. Sometimes we find dice: rolling them would refer to preestablished phrases in a list of predictions.[60] That is akin to bibliomancy when the lot picks up a verse from a prewritten corpus, also known in Christianity.[61] There is abundant evidence from southwestern Anatolia dating to the second century that seems to reflect later regional developments and may not relate to earlier practices; fifty-six oracles inscribed on the sides of a statue of Hermes that were positioned in an agora constituted such a corpus. The sum of the numbers achieved through the roll of five astragals would correspond to a specific prophecy and a named god.[62]

---

[54] Suidas, s.v. *Pytho* with Holland (1933) 203.
[55] Parker (2015).
[56] Robbins (1916); for the unsupported suggestion that Themis is gazing into a bowl full of water (*lekanomanteia*) see Dillon, Eidinow, and Maurizio (2017) 269; for further references, 312n33. Cf. Maurizio (2019) 113, who mentions such options and prefers to understand the Pythia as pouring a libation. However, her sitting position and her attitude, while it may point to a potential ritual, does not seem to concern an actual libation. I thank Milette Gaifman for advice on this point (with Gaifman 2018).
[57] Cf. Gaifman (2018). There one explicit, albeit very late reference: Gregory of Nazianzus 5.32 and 39.13 (following Nonnos) refers to Apollo himself shaking the lots. Suidas suggests that after lots are drawn (no agent is named), the Pythia becomes possessed by using them (inspirational prophecy).
[58] Amandry (1950) 31–32. Flacelière (1950), who believes mostly that the inspired prophecies were the rule, prefers the sense of the middle voice here: the Pythia trembled, or made tremble, herself and the tripod.
[59] Johnston (2008) 169–170. Cf. Ps. Lucian *Amores* 16 for knuckle bones of a gazelle.
[60] Johnston (2008) 99–100; Brixhe and Hodot (1988) 134–164; Donnay (1984). For Asia Minor, see Nollé (2007).
[61] On a bridge in Istanbul, I once encountered a modern version: the itinerant oracle monger has a kind of a tray with hundreds of preinscribed prophecies; a little white rabbit then pulls out a prophecy at random, which is then read to the consultant.
[62] Johnston (2008) 99; Graf (2005): 84–94. Christianity: Aune (1983).

Figure 2.2 Themis, as the prototype of the Pythia, seated on the Delphic tripod, consulted by Aigeus. Attic red figure, attributed to the Kodros Painter, ca. 430. Antikenmuseen, Berlin F2538 (Beazley Archive no. 217214). Illustration from "Illustrerad verldshistoria utgifven av E. Wallis. Volume I." 1875. Photo of illustration by Ernst Wallis et al. (own scan) [Public domain], via Wikimedia Commons.

Figure 2.2 shows the Goddess Themis, probably the "first Pythia."[63] Some Delphic mythologies consider Themis as one of the possessors of the oracles before Apollo, and according to Aeschylus, she had won Delphi by lot (see below). She was also worshiped at the oracles of Gaia (Earth) and those of Zeus at Dodona and Olympia.[64] Her name, Themis, is significant as its changing functions marked the transition to democracy in the late sixth century. According to Martin Ostwald, it was a transition from the concept of the law as *themis*, "something placed / laid down" (*thesmos*, from the verb *tithemi*), to mutually accepted, even equal, norm, *nomos*. It was a transition from the "top-down" vision of society to the horizontal one. Themis and *thesmos* retain a visual association of something "from above" "laid down," whereas *nomos* is a human norm to be viewed laterally and deriving its authority from the mutual recognition of the members of the

---

[63] Here I concentrate only on the role of Themis at Delphi.
[64] Pindar *Isth.* 8.30–45; Aesch. *PV* 209; Paus. 5.14.10; and Johnston (2008) 59; Dakaris (1996) 52–53; Parke (1967) 180. Themis can mean "oracle": *Od.* 16.403; *themisteuo*, give an oracle: Eur. *Ion* 371; Themis as the direct predecessor of Apollo: Eur. *IT* 1259–1269.

community.[65] *Nomos*, as noted, has its origins in "assigning portions" (*nemo*),[66] and "equal portions" would become "equal law," *isonomia*, the first term to denote democracy.[67]

Yet *themis* in the sense of "what is established" appears in Homer and the Homeric Hymns as a goddess of assemblies, of that which humans establish, namely a decision about a course of action, a choice between alternatives.[68] This role of *themis* would become less frequently mentioned as the transition from *thesmos* to *nomos* progressed. Themis, in the plural, can mean oracles.[69] "What does it mean," asks Sarah Iles Johnston, "that a single goddess watches over both human assemblies and oracular knowledge?" The human and the divine are not mutually exclusive,[70] which brings us back to the misguided dichotomy between "the city of reason" and divination. Both oracular *themis* and the *themis* of assemblies existed on the same spectrum, with shifting emphasis from the vertical ("from above") to the horizontal (laterally, among people).

2.5 Delphi: Beans used as lots

The Byzantine encyclopedia, the Souda (tenth century CE), seems confident about the role of the Pythia in drawing lots: "Near the city (Delphi) was a temple of Apollo, called Pytho. In this, a brazen tripod was set up, and above this was a basin that held the prophetic lots. Whenever those who were consulting the oracle asked a question, some were drawn out, and the Pythia, employing them, or becoming possessed, declared that which Apollo revealed." However, the Souda connects the lots with the Pythia's possession, which does not seem to have been the case. Accessibility and frequency matter; since the Pythia was usually unavailable, there must have been lot oracles independent of her presence and direct involvement. We must remember that the Pythia was accessible for consultation during the archaic period first, one day a year, and then one day each month for nine months a year.[71] Lot oracles may have been conducted on a more regular basis by the Delphic priests, and beans seem to have been used for two types of oracular divination.

First, beans were used for selection from among several alternatives. The Thessalians (described later) submitted names of candidates for the kingship

---

[65] Ostwald (1969) 12–56, cf. Hölkeskamp (2000) 79–80.
[66] Chantraine (1968–1980) 755, for *nemo*, 742; Beekes (2010) 1023, for *nemo*, 1006. Cf. Laroche (1949).
[67] For the appearance and meaning of *isonomia*, see ch. 8.2.
[68] *Il.* 15.87–95; 20.4–6; *Od.* 2.68; Hymn 23.2; *Cypria* = Proclus *Chrestomathy* 1; *Od.* 9.112–115.
[69] E.g., *Od.* 16.403, *themisteuo* means to give oracle Eur. *Ion* 371.
[70] For the quote and excellent observation, see Johnston (2008) 59.
[71] Plut. *Mor.* 292e-f, 398a. Holland (1933); Parke and Wormell (1956) 1:30–34.

inscribed on beans, from which the Pythia was to choose one. The Aitolians may have done the same with their archons, and Cleisthenes the Athenian may have used beans when he submitted one hundred names of Attic heroes to the Pythia from which to choose. It would appear that the Pythia had a direct role in such selective lotteries by beans.

Aside from selection, an oracle of "two beans" seems to have been used for yes/no answers.[72] The use of beans as lots for oracular procedures seems well attested at Delphi. An inscription dating to the fourth century concerning Delphi and Skiathos demonstrates that those consulting the oracle sometimes came to Delphi "for the consultation of the two beans"; there was also a relatively high price for such a consultation: a high state fee for the *pelanos*, a sacrificial cake.[73] Bean oracles probably provided yes/no answers; the two beans are probably analogous to the use of beans in the choice of archons at Athens by lot, where black and white beans were used. Similarly, the Aitolians are said to have chosen their "archons" by such beans.[74]

Why beans? Did the beans perhaps have "souls" directing or being directed to an answer? One is reminded of the Pythagorean belief in a "soul" (*psyche*) of beans, which may be relevant to their use as lots, but there is no way to verify it.[75] Otherwise, we hear of beans as an instrument, efficient for their low price and the relative equality of size and shape: Hesychius, a Greek grammarian (fifth–sixth centuries CE), defines *phryktos* (bean) as a divining token, "lot," torch (*mantis, kleros, symbolon,* and *pyrsos*). Specifically, the *phryktos delphis* is "a lot (*kleros*)." At Olympia, the inquirers "used lots for divination (*echronto de tois klerois manteuomenoi*)."[76]

---

[72] Maurizio (2019) does not distinguish between the two types and considers the selective lottery by beans as a contradiction, whereas it is simply a discrete mode of divination by lot. She prefers to see lot oracles confined to Mount Parnassus. However, whereas she rightly brings some examples where yes/no answers may seem insufficient, both at Delphi and Dodona, that does not seem to be the general situation. The point is arguable and is contradicted by most of the fourteen hundred inquiries discovered at Dodona, among which we may find some exceptions. Relying on the forever mentioned Azande and Evans Prichard for "parallels" is at best suggestive. Greaves (2012) 195–196, relying on ethnographic comparanda, suggests that several throws of astragals could produce complex answers beyond yes/no. That may be possible, but we need evidence for the archaic period.

[73] Amandry (1939); (1950) 33; Parke (1967) 109. The text concerns Skiathos and the rather steep fee to be paid for the oracle by the two beans: Amandry (1950) 184 ll. 15–19. There is a different price for private or state consultation. Amandry takes *epi phrykto* as a dative dual, "two beans." Sokolowski (1949) prefers to read it as a dative singular, referring to the sacrifice of a cake made from beans. However, Amandry rightly links it with the story of how the Thessalians attempted to select their king with a bean oracle (Plut. *Mor.* 492a-b; see below). Maurizio (2019) 120), whose interest is not lot oracles as such but whether it was the Pythia who used them, doubts Amandry's position (who is careful when associating it with the Pythia). Moreover, she does not consider the steep price demanded as a state fee (one Aeginetan stater), which further supports Amandry's position.

[74] Hdt. 6.109; Thuc. 8.66.1; *Ath. Pol.* 8.1; and further references Amandry (1950) 33 n.1. Aitolians: Hesych., s.v. κυάμῳ πατρίῳ, with reference to Soph. *Meleager*; see also section 8.2.3.1 in this volume.

[75] Onians ([1951] 1988) 112.

[76] Please note that *phryktos* literally means "roasted" and signifies a "roasted bean" used for the lottery. Sometimes the "roasted bean" is referred simply as "bean": *kaunos*. Therefore, *phryktos* and

Selection by lot was probably less frequent, with a dramatic allure that prompted stories about manipulations; according to Plutarch, the Thessalians selected their king by a bean lot oracle.[77] These must have been beans inscribed with a name or a symbol, not the black/white, yes/no type.

> When the Thessalians sent some bean-lots (*phryktoi*) to the oracle at Delphi, to enquire by them who should be their King, his uncle stole in one lot privately in the name of Aleuas; the priestess answered from the oracle, that Aleuas should be King. His father being surprised averred that there was never a bean-lot (*phryktos*) thrown in for Aleuas that he knew of; at last all concluded that some mistake was committed in putting down the names, whereupon they sent again to enquire of the oracle. The priestess, confirming her first words, answered:
> I mean the youth with reddish hair,
> Whom dame Archedice did bear.
> Thus Aleuas was by the oracle, through his uncle's kind policy, declared King. (trans. W. W. Goodwin)

The story exemplifies human-divine collaboration with a "trick" on the human side. It is a selective lottery; hence one need not expect "two beans." It is remarkable that, in this anecdote, the first phase is cleromancy; the second "rises" to an inspired prophecy needed to confirm the first. The first order of importance was accorded to the lot, and inspiration came in second. Such order of importance depended on the specific context: the Thessalians were the ones to initiate the cleromancy, as their custom had been. Had there been no challenge, there would be no need for the Pythia's spoken words.

The story about a choice made by Delphi from a presented list may be indirectly supported by the reforms that created a regime opposite to kingship, the Athenian democracy. When founding the democracy (ca. 508), Cleisthenes created a hugely complex system of mixing the citizens by lot, including creating ten new "tribes" of Athenian citizens. There is no doubt that Cleisthenes established the new tribes of Athens and that he composed them through the lot. Such issues are discussed later (ch. 8.2.2).

Here it is essential to note the theme of the lot: the older, traditional four Athenian tribes had eponymous heroes; Cleisthenes needed ten new ones for the

---

kaunos are used interchangeably throughout the Greek corpus. Cf. Hesychius, s.v. *diakauniazo* (ad Aristoph. *Peace* 1081): "*kaunos gar ho kleros*"—for *kleros* is *kaunos*. "To make a selection by the beans" and note the verb *kuameuo*, which is close in meaning (*kuamos* is another word for *kleros*; see also *kuamobolos*), and were commonly used in fifth-century Athenian democracy, e.g., *Ath. Pol.* 8.1, 22.5, 24.3, and 32.1.

[77] Plutarch, *On Brotherly Love* 21, 492a–b. See Helly (1995) 121–124 for discussion. Cf. Di Salvatore (2001).

ten tribes he established. He sent the Pythia a list of a hundred founding heroes, *archegetai*,[78] and asked for a choice of ten heroes. It is the only aspect of his complex reform for which he had asked for Apollo's involvement; by selecting the ten eponymous heroes, Delphi, by implication, sanctioned Cleisthenes's entire reform. A highly probable inference is that the Pythia used lots for this selection of heroes, "picking up" ten names.[79]

Athens had close relations with Delphi. Probably relying on the authentic practice of the state turning to Delphi to choose names from a list, Plato writes about the choice of religious interpreters (*exegetai*) "whom the oracle names."[80] Delphi also makes such choices when Plato imagines the process in his future state of how to attach citizens to allotments, preserving the unity of the *kleros* by allotting it only to one son (see ch. 7):

> And from the sons of citizens who happen to have more than one son over ten years old, ten shall be chosen by lot (*kleroö*) ... and the names thus chosen (the verb is *lanchano*) shall be sent to Delphi; and that man whom the oracle names (*anaireo*, "picks up") shall be established as the allotment-holder in the house of those departed. (Plato *Laws* 856d–e, trans. R. G. Bury)

2.6 Delphi: Mythical history and oracular procedure

The lot plays a significant role in Delphi's history, especially in how the oracle functioned. In the prologue to *Eumenides*, Aeschylus says that it was by the "third allotment" that Themis transferred Delphi to Phoibe and hence to Apollo. The word "third" implies that the entire chain of the transfers of Delphi from one god to another was effected by lot.[81] Elsewhere in the play, *moira* is "spinning" the lot, *lachos* (334–335). Aeschylus disregards the better-known version of the *Homeric*

---

[78] Cf. M. Guarducci, *Insc. Creticae* III.3.A, where the heroes and the *archegetai* of the land are distinguished from each other: "All the gods and Goddesses, to the *archegetai* and to the heroes as many as they have under their protection the city and the country of the Rhodians."

[79] See ch. 8.2.2.2. Cleisthenes: *Ath. Pol.* 21.6; cf. Pollux *Onom.* VIII.10. See Bowden (2005) 99–100; Kearns (1989) 87–90; Parker (1996) 118; Kron (1976). Whether he manipulated the list or the result because of the influence of the Alkmaionidai at Delphi is beside the point here; what matters is the notion that Apollo had *chosen* from among Attic founder-heroes. Some of the heroes chosen might seem too convenient politically (e.g., Aias of Aegina), but we need to remember that all we have is hindsight. We know too little about the importance of the heroes who were not chosen, such as Araphen, the only name we have from the ninety not picked up. See also Malkin (1987a) 244.

[80] Plato *Laws* 865d; cf. 759d.

[81] Unless Aeschylus here refers to the more comprehensive allotments of the successive Olympian generations (Robertson 1941), which seems speculative (Ouranos is definitely not mentioned here). Themis was the daughter of Ouranos and Gaia; *Phoibe* ("bright", note Apollo's epithet *Phoibos*) was the mother of Leto, Apollo's mother and Themis's sister. Hes. *Theog.* 135–136. Cf. Robertson (1941).

Hymn to Apollo, where the god conquers Delphi by force.[82] Aeschylus has the Pythia proclaim,

> First, in this prayer of mine, I give the place of highest honor among the gods to the first prophet, Earth; and after her (*deutera*) to Themis, for she was the second to take this oracular seat of mother, as legend tells. *And in the third allotment (en . . . trito[i] lachei* [ἐν δὲ τῷ τρίτῳ λάχει]), with Themis' consent and not by force, another Titan, child of Earth, Phoibe, took her seat here. She gave it as a birthday gift to Phoibos, who has his name from Phoibe.[83]

Lanchano must signify here "getting by lot," otherwise the words "second, *deutera*," and "in the third" would make no sense. The phrase has "a certain formal solemnity."[84] Aeschylus, therefore, conceived of the rotating possession of the Delphic Oracle as practiced by drawing lots, a rotation that has ended (so far?) with Apollo.

Note that what is at issue is not a presence at Delphi's *sanctuary* but who owns the *oracle*. The overlap between the two institutions is only partial. Greek sacred precincts (sanctuaries) could contain cults to several divinities and heroic figures. Hera's temple at Olympia, for example, is older than that of Zeus, the quintessential god of Olympia. Apollo's temple at Delos, his birthplace, had a shrine of the local hero Anios.[85] Gaia had a shrine at Delphi,[86] as did Athena, and the god Dionysos was present at the sanctuary three months every year when Apollo went to spend his vacation among the ever-happy Hyperboreans.

Specifically, the Furies (Erinyes) who chase Orestes got their province too as a *lachos*, an "allotted office" or "apportioned lot."[87] Their defined province of power is equivalent to the distribution of other *timai*, "honors" (provinces of power), also distributed by lots to the gods, as we saw. At some point, Athena announces she had installed *daimones* in the land "for they have been appointed (or "allotted," *lanchano*) to arrange (*diepein*) everything among mortals" (*Eumenides* 930). As noted, the word *daimon*, loosely translated as "divinity," derives from *dateomai*, the verb for distribution and allocations.

What is remarkable is that the institution of the Delphic oracle itself was partly run by drawing lots. The order of consultation with the Pythia was managed by drawing lots, as is further evidenced just a few verses down in the *Eumenides*

---

[82] For more violent versions of how Apollo got Delphi, see the *Homeric Hymn to Apollo*; cf. Eur. *IT* 1249ff.
[83] Aesch. *Eum.* 1–5, trans. H. Weir-Smyth (1926; Loeb ed.). Cf. Paus. 20.5.6.
[84] Robertson (1941) 69.
[85] Robert (1953).
[86] Plut. *Mor.* 402c–d.
[87] Sommerstein (1989) 307–308; Pironti (2011) 96. Cf. Thalmann (1978) 78; Lebeck (1971) 150–159.

(30–32). Historically, Delphi could declare the status of *homoklaroi*, apparently allowing such inquirers to be "equal before the lot" that determined the order of consultation.[88] Since the oracle was a pan-Hellenic institution, it is clear that the convention of sortition (here to determine the queue) was familiar and acceptable to all Greeks coming from all over. It was a pan-Hellenic *nomos*. In the prologue the Pythia addresses the consultants gathering outside the temple:

> And if there are any from among the Hellenes here, let them enter, in turn, by lot, as is the custom (*iton palo[i] lachontes, hos nomizetai*).[89]

The emphasis on "as is the custom" in an early-fifth-century play makes it an explicit testimony that it was a universally familiar convention, and the combination of *pallo* and *lanchano* leaves no doubt about the use of lots. In another play, *Ion* by Euripides, the hero is an attendant at the temple of Delphi, so Delphic information and associations are plentiful. Euripides explicitly says that Apollo delivers his oracle by lot. However, some modern commentaries assume something was missing in the text and suggest the words have to do with the order of entry and consultation.[90] That is the danger of vague translations, such as (*Ion* 908, trans. R. Potter), "Oh! Son of Leto, I invoke you, who sends forth your holy voice from your golden seat."[91] But what the text says is, "You (Apollo). . . / who allot your oracles (*kleroö*) (literally: "*deliver an oracle by lots*," [LSJ] / to those who come to your golden seat."[92] So the "golden prophetic voice" (*omphe*) of Apollo may have expressed itself through the lot (*omphan klerois*), conforming to the "single process" view: first the lots are shaken, and then the Pythia prophesies. Another possibility is that the lot determines whom Apollo should speak to, which is closer to the meaning of a queue of participants.

While reading Greek tragedies in translation, especially older ones, one might miss the lot entirely, as the following illustrates: about to enter the oracle, one character (Xuthus) says, "Good; I have everything I need. I will go inside; for, *as I hear, the victim has been sacrificed for foreigners*" (*Ion* 420). However, a more accurate translation would be, "for, I hear, the oracular lot has been cast (*chresterion peptoke* [derivative of *pipto*]) for foreigners." *Chresterion* usually means "an oracle," and the verb *pipto*, while it can be used for sacrifice, really means "to fall,"

---

[88] *Syll.*³ 295; cf. Pouilloux (1952) 493–499. Thourioi is to be *homoklaros* with Taras.
[89] κεἰ παρ' Ἑλλήνων τινές, ἴτων πάλῳ λαχόντες, ὡς νομίζεται. Aesch. *Eum.* 30–32.
[90] Owen (1939) 130, *ad loc*.
[91] Euripides, *The Complete Greek Drama*, edited by Whitney J. Oates and Eugene O'Neill Jr., in two volumes. 1. *Ion*, translated by Robert Potter (New York: Random House, 1938).
[92] Kovacs (1999) 425. Lee's translation (1997) of verse 908: "I call on the son of Leto, who gives response by lot at the golden seats and the throne at the centre of the earth."

or since *pipto* is one of the verbs used in cleromancy, perhaps relates to the *kleros* "falling out."[93]

Aside from the order of the queue of inquirers, the personnel at Delphi are said to have been chosen by lot. That may not be surprising: in another major sanctuary of Apollo, Didyma, the *prophetes* was selected by Apollo himself by lot, as shown in an honorific decree for one of them, who was three times drawn by "pious lots" (*eusebesin klerois*) and garlanded by "immortal crowns."[94]

The Pythia was chosen from among Delphic women, probably (that is not explicit) by drawing lots. In Euripides's *Ion*, the Pythia presents herself saying, "I am the priestess of Phoebus... chosen from all the women of Delphi." Specialists may discuss the specific roles of prophets, priests, and a body of priests called *hosioi* at Delphi,[95] but for our purpose the explicit mention of the lot as a tool of selection of officeholders at Delphi is sufficient. In Euripides's play *Ion*, the young man appears as a servant at the Oracle. (*Ion* 415, Ion speaking:) "I am, outside; within, it belongs to others seated near the tripod, stranger, the best men of Delphi, *chosen by lot* (*hous eklerosen [kleroö] palos*)." A choice of priests at Delphi by lot is also evident in a passage where the text is sufficiently corrupt so as to prevent its full understanding yet sufficiently clear to evidence the explicit use of the lot to select a priest or priests. This is how Frank Babbit (1936) translates the passage but relying on emendations and editorial conjectures:

> (Plutarch, *de e apud Delphos* 16; *Moralia* 391d) On the sixth day of the new month, namely, when the prophetic priestess is conducted down to the Prytaneion, the first of your three sortitions (*kleroi*) is for five, she casting three, and you casting two, each with reference to the other.

As the action takes place in the Prytaneion (the Council House) of Delphi, the passage seems to relate not to the oracle but to a choice of priests or magistrates at the council house of Delphi-city.[96] The numbers and their relations to the procedure seem vague, and some have tried to connect this with Orphic or Pythagorean traditions (discussed by Plutarch a little earlier). The precise meaning is beyond redemption, but it seems clear that the practice of sortition is confirmed for our purpose. "The best men of Delphi, chosen by lot" of Euripides's *Ion*, mentioned in a fifth-century play, seems confirmed by the learned Plutarch, who lived some six hundred years later. He was a specialist in Delphic matters and served as a

---

[93] Amandry (1950) 106.
[94] *Miletos* 455; *I Didyma* 282. Were lots used in archaic Didyma? Greaves (2012) plausibly argues they were, using astragales (esp. at 195). Inspired prophecy at Didyma, he argues, is mainly a Hellenistic phenomenon.
[95] Parke (1940) 87; Amandry (1950) 115–125; see also section 8.2.4 in this volume.
[96] Flacelière (1950) 320.

priest at Delphi for some thirty years until his death.[97] Specifically, although vague, the description seems to fit "pairing" oracles, that is, pairing a name from a list with oracular results.

We have one remarkable description of an inquiry at Delphi by the Athenian state, with a double- or triple-blind process.[98] In the mid-fourth century, the Athenians wished to decide whether to cultivate some of the "sacred lands" by Eleusis; having debated and passed a public resolution on the matter, they deferred the decision to the Delphic Oracle. A long inscription details the background and decrees what is to be done: "The secretary of the council is to write upon two pieces of tin which are equal and alike (*iso kai* [*homoio*]), on one, "is it preferable and better for the Athenian people . . . (to till the land)"; on the other is written the reverse outcome (the land to remain untilled). The two identical tin foils are then folded and tied with wool (by different functionaries) and placed in a bronze jug full of water "in the presence of the people." In a public ceremony, the priest blindly pulls out one tin foil and places it in a silver jug, then repeats the action with the other, putting that one in a gold jug. The pitchers are then formally sealed, and any Athenian may add his seal; the treasurers then take the pitchers to the Acropolis of Athens.[99]

Then the people choose three men, one from the council and two from "all Athenians," to lead the expedition that goes to Delphi "to ask the god according to which of the two written messages the Athenians should act . . . whether that from the gold water jug or that from the silver water jug." Neither the Athenian delegates nor the priests at Apollo's temple know which foil is in which jug. Once Apollo indicates one of the jugs, the expedition returns to Athens. The final revelation of the gods will happen not at Delphi but at Athens: it happens publicly with a strong performative—one might say, theatrical—display when the seal is broken, and the contents of the chosen tin foil are read out.

Distrust is a key concept here. The blinded process of consultation and the blind placement of lots at Athens and their selection at Delphi implies, *a priori*, an attitude of distrust toward the human agents involved. Yet the purpose is to *create trust* in the process. Neither an Athenian nor a Delphian nor anybody en route could tamper with the lots.

---

[97] *Table Talk* 7.2, 700e; *An seni*, 17, 792f. Cf. Obsieger (2013) *ad loc.*

[98] RO 58 (IG II² 204) with translation and excellent commentary. On the sacred *orgas* in Athens, see Papazarkadas (2011) esp. 244–259.

[99] Cf. the procedure, ca. 100, at Thessalian Korope, *IG* IX, 2 1109 (Thessaly), where inquiries on small tablets were kept in sealed jars overnight. Parke (1967) 106–108 translates: "When the consultation has been completed, having placed the tablets in a jar, they are to seal it with the seal of the generals and guardians of the laws and likewise with the seal of the priest and are to let it remain in the sanctuary. On the following day the secretary of the god is to bring forward the jar and show the aforementioned seals and open it and give back the little tablets to each, calling them up in accordance with the record."

"Whether it is better and advantageous" is a standard formula in oracular inquiries. It implies a choice between two alternatives formulated by the inquirers: "preferable" or not. Not all questions addressed to the oracle were of that nature. For example, Delphic colonization oracles are formulated openly: "to which land should I go?" With his divine, panoptic knowledge of the world, Apollo would then provide the answer, often in terms of itinerary or topography.[100] On the other hand, especially since a significant percentage of oracular inquiries at Delphi concerned cult issues, such yes/no answers were quickly and efficiently answered by a lot oracle. Consider too, as noted, that during the archaic period, the Pythia supposedly was accessible for oracular business one day per month and only nine months a year,[101] so "better and preferable" questions could be disposed of rapidly, aside from, or in conjunction with, inspired utterances by the Pythia.

Had we not had the Athenian inscription, we could still rely on comments from ancient historians who merely report that "the sanctuary had responded: it was more profitable and better if they left them untilled."[102] It is noteworthy that the Athenians, having received their answer, copied the text they had written before the consultation into a direct quote from the oracle. Without the inscription, a rare find, one might have assumed this was a straightforward, inspired answer from the Pythia. Do other such reports imply parallel or identical procedures of lot oracles? How exceptional or representative is this Athenian inquiry about the sacred fields?[103] The procedure seems exceptional, probably because sacred borderlands are concerned, yet reflects normal Athenian state consultations at Delphi.[104] However, it does express the main use of lot oracles: deferring a decision, with the options blind to the participants but not to Apollo. As for what is representative, it is hard to tell when our evidence is so patchy. I suppose that gold and silver jugs and the very place of revelations, Athens (not Delphi), constitute exceptions. Still, as for the "blind inquiry" itself, resolved through a single choice between two options, it seems to have been quite common, as the evidence from Dodona also suggests. Finally, this is a clear case where the formulation of the question by the inquirer is answered back as a direct prophecy.

---

[100] Malkin 1987a ch. 1.
[101] Plut. *Mor.* 292e–f; 398a; Parke (1943).
[102] RO translate ll. 28–30: "it is preferable and better for the Athenian people that the parts of the sacred *orgas* currently being cultivated outside the boundaries be left to the two goddesses untilled." Philochoros and Androtion *FGrHist* 328 F 155 with Bowden (2005) 92.
[103] Parker (1996) 111 reasonably suggests that the clients usually devised the means of inquiry themselves.
[104] See Bowden (2005) 88–95.

2.7 The oracle of Dodona

At one point in Sophocles's tragedy *Women of Trachis* (verse 169), Deianeira mentions Herakles, who got an oracular tablet from Dodona, where an alternative to his impending death is offered: if he survives a year and three months, he shall not die. Here too, "fate" is not a single course, as we have seen with Achilles, who might have chosen not to go to Troy and instead grow old and die an old and happy, albeit obscure, grandfather. The remote oracle at Dodona in northwestern Greece was sacred to Zeus and the goddess Dione. Its status was on a par with Delphi in terms of antiquity and reputation, but much less frequented because of its location in Thesprotia in northwestern Greece, not far from modern Albania. Ancient myths were associated with its oracle.[105] In the *Iliad*, Achilles sings to "Pelasgian Zeus" of Dodona (*Il.* 16.231–235), and the Graikoi, the people living around it, were "the most ancient of the Greeks," as Aristotle says. They could be partly responsible for the English word "Greeks," *Graeci* in Latin (Thesprotia faces Italy), but *Hellenes* in Greek.[106]

Before the advance of archaeological work at the site, the use of lots at Dodona was attested only in a story told in Cicero's essay *On Divination*, which was based on Callisthenes, a historian who lived in the fourth century.[107] Before the battle of Leuktra of 371, in which they were severely defeated, the Spartans came to consult the oracle. The vessel with the lots stood ready, but suddenly the pet monkey of the king of the Molossians (who was personally present, apparently) overturned it, throwing the lots for divination into shambles.

> The Spartans sent to consult the oracle of Zeus at Dodona as to the chances of victory. *After their messengers had duly set up the vessel in which were the lots*, an ape, kept by the King of Molossia for his amusement, disarranged the lots and everything else used in consulting the oracle, and scattered them in all directions. Then, so we are told, the priestess who had charge of the oracle said that the Lacedaemonians must think of safety and not of victory (Cic. *De Div.* 1.34.76)

What did the monkey disturb? The "lots" (*sortes*) "and everything else" probably included the urn holding the lots and perhaps some other paraphernalia. Because "how" is an open-ended question, the original inquiry may have offered several options with corresponding lots, demanding more than a yes/no answer. But it might have been something like, "Should we force a battle?" Answer: yes/

---

[105] Soph. *Trach.* 169; Hom. *Od.* 11.488–491. Cf.
[106] Arist. *Mete.* 352b2–3. Cf. Malkin (1998) 147.
[107] Cic. *De Div.* 1.34.76 = Callisthenes *FGrH* 124 F 22 (a) = BNJ 124 F 22a. Parke (1967) 83–85, 108–111. Dieterle (2007) 61–62; 83; Georgoudi (2012) for other forms of divination at Dodona.

no. Perhaps the monkey disturbed just two lots, but his intervention was sufficient to cause scandal.[108]

That lots were used and recognized as such is clear from a recurrent expression in inscriptions.[109] The random order (random to the eyes of humans) in which the priestess took lots out from the jar of inquiries was itself significant since the priestess was probably supposed to draw "yes/no" lots from another jar simultaneously.[110] In later periods, "ticket oracles" from Ptolemaic and Roman Egypt provide a parallel: inquiries written on papyri and submitted with two alternatives.[111] Although hidden from human eyes, the god supposedly knows what is written when expressing his choice between two possibilities. This kind of consultation has the advantage not only of allowing the inquirer to frame the question and limiting the range of the answer. It also gives the process a sense of "objectivity": hiding the effect desired by the inquirer so as not to influence the prophecy.

Discoveries of small, inscribed lead tablets have considerably enriched our knowledge about using lots at Dodona. Now we have over four thousand at our disposal, mostly from private inquirers. They provide rich information about what inquiries were about, their concept of risk, the method of consultation, and the identity of inquirers.[112] The varieties in handwriting, alphabet, spelling, and grammar indicate that the individuals did the writing. Once inscribed and folded up, a mark or a name was written on the outside of the lead tablet so that one could identify the lot without needing to unfold it.

The verb "to pick up a lot" is relatively current in those tablets: for example, no. 3128 states, "If farming the plot will be beneficial for Apollonides, may this lot (klaron) come out for me (ἄνελ(ε) τὸν κλᾶρον) (anele [a derivative of anaireo] ton klaron)" or, literally, "Oh God, pick up the lot!" So the verb anaireo (and haireo) may mean both "choose" (by picking up) and "answer," since the choice becomes equivalent to the answer.[113] Inquiries vary, with many expecting a yes/no answer. For example, "Good luck. Parmenides asks Zeus Naios and Dione whether he will fare better if he stays home."[114] Other inquirers ask about moving to a colony or choosing a wife, mostly with a yes/no answer. "God. Good fortune.

---

[108] Parke (1967) 85–86 complements the "missing" noun in Demosthenes, 21, 53 as the "[kleros] of Zeus in Dodona signifies" and refers to St. Byz., s.v. Δωδώνη, as quoted by Strabo (7 fr. 1 Loeb): "Zeus used to utter oracles not by words but by certain tokens, just as the oracle of Ammon in Libya." See also Parke (1967) 108–110.

[109] Eidinow (2007) 68–71 and especially the "Catalogue and Summary of Published Questions by Individuals and Responses from the Dodona Oracle."

[110] Parke (1967) 109.

[111] Parker (2015) 111.

[112] Lhote (2006); Dakaris, Vokotopoulou, and Christidis (2013).

[113] LSJ, s.v. III. Cf. Parker (2015). Berman 166 cf. *ad sortes tollendas* = to consult the oracle.

[114] Parke (1967) 22; *Ep. Chron.* 1935: 255, 13; fifth to fourth century.

Polemarchos asks Zeus Naios and Dione whether he will have a share in something good and trustworthy from this woman?"[115]

Some inquirers ask about a cult, and the answer, in the form of lists of tailor-made deities, was very probably arrived at by lot. For example, a man named Hermon asks which god he should propitiate "in order to get children from a woman Kretaia."[116]

Cleromancy could also be used for settling ritual norms and proscriptions inside a sanctuary. We have some evidence from another sanctuary: an inscription from a sanctuary of Asklepios in Apollonia (ca. 425–375)[117] mentions a form of cleromancy linked with interdictions about what may not be brought into the sanctuary. The extant text does not contain sufficient information on the exact nature of the use of the lots. One possible translation would be, "The People of Apollonia [have decided:] the prophetess forbids, following the casting of lots, that Asklepios receive...."[118]

One wonders what these inquiries implied: unlike the Athenian consultation with the gold and silver water jugs, there is no indication that alternative yes/no inquiries were provided on *two* separate lead tablets at Dodona.[119] Perhaps two contradictory answers were thrown in a jug, and only one would be picked up blindly. Opinions vary. One may assume that the inquirer was given a yes/no answer, perhaps using white and black beans for affirmative or negative replies. The text, usually on folded lead tablets or foil, was supposedly known only to the inquirer and the gods. If the question concerned a choice from a list (e.g., "to which god or hero should I sacrifice?"), then perhaps variously colored beans were used,[120] or the lot might have somehow "stopped" at a name (read out or inscribed), analogous to a roulette wheel. Another possibility is that the answer to the question "To which god?" was given by inscribing the names of a few deities on separate lots and then picking one up. That may have been the case at Himera, where small bronze spheres were discovered bearing the names of Herakles, Leukathea, and Zeus Soter. One inscribed sphere dates from the late sixth century, and the other three from a century later.[121]

---

[115] *SGDI* 1568b; Rhodes or Rhodian colony. See Eidinow (2007) 86.

[116] Carbon (2015) 83: "It is remarkable that the response of the oracle was substantially tailored to the question, to the origin of an individual, or to the needs and concerns of a group. So, an Athenian received an answer mentioning Erechtheus (no. 2), someone concerned with debts or material possessions was told to propitiate Zeus Ktesios and other related gods."

[117] *CGRN* 40.

[118] I am closer to the French version proposed by the editors of *CGRN*, which is slightly different from their English rendering: "*Les Apolloniates [ont décidé]. La devineresse interdit, à la suite du tirage au sort, qu'Asclépios reçoive....*" "The female seer from the lots (drawn) forbids that Asclepius receive...." Cf. Cabanes (1995–2016) 51–53 no. 2.A3.

[119] Parker (2015), on the analogy of ticket oracles in Egypt, thinks this may have been the case.

[120] Parke (1967) 110.

[121] Manni Piraino (1974) 267–269 no. 4; (1984–1985) 254 nos. 2 and 3; Brugnone (2011b).

WHEN DOES THE LOT REFLECT THE WILL OF THE GODS? 129

Figure 2.3 Cassandra drawing lots with her right hand and predicts the downfall of Troy. *Vaticinio di Cassandra*, Museo Archeologico Nazionale di Napoli (inv. nr. 111476), affresco da Pompeii (I, 2, 28), III stile pompeiano (1-cd d.C.). Cassandra (center) drawing lots with her right hand and predicts the downfall of Troy in front of Priam (seated, on the left), Paris (holding the apple of discord), and a warrior leaning on a spear, presumably Hector. From the House of the Metal Grill (I, 2, 28) in Pompeii. https://commons.wikimedia.org/wiki/File:Cassandra_prophecies_MAR_Naples.jpg. Permission: Naples Archaeological Museum.

Late frescoes from Pompeii (and one relief vase), perhaps following an earlier painting, show a tripod in the background and a prophetess (perhaps, but not definitely, the Pythia) with her hand over a jug, looking away, apparently so as not to see what her hand was about to do once she plunged it into the vase to "pick up" the lot (Figure 2.3).[122]

Since so many lead tablets were found at Dodona, it is unlikely that inquirers took their answers back with them. The evidence indicates that new inquirers smoothed out and reused lead tablets. One may infer a minor, local source of income for selling or renting out such tablets. Incidentally, the implications for the extent of widespread literacy and "numeracy"[123] become manifold: all those thousands of nonaristocratic inquirers who came to Dodona were literate. Written by their own hand, their original inquiry was then smoothed over and reinscribed by other literates. We need to infer a few more inquirers practicing the same type of lot divination for every lead tablet found, used, and reused.[124]

2.8 What is religious about lot oracles?

In sum, Greeks used lot oracles both for *selection* by drawing lots (e.g., the Athenian eponymous heroes) and to attain prophecies. Otherwise, drawing lots in oracular institutions seems to have parallels in the civic sphere: procedure (e.g., the queue) and personnel selection. With lot oracles, both the decision to inquire and the formulation of the yes/no inquiry depend on the human inquirer. So, we are back to the question of lotteries as revealing divine will: are lot oracles a discrete category, distinct and perhaps even contrary to the other types of drawing lots we have observed? Turning to the gods for an oracular response falls under our category of "religion." However, we need to remember that the ancient Greek language (as many other languages, e.g., Hebrew) had no comprehensive word for "religion." An often-quoted passage from Jonathan Z. Smith, recently by Jennifer Larson, goes as far as to claim that

> While there is a staggering amount of data, phenomena, of human experiences and expressions that might be characterized in one culture or another, by one criterion or another, as religion—there is no data for religion. It is created

---

[122] There are two images in Amandry (1950) 74 Plate V. Badly reproduced. Taken from Juliette Davreux (1942), *La légende de la prophetesse Cassandre d'après les textes et les monuments* (Paris: Droz). Pompeii, fresco Davreux no. 43 Vse relief: Davreux no. 42 fig. 25 Hektor in the *Iliad* also looks away while conducting the lottery. Parke (1967) 111–112.
[123] Netz (2002).
[124] For late antiquity, see Duval (2016).

for the scholar's analytic purposes by his imaginative acts of comparison and generalization.[125]

The first point to note is that when classifying any use of the lot as "religious" and assuming it expresses a divine will, we must first understand its context and *raison d'être*. Our question should be *when* and in which contexts do we find drawing lots identified with the gods. When an inquirer approaches the god and uses a lot oracle, "religion" is explicit. But lot oracles seem to form a discrete category and always deal with specific questions with alternative answers. As such, they are distinct from other contexts and modes of using lots. An invocation of the gods (not an oracular inquiry) is what we mostly find in distributive (e.g., booty), selective (e.g., colonists), or procedural (e.g., taking turns) lotteries. Posing the question to an ancient Greek might have forced out an answer that everything is "gods' willing," but that answer would come because solicited. The fallacy of getting a response in Western terms to a hitherto nonformulated question is a familiar problem in ethnology.

So what is religious about lot oracles? First, of course, are the gods. Gods are human projections, but trivial they are not. People do not project the trivial or mundane onto the divine, and lotteries are anything but trivial. Lotteries were an essential concern for the Greek mindset, present—as we have seen—in the poetic imagination of Homer, with the gods sharing the world by lot, in division and distribution, and in establishing "turns." All such lotteries exclusively define the community of participants as "sharers" of *moirai* and *kleroi* and "mixing" or "reshuffling" the group at the same time. Because they were a significant phenomenon, lotteries deserved their gods, notably Lachesis and Hermes. Yet Hermes neither determines nor intervenes with the lots, and Lachesis is either the lottery itself or perceived as presiding over it. Specifically, we have seen how lotteries were imagined or expressed through those gods or gods who prophesied employing lots, such as Apollo at Delphi or Zeus and Dione at Dodona.

That does not signify that Greeks thought the gods were determining the actual result of any lottery except in the case of oracular lot divination, where they certainly did. There were conflicting opinions also in antiquity. In a discussion between two Romans, Marcus T. Cicero and his brother Quintus, the former attributes the results of the lot to chance, whereas Marcus thinks it expresses the will of the gods.[126] We need always remember that the same things might have meant different things to different people at various periods, so any generalization can be no more than an indication of where we should be looking. Lotteries constituted, to return to Eidinow's formulation, "a mental pattern of connections

---

[125] Smith (1982) xi; cf. Larson (2016).
[126] Cicero *De Div.* ii.85–87 with Grottanelli (2005) at 131.

[or "mindset," in my terminology], a network of associations, dependent on both the context of their use and the experiences of those using and apprehending the terms.[127]

What about randomness, the question with which we started this chapter? A contemporary physicist might claim that nothing is ever truly random aside from the quantum dimension. But this is primarily an irrelevant observation for a historian who, even today, might find herself standing in line behind such a physicist to buy a lottery ticket—*a fortiori* in antiquity, when the randomness of the lot was regarded as self-evident and being random was its main attraction.

2.9 One's portion in life: *Moira* between the concrete and the abstract

Most studies of *moira* are conducted within the framework of "Greek religion." In such studies, the abstract, poetic, and metaphoric uses of *moira* often take precedence over the concrete sense of "portion" or "part."[128] Yet the implications of the overlap in meaning are highly significant, illustrating *reciprocal* relations within a society that applied the notion of "portion" to a broad spectrum of activities. This becomes especially evident in the framework of drawing lots and the subsequent distribution of portions. A portion implies something "delimited" in relation to some other portion, all being part of some "whole." Thus, in terms of human relations, *moira* becomes "the right measure," indicating what is appropriate. The expression *kata moiran* may describe a "proper" division, for example, of meat (*Od.* 3.66). One may also divide up spoils *kata moiran* (*Od.* 16.385): the suitors in Ithaka contemplate murdering Telemachos, "and his property let us ourselves keep, and his wealth, dividing them fairly (*kata moiran*) among us."[129] However, this example also illustrates the overlap between the metaphoric "fairly" and the concrete, "each man gets a *moira*, portion by portion." In other words, because there is a portion for each person, the process is appropriate and fair, and "dividing up according to portions" turns into the abstract "fairly" or even "properly."[130]

This becomes especially significant when portions are equal and distributed by lot. We may never find out whether the values or the practice came first: were portions of sacrificial meat or land distributed equally, by lot, because people

[127] Eidinow (2011) 9.
[128] On Moira as a "*Déesse du partage, du lot*," see Chantraine (1968–1980), s.v. μείρομαι.
[129] δασσάμενοι κατὰ μοῖραν ἐφ' ἡμέας.
[130] See Eidinow (2011) 32. Note the proper fitting of oars *kata moiran* (*Od.* 8.54). *Moira* may also function in the sense of "sections of time": when Penelope explains why humans cannot stay awake for a long time, since "the immortals have set a proper time (μοῖραν ἔθηκαν) / for everything that mortals do on earth" (*Od.* 19.592–593). I thank Hila Brokman for the reference.

were implementing some value of equality? Or did "equality" become a value because they kept practicing equal apportionment by lot (i.e., equality of chance and equality, or equivalence, of portions)? Since the lottery primarily involved "equality before the chance," the idea of "luck/fortune" probably became attached to *moira*. It probably came to be perceived as the agent of the lot ("fate/luck/fortune") instead of just its object.[131]

Practices involving equal portions became social metaphors about doing things "according to *moira*" (*kata moiran*), signifying, according to context, "in order," "appropriately," "in the right measure," "in a balanced way," and "fairly." A key term is *moira*: "part, portion," since the idea of "portion" was also perceived as impersonal: some power (*moira* as a subject) was allocating a "portion of life" (*moira*, now as an object) to a human being. *Moira* acquired other abstract expressions: the *Moirai* were goddesses with some presence in myth but were also perceived as impersonal, superhuman powers, often translated as "destiny" or "fate." Thus, the same word, *moira* (and derivatives), stood for both a tangible portion and abstract fate.

This indicates a wide semantic range; concretely, one could refer, for example, to a "portion" (*moira*) of meat, a piece weighed equal to another portion and distributed by lot. But "portion" (*moira*) can also be "one's lot in life," namely, "fate." My emphasis here is not a discussion of fate and destiny in Greek thought but to point out how the notion of the concrete portion overlaps with the abstract "portion of life," revealing a significant aspect of the archaic Greek mindset. What is apparent is the stress on the equality of chance: to get the best-quality portion (e.g., a gold cup instead of a bronze one as a portion of all the booty). Sometimes, for example, with portions of land or sacrificial meat, Greeks attempted a close overlap between quality and quantity (equally measured portions).

To understand a mindset, we need to enter the field of connotations: semantic fields, overlaps in meaning, implications, and metaphors can be more relevant than the transparent and the explicit, which are often the focus of scholarly concern. The modern tendency to overcategorize and sharpen boundaries can be misleading, while the opaque and the implicit may reveal more.[132] I, therefore, wish to avoid the distinction between *moira* (portion, part) and the capitalized *Moira* (e.g., "fate").[133] Ancient Greeks would have known the difference according to context, but I doubt that the difference mattered in the way it does to modern scholars.

---

[131] It is not my purpose here to discuss *moira* in its various manifestations (e.g., as personification, the imagery of spinning [one's duration of life or one's fate]). See Pironti (2009); (2011). My focus is on its primary meaning as "portion." Cf. Edwards (2011).
[132] As rightly observed by Versnel (2011) 167.
[133] Eidinow (2011) writes persuasively on this issue; on "M/moira" see 27–30.

Someone's "life" is perceived as a "portion of Life" in general. There is such a thing as "Life," and each one of us gets a "portion" of it. The thread of life spun by the "Spinners" (Klothes) and provided at birth is equivalent to one's life span but not necessarily to what will happen in that life. In other words, that approach holds that *moira* determines how long we shall live, but not our choices during that life. In cult the Moirai appear as a triplet; their myths vary, but their names are constant: Klotho, the spinner; Lachesis (*lanchano*, again), the allocator of lots; and Atropos, who cannot be turned. We observed that Lachesis, who presided over the oath of the gods when Helios, having missed the distributive lottery among the gods, got Rhodes as his special prize; in the Platonic myth, the souls get their lots from Lachesis.[134] The idea of life as an allocated lot may explain why in poetry *moira* is linked with birth and death and with the latter, "death," acquiring the extra sense of "fulfilling one's *moira*"—hence the idea of "fate," overlapping one's *telos* in the sense of purpose ("what had led one to this point") with *telos* in the sense of "end."

Somehow, the notion of equitable "portions and lots" became equivalent to good order and harmony in the universe—specifically so in the city,[135] as in democratic Athens and its "lotacracy." We find it also in earlier times: in a poem ascribed to Simonides of Keos, the poet asks the *moirai* for peace and order on behalf of the city. *Moira* is associated with balance, the right order and measure of things. In Hesiod's *Theogony* the *moirai* have a genealogy that is directly linked with divinities responsible precisely for those aspects (*Theog.* 901ff.): Themis, identified with divine law (literally, "that which is put in place"), was their mother. Themis is associated with fairness, order, assemblies, law, and custom. Once, as we saw, she had been one of the possessors of the Delphic oracle. The *Moirai*'s sisters all conform to ideas of structure and order: the Horai (hours, seasons), Dike (justice), Eirene (peace), and Eunomia (good order). The *moirai*'s role is specified as giving "good and bad" to men. Yet Hesiod also preserves the ambivalence and fear associated with the *moirai*. He provides an alternative genealogy (*Theog.* 207ff.) where the *moirai* are daughters of Night, and mothers of such figures as Moros (appointed doom, fate, or destiny), Ker (a goddess of death or doom), Momos (blame), Thanatos (death), Hypnos (sleep), Oizus (misery), and Nemesis (retribution). The three *moirai*, Klotho, Lachesis, and Atropos, again "give good and bad" to men, but now it is explicitly "at birth." Yet the gods, too, are somehow under their supervision: Together with the Keres "they pursue men and gods when they transgress their limits."[136] The idea of limits seems essential to the concepts of right/good measure, implied in the general perception

---

[134] For the connection between Lachesis, *moirai*, and sortition, Guidorizzi (2001) 42–44.
[135] Eidinow (2011) 42.
[136] Hes. *Theog.* 220.

of the Moirai. The gods also need to respect the right measure to preserve divine order and harmony.

The overlap between concrete and abstract portions, and the fact that both are manifested in so many aspects of Greek thought and practice, reveal a lateral mindset of relating "portions to wholes" within a society, with no external authority to impose a distribution of portions. Such a "whole" may be concrete, such as a heap of booty to be divided into portions for distribution by lot, by the band of warriors or for them; or they may be abstract, such as one's personal "portion of the whole of life," that is, one's *moira*. Thus, we observe again the lack of a top-bottom authority to distribute portions. The Olympians too are subject to *moira*, and *moira* (or "the *moirai*") as such are very specific; they are not Olympian goddesses with allotted *timai*, or domains. The idea of *moira* belongs to the category of distributive lotteries where "portions" imply both belonging to—and the definition of—the "community." That is not self-evident for human societies as it implies *a priori* a relational society where portions relate to each other and not to an external authority that allocated them.

Associated with *moira* ("part") are other concepts or personifications that are also linked with notions of "parts" or "allotted shares," and, like *moira*, with various associated ideas of fate, social and divine order, and justice. The language is illustrative: the root verb of *aisa*, which often overlaps with *moira*,[137] may be *isasthai*, Lesbian for *klerousthai*, a word implying the idea of division into equal shares by *kleroi* (lots) and about *kleroi* (the portions received, e.g., land for new *oikos* or an inheritance, also called *kleros*).[138] It seems probable that in Homeric Greek *aisa* may relate to "portion of booty due," thus linking the particular application of "portions" with more general concepts and values associated with equal parts and the lottery.[139] *Aisa* is also connected with the term *aisymnetes*. In Homer an *aisymnetes* may be a judge for the dance at the court of Alkinoos, [140] and in some Greek cities, such as Naxos and Miletos, the *aisymnetes* was an official title of a magistrate. The term could also mean legislator or tyrant holding a supreme position. Thus, we observe an entire spectrum, from the concrete to the political: *aisa* means both "part/portion" and "fate" and is associated with judgment and legislating. "But all the different senses can be traced to the original meaning of 'one who distributes, gives, or directs the portions.'"[141] Finally, to stress the link between equality, portions, and the lot, *aisa* may be linked

---

[137] Dietrich (1962) 87: *moira* and *aisa* are interchangeable, but *aisa* does not possess a personal force. Cf. Greene (2008).
[138] Etymology Bianchi (1953) 3 nn.2, 3; and comprehensively 1–10. Dietrich (1965) appendix 2, p. 339. Cf. De Mauro (1985).
[139] Bianchi (1953) 1–10.
[140] Hom. *Od.* 8.258.
[141] Dietrich (1965) 339.

with *isos*,[142] "equal," and in some inscriptions, it denotes a portion of sacrificial meat.[143]

There are other terms associated with the idea of "portion." Except for *potmos* (below), *moros, morismos, aisa,* and *heimarmene,* all have their root in the concept of allocation and the lot and carry associations with social and cosmic justice. All originate from *meireo*—to "take one's portion"—and the passive *meiromai*— to be allotted one's due.[144] *Potmos* is another term associated with "fate," which is of particular interest since it seems explicitly connected with the practices of a lottery. Its root verb is *pipto,* which we have observed with the lot "jumping out," for example, in the lottery determining who will fight Hektor. Its use became increasingly rare after the classical period,[145] which may indicate that in the archaic period, the mental association with practices of the lot was especially close. In the *Iliad*, for example, *potmos* is associated with death, "encountering one's fate," and, like *aisa,* it may signify the duration of one's life.[146] *Potmos* provides another illustration of the ambivalence around the idea of "fate," whether it means the extent of one's life or its contents (or both). For example, whereas Pindar says, "The *potmos* that is born along with a man decides in every deed," Aeschylus seems to understand it as the length of one's life: "For many calamities from the sea, many from the land, arise to mortal men if their span of life (*potmos*) is extended far."[147] What is noteworthy is the negative adjective *apotmos* (or *panapotmos*). Just like *ammoros* ("having no part"), it denotes someone who is *unfortunate,* to whom no (good) lot has befallen.[148] In other words, through a negative, an aspect of how Greeks perceived "luck" is revealed: having a "part" versus not having one.

We may ask again, how is *moira* as "fate" linked with *moira* as "portion/share"? Some prefer to argue against a real connection. B. C. Dietrich's *Death, Fate, and the Gods,* published in 1965, assumes a progressive approach to religion and likes to keep matters discrete; my approach is closer to that of Versnel. The *moira* of "popular religion," or the *moira* as a "chthonic power," are discrete categories separated from the literal meaning of *moira* as "portion/share." There is also an assumption of progress: The *moira* of the *Odyssey,* for example, is more "evolved" and abstract. In other words, the scholarly preoccupation with "origins" and evolvement in the history of religion has led some to look for what *moira* stood for *initially* and how it has evolved.

Yet I see no reason to avoid the alternative, "simultaneous" approach, which does not force prioritization on various aspects of *moira.* A word can have a

---

[142] Bianchi (1953) 3–4 n.4.
[143] *CGRN* 223, l. 12; Bianchi (1953) 2; 7 n.6; Dietrich (1965) 12 n.1; 339.
[144] Eidinow (2011) 42; Dietrich (1965) 11; LSJ, s.v. *moros.*
[145] Dietrich (1965) 12; Eidinow (2011) 43.
[146] Hom. *Il.* 1.416; *Od.* 1.217; 20.140.
[147] Pind. *Nem.* 5.40; Aesch. *Persians* 709.
[148] Eur. *Hip.* 1143.

simple, concrete reference while serving as a metaphor in another context. That metaphors "derive" from words does not indicate stages in development. The interplay between practice, myth, and belief is never one-sided and has been debated for quite some time. I prefer to see practice, metaphor, and myth coexisting in a "network" that involves mental frameworks and concrete rituals. For example, cutting up meat, providing a *geras* to the guest of honor or the priest, and then dividing the rest of the portions for the "equal feast" are a practice, a ritual, and a social value. The jump from the concrete idea of distributing portions to the metaphor of distributing "portions of life" is not too hard to grasp. If we follow Ernst Cassirer's analysis of how a metaphor translates into myth (adding a story to the image and filling up its characters),[149] the *myths* of "the three *moirai*," Klotho, Lachesis, and Atropos, follow, but not necessarily in order of "first and last." There is no linear progression here: all three levels—concrete practice, metaphor, and myth—may be simultaneous and reflect on each other. Once in place, the mental framework of drawing lots and portioning, combined with some practice (e.g., partible inheritance by lot), would encourage the further application of "portioning" (sometimes explicitly *equal* portioning). This practice and its conceptualization might have informed, for example, the myth of how the gods divided up the world by lot or could impact the new practice of dividing up plots of land in a colony. In short, ritual, metaphor, and myth coexist and are mutually reflective.

Unlike the *moirai*, perceived as external powers, most practices of portioning and distributing by lot depend on human sovereignty. The lottery is conducted within and for the community, as in communal sacrifice. Already in Homer *kata moiran* has its metaphoric meaning as rightly, according to custom, while also retaining the idea of "in order," one by one. *Kata moiran*, following certain limits and order, expresses the idea of custom, which will be replaced by *kata nomon*. *Nomos* (law, custom) too is linked with *nemein*, assigning "portions." With *isonomia*, "equal portions of law," the overlap with the political would reach its full extension.

---

[149] Cassirer (1953).

3
Sacrifice and Feast: Social Values and the Distribution of Meat by Lot

3.1 The lot and the sacrifice: Frequency and ubiquity

The more we observe the lot among Greeks of the archaic period, the more ubiquitous its use appears, touching all aspects of life (and death). It is one thing to find sporadic references to lotteries, but by observing the frequency and wide range of the lot's use, we can begin to grasp how pervasive the lot and the associated values were in the Greek mindset.

The use of the lot, far from exceptional, was interlaced with practices and values that had shaped that mindset. Salient traits included emphasizing equality and fairness among group members and the group's sovereignty to hold a distribution by lot. Those belonging to the group were *sharers*. The "groups" could be anything from small families in partible inheritance by lot—a *genos* sharing a sacrifice—or larger ones, such as groups of colonists who distributed equal portions of the land by lot among themselves. In Homer, the group is as large as the entire army that shares booty by lot, both among those who fight and those who stay behind.

An entire practical and mental network is revealed: the vocabulary of lottery and distribution appears consistent. What is noteworthy is that using the lot and thinking in terms of "portions" was the expected norm. However, the question of frequency arises: did Greeks apply the lot only for singular occasions? Victories in battles (and consequent distribution of booty) or the death of a head of a household were one-off affairs. Similarly, Greeks usually intended to found a colony only once (there were exceptions), as were the allotment of the First (equal) Lots.

However, that is not the case with the distribution of sacrificial meat or meat at a banquet. Here we get a chance to glimpse beyond the singular, exceptional occasion, such as the division of the cosmos by lot among Zeus, Hades, and Poseidon. Eating meat was generally ubiquitous, and the rites associated with it were normative. Moreover, unlike special occasions, meat distribution was frequent, planned, and expected. Greeks had numerous occasions for sacrifices of all kinds in various contexts, from the family to the city. As is evident since

Homer, they also ate meat at the banquet, the *dais*, a term linked to the verb *dateomai*, the distribution by and for the group.[1]

Moreover, the convention of sacrifice and distribution cut across the entire society, especially when participation in sacrifice was universal. As I insist from the start, to study only specific uses of the lot might be misleading: we lose the canvas for the pixels. However, seeing how wide-ranging the lot was in various contexts explains the *idées reçues* at the end of the sixth century when Athens implemented its version of equal sharing of "political" portions, *isonomia*.

3.2 Sacrifice, equality, and sharing in the city

My purpose here is not to discuss theories of Greek sacrifice. Debates sometimes revolve around emphasis: Should we concentrate on the emotions evoked by killing? Should one focus instead on what accompanies the sacrifice, such as prayers? Alternatively, we could focus on the priests performing the sacrifice and their perquisites. Might we rather privilege aesthetic values, beauty, decorum, olfactory qualities, and performance? The Paris School, notably the scholars participating in the Cuisine of Sacrifice project, prefer to concentrate rather on feasting and the distribution of meat as an expression of civic solidarity and the spirit of *isonomia*: "From Homer to Plutarch, for nearly ten centuries, the egalitarian meal functions, through sacrifices and public banquets, as an institutional practice in solidarity with the social relations that underpin the isonomic figure of the City."[2]

That is an ideal distillation of both "the city" and the notion that, although ahistorical (Plutarch too is evidence for a change), retains the specific emphasis on equal sharing of meat in terms of mindset and practice. In an essay titled "Table Talk," Plutarch complains that ever since luxury has crept in, "the custom of equal share for all (in a feast, *isomoiria*) was abandoned" (644c). However, he continues that equality is still preserved in public and traditional rituals: "Even now at sacrifices and public banquets (*thusia kai ta demosia deipna*) . . . each guest is still served his equal portion of the meal." The learned Plutarch, writing at the turn of the first century CE, had a vast repository of ancient texts at his disposal. He was sensitive to the equality of portions and the lot as the means of distributing them, especially at rituals; he was also a priest at Delphi for some

---

[1] Cf. Rundin (1996) 182, 184. On sacrifice see Bremmer (2008); cf. Osborne (1993).
[2] Detienne, Vernant ([1981] 1989); Loraux (1981); Detienne and Svenbro (1979) 222: "*Mais d'Homère à Plutarque, pendant près de dix siècles, le repas égalitaire fonctionne, à travers les sacrifices et les banquets publics, comme une pratique institutionnelle solidaire des rappnaorts sociaux qui soustendent la figure isonomique de la Cité.*" Naiden (2013) 12–14 et passim; Ekroth (2020).

thirty years.[3] Just a few lines before, he says (644b), "The Goddess Portion (*Moira*) and Lot (*Lachesis*) presides with equity (*isoteti*) over dinners and drinking parties."[4]

Equality of distribution of portions of meat, whether at the banquet or the sacrifice, follows the same principles we can observe with the distribution of booty and land: striving to distribute the "whole" into equal portions to a defined group while reserving choice portions to a king, such as Oedipus.[5] This combination of equality and hierarchy continued through the classical and Hellenistic periods and was variously expressed.[6] In the archaic and classical periods, with no kings around (except Sparta, whose kings got double portions), such special portions were reserved for a priest or a God. Otherwise, aside from the *geras*, whether at a feast or a sacrifice, meat is somehow divided into equal portions and distributed (sometimes we hear about it explicitly) by lot.

The feast must be equal and, as Homer says, no one should be "denied the equal feast," a formulaic expression.[7] Since the distribution of portions and eating are standard features of the feast (private or public) and the sacrifice, there are clear overlaps between them. For example, in the *Iliad*, Agamemnon hosts seven heroes who sacrifice to Zeus, leave aside a choice portion for the altar, and then (*Iliad* 2.402–232) "feasted, nor was anybody's hunger denied the equal feast." On a different social scale, the swineherd Eumaios (*Od.* 14.418–438) divides the meat of a sacrificed boar into seven portions, sets aside one for Hermes and the Nymphs, honors (*gerairo*) Odysseus with a special portion, and distributes the other portions to each of his companions. The first public sacrifice appears in the *Iliad* when Odysseus, together with twenty rowers, returns Chryseis to her father and performs a sacrifice in which *all* are involved and, again, "they feasted, nor was anybody's hunger denied the equal feast" (*Il.* 1.468). Wine, too, was distributed to everyone (*Il.* 1.471).[8]

Such rituals and sacrifices are also performed *ad hoc*, for example, on a hero's death or a public funeral. They obviously cannot depend on fixed days, such as

---

[3] The probable dates of his service according to Plutarch's own testimony are around 90–120 CE. Cf. Plut. *An seni* 792f.

[4] He continues in his learned fashion: "Moreover, dinners were called *daites* 'distributions,'" the guests *daitumones*, "those to whom distribution is made" and servers *daitroi* "distributors" (the Greek words are in the accusative). Plutarch 644b–c *Table Talk II*. 10.2, trans P. A. Clement and H. B. Hoffleit, LCL.

[5] *Thebais* fr. 2 (Bernabé 1996), in Athenaeus *Deipn.* 11.14.465e.

[6] Cf. Ekroth (2011) 28–33.

[7] Rundin (1996) 188 supposes the expression applies only to high-ranking people, equal among themselves.

[8] Rundin (1996) 187. Seaford (2004) refers to *Il.* 1.602; 1. 431; 7.320; 23.56; *Od.* 16.479; 19.425. "Equal feast" also occurs at *Il.* 4.48; 9.225; 15.95; 24.69; *Od.* 8.98. See also *Od.* 20.281–282, 293–294. In addition to the role of the middle in sacrifice and distribution, Sarah Hitch points out the role of the middle as neutral, common ground, e.g., between Greeks and Trojans before taking an oath). Hitch (2009) 78–80 with n.56.

festivals, where sacrifice is prominent. *Ad hoc* sacrifice is akin to the distribution of booty, which is also occasional.[9] A public sacrifice is evident in a scene at the start of the *Odyssey*, when Telemachos, seeking news of his father, arrives at Pylos with his companion. He finds all the Pylians sacrificing on the beach (i.e., not in a demarcated precinct), arranged in nine groups (each comprising five hundred men), and sacrificing nine bulls to Poseidon (*Od.* 3.5–8). It is the community of Pylos that performs the sacrifice, the "assembly and seats of the Pylian men" (*Od.* 3.31). The strangers are welcomed and given shares of the innards and wine (*Od.* 3.65–66): "dividing shares (*moiras*), they held their communal high feast," as Lattimore translates. Richard Seaford rightly observes that, in the Greek original, "in fact, every word except the penultimate derives from a root meaning divide up": *moira* (portion); *dassamenoi* (distribute among themselves); *dainumi*, which also means to distribute; and the word for "feast," *daïs*, which also belongs to the semantic range of distribution (*dateomai*). The vocabulary is relational, just as in other contexts of distribution by lot, such as inheritance, land for settlement, and booty. Equal distribution to all and collective participation are consistent in group rituals. Sacrifice binds the community and defines it through control of access and recognizing those who deserve a portion.

3.3 Expressions of citizenship and belonging

Citizenship and belonging are generally expressed in terms of sharing in *hosie* and sacrifices.[10] For example, the "Naupaktos foundation decree" (ca. 500) speaks of religion as the primary "foundational act" of the new community. It sets down the terms and rights of colonists vis-à-vis their mother city. It is especially noteworthy since the colonist remains a member of his home cult community. To confirm one's participation and sharing, the decree uses the verb *lanchano* twice in the sense of "receiving (due portion) by lot."

> The *apoikia* (goes) to Naupaktos on these terms. It is permitted that a Lokrian of the Hypoknemidians, when he has become a Naupaktian, being a Naupaktian, receives his due portion by lot (*lanchano*) and sacrifices (*thyein*) where / in the way it is *hosie* for a stranger, when he happens to be (in Lokris) if he so wishes. If he so wishes, he may sacrifice and receive his due portion (by lot) of the *demos* (*damos*) and of the (sub)groups (*koinanoi*), he himself and his descendants, forever. (ll. 1–4, trans. Blok [2018] 90)

---

[9] Seaford (2004) 42 claims that booty is occasional, whereas ritual and sacrifice depend on fixed days. These examples seem to refute the distinction. See also Seaford (1994).

[10] This is a major theme of Blok (2018) 90–91 with n.44; Blok (2011); Peels (2015). Blok interprets it not as a neuter plural but as a singular feminine (and changes the accent accordingly).

The use of the lot enables full integration into the new, equally based society. Josine Blok makes the critical observation that "At this communitarian level (i.e., the sharing of sacrificial meat), the decree does not make any distinction between the elite and the ordinary citizens, but defines the *polis* by distinguishing between insiders and outsiders in terms of sacrifice."[11] As noted already, not only the result (sharing sacrificial meat), but the "mechanism" of the lot and the *access* to its use defines the group of participants even before they had eaten their first morsel. Aside from defining the "perimeters" of society in terms of outsiders and insiders, the lottery also "mixes" the insiders, that is, the entire community, whose members are to be equal concerning that which expresses their belonging, their share in the sacrifice.

Sacrifice represents what is normal: outside human geography, for example, on the island of Calypso, there are no sacrifices.[12] "Sacrificial distribution in Homer is a publicly visible ritual, with traditionally regulated and accepted procedures, in which nobody is denied an "equal share," as Seaford rightly observes. Sometimes booty and sacrifice overlap: having captured goats, Odysseus then divided that booty by lot; each of his twelve ships got nine goats, but his companions gave Odysseus an extra one. On another occasion, Odysseus received a ram as an extra portion (a *geras*?). He sacrificed the ram, and all the companions presumably got a share of the meat;[13] effectively, the entire group also shares in the extra portion. The goats are for future nourishment and sacrifice.

3.4 Honorific shares

We have seen old Oedipus cursing his sons for depriving him of his *geras*, the choice cut of meat. Remarkably, at Sparta, each of its two kings deserved a double portion of meat, probably because of their function as priests of Zeus.[14] However, kings hardly existed in archaic Greece, and choice cuts were reserved for the priests (who often got the hides of the slain animals as well). Gunnel Ekroth notes that sometimes tables for the gods were set aside and that a priest or priestess would often take what was on these tables. The term *hiera moira* (sacred portions) may appear among the priestly prerogatives.[15] The word for the choice portion is the same as in the case of Homeric booty: *geras*. Characteristic of this removal from the heroic sphere to communal ritual, the *geras* became an

---

[11] Blok (2018) 91.
[12] *Od.* 5.101–102. See Vidal-Naquet ([1970] 1986) 15–38.
[13] *Od.* 9.159–160: "The ships that followed me were twelve, and to each nine goats fell by lot but for me alone they chose out (*exelon—exaireô*) ten" (trans. Murray). *Od.* 9.548–552 (the ram).
[14] Hdt. 5.56.
[15] Ekroth (2008b) 259; cf. Ekroth (2008a); Naiden (2013) 185–201.

extra payment to the priest and synonymous with *hierosyne* (a word signifying the payment for the priest and later simply "priesthood").[16] It is important to stress that it was the group as such, not the priest (as mediator), that gave the offering to the god.[17] A priest would sacrifice on behalf of the *polis*; his *geras*, like the Homeric king's, would come *from* the people.[18]

Matthieu Carbon rightly observes that "honorific shares . . . played with a dialectic of hierarchy and equality that is characteristic of Greek sacrifice as a whole: some honors particularly stressed sharing and commensality, while others emphasized privilege and a special relationship with the god and the ritual; occasionally, both aspects could be at play. Sometimes extra portions could be provided to others to mark a distinction, such as the girls at the Little Panathenaia at Athens (the *kanephoroi*, carrying baskets) who received special portions of meat. Such distinctions only emphasize the equality of the rest."[19]

The most direct evidence is that of inscriptions. Let us observe an inscription from Miletos, ca. 400, concerning the sale and privileges of priesthoods. It is important to note that such regulations may reveal general patterns but also concern aspects peculiar to the given situation. Aside from the particular portions that were set aside, the rest was distributed by lot, as implied by the term "portion by lot": "Portion by lot (*apolochon*): the legs and the meat and the stomach (or: little stomach) and (line 10) the large intestine."[20] Whereas the word *apolochon* is not attested elsewhere, it derives from *apolanchano*; the meaning seems to point directly to the lot in the context of general distribution.[21] Perhaps the *apolochon* refers to quite a few special portions divided by lot among the group of priestly attendants and not among the public. Equality is implied, although not explicitly: we cannot be sure that the other portions in this case were equal, although it would be a reasonable assumption, but the lot at least ensures equality of chance to the participants.

In an earlier inscription (ca. 460),[22] we find regulations of the Attic deme of Skambonidai. It concerns (the text is fragmentary) "the distribution (*nemo*) of meat until the sun [sets]." It continues,

---

[16] Dignas (2002) 248.

[17] Ekroth (2008b) 266.

[18] Dignas (2002) 250. Cf. *id.* "Standard characterizations of Greek priests stress how much they were institutionalized within the secular life of the Greek *polis*, how much their office lacked expertise and dogma, and how negligible their political impact as a homogeneous group was" (248). Dignas also stresses the lucrative aspect of being a priest and the personal interest of persons wishing to become that.

[19] Carbon (2018); cf. Paul (2018) 332. Cf. Schmitt-Pantel (1992) 127–128; cf. Schmitt-Pantel (1990). See also *Kanephoroi RO* 81 at B 1–26.

[20] *Collection of Greek Ritual Norms* = *CGRN* 39 (http://cgrn.ulg.ac.be text, translation, and commentary); *LSAM* 44.

[21] See the definition in *DGE*: *porción sorteada* (an allotted portion). On Perpillou's position, see ch. 1, Endnote 2.

[22] *CGRN* 19 text C; Sokolowski *LSCG* 10.

Established rites [of Skambonidai]: the [demarch] and the [*hieropoioi* are to sacrifice] (5) an adult animal to Leos; assignment by lot [of the meat] (*lechsis*),[23] [from the] spits to [each] of the Skambonidai, and the resident aliens are also to receive a share by lot, in the agora (10) of Skambonidai. For the ... sacrifice [an adult animal (?)], and distribute [the meat].

The meat distribution is public, happens in the *agora*, and is probably conducted by lot ("from the spits"). It includes all residents of the deme, both Athenian citizens and the metics (resident aliens). So the "group" is exclusively defined, this time in terms of the boundaries of the deme, including citizens and resident aliens. Again, equality in the distribution is implied, not stated, yet retains the aspect of equality of chance before the distribution.

3.5 The lot, the victim destined for sacrifice, and the priests

Especially interesting is that before all that, the choice of the sacrificial animal is sometimes made by lot. This is curious, for it implies either the existence of a public herd or a contribution by some wealthy citizen, with the animal selected by lot (by officials) from his herd. The lot (here explicitly) makes sense for three different types of prevention. If a rich person wished to show off with a particularly "beautiful" (*CGRN* 92) animal, he could not have ensured this because of the lot; conversely, had he been a miser, he could not have explicitly chosen an animal of inferior quality. Finally, no official could force such a person to contribute his best animal that might appear especially attractive to those conducting the selection. It is a measure of fairness.

In an idyll by Theocritus (no. 4), it is evident that bulls were allotted to each *demos* by lot. Theocritus presents both speakers as if they hate their neighboring *demos* and wish it to get by lot a thin bull at the sacrifice to Hera (this is a public sacrifice, where the *polis* provided many cows).

> The bull's thin too—the ruddy one. I hope Lampriadas's folk may get by lot such another (*lanchano*) when the demesmen sacrifice to Hera—they're [rascals] in (?) that deme. (Trans. A. S. F Gow, adapted)

---

[23] For *lexis* cf. *CGRN* 201 (Molpoi). The "basileus" (not a "king" but a priestly title) "receives *by lot* (*lanchano*), a portion of the meat equal to ("no greater") than the other Molpoi" (*ll.* 23–24). The "crown-bearers" (*stephanophoroi*) get "an obtaining by lot of a portion" (*moires laxis*, l. 35). The same right of "obtaining by lot" (*laxis*) is also given to the herald, who gets a portion of entrails from each of the sacrificed animals (l. 44). Cf. Hdt. 4.21; Plato *Laws* 740a, 747e; *Crit.* 109c, 113b.

SACRIFICE AND FEAST   145

The lot, therefore, plays a role in choosing which animal to sacrifice and, second, in how the meat gets distributed. However, there is a third sphere: in democratic Athens, the lot could also determine who performs the sacrifice. In an Athenian decree of ca. 421, among regulations that concern the festival to Hephaistos, we read (*CGRN* 43) about the officials responsible for the sacred rites:

> The *hieropoioi* should choose by lot ten men to make the sacrifice, from the judges, one from each tribe from the [The]archs should organize the selection by lot (*diakleroö*) together with those of the Council and perform the lot-drawing in the presence (20) of the Council. Those chosen by lot *l[ach] ontes* (*lanchano*) receive wages exactly as [the councilors do while they] take care of this.... The Council must choose by lot among themselves ten men as *hieropoioi* one from each tribe.[24]

The cult officials (the *hieropoioi*) are to be chosen by lot: ten from the pool of judges (selected annually by lot) and ten more from the five hundred members of the council that was made up of fifty representatives, chosen by lot, from each of the ten Athenian tribes. It appears that the lottery was conducted within each unit of fifty members to select its single representative. The same salary expresses the notion of equality as that of the members of the Council. What is remarkable is that should the priest responsible be absent, the deputy-priest too is to be selected by lot. It is unclear from which specific group the replacement might have been chosen. However, it may plausibly be suggested that the group was selected by lot, as we see in the inscription.[25] Finally, the drawing of the lots is represented as an official, public ceremony, as it takes place with all members of the council present.

The functions of distribution and selection sometimes overlap. An inscription from Chios[26] (*CGRN* 50) from about the first half of the fourth century concerns a priesthood of Herakles from a *genos*. Following a list of what is owed to the priest (such as the entrails, a double portion of meat to be placed in the arms of the cult statue), "The one sacrificing is to call out (10) to the priest, and if the priest is not present, one of those *assigned by lot* is to act as deputy-priest." This time the well-defined group from which the deputy priest is allotted is, as often, a *genos*. Still, the same notion applies: access to the lot expresses a definition of the group with equal chances for its members. It is important to note how an entire spectrum of the lottery is present in some sacrifices both in terms of the

---

[24] *CGRN* 43; Sokolowski *LSCG* 13.
[25] *CGRN* 43. In their commentary Jan-Mathieu Carbon and Saskia Peels suggest that such a selection of candidates implies divine sanction. This interpretation relates to the general question of the role of the divine in lotteries. See ch. 2.
[26] *CGRN* 50; Sokolowski *LSCG* 119.

146 DRAWING LOTS

personnel (chosen by lot), the animal (also thus chosen), and in the equality of chance (and of portions) of the meat that this personnel distributes. The sortition to select priests is consistent with the values we note in partible inheritance and the conscription of soldiers and colonists: group members (actual brothers, or as here, *genos* members) are *interchangeable*; they all have the same qualifications concerning the issue at hand.[27]

The use of the lot for selecting priests, known mainly from Athens, is discussed further in the context of the working of democracy. At this stage, it is essential to note that the entire sacrifice experience could involve the lot at all stages. The same mindset is apparent both in the choice by lot of priests and in the distribution of portions. A fascinating Hellenistic inscription from Miletos concerns the Molpoi, a "college" of priests-musicians-politicians that existed in several (mostly) Ionian cities and Milesian colonies, such as Olbia.[28] They go back at least to the sixth century, and many regulations seem to go back to the archaic period. Let us briefly note some relevant ones:[29] It is stated that the "basileus" (not a "king" but a priestly title) receives *by lot* (*lanchano*) a portion of the meat equal to ("no greater") than the other Molpoi (*Ll.* 23–24). The "crown-bearers" (*stephanophoroi*) get "an obtaining by lot of a portion (*moires laxis*) (l. 35). The same right of "obtaining by lot," which we noted in the Skambonidai inscription—*laxis-lexis* (a derivative of *lanchano*)—is also given to the herald, who gets a portion of entrails from each of the sacrificed animals (l. 44).

3.6 The equal feast

Equality, again, is a crucial term. Aside from extra or especially choice portions, distribution at the "equal feast"[30] and at a public sacrifice was apparently equal. The meat was divided into equal portions: supposedly equal parts (*isomoiron*).[31] Dosiadas, for example, relates that in Crete (in the *andreia,* the men-citizen "clubs"), "an equal part . . . is distributed to each person."[32] This equality of distribution seems to conform to the stipulation expressed in an inscription from Mykale (near Priene) of ca. 400–350, where the distribution of meat is to be

---

[27] Cf. *CGRN* 84 ll. 17–23 and Blok's discussion 7.2.2, For differences distinguishing eligible groups that became more marked in the Hellenistic period, see Paul (2018).
[28] *CGRN* 201; Sokolowski *LSAM* 50 with Herda (2006).
[29] On Molpoi see Gordon (2012); cf. Chaniotis (2010); Graf (1974); Molpoi (Miletos) *LSAM* 50, 34–36. The earliest known reference to the Molpoi at Miletos contains the list of these officials, which provides their dates for the late archaic and classical periods (*Milet* I.3 122 / Miletos 103, running from 525/4 to 522/1 according to PHI to 311/0 BC).
[30] *Dais eise Il.* 1.468; 7.320; 9.225; *Od.* 8.98 ; 19.425.
[31] Suda: *daitros*: *Daitos eises*; *isomoiron trophes*.
[32] *FGrHist* 458 F 2 = Athenae. 143e with a detailed discussion by Berthiaume (1982) 44–53.

made "by heads," namely, man to man.³³ An inscription concerning privileges of priests and priestesses from the deme Aixone in Attica mentions several times equal portions of meat, besides their special portions or remuneration in money.³⁴

It is not clear how Greeks measured equality. In some sanctuaries, evidence of weights may indicate that meat was distributed perhaps raw, by weight, according to households, or individually.³⁵ Otherwise, there is evidence (and it seems more likely) that boiled meat could be distributed in identical-sized bowls on the occasion of the sacrifice. We may have less information about cooked (boiled) meat because cooked was less prestigious than roasted and usually came after roasting certain parts.³⁶ The verb *lanchano* appears in such contexts, mainly in inscriptions, and one needs to decide whether the meaning retains the association with the lottery in each case. There was also an *a priori* reason to support the use of lots, quality: even identical bowls of cooked meat could vary in the quality of their content. The lot evens out the chances.

---

[33] *CGRN* 81 350 Thebes near Mykale: Sokolowski *LSAM* 39 νέμειν μερίδας κεφαληδὸν.

[34] *SEG* 54, 214; *CGRN* 57, ca. 400–375. Cf. Scullion (2009).

[35] Ekroth (2008b) mentions portions large enough for an entire household as well as small weights (e.g., at Olympia and Ephesos were found weights of 150–200 grams) that seem to indicate individual distribution. But experienced butchers, she adds, do not need weights.

[36] Ekroth (2008b) 270, 274. She also notes debris from sanctuaries that indicates the use of bowls. For boiling as the preferred cooking method, see Ekroth (2008b) 274–276; Ekroth (2007) 266–268; Ekroth (2008a) 98–100. Cf. Berthiaume (1982).

Irad Malkin

PART II
EQUAL AND FAIR
Inheritance, Colonization, and Mixture

4
Partible Inheritance by Lot

4.1 Brothers sharing an inheritance

Telemachos, Odysseus's only son, grew up knowing he would not have to share his father's inheritance with a brother. In contrast, Oedipus had two sons, Eteokles and Polyneikes, and their inheritance was partible and divided up by lot. The curse of their father and their quarrel over the inheritance that was divided up by lot became the stuff of poetry and tragedy, known primarily in a long fragment of the sixth-century Sicilian poet Stesichoros, in Aeschylus's play *The Seven against Thebes*, in Euripides's *Phoenician Women*, and another fragment by the historian Hellanikos.[1] Versions vary in detail, but the inheritance issue generally seems clear and consistent with fifth-century Athenian conventions regarding partible inheritance. Before determining who gets what, the brothers decide what constitutes the equal/equitable portions of the estate (the adjective is *isos*, which could have both meanings). The procedure thus encourages the self-interest of both brothers to agree on equitability. In case there is no agreement, an arbitrator may make the decision. Having determined the portions, a drawing of lots then takes place. The evidence, especially from the Athenian law courts, suggests that the procedure implies *hairesis*, a personal choice. The lottery does not "pair" but establishes *turns*: for example, Brother A, whose lot came up first (or who "picked it up," hence *hairesis* cf. ch. 2), then declares his personal preference. Brother B then gets the alternative. Here we see a combination of blind luck with personal intention and will, probably similar to how sometimes lotteries were conducted in colonies to allocate *kleroi*. No god determined the outcome. The inheritor got a *moira* (portion) of the inheritance, but he was not destined ("it was not his *moira*") to choose it.

The custom of partible inheritance is attested already in Homer to be distinguished from primogeniture, where the eldest might take all. We also find partible inheritance by lot in the Ancient Near East, but primogeniture is there sometimes acknowledged with the eldest getting a double portion.[2] Greek partible inheritance presupposes interchangeability and the equality of status

---

[1] Stesichoros (*PLille* 76 A ii + 73 i), Aesch. *Sept.* 711, 727, 914; Eur. *Phoen.* 80; Hellanikos *FGrH* 4 fr. 82.
[2] Westbrook and Beckman (2003) 57–58. Cf. Jackson (1978).

Drawing Lots. Irad Malkin and Josine Blok, Oxford University Press. © Oxford University Press 2024.
DOI: 10.1093/oso/9780197753477.003.0005

among brothers, as we also saw with the use of a selective lottery to choose among brothers for conscription for military service or for settling new colonies. It is comparable to other distributive lotteries among members of a predefined group; all are equal before the lot, such as settlers sharing out land or soldiers distributing booty. The three Olympian brothers, sharing out the world by lot among them, overlap in this respect: they share the spoils of the cosmic victory, which also happen to be their "inheritance" from their vanquished, albeit immortal, father Kronos. Theirs was not an inheritance in human terms following a death (gods are immortal). Yet the conventions of distributive lotteries in general (e.g., booty, catch, land)—and those of partible inheritance in particular—seem to have shaped the Homeric story of the divine, distributive lottery, which we observed earlier.

Historians discussing conventions of ancient Greek inheritance face fragmentary and uneven sources, blatant contradictions, and a seemingly irresistible urge to form a linear story where there might be none.[3] Cameron, for example, postulates a time when the land was given to the oldest son and was indivisible and inalienable, whereas, in later periods, lands granted by will or dowries were allowed.[4] However, we cannot know if the conventions of inheritance "developed" from one to the other. A safer assumption would be that although following similar values, various modes of bequeathing and transferring property (sale, gift, dowry, and inheritance) existed concurrently or, when not concurrently, in different places in the Greek world. For example, note the change of emphasis in the quasihistorical story discussed later of how the three Herakleidai brothers cast lots for the Peloponnese; Chresphontes cheated and received Messenia (see ch. 6.3.6). However, in another version preserved by Pausanias, writing under the Roman Empire, the gist of the story is the same except that, at first, Chresphontes tries to claim Messenia *because* he is eldest, an apparent anachronism of Pausanias's time (second century CE). The claim fails, and the brothers then resort to the lot.[5]

I do not intend to provide yet another assessment of the history and nature of Greek inheritance but discuss one of its earliest, ubiquitous forms: inheritance by lot and its implications. We may be justified in speaking of "Greek" customs of

---

[3] For a convenient introduction, see Maffi (2005). See also Asheri (1963); Lane Fox (1985); Berman (2007) ch. 4.

[4] Cameron (1970).

[5] Paus. 4.3.3–5. When the Dorians assigned Argos to Temenos, Chresphontes asked them for the land of Messenia, in that he was older than Aristodemos. Chresphontes, wishing to obtain Messenia as his portion at all costs, approached Temenos, and having suborned him pretended to leave the decision to the lot. See also on Chresphontes : Apollodorus *Bib.* 2.8.4–5; Paus. 4.3.4–5; Polyaenus *Strateg.* 1.6 (stones do not float; perhaps drawing by hand?). Cf. Soph. *Ajax* 1283–1285 with scholiast; Plautus *Casina* 307, 398f. Cf. Soph. *Ajax* 1285. Pheidon is said to have (re)conquered the lot of Temenos; Ephoros *FGrHist* 70 F 115. The division is mentioned in a lost play of Euripides: Strabo 8.5.6 = fr. 1083 N_2 pp. 252–257 assigns the fragment to the *Temenos*. Malkin (1994a) ch. 1.

inheritance since conventions and procedures relating to inheritance were similar. An heiress at Gortyn in Crete might get more than an heiress in Athens. Still, the general criteria of division and distribution were basically the same, with certain variations from region to region and from time to time. What other modes of property transfer between generations existed alongside partible inheritance by lot is a question left to other historians.[6] There are two notable commonalities I observe at both ends of the chronological spectrum: on the one hand, the poems of Homer and Hesiod (ca. 700), and on the other, court speeches from fourth-century Athens.[7] The first common feature is a general lack of special rights to a "firstborn"; the second is the attested existence of partible inheritance by lot.

4.2 Equality versus primogeniture

The general absence of primogeniture is a well-known fact.[8] Even Plato, when arguing for a single-heir system, recommends giving the property not to the eldest but to "whichever one of his own children is especially dear to him."[9] Ideally, primogeniture affects all of society since it should prevent conflict and especially resentment because nobody would contest the rights of the firstborn unless murdered precisely for that reason.[10] I am not sure that princes in the Ottoman Empire, often murdered upon the succession of a brother, appreciated the point of non-resentment. However, lottery in partible inheritance achieves the same goal much more efficiently: a lack of resentment at an outcome while avoiding the dangers facing the firstborn because he had been singled out, *a priori*, by nature. As we shall see, Aeschylus's *Seven against Thebes* revolves around scandalous resentment between brothers, the sons of Oedipus, following the refusal to follow up on what the lot determined.

A division into relatively equal portions of a parent's estate into discrete units can only work for one or two generations, after which the plots would become too tiny.[11] Mostly two standard solutions were practiced:[12] either let several sons

---

[6] A single-heir convention instead of partible inheritance is sometimes mentioned too; see Berman (2007) 121–122 with Asheri (1963) on the *pastas* as sole heir in the Gortyn law code.

[7] E.g., Isaeus 6.25: patrimony to be divided equally among sons *isomoroi*; Dem. 43.51: *moiran lanchanein* followed by *lanchano* again. According to Isaeus the law ordains that all the legitimate sons have an equal right to share in their father's property

[8] On primogeniture see Beauchet (1897) 450–457. Cf. Blok (2017) 137, who notes the exception of the Spartan kings, to which may be added the kings of Cyrene (Hdt 4.160; cf. Plut. *Bravery of Women* 25) and the traditions about Corinth: Synkellos 337.7f. "After Aletes's death, the eldest of his posterity always reigned, up to the tyranny of Kypselos."

[9] Plato, *Laws* 740b6–8; cf. 923a–d; cf. 740b–c.

[10] See Jackson (1978).

[11] Although Aristotle (1265B2–3) might claim that no one is destitute because of subdivisions, he contradicts himself: too many people spell poverty and social tensions (1265B10–12).

[12] Cf. Lane Fox (1985) 217; Cox (1998) 109 (for disputes among brothers, ibid., 109–114). It was sometimes possible to combine *kleroi* by marriage, hence the preference for cross-cousin marriage

inhabit the same *kleros*, or for a son to depart and found a new *oikos/kleros* "away from home," literally becoming an *ap-oikos* ("colonist"). The *Odyssey* avoids the issue of inheritance and potential conflict since both Odysseus and Telemachos were only sons. But the *Odyssey* still mentions partible inheritance and is the earliest source to do that explicitly (it is hinted at also in the *Iliad*). It also mentions the second option when Odysseus speaks of potential colonization on an offshore island facing the Cyclopes. The text implies that colonization (and the establishment of new *oikoi/kleroi*) were viable options.

Robin Lane Fox rightly criticizes the conventional paraphrase of a famous passage in Hesiod as if the poet (ca. 700) recommends having only one son. While Hesiod suggests a man marry late, not before the age of thirty, he advises having plenty of sons. Perhaps Plutarch created some confusion in modern scholarship because he misrepresented Hesiod: "Hesiod does not well in advising 'an only son to inherit his father's estate.'"[13] What Hesiod says is

> There should be an only son to feed his father's house, for so wealth will increase in the home; but if you leave a *second son* you should die old. Yet Zeus can easily give great wealth to a greater number. More hands mean more work and more increase. (*WD* 375–380, trans. Hugh G. Evelyn-White)

So, what would happen to the extra sons? Lane Fox indicates contradictions and inconsistencies in our sources, which are only to be expected, especially if we assume (as I do) that several methods of dispensing with an inheritance could coexist and need not evolve from one to the next. Clearly, for Hesiod having more than one son meant a chance for long life and more wealth. Lane Fox, relying on anthropological comparisons and Athenian court cases, points to cases of several sons residing in an *oikos*, sometimes hiring out the extra children and sometimes nominally breaking up an estate into smaller units to avoid liturgies (a kind of tax).

One could further mention the poetic metaphor for "brothers," *homoklaroi*, or "*equal sharers of the kleros/oikos*."[14] This could mean having split equal shares of the same *oikos*, or equally sharing the one whole *oikos*. Apollo and Artemis, brother and sister, are *homoklaroi*, probably because they were born in Delos, sharing the same ancestral home.[15] The term keeps its lottery association in other

---

(Cox 1998, 34 with n.102). I thank Josine Blok for the reference. Another option was to marry a neighbor's daughter and move to her *oikos*. See ch. 6.3 for warnings against augmenting property by joining *kleroi* by means of marriage and dowries.

[13] *WD* 695–696; Plut. *On Brotherly Love* 480f., trans. W. C. Helbold.
[14] Pindar *Ol.* 2.49.
[15] Pindar *Nem.* 9.5; cf. *Ol.* 2.49.

contexts. A Delphic inscription recounts how the Thourians asked to renew their right of consultation at Delphi, the *promanteia*. Delphi declared them "*homoklaroi* with the people of Taras," apparently allowing them to be "equal before the lot" that determined the order of consultation.[16]

Yet Hesiod did not wish to live with his brother, and it is Hesiod himself who attests to the existence of *partible* inheritance since he had to share his inheritance with his brother Perses. Hesiod complains that Perses took more than he deserved. Since his complaint relates to what happened after the estate division, he is probably referring to the moveable wealth of the inheritance (for which there are special provisions in later sources), judged by corrupt arbitrators to belong to his brother. He uses the same verb (*dateomai*), which we observed earlier.

> For we had already divided our *kleros* (*kleron edassameth'*) but you seized the greater share and carried it off, greatly swelling the glory of our bribe-swallowing lords who love to judge such a cause as this. (Hes. *WD*. 37–39, trans. Hugh G. Evelyn-White)

Several centuries later, Plutarch, quoting Plato, refers to the same issue, recommending an arbiter in case brothers cannot work it out, especially concerning the moveable property. He adds the notion of value since the use of the lot in such cases is defined *as justice*:

> Plutarch *On Brotherly Love* 11 (483d) And when they seek to divide their father's goods, they should not first declare war on each other. . . . Let them preferably assemble alone by themselves; otherwise, let there be present some common friend as a witness equally friendly to both, and then "by the lots of Justice," as Plato (*Critias* 109d) says, let them, as they give and take what is suitable to each and preferred by each (and not grab each other's slaves, etc. Trans. W. C. Helbold)

4.3 The *oikos* and the *kleros*

Possessing a plot of land, a *kleros*, which would sustain a household and provide for a full-fighting community member, became a personal ambition that would also serve the community. The move for single households (one *oikos* / one *kleros*) seems to have happened sometime in the eighth century. It was a major pushing force encouraging Greek colonization since new *kleroi* were available overseas. "The Greek city was already by the eighth century conceptualized essentially

---

[16] *Syll.*³ 295, cf. Pouilloux (1952) 493–499.

as a union of property-holding households," observes Sally Humphreys, and continues to note that in new settlements, the *kleroi/oikoi* were free from claims by kin, thus implying an even stronger emphasis on the discrete nature of the new *oikos/kleros*.[17] Even when there may have been several brothers, one wished for the desired situation of a single person who would head a personal *oikos* that would be established over a single *kleros*. Lane Fox suggests that extra sons could be hired out to neighbors (hence less pressure to depart overseas), which is certainly plausible. Still, this outlet may have become blocked by other factors, such as slave labor, attested to in Homer and Hesiod. In short, parallel to partible inheritance, there emerged an inherent need to get away and carve out one's *kleros*.

But would not the problem of partible inheritance rise again in the new colonies? Would not inheritance claims of kin from "the old country" surface now and then, despite Humphreys's claim of the colonial *kleros* being kin-free? The issue of partible inheritance probably did come up already with second-generation colonists, but our knowledge is too fragmentary. Some portions of the reserved land were likely kept for extra sons of colonists, but that would not be a solution in the long run as additional migrants probably would arrive too. This type of *stenochoria*, shortness of available land (literally, "narrowness of space"), is one plausible, albeit partial, explanation for the foundation of many "colonies of colonies."[18]

What would happen when tensions in a new colony get to a dangerous point, seemingly because of the lack of *kleroi*? Plato recommends further colonization as the solution:

> Moreover, as a final step,—in case we are in absolute desperation about the unequal condition of our 5,040 households, and are faced with a superabundance of citizens, owing to the mutual affection of those who cohabit with one another, which drives us to despair,—there still remains that ancient device which we have often mentioned, namely, the sending forth, in friendly wise from a friendly nation, of colonies consisting of such people as are deemed suitable. (*Laws* 740e, trans. R.G. Bury)

Plato, too, recommends that a *kleros* remain intact (*Laws* XI 923d), and, like Philolaos and others before him, Plato suggests the adoption of extra sons into destitute households. Philolaos (fifth century) allowed the adoption of sons into "empty" households so that the number of households could remain constant.[19] Keeping a viable number of households was a perennial problem for Greek cities.

---

[17] Humphreys (1978) 162-4.
[18] On colonies of colonies see Costanzi (2010).
[19] Arist. *Pol.* II 1274b2–5.

For example, Solon apparently legislated that a man with no sons (*apais*) can adopt (postmortem?) the husband of an heiress.[20] To ensure the progeny and continuity of the *oikos*, Solon also instituted that having married an heiress (*epikleros*), a man must have intercourse with her three times a month "at all costs" (*pantos*). If not, she can choose a replacement.[21]

The historical case of the mid-seventh century Thera illustrates the desire for the formula one *oikos* = one *kleros*: any household with more than one son participated in a comprehensive drawing of lots of the entire political community of Thera. The lot determined which brother would go to settle in Cyrene.[22] The implication is that in the case of two sons, the one allotted to stay home would now be the sole owner of his father's *kleros*. We see, therefore, two opposing tendencies that developed probably concurrently: on the one hand, a division of inheritance (by lot) among at least two sons; on the other, a desire to possess a large enough *kleros*, which could be fulfilled in the foundation of new settlements or by joining one at a later date. So from the perspective of the mother city, colonization could solve both the problem at home and abroad: To keep the *kleros* intact in the mother city, a new *kleros* was available overseas, which was then to become a First Lot (*protos kleros*), supposedly inalienable, in its own right (see ch.6.2.2). The drawing of lots, so essential to Greek inheritance practices, had evolved but was still consistent in its purpose and method. Instead of dividing up by lot one *kleros* between two brothers, the lot now divided and separated the two brothers while assigning each a whole *kleros*, one in the mother city, the other in the colony (see Figure 4.1).[23]

4.4 Inheritance at home and abroad

There must have been complications. What would happen, for example, when a father in the metropolis lost a son in some battle while his other son had already departed for a colony? Did his *kleros* remain empty?[24] Sometimes we find provisions for that: at Naupaktos, a colonist-son could reclaim his father's inheritance back home, provided he left someone responsible for his *oikos/kleros* in the colony. I noted the combined aspect of religion and society, with the latter

---

[20] Interpretation: Lane Fox (1985) 224 with Dem. 46.14.
[21] Plut. *Solon*, 20 = fr. 52a LR.
[22] Hdt. 4.153.
[23] Plato (*Laws* 856d–e) prefers to keep a *kleros* whole, imagining a decision by a lot oracle among brothers: "And from the sons of citizens who happen to have more than one son over ten years old, ten shall be chosen by lot (*klerosai*) . . . and the names thus chosen (the verb is *lanchano*) shall be sent to Delphi; and that man whom the oracle names (*aneilei*, "picks up") shall be established as the allotment-holder in the house of those departed (trans. R.G. Bury). See also ch 2.
[24] Cf. Cox (1998) 155–161.

Partible inheritance: Two brothers, each getting half a *kleros*

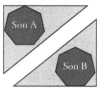

Colonization: Two brothers, each getting a whole *kleros*

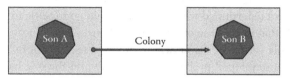

Figure 4.1 brothers and *kleroi*
(1) Partible inheritance by lot: two brothers, each gets half a *kleros*; the lot either determines which brother declares first for his preferred half or "pairs" a brother and the specific half-*kleros*.
(2) Colonization: Each brother gets a whole *kleros*, one brother at home and the other abroad; the lot chooses between the brothers and determines who will depart.

defined as a political community in terms of the former. The case of Naupaktos, a colony of the Eastern Lokrians, founded ca. 500–460, illustrates how issues of inheritance and continuity were of the utmost importance to both mother city and colony.[25] The inscription demonstrates the cult's role in defining a community (discussed earlier) and prescribes a general right of return in case of the colony's failure. It also allows a returning or visiting son a right to participate in cults and sacrifices.

The decree specifies that individually, if anyone wishes to return, he can do so provided he left a son or an adult brother behind—that is, to maintain the household. What happens if a settler then dies without heirs? In that case, "If there are no descendants or heirs of a Hypoknemidian Lokrian colonist in Naupaktos, the nearest relative from the Lokrians (the 'mother city') will take possession of the inheritance (within three months)." In other words, he would have to leave Lokris to take possession of the *kleros* in Naupaktos so that the household in Naupaktos would continue to exist. The point is then repeated in more detail, with a different emphasis: it specifies that a Lokrian brother (who had presumably never left), as an heir, "shall take everything he is entitled to, according to the laws in Hypoknemidian Lokris." It is unclear which inheritance is referred to; it might have been the inheritance both brothers were expecting from their father,

---

[25] Graham (1983) 54–55.

not the property in Naupaktos for which we saw the earlier provision. Finally, the focus shifts yet again to the departing son: "Anyone who leaves his father, leaves him part of his property; in case of a father's death, the colonist in Naupaktos will recover that part." This clearly shows concern for the state of the household at the mother city. At the time of departure to the colony, the "part" of the son is reintegrated with the *kleros* of his father, thus enhancing its chances to be viable and prosperous. We have no idea how the Naupaktian son's property rights were to be affected. Still, the fact that they were illustrates the ongoing individual worries that kept a colony and a mother city connected regarding property rights and marriage. Plato even recommends importing a colonist to marry a daughter at the home community to preserve an *oikos*.[26]

Inheritance is often called *kleros*; one inherits a "portion," or "part," a *meros*; what one gets (*lanchano*) may be a *lachos*, which means "that which one gets by lot." Significantly, the verb describing sharing the land by the prospective colonists of Cyrene is *apo-lanchano*. Note how the same word (*apolanchano*) also appears in conjunction with another lottery-associated verb of "throwing," *epiballo*. Observe Herodotus's story about what the Amazons tell their Scythian men-consorts:

> (Amazons) If you want to keep us for wives . . . go to your parents and let them give you the allotted share of their possessions (*apolaxete ton ktematon to meros*) (Hdt. 4.114.4) . . . when they had been given the allotted share of possessions that fell to them (*apolachontes ton ktematon to epiballon*) and returned to the Amazons. . . (Hdt. 4.115.1)

The subject of inheritance has mostly slipped under the radar of historians who study the phenomenon of Greek colonization yet disregard the continuing relations between settlers and their home community, which often revolved around inheritance and marriage. Scholars discussing Greek colonization in abstract or sociological terms might overlook the life experience of the actual settlers, with family members spread across the water at both the metropolis and the colony. For at least three generations after any foundation, property issues must have concerned remaining parents, brothers, and sisters, and the *apoikoi*, the settlers who went overseas (not to mention individual migrants, *epoikoi*, who kept coming in later periods).

Our evidence is scanty, but enough of it illustrates the case. The foundation decree of Naupaktos explicitly states that a son may return to the mother city and inherit, provided he leaves his son (or an adopted one?) to maintain the *oikos* (and the implied *kleros* that goes with it). In such a case, each community, that

[26] *Laws* 11.925.

of the mother city and that of the colony, supposedly keeps its number of citizens "constant," according to the number of *kleroi* and *oikoi*. As noted, Plato recommends asking a colonist (preferably, but not necessarily, kin) to marry a local woman. The fact that Plato sees such an option as natural only helps to underline the *ongoing* personal connections between members of the same family or close community, keeping up their links with their relatives.

The lot must have played a significant role in both personal and collective memory: it was sometimes used when selecting settlers; the moment when a brother was to be separated from a brother and a father torn away from his son must have been both traumatic and momentous, as were the first days in the new settlement, the memorable days of "foundation," when lands were marked out and allocated by lot.

Foundations are "dramatic" events and puncture time by articulating a moment of sudden creation: the foundation of a new city, a new community together with its gods, to be annually celebrated in the form of a heroic cult to the founder.[27] However, the arrival of *epoikoi*, later immigrants, is much less spoken about for understandable reasons: they were not news, nor were they generally linked with any dramatic, memorable event. And yet everyone expected them: colonies kept land in reserve precisely for such cases. Aside from Plato's comment about a colonist returning to marry, there is also evidence from the Oracle of Dodona. For example, one private individual inquires whether to join a colony; another asks whether it is better for his wife and family to live in Kroton. Another inquirer asks if he should move to Orikos or stay. Ariston (early third cent.) wants to know if he will fare better if he joins a colony of Syracuse at a "later" stage. Another person asks about emigrating to Pharos, a colony of Paros. Yet another wishes to change residence or registration between Taras and its colony Herakleia, perhaps moving back to Taras for personal reasons (e.g., inheritance; the two cities are mere ca. thirty kilometers apart).[28]

What is common to both systems—partible inheritance by lot, and a single occupier of a *kleros*—is that both share the preference for the formula of "one household = one *kleros*."[29] With partible inheritance, the result would be as many new *kleroi* as there were sons; in colonization, there were as many new *kleroi* as there were colonists (such as the brothers of those left behind by lot). Once partible inheritance becomes ineffective (i.e., if the inherited *kleros* is too small because of too many cycles of inheritance), either as a reaction to *ad hoc* situations

---

[27] Malkin (1987a) Part II; cf. Leschorn (1984).
[28] Eidnow (2007) "A Catalogue and Summary of Published Questions by Individuals and Responses from the Dodona Oracle," nos. 5, 4, 17, 14, 11. See discussion of the lot oracle at Dodona (ch. 2.7) Parke (1967); Dakaris (1996); Parker (2015); Carbon (2015).
[29] Cox (1998) 132 on the *oikos* understood as a "nuclear family."

or in such that were easily foreseen, settling overseas became the best option both for those staying home and for those departing.

Although generally studied as distinct subjects, inheritance and colonization reflect closely on each other. From the colonial perspective, I return to their overlapping features in chapter 6. Here let us note the following points:

- Inheritance and colonization are contemporary historical issues.
- Both are concerned with allocating individual *kleroi*.
- Both employ a drawing of lots for that purpose.
- The drawing of lots either "pairs" an individual with a predefined *kleros* or the lot decides which brother, or which colonist, will be the first to declare his choice between predetermined portions (see also ch. 5 for those features in Greek drama).
- Both share notions of equality of chance and outcome.

4.5 Poetry and myth

In one of his realistic lying tales, Odysseus appears as a raider, a bastard, who did not get an equal share of inheritance with his brothers.

> His proud sons divided among them his property (*zoe*) and cast lots therefor (*epi klerous ebalonto*). To me they gave (*dosan*) a very small portion, and allotted (*eneiman*) a dwelling.[30] (*Od.* 209–210, trans. A. T Murray)

The statement spells out an expected norm: partible inheritance among legitimate sons employing the lot. The same norm is implied in Pindar's story (early fifth century) about the three grandsons of Helios, the god of Rhodes, dividing up Rhodes among them. A keyword is *moira*.[31]

> And there he (Helios), and begat seven sons . . . ; and of these one begat Kameiros, and Ialysos the eldest, and Lindos. Each had his own separate share of cities (*asteon moiran*) in their threefold division (*tricha dassamenoi*, thus *dateomai*, again) of their father's land, and their dwelling-places were named after them.

---

[30] *Od.* 14.209–210.
[31] Pind. *Ol.* 7.74–76. Thalmann (1978) 64: "The word *moiras* may well imply the sons' use of the lot."

Myths sometimes articulate conventions. Euxanthios, son of the mythical king Minos (but not of Pasiphae, Minos's wife), gave up the equal part, a seventh, of the inheritance in Crete, perhaps because he too, like Odysseus the liar, was a bastard.[32] What he gives up is his *kleros* (*klaros*), now in the sense of both "inheritance" and "estate." Instead, he prefers his small *kleros* at home, which he got apparently by lot (*lanchano*).[33] Euxanthios is not simply a home-loving person: he does this to avoid strife with his brothers, which is what does happen in Aeschylus's *Seven against Thebes* (see next chapter). "To me," he says in Pindar's voice, "has been given a small (portion?).... But I have been allotted (*lanchano* again) no sorrows, no civil strife." Pindar seems to play with the semantic field of *lanchano*: the concrete "getting by lot" and, metaphorically, one's lot may be a "share" of troubles and civil strife. By avoiding the inheritance lottery in Crete, Euxanthios also "gives up" his share of problems.

Equality of chance and portions (a "seventh") is implied in Pindar's *Paian*. Already in Homer, we note awareness of the equality of land portions. This is spelled out in a simile concerning the division of a land (*Il.* 12.421–423): "As two men with measuring-rods in hand ... in a narrow space contend each for his *equal share* (*peri ises*)." Clearly, they were arguing about where the division line marked equal plots. The Spartans were about to use such "measuring rods" if they defeated Tegea and took over its land.[34] They were perhaps employed already in the last third of the eighth century at Megara Hyblaia in Sicily, where the planned "blocks" and even the houses themselves appear obsessively equal (see ch. 6.2).

Throughout the history of partible inheritance by lot we note a consistent emphasis on fairness and equality based on mutual agreement or, if not, on arbitration. In the fifth century, on the Athenian stage, one could present a play such Aeschylus's *Seven against Thebes* in front of thousands of spectators. They all knew the values, customs, and the traditional framework of partible inheritance by lot, and they could all be shocked by their abuse.

---

[32] Pindar's fourth *Paian* for Keos.
[33] See Demont (2000) 313.
[34] Hdt. 1.66.

5
Drawing Lots on the Athenian Stage

5.1 Inheritance, sortition, booty, captives, and military procedures

(Jocasta) Why, my son, do you so long for Ambition, that worst of deities? . . .

It is better, my son, to honor equality, *isotes* who always joins friend to friend, city to city, allies to allies; for equality is naturally lasting among men; but the less is always in opposition to the greater, and begins the dawn of hatred. For it is equality that has set up for man measures and divisions of weights, and has determined numbers; night's sightless eye, and radiant sun proceed upon their yearly course on equal terms, and neither of them is envious when it has to yield. Though both sun and night are servants for mortals, you will not be content with your equal share [*isos*; some would translate "fair"] of your heritage and give the same to him? Then where is justice (*dike*)?

Euripides, *Phoenissai* 531–548 (trans. E. P. Coleridge)

In classical tragedy, the language of the lottery is pervasive. Over the fifth century, Athenian audiences in the theatre, numbering in the tens of thousands, shared the mindset and understood the broad spectrum of lottery-related procedures and overlapping evocations and resonances. The lot had been an integral part of their frame of reference in previous centuries, and its application to civic and political life constituted a significant feature of their democracy.

Lottery-related metaphors and images also abound in Athenian tragedy. For example, in Aeschylus's *Persians*, two sisters appear in a dream: "to one had been assigned by lot the land of Hellas, to the other that of the barbarians."[1] For a contemporary member of the audience, the sisters' dream probably evoked at once "literary" associations (such as allusions to Homeric lotteries), myths of primordial territorial divisions (e.g., the Herakleidai and the Peloponnese), and concrete customs and practices concerning division and distribution of an inheritance,

---

[1] Aesch. *Pers.* 185–187.

all familiar and current in the fifth century. Thus, for example, Euripides refers to partible inheritance by drawing lots yet makes it a primordial event: the two sons of Theseus received their portions "by the drawing of lots (*klero[i] lachontes [lanchano]*).²

Athenian playwrights used the lot as a narrative device, an idiom, and a poetic metaphor while relying on a mental frame of reference that recognized lotteries as something ubiquitous in the experiences of life and death. The language of drawing lots moves between the concrete and the metaphoric, playing with the overlapping meanings of *lanchano, kleros, epiballo, palos,* and some *moira*-related words. The *kleros*, for example, appears as a "lot," "plot," "portion," "estate," "inheritance," and even "fate."

The theme of lotteries was traditional and well known from a common store of Greek myths while also reflecting contemporary issues. For example, Sophocles repeats the story in the *Iliad* about the lottery that determined who would fight Hektor; the lot of Aias, the hero of Sophocles's tragedy *Ajax*, jumps out:

> The lot (*kleros*) which he cast in was not the kind to flee the challenge; it was no lump of moist earth, but one which would be the first to leap lightly from the crested helmet! (Soph. *Ajax* 1285, trans. R. Jebb3)

Aias's lot exemplifies the problematics of historical interpretation: Sophocles knew his Homer, as did the audience. So when Sophocles mentions Aias's lot, aside from reflecting the expectation that the story was familiar to the thousands in the audience, does it reflect anything beyond a literary allusion? The fifth-century audience was quite undoubtedly familiar with the general framework of practicing lotteries, as those were employed daily in Athenian democracy. Moreover, Sophocles lets fly a contemporary allusion to Sparta's constitutive myth of the division of the Peloponnese by lot, which has nothing to do with Homer. These were contemporary issues: Sophocles alludes to the Herakleid charter myth of the primordial division of the Peloponnese and Sparta's right over its divinely promised land (specifically the allusion to the cheating by Chresphontes see 6.3.6). Sophocles uses the term "a runaway (*drapetes*) lot" (for the dissolving lot) as if this was a familiar term for lotteries and, one suspects, games of chance.

Guards have a special link with lotteries, especially since turns for guard shifts were arranged by lot. The guard shift is articulated as *moira*, a "portion" of the total guard duty, articulated also as "the shift as determined by the lot" (*klerou kata moiran*).³ Sophocles returns to the selective lottery of "one out of some" in

---

² Eur. *Heracl.* 31–37 (*klero[i] lachontas*).
³ Eur. *Rh.* 545.

his *Antigone*: the guard bearing the bad news to Creon that someone had buried Polyneikes against his express orders was chosen for this dangerous mission by lot (*palos*, v. 274). However, the second time, having caught Antigone red-handed, no lottery was needed to select him as the bearer of the good news. "This time there was no casting of lots (*kleros*). No, this *kleros* has fallen (*epalleto*) to me, and me alone" (ll. 396–397). Sophocles uses *kleros* here with the twist: it is a *kleros* without a *klerosis* (lottery), hence most would translate *kleros* here as "luck": "This is *my* luck/chance"![4]

So the guard's *kleros* became personal, his alone, and his chance. In general, it is choice, not the lot, that gives individual action a significance that goes beyond the execution of some task or even the loss of one's life. To be able to set out with the fleet from Aulis, Agamemnon needs to sacrifice his daughter.[5] But he has more than one; why should Iphigeneia, specifically, be sacrificed? Euripides in *Iphigeneia in Aulis* has Clytemnestra railing against Iphigeneia's selection to be sacrificed, but a solution is suggested: instead of marking out Iphigeneia, a lottery will decide which daughter will be sacrificed (l. 1198). But Iphigeneia rejects this "fair" arrangement precisely because such a selection would rob her sacrifice of meaning and reputation: her own choice to die for the sake of Hellas (l. 1554–1556).

In his *Trojan Women* Euripides describes how the captive Trojan women get assigned to their new masters by lot. Hecuba, Priam's enslaved widow, learns of the fate of the other Trojan women from a messenger. In another play, *Hecuba*, Euripides presents the messenger himself as an allotted slave: "Hecuba, I have hastened away to you, leaving my master's tent, where *the lot assigned* (kleroö) me as his slave."[6] In the *Trojan Women*, as elsewhere in the play, the practice of the lot and its vocabulary (*lanchano*, *potmos*, and especially *kleros*) is consistent and conforms to Homeric notions of how booty was to be distributed.

The general theme of assigning the booty, the captured women, to the victors is stated at the beginning of the play, followed later with more specificity:

> Scamander's banks re-echo long and loud the screams of captive maids, as they by lot receive their masters. . . . And such of the Trojan women as are not portioned out (*akleroi*) are in these tents, set apart (*exaireo*) for the leaders of the army. (*Trojan Women* 29, trans. E. P. Coleridge)

---

[4] It is noteworthy that *kleros* can indeed function the way one would use "chance" in English both as "luck" and "opportunity": "I had a chance to do it, so I did"; "She saw an opportunity and took her chance."
[5] Eur. *IA* 89–93 (Kalchas's prophecy). Cf. Papadodima (2014).
[6] Eur. *Hec.* 99, trans. E. P. Coleridge. Cf. Schirripa (2001).

It seems clear that among the women, a particular group had been preselected (*exaireo*) for distribution by lot among the princes of the army. It appears Euripides understood that the lottery was about deciding which turn a hero may declare his personal choice, as Agamemnon chose Cassandra. It was not a blind pairing but a mixture of randomness and personal choice. The vocabulary is consistent with other areas of drawing lots that we have seen. For example:

TALTHYBIOS: Each warrior took his prize in turn; ye were not all at once assigned (*lanchano*).
244] HECUBA: Whom hath the lot assigned us severally? ... (*lanchano*)
HECUBA: Then tell me, whose prize is my daughter, hapless Cassandra?
TALTHYBIOS: King Agamemnon has chosen her out (*exaireo*) for himself.

As noted, a major function of the lottery is procedural: establishing turns. In Euripides's *Rhesos*, the turns of a military guard shifts are determined by lot: "Is it not then high time we went and roused the Lykians for the fifth watch, as the lot decided?"[7] The guard shift is articulated as *moira*, a "portion" of the total guard duty—hence the expression *klerou kata moiran*, "the shift as determined by the lot."[8] Since guard shifts were a matter of routine, their use of the lot reminds us how common and self-evident the place of the lot was in the Greek mindset. We have seen how the order of the chariots in the Homeric chariot race was established by lot (Antilochos won the first lot and thus the innermost lane).[9] Sophocles refers to a chariot race in similar terms: "Having taken up position (in the places) where the appointed umpires, drawing lots for them, stationed their chariots."[10] In Homer, we find the Trojan allies positioned by lot: "And towards Thymbre fell the lot of the Lykians and the lordly Mysians, and the Phrygians that fight from chariots and the Maionians, lords of chariots" (*Il.* 10.430).

Historically, outside the contemporary theatre stage, the lot is also apparent in the distribution of positions and areas of military command. Perhaps anachronistically, Herodotus reports that just before the battle of Marathon, when the supreme command was rotated daily among the generals, they waited for the turn of Kallimachos, who got his post "drawn by lot by the bean."[11] Thucydides reports that during the siege of Sicily, "the fleet was divided into three squadrons, and one of them assigned by lot (*kleroö*) to each of the three generals."[12] Apparently,

---

[7] Trans. E.P. Coleridge. For turns in standing guard, see also section 7.2.4 in this volume.
[8] Eur. *Rh.* 543–545; 562–564. See Liapes (2012) *ad loc.*
[9] Hom. *Il.* 23.353–354, and cf. Xen. *Cyr.* 6.3.34 determining the placing of the chariot units.
[10] Kells (1973) on Soph. *El.* 709. At Olympia the lot was used in wrestling; Lucian Hermotimus 40 and *IvO* 225 (49 CE), honorary inscription, ll. 14–19. See Ajootan (2007).
[11] Hdt. 6.109–110: ὁ τῶι κυάμωι λαχὼν. For the questions this clause raises, see section 7.2.5 in this volume.
[12] Thuc. 6.42.1, trans. Hornblower (2008) *ad loc.* Cf. 6.62.1. See also section 7.2.5 in this volume.

this was a normal pairing procedure since the Athenian Aegean fleet was also divided by lot for *ad hoc* operations, "drawing lots (*diakleroö*) for the respective services."[13] Similarly, in Aeschylus's *Seven*, positions are allocated by lot. Using several lottery-related words (*kleros, palos, lanchano*) Aeschylus has the messenger say, "I left them (besiegers of Thebes) casting lots to decide how each commander, his post assigned by *casting lots*, would lead his regiment against the gates."[14]

Perhaps the most dramatic of such allotments occurred just on the eve of the battle of Salamis (480) after Athens-city had been abandoned and Themistokles published a "decree-before-battle," a late copy of which was found at Troizen. Whether it is a genuine copy or not, an embellished version, or even an outright forgery has been variously debated. The text implies that Themistokles and the anxious Athenians considered the lot as best serving their purpose: the decree instructs to pair warships with commanders (trierarchs) by lot.[15] Even if the inscription is a forgery, it is remarkable that Greeks of the fourth century accepted drawing lots for trierarchs on the eve of battle as solid fact, conforming to their mindset and standard practices.[16] That was their reality: assigning trierarchs to warships by drawing lots is well evidenced in fourth-century Athens. The Athenians even had a term to denote a warship as yet unassigned by *epiklerosis* (drawing lots): *anepiklerotos*.[17]

Thousands of Athenians in the theatre listened to the chorus in Aeschylus's *Eumenides*, which sang about how the possession of Delphi's oracle moved from one divinity to another by lot (ch. 2). In a series of allotments, the oracle, described as a *lachos* (that which one gets by lot, cf. *lanchano*), shifted from hand to hand, starting with Gaia, then Themis, and, "by the third allotment," Phoibe, who then gave it (i.e., not by a lot) to Phoibos Apollo. The "it" seems to be the physical seat, the geographical "place" of the Oracle at Delphi, and the prophetic, oracular function tied directly with Delphi. We also noted, especially regarding Euripides's *Ion*, that the order of consultation was determined by lot and that Delphi's personnel could also be selected by lot. When shifting our gaze from

---

[13] Thuc. 8.30.1. Compare the use of the lot for Roman military positioning in Polybius 6.35.11, 6.36.1 (cavalry-men doing allotted rounds), and especially Jos. *BJ* 5.510–511.

[14] Aesch. *Sept.* 55–56, trans. H. W. Smyth: κληρουμένους δ' ἔλειπον, ὡς πάλῳ λαχὼν / ἕκαστος αὐτῶν πρὸς πύλας ἄγοι λόχον.

[15] This detail appears weird to some scholars. For example, Chambers (1962) 311 states, "And why should generals, in appointing trierarchs for the fleet, not do so directly, without recourse to the lot as commanded in the decree? ... It would seem that this purported allotment is a retrojection of practices from the fourth century, when the lot was used to appoint all manner of Athenian magistrates." However, *ad hoc* selection for commanding a warship was not a magistracy, so the analogy does not work.

[16] See van Wees (2004) 307 n.25 who considers it traditional and hence plausible.

[17] See Gabrielsen ([1994] 2010) 80–83 for *epiklerosis*, randomly assigning warships to trierarchs; see also section 7.2.3 in this volume.

Delphi to the Athenian audience, we change the emphasis from drawing lots at Delphi to its mass *reception* elsewhere. As the lot oracle was prominent at Delphi and employed by Athenians, the play speaks directly within a familiar and well-established frame of reference.

Athena herself appears on the scene, proud to have received a *lachos*, a portion of the booty dedicated to her, "while I was taking possession of the land, which the leaders and chiefs of the Achaians assigned to me, a great portion of the spoil their spears had won, to be wholly mine forever, a choice gift to Theseus' sons."[18] The language is supposedly Homeric, but there is a significant difference: No tithe, *dekate* to the gods from the spoils, exists in the *Iliad* and the *Odyssey*. Moreover, although spoken of in Homeric terms, the *lachos* is not a Homeric *geras*, a singular honorary gift to the leader by the army, but a "tenth" (*dekate*), a tithe, perhaps set aside from the booty by lot. However, such a tithe would fit the framework of expectations of an Athenian audience in the fifth century (see ch. 1).

The role of the Erinyes (their *lachos*) was to punish the homicide of kin. It was "spun" for them by Moira, a common metaphor, mixing cause and result: *moira* is the cause of their having this task, but that is also their *moira*, their assigned portion of divine jobs.

> For this is the office (*lachos*) that relentless Moira spun for us to hold securely: when rash murders of kin come upon mortals, we pursue them until they go under the earth; and after death, they have no great freedom. (Aeschylus *Eumen*. 316–320; 334, trans. H. P. Smyth)

Similarly, in [Ps.] Aeschylus's *Prometheus Bound* (45–50), Hephaistos is unhappy with his job: "I wish it [his special *techne*] had fallen to another's lot (*allos ophelen lachein*)!" Despite the term *lachos*[19] we do not hear elsewhere of the Erinyes as having participated in the primordial lottery, but Hesiod tells us that some of the "old gods" (e.g., Hekate) kept their *timai* which they had received through drawing lots that had taken place earlier (*Theog.* 421–426 and ch. 1). The Erinyes have their allotted office (384; *lache*) and complain of their distance from the other gods and that they have "neither lot (*kleros*) nor portion (*moiros*)" in ritual:

> This office was ordained for us (*lache*) at birth; but the immortal gods must hold back their hands from us, nor does any of them share a feast in common with

---

[18] Aeschylus *Eumen*. 399–401 (trans. Herbert Weir Smyth).
[19] See too 715 *ou lachon*: "when that is not your allotted province."

us; and I have *neither lot nor portion (akleros, amoiros)*[20] of pure white ceremonial robes. (Aeschylus *Eumen.* 347–352, trans. H. P. Smyth)

Athenian tragedy covers much of the spectrum of the uses of the lottery. It follows Homeric conventions of distribution of booty, honors, and captured land. There is one play in particular, more than any other extant tragedy, where the drawing of lots takes center stage.

5.2 The lot and Aeschylus's *Seven against Thebes*

The sons of Oedipus fight each other because of the abuse of their inheritance agreement. Polyneikes besieges his brother, Eteokles, at Thebes with its seven gates. The sortition that allocates gates to heroes forms a significant section of the *Seven against Thebes* (*Sept.* 55–56; 126; 376; 423; 456). The messenger's speech recounts the drawing of lots at length and describes the heroes' shields. He opens with the statement

> I left them casting lots (*kleroö*) to decide how each commander, his post assigned by chance (*hos palo lachon* [*lanchano*]), would lead his regiment against the gates. (Aeschylus *Seven* 55, trans. H. P. Smyth)

In a brilliant analysis of the play, Paul Demont observes how Aeschylus uses the lot to distinguish between the political character of each brother.[21] Polyneikes, the besieging brother, is more "democratic": the lot, well-known to an Athenian democratic audience, is used to pair heroes with gates: to select which hero (there were seven) should face each of Thebes's seven gates. By contrast, the tyrannical Eteokles nominates (top-down) the counterparts.

More specific descriptions of the allocation of gates by lot follow in the play, employing words commonly used in lotteries, notably *kleros, kleroö, lanchano*, and often in combination with *palo*, such as "acquiring by lot," *palo lachontes* (126; 376; 423; 456). The lottery is practiced Aias-style by placing markers in a helmet: "his lot (*palos*) jumped out of the bronze helmet" (457–459). The messenger insists (375) that every one of the heroes participated, thus emphasizing the role of predefined lists.[22]

A significant theme of Aeschylus's *Seven against Thebes* revolves around the issue of inheritance (e.g., 727; 914). It is crucial to the plot: the two sons of

---

[20] See Sommerstein's (1989) note for this correction in the text (contra Muller's ἀπόμοιρος ἄκληρος).
[21] Demont (2000) 316 et passim.
[22] Demont (2000) 317 with reference to *Ath.Pol.* 8.1; Cf. Berman (2007) 155.

Oedipus kill each other because of conflicting claims over their partible inheritance by lot. Again, primogeniture is not an issue; the sources are contradictory about which brother was the elder.[23] The plot's framework mattered: Athenian drama mainly dealt with familiar narrative frameworks, and the story was no surprise to the audience. No tragic irony could have been possible (say, in *Oedipus Tyrannos*) if the audience shared the protagonist's ignorance. Oedipus's curse upon his sons, their duel over their inheritance, and their death at each other's hand were known to all. But were the conventions of inheritance and the values implied in them in the fifth century traditional too? The links between the mythical inheritance and familiar historical reality in *Seven* have been studied by others, convincingly concluding that Aeschylus did not invent partible inheritance; it was one realistic option known to contemporary (and earlier) Greeks.[24] Such conventions were as traditional as the common mythical frameworks (first attested in Homer), shared among all (not just Athenian) Greeks.

In *Seven*, a lottery determines which brother gets the moveable property, departs, and who stays and inherits the immoveable property (the kingship is implied). One version of the myth mentions rotation, perhaps to shift the blame from one brother to the other, but that is beside the point here.[25] Depending on the version, the two brothers agree on the inheritance's equitable portions. Eteokles allows his brother to make a choice (for Hellanikos's version, see below), or an arbiter (Jocasta, their mother) defines the equitable parts before the lottery takes place (Ares and "Iron" are metaphoric arbiters too). As it seems, once the division is decided upon, the lot then chooses which brother declares his first choice; thus, the lot is not quite "blind," pairing a brother with a specific unit of the partible inheritance, but leaves room for choice and free will. It prioritizes, arbitrarily, one brother over the next. The procedure has its historical parallels in inheritance and colonization (see ch. 4), and the play may thus serve as further evidence for the practice and, indeed, for the mindset.[26]

In a version of the myth told by the fifth-century historian Hellanikos of Lesbos, Eteokles divided the shares and asked his brother Polyneikes to choose between them.[27] That Eteokles made the primary division means the portions were considered roughly equal.[28] The practice (discussed in ch. 4 for the archaic period) is known from Athenian courts of the fourth century: brothers may agree among themselves about equitable division of their deceased father's property or employ an arbiter to make that decision before the lottery takes place. In an

---

[23] Polyneikes is older in Soph. *OC* 375; 1294; 1422, and the younger one in Eur. *Phoen.* 71.
[24] Borecký (1983); Berman (2007); Demont (2000); cf. Cameron (1970).
[25] Euripides *Phoenissae* 474–484. Polyneikes complains that his brother not only reneged on his oath but also kept his (Polyneikes's) portion of the inheritance, his *meros*. See Gantz (1993) 505–517.
[26] Cf. Berman (2007) ch. 4.
[27] *FGrH* 4 F 98.
[28] Thalmann (1978) 68.

Athenian law court, the lottery is not conducted by pairing a brother with a portion but determines order: the brother whose lot comes first makes a choice.[29] Euripides makes a similar reference. In the *Children of Herakles*, the word *kleros* also signifies the estate or the inheritance itself.[30] Herakles's sons say,

> It is said that Theseus' two sons dwell in the plain of this land, which they received *by the drawing of lots* among the descendants of Pandion. (*Children of Herakles* 34–35, trans. David Kovacs)

An inheritance may be "partible" by cutting the land in two halves and dividing up the moveable property and money. Alternatively, a brother may depart with (some of?) the moveable wealth and "his father's gold." *Seven* moves from partible inheritance determined by lot in the second sense (one stays, the other does not) to partible inheritance in the first, concrete sense: dividing up the *kleros* with both brothers staying on it. But this is a tragedy after all. At the end of the play, the brothers kill each other, and their inheritance becomes partible indeed: they finally share the same *kleros,* which happens to overlap with their metaphoric destiny and the actual tiny piece of land now "shared" between them: their grave. Its surface is tiny, but its depth is endless. The chorus is explicit:

> They hold in misery their *allotted portion* of god-given sorrows. Beneath their corpses there will be boundless wealth of earth. (*Seven* 945, trans. Herbert Weir Smyth)

In *Seven* the lot, with the verb *lanchano*, functions on various overlapping levels: it involves establishing order and turns (assigning positions in the field to heroes); dividing and assigning, mostly of inheritance; a metaphoric lot, destiny, death.

The myth is old, first alluded to in the *Iliad* and the *Thebaïs*, a lost epic.[31] In a fragment of the sixth-century poet Stesichoros of Himera, Jocasta appears as a kind of arbiter, suggesting equitable parts and the lot as the means to decide between her sons. She wants to avoid *potmos*, one's fate:

Hear, I will make a way clear out for you. / One of you, taking possession of the halls, inhabits paternal Thebes / And the other goes away, / Having the gold and all possessions of your dear father, / Whoever is chosen by lot first / By the will of the *moirai* (*klaropaledon hos an pratos lachei hekati moiran*).[32]

---

[29] Dem. 36.11; 48.13.
[30] Wilkins (1993) *ad* Heracl. 876 is unique in Euripides. Cf. Demont (2000) 313–314.
[31] Hom. *Il.* 4.378–398; cf. *Thebais* fr. 2 *PEG.* fr. 3 (Athenae 11.465e).
[32] κλαροπαληδὸν ὃς ἂν πρᾶτος λάχηι ἕκατι Μοιρᾶν, trans. Berman (2007) 154.

The word *klaropaledon*, "chosen by lot," is unique in extant Greek,[33] but its lot meaning is clear, especially in combination with the verb *lanchano*. But what are the *moirai* doing here? Do they direct the result? Thalmann claims that "the phrase *hekati moiran* strongly supports the argument "that allotment was not considered random but was associated with fate or destiny."[34] This articulation is evasive, however, since "associated" is too open-ended to be meaningful. An ancient Greek would not have conceived of anything *not* associated somehow with the gods. Do the *moirai* direct the decision, or is the lottery considered a ritual merely under their aegis, just by their being *Déesses du partage, du lot* (as we noted with the *moira* Lachesis (cf. ch. 2.9)[35]

Alternatively, the translation could be more literal: "Whoever is chosen by lot first / for the sake of the portions (*moirai*)." In the *Homeric Hymn to Hermes*, the young god divided the sacrificial meat into twelve *moirai*, "portions." Moreover, in Jocasta's speech, the Greek for "chosen by lot, *klaropaledon*," appears nowhere else (a *hapax*) ; however, with Hermes we also encounter "the *moirai* = portions chosen by lot (*kleropaleis*)."[36] In the *Homeric Hymn* the literal meaning of *moirai* as "portions" is straightforward and uncontroversial. Why not here too? Jocasta does not turn to "the *moirai*" as goddesses who regulate (or determine) the lot. They are not even alluded to here. What she says is conventional: the lot chooses which brother will be the first to declare which of the two "portions" of the inheritance he prefers (Thebes and the kingship or the gold and moveable property). This interpretation of *moirai* conforms better with Athenian practices of inheritance, where brothers agree in advance, amicably or through an arbitrator, on what are equitable portions and then hold a lottery to see who is the first chosen to declare his preferred portion.

The curse of Oedipus was too powerful, and the sortition/arbitration went horribly wrong. The curse prevented his sons from indeed dividing up their inheritance. Instead of a peaceful division, they will fight each other (with iron).

> (*Seven Against Thebes* 785) Next he [Oedipus] launched brutal, wrathful words against the sons he had bred—ah! curses from a bitter tongue—that wielding iron in their hands they would one day divide his property. (*dia . . . lanchano*)

The keyword, *dialanchano*, means literally "divide by casting lots," says Thalmann, "... thus the wording of the curse apparently implies that the brothers normally *would be expected to cast lots peacefully* to divide the possessions they

---

[33] Berman (2007) 155.
[34] Thalmann (1978) 386.
[35] Chantraine (1968-80) s.v. μείρομαι; Beekes (2010) 922–923 s.v. μείρομαι.
[36] *Homeric Hymn to Hermes* 4.129.

inherit, but that they are doomed instead to share their patrimony by hostile means." . . . "The brothers do, in fact, share their inheritance by the sword."[37] This is repeated in Euripides's *Phoenician Women*: Oedipus, imprisoned by his sons, keeps cursing them:

> (68) Afflicted by his fate, he makes the most unholy curses against his sons, praying that they may divide (*dialanchano*) this house with a sharp sword. (Trans. E. P. Coleridge)

In the *Seven*, the Messenger, then the chorus, is explicit:

> (815–817) Yes, so all too equal was their destiny to them both. . . . The leaders, the two generals, have divided the whole of their property (*dialanchano*) with hammered Scythian steel. They will possess only that land they take in burial, swept away as they were following their father's curses.
>
> (906–910) In their haste to anger they apportioned their property (*moirao*) so that each has an equal share (*host' ison lachein*) (*lanchano*).

"Apportioning" (*moirao*) and "having an equal share" express the overlap between the notions of "portion" and "fate."[38] All the keywords—*moirao* (*moira*), *lanchano*, *isos*—point to the terminology of partible inheritance, done by lot, the result of which is supposed to be "equality," or rather, in practice, "equitability" (*isos*).[39] The guiding *value* is equality: interchangeability of brothers (no *a priori* hierarchy among them), the equal chance before the lot, and the equitable portions of the inheritance.

When brothers disagree about what constitutes equitable parts, an arbitrator may decide. This was formalized in classical Athens, where one of the archons was responsible for lawsuits concerning the inheritance of *epikleroi* and orphans.[40] We noted the way Plutarch, quoting Plato, recommends having an arbitrator in the form of a friendly witness:

> Let them preferably assemble alone by themselves; otherwise, let there be present some common friend as a witness equally friendly to both, and then "by the lots of Justice," as Plato says (*Critias* 109b6), let them, as they give and take what is suitable to each and preferred by each.[41]

---

[37] Thalmann (1978) 62.
[38] Thalmann (1978) 70.
[39] Ostwald (1996) 53 ; LSJ, s.v. ἴσος.
[40] *Ath.Pol.* 56.6; Dem. 43.75.
[41] Plut. *On Brotherly Love* 11 (483d), trans. W. C. Helmbold. The reference is to Plato *Crit.* 109b.

In the *Seven*, the arbitrator is the one who divides and distributes, *datetes*. That is another word related to *dateomai*, denoting a distribution by—and among—a predefined group.[42] He is also a *diallakter*, a political term for a mediator or arbitrator (908). A loose image of the god Ares as arbiter appears (414, cf. 906-908, 943-944); "Ares will decide the result with dice" may allude to what such persons usually did: conducting the lottery.

The figure of Ares moves between the metaphoric and the concrete. Representing strife and war, "Ruthless, too, was Ares, the cruel divider (*datetes*) of their property, who made their father's curses come true" (940-944). By this point in the play, it is no longer clear who the "arbiter" is since the poetry takes over. Just preceding the word "iron" is the arbiter who "resolved" the fight between the brothers: Chorus: [940] "Ruthless is that which resolved their strife, the stranger from across the sea, sharpened iron rushed from the fire." So "iron" becomes the bitter arbiter:

> Chorus: A stranger (*apoikos*) distributes their inheritance, a Chalybian immigrant from Scythia, a bitter divider of wealth, savage-hearted iron that *apportions land by lot* [the verb is *diapallo*] for them to dwell in, as much as they can occupy in death when they have lost their share (*amoiros*) in these wide plains. (728-732; trans. H. W. Smyth adapted)[43]

Being an *amoiros* (cf. *moira*), having no "portion," is yet again related to practices of land distribution that we observe in colonization, where the same criteria and practices were operating. Perhaps it is not by chance that Aeschylus chose the word for a "colonist," *apoikos*, in its rarer and narrower meaning of "stranger, away from home."

The advantage of the present study is that it provides a broad context for drawing lots in the Greek experience. When we observe the widely applied, consistent vocabulary and terminology of lotteries and distribution, we may better understand specific cases and have more confidence in the meaning of lottery-related words, such as *lachos* or *kleros*, which otherwise might have been understood differently.[44] We observed, for example, a remarkable similarity between the status of sons in partible inheritance and that of Greek colonists and land distribution (ch. 4.4). So we now have a context of plausibility: we have an ancient mythical framework revolving around inheritance and conforming to traditional norms and actual practices. There is no anachronism here since the same concepts, values, terms, and practices concerning the lot seem consistent

---

[42] Cf. ll. 711, 729 with Thalmann (1978) 75.
[43] Demont (2000) 322 rightly says that the use of *diapallo* should leave no doubt as to the implication of the lot.
[44] See Appendix.

from Homer (eighth century) to Isaeus and Demosthenes. The values expressed or implied are precisely the same values that seem to guide the parcellation and distribution of land among Greek colonists: no *a priori* hierarchy, equality before the lot that selects the settlers, equality before the lot for land distribution, and finally, equal-size portions of land distributed to all.

6
Founding Cities and Sharing in the *Polis*: Equality, Allotment, and Civic Mixture

6.1 Introduction

The distributive drawing of lots is a device; it is not a value in and of itself. The values of equality of chance and, when possible, equality of results are typical of Greek distributive lotteries, the purpose of which is the distribution of equal or equitable portions to each member of the predefined group. Distributive lotteries are a "subset" of communal "distribution," and no lotteries were used on the rare occasions when portions were of precise, equal value, such as "ten drachmas" for each citizen. Occasions for precise distributions without the mediation of drawing lots were rare, since aside from gold, silver, or coin, most "goods" in the archaic period—such as portions of booty, meat, or inheritance—did not have a precise, "fiscal" value. Therefore, although a subset of the general category of communal distributions, distributive lotteries, used for equity and equality, were much more common than distributions of portions of an exact value when drawing lots was unnecessary.

A few cases of exact equivalence illustrate how distributive lotteries expressed an egalitarian mindset and set of practices. The Phokaians considered the revenue from the silver mines in Spain as belonging to all the Phokaians, not specifically to those who met King Arganthonios in Spain. They used it to build a massive defensive wall against the Persian threat. They also tried, *as a collective*, to buy the islands of Oinoussai, which indicates a mindset of collective ownership. That was similar to what we shall see at the "communist" pirate community Lipara, whose members rotated, dividing up spoils and possessing *kleroi*.[1]

Herodotus tells of someone called Kolaios from the island of Samos, who, in the mid-seventh century, was a captain-trader of a ship that reached the silver mines of Spain and struck it rich. In gratitude, "the Samians" (not Kolaios personally) dedicated a tithe to Hera, their primary goddess. The transition from the private Kolaios to the entire political community, "the Samians," is remarkable and testifies, yet from another angle, to the practice of egalitarian (here actually

---

[1] Hdt 1.163.

equal) communal sharing. It indicates that the gain belonged to all without special mention of the captain.[2]

The attested, comprehensive community distributions in the archaic period indicate a strong sense of membership on equal footing in the community. All members deserve individual portions. When possible, with exact sums, they get them; when not, the community draws lots so that each portion is equal (*isos*) or at least "like" the next portion (*homoios*). I discuss the recurrent formula *isos kai homoios*, "equal and like," further below (6.3.9).

About a century later (mid-sixth century), the gold and silver mines at the island of Siphnos enriched the entire island community: "The Siphnians" (a term denoting the state) invested in decorating their agora and their prytaneion with Parian marble and dedicated a *dekate* (tithe) in the form of a treasury at Delphi. In addition, the Siphnians "divided among themselves each year's income."[3] Similarly, some fifty years later, a rich vein of silver was discovered at the mines of Laurion in Attica. It was proposed to share the income among all Athenian citizens *individually* (ten drachmas per citizen):[4] "When each man was to receive ten *drachmai* for his share, Themistocles persuaded the Athenians to make no such division but to use the money to build two hundred ships for the war."[5] Although the Athenians voted for building a navy, the proposal still reveals the conventional expectations about the comprehensive nature of the community and "sharing in the city" in a concrete sense of getting individual portions.

Therefore, the distribution of *kleroi* in Greek colonies is a subset of a Greek mode of collective distribution. When asking about the equal distribution of lots of land in Greek colonies, the question should not be viewed in isolation. "Equal distribution," whether by drawing lots or not, was a ubiquitous Greek practice, relevant to a broad spectrum of issues and sharing the same vocabulary. In short, land distribution in newly founded *poleis* is not primarily a question of distributing "land and property" but of egalitarian "distribution" *tout court*.[6]

---

[2] Bravo (1984) 115–119. Sally Humphreys (1978) 168 suggests that "the Samians" refers to the ship's crew, but the expensive *dekate* at the Samian Heraion seems to have been a state affair, as Herodotus implies. Note that Herodotus (4.152) frames the story about "the Samians" within the foundation story of Cyrene and concludes, "What the Samians had done was the beginning of a close friendship between them and the men of Cyrene and Thera." In other words, I doubt he had changed the meaning of the subject in mid paragraph; it is "the Samians" throughout.

[3] Hdt. 3.57. Herodotus says, "At this time the marketplace and town-hall of Siphnos were adorned with Parian marble," which I see as implying communal expenditure from those public revenues.

[4] Hdt. 7.144; as in the case of Siphnos, the verb is *dianemo*; cf. *Ath.Pol.* 22.7; Plut. *Them.* 4; Nepos *Themistocles* 2.2. Cf. the equal distribution of Egyptian wheat: Schol. Aristoph. *Vespae* 718a–b; Philochoros *FGrHist* 328 F 119.

[5] Hdt. 7.144.

[6] Generally, there seems to be a terminological confusion between "distribution" and "redistribution." It could be argued that any distribution is, by definition, a redistribution. Asheri (1963) notes that sometimes a distinction can be made between *dasmos* (distribution) and *anadasmos*

Comprehensive distributions imply a well-defined "community." Outsiders do not merit shares. The size may vary from the tiny group of brothers sharing an inheritance, a cult community sharing by lot equal portions of sacrificial meat, a Homeric army sharing booty by lot, or a group of colonists sharing equal lots (portions) of land. How did archaic Greek colonists do that? By drawing lots, I suggest. The question is significant: colonization is a huge phenomenon, responsible for the foundation of about one-third of all Greek *poleis* in the archaic period. We have no explicit, contemporary evidence to explain the equal size of plots of land archaeologists have exposed in some early colonies (eighth-century and seventh-century). Yet we observe precisely the same pattern of equal plots of land at the other end of our chronological spectrum in the fourth century, but this time we have explicit words about their being equal and distributed by lot to the settlers. Moreover, various sources—philosophical, historical, quasihistorical, mythical, and poetic—address the issue and consistently support the notion of equal plots of land distributed by lot, never suggesting alternative modes. However, they too mostly date to the classical period and later. To what extent may we assume consistency of mindset and practice reaching back to the early archaic period?

We have concrete evidence on the ground for equal parcellation of plots of land in eighth- and seventh-century settlements about which our meager and lacunose sources are silent. However, once we acknowledge the egalitarian mindset and the practice of communal distribution by drawing lots in other areas, as we have seen in previous chapters, we can become more confident that communities of new settlers did the same.

Our sources are varied, and many are quasihistorical, that is, concocting stories as if presenting an actual historical account while following conventions of real historical writing. Such would be, for example, the story about the invasion of the Herakleidai and the Dorians into the Peloponnese and the distribution by lot of the Peloponnese among the victors. The foundation of the Spartan regime is also told in terms of nine thousand equal plots of land distributed to nine thousand Spartiates, thus forming the body of the Spartan *homoioi*, the "equals" or "peers." Such quasihistorical stories tell us a lot about Greek conventions and the Greek horizon of expectations. Not surprisingly, they are all consistent.

Never does any ancient source of whatever genre imagine any alternative distribution manner. What people do not care to invent is just as important as what they do: it tells us much about their mindset and norms. The entire spectrum of

---

(redistribution) but acknowledges that Greeks often used *anadasmos* for both. As Lucia Cecchet illustrates in a dedicated study of *ges anadasmos* (2009), the term applies both to an initial "colonial" situation ("distribution") and to social and political demands for "redistribution." In the classical period, the demand for *ges anadasmos* often overlapped with a demand for the cancellation of debts, but that need not have been the case earlier.

sources, from poetic fancies to foundation inscriptions, follows the basic scheme of a founder presiding over the distribution by lot of equal plots of land to the settlers of the first generation. Those had a special status as "First Lots" (*protoi kleroi*) and constituted the minimum token of sharing in the new *polis*. We do not always get all the elements in a single account, but they often complement each other.

The exceptional status of a Greek colony's founder (*oikistes, ktistes*) also testifies to an egalitarian mindset and its application. The sources are unanimous about the unique, heroic cult of the founder after his death: he would be exceptionally buried in the agora and receive cult as a hero. There is even some archaeological support for the existence of such cults. A founder's supreme, incomparable authority thus expresses another aspect of egalitarianism. His position was unique and *ad hoc*. His status was not passed on to his descendants (except Cyrene and some Sicilian tyrants), and his hero's cult elevated him to a level no one else could claim. The heroization of a founder would have emphasized the equality of status of everyone else in reference to him.[7]

As we shall observe, there is no indication of any exceptional estates among the equal First Lots. I shall argue that colonists of the first generation were mostly equal and that social and economic differentiation and the emergence of elites are mostly observable after the second or third generation postfoundation.[8]

Egalitarianism and equality are not synonyms. Greek colonists did not have a communistic vision of a society where all property should be equal. Nor was egalitarianism an "ideology": the equality of the First Lots was the lower limit, the minimum holding for a new household (*oikos*) to be set up on the new *kleros* (= plot of land), received through the lot (*kleros*, yet again). Settlers were free to bring individual wealth and equipment (*chremata*), and there was no limit on further expansion, annexation, or personal purchase of more lands. Yet the initial equal plotting of the land and the distribution of individual *kleroi* expressed a powerful egalitarian, social, and economic vector of archaic Greek society.

Our sources are varied and include inscriptions containing the texts of "foundation decrees" of new settlements. Public decrees about founding a new colony were made in the mother city and are an excellent source for how Greeks imagined an unrealized settlement's future. Foundation decrees do not describe reality but *prescribe* it in terms of "equal and fair terms (*isos kai homoios*)," expressed in land distribution by lot and even in terms of selecting the colonists by lot at the mother city. Foundation decrees illustrate a mindset and accepted conventions. The extent of realization probably depended on *ad hoc* circumstances, and one

---

[7] Malkin (1987a) Part II. Cf. Lane (2012).
[8] See the discussion of social classes, status, and wealth in de Angelis (2016) 146–173, esp. 158. See further below.

should be very careful before pointing out archaeological "contradictions" with specific stipulations in foundation decrees. We have, for example, an Athenian foundation decree for a colony at Brea, but we know nothing of what happened later. Intentions reveal a mindset, yet they can never be observed archaeologically when they remain unrealized.

Why invest an effort in interpreting Greek conventions of how to found a colony? Historians must recognize that historical phenomenon as enormous by any standard. It applies to some 30 percent of all Greek city-states, a total of 1,035 *poleis*, founded before ca. 323 and stretching from the western Mediterranean to the Black Sea.[9] Regardless of local particularities, all of them faced the issue of allotting plots of land to the settlers. I argue that the most probable inference from archaeology and written texts is that most Greeks accepted, applied, and practiced the egalitarian notion of equal distribution of portions of land by lot. It was a Small-World phenomenon since both the conventions and the practices of distributive lotteries are observable throughout the Greek world. A line of continuity, I maintain, may be drawn between Megara Hyblaia in the eighth century and Black Corcyra in the fourth.

The equal portions of land we observe are the earliest, most concrete expression of equality and sharing accessible to historians of the archaic period. The First Lots in colonies were not an isolated practice but were contemporary and compatible with other attested methods, especially those of partible inheritance by lot; the two were linked and overlapped. The equal shares of land we have observed in the practice of partible inheritance-by-lot match the *contemporary* equal shares of land in the foundation of new colonies.[10]

When two brothers were sharing, equally and by lot, an entire inheritance, they were doing on a family scale what Greek colonists, sometimes probably the actual brothers of those left behind to inherit, were doing on a community scale. Both would wish for an independent *oikos*: the term *apoikia*, "colony," connotes the *oikos*. A Greek colony was called, explicitly, an *ap-oikia* (a home away from home), and its founder was an *oikistes*: "a founder of a home (*oikos*)."[11] In terms

[9] Hansen (1999) 84. Cf. Malkin (1994b).
[10] Matthew Fitzjohn (2007) casts doubt on colonial equality: first, equally sized plots of land are not, in fact, equal in value or access, he says. However, as I argue here, that is the point: forced equality in formal (size) outcomes, but not in value. Second, if the land was forcefully taken from non-Greeks, then "equality was born of inequality and oppression" (followed by a qualification. "In reality, this is an oversimplification" (Fitzjohn [2007] 219). However, that is moralizing and speaks of equality in the modern sense as a *universal* value, and hence anachronistic. The settlers living in the eighth century were probably alien to this thinking. See further discussion in Malkin (2017a).
[11] Alternatively, a colony would be a *ktisma* and its founder a *ktistes*. A common mistake is to claim that the term "colonization" is inappropriate and anachronistic when applied to ancient Greek migration and the foundation of new *poleis*. However, a glance at the vocabulary of Greek colonization is enough to refute what had become an entrenched notion. Greek colonization had not one but *two* sets of vocabularies: the one stressing the departure (*apoikia, oikeo-oikizo*-related) and the other stressing possessing and tilling the land (*ktizo*-related). This second set of colonization vocabulary stresses not the origins but the working and cultivation of the (newly acquired) land. It carries

of modes of distribution (equality before the lot) and equal outcomes (equal or equitable plots of land), there is not much difference. Partible inheritance by lot could be understood as a "fractal" of partible territory by lot in Greek colonies.

How could a territory be defined as such, ready for parcellation and distribution to settlers? Unlike inheritance, the new land supposedly belonged to nobody: it was "empty land," *eremos chora*. Upon taking possession of a colonial site, it was as if the initial territory was one "whole" to be divided among the settlers, precisely like the division between brothers in partible inheritance by lot, and very close to practices of dividing up and distributing booty. The *hetairoi* of the founder were like "brothers" dividing up the initial territory into equal parts and then distributing them by lot,[12] or like soldiers similarly dividing up booty; conquered land was immovable booty.

What made it possible to perceive the land for settlement in terms of demarcated "territory" available for equal parcellation and redistribution was that it was perceived as "empty." For example, according to the commonly accepted historical myth, when the Dorians conquered the Peloponnese, they treated it as empty: "The Dorians had this further advantage, that they were free from all dread of giving offense so that they could divide up their land without dispute."[13] Settling an empty land (*eremos chora*) is a familiar *topos* of colonization and foundations throughout history.[14] For example, the foundation story of the medieval monastery at Fulda, east of the Rhine, was told in terms of arrival in a "desert." In reality, it had been inhabited previously.[15] Ancient Greek paradoxographic writings, like modern utopias, prefer islands that sometimes afford true emptiness.[16] Such is the "land-good-to-settle" (an empty goat island) that faced the land of the Cyclopes in the ninth book of the *Odyssey*. Names can be significant for perceived emptiness: Thera was an island of "wild animals," or "hunting island," Pithekoussai was "monkey island," Arktouronesos "bear island," Ophioussa, "snake island," and so on.[17]

The perception of land as empty likely contributed to the egalitarianism within the group of settlers. The (modern) Latin equivalent, *terra nullius*, stresses

---

the same semantic range as *colere* in Latin; in that sense, a *ktisma* is close to the Latin meaning of *colonia*. See Casevitz (1985). Finally, Greeks commonly translated the Latin term *colonia* as *apoikia*. See Costanzi (2020).

[12] Interestingly, in Biblical Hebrew the expression "to inherit the land" (לרשת את הארץ) means "to conquer" it (and, similarly to ancient Greeks, divide it up by lot). See Londblom (1962) now with Bar-On (2020).
[13] Plato *Laws* 684d.
[14] Moggi (1983); cf. Malkin (1994a) 96–97 on "empty islands." For the idea of *eremos chora* as a "reset," see Diod. 16.82.5; cf. Nepos *Timoleon* 3.1–2.504; Plut. *Tim*. 23.6–7; Plato *Laws* 684d–e, 736c–d.
[15] Algazi (2005); von Nahmer (1972); cf. Le Goff (1988).
[16] Cf. Gabba (1981); cf. Lombardo (2012).
[17] On "place-names and attitudes," see Malkin (1994a) 95–98.

people and the lack of property rights, "nobody's land." By contrast, the Greek term *eremos chora* disregards people altogether, raising a mental image of empty space. However, more often than not, emptiness is in the eyes of the beholder. The founders of Syracuse (733) certainly knew there had been inhabitants on the conquered islet of Ortygia. They were the ones to make it empty and leveled to the ground its previous oval-shaped buildings to impose their regular plan on the site.[18] This vision and practice, namely, seeing a territory as "blank" and available for redistribution *ex novo*, is highly significant for many points throughout Greek history, especially when revolutionary calls for redistribution were framed in terms of a return to an original "blank" state and equal sharing of plots of land.

6.2 Section I: Things done

6.2.1 The setting: Greek colonization

When the Greeks founded new settlements, they faced the question of how to distribute plots of land to individual settlers. The scale of new foundations is astonishing (Figure 6.1): "From the River Phasis (Georgia in the eastern Black Sea) to the Pillars of Herakles (Gibraltar)."[19] There was no central direction, and settlers came from numerous mother cities. Soon some of the cities they were founding became mother cities themselves. Although the Greeks joining new settlements were of varied sub-ethnicities and local traditions, their guidelines and conventions seem similar, especially when settling and allocating land. When explicitly articulated, the general scheme is consistent from Homer (eighth century) through Plato and Aristotle (fourth century), down to Diodorus (first century CE): The founders would treat the new territory as *eremos chora* (empty land); they would carve out a section of the newly acquired territory and divide that section into private, public, and sacred areas.[20]

Most Greek foundations were just that, Greek. It was a reciprocal process since colonization, as such, contributed to Hellenic self-awareness.[21] "All the Greeks," or *ho boulomenos*, "whoever wishes" (provided he was a Greek), could join a nucleus of founders or an existing settlement.[22] For example, at the Spartan colony

---

[18] Cf. ch. 6.2.7. Thuc. 6.3; Voza (1999) 93; Fischer-Hansen (1996) 334–336.

[19] Plato (*Phaido* 109a–b) regards the Black Sea and the Mediterranean as a single sea. On mobility and colonization see also Morel (1983); Bernstein (2004); Capdetrey and Zurbach (2012); Mauersberg (2019); d'Ercole (2012).

[20] The following passages present some general points about Greek colonization, some of which are disputed. See Morris (1997); de Angelis (2020); Tsetskhladze (2006–20008); cf. Stazio and Ceccoli (2001).

[21] Malkin (2011). See Malkin (2017a). On "hybridity" in Greek colonization, Malkin (2017b).

[22] On the notion of "foundation," see Malkin (2009).

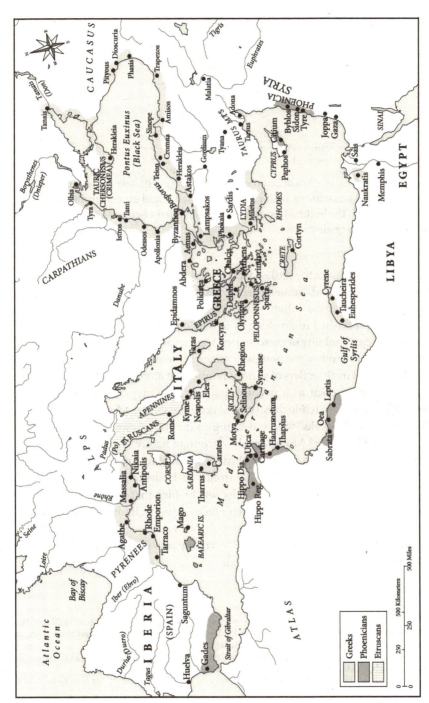

Map 6.1 Map: Greeks, Phoenicians, and Etruscans in the Mediterranean (from Malkin 2011).

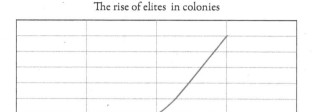

Figure 6.1 The rise of elites in colonies, a schematic graph: Relative equality in the first and second generations, with a sharp rise in social and economic differentiation toward the third. The bottom line illustrates the number of generations. The curving line marks the inequality rate.

of Herakleia Trachinia the settlers were *perioikoi* and *anyone who wanted* except Ionians, Achaians, and "some other people."[23] When the Corinthians planned a colony for Epidamnos, they "gladly sent the desired aid to Epidamnos, inviting whoever wished to go along as settlers on equal and fair terms."[24] There was a significant mobility of mercenaries, traders, artisans, and so on, who could join too.[25] Aside from some non-*polis* mixed settlements, the mixture occurred mainly among Greek settlers of various origins, not among Greeks and "natives." The point is as explicit as it is consistent in various types of accounts and is attested as early as Archilochos (mid-seventh century), who complained that "the misery of all-Greeks" was converging on the colony of which his father was the founder (Thasos).[26] Moreover, the corporate nature of Greek religion and society encouraged the exclusion of those not belonging to the corpus. Although the gods were ubiquitous, cult, aside from pan-Hellenic sanctuaries, was usually exclusively communal. Greek cults set the idea that the size of the social body—an *oikos*, a phratry, a *genos*, even a *polis*—must be limited, unlike imperial societies in the ancient Near East.

Founding a city was a sacred act:[27] A colony was prophesied by the Oracle of Delphi, which also named the founder and specified the place of settlement.

---

[23] Thuc. 3.92.5.
[24] For calling on "anyone [Greek] who wished" to join a colony, cf. Thuc. 1.27.1: "The Corinthians . . . gladly sent the desired aid to Epidamnos, inviting whoever wished to go along as settlers on equal and fair terms" . Cf. Malkin (2017a) and Hall (2004).
[25] Plato *Laws* 8.847e–848c, referred to by Gras, Tréziny and Broise (2004) 577. See also Giangiulio (1996); Luraghi (2006); Purcell (1990); Antonaccio (2007); Figueira (2008) 484.
[26] Archilochos 102 (Gerber). For Thasos, see Graham (1978); Owen (2003). For Greeks in general joining nuclei of colonists see Malkin (2017a).
[27] Cf. Scully (1990).

The first order of foundation was to set up a community of cult and a "covenant" with the gods.[28] The gods, especially those who "hold (*echein*) the *polis*," such as Athena Poliouchos, needed to accompany the colonists and settle down with them. The foundation probably involved rituals (the land lottery was probably among them), and we have evidence that sometimes the founders were accompanied by seers (*manteis*).[29] Greek cult required a sacred precinct and an altar (temple buildings were an addition), and the gods were provided with sectioned-off areas. A founder would also section off a public space (an agora), reserve space for roads, and, most significant for us, divide up the agricultural land into supposedly equal plots named *kleroi*, literally, "lots," or "plots assigned by lot,"[30] while reserving more land for future parcellation and distribution. As we shall see, the lots were considered "First Lots" (*protoi kleroi*), and were supposed to be kept inalienable. The distinctive status of the First Lots, forming an integral part of the sacred foundation acts, may explain why Plato regarded such *kleroi* as "divine."[31] Colonists were expecting to "sail on equal and like/fair terms" (*isos kai homoios*) with each expecting an equal *kleros* at the end of the voyage. After all, being "a man with no *kleros*" (*akleros*) is the lowest social position, according to Achilles (*Od.* 11.490), or in the parallel world of the gods, Helios was not to remain *aklaroton*, "*kleros*-less."[32]

How would a group of settlers cohere into a *polis*? A founder needed to establish (*tithemi*) the *nomima* of the new community, those markers of collective identity (e.g., the number and names of tribes, *polis* magistracies, and institutions), expressly acknowledged as such by ancient authors.[33] Sets of *nomima* were probably "transferred" from the mother city and then accepted by *all* settlers, both the organized nucleus and the other colonists, and created a more cohesive collective identity. Greeks needed their gods and goddesses, and a single sacred calendar (an essential part of *nomima*) to celebrate them was de rigeur. It was through *nomima* that settlers who joined the organized nucleus integrated into the new community, and after one generation, all would become, say, "Chalkidian colonists."

After ca. 500, Greek colonization continued through the classical period, retaining many of the older, archaic patterns and conventions (but not always the

---

[28] Blok (2018) 88 illustrates this with the opening lines of the foundation decree of Naupaktos (ca. 500). See below
[29] See Malkin (1987a) chs. 1–4 for discussion of the role of religion in colonization. Aside from Delphi, other oracles were probably involved (Apollo's at Didyma), but we lack sufficient information.
[30] For the various other elements in a territory, see Endnote 3.
[31] Plato *Laws* 741b5.
[32] Pind. *Ol.* 7.58 and see ch. 1.
[33] See my discussion in Malkin (2011) ch. 6. See also Hanell (1934); Jones (1987); Knoepfler (1989); Antonetti (1997); Hadzis, C. (1995); Trümpy (1997); Quantin (2011); Robu (2014); see also Martin (1987); Jones (1975); (1987). The field of *nomima* is still open for further study. Note especially Thuc. 6.3–5 and 7.57.2.

purpose). Continuities with the archaic period and some significant deviations are apparent.[34] Some continuities are evident through Hellenistic colonization but now with some important differences. Toward the end of the fourth century, beginning with Alexander the Great, colonies were now mostly *katoikiai*, established *within* already-controlled territories; the implied "from" in *ap-oikiai*, stressing identity in relation to a mother city, has disappeared, as did the specific mother cities. Hellenistic colonies were often mixed veteran colonies, founded "from above" by monarchs within already-controlled territories, and I do not discuss them here.[35]

Continuities between archaic and classical periods are important, as they allow us to put more faith in some of our sources regarding practices and conventions that appear traditional. It also helps to understand that expressions of equality were not a fifth-century invention but had a long history before that. Open-ended horizons for settlement encouraged egalitarianism. Unlike modern colonialism, no empire directed the archaic colonization, the mother cities were numerous, and most new settlements acquired the form of the city-state. In their turn, many *apoikiai* also became mother cities. Traditions about the new foundations (some based on fact, some fictitious) all emphasize the existence of a "mother city," thus distinguishing "colonization" from traditions about the earlier Ionian and Dorian mass migrations, which were perceived as *exodus*. However, the preferred sites for occupation seem consistent in both the early Iron Age (the "Dark Ages") and archaic periods: mostly offshore islands and headlands, demonstrating the maritime perspective, "from ship to shore," that most Greeks shared. These could serve as temporary or permanent pirate havens or settlements with naval advantages.

In contrast to Hellenistic colonies, the earlier classical colonization shares significant commonalities with the earlier archaic colonization. Gabriel Zuchtriegel's study of classical colonization demonstrates that not only did it exist but it also did so on a significant scale with apparent continuities of conventions and practices.[36] Colonization continued throughout the fifth and fourth centuries, and the number of new colonies in the helpful list he produces is impressive and convincing (for example, between ca. 470 and 430, seventeen new colonies were founded).[37] Yet there are also some significant differences: some classical

---

[34] See the excellent observations of Zuchtriegel (2018). Cf. Cargill (1995); Figueira (2008). Robin Osborne (1998) suggests that stories about archaic foundations are anachronistically dependent on what he calls the "Classical model." *Contra*: Greco and Lombardo (2012); Malkin (2002; 2003; 2009; 2016). However, deviations (e.g., the founder no longer staying in a colony) were considered as such and were regarded as aberrations precisely in the classical period. In fact, there never was a classical "model" of founding colonies distinct from an archaic one.

[35] Cohen (1995; 2006; 2013).

[36] Zuchtriegel (2018). As his main subject is not continuity but subaltern populations in colonies, Zuchtriegel places caveats about what we actually know but substantiates, explicitly, such continuities.

[37] Zuchtriegel (2018) 34–45.

colonies were settled with a clear strategic purpose on the part of the mother city, such as Herakleia Trachinia and Herakleia Lucania, founded by Sparta and Taras (in 426/5 and 432/1), respectively.

There was also a shift in focus and collective identity: the three founders of the Spartan colony Herakleia Trachinia (Leon, Alkidas, and Damagon) remained "Spartans" (they did not become Herakleian) and left their foundation, as did Hagnon, the Athenian founder of Amphipolis. These were all deviations from earlier conventions; the citizens of Amphipolis were furious at the Athenian Hagnon, who did not respect his foundation sufficiently to remain and die there as expected. They chose the Spartan Brasidas as an alternative founder, buried him in the agora, and accorded him annual heroic honors, as had been the general Greek custom.[38] Because of such deviations, classical-era colonies—such as Herakleia Lucana, Amphipolis, Thourioi, Athenian klerouchies, or colonies founded by Sicilian tyrants—could not possibly have constituted a historiographical model for reprojection onto a colonial past.

The foundational actions of some Sicilian tyrants in the fifth and fourth centuries illustrate the personal ambition of tyrants to be acknowledged as "founders" *à l'ancienne* (!). Their practices of founding colonies kept some archaic patterns (such as the allotment of *kleroi*) while widely deviating from earlier practices in terms of the purpose and composition of settlers.[39] In general, the scale could be massive and sometimes (not only with tyrants) involved entire communities that had become refugees, such as those of Katane and Kamarina or Melos and Delos (due to Athenian imperialism).[40] Both Athenian-organized colonies (such as Thourioi and Amphipolis, both mixed),[41] and those of the Sicilian tyrants involved thousands of people, not just a few hundreds. It was not only done by Greeks: for example, at Adramyttion in Asia Minor (southern Troas), the Persian Pharnakes settled Delian refugees and others at the Tauric Chersonese.[42]

As often, abuse and exceptional cases reveal the norm. When the Sicilian tyrant Dionysios "reshuffled" the state of Syracuse in 397,

> Dionysios picked out the best of the territory of Syracuse and distributed it in gifts to his friends as well as to higher officers, and *divided the rest of it in equal portions (ep' ises)* both to aliens and to citizens, including under the name of

---

[38] Thuc. 5.11.1; Malkin (1987a) 228–232; cf. Mari (2010).
[39] Jacquemin (1993) elaborates on the tension between western colonies' egalitarian character and the tyrants' supreme role. Cf. Vattuone (1994).
[40] See Figueira (2018) 486.
[41] Zuchtriegel (2018) 21 with Hdt. 7.114; Thuc. 4.102–108; Diod. 12.32; 12.68. Cf. Herakleia Lucana: Diod. 12.36.4.
[42] Thuc. 5.1; 5.32.1; 8.108.4; Diod. 12.73.1; Ps. Scymn. 822–830. See Carter (2003) 22; Zuchtriegel (2018) 27.

citizens the manumitted slaves whom he designated as New Citizens. (Diod. 14.7.4, trans. C. H. Oldfather)

Reserving the best lands for himself and his retainers is certainly abuse and a tyrannical exception. The scandal of manumitted slaves as new citizens is probably why we even hear about this.[43] However, founding a city with equal lots for all new citizens (they become citizens by owning those lots) addresses the norm. Pericles's reaction after the fall of the tyrant at Sinope in the Black Sea illustrates the point:[44]

Pericles got a bill passed providing that six hundred volunteers of the Athenians should sail to Sinope and settle down there with the Sinopians, dividing up among themselves (*nemo*) the houses and lands which the tyrant and his followers had formerly occupied. (Trans. B. Perrin).

6.2.2 Equal chances and equal outcomes: Kleros, inheritance, and colonization

Scholars tend to discuss distribution within separate categories: inheritance may be a juridical or a "property" issue; sacrificial meat is "religion"; the booty is "warfare"; lands distributed to settlers—a matter for historians and archaeologists of Greek colonization. Let me reiterate: all these were contemporary matters, approached with the same mindset and vocabulary of drawing lots. Inheritance is an especially close issue: around 660, upon coming of age, two brothers growing up on the island of Thera probably knew what to expect upon their father's death. They would be dividing and distributing the family estate (their *kleros*) by lot (*kleros*), with each one getting roughly an equitable half (see ch. 4). But halving properties had its apparent limits. Having a viable *kleros* was not just a private matter: Greek communities, as we shall see, would want a critical mass of sustainable households supporting a corps of fighting men.

The limiting factor of partible inheritance was probably one reason for encouraging young men to leave home. There were others: years with little rainfall,

---

[43] The Sicilian tyrants aimed at mixture on a grand scale. For example, in 480, Gelon captured Himera and sent new settlers "both Dorians and others who so wished" (Diod. 11.49.3). Hieron abolished Katane, became a founder of Aitna (thus celebrated by Pindar), and settled it with five thousand Peloponnesians and another five thousand from Syracuse. "He portioned out allotments, up to the full sum of 10,000 settlers" (Diod. 11.49.1). From 466 to 461, those expelled were allowed to return, expelling in their turn the settlers at Aitna and Naxos, and the land was redistributed (Diod. 11.76.4).
[44] Plut. *Per.* 20.2. Cf. the expulsion of landowners and redistribution of lands at Sybaris, Kroton, and Kyme. Zuchtriegel (2018) 133 with Robinson (1997) 37–38;,76.

bad harvests, and abandonment, which recur in the Aegean throughout history.[45] Some such crises befell Thera around the middle of the seventh century. The Theran community took a comprehensive step: every household numbering at least two sons held a "home lottery" to choose who would depart. It was considered part of a simultaneous "statewide" lottery all over the seven districts of Thera. The lottery determined who stayed and who went away.

The values and modes of division and distribution of land overlap significantly in both practices of inheritance and colonization, especially concerning equality and the use of the lot that expressed it. Within vast horizons and a relatively short time, Greeks of various mother cities and sub-ethnicities faced the same issue: how to distribute lands to settlers. It was a Small World phenomenon responsible for the rapid emergence of pan-Hellenic commonalities of value and practice.[46] Adopting conventions from distribution of inheritance and booty, the answer to the question of what to do with land was readily available: distribute equal, *individual* portions by drawing lots.

Why individual? By the late eighth century, something fundamental has changed in the relations between a person, the land, and the community. There seems to have emerged a preference for the formula "one man / one *oikos* (household)." In the early archaic period, most Greek men aimed to head an *oikos* and own a personal *kleros*, not to be an *akleros* or a *thete*, a hired day laborer. As noted, since partible inheritance was a solution with a built-in expiration date (once portions become too small),[47] it implies an automatic "overpopulation."[48] As we saw in the *Odyssey*, four sons split up their inheritance by drawing lots, leaving the fifth brother, a bastard, with very little, so he sets out to raid and makes his fortune. However, during their father's life, several sons may live together on an estate: Homer speaks of estates (e.g., Nestor's) where the master, his companions (*hetairoi*), his family and sons, and sometimes his chattel all live together (see ch. 4).[49]

As the two (hypothetical yet realistic) Theran brothers illustrate, what happens to the one also happens to the other, albeit in different contexts. I have already pointed out several features common to inheritance and colonization (ch. 4). Let me highlight the *kleros* aspect: In partible inheritance by lot, each brother gets a *kleros* equal, or equitable, to what his brother gets. That is also what a brother would get in a colony: a *kleros* equal or equitable to what his fellow settlers would get (ch. 4, Figure 4.1). Note that both would probably happen within the lifetime

---

[45] Kolodny (1974).
[46] Malkin (2011).
[47] Cf. Arist. *Pol.* 1270b1: "Yet it is clear that if a number of sons are born, and the land is correspondingly divided there will inevitably come to be many poor men."
[48] Cf. Plato on *stenochoria*: *Laws* 708b.
[49] Hom. *Od.* 3.353–355. In Latin we find the equivalence with the word *familia*: a *famulus*, for example, a "family member," actually meant a slave. Lewis and Short, s.v. *familia*.

of the two brothers. In terms of probability, it is doubtful that entirely different values (equitability) and modes of distribution (drawing lots) were applied at home and abroad to the same family members. Each of them was about to get a *kleros* of their own. As noted, it becomes even more probable since land distribution is a subset of the "distribution of goods by lot," with the same values and practices applied. As we shall see, we do not have to rely on probability alone.

6.2.3 The archaeology of *kleroi* in the archaic period

Colonization did as much for the rise of the *polis* as vice versa. Young men, less constricted by home traditions,[50] now faced the need to make an abstraction of their society and needed to *prescribe* in advance what they would be doing. They did not grow up in a given situation but had to formalize a new one. The need to "imagine the *polis*" was particularly acute in colonies, and there is perhaps good reason why the earliest comprehensive lawgivers (Zaleukos of Lokroi and Charondas of Katane) are reputed to have come from western colonies. Emily Mackil observes that emergent states "from Massalia to Cyprus, from the Black Sea to Crete" felt the need to regulate property claims.[51] In colonies, especially with the Greek vision of sites as empty, we first find evidence for comprehensive planning according to apparent criteria of equality.

For the eighth and seventh centuries, our best, sometimes only, evidence comes from Sicily and Italy. Comprehensive planning, orthogonal when possible, with equal blocks and a reserved space for an agora, seems evident in varying degrees at Syracuse (Ortygia), Megara Hyblaia, Naxos, Himera, Selinous, and Akragas; Gela, Zankle, and Katane also indicate such planning, but the information is less accessible.[52] Traces of city perimeters are sometimes evident as well.

In general, settlements appear to have had three initial phases: possession and temporary habitations (tents or huts), primary organization and allotment, and development into more of a "city," filling up house plots and *kleroi*. Archaeologically what we can observe better is the last phase (e.g., mid-seventh century at Megara Hyblaia). Following the excavators of Megara Hyblaia in their most recent publications, we need to see this last phase in terms of the development and implementation of the planning and allotment that started at the time of Megara's foundation. Similarly, Selinous, which was founded from Megara Hyblaia, began around the shore near the river estuaries; it became an entirely

---

[50] Cf. Link (1991a) 168–169.
[51] Mackil (2017) 69.
[52] De Angelis (2016) 76–82.

planned city during the first twenty-five years of the sixth century, about a generation after its initial foundation.[53]

6.2.4 Egalitarianism and equality in a Greek colony

Absolute equality had never been on the horizon of the expectations of Greek colonists. The exception was a "first lot" (*protos kleros*), which each colonist would get as the entry ticket for sharing in the community. Colonists had known their own social and economic differences, probably right from the start. To illustrate, as we shall see at Megara Hyblaia (established ca. 728), whereas the plots of land were equal in size, the houses built on them were individual. Some settlers must have been better off than others, coming with moveable wealth (*chremata*) and bringing (or buying on the spot) equipment and animals.[54] Plato was aware of the problem:

> It would indeed have been a splendid thing if each person, on entering the colony, had had all else equal as well. . . . However, [this] is impossible, and one man will arrive with more money and another with less. (Plato, *Laws*, 744b, trans. R. G. Bury)

Except for the First Lots there was no limit on personal enrichment. Egalitarianism has been more prominent in the first and, to a lesser extent, the second generation. Unequal land acquisition often developed within two or three generations after the foundation of a settlement (Figure 6.1).[55] That was not a deviation from any standard since nobody had ever claimed that *all* lands ought to have been equal. Archaeological surveys often indicate that, over time, a variety of land holdings and land uses may be observed (see Endnote 3). However, archaeologists and historians may be observing two distinct phenomena that complement rather than contradict each other. The egalitarian spirit was indeed there and was expressed in the equal First Lots, as in other distributive lotteries I have discussed. Theirs was not an ideology of primitive communism, and total equality was never the aim. The equal *kleros* was a *minimum* qualification to be a sharer or "citizen" who could then get more alienable lands (*autokteta*) as a private person.[56] The latter does not contradict the former. As I shall point out,

---

[53] De Angelis (2016) 73–76. Cf. Mertens (2010); (2003).
[54] On the category of *chremata* in Cretan laws see Link (1991a) 107–112. On houses see Hoepfner et al.(1994).
[55] Zuchtriegel (2018).
[56] The "either/or" debate over the inalienability of land does not take sufficiently into consideration the distinction between the inalienable First Lots (the *minimum* holdings of first settlers) and other types of land (bibliography: Morakis [2015] 37n32).

material evidence for inequality that often ranges over centuries cannot refute the initial equality of *kleroi*. However, the question remains: can archaeology confirm initial equality among settlers?

Archaeologists do not necessarily see their task in terms of correlation with, or the confirmation of, textual statements. On the other hand, historians should be able to use material evidence to make their assessments. As noted, a strictly archeological approach cannot reveal unrealized intentions or the kind of prescriptions we read in foundation decrees. Whereas it is perfectly acceptable that archaeology can expose "practices," it can only make conjectures about "ideals and concepts"; it cannot know anything about professed intentions and a mindset without words articulating them in the form of written evidence.[57] On the other hand, if "things done," such as precisely equal plots of land in an eighth-century colony, conform to what all available sources consistently say (and none denies), they may appear as confirmation with a high degree of probability.

6.2.5 Territories and grids

The archaeological evidence for equal plots of land usually relates to the initial settlement, not the unequal land possessions that appeared somewhat later. Noteworthy already, Megara Hyblaia (last third of the eighth century), a grid "town plan," and perhaps the military character of secondary settlements indicate a comprehensive grasp and central planning. That is especially apparent at Sicilian Kasmenai, which was almost certainly founded and planned at one stroke with a "state hand" behind it.[58] But territories beyond the initial settlement were a different matter: in Sicilian colonies, for example, territories varied between four hundred and twenty-five hundred square kilometers, and over the centuries, various types of uses of the land would emerge, such as farmsteads, small villages, fortified outposts, and even trading stations.[59] Moreover, "borders" were fluid and not predefined, especially in the colonies. Coasts were the only clear border-"lines," whereas the hinterland was more of an open frontier.

Syracuse, for instance, expanded rapidly. Starting from the islet of Ortygia in 733, by the end of the first generation, Syracusans occupied the "mainland"

---

[57] See Hall (2014) esp. at 212–219. Cf. MacSweeney (2009). Specifically, by analogies with anthropological models, one could infer social structures, perhaps even "attitudes"—e.g., Hall (2014) 214. I am not trying to discuss the entire issue of the relation between material evidence and written texts, only to indicate the limitations of archaeology in the context of this specific issue.

[58] Moreschini (1992); M. Melfi, cited by de Angelis (2016) 164 (unavailable to me) casts doubt about the "military nature" of Kasmenai. He is probably correct: Kasmenai has almost no cross streets, probably adhering to the notion of "row" (*stoichos*); cf., Gras Tréziny, and Broise (2004) 561–563. Therefore, the town plan does not confirm a military character per se.

[59] Zurbach (2017) 729 based on Vallet (1968) and Lepore (1968). De Angelis (2016) 95 and 96, Table 1.

across and kept expanding while founding more settlements, such as Heloros, Akrai (664), and Kasmenai (643) and finally taking over Kamarina (598).[60] Native sites, such as Monte Finocchito and Pantalica, were abandoned around the same time.[61] Or take Gela, founded in 688 by Antiphemos of Rhodes and Entimos from Crete: we hear of Antiphemos conquering Omphake and probably Ariaton, followed by the foundation of Maktorion. Mythology seems to have legitimized conquest: Antiphemos recovered at Omphake a statue once made by Daedalus (Daidalos) after he fled Crete and King Minos. The statue was probably meaningful to all Greeks but especially to the Cretan colonists whose ancient King Minos was supposedly murdered in Sicily when he was chasing Daedalus.[62]

In short, we are still determining how Greeks took possession of lands in periods later than the generation of foundation. However, that is the relevant generation since, as Cahill says,

> Cities throughout the Greek world were laid out on a grid plan, with standard house-plots distributed among the citizens. This convention of building adjoining houses on lots of identical sizes was common to most Greeks.[63]

Few would argue with this general statement by Cahill concerning the classical period. Cities founded in the classical period, such as Olynthos or Thourioi, confirm the model. How early can we observe the guiding values of equality of chance and distribution evident at Olynthos and elsewhere? Equal plots and orthogonal panning, in and of themselves, signify little without a vocabulary to articulate their meaning. The argument is familiar but worth restating here: the same material phenomenon can mean very different things. Orthogonal (grid) planning does not necessarily imply an egalitarian mindset. There is "an implicit misunderstanding of how egalitarian principles in one social practice may—and often do—co-exist with highly stratified realities in another."[64] To illustrate with an example in the context of the colonial grid, let us note a plan of a city founded by King Edward I in the thirteenth century CE: Montpazier in France (founded 1284; Figure 6.2). It is laid out in a grid plan, similar to grids in a Greek colony. However, in the Greek world, as all extant texts explicitly indicate and none arguing the reverse, the grid signifies a *homoioi* (equals, peers) type of equality and the community's sovereignty to make decisions about itself; the Edwardian

---

[60] De Angelis (2016) 93 n.117. Luraghi (1994) 216 rightly observes that sixth-century colonies took control over the territory not progressively but immediately.
[61] De Angelis (2016) 163.
[62] Paus. 8.46.2; 9.40.4 with D'Asaro (1991). For mixed areas under Gela, see de Angelis (2016) 165.
[63] Cahill (2002) 200; cf. de Angelis (2016) 86: "The construction of private dwellings took place on land demarcated for that purpose; property rights and land ownership are presupposed by this very act."
[64] Smith (2013) 136. Cf. Grant (2001).

Figure 6.2 Montpazier (founded 1284 CE), following Lilley (2009); with the permission of Keith Lilley

grid signifies the exact opposite. "The absent ruler's omnipresence was carved into the very environment of his subjects.... The grid, or rather the predictability of the *bastide*, signals a coherency, a hidden power controlling the environment. The *bastide* is an image of divine rule. As such, it is a substitute for the body (or one of the bodies) of the absent king."[65] The modern city of Philadelphia (USA) offers yet a very different set of "concepts and practices" while presenting the same kind of orthogonal grid (Figure 6.3). Had we no literary evidence for the ancient Greek, the Medieval English, or seventeenth-century Philadelphia, how

---

[65] Randolph (1995) 306. I am grateful to Keith Lilley for directing me to this information and quote. Cf. Lilley (2011) chs. 2, 4.

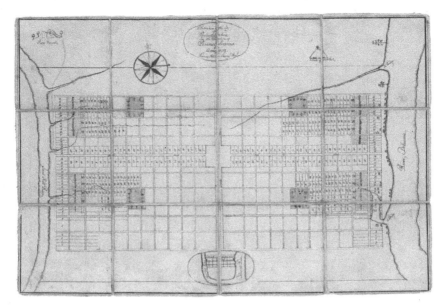

Figure 6.3 Philadelphia: *Map illustration from The Independence Square Neighborhood. Published by The Penn Mutual Life Insurance Company, Philadelphia, 1926.*

would one assess the distinct and opposite "ideals and concepts" implied in an orthogonal grid?[66]

In contrast to those examples, what sources from the classical period say, and what they never even imagined—such as a "King Edward type" of imposed equality—indicate that the Greek colonial grid plan did express an egalitarian mindset. Let us first observe the earliest Greek colony where equal plots are apparent.

6.2.6 Equal lots: Megara Hyblaia

The settlers were a group of migrants from the *polis* of Megara Nisaia between Athens and the Peloponnese.[67] Around 735, they set out for Sicily, but Lamis,

---

[66] Grant (2001) provides a historical overview according to which "the grid emerges in some societies seeking to diffuse authority among citizens, but appears most commonly in societies which are centralizing or globalizing power." Cf. Hurt (1992); Rose-Redwood and Bigon (2018). As noted, Sicilian tyrants provided equal plots but gave much more to their own narrow circle.

[67] Thuc. 6.3, probably based on Antiochos of Syracuse's account of Sicilian history with Hornblower (1991) *ad loc.*

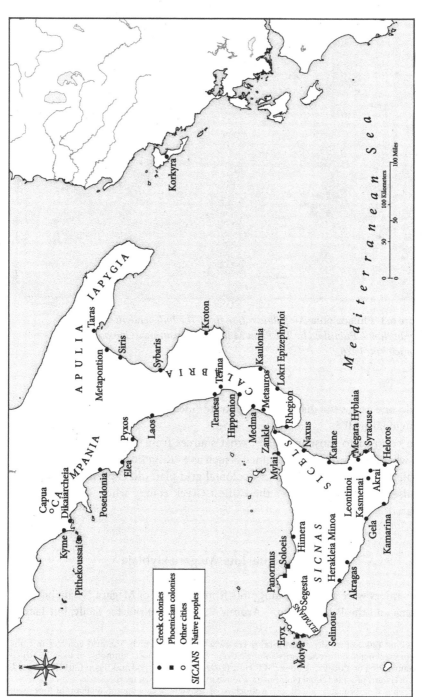

Map 6.2 Major sites relevant to archaic and classical southern Italy and Sicily (from Malkin 2011).

their founder (*oikistes*), died before founding a colony. After several failures, a local king, Hyblon, who might have been worried by the foundation of Syracuse to the south, eventually invited the weary Megarians to settle down in his kingdom. He gave them an undefended flat ground with no possibility of an acropolis, the typical elevated area where the defense of a *polis* and temples to the gods would generally be concentrated.[68] Thus, all Greek *polis* elements had to be expressed by an arbitrary spatial organization with few natural features to guide the planners. Reserved at the outset, there were sacred areas, a trapezoid public area (probably a kind of agora—the political, commercial, and civic heart of a Greek *polis*), roads, and equally sized "blocks" of houses with varied orientations, perhaps expressing distinct sub-identities (yet all sharing the same public and sacred areas).[69] The later seventh-century houses all follow the alignment of the original plan[70] (Figures 6.4a, 6.4b) Generally speaking, the emphasis on orientation in various Greek colonies indicates "a preoccupation, if not obsession, with *orientations* [emphasis in original].... The very existence of such orientations reflect a communal spirit."[71]

> Town plans represent a first attempt on the ground to delineate the community and to structure it and its institutions internally in a way which the community regarded as rational and meaningful. The Sicilian Greeks were presented with a unique opportunity to organize themselves in landscapes that presented few natural and human hindrances. This is a conclusion that emerges from all the Greek cities, but it is clearest in those cases, like Megara Hyblaia, Gela, and Selinous.... In founding these cities, the settlers cleared the land, organized the space in a new way, and had free rein to establish their societies and economies as they saw fit.[72]

Megara Hyblaia existed for 246 years when its Greek neighbor Syracuse destroyed it. It had a later life, but much of the site was abandoned until archaeologists of the French School in Rome conducted a wide-ranging excavation. The destruction of an entire city, with the bonus of no resettlement in later periods, is the kind of site archaeologists dream of. Such a site affords a comprehensive vision within a limited period that also involves understanding the relations between the elements discovered (houses, temples, agora, streets, cemeteries, etc.). To illustrate what happens when this is not the case: the city of Marseille, which was

---

[68] Cf. Graham ([1988] 2001); Mertens, Greco (1996).
[69] *Régulier hétérogène* is how Henri Tréziny expresses regularity within sectors which exist in different orientations in the same city, sometimes for topographical reasons (Tréziny 2002); cf. Tréziny (1999). On distinct groups from Megara (Nisaia): Svenbro (1982); Gras and Tréziny (2017).
[70] Gras, Tréziny, and Broise (2004); Tréziny (2016).
[71] Fischer-Hansen (1996) 320.
[72] De Angelis (2016) 85.

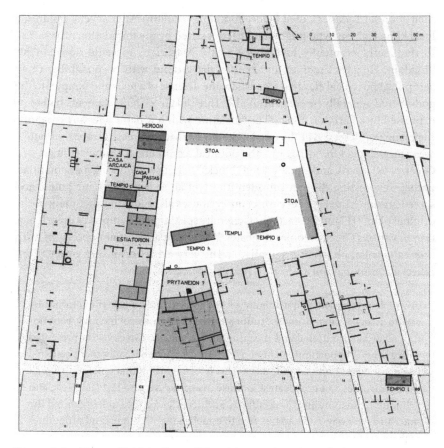

Figure 6.4a *Megara Hyblaia, "agora."* Fom Mertens (2006). With the permission of Dieter Mertens.

initially a Greek colony (Massalia, founded ca. 600) and has known continuous habitation since, is a busy, modern megalopolis.[73] It is impossible to excavate the ancient Greek city, and only patchy rescue excavations sometimes bring a spot to light, as happened when the municipality conducted works in the area of the Bourse. By contrast, the comprehensive nature of what has been unearthed so far at Megara Hyblaia allows us to be more confident about the strict implementation of equality.

This comprehensive nature of Megara Hyblaia's planning is emphasized by the fact that the divisions inside each block were contemporary with the

---

[73] See Hermary, Hesnard, and Tréziny (1999) and the volumes of *Études Massaliètes*.

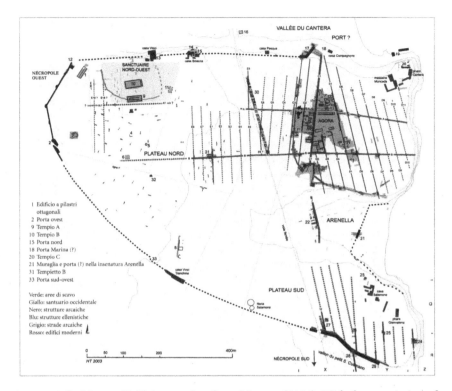

Figure 6.4b Megara Hyblaia overview from Mertens (2006). With the permission of Dieter Mertens.

overall setup of the roads and the blocks themselves (all eighth century). Megara Hyblaia's colony Selinous would be much better planned (Figure. 6.5); Shipley comments that "strip planning" comes "long after" foundation. He is right: second-generation colonies were better planned; they were not inventing but implementing and improving on the same notions shared by the first generation of settlers of Megara Hyblaia.[74]

Here is what the excavators, revisiting the site time and again, have to say about it:

> The rationality of the Greek city allows us to link the institutional and philosophical dimension to the urban one. Everything in Megara Hyblaia speaks of

---

[74] Shipley (2005) 347: "The layouts of colonies imply that there was already an idea of what a *polis* should be." "An overall scheme of the site existed in the minds of some person or persons." Cf. Murray (1993) 114: "No colonial site has yet produced evidence of an irregular original plan."

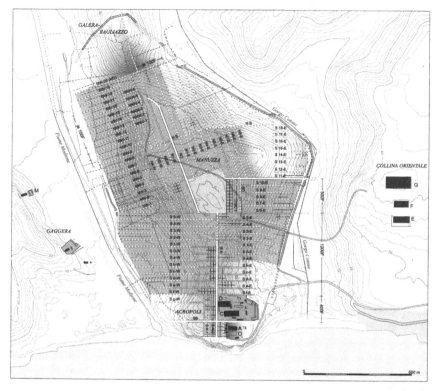

Figure 6.5 Selinous (founded 628) from Mertens (2006). With the permission of Dieter Mertens.

rationality. The urban space was built collectively as a political space, and all the constituent elements of the city contributed to this construction.[75]

The French excavators are writing within the context of the debate over "cities of reason," which is not necessarily the point regarding privilege here.[76] Megara Hyblaia, with its spatial organization and *nomima*, imported from the mother city—with its public and sacred areas, planned territory, and equal plots—appears as a planned, coherent *polis*. Yet some scholars interpret all new colonies/*poleis* of the archaic era as "organic," the result of a slow, haphazard trickle

---

[75] Gras and Tréziny (2017) 164: "*La rationalité de la cité grecque permet de relier la dimension institutionnelle et philosophique à la dimension urbaine. Tout à Mégara Hyblaia parles de rationalité. L'espace urbain fut construit collectivement comme un espace politique, et tous les éléments constitutifs de la cité contribuèrent à cette construction.*"
[76] Murray (1990; 1996) and my Introduction in this volume. .

of immigrants evolving into communities living in the gridlike city plan only at a much later stage.[77] Since the entire layout and the first houses belong to the last third of the eighth century, Megara Hyblaia seems to be a glaring refutation of that position. The unconvincing strategies to face that refutation involve either denying the conclusions of the French archaeologists, or accepting equal plots but suggesting that one person could own more than one equal plot, or accepting but contending that Megara Hyblaia is somehow not "representative." I find such strategies desperate attempts to save some preconceived notions about archaic Greek history.

Equality at Megara Hyblaia seems almost obsessive in its implementation along the layout set down in the eighth century: house blocks measured 120 or 135 square meters (in two sections).[78] Houses were built facing one street and sharing the median line of the block, with the back of another house facing a parallel street. The inner divisions of a city block were contemporary with the roads, so it all goes back to the time of the foundation.[79] The back wall of both or the reserved space between (a distance of 0.45 meter) was reserved for the median wall and the curbstones facing the street) divides the plot of land precisely in the middle; the blocks are equal.

Egalitarianism was not equivalent to absolute equality among settlers as expressed in the equal house plots (and the equal chances of the presumed lottery to distribute them). Whereas house plots were equal, the houses were not. There were means to express inequality, such as forms and content of burials, changes in size and degree of luxury of the houses, or the use of expensive polychrome pottery with some specific shapes. The difference is significant: equal plots emphasize the *relational* aspect of land distribution: how each plot of land is compared, or relates, to another in an overall scheme. The individual houses, by contrast, are indeed individual.

The implications of the archaeological findings at Megara Hyblaia tend to confuse scholars who generally stress the "elite vector" as typical of archaic Greek society. My position is that whereas the elite vector often took over within each political community, archaic Greek societies kept experimenting with "restarts" following the egalitarian vector. However, the presupposition of an "aristocratic society" might muddle the issue. The excavators, too, seem misguided here: "In an archaic, aristocratic society, based on solidarities and hierarchies between and within groups, the definition of the individual, equal lots may seem paradoxical. The lots are probably regrouped in larger units of 'lot-groups' which reflect social

---

[77] Notably Osborne (1998) and Hall (2007; 2014) 107–110 (a brief discussion of Megara Hyblaia in the framework of a textbook). Cf. Delamard (2014).
[78] De Angelis (2016) 86 rightly claims that the difference is negligible. Cf. de Angelis (2003)
[79] Summary of the evidence in Shipley (2005).

reality."[80] In other words, to fit the frequently stated *unequal* image of early colonial society with equal plots, they suggest that one person could own several *equal* plots.

That is highly unlikely. First, how justified is the assumption of an "aristocratic" society, especially in colonies where the only "aristocrat" seems to have been the *oikistes*? Specifically, at Megara Hyblaia, the later social differentiation was material, not blood-oriented. When discussing Gelon (ca. 483), Herodotus distinguishes between the Megarian *demos* and the Megarian "fat ones," *pacheis*, clearly a materialistic criterion.[81] Specifically, the suggested sequence makes little sense: The settlers after first taking extreme care to measure, precisely, equal lots; then insisting that the backs of their plot houses fit equally down the median line within any single block; then, finally, they forget all that and "group" the equal plots together so that the resulting grouping is *unequal*. This self-contradictory sequence is a mere guess to save a preconceived assumption about the "nature" of archaic Greek society. There is no evidence for such a practice, which is unparalleled elsewhere. When we get some specifics in later sources, an individual settler always receives a single *kleros*, not some "grouping." In the foundation decree of Black Corcyra, we even get individual names for each of the settlers.

Remarkably, we can find the original layout and even some fourteen eighth-century houses built during the first generation of foundation when most settlers probably lived in temporary dwellings or tents (*campements*).[82] Tents or huts for the first generation are a typical colonial phenomena throughout history. For example, at the site of the future New Orleans (USA), the two hundred people who were sent to build a town were "camped on the banks of a great river, where they have only dared to put themselves in shelter from the weather while waiting to have a plan drawn for them so they might have some houses built."[83] The "tent generation" is invisible archaeologically, yet tents, as such, are significant. Note that when Xenophon was suspected of trying to found a city and prevent the mercenaries from returning home, "The men took up quarters (*eskenoun*) on

---

[80] Gras, Tréziny, and Broise (2004) 546 (cf. 584, no doubt that *isomoiria* was practiced) : "*Dans une société archaïque, aristocratique, fondée sur les solidarités et les hiérarchies entre les groupes et à l'intérieur de ces groupes, la définition des lots individuels égaux peut sembler paradoxale. Il est probable que ces lots sont en fait regroupés en entités plus vastes, en 'group des lots' qui reflètent une réalité sociale.*" Two of the authors do not repeat this idea, which is entirely circular, in Gras and Tréziny (2017).

[81] Hdt 7.156 and see below 6.3.4.

[82] Gras, Tréziny, and Broise (2004), 465–466; 523–526; cf. Tréziny (2016). We may never know enough about "clusters of families" as suggested by the excavators at Megara Hyblaia (Gras, Tréziny, and Broise 2004) 584 pointing out circular platforms that could imply cults common to a few families. Their general conclusion is that there should be no doubt that *isomoiria* was practiced, but that does not signify social equality, as I, too, claim regarding First Lots and personal *chremata*.

[83] Letter of January 22, 1722, quoted in Dawdy (2008) 64.

the beach by the sea, refusing to encamp on the spot which might become a city." *Skenein*—setting up tents—was how a city started.[84]

The number of houses discovered so far and dating to the first generation is assessed as fourteen, apparently built while the tent generation settled and planned their settlement site. Since seventh-century houses followed precisely the exact alignments and the reserved public area stayed unbuilt, the implication of comprehensive perception and equality among the settlers seems highly probable. It fits what Greeks called (at least from the fifth century and probably much earlier), "equal and fair terms" (*isos kai homoios*). Let there be no mistake: by accepting the equality of individual lots with the ratio of "one *oikos*: one *kleros*," I am not claiming that Megara Hyblaia was a democracy in the making. But when we try to understand how egalitarian ideas were later translated into a democracy, one cannot avoid the *isomoiria* of the early archaic period.[85]

At Megara, we may note other indications of initial egalitarianism versus later social and economic differentiation. No arms were found in the tombs, and the only outstanding nontemple building at Megara Hyblaia is the *heröon* facing the agora, which may have been the burial site of the founder (two such burials were discovered in the agora of Selinous, Megara's colony).[86] No other house is comparable, which brings me back to the argument concerning the cult of the founder and equality: the exclusive heroic status says something far more humbling about the rest of the settlers. A kind of equality is implied in the superhuman elevation of one person vis-à-vis the "equal" rest.

Another early communal aspect concerns food storage. At Megara Hyblaia, its colony Selinous, and Himera, archaeologists discovered circular stone structures that served as granaries, built even before the houses and placed at separation points between blocks. A plausible connection has been suggested between their existence and the term *homosepyoi*, "those who eat from a common granary, sharers of the bread basket," that is, equality of the *homoioi*-type ("peers," equal in specific respects), as at Sparta. A sacred law from mid-fifth century Selinous specifies *homosepyoi* as sacrificing *together*. Aristotle attributes the term (*homosepyoi*) to Charondas of Katane, an early lawgiver from Sicily, who defined it as members of the same *oikos*.[87]

---

[84] Xen. *Anab*. 6.4.7. Zuchtriegel (2018) 62–68 is the one to point out the relevant passage in the *Anabasis*. Cf. Tréziny (2016) on *campements*.

[85] McInerney (2004). Cf. Rausch (1999) 64–67, comparing the establishment of Athenian tribes to colonial projects. See also Endnote 2.

[86] Gras, Tréziny, and Broise (2004) 419–421; cf. Mertens (2003) 413–418; (2012) 1160–1161; (2019). Cf. also Malkin (1987a) 134–144.

[87] *SEG* 43.630. Cf. Guzzo (2013); de Angelis (2016) 138; Zuchtriegel (2018) 63. For Selinous: Jameson, Jordan, and Kotansky (1993) 14, col. A, l. 3; 20; Robertson (2010) 46–49. Arist. *Pol*. 1252b14, who compares him to Epimenides's *homokapoi*; for Charondas, cf. Arist. *Pol*. 1274a23. Cf. Robu (2014) 157. Cf. *homometrioi homo-patrioi, homo-galaktes*.

6.2.7 Syracuse

Syracuse was founded initially at the site of the islet Ortygia by Corinthian colonists under Archias the Bakhiad in 733. Much denser than Megara Hyblaia because of topographical constraints, the streets were equally spaced; sacred areas (the temples of Apollo and Athena) were reserved from the outset; and the lots for buildings were adhered to (Figure 6.6). The urban "plan" firmly belongs to the mid-seventh century. However, we know too little about what the settlers did after deliberately destroying the native houses to make Ortygia an *eremos chora*. About twenty-four meters wide, the blocks were separated by streets, about three meters wide (as at Megara Hyblaia and Kasmenai, Syracuse's foundation [643]).

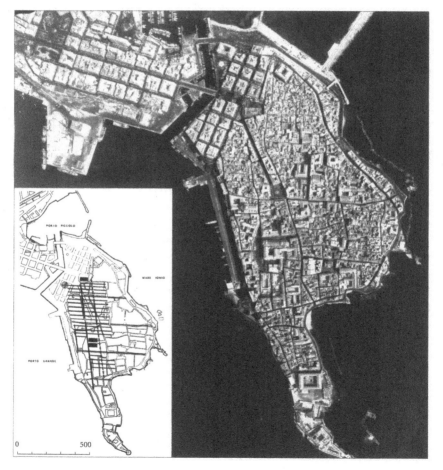

Figure 6.6 Syracuse. from Mertens (2006). With the permission of Dieter Mertens.

An even more straightforward layout is remarkable at Syracuse's foundations at Akrai (664) and Kasmenai, as well as Kamarina (598, and see further 6.2.8).[88]

6.2.8 Himera

Let us observe another example. Himera is a good illustration of the distinction between equal plots and the rest of the land. Its immediate hinterland covers some fifty square kilometers, whereas its entire territory stretched to some seven hundred square kilometers. In the immediate hinterland were a few rural settlements and border fortresses. Within the greater territory, there were also some non-Greek settlements. Neither the greater territory nor the immediate hinterland was divided into equal *kleroi*. However, that is what precisely happened in the center. Himera was founded by another colony, Zankle (founded by Chalkidians), in 648. It had three founders, two probably from the respective mother cities.[89] A group of Dorian exiles from Syracuse, the Myletidai, joined the Chalcidic-Ionian settlers. As a result, notes Thucydides, the dialect of Himera was mixed, but the *nomima* that prevailed were Chalkidian.[90] It is an excellent illustration of the role of *nomima* (e.g., terms of magistracies, "tribal" divisions, sacred calendars) in consolidating a community and its identity. The Greek *polis* was founded on a covenant with the gods,[91] and the reciprocal relations with the gods, punctured by days of sacrifice, were of the essence. One could not have, for example, conflicting Dorian and Chalkidian sacred calendars. But dialect was not such a marker of identity, and Himera became a mixed, homogeneous community, speaking a mixed Dorian-Ionic dialect while following Ionian *nomima*.[92]

Himera was established on a hilltop and a coastal location, which may partly explain why some plots are almost 50 percent larger than those in the lower city,[93] reflecting the status of different waves of settlers. A fascinating inscription, dating to 493, provides for plots of land to be allotted to exiles from Zankle, Himera's mother city. According to Antonietta Brugnone's convincing restoration of the text, the assembly decrees that each new *epoikos* (often this means an additional settler who comes after a foundation is accomplished) will get half a *schoinos*

---

[88] Voza (1999) 93. Fischer-Hansen (1996) 334–336. Cf. Belvedere (1988).
[89] Eukleides, Simos, and Sakon (Thuc. 6.5.1). Thucydides says it was a *nomos* to invite a cofounder from the mother city (Thuc. 1.24.2). Denis Knoepfler thinks he was one of the Myletidai, based on the name found at Selinous and around Gela (2007: 95). See also Strabo 6.2.6. A native origin has also been suggested as a possibility: de Angelis (2016) 166.
[90] Thuc. 6.5.1; cf. Strabo 6.2.6.
[91] Blok (2018) 88.
[92] Thuc. 6.5.1.
[93] De Angelis (2016) 85–86.

but none of the *oikopeda*.⁹⁴ It further decides to create a new tribe, Danklaioi (= Zanklaioi, the exiles from Zankle), once the phratries have published registration.⁹⁵ The lot as the means for the equal distribution of plots is not mentioned (as it is, explicitly, in Hellenistic inscriptions integrating new citizens); apparently it was self-evident. The plots themselves were small, providing a place for a house and some agriculture.

The pattern, first seen here, is consistent: In the fourth-century Chersonese (in the Black Sea), aerial photography and survey archaeology of the agricultural countryside (*chora*) have revealed a landscape division into equal plots of 216 square meters each. It is remarkable that without modern land surveying instruments, such measurable equality was achieved and implemented in antiquity.⁹⁶

* * *

One notes a significant enlargement of properties and houses in the second or third generation after a foundation. At Naxos, for example, the settlers started at the eastern end of the peninsula (some ten hectares), and by the second generation, the settlement was enlarged to some forty hectares. Aside from Megara Hyblaia, some orthogonal planning is evident throughout these processes: at Naxos, Syracuse, Selinous, Himera, Akragas, and probably Zankle, Katane, and Gela. They all include an agora, the public space reserved *a priori*, indicating the existence of a self-recognized community careful to separate the private and public areas.⁹⁷ "The respect for private, public, and religious zones implies a communal recognition of this egalitarian ethos from the beginning."⁹⁸ With growth, colonies often show direct continuity with the layout of the initial planning, as one may observe at Gela. The study of a five-kilometer radius around Kamarina indicates that the city and countryside were "simultaneously and closely developed," with "city streets" as the starting lines for roads in the countryside. Plots of land (ca. 265 by 210 meters) and, later, individual farmsteads were oriented accordingly.⁹⁹

---

⁹⁴ The exact size is controversial and varies in ancient sources from thirty to sixty stades (between five and ten and a half kilometers). See Jansen-Wilkeln Karl (2006) in *Brill's New Pauly*, s.v. *schoinos* http://dx.doi.org/10.1163/1574-9347_bnp_e1104170.

⁹⁵ Brugnone (1997); Lombardo, Aversa, and Frisone (2001) 120–121. Cf. the quarter named "Phokaia" at Leontinoi, probably made up of fugitives from Phokaia in Asia Minor. Thuc. 5.4.4,. with Frasca (2009) 60. See also Brugnone (2011a; 2011b).

⁹⁶ Note the ancient farms and land-plots on the Chora of Chersoneses Taurike Saprykin (1994). Cf. Müller (2010) 125–136. Cf. Carter, Crawford, Lehman, *et al.* (2000); Gavrilov (2006).

⁹⁷ De Angelis (2016) 74–83. Map nos. 5–11. 99: "Overall allocation of space occurred from the start; the community clearly maintained control of land, regulating where and how private and public space was used."

⁹⁸ Smith (2013) 137.

⁹⁹ Mertens (2006) 353; quotes from de Angelis (2016) 114, 119–120.

6.2.9 Perimeters

The perimeter of Greek colonies is another indication that Greek colonists had, *a priori,* an idea of their settlement as a *unit,* in contrast to slowly evolving settlements. The concept of a perimeter is, therefore, significant. One of the constitutive actions of the Homeric founder of Scheria was to create a perimeter: "About the city he (Nausithoös) had drawn a wall" (*Od.* 6.6–10). Perimeters developed into city walls (better known are Naxos, Katane, Gela, Akragas, and Selinous) by the time of the third or fourth generation of settlers. What seems remarkable is that space for walls appears to have been reserved from the outset, just like space for roads and public areas.[100] Megara Hyblaia and Leontinoi first had a temporary wall (ca 750–700), an earth rampart made from the earth of the ditch in front, which was replaced by a stone city wall in the third phase ca. 525–500.[101] With the advance of archaeology, the walls have become less of an "idea of a wall" and something more concrete. Such walls are not there to define the general territory but the area of the actual settlement, within which equal house plots were planned. Walls also express the comprehensiveness of the foundation and the idea of "portions" of land *within* the marked space of the walls. Since it now seems clear that their space had been reserved *a priori,* walls provide an excellent illustration of the communal, more cohesive aspect of the organized foundation and the political community.

To sum up so far: The time span of a "foundation" should be understood as overlapping with the first generation of settlers, that is, the life span of an *oikistes* (founder), say, thirty to forty years.[102] That first founding generation was busy taking over the settlement site, setting up temporary habitations, negotiating their situation versus non-Greek local peoples, implementing *nomima* and establishing cults and sacred precincts, conducting the distribution of the First Lots, starting to build permanent dwellings, and finally burying the founder in a central public place with an annual heroic cult. What is at stake is that early settlements were planned, that they were planned with an egalitarian framework in mind, that initial *kleroi* were equal, and that their mode of distribution was by lot. Not all of those aspects can be confirmed or refuted archaeologically. As noted, whereas archaeology can observe a category of human actions with "things done," *intention* and *verbal representation* of values and the significance of actions are much more problematic.[103] At Megara Hyblaia and other

---

[100] De Angelis (2016) 92–94, 98; cf. Frederiksen (2011) 105.

[101] Frederiksen (2011) 162–163 (Megara), 115 (Leontinoi). For the other city walls see Frederiksen (2011), s.v. (cities are presented alphabetically). See de Angelis (2016) 93n107. One wonders to what extent such walls were used to keep animals *inside* the perimeter.

[102] Malkin (2009) 375.

[103] See Endnote 4. Specifically, by analogies with anthropological models, one could infer social structures, perhaps even "attitudes"; e.g., Hall (2014) 214. I am not trying to discuss the entire issue of material evidence and written texts, only to indicate the limitations of archaeology in this particular context.

settlements in Sicily, the archaeological evidence shows that the first plots of land were equal in size and formed part of an overall "urban" plan within a predefined perimeter. That these constituted the First Lots (distinguished from personal wealth, *chremata*, individual purchase of land, and further conquered territories) becomes highly probable once we observe explicit Greek expressions concerning the relation between *kleroi* and the *polis* (see 6.3).

6.2.10 Classical colonization

The archaic patterns and some of the salient features we have observed seem consistent throughout centuries of Greek colonization, including the classical period (fifth–fourth centuries),[104] as one can beautifully observe at Olynthos.[105] The dividing line distinguishing between archaic and classical colonization is misleading, as Gabriel Zuchtriegel convincingly demonstrates. In some cases, we note a "refoundation" in the sense of a new organization of the colony's space. Kamarina, for example, was re-founded in 461 by settlers mainly from Gela who "apportioned out the land by Lot (*katekolerouchesan*)."[106] The portions of land (270 by 210 meters) were oriented following the town grid. To compare, at the Tauric Chersonese, about four hundred plots were identified around 300 BCE (but going back to the time of foundation, ca. 420). They were larger plots, measuring 630 by 420 meters.

In 1987, some 158 standardized lead tablets were discovered at Kamarina, with an exemplary publication by Federica Cordano.[107] On each tablet is inscribed the name of a citizen and his patronymic (a numbered phratry appears on the reverse side, apparently the one to which the person is assigned). Several interpretations are possible, acknowledged by Cordano. One likely possibility is that they were the tokens of drawing lots for the land distribution and, at the same time, tokens affirming citizenship ("effectively the same thing").[108] They may be related, claims Cordano convincingly, to Diodorus's statement, "The people of Gela, the old settlers of Kamarina, distributed it out by lot."[109] That was a general state of affairs: "nearly all the cities cast off the constitutions that had been given over to foreigners and distributed out their territories by lot to

---

[104] This is a major, convincing claim by Gabriel Zuchtriegel (2018). Note his table of foundations at 34–45.
[105] Cahill (2002).
[106] Diod. 11.76.5.
[107] Cordano (1992) and especially 91–102. *SEG* 42.846; Robinson (2002); Dubois (2008). For a recent reappreciation and discussion, see Faraguna (2017); cf. Murray (1996). Cf. Cordano (2001).
[108] Murray (1996) 498; Walthall and Souza (2021) 372.
[109] Diod. 11.76.5; Cordano (1992) 100–101.

all their citizens."[110] At Kamarina, their deposit in the temple of Athena Polias may support this interpretation since there seems to have been a public interest in preserving the lead tablets as a category. If that is the case, they may imply the special status of *protoi kleroi*. Each phratry is numbered (it does not have a name), suggesting an artificial creation for the new civic order needed for mixing and homogenizing settlers of mixed origins, a feature of fifth-century Sicily that had known massive relocations under the tyrants. The numerical notations further imply "that Kamarina was geometrically laid out and that the phratries were distributed geographically."[111]

Finally, let us observe Metapontion, which no longer exemplifies land divisions and distributions going back to the time of foundation, with grid lines extending from the planned center into the countryside. With the current revised view, the landscape's rearrangement belongs to the end of the sixth century and the beginning of the fifth. Joseph Carter sees the division lines as evidence for (re-?)distribution based on egalitarian principles belonging to ca. 525–475.[112]

Unlike Kamarina, colonies established as new projects continued to be founded in the classical period as they had been formerly in the archaic period, with distinct features of continuity in the modes and patterns of foundation. The difference consisted instead of their purpose and scale. Mother cities now founded new colonies to further the interests of the *metropolis* or a tyrant. Herakleia Lucana (established from Taras in 433) or Herakleia Trachinia (from Sparta in 426) are good examples. There was also a difference of scale: whereas in the seventh century, an initial settlement or a bridgehead by around two hundred men would be conceivable; in the classical period, we hear of numbers reaching up to ten thousand. Also new are the expulsion, mixture, and (sometimes) resettlement of entire Greek populations on a grand scale, as was done by Athens at Melos and Delos and by some tyrants in several cities in Sicily.

The scale of the mixture (often forced) among colonists had grown significantly in the classical period, especially with more relocations and fugitive communities.[113] Moreover, whereas, in the archaic period, founders were at

---

[110] Diod. 11.76.6, quoted by Walthall and Souza (2021) 372 n.41.
[111] Faraguna (2015) 658 with Cordano (1992) 100–102; Pelagatti (2006).
[112] Carter (1990); (2000); De Siena (2001); (2006) ch. 3; cf. Gavrilov (2006); Zuchtriegel (2018) 124–136 with references. Cf. Belvedere (1987); Guldager Bilde, Stolba (2006). The case of Metapontion first seemed promising: The lines dividing the countryside into field blocks (possibly as irrigation channels) that seemed to be the direct continuation of the "street lines" in the city itself now seem to belong to a later reorganization of the chora. I thank Lin Foxhall for her advice on this.
[113] To illustrate: Gelon captured Himera in 480 and sent new settlers "both Dorians and others who so wished" (Diod. 11.49.3); Hieron founded Aitna (Katane) with five thousand Peloponnesians and five thousand from Syracuse: "he portioned out allotments, up to the full sum of 10,000 settlers." Diod. 11.49; in 466–461 the expelled were allowed to return, expelling in turn the settlers at Aitna and Naxos and with the land redistributed. Cf. Jacquemin (1993). Diod. 11.76.4; Gelon deported the people of Kamarina in 484 and they returned in 461/60 with the help of Gela. Diod. 11.76.5.

the core of a colony's identity through their annual cult around their tomb in the agora, classical founders sometimes did not stay and were identified instead with the mother city (e.g., Hagnon left Amphipolis to return to Athens, Leon, Alkidas, and Damagon left Herakleia Trachinia to return to Sparta). No wonder this kind of behavior, flaunting the values of the archaic colonization model, was resented.[114] Finally, some foundations, such as Athenian klerouchies or the aborted Corinthian colony to Epidamnos, had distinct aspects differentiating them from the archaic model: Athenian settlers retained Athenian citizenship and sometimes even remained in Athens, drawing revenue from the *kleroi* in the *klerouchia*. In contrast to the archaic, colonists in the classical period could be perceived as shareholders and investors: When the Corinthians announced the colony to Epidamnos, settlers who wished to remain at home could invest fifty *drachmai* and have a "share in the colony" (*metechein . . . tes apoikias*).[115]

On the other hand, the salient aspects of taking over and distributing land (*kleroi*) were directly continuous from archaic practices, as were practices of partible inheritance by lot: first, equality before the chance and equality of the size of the First Lots; second, which is not self-evident, the concentration of settlers at a single site instead of spread-out farmsteads. Gabriel Zuchtriegel convincingly argues that the egalitarian vector (to use my term) was far more prominent as long as settlers were concentrated at a single site. Once they spread out and individuals acquired more lands, something changed: classical foundations reflect, he says, "the egalitarian ideology of Classical Greek colonists. On the other hand, the spread of farmsteads and rural necropoleis is not due to democratization . . . but simply to the break-up of the egalitarian structure that characterized the first two or three generations"; "the notion of equality was applied . . . also to the place of residence, which had to be the same for all."[116]

In other words, both archaic and classical colonies followed the same trajectory in their development: the first and second generations of settlers were concentrated in a nucleus (the same for all) that gradually expanded outward, what Roland Martin calls "centrifugal" cities (see 6.3 with Figure 6.7). Although all *protoi kleroi* were equal in size in the initial settlement site, some social differentiation was probably already apparent yet expressed differently (e.g., *chremata*). However, with better opportunities for the purchase and annexation of lands, the initial equality was rapidly disappearing. In short, the egalitarianism of the first generation, concretely expressed in the equal plots of land and abstractly defined as "equal and fair," gave way to the rise of elites (figure 6.1).

---

[114] Thuc. 5.11.
[115] Thuc.1.26.1 with Zuchtriegel (2018) 116.
[116] Zuchtriegel (2018) 113. As archaic colonization is not his subject, he is careful (on 116) not to commit to the "continuity" of egalitarianism, although that is precisely what emerges from his work.

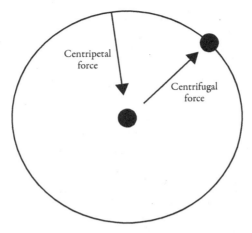

Figure 6.7 Centripetal forces, illustrative, e.g., of *synoikismos* (arrow pointing to the center of the radius) vs. centrifugal forces, illustrative of a colony's expansion from a central point of settlement.

6.2.11 Athenian klerouchies

At the end of the sixth century, the Athenians came up with another term for colonization, reserved for Athenian settlements overseas: klerouchies.[117] The salient features of colonization continue to be evident: the allotments for each settler were equal, and the selection of settlers was by lot (unlike Thera, it was probably from among volunteers).[118] The word, perhaps not surprising by now, combines "having, possessing" (*echo*) and the object of possession, the *kleros*. In some cases, there seems to be little or no difference from other types of colonies. However, unlike archaic colonists, Athenian colonists ordinarily remained Athenian citizens—like the *Français outremer* of French colonialism—and served in the Athenian army.[119] The difference is of minimal significance for our purpose since dividing up equal *kleroi* among members of a predefined group followed the same principles in colonization and partible inheritance. There is a difference in aspect: *apoikoi* ("colonists") were defined in terms of "away from" (*apo-*) the home community; *klerouchia*, like *ktisis* ("foundation"), points instead to what would happen at the actual site of a settlement.[120] The *kleroi* would be

---

[117] Salomon (1997); Igelbrink (2015).
[118] Figueira (2008) 479.
[119] See the comments by Figueira (2008) 435–438; the distinctions between *apoikia* and klerouchies "fell out of use": (2018) 464.
[120] For an Athenian distinction between *klerouchia* and *apoikia* see IG I³ 237 (410–404?). See Casevitz (1985) with Malkin (2016).

either settled directly by Athenians or, sometimes, remain in the possession of their original owners, who paid their Athenian masters for the privilege.

The first *klerouchia* was a straightforward affair of conquest and annexation. The young democracy in Athens, just born (508/7), had to face the military reactions of its neighbors—the Boiotians and the Chalkidian aristocrats, the Hippobotai ("horse breeders")—on the island of Euboia, just across the maritime strait to the west. The Athenians crushed both enemies with fervor analogous to the French or Soviet victories after their successful revolutions. This is how they treated the land captured from the Euboians:

> [the Athenians] crossed to Euboia where they met the Chalkidians too in battle, and after overcoming them as well, they left four thousand *klerouchoi* on the lands of the horse-breeders (the nobility).... Moreover, they made a dedication of a tenth part of the ransom (to Athena).[121]

In this case, the Athenian settlers do not seem to have been absentee masters. Similarly, the first Athenian colonists to Salamis, a few years after the reforms of Cleisthenes in 508, were explicitly forbidden to engage in renting out the lands they received.[122] When Eretria (also in Euboia) asked the Athenians for help against the invading Persians, "The Athenians did not refuse the aid, but gave them for defenders the four thousand tenant farmers who held the land of the Chalcidian horse-breeders."[123]

It was not coincidental, in my view, that cutting up the territory into *kleroi* and distributing them to settlers took place at the same time as the revolution that brought *isonomia* ("equality of law," the first name for "democracy") to Athens. The term *isonomia*, as we shall see, retains the notion of "equal distribution, allocation," which functions in the same semantic range as *isomoiria*: individual, equal "portions" of either something concrete (land) or abstract ("law"), and it was all happening, as it were, at the same time.[124]

Klerouchies is not our subject but let us observe one more example from almost a century after the Athenian *klerouchia* in Euboia. Reporting on the punishment the Athenians had inflicted on the rebel Methymnians on the island of Lesbos, Thucydides says,[125]

---

[121] Hdt. 5.77. Cf. Aelianus *Var. Hist.* 6.1. These klerouchoi were forced to retreat to Athens before the battle of Marathon (Hdt. 6.100).

[122] ML 14 (*SEG* 10.1). The word "klerouchoi" is restored (κλερόχ]ος) but highly plausible; see AIO, text and comm.

[123] Hdt. 6.100.1.

[124] For the implementation of a much wider participation in the *polis* in Cleisthenes's system, and the appearance of *isonomos* perhaps in these same years, see section 8.2.2.1 in this volume.

[125] Thuc. 3.50.2; cf. *IG* I 3.66, cf. Antiphon 5.77; Diod. 12.55.10.

They divided the whole island, except for the territory of Methymna, into three thousand allotments, of which they dedicated three hundred to the gods; they let out the rest to *klerouchoi* taken from their own citizens, *whom they chose by lot*[126] and sent to Lesbos. The Lesbians undertook to pay them a yearly rent of two *minai* for each allotment and cultivated the land themselves.[127]

The Lesbian case, where the original inhabitants were permitted to stay and work the newly divided *kleroi*, reminds us of the more somber aspects of equal sharing: citizens appear as masters, equal among themselves, but riding on the backs of the less fortunate others. We shall further note parallel cases where equality among some colonial "class members" coexists with them becoming a class of masters, such as the Gamoroi ("those who hold portions of the land") at Syracuse and the Herakliots of the Black Sea. In Lesbos the land had become a booty, divided equally among three thousand Athenian landowners who were themselves chosen by lot. One may assume the plots were assigned to the Athenian individuals also by lot, but the text is silent on this. There is no hiding the fact that they were the masters. "Between the slave and the free" is how Pollux, a tenth-century Byzantine author, sums up the situation of conquered, dependent people attached to plots of land and owing revenues to their masters.[128] The Spartans planned to do the same to the Tegeans: to measure the fields with the measuring rope and enslave the Tegeans to work those fields. Most significantly, we hear of the comparable *klarotai* (apparently dependents attached to a *kleros*) in Crete: "Ephoros (fourth-century) . . . says that the Cretans call their slaves *klarotai* from the lots (= *kleroi*, or *klaroi* in dialect) to which they were attached."[129]

In his comedy *Birds* of 414, Aristophanes makes fun of Athenian imperialism. At the same time, he attests to the norm, very familiar to his audience, of cutting up territory into *kleroi*. In *Birds* we meet two Athenians who leave their city to found a *polis* of birds in the sky. In a few scenes, Aristophanes mocks specialists of colonization, such as a poet who comes with a prepared foundation poem,

---

[126] Alternatively (but not convincingly), Dent (Loeb-ed1910) translates, "The rest (of the *leroi*) they assigned by lot (*lanchano*: κληρούχους τοὺς λαχόντας).

[127] Thuc. 3.50.2, trans. Hornblower (1991) ad loc.

[128] Pollux *On.* 3.83. Cf. Gauthier (1966); (1973).

[129] Pollux *On.* 3.83 mentions the Helots in Sparta, the Maryandinoi, subjects to the citizens of Herakleia on the Black Sea, the Penestai in Thessaly, and several others. Ephoros *FGrHist* 70 F 29 = Ath. 263e. Cf. Zelnick-Abramovitz (2012) 106. David Lewis (2018) 147 n.2, offers another possible translation: "after the lots cast for them," i.e., "slaves distributed by lot as booty." Cf. Arist. *Pol.* 1271b41–1272a1 (Cretan *perioikoi*); but Arist. fr. 586 (Rose) = 613.1–2 (Gigon) speak of Cretan *klarotai*. Cf. Callistratus *FHG* 3.257 = Ath. 6.263f: "the Klarotai are so-called because they are allotted" (but this may be part of the fragment).

an oracle monger, and a town planner, fulfilling a task that was conventional in Greek colonization but now serving an empire:

METON (THE TOWN PLANNER): (995) I want to survey the plains of the air for you and to parcel them into lots. . . .
PISTHETAERUS (THE FOUNDER): What are these things?
METON: Tools for measuring the air. . . . Do you understand?
PISTHETAERUS: Not in the least.
METON: With the straight ruler I set to work to inscribe a square within this circle; in its center will be the market-place, into which all the straight streets will lead, converging to this center like a star, which, although only orbicular, sends forth its rays in a straight line from all sides.
(THE FOUNDER HAS HAD ENOUGH) PISTHETAERUS: A regular Thales! . . . We are agreed to sweep all quacks and impostors far from our borders. (trans. Eugene O'Neill)

In *Clouds* of 423, a satire on sophists such as Socrates, he goes even further (202ff.):

STREPSIADES (THE "AVERAGE" ATHENIAN CITIZEN): But what is this?
DISCIPLE (OF SOCRATES): Geometry.
STREPSIADES: What then is it good for?
DISCIPLE: To measure out the land.
STREPSIADES: A land that belongs to an allotment? (*ten klerouchiken*)
DISCIPLE: No, but the whole earth. (trans. W. J. Hickie)

6.3 Section II: Things said: The lot, the "first plot," equality, and the unity of the *kleros*

Examining the question of how lands were distributed merely in terms of landed property misses the larger canvas of the distribution of "goods" in Greek society. Greeks seem to be consistent in what they kept saying explicitly, while applying the same vocabulary since the time of Homer: "goods" (e.g., booty, land, meat, inheritance) are distributed to all sharers, by lot (except for revenues from mines; see above), and equally: equality before chance, and when possible numerical equality of the result, "an equal portion" [F]*isFo moir*[*on*], as an early Cretan inscription expresses it for the share of an inheritance.[130]

---

[130] F]ισϝό μοιρ[ον *IC* IV 20 (*LAC* G20 ca. 600–525); *IC* IV 72 (*LAC* G72.10.53 ca. 450?), both concerning part of the inheritance in the context of adoption.

Land, as noted, was "immovable booty" ready for distribution. If one doubts this, one must be able to demonstrate some alternative mode of ancient Greek thinking and terminology about the distribution of goods by lot within the community. I have not found any.[131]

I shall now concentrate on what Greeks were saying and how early they were saying it, with some commentary on what they were doing. The declarative, the prescriptive, and the descriptive should all point to the same conclusion. The *protoi kleroi* (First Lots, a discrete category) were equal in size, they were distributed by lot, and their purpose was to create a community whose members settled according to the guideline "one *oikos* per one *kleros*." The First Lots expressed, I claim, the notion of *isomoiria* ("equality of land-portions") and the terms implied in *isos kai homoios* ("equal and like/fair") for sharing in the new community.[132]

Let us listen to what some Greeks had to say. As repeatedly emphasized, never did any Greek imagine an *alternative* to the model presented here. What people do not bother to invent reveals the *framework* of what was traditional and expected. For example, no Greek had ever recounted or imagined that a founder could be allotted more land than any other settler, nor, with very few exceptions, did Greeks accord the family descendant from a founder any special privileges.[133] That is a constant mental framework. By contrast, when Plutarch (a late moralizing biographer with excellent sources at his disposal) imagined Rome's early history, it was clear to him that an aristocrat would get far more than the commoners would.[134] That was not a Greek scenario.

We saw above how very similar town grids could signify a whole spectrum of meanings, so we need some words in Greek sources to make sense of the equal plots discovered in colonies. Ideally, a single household (*oikos*) would own a single *kleros*. That ideal does not refer to the sacredness of private property but to the relationship between *oikoi, kleroi,* and the "whole" *polis*. "The Corinthian Pheidon, in fact, one of the most ancient lawgivers, thought that the households and the citizen population ought to remain at the same numbers," as Aristotle tells us in the *Politics*.[135] Pheidon was a historical figure attributed to the seventh century, and he was the contemporary of several *oikistai*, founders of colonies; they were all facing similar issues. Pheidon was probably reacting to his

---

[131] See Hennig (1980); Ménager (1987).
[132] For *isomoiria*, see Endnote 2.
[133] Plut. *Them.* 32.5 recounts that Themistocles's descendants still enjoyed privileges in the province the Persian king had given to the Athenian leader. However, this was a Persian king doing the giving, top-down, which illustrates precisely the contrast with Greek practices and conventions relevant to Greek land distribution. Cyrene, as noted, is the other notable exception.
[134] Plut. *Publ.* 21.6 [6]; cf. App. *Reg.*12 and see below.
[135] Arist. *Pol.* 1265b12–14, trans. Rackham (1944); for Pheidon's views on the relation between the number of citizens and *oikoi*: Link (1991a) 49–56. Cf. Hölkeskampf (2015).

changing reality, which deviated from the ideal schematic equivalence between landholders and citizens. But determining what people consider ideal is no less critical. Each *kleros* was also regarded as an equal "portion" (*moira, meros*) of some "whole." The colonial land division into *kleroi* and the attachment of each *kleros* to one *oikos* and the male citizen expressed the equal sharing in the community and its fighting corps.[136]

Pheidon was one of many in thinking about land and the *polis*. As Aristotle reports, demands for the redistribution of lands were acute in the Greek mainland. They imagine a "restart" of the community based on *isomoiria*, equal *kleroi*. Referring to Tyrtaios, a Spartan poet writing around the middle of the seventh century, Aristotle says, "It happened too in Sparta in the course of the Messenian War, as is clear from the poem of Tyrtaios called *Eunomia*: For some, hard-pressed because of the war, demanded a *redistribution* (*anadaston poiein*) of the land."[137] Theognis too complains that people no longer make a fair distribution "from the middle."[138] In the fifth century, the revolution against the elite at Leontinoi was equally articulated in terms of the redistribution of lands (*anadasmos*).[139] The rise of political communities in the archaic period involved confronting issues of land and demands for (re)distribution as early as the seventh century.[140] Aside from Tyrtaios, Solon (late seventh–early sixth centuries) was proud to have refused demands for equal (re)distribution of lands, *isomoiria*.[141] Solon was not an egalitarian reformer (I do not wish to imply that). His rejection of the demands for *isomoiria* is not evidence of what Solon did, but it is evidence that such demands existed.

A Lokrian inscription of ca. 500 mentions land kept in reserve (*anadaithmon*) and threatens infringements with severe penalties.[142] In colonies, because land for settlement was considered "empty," we can observe more clearly a fuller spectrum of the exercise of the power of the community to make decisions about property and territory. Land reserved for future settlers was a common feature of Greek colonization.[143] Moreover, as Roland Martin observes, colonies developed centrifugally (from a center radiating outward), whereas many cities in

---

[136] See Parker (2005) 32–35.
[137] Arist. *Pol.* 5.1306b36–1307a2 = Tyrt. Gerber fr. 1; cf. Hodkinson (2000) 76.
[138] See *Introduction*, 7. Solon fr. 34, 6–9 West; Arist. *Pol.* 5.1306b36–1307a2 = Tyrt. Gerber fr. 1; Theogn. 678. See Cerri (1969).
[139] Thuc. 5.4.2; cf. for Syracuse ca. 357/6, Plut. *Dion* with Fuks (1968), Consolo Langher (2005); for Herakleia Pontike, Justin *Epit.* 16.4.1.
[140] Link (1991) 49–56, 62–67.
[141] Solon fr. 34, 6–9 West.
[142] *Nomima* vol. 2 no. 44: 187–192; ML 13 The Lokrian law seems to relate to a second phase in the life of the settlement when the nonpartitioned land is divided up among the citizens. The law expressly recognizes lands reserved by the community and it is about the partitioning of the plain, "as yet not-allocated" (*andaithmon*).
[143] Graham (1982).

"the old world" converged centripetally to form political entities (*synoikismos*; See Figure 6.7).[144] With the latter, it is much harder to observe changes on the ground because of precedents, unlike the colonial world's idealized "empty land." Reserved land depends on the orientation of a settlement's expansion. I noted above Gabriel Zuchtriegel's remark, which is also relevant here: in their early years, colonies tended to be "urban" centers where *kleroi* were adjacent, and people could exercise a measure of political power (*Ackerbürger poleis*), whereas in the later period, we find more farmsteads with the accompanying loss of involvement and political power because of distance from the center.[145]

As we saw, ideally, the number of *kleroi* and *oikoi* should be the same.[146] At Sparta, full Spartan citizens were supposedly *homoioi* ("equals" or "peers") in both their political and military status and in the size of their *kleroi*. The quasihistorical founder-legislator of Sparta, Lycurgus, supposedly distributed nine thousand lots to nine thousand Spartiates (see Introduction, 7). Those *kleroi* were forever to be fixed, unsold, and inherited whole, not to be given away as a dowry, while keeping constant the relation of one *oikos* per one *kleros*.[147] Like Lycurgus, the fifth-century lawgiver from Thebes, Philolaos, wished expressly "to preserve the number of lots" (for example, by adopting a son) and legislated against increased landholdings. Phaleas of Chalkedon (early fourth century) argued for equalizing the property of citizens either in the context of a newly founded city or by regulating dowries in existing cities.[148]

It did not work quite that way in Sparta. Lycurgus may be shrouded in myth, but Sparta was a *kleros*-based society. The *kleros* allowed a Spartan citizen to contribute to the public mess he belonged to; inability to contribute meant demotion or even the loss of one's citizen status. The reality, however, was different from the ideal, fixed image of the formula "one *oikos* per one *kleros*." Sparta kept suffering from a "paucity of men" (*oligandria*) after many had lost their full citizen status.

---

[144] Martin (1974); cf. Fischer-Hansen (1996) 320; Moggi (1976).

[145] Zuchtriegel (2018) 117–124; cf. 132, 154. A high number of rural dwellers, he says, "is not a feature of a democratic, but of aristocratic and oligarchic societies." Concerning Herakleia, for example, he says that the equality phase is when settlers live in the city and own lands outside of it. The inequality intensifies when people move out to farms (2018: 113). "As I argue here, the settlement pattern that emerges from the study of Heraclea and its territory reflects the egalitarian ideology of classical Greek colonists. On the other hand, the spread of farmsteads and rural necropoleis is not due to democratization and development, but simply to the break-up of the egalitarian structure that characterized the first two or three generations." Cf. Bintliff (2006); Boyd and Jameson (1981).

[146] Arist. *Pol.* 1265b13–16. Cf. Is. 7.30. For similar views of Phaleas of Chalkedon, see Arist. *Pol.* 1267b10. Cf. 1265a38ff.; 1266b14–24; Plato *Laws* 740a. Adoption to preserve the integrity of the *kleros*: Arist. *Pol.* 1309a23–6; Plato *Laws* 740c. The needs of a new community were not merely agricultural. Some of the equal lots were perhaps given to artisans, not farmers. At one point, Plato recommends providing artisans with lots in each of the *mere* (parts) of his invented colony: Plato *Laws* 8.847e–848c, referred to by, Gras, Tréziny, and Broise (2004) 577.

[147] Plut. *Lyc.* 8.1 and see below.

[148] Arist. *Pol.* 1266b1, 1274b2. The survey of these views: Arist. *Pol.* 1266a–b. Cf. Lane Fox (1985) 215.

There were fewer than one thousand full *oikos*-holding citizens in the fourth century.[149] So whether the ideal image of nine thousand fixed *kleroi* had much to do with reality, eventually, the *kleroi* did not remain in their original state. Over time in colonies, too, reality did not always match the ideal guidelines when the elitist vector overshadowed the horizontal one.

Sparta provides an excellent illustration of the distinction between what people do and what they say they do. Each Spartan had to contribute to his common mess, the *syssition*. Supposedly everyone ate the same at the *syssition*—demonstrating how *homoioi* were equal to each other. Xenophon remarks that members of a *syssition* would "add" to its meager menu shared equally among them, as prescribed in primordial times: "But many extras are supplied from the spoils of the chase; and for these rich men sometimes substitute wheaten bread,"[150] thus making the fare luxurious despite the image of frugality. However, he still insists on the equality of portions, even for the extras.

The initial *kleroi* at Sparta as elsewhere were distinguished from other landholdings and were sometimes known as *protoi* (first), or *palaioi* (old), or (at Sparta) *archaia moira* ("the ancient portions, or sections"). Often, as at Sparta, these were supposed to be inalienable and were to remain undivided. "To sell land is considered shameful by the Lakedaimonians, but from their ancient portion (*archaias moiras*) it is not permitted."[151] Over the centuries, this did not hold. Herodotus has Demaratos claim that the number of Spartiates was eight thousand; in contrast, a century later, by Aristotle's time, there were less than one thousand, and Aristotle was blaming inheritances and dowries for the scarcity of Spartans.[152]

So, where do we place the emphasis? Was it an equal society (in terms of its self-reflection and ideals), or a highly unequal one "in reality"? The issue here is

---

[149] Arist. *Pol.* 1270a30; Xen. *Resp. Lac.* 1.1.

[150] Xen. *Lac.Pol.* 5.3, trans. E. C. Marchant and G. W. Bowersock.

[151] Arist. fr. 611.12 (Rose; Arist. *Lac.Pol.*). On the *archaia moira* at Sparta, Heraklides Lembos fr 12 (Dilts 1971), *De reb. publ.* II.7. Cf. Plut. *Mor.* 238e = *Instituta laconica* no. 22). Cf. F. J. Lazenby (1995), who believes that *archaia moira* was not land but a tribute paid by the Helots. Hodkinson, who used to accept *archaia moira* as a distinct category at Sparta, now favors Lazenby's hypothesis (which suffers from the fact that such tribute was called something else entirely, *apophora*) (Hodkinson [2000] 85–90). Both scholars miss the larger framework: they treat this as a *Spartan* subject (it is not) with little comparative evidence from the Greek world. This is misguided, I think, since both vocabulary and explicit statements about "First Lots" in colonies provide a better frame of reference. Van Wees (2018) claims that the ancient lots were a late invention; I take a different view. For example, he quotes Plutarch *Agis* 5.4 that says explicitly that *before* the reforms there were one hundred Spartans with both land and a *kleros*, and six hundred with merely a *kleros*. The distinction between land and a *kleros* points rather to its existence as a precedent category.

[152] Hdt. 7.234.1–2; Arist. *Pol.* 1270a31. Moreover, because of the special status of heiresses at Sparta, Aristotle is shocked to observe huge amounts of landed property at Sparta in the hands of women, a measure originally designed to keep a *kleros* intact; *Pol.* 1270a23–25. Cf. Plut. *Agis* 5 on the reforms of Epitadeus. Polybius 12.6b.8 claims that several men (perhaps brothers?) could marry the same woman at Sparta, supposedly for the same reason: to keep a *kleros* whole. See also David (1981).

not Spartan history but the recognition of the apparent contradiction between what people do and what they say about it. Much depends on time: an initial situation of equality often develops into one of inequality. In time, there were indeed wealthy Spartans and colonists with landholdings more extensive than others. Yet the idea of equal *kleroi* expressing what it meant to be *isos kai homoios* (equal and like) and actual inequality existed side by side, representing the constant tension between the egalitarian/horizontal and the elitist/vertical vectors.

6.3.1 The First Lots articulated

In time the distinction between the primary parcellation and distribution of equal lots by lot and other types of alienable lands led to the juridical distinction between *ta patro[i]a* and lots that were *autokteta*, "for sale."[153] But what were those First Lots, and how large were they? To reiterate: the equal *protoi kleroi* did not constitute the *limit* of how much land one could own. Instead, a First Lot constituted the minimum to qualify as a sharer or citizen. The land portion was concrete, fixed, and often surprisingly small. There were probably practical reasons for that, especially since colonies usually started as small, often planned centers from which people could walk to their fields. Considerations of defense and esprit de corps were probably significant: protecting *together* relatively small, nearby fields that were still sufficient for essential livelihood. It would have been difficult at the initial stages to control broad areas.

Michel Gras compares Greek First Lots with Roman quasihistorical traditions about settlers getting *bina iugera* each. He points out that the *protoi kleroi* may seem small, but they also conform to what is found on the ground. At Megara Hyblaia, ca. 700, the size of a *kleros* was around 3,000 square meters. At Zankle, toward the end of the sixth century, the urban blocks were approximately 168 by 42 meters, or 7,000 square meters. Himera (founded by Zankle ca. 650) provides further information: in the lower town, the lots are equal in size to those from its mother city, Zankle; in the upper town, the blocks are 5,120 square meters (160 by 32 meters). Michel Gras convincingly suggests that Roman traditions, casting Romulus in the guise of a Greek *oikistes*, provided each citizen with *bina* (two) *iugera*, which comprise around ca 5,000 square meters (discussed further below). Varro explicitly refers to this as *heredium*, probably reflecting the Greek notion that a *protos kleros* must not be split up or sold, hence inherited whole.[154]

---

[153] Asheri (1966) 21.
[154] Gras (2019/21) 6 with reference to Varro, *Rust.* I 20.2 with Plin. *Hist. Nat.* 18.7.

There may have been another implied reason: Since land could serve as security for a debt, it was often liable for confiscation or seizure.[155] Ancient thinkers and lawgivers, who could observe how wealth could concentrate in fewer hands, warned against or prohibited the practice. With his researched knowledge of ancient Greek institutions, Aristotle mentions various laws limiting the size of lots. As noted, in his discussion of agricultural communities, he says, "In early times . . . *in many states* there was even legislation prohibiting the sale of the *original allotments*."[156] In the same passage, Aristotle mentions others who limit only those plots of land "lying between a certain place and the citadel or city," implying no such limits on others.

The *minimum* aspect of the First Lot is implied in a law attributed to Oxylos of Elis, "with some similar provision, forbidding loans secured on a certain portion of a man's existing estate."[157] The "certain portion" constitutes a minimum: Limitations were perhaps intended to curb greed, but it was imperative to guarantee a small minimum of land. Colonial First Lots share this aspect with plots of land in the "older" Greek world: a minimum specified by size, fulfilling the purpose of "sharing in the *polis*." One probably wished to avoid using those as securities for loans. Small *kleroi* could only secure small loans, which were easier to repay. Perhaps this is why, in the foundation decree of Black Corcyra, the First Lot (*protos klaros*) is distinguished from the inalienable *katanomon*, calculated apparently as precisely half the size of the First Lot.[158]

Something of that nature seems to be indicated in the laws of Aphytis: "the citizens of Aphytis, although numerous and possessing a small territory nevertheless are all engaged in agriculture, for they are assessed not on the whole of their estates, but on divisions of them so small that even the poor can exceed the required minimum in their assessments."[159] This is another illustration of the direct, explicit relationship between "sharing in the community" and, ideally, owning and keeping a First Lot or its equivalent. We do not know whether the Aphytians used the term *protoi kleroi* or *archaia moira*. Still, the function of the divisions was the same, indicating a general Greek pattern of thinking about this relation. This pattern may have been responsible for the emergence of the *protoi kleroi* in colonies in the first place.

Leukas, a Corinthian colony, also used to have laws "to preserve the old allotments." At some point, those were repealed, and Aristotle was unhappy with the exaggerated democratic result: there were no more property qualifications for holding office at Leukas. Aristotle's unhappiness testifies to the antiquity of

---

[155] Zurbach (2015).
[156] Arist. *Pol.* 1319a10–11 (emphasis added).
[157] Arist. *Pol.* 1319a13 with Link (1991a) 145–149.
[158] See below on Black Corcyra. This is also the view of Dittenberg *ad loc.* Cf. Zurbach (2017) 701 n.90.
[159] Arist. *Pol.* 1319a16–19.

the *protoi kleroi*. Scholars sometimes claim an "invention of the past" in a (late) source for contemporary political reasons. Yet here we have the reverse situation concerning how we read an ancient source: that Aristotle is unhappy with the fact that the inalienability of the First Lots at Leukas had been *repealed* by his day attests to their antiquity, most probably going back to the time of Leukas's foundation. Moreover, as with other cases cited by Aristotle (his school researched dozens of *politeiai*), we are not dealing here merely with "ideas of fourth-century philosophers" but with researched historical precedents cited by a fourth-century master.

Plato recommends keeping the *kleros* intact and letting only one son (not necessarily the eldest) inherit to preserve the constant number of allotments.[160] Reflecting further on the problem, Aristotle succinctly links the issues of equality, a preference for "one son" (so the land need not be divided), the unity and sustainability of the *kleros*, the danger of accumulation of wealth in the hands of the few, the "old *kleroi*," and the well-being of the state. Aristotle here refers to (apparently futile) attempts to limit landholdings in general, while these possessions are distinguished from the First Lots:

> That when regulating the amount of property legislators ought also to regulate the size of the family; for if the number of children becomes too large for the property, the law is quite sure to be broken.... There is the legislation of Solon, and other states have a law prohibiting the acquisition of land to any amount that the individual may desire; and similarly there is legislation to prevent the sale of estates, as at Lokroi there is a law [20] that a man shall not sell unless he can prove that manifest misfortune has befallen him and also there is legislation to preserve the *old allotments*....[161]
>
> But it is possible that *equality* of estates may be maintained, but their size may be either too large and promote luxury, or too small, causing a penurious standard of living; it is clear therefore that it is not enough for the lawgiver to make the estates *equal*, but he must aim at securing a medium size.[162]

The insistence on *isomoiria* (equal portions) may have been partly responsible for the foundation of numerous "colonies of colonies."[163] Founding colonies provided an outlet from the smaller holdings of partible inheritance at home, but such problems would reappear in colonies, hence another impetus to found yet more settlements. An elite of first settlers would tend to preserve privilege and become a kind of oligarchy, with an ethos perhaps similar to the Spartan

---

[160] Plato *Laws* 11.923c; cf. *Laws* 5.741c.
[161] Arist. *Pol.* 2.1266b10–22.
[162] Arist. *Pol.* 2.1266b24–28.
[163] Cf. Costanzi (2010).

homoioi, hesitant to share all with either newcomers or with the second and third generations of sons. Sons of new colonial elites that had acquired more land may not have felt the land pressure, but those who remained poor probably did. The general birth rate probably rose since migration studies indicate that the first generations of settlers tend to produce more children. Within a century of their foundation, the Megarian Hyblaians in Sicily probably thought their offsprings were too many to become *oikos* owners, which encouraged the foundation of Selinous. Plato expressed the idea of "too many" as limited space, or *stenochoria*, "place too narrow," a reason to leave and colonize.[164] Consider too the ideal of "one *kleros* per *oikos*": sons may have been encouraged to imitate their grandparents or parents and establish a new settlement where they, in turn, would enjoy full privileges of *isomoiria*.

6.3.2 First Lots: Inclusion and exclusion

First Lots were distributed by lot among the first settlers. As with any distribution of booty, those who share form a predemarcated group that, by definition, would not let others participate. This consideration would imply that at the initial stages of the foundation, no "natives" participated as full members. Even in rare cases when a colony was founded peacefully, only Greeks were the settlers, as seems to be confirmed at Megara Hyblaia. It was founded peacefully at the invitation of the local king Hyblon and named "Hyblaia" after him, a true rarity among the names of colonies.[165] This peaceful nature was exceptional since most other foundations involved violence, conquest, the expulsion of locals, and territorial annexation. Mimnermos of Kolophon was not ashamed of the *hybris* (violence) involved in the foundation of his native city,[166] and Archilochos sang,

> They founded (*ektisen*) another house and another orchard—they had evacuated so many acres of land (*gyai*) without arousing anyone's pity."[167]

---

[164] Plato *Laws* 708b.

[165] Peaceful relations, colonization "by invitation," Thuc. 6.3; lack of non-Greek settlers at Megara Hyblaia: see the superb analysis by Bérard (2017). Although the story might seem an *aition* (explaining the name Hyblaia), the site itself (flat and defenseless) corroborates Thucydides's account. Colonies were often named after natural features (e.g., Zankle), and Taras (a river's name), not after non-Greeks like Hyblon.

[166] Mimn. fr. 9 (West) [Strabo 14.1.4].

[167] See Archilochos fr. 1 Gerber. For the compounds with *gyai* designating land portions, see Hom. *Od.* 7.113; *Il.* 9.579. Cf. Hes. *WD* 425, 434. See Archilochos fr. 264 Lasserre (1968): "*Alors, sur ce sol riant, ils fondèrent (ektisen) une autre demeure et un autre verger – ils avaient évacué tant d'arpents de terre (gyai) sans éveiller la pitié de personne.*" Gerber (fr. 94, l. 5) (*gyai*) does not accept *ektisen* and translates, "for so much land did [Gerber misses the more precise meaning of *gyas*] it give up." Zurbach (2008) 94 does not cite the alternative reading.

As mentioned earlier in the discussion of "empty lands" (cf. 6.1), Thucydides's description of the settlement of the islet of Ortygia (Syracuse) and Strabo's description of the founding of Corcyra are typical: "Syracuse was founded," says Thucydides "by Archias . . . who began by driving out the Sikels from the island upon which the inner city now stands." "Chersikrates . . . ejected the Liburnians, who held possession of the island (Corcyra), and colonized it with new settlers."[168] An "empty land" would thus be created, and the Greek community, disregarding previous patterns of ownership (had there been any), imposed and implemented its mode of land allotment. This taking possession tallies well with what Julien Zurbach calls "confiscation," parallel to what was going on in the Greek world at large, with "non-colonial" Greeks expanding and "confiscating" (in fact, annexing) territories, as did Argos, for example.[169] "I will give you to beat with your feet in dancing, and its fair plain to measure with a rope," said Apollo (misleadingly) to the Spartans (Hdt. 1.66.2), thus revealing their expectations: capturing land as booty and measuring it with a *schoinos*, "rope" (a term that also served as a measuring unit of plots of land for colonial distribution).[170] Why measure the "land booty" if not for the sake of distribution of *kleroi*?

By the end of the eighth century, a newly established Greek community could have a comprehensive vision of itself, expressed in an initial territory and regarding it as available plow land (*aroura*) for distribution into *kleroi*. The violent character of occupation resulting in "empty lands," divisible as booty, seems to support this view. The mode of land distribution to individual colonists (one *oikos*/one *kleros*) follows the terminology, values, and modes of distribution of other types of "portions" that we have discussed. The allotment of equal portions of land as fixed, perpetual booty to be shared by all group members highlights the egalitarian vision behind it.

6.3.3 First Lots and equality: Was there an aristocracy among Greek colonists?

The question came up before, yet it needs more focus. The short answer is no:[171] to the best of our knowledge, only the *oikistes* was of higher standing, and as noted earlier, his unique status was marked only after his death, and his

---

[168] Thuc. 6.3.2; Strabo 6.4.2.
[169] Zurbach (2015; 2017) 39 stresses the "imperialist" aspects of Greek colonists and *doriktetos gê*, the land won by the "right of the spear."
[170] On Black Corcyra, see 6.3.10. Cf. Hdt. 2.6.2.
[171] The concept of "aristocracy" in archaic Greek history has been fundamentally revised in recent years. See Fischer and van Wees (2015); Duplouy (2006); Ma (2016); Giangiulio (2016), and section 7.1.2 in this volume.

descendants were not privileged. In some cases, the *isomoiria* of the first generation of founders resulted in an "elite of first settlers," which could result in further colonization.[172] Note that this is not an elite *among* the first settlers, but the colonists have become an elite. Such elites of first settlers imply *isomoiria*: they rose together, as it were, *en bloc*.[173] Aristotle refers explicitly to this phenomenon, defining *eugeneia* ("well-born") in terms of belonging to the first generation of colonists when describing the situation in Adriatic Apollonia and Thera:

> Neither is it a democracy if the free being few govern the majority who are not of free birth, as for instance at Apollonia on the Ionian Gulf and at Thera for in each of these cities the offices of honor were filled by the specially well-born (*eugeneia*) families who had been the first settlers of the colonies (*protoi kataschontes tas apoikias*), and these were few out of many.[174]

The situation of sharing in the initial *dasmos* (division) of the land probably gave rise to the elite of first settlers at Syracuse, called *Gamoroi*, "having shares (*moroi*) in the land (*ge*)."[175] Although its origins are unknown to us, the elite at Samos was likewise named *Gamoroi*. What characterizes such an elite is the initial equality (defined in terms of equal portions of land) among all and a sense of collective superiority toward the rest. Specifically at Syracuse, some of "the rest" consisted of non-Greek tenants, called *Kyllyrioi*, and perhaps some other Greek settlers who joined Syracuse beyond the initial nucleus.[176] However, aside from such a precise definition of a class, belonging to the first generation was a mark of pride, as the Sicilian *Deinomenidai* (tyrant rulers of Gela and Syracuse) and *Emmenidai* of Sicilian Akragas illustrate. Although Archias, the founder of Syracuse, was an "aristocratic" Bakchiad, what counted in the later period was

---

[172] Cf. McInerney (2004) 30; Sartori (1980–1981) 265–266.

[173] Contra Gallo (2009); see Endnote 2.

[174] Arist. *Pol.* 4.1290b13–14: κατ' εὐγένειαν καὶ πρῶτοι κατασχόντες τὰς ἀποικίας, ὀλίγοι ὄντες, πολλῶν. Thera was considered a Spartan colony, a point that should be taken more seriously than is sometimes the case; Malkin (1994a) 67.

[175] Hdt. 7.155; Arist. fr. 586 (Rose); Timaios *FGrHist* 566 F8; Diod. 8.11; cf. Arist. *Pol.* 1303b20; Plut. *Mor.* 825c; Photius; Suda; Hesych., s.v., *Kallikyrioi*. See Bravo (1992); Luraghi (1994) 281–288. Sappho may have found refuge among them: Jacoby *FGrHist* 239 F36 = Marmor Parium A36, but the lacuna between "Sappho" and *gamoroi* is quite large. "From the time Sappho sailed from Mytilene to Sicily, fleeing ..., when the elder Critias was [arch]on in Athens, and in Syracuse the landowners seized power" (trans. Rotstein 2016). At Syracuse, they seem to have evolved as an oligarchy later than the time of foundation. The Gamoroi were chased by the Syracusan *demos* together with the Kyllyrioi in 492; Gelon had them return in 485 from Kasmenai to Syracuse (Hdt. 7.155). *Geo-moroi* (*gamoroi*) at Samos: Plut *Mor.* 303e–304c; Thuc. 8.21; Shipley (1987) 39–41; Mariaud (2015) 259–286; Marcotte (1994). For a review of the scholarship, see Morakis (2015) and my remarks in Endnote 2.

[176] Hdt. 7.155.2; Dunbabin (1948) 111–112; 400; 414–415; Leighton (1999) 233 suggests that as a class they emerged in the first half of the seventh century, i.e., by the time of the second and third generation of Syracusans. See Bravo (1992). Cf. Timaios *FGrHist* 566.8; Aristotle fr. 586 Rose (= Photius; Suda, s.v., *Kallikyrioi*). Cf. Hesychius, s.v. *Kallikyrioi*; Zenobius 4.54.

not individual *eugeneia* but the "horizontal" belonging to the Gamoroi. By contrast, in the only colony founded with kings, Cyrene, being a direct descendant, Battos I was a point of great pride for the Cyrenaian poet Callimachus.[177]

On a grander scale, this is precisely the story of the Spartans. The Spartan "Equals," *homoioi*, supposedly with their "9,000 *kleroi*," were an "aristocracy of first conquerors-settlers." Having taken possession of "the land taken by the spear" (*doriktetos ge*),[178] the land then becomes "free," or "empty" and "uninhabited," and ready for a primary division as fitting the "colony of the Dorians."[179] All Spartan *homoioi* then form an upper class in relation to the "dwellers around," *peri-oikoi*, the dependent yet autonomous cities, with their "30,000 *kleroi*," and the enslaved tenants (*helots*) in Messenia and some other areas.[180]

One exceptional case from the classical period illustrates the prerogatives of first settlers, the position of women, and the "old *kleroi*" in relation to newcomers.[181] Sybaris, the ancient Greek city in southern Italy, was founded ca. 720; it was destroyed and occupied several times by its Greek neighbor Kroton. In 446/5, Pericles initiated an ambitious new colony, pan-Hellenic in character, to be founded on the site of ancient Sybaris together with the displaced Sybarites. It was an exciting venture, with people like the philosopher Protagoras, the historian Herodotus, and the famous town planner and utopian thinker Hippodamos of Miletos joining the new foundation, now named Thourioi. However, soon after its foundation, the settlement was torn apart by quarrels between the Sybarites and the newcomers.

> The *land* lying near the city *the Sybarites were portioning out in allotments* among themselves, (*katakleroucheo*) and the more distant land to the newcomers." (Diodorus 12.11.1, trans. C. H. Oldfather)

This did not end well. The new settlers massacred and expelled the former ones and then,

> Since the countryside was extensive and rich, they sent for colonists in large numbers from Greece and to these they assigned parts of the city and distributed the land equally (*ep' ises enemon* [*nemo*]).[182]

---

[177] Callimachus epigram 35 cf. 21.
[178] Zurbach (2015; 2017) 39, LSJ, s.v. δορικτητός. However, Zurbach exaggerates when he says that colonization was a "typical imperialist act," not distinguishing between forceful, "independent" occupation and "imperialism" (that supposedly serves another entity, not directly involved on the spot).
[179] Pind. *Isthm.* 7.12–15.
[180] Plut. *Lyc.* 8; cf. Cartledge (1996).
[181] Diod. 12.11.1–2; 14.7.4–5.
[182] Diod.12.11.1–2, trans. Oldfather, adapted. See Ehrenberg (1948); Lombardo (1993b); Rutter (1973). For comparable troubles with new waves of settlers, see Arist. *Pol.* 1303a26.

The quarrels arose precisely because of what the new settlers regarded as the abuse of equality in several areas. First, the expectation had been that the allocation of *timai* (positions in the state) would be equal, most likely by drawing lots (Thourioi was a democracy modeled on Athens). The second complaint concerned the equality of access to ritual, specifically the equality of citizen rights for women.[183] Finally, the land: the complaint about nearer and more distant *kleroi* signifies that the available agricultural territory was not viewed as an *entire entity*, an *eremos chora*, precisely what was to be expected if equal chances were followed by distribution by lot on an equal basis.

The link between equal *kleroi*, distributed by equal chance, and the notion of the community as sharers is well illustrated by the case of Sybaris and Thourioi. Other historical (nonlegendary) practices of Greek colonists further substantiate this notion of "sharers," owners of "portions." This practice of equal plots distributed by lot was commonly Greek. It was implemented in hundreds of settlements established over vast distances by Greeks of different origins and speaking various Greek dialects. The "lot-equality-fairness-sharing of portions" cluster was implemented concretely while expressing abstract values of sharing and membership. It is no wonder that Aristotle would later conceive of the state as a "partnership," *koinonia*.[184]

A quasihistorical Roman example illustrates how Greek expectations could be different from Roman ones. It is the story of *unequal* land allotment for an "aristocrat." Appian says that "Claudius, an influential Sabine of the town of Regillus, . . . took refuge in Rome with his relatives, friends, and slaves, to the number of five thousand. To all these, the Romans gave a place of habitation, land to cultivate, and the right of citizenship. Claudius, on account of his brilliant exploits against the Sabines, was chosen a member of the Senate, and the Claudian *gens* received its name from him." Plutarch provides further details about the land allotment: "For he at once incorporated the families in the Roman state, and gave each one *two acres* of land on the river Anio. To Clausus [= Claudius], however, he *gave twenty-five acres* of land and enrolled him among the senators. . . . The Claudian family, descended from him, is no less illustrious than any in Rome."[185]

We never hear such a story (not even a concocted one) concerning a Greek founder. Aside from reserving public and sacred spaces, the First Lots were equal. But there were also exceptions in the Greek world that indicated the norm because of its abuse. After 404 (the peace with Carthage), the tyrant Dionysios

---

[183] Blok (2017) 33. On women and colonization, see Malkin (2020) discussing earlier work and Endnote 3.
[184] Arist. *Pol.* 1.1 1252a.
[185] App. *Reg.* 123; Plut. *Publ.* 21.6 [6]. Gras (2019/21) 6 with reference to Varro *Rust.* 1.20.2 with Plin. *Hist. Nat.* 18.7.

of Syracuse divided up the territorial space of his rule into three: (1) the fortified Ortygia, where he resided; (2) the best parts of the *chora* were singled out and given to friends and commanders of Dionysios; (3) the rest was divided up into equal lots and distributed to everyone else, both citizens, *xenoi,* and freed slaves. Exceptional are the first two categories. The last conforms to modalities and the general purpose of colonial land distributions by lot: equal status at the initial stage and a mixture of the entire population.

To what extent does the notion of "elites" contradict egalitarianism? The common image of elites as typical of archaic Greek society has been deconstructed in current research that has moved away from considering elites in terms of blue blood with a greater emphasis on the acquisition of wealth, prestige, and social mobility.[186] Alain Duplouy, in particular, has rightly drawn attention to what mattered most in the fluctuating circumstances of the formation of political communities, notably a distinction between who is in and who is out, that is, the criteria of inclusion and exclusion. However, social and economic elites did emerge, with porous distinctions and practices, such as *symposia*, to set them apart.[187] Colonies, in particular, seem to support the priority of the inclusion issue (who would merit sharing in the *kleroi*?), especially since newly founded colonies show no sign of elites among the first generation of settlers.

There were probably distinct elites in the eighth century in the style of Odysseus and his *hetairoi* (companions) musing about ideal colonization sites, as Odysseus does in the ninth book of the *Odyssey*. Perhaps anachronistically, the Foundation Decree of Cyrene also refers to colonists as the *hetairoi* of the founder.[188] By the end of the eighth century, some Homeric-style "princes" celebrated in Homeric-style burials that revealed their distinction from the rest of society. Such princely graves existed for about one generation with no precedent or continuity.[189] Such tombs were found across the Mediterranean at Cypriote Salamis, the West Gate of Eretria in Euboia, and Kyme in southern Italy. The princely tomb disappeared in tandem with the rise of the equalizing forces of the new communities.[190]

---

[186] The literature is vast. See especially Morris (2000); Duplouy (2006) esp. 11-35; E. Kistler et al. (2015); Duplouy (2019). Cf. Zurbach (2008); Fisher and van Wees (2015); cf. de Angelis (2016) 146.

[187] See, e.g., Murray (2018); Węcowski (2014).

[188] *SEG* 9.3. The Foundation Decree of Cyrene (the agreement of the founders) *SEG* 9.3; ML 5; quoted and trans. by Graham (1983) 224–226. Cf. Ruzé (1998) 182. See further below on its implications.

[189] Coldstream (1979) 341–357; contra Antonaccio (1995). Luraghi (1996) views the princely tombs as an argument against egalitarianism; however, the exceptionality of those burials seems to indicate the last gasp for extraordinary recognition by self-styled *basileis*. The Lefkandi "heroic" burials are far too early to constitute a precedent for an argument relating to the end of the eighth century.

[190] Crielaard (2000); Walker (2004) 76–86, 115–118; d'Agostino (2006), 232–234. For a review of mainland Greece's rich burials, see de Polignac (1995b). Cremations with bones were placed in silver

By contrast, as noted at the beginning, founders (*oikistai*) of colonies did not celebrate themselves but were heroized by the community after their death, an honor that was singular by definition and did not express any "class-elite" aspect. Thoukles may have had aspirations to be a "prince": he tried to be the founder of more than one colony in Sicily but had his wings clipped. Katane rejected his status and chose an alternative founder.[191] Thoukles was the last of the princes: Never again do we hear of any founder trying that. In my view, the years around 700 mark the change of emphasis: the *hetairoi* became much more prominent and so does the egalitarian vector.

In short, single, named founders with "companions," not "elite groups" with their dependents, founded the colonies; significant differentiation in wealth usually appears not before the second or third generation after a colony's foundation (Figure 6.1). The founder was often the only "aristocrat" among the settlers (e.g., Archias the Bakchiad,[192] Philippos of Kroton).[193] For example, Antiphemos, the cofounder of Sicilian Gela (founded ca. 688), was accorded heroic cult for which we have independent evidence (a cup bearing personal dedication with the founder's name and the name of the dedicator) dating to the fifth century.[194] To reiterate: The cult was the *geras* of the *oikistes*; the community of equals, namely *all* the first settlers, elevated him to heroic status. As suggested earlier, the unique hero's cult meant that no one (unless a tyrant) could claim supremacy above the other sharers in the community.[195]

One significant difference between the Homeric and archaic periods concerns leaders and gods. As noted in chapter 1, in Homer, while the human leader gets a special prize (*geras*), the gods do not receive a tithe (*dekate*) (a common practice in historical periods). When colonizing, the unique portion previously reserved for the king was transformed into discrete land portions (a *temenos*) set aside to serve as sanctuaries to the gods.[196]

---

urns inside a bronze *lebes*, often covered with bronze shield, and placed in a stone cist grave. Luraghi (1996) 218 rightly observes that Kyme's princely tombs do not indicate "equality." However, Kyme is one of the earliest settlements (mid-eighth century), about a generation before Thoukles. Moreover, my point is not material equality but equality of First Lots, as I shall argue. Cf. Shepherd (2015b) 357–370 for varied strategies of displaying wealth and status in western colonies, with significant developments in the sixth century, long after the foundation.

[191] Thuc. 6.3.3.

[192] This is true of both historical and mythical accounts. Specifically, stories about Archias explicitly referred to as a Bakhiad only to emphasize that he had left alone with a group of followers, perhaps from Tenea in the land of Corinth, or with his brother who split off and founded Corcyra. See discussion in Malkin (1987) 41–43.

[193] Hdt 5.47. Cf. Figueira (2008) 429. He uses the term "patronal colonization" also referring to Miltiades at the Chersonese and Lemnos.

[194] *Mnasithales anetheke Antiphamoi;* Ciaceri (1911) 311; for the inscription see Guarducci (1967) 1:254–255, with bibliography. Dubois (1989) 1:135, 159–60. Also Orsi (1900).

[195] Malkin (1987a) 189–261.

[196] The exception is Cyrene, where there was apparently an overlap between the royal and the divine *temenos* (Hdt. 4.161).

Homer is our earliest source for the activities of a founder that reveal a comprehensive vision of the land, the community, and its gods. The gods received delimited, sacred plots of land (a *temenos*) and the settlers a *kleros* each. In the *Odyssey* we hear about the mass migration of the Phaiakians fleeing the constant harassment of the ferocious Cyclopes, and the eventual foundation of their new settlement: Phaiakia (or Scheria), where the weary Odysseus found shelter. It was founded by the father of Phaiakia's present king, who is still "Homeric" when (unlike historical founders) he gets a private *temenos* (see ch 1), but he is already closer to historical *oikistai* as a founder of temples:

> [*Odyssey* 6.6--0] From thence Nausithoös, the godlike, had removed the Phaiakians, and led and settled them in Scheria far from men that live by toil. About the city he had drawn a *wall*, he had built *houses* [10] and made *temples* for the gods, and *divided the ploughlands*.

The "wall" seems virtual, as hardly any Greek colony was surrounded by walls in its first generations,[197] but it does seem to emphasize the perception of the settlers as a bounded community. Only among members of a predefined community can a collective distribution have any meaning. Homer speaks of the activities of this founder in concrete terms. Sacred lands are implied in the "temple to the gods." The "houses" seem to correspond to *oikoi*, households, and to the practice of allotting a "town plot" as well as an agricultural plot (hence "plow land," *aroura*). The word Homer uses for the act of distribution of the plow land (*edassate arouras*) is the same as we have observed when discussing the division of spoils (*dateomai*) and points to the same range of meaning: under the leader's direction, the group divides the spoils—in this case, permanent spoils (land)—to its own members.

6.3.4 First Lots and equality: Social and economic differentiation

Equality in Greek colonies was not an ideology but a frame of reference that transformed the *hetairoi* code of Odysseus's companions for sharing booty by lot to a more formal and concrete equal division of land-booty to colonists who were sometimes chosen by lot at home.[198] There was a contradictory vector in the

---

[197] Frederiksen (2011). See (see 6.2.9) and on Megara Hyblaia and its temporary initial wall. It is not always clear whether such initial perimeters were designed to keep animals in rather than infiltrators (including animals?) from outside.

[198] I would like to acknowledge conversations with Nicholas Purcell, who gradually convinced me of the initial "piratical" nature of early Greek colonization, according to my understanding, for which he is not responsible.

archaic period: Greek *poleis*, colonies included, saw the emergence of economic and social differentiation, which went against the grain of an egalitarian mindset. As noted, the two contradictory vectors coexisted as expressed in the repeated demands for *ges anadasmos* (redistribution of lands) down to the Hellenistic period. These calls indicate that grievances kept being addressed precisely in terms of a "reset" based on equal and fair distribution.[199] Interestingly, authors writing in Greek under the Roman Empire speak of the revolutionary aspects of the Roman tribunes, the Gracchi, in terms of *ges anadasmos*.[200]

Moses Finley argued that in ancient Greek Sicily, differentiation in social classes happened only in the second half of the sixth century.[201] He was late by about one century: whereas some inequality at Megara Hyblaia is evident right from the start, significant differentiation is noteworthy in the archaeological record from around the mid-seventh century.[202] Herodotus expressed this differentiation at Megara Hyblaia in his account of Gelon (ca. 483) as a distinction between the Megarian *demos* and the "fat ones," *pacheis*.[203] Even if perhaps derogatory, the term describes wealth, not high-born descent. It has nothing to do with any semblance of a heroic genealogy (there was no [*i*]*dai* suffix, such as *Bacchia-dai*, *Herakle-idai*, *Eupatr-idai*).[204] Aside from the *pacheis*, such descriptive terms that are based on economic status are found elsewhere in Sicily: the *Gamoroi* (owners of the portions of land) at Syracuse, the *hippeis* at Leontinoi (probably a property class), and "those bearing the purple (*periporphyra echein himata*)" at Akragas.[205] All such terms appear to have evolved from differentiation in economic status that developed locally. They seem to point to the reverse image of a well-entrenched aristocracy, arriving *as an aristocracy* in a new world and replicating their status in their former home communities.[206] Becoming a citizen of a new colony during the first generation did not depend on descent (usually the major criterion for citizenship), which also argues against descent-oriented "aristocracy." Aristotle noticed the difference between citizenship dependent on descent and citizenship in colonies, where all first settlers are citizens by being sharers in the new community: "it is clearly impossible to apply the

---

[199] Cyrene: Hdt. 4.163; Leontinoi: Thuc. 5.42; Syracuse: Plut. *Dion* with Fuks (1968); Herakleia Pontike: Justin *Epit.* 16.4.1.
[200] Diod. *Sic.* 35.33.6; Plut. *Tib. Gracchus* 9.3.
[201] Finley ([1979] 1987) 38.
[202] De Angelis (2016)152–154, 177, noting indicia such as tombs, houses, and expensive utensils.
[203] Hdt 7.156.
[204] Cf. Gras and Tréziny (2017) 159; cf. Duplouy (2010).
[205] Cordano (1986) 126–127.
[206] I agree with the line developed especially by Alain Duplouy and the general argument of Fisher and van Wees's Introduction (2015). Contra (replication in colonies of elite status "at home") Figueira (2015), stated, not argued.

qualification of descent from a citizen father or mother to the original colonizers or founders of a city."[207]

In sum, there was no "aristocracy" among the first settlers. Later, by the sixth century, we may speak more confidently of Sikeliote Greeks as a moderate, economic class–based society based on a proportionate set of duties and privileges under the name of the lawgiver Charondas of Katane. His "laws" articulate the differentiation of wealth in terms of property classes (not an "aristocracy" of birth), differences that had been developing since the early history of each settlement. True to network dynamics of the spread of regional commonalities among the Greeks living in Sicily (*Sikeliotai*) and elsewhere,[208] Charondas's laws were also adopted by Leontinoi, Zankle, Naxos, and cities in southern Italy, as well as distant Kos.[209] As we noted with the implication of terms such as "the fat ones" (*pacheis*) at Megara Hyblaia, Charondas's laws illustrate how such wealth differences eventually crystallized.[210]

The equality that a settler could expect was equal chances before the lot and equal portions of land as a minimum starting point; the economic and social differentiation was usually apparent by the second and primarily third generations of colonists. Even in the classical period, "equal and fair" referred only to equality in specific respects, not equality *tout court*. "It begins to look increasingly as if a sentiment in favor of one's just entitlement was the limit of egalitarianism in early Greek society."[211]

When observing several centuries of Greek history, it appears that material equality, based on the yardstick of equal land distribution, was supposed to ensure the state against dissension and civil strife (*stasis*), "for generally the motive for *stasis* is the desire for equality."[212] In other words, equal plots signified balance, hence also the revolutionary cries in the fourth century to redress it by calling for *ges anadasmos*, a "restart" of land distribution. In the *Laws* Plato says that the "lawgiver" should be careful about "the distribution of lands and houses" (*dianome tes ges*).[213] Having established the total number of citizens and completed a division into "parts," Plato's utopian founder "must distribute, as equally as we can (*malista isas*), both the land and the houses."[214]

---

[207] Arist. *Pol.* 1275b32–. Historically, citizenship in western colonies had its own history, beyond the founding generation, with local specificities. See Lomas (2000) and the unpublished Sranford Ph.D. thesis by Trinity Jackman (2005).

[208] Malkin (2011) ch. 3.

[209] The laws of Kos went back ultimately to Charondas of Katane; Arist. *Pol.* 2.1274a–b; Herondas *Mim.* 2.48.

[210] Gagarin (1986) 64–5; cf. Dreher (2013) 63–78.

[211] Shipley (2005) 350; Luraghi (1996) 217; see discussion below on *isos kai homoios*.

[212] Arist. *Pol.* 5.1301b28.

[213] Plato *Laws* 737b.

[214] Plato *Laws* 737c. Cf. Macé (2019), who discusses proportionate and absolute equality in Plato, claiming that the combination of the two allows for a viable political community. Cf. Morrow (1993).

Concerning new settlements, all sources are consistent in claiming that land division and distribution of *kleroi* took place at the initial stages of the foundation. The wording is often linked with other words that connote the lot, notably *lanchano*, "to get by lot." For example, the verb used to describe land held in reserve for future settlers in Cyrene is *apolanchano*.[215]

6.3.5 Things said: The *kleros* and the *polis*

Ideally, each settler would keep only one *kleros* equal in size to his fellow settlers, and the number of *oikoi* was maintained identical to the number of *kleroi*. As we saw, that is how several Greek thinkers thought, despite being unrealistic and often unreal. One of the perennial problems of Greek cities, down to the late classical period (fourth century), was retaining the ideal proportion of one male per one *oikos/kleros*.[216] The vector pulling toward social and economic differentiation, on the one hand, and the vector pointing to a community of *homoioi* (to borrow the term from Sparta), on the other, was something that Greeks kept experiencing. Too many sons, inheritances, and dowries were perceived as a danger to the state; Aristotle recommends regulating the size of the family, forbidding the sale of a *kleros*, preserving the "old allotments" (First Lots), and supporting sustainable equality.[217] The "state" saw as its concern what happens to "private" property, implying that land was not "private" in our sense.[218] The welfare of the *polis* depended on a viable, functioning number of *oikoi*. One household (*oikos*) per one *kleros* was a concept that could be realized in a new colony. From the point of view of the individual settlers, the entire movement of Greek colonization was about creating new *kleroi* for new *oikoi*.

What were the Greeks saying about the distribution of land by lot? Let us repeat the warning that some of our sources, such as inscribed foundation decrees or the writings of Plato and Aristotle, are mainly prescriptive. We need to learn much about the specifics of territorial possession, especially for the archaic period. Still, the few pointers from texts, archaeological surveys, and excavations indicate that we may connect the dots in a way that shows consistent criteria applied down to the classical period. By the fifth century, some conventions were diluted, while others were abused. Yet the frameworks, especially the values of equality and fairness, appear consistent in verbal texts (literary and epigraphical). What cannot be emphasized enough is that no alternative to the combination of

---

[215] *SEG* 9.3.33.
[216] Is. 7.30.2; cf. Parker (2005) 32–36.
[217] Arist. *Pol*. 2.1266b9.
[218] Cf. Blok (2018) 98; cf. Asheri (1963).

the elements of lottery, equality, and distribution is ever conceived in any ancient source.

When Aristotle formulated his recommendations for the territorial division of the state in the fourth century, he relied on well-researched evidence from the entire Greek world. Interestingly, he also stressed the advantages of the institution of common messes for the citizens, familiar to us mostly from Sparta and the Spartan *homoioi*, indicating again the awareness of the predefined group, which would share in the *polis*.[219] Most significantly, Aristotle also sees a direct link to issues of equality and "justice," perceived in terms of "fairness," of someone "being like another" (*homoios*).

Aristotle follows the traditional distinction between public, private, and sacred lands, also attributed to the most famous town planner in antiquity, Hippodamos of Miletos: "sacred lands" (*hiera*), "public (*demosia*) or common (*koina*) land," and private (*idia*) land.[220] Aristotle thinks that public lands should pay for the public messes and the sacred lands should pay for the "expenses connected with the gods (that) are the common concern of the whole state." Finally, "of the land in private ownership, one part should be the district near the frontiers, and another in the district near the city, so that *two plots* may be assigned to each citizen and all may have a share in both districts. This arrangement satisfies both *equity* and *justice* (*to ison . . . to dikaion*)."

Long before Aristotle's time, equal division of *kleroi* was articulated on a private level, in practices of partible inheritance (land) by lot. Homer has the earliest reference to the expected equality: he compares static battle lines facing each other to the equal measuring of fields. We are not told explicitly that the context is inheritance; they could also be neighbors settling a dispute. Still, it is the likelier explanation in a private sphere with no judges, the kind we find in the Shield of Achilles scene.[221]

> But as two men with measuring rods in hand strive about the boundary-stones in a common (*epixuno*) field, and in a narrow space contend each for his *equal share* (*peri ises*); even so did the battlements hold these apart.[222]

In the *Iliad*, the *Odyssey*, and generally in archaic and classical Greece, the acquisition of a *kleros* by lot (inheritance, colonization) seems to be a one-off affair. Like the Homeric *temenos*, cut up and donated by the community to a hero, which then becomes privately inherited property, the *kleros*, once obtained

---

[219] Figueira (1984) 198n51.
[220] Arist. *Pol.* 2.1267b34; cf. *Pol.* 7.1330a9–14. Crete: 2.1272a18.
[221] Hom. *Il.* 18.478–608.
[222] Hom. *Il.* 12.421–423. The word ἐπίξυνος may need further discussion (a poetic form of ἐπίκοινος, "common, equally shared").

and inherited, becomes private and loses its connotations of drawing lots. It even came to mean "inheritance" *tout court*.[223] Hector, for example, fights for his *kleros*, which means simply his land, and Hesiod speaks explicitly of selling or buying land, a *kleros*: "and so you may buy another's *kleros* and not another yours."[224]

Assigning land by lot was prominent in the general Greek mindset and found its extended expression in poetry. For example, in his tragedy *The Persians*, the Athenian playwright Aeschylus tells of a dream by the Persian queen in which "Hellas" (Greece) and the barbarian lands were assigned by lot:

> (184) I dreamed that two women in beautiful clothes, one in Persian garb, the other in Dorian attire, appeared before my eyes . . . flawless in beauty, sisters of the same family. As for the lands, in which they dwelt, to one had been assigned *by lot* the land of Hellas, to the other that of the barbarians. (trans. H. W. Smyth)

Normative practices are rarely mentioned in historical sources (who would want to bore the readers with what they already know and expect?). However, an exception, a challenge, or abuse may mark them as worthy of note by an ancient source. A fascinating story about a communist pirate society may illustrate the issues involved. Feeling themselves under the pressure of the Anatolian kingdom of Lydia, Greeks from the islands of Rhodes and Knidos sailed to settle overseas in Sicily. Once there, they became entangled in a local war, their leader was killed, and the soldiers-settlers decided to return home. They stopped en route at the Aeolian Islands (Lipari), where the small community of inhabitants convinced them to join them, settle down, and defend them against marauding Etruscans.[225]

> (Diod. 5.9.4–5) They fitted out a fleet and divided themselves into two bodies, one of which took over the cultivation of the islands which they had made the common property of the community, whereas the other was to fight the pirates; their possessions also they made common property, and living according to the public mess system, they passed their lives in this communistic fashion for some time.

---

[223] Frisk (1960); Beekes (2010).
[224] Hom. *Il.* 15.498; Hes. *WD* 341.
[225] Thuc. 3.88.2; Antiochos *FrGHist* 555 fr. 1 = Paus. 10.11.3–4; Strabo 6.2.10 with Fischer-Hansen, Nielsen, and Ampolo (2004) 211–212; cf. Buck (1959); Figueira (1984). Porciani (2009) 316 supposes that "communism" was a later phenomenon. He does not quite substantiate the notion (the paraphrase of Antiochos of Syracuse via Pausanias does not carry the weight of the argument). He also relies on general assumptions about the nature of Greek colonization.

At a later time, they apportioned among themselves the island of Lipara, where their city also lay, but cultivated the other islands in common.

And in the final stage they divided all the islands among themselves for a period of twenty years, and then *they cast lots* for them again at every expiration of this period. (trans. C. H. Oldfather)

The "public messes" refer to the institution of "dining together" (*syssition*), which is well known from Crete and especially Sparta, where it served both as a men's club and a fighting unit. The ethos is that of a men's warrior band: comrades at a barrack, eating together, and supposedly equal to each other in status and fighting, as the poet Tyrtaios expresses it: "Setting foot beside foot, resting shield against shield, crest beside crest, helm beside helm."[226] He refers to the Spartans as "peers," equals, *homoioi*. The significant point reminds us of the communal aspect of fighting in interdependent ranks. Expecting equal shares seems apt with such an ethos of equal stations.[227]

The Liparans were not that different from the gods, who divided up the world by lot but retained Olympus and Earth as their common ground. Similarly, common lands are a norm in the Greek *polis*, either for sacred uses or for common concerns such as pasture or future parcellation into individual plots. Because several islands are involved in the Aeolian Islands, the distinction between "apportioning" land into individual plots on Lipara Island and the other common islands becomes more concrete. Such islands could be used for agriculture or keeping herds, a common practice in the Aegean today. In the third phase, we see a rotation every twenty years, when half of the men (supposedly supported by the common messes) exchange positions with the farmers, and the entire landed property on Lipara is redistributed by drawing lots (this is explicit). I stress again the "mixture" aspect, or even purpose, of some lotteries: The lot reshuffles the deck of the entire community and re-homogenizes it. Such a mixture, as we shall also see later, is a prominent aspect of ancient social and political lotteries.

Exceptional here are the special circumstances of the foundation, piracy, and twenty-year cycle of rotation. Otherwise, the norms and the values are commonly Greek: the lot, equality, and fairness. As with other colonies, there seems to have been a shared recognition that all the land belongs to all the Liparan community and that a *kleros* is neither held in perpetuity nor should it be possible to divide or sell it. What made this possible for the Liparans, it seems, was the common mess system as well as the flow of booty that helped pay for it. We are not told how the spoils were distributed, but the community certainly took

---

[226] Fr. 11.31–33 (Gerber); Stobaeus 4.9.16.
[227] Cf. above on *homosepyoi*.

responsibility for all the spoils: it dedicated to the gods "a tenth part" (a tithe) on behalf of the political community:

> After effecting this organization they defeated the Tyrrhenians (Etruscans) in many sea-fights, and from their booty they often made notable dedications of a tenth part, which they sent to Delphi. (Diod. 5.9.5, trans. C. H. Oldfather)

The story of Lipara also illustrates the pitfalls of generalization: it is a unique case, yet develops from common practices of apportionment and sortition and a common attitude to both land and communal windfall, as we noted for Samos and Kolaios, and with Siphnos and Athens and their mines. These were the concerns of the entire community.

This notion of communal sharing in booty is made explicit in a remarkable inscription from ca. 450 that contains the arbitration by Argos as a mother city between Knossos and Tylissos in Crete (fragments of the copies were discovered both at Argos and Knossos). It, too, affirms the notion of communal booty, apparently to be shared by citizens. "As to the booty which we win both together from the enemy, in the division, they [the Tylissians] shall have the third part of everything taken on land, but a half of everything taken on the sea."[228]

At Lipara, the community comprises people entitled to portions or shares in the land. The primary *kleroi* cannot be bequeathed arbitrarily in personal wills: they revert to the community for further rotation. We shall see how wills and dowries became a significant concern for Greek lawgivers, most of whom did not take kindly to the idea that one's *kleros* was private.

Conquest, expulsion, and possession with precisely measured plots of land are alluded to already by the poet Archilochos. Writing in the mid-seventh century, he mentions, as we saw, lost *gyai*, a term that denotes precise land measurements and implies a context of a new foundation and the forceful expulsion of local inhabitants.[229] Elsewhere Archilochos makes fun of a settler who, a few decades before the poet's time (ca. 733), had sold his prospective *kleros* (or, as I shall suggest, his allotted turn to choose a *kleros*) in the future colony of Syracuse while still on board the ship bound for Sicily.[230]

> When this man Aithiops was sailing with Archias when he [Archias] was intending to found (*emellen ktizein*) Syracuse he sold[231] the *kleros* which he was

---

[228] Trans. Graham (1982) 238, slightly modified; cf. OR no. 126 at p. 151. The arbitration works *as if* Argos had been, in fact, the mother city, which is what matters here. On arbitrators see Piccirilli, Magnetto (1973).
[229] Archilochos fr. 1 Gerberf cf. 6.3.2.
[230] Archilochos's *kleros*: fr. 293W = Demetrios of Skepsis fr. 73G = Ath. *Deipn.* 4.167d.
[231] See below on what it meant to "sell" a *kleros*, which was supposed to be inalienable. Cf. Asheri (1974).

about to get in Syracuse by Lot [probable meaning: which he will get after he has participated in a lottery in Syracuse] to his mess-companion, for a (mere) honey cake, the *kleros* he drew by lot.[232]

Archilochos plays with the tenses, but it seems that the lottery for the *kleroi* was expected to take place once having arrived at the site of Syracuse.[233] The passage illustrates the horizon of expectations of a settler: it was focused on the *kleros*, which enabled subsistence and the income to afford the time for training and fighting. Moreover, the owner would be a "citizen," at least in the sense of having a "share," a "portion" of the community. Apparently, the notion of distributing equal *kleroi* was very much on the minds of seventh-century Greek colonists; around 606, "When the inhabitants of Mitylene offered to Pittacus the half of the land for which he had fought in single combat, he would not accept it, but arranged to assign to every man by lot an equal part, uttering the maxim, 'The equal share is more than the greater.'"[234]

6.3.6 Quasihistorical accounts: Sparta and its colony Thera

Myths and foundation stories articulate authentic Greek principles and practices while avoiding particulars that were inevitably messier on the ground. The constitutive historical myth of the foundation of Thera's mother city, Sparta, by the descendants of Herakles and the Dorians illustrates a conventional Greek pattern.[235] It is a quasihistorical account about the conquest of the Peloponnese by Dorian Greeks and its division into states, such as Argos, Messenia, and Sparta, and the parcellation of land specifically at Sparta. It is also a story about the legendary founder and lawgiver Lycurgus, who divided up the land into the *kleroi* that formed the basis of the Spartan regime. Several sources tell the story,

---

[232] Ath. *Deipn.* 4.167d; Archilochus fr. 293 (Gerber) = Demetrius fr. 73 (Gaede) "τοιοῦτος ἐγένετο καὶ Αἰθίοψ ὁ Κορίνθιος, [ὥς φησι Δημήτριος ὁ Σκήψιος (fr. 73 Gaede)· οὗ μνημονεύει Ἀρχίλοχος.] ὑπὸ φιληδονίας γὰρ καὶ ἀκρασίας καὶ οὗτος, μετ᾽ Ἀρχίου πλέων εἰς Σικελίαν ὅτε ἔμελλε κτίζειν Συρακούσας, τῷ ἑαυτοῦ συσσίτῳ μελιτούττης ἀπέδοτο τὸν κλῆρον ὃν ἐν Συρακούσαις λαχὼν ἔμελλεν ἕξειν"

[233] Gerber (1999) translates differently: "Aithiops . . . sold to his messmate for a honey cake the share (*kleros*) which he had drawn by lot and was to have in Syracuse." Gerber's translation is a little ambiguous about the tenses, especially the aorist participle. The sentence has a clear structure: main clause: οὗτος . . . πλέων (when he was sailing, simultaneously with *apodidomi*) . . . ἀπέδοτο τὸν κλῆρον; relative clause: λαχὼν (after he will draw—prior to *echo*, that will happen in the future, but not necessarily prior to him sailing, which would be parallel to the lottery selecting colonists at Thera). ἔμελλεν ἕξειν: he gave up the *kleros*, which he intended to get after drawing lots in Syracuse.

[234] Diod. 9.12.1: ὅτι τῶν Μιτυληναίων διδόντων τῷ Πιττακῷ τῆς χώρας ὑπὲρ ἧς ἐμονομάχησε τὴν ἡμίσειαν οὐκ ἐδέξατο, συνέταξε δὲ ἑκάστῳ κληρῶσαι τὸ ἴσον, ἐπιφθεγξάμενος ὡς τὸ ἴσον ἐστὶ τοῦ πλείονος πλεῖον.

[235] I discuss in detail various aspects of both Spartan and Theran history and in particular the "colonial chain" of Sparta-Thera-Cyrene in Malkin (1994a) ch. 3.

including an attempt to cheat in the lottery.[236] It is "historical" as a mental fact of an ancient Greek's horizon of expectations regarding land and the community.[237] Here is the succinct version of Apollodorus (2.8.4):

> When they had made themselves masters of Peloponnese, they [Dorians] set up three altars of Paternal Zeus, and sacrificed upon them, *and cast lots for the cities*. So the first drawing was for Argos, the second for Lakedaimon [Sparta], and the third for Messene.
>
> And they brought a pitcher of water, and resolved *that each should cast in a lot*. Now Temenos and the two sons of Aristodemos, Prokles and Eurysthenes, threw stones; but Chresphontes, wishing to have Messene allotted to him, threw in a clod of earth. As the clod was dissolved in the water, it could not be but that the other two lots should turn up. The lot of Temenos having been drawn first, and that of the sons of Aristodemos second, Chresphontes got Messene. (Trans. Frazer 1898)

As we have seen elsewhere, the story implies no primogeniture; all brothers are equal before chance.[238] The claim that one brother had cheated in the lottery became a historical *casus belli* to legitimize Sparta's conquest of Messenia and the subjugation of its population and to justify conquests by Dorian Argos.[239] The story and its use may seem preposterous and cynical, made up to justify military intervention because of "cheating." But why did the Spartans think anyone would take that seriously? We need to understand its force in the context of the archaic Greek mindset. Conquests of lands, foundations of cities, and the distribution of *kleroi* along the same criteria were precisely what Greeks were doing, intensively, along the coasts of the Mediterranean and the Black Sea when founding approximately three hundred new city-states. It was a familiar issue, integral to the Greek mindset. The Spartans regarded as self-evident the outrage following

---

[236] Surprisingly there are very few stories about cheating. See Aul.Gell. *NA* 5.9.5–6: "For when in a sacred contest the casting of lots between the Samians and their opponents was not being done fairly, and he had noticed that a lot with a false name was being slipped in, he suddenly shouted in a loud voice...").

[237] See my detailed discussion in Malkin (1994a) 15–45.

[238] In the Roman world of Pausanias, this did not make sense. In his version, Chresphontes demands first choice because he is older than his brother's sons are; the brothers disagree, and the lottery is then conducted (Paus. 4.3.3–5).

[239] "When the Dorians assigned Argos to Temenos, Chresphontes asked them for the land of Messenia, in that he was older than Aristodemos.... Chresphontes, wishing to obtain Messenia as his portion at all costs, approached Temenos and having suborned him pretended to leave the decision to the lot. " See also Chresphontes etc.: Apollodorus *Bib.* 2.8.4–5; Paus. 4.3.4–5; Polyaenus *Strateg.* 1.6 (stones do not float; perhaps drawing by hand?). Cf. Soph. *Ajax* 1283–1285 with scholiast; Plautus *Casina* 307, 398f. Cf. Soph. *Ajax* [1285]. Pheidon is said to have (re)conquered the Lot of Temenos; Ephoros *FGrHist* 70 F 115. The division is mentioned in a lost play of Euripides: Strabo 8.5.6 = fr. 1083 N pp. 252–257 assigns the fragment to the *Temenos*. Malkin (1994a) ch. 1. See also. Ch 4.

the cheating in a distributive lottery. Distributive lotteries were familiar to all Greeks, and fairness at distributive lotteries was the expected norm, not its abuse.

The division of the Peloponnese by lot among the Dorian states has its parallel in the specific land parcellation and distribution within one of them, Lakonia (the "country" of Sparta), where the legendary lawgiver Lycurgus is said to have divided up the land in equal plots. According to one tradition, the Spartans also defined and reserved unoccupied land for future allotments.[240] Plutarch adds details that, aside from the moral purpose he attributes to the lawgiver, seem to conform to what Spartans liked to think about their state:

> Plutarch, *Lycurgus* 8.1 [1] a second . . . measure of Lycurgus, is his (re)distribution (*ges anadasmos*) of the land. . . . [2] he persuaded his fellow-citizens to make one parcel of all their territory (literally, to bring it to the middle, *es meson*, as one did with heaps of booty) and divide it up anew (*ex arches*), and to live with one another on a basis of entire uniformity and equality . . . [3] Suiting the deed to the word, he distributed (*nemo*) the rest of the Lakonian land among the *perioikoi* (allied, dependent non-Spartans, living in their own communities) . . . in thirty thousand lots (*kleroi*), and that which belonged to the city of Sparta, in nine thousand lots, to as many genuine Spartans (trans. Bernadotte Perin 1914) (See also Introduction 7; ch. 6.3.)

We have no idea whether there is any truth in the traditions about Lycurgus. However, the idea that all Spartans possessed equal plots of inalienable land that were created in the first days of settlement (the First Lots) and that this was the basis of Spartan society had an effective long life, serving as a standard for what Sparta ought to have been. Polybius, for example, is explicit about Spartan equality: "The peculiar merit of the latter is said to be its land laws, by which no one possesses more than another, but all citizens have an equal share in the public land."[241] In later periods, Spartans resented the growing concentration of land in a few hands while horrified at the shrinking number of Spartan citizens (citizenship depended on possessing a *kleros*).[242] As in other *poleis*, revolutionaries at Sparta kept demanding reparceling of the land and a new apportionment (*ges anadasmos*).[243] In other words, they were calling for a "restart," back to the supposed moment of the "colonial" foundation of Sparta, the "colony

---

[240] Pausanias says that until the end of the rebellion, Sparta decreed that the lands west of the Taygetos remain uncultivated (4.18.1–3).
[241] Polyb. 6.45, trans. Evelyn S. Shuckburgh.
[242] Sparta: less than one thousand in the 4th cent.: Arist. *Pol.* 1270a30; Xen. *Resp. Lac.* 1.1. Cf. Cartledge (2004).
[243] Cartledge (2009) 110–119.

of the Dorians,"[244] and a *remixture* of the Spartan political community, effecting full citizen rights to the disenfranchised.

The foundation decree of Cyrene, a colony of Thera in Libya (founded between 640 and 631), projects a need for further distribution by lot of lands for later arrivals from the metropolis (*gas tas adespoto apolanchanen*).[245] This projection was fulfilled, but on a grander scale: about two generations after its foundation, there was a need for many more settlers. Cyrene turned to the pan-Hellenic oracle at Delphi, which had prophesied its foundation, and received an oracular prophecy calling this time on "all Greeks" to come to Cyrene and goading them to hurry up:

> Hdt. 4.159.2: The Pythian priestess warned all Greeks by an oracle to cross the sea and live in Libya with the Cyrenaeans; for the Cyrenaeans invited them, promising a distribution of land (*ges anadasmos*); [3] and this was the oracle:
> "Whoever goes to beloved Libya after
> The division of the land
> (*ges anadasmos*), I say [= Apollo is speaking] shall be sorry afterward."
> [4] So a great multitude gathered at Cyrene, and cut out great tracts of land from the territory of the neighboring Libyans.[246] (trans. A. D. Godley)

Libya was open-ended, it seems, for an exceptionally sizeable application of *ges anadasmos* for Sparta's "granddaughter," Cyrene.[247] We must recall that Cyrene's colonial charter from Delphi had covered all of "Libya," not merely the city of Cyrene. Accordingly, Cyrene never inquired at Delphi about its new foundations in Libya. Therefore, the idea that redistribution of lands on a vast scale, while applying a compound of the verb *lanchano* (*apolanchano*), seems to have been well anchored in the Cyrenaian mindset. In fact, according to Herodotus, it goes back to the *ktisis,* "foundation story," of when Sparta had founded Thera.[248]

Spartan traditions about their early days contain further references to the issue of land division and social and political integration that link it with Cyrene's mother city, Thera. One tradition originates from the myth of the Argonauts: when Jason and the Argonauts set out to the Black Sea in search of the Golden Fleece, they stopped at the island of Lemnos. The island was populated only by widows and orphan girls since the women had murdered all the males. When the Argonauts continued their journey, they left many pregnant women

---

[244] Pind. *Isthm.* 7.12–15.
[245] *SEG* 9.3.33–34.
[246] Later, an ousted king, Arkesilaos, tried to get himself an army at Samos. Hdt. 4.163: "collecting all the men that he could and promising them a new division of land (*ges anadasmos*)"
[247] Malkin (1994a) ch. 3.
[248] Malkin (1994a) 106–114.

behind; eventually, their descendants were expelled from Lemnos and came to Sparta, since some of them had hailed from there. They said that

> Hdt. 4.145.4: Having been expelled (from Lemnos)... they had come to the land of their fathers, as was most just; and their wish was to live with their fathers' people, sharing in their rights (*metecho*) and receiving *allotted* pieces of land (*apolanchano*).[249] [5] The Lacedaemonians were happy to receive the Minyai (that was their collective name) on the terms which their guests desired... so they received the Minyai and gave them land and distributed them among their own tribes. The Minyai immediately married, and gave in marriage to others the women they had brought from Lemnos.

The story emphasizes the integrated overlap of sharing in "rights" (literally, "portions," *moirai*, and "honors," *timai*) and receiving allotted portions of land, all in the framework of the vocabulary of the lot (*apolanchano*), which is the same as in the foundation decree of Cyrene that was independent of the account by Herodotus.[250]

Another relevant tradition concerns why Spartans went to colonize overseas so early in their history.[251] Their war for the conquest of Messenia (justified, as we have seen by claiming deceit at the original lottery) was going poorly and slowly. The men swore not to return home until it was over. As this took some twenty years, the frustrated women left at home had sexual intercourse with slaves, so when their husbands finally returned, they found a whole *classe d'âge* composed of young men, legitimate as sons of Spartan women yet illegitimate as sons of slaves. Like the Minyans, they demanded a full share in the state. As Herodotus explicitly says (in the Minyan *ktisis*), having a share (*metecho*) meant a share in *timai* and allotted portions of land. Their requests denied, the young men were sent out to found the *polis* of Taras (Tarentum, Taranto) in southern Italy around 706. However, they were promised that should their colonization fail, they would have the right to return home and receive "one-fifth of Messenia."[252] In other words, social and political integration was expressed as having a share in the whole (the land). "Portions" of the whole of the territory overlapped with the members of the community, all "sharers" in the state. It is no wonder that in Greek, the word *demos* can mean both "land" (territory) and "people."[253]

---

[249] Hdt 4.45.4: δέεσθαι δὲ οἰκέειν ἅμα τούτοισι μοῖράν τε τιμέων μετέχοντες καὶ τῆς γῆς ἀπολαχόντες.
[250] Independence: Graham (1960); cf. Malkin (1994a) 76–77; 88.
[251] I discuss this at length in Malkin (1994a) 115–142.
[252] Ephoros *FGrHist* 70 F 216; Malkin (1994) ch. 4.
[253] Donlan (1975); (1999) 308; Werlings (2010) claims that *demos* defines a certain type of community whose unity is thought of in relation to the territory it occupies; cf. Blok (2018) 98, and section 7.1.2 in this volume.

6.3.7 Quasihistorical accounts: The great migrations

The terminology and description of practices concerning equal land division by lot seem consistent in most accounts, whether historical or not. It is a testimony to a mindset, especially when no other manner of telling is evident in the sources. When Greeks started re-creating the history of their earliest migrations to the Aegean and Asia Minor (eleventh to the eighth centuries), they seem to have had at their disposal only vague traditions.[254] They still needed to tell detailed migration and foundation stories, often inventing an eponymous founder whose name derives from a place name. Tenedos, for example, an island mentioned by Homer,[255] acquires a human founder named "Tenedos" after whom the island is supposedly named. What is more significant, however, is that conventions and patterns of the well-known foundations of the archaic and classical periods were projected onto obscure times. In other words, an anachronism in historical accounts can be a good thing: it tells us much about actual practices that serve as the model for the invention.[256]

Here, again, Didodorus (first century) imagines the prehistory of the eastern Mediterranean (the Aegean), when the legendary king Minos of Crete ruled the waves.

> While in ancient times the Cyclades were still *uninhabited*, Minos, the son of Zeus and Europe, who was king of Crete and possessed great forces both land and naval, was master of the sea and sent forth from Crete many colonies, and he settled the greater number of the Cyclades, *portioning the islands out in allotments* among the folk, and he seized no small part of the coast of Asia. (Diodorus 5.84.1, trans. C. H. Oldfather)

As we saw with Nausithoös (ch. 1), the leader of the Phaiakian migration who presided over the distribution of the farmland, a common and consistent theme in Greek foundation stories (*ktiseis*) is the role of the founder (whether a legendary king or a historical *oikistes*). After finding a suitable, preferably empty, site, he oversees the apportionment and allocation of lands. Thus, for example, it is said that the eponymous hero Xanthos (a city in Lykia in southern Asia Minor), who was not a Greek but a "Pelasgian" (supposedly belonging to pre-Greek inhabitants), "crossed over to (the island of) Lesbos, which was *uninhabited*, and *divided the land* among the folk."[257] Somewhat later, someone called Makareus

---

[254] MacSweeney (2013).
[255] Hom. *Il.* 1.38, 1.452, 11.625, 13.33; *Od.* 3.159.
[256] In contrast, classical sources did not use a discrete and distinct "classical model" to project backward (Osborne 1998) because such a model never existed (Malkin 2002; 2003; 2009; 2016).
[257] Diod. 5.81.2, trans. Oldfather.

takes over the island with a mixed bag of immigrants; then Makareus "won for himself the neighboring islands and *portioned out the land* which was *uninhabited*." Finally, Lesbos acquires its present name and becomes Greek: someone named "Lesbos" marries the daughter of Makareus, and "he named the island Lesbos after himself and called the folk Lesbians" (Diod. 5.81.6). By now, the island had been inhabited, so no more land division is mentioned.

Or take the story about the island of Samos: Makareus "dispatched another son... to Samos, where he settled, and *after portioning out the island in allotments* to the colonists, he became king over it." A few generations later, someone called Tennes, "gathering together colonists and using as his base the mainland opposite to it, he seized an *uninhabited* island called Leukophrys; this island *he portioned out in allotments among his followers*, and he founded a city on it which he named Tenedos after himself" (Diod. 5.81.8, 5.83.2).

6.3.8 Religion and the distribution of *kleroi*

Direct evidence of how the land was measured, divided, and distributed comes to us only in classical inscriptions. Around 440–432, the Athenians decided to send a colony to Brea, in a region probably not far from Thrace. The Foundation Decree says that "ten men shall be chosen (*haireo*) as land-distributors (*geonomoi*): let these distribute (*nemo*) the land.... The sacred precincts which have been set aside shall be left as they are."[258] The decree illustrates the combination of human and divine settlers, all sharing the new settlement land. The sacred precincts fall under different criteria: they are an integral element of the overall distribution but distinct. The process was to be based on the survey under the charge of the *geonomoi* to ensure equal distribution, but the distribution method is not specified.[259] It appears that what may be the Athenian novelty of the fifth century is not the function of the *geonomos* as such (someone fulfilling his role must have done the work) but the number "ten," typical of the boards created under the Athenian democracy.[260]

Greeks saw the foundation of a colony as a comprehensive action involving lands distributed to both the gods and the human settlers. Since the foundation of a city was a sacred act, it means that procedures such as drawing lots, were also under the auspices of the gods. The foundation itself, as we can see with the explicit example of the foundation decree of Naupaktos (ca. 500), was the

---

[258] For what those were see Malkin (1984) on *SIG*³ 67; *IG* I² 45; *IG* I³ 46; ML 49; OR 142.
[259] Graham (1983) 59.
[260] Phryn. *Praep.Soph.* 57: "A *geonomes* is the one who distributes/allots in a colony a *kleros* to each one, whereas a *geometres* is the one who measures the *kleroi*."

244 DRAWING LOTS

establishment of a "covenant" with the gods.[261] The gods, too, were immigrants, settling together with humans to "hold and obtain" the land (*echo ten gen*).[262] The formal expression of belonging to the new community is cult (*hosie*, or *hosia* in the inscription's dialect) and the right to obtain portions of sacrificial meat by lot, mentioned twice with regard to the settlers and their home communities (cf. ch. 3.3)). "Crucial here is that in the first clause of the foundational document, the colonists constitute themselves as a community *vis-à-vis* their *polis* of origin (Lokroi) in terms of *hosie*," says Josine Blok. Greeks conceived of colonies and mother cities as sharing a cult community.[263]

> The *apoikia* (goes) to Naupaktos on these terms. It is permitted that a Locrian of the Hypoknemidians, when he has become a Naupaktian, being a Naupaktian, receives (*lanchanein*) his due portion (by lot) and sacrifices (*thyein*) where / in the way it is *hosie* for a stranger, when he happens to be (in Lokroi) if he so wishes. If he so wishes, he may sacrifice and receive his due portion (by lot) of the *demos* and of the (sub)groups, he himself and his descendants, for ever. Those of the Hypoknemidian Locrians who live in the *apoikia* will not pay *telos* among the Hypoknemidian Locrians, until someone has become a Hypoknemidian Lokrian again (etc.).[264]

In short, an *oikistes* with a charter oracle in hand was endowed with the religious authority to implement a whole set of actions in the new foundation. All other "religious" acts, such as rituals by accompanying *manteis*, were already implied in the foundation oracle.[265] In other words, this is the extent to which we may attribute an active role to the gods in the distributive lottery of *kleroi*: a general, *a priori* (Delphic) blanket sanction within which all foundational procedures, including land lotteries, were conducted. Neither in historical accounts nor concocted foundation legends do we ever hear of *ad hoc* divine intervention determining the results of a lottery in colonial foundations.

---

[261] Blok (2018) 8--90.
[262] Malkin (1987b).
[263] Blok (2018) 8--90. A fact that may explain the absence of colonies and mother cities in proxeny decrees since they were related "as parents to children" (Polyb. 12.9.3, following Timaios). Cf. Plato *Laws* 6.754a–b; Diod. 10.34.3: "Now children, when they are being ill-treated, turn for aid to their parents, but states turn to the peoples who once founded them." For proxenies see the lists in Mack (2015).
[264] Trans. Blok (2018) 90. Cf. Walter (1993) 129–130. See my discussion earlier in the context of the distribution of sacrificial meat (ch. 3.3). At this point, what is noteworthy is the combined aspect of religion and society, with the latter defined as a political community in terms of the former.
[265] Malkin (1987a) chs. 1–4.

6.3.9 Equal and fair: *Isos kai homoios*

Abstract, social concepts of "equality and fairness" would serve as the guidelines for distribution and for "sharing in the community."[266] Those concepts are explicit in the extant sources since the early fifth century (or since the mid-seventh, depending on one's view of the authenticity of the foundation decree of Cyrene). They were consequential for the general development of political morality and the notion of "law" as a "fair portion." The means to achieve equality and fairness were the equal chance afforded by the lot and, when possible, equality in outcomes. In our context, the plots of land in new settlements were equal in size, although the quality of soil and location could still differentiate them. Hence, they were "arithmetically equal" (*isos*), but each plot was only "like" another (*homoios*). "Fairness," in other words, was perceived as equality.[267] That is not self-evident: as we saw with Henry Morgan's Code, or with Clausus/Claudius, who received twenty-five acres but his followers only two each, another view of fairness is "to each his due." Namely, an aristocrat deserves to get more than a commoner (fair) but not less than another aristocrat (unfair).[268] But this is not the case in Greek colonies where even the founder and his descendants had no unique material or cultic privileges.

Here we arrive at one of the significant implications of ancient lotteries. The two major Greek terms for what we translate as "fairness" and "equality" need some explanation. One may translate *isei kai homoiai* as "on equal and like terms." In the imaginary foundation of Plato's Cretan city, the founder urges the colonists to honor *homoiotes* (equality/likeness) and *isotes* (equality *tout court*) by not purchasing or selling the *original lots*, the distribution of which was to be considered a divine act.[269] The adjective *isos*, "equal," is relatively straightforward. *Homoios* denotes a more subtle shade of equality: one is *like* another. Equality and identity are not the same, for being "equal and like" signifies equality only in *some* respect. Rich and poor citizens are unequal, but they are "like each other"

---

[266] Generally, the formula is *ep' ise(i) kai homoia(i)* (Attic Greek), or *ep' isa(i) kai homoia(i)* (Doric). Note that the formula usually appears in the feminine singular form. However, sometimes we observe it in neutral plural dative or in nominative without *epi*.

[267] Cf. Plato *Laws* (757b): "For there are two kinds of equality which, though identical in name, are often almost opposites in their practical results. The one of these any State or lawgiver is competent to apply in the assignment of honors—namely, the equality determined by measure, weight, and number—by simply employing the lot to give even results in the distributions."

[268] "Fair" in the sense of "proper," "fitting," "equity" is better expressed in Greek by ἐπιείκεια, ἐπιεικής. Cf. Todd (1993) 58–63; LSJ, s.v. ἐπιεικής. It usually means "fair" (morally) as opposed to the strict law; Bailly (2020), s.v. ἐπιεικής; Isocrat. 18 in *Callimachum* 34; Isocr. 7. *Areopag*. 33 "fitting" (the social norms) Hom. *Il*. 19.146–148; or "reasonable" (Thuc. 3.9.2); it is most frequently used in legal language, e.g., Arist. *Rhet*. 1.13.19.1374b: "for the arbitrator keeps equity in view, whereas the dicast looks only to the law, and the reason why arbitrators were appointed was that equity (*to epieikes*) might prevail."

[269] Plato *Laws* 5.741b.

with respect to their equal citizen rights. One may advance a claim that there is no functional difference between the two terms of "equality" and "likeness" since equal citizens (note the Spartan *homoioi*) are in any case equal only in certain respects, as "peers." So what could Greeks mean by *isei kai homoiai*, two words that might seem redundant?[270]

In ancient Greek, the word "and," *kai*, may also mean "and especially, particularly," or even "namely": "on equal, *namely*, on like terms." *Isos* standing alone can also refer to arithmetical exactitude. To take a related example: attempting a *synoikismos* between Lebedos and Teos, King Antigonos wrote a letter, saying, "We thought it best that a building lot [be given] to each of the L[ebedians] among you equal to (*isos*) that which he leaves behind in Lebedos."[271] This is compensation *ad hominem*, since each house had a different value. This may be contrasted with inscriptions granting citizenship or reintegration of exiles where the formula insists on equality, *isei kai homoiai*.[272]

The combination of those two words (literally, "equal and like") probably involved a notion of "fairness," a concept that stresses not the result, "equal" (*isos*), but the expectation of the equal share of what one deserves, *fairly*. It is in this spirit that a later Greek author conflates "equal/like" with "just": the Corinthian Timoleon "invited Syracusans and any other Sicilian Greeks who wished, to people the city with free and independent citizens, allotting the land among them on *equal and just* terms (*ep' isois kai dikaios*)."[273] In other words, it is "just" for a *homoios* to be *isos*. On the ground, fairness is the yardstick by which "equal distribution" (*iso-nomia*, a word that becomes "equal law" or "democracy" in a later period) is to be practiced by *geo-nomoi* who survey and parcel out the land.[274]

"They shall sail on *equal* and *fair* terms (*epi isai [isei] kai homoiai*)." These words constitute a formula, repeated in various contexts in Greek sources (sometimes *isoi kai homoioi*).[275] The formula appears in a complicated document, a fourth-century inscription from Libyan Cyrene that quotes the original foundation decree that the people of Thera proclaimed before 631. Such decrees are familiar to scholars, but none date before the early fifth century. However, since the fourth-century inscription quotes the text of the foundation decree that dates to the mid-seventh century, the question facing scholars has been whether we can treat this as an original document (paraphrased at some points) or whether what we have is a fourth-century forgery, made up for the *ad hoc* reasons of admitting into Cyranaean citizenship citizens from the mother city. The latter

---

[270] Cf. Cartledge (1996).
[271] *Syll.*³ 344 ll. 4–5.
[272] *IG* XII IV 1:130, *IG* XII IV 1:131, *IG* XII VI 1:98, *IG* XII VI 1:101, *IG* XII VI 1:112, et al.
[273] Plut. *Tim.* 23.2–3; cf. Nepos *Tim.* 3.1.
[274] *IG*³ 46.
[275] Hdt. 9.7; Thuc. 1.145.1; 5.79.1; Xen. *Hell.* 7.1.1, 7.1.13.

point is explicitly stated as the reason for quoting the original "Agreement of the Founders." The case for a forgery is partially based on exposing anachronisms.[276]

Sailing on "equal and fair terms" has been seen by the skeptics as proof of such anachronism in the Cyrene Foundation Decree.[277] Such notions, it was argued, cannot possibly belong to the (presumably elitist) society of the seventh century since they are explicitly attested in much later periods. However, as often with *a priori* arguments (here, claiming a negative), one piece of evidence to the contrary can render the entire case invalid. In our case, we are lucky to possess much more: a whole early colony, Megara Hyblaia, discussed above, dating to the last third of the eighth century, that is, a century *before* the foundation of Cyrene, which has been surveyed and excavated, as we saw, with surprising results concerning planning, allotment, and equality, with parallel cases elsewhere.[278]

6.3.10 How to found a colony? Late archaic and classical inscriptions

Inscribed "foundation decrees" are an excellent source for observing mindset, values, and general practices. However, they can never be used as evidence for what happened, only for what should have happened (prescriptive function). The communities that drew the colonial "charters" probably knew that reality might not overlap with prescription. For this reason, foundation decrees often include dire warnings against deviation or transgression.[279] To illustrate this point: an inscription dating around 525–500 that originates from Lokroi[280] contains terrible warnings against anyone trying, now or in the future, to make changes to the division of land plots:

> Whoever proposes a division (of the land) or puts it to a vote in the Council of Elders or in the city . . . or who wishes to create civil discord relating to the distribution of land (*peri gadaisias* l. 11). That man shall be accursed to all posterity, and

---

[276] Graham (1960) argues for authenticity; accepted by ML 5 as authentic. Contra Osborne (2009) 8–15, who challenges the claim for authenticity mostly on the political level of *cui bono* (see Endnote 1). However, most of Graham's other arguments, especially the case that the fourth-century inscription did not follow Herodotus (who wrote about one century earlier) are not discussed by Osborne. See also Malkin (2003). Here I concentrate just on the formula. My own addition to the debate is to point out that the "right of return," which those denying the authenticity proclaim as an excuse invented for the *ad hoc* admission of Therans to Cyrene, had in fact been implemented one century *earlier* than the date of the inscription and concerned the reverse direction: Cyrenaians founding refuge in their mother city, Thera (Malkin 2016).

[277] Dušanić (1978).

[278] On the overlap of essential points between Herodotus and the text of the inscription, see the next section.

[279] Cf. Zurbach (2015).

[280] ML 13; *IG* IX 1² 3, no. 609. Cf. Asheri (1965); Maffi (1987); Link (1991b).

his property shall be confiscated and his house leveled to the ground in accordance with homicide law. The covenant shall be sacred to Apollo. (trans. Charles Fornara [1983] 33)

Similarly, the Foundation Decree of Cyrene ends with an account of a public oath and horrible magical curses taken by men, women, and children.[281] It also warns that "He who is unwilling to sail when the city sends him shall be liable to punishment by death and his goods shall be confiscated. And he who receives or protects another, even if it be a father his son or brother his brother, shall suffer the same penalty as the man unwilling to sail."[282] The decree to send the Athenian colony to Brea forbids putting a motion to a vote or for a speaker to suggest changes: "(ll. 24–30): He shall be *atimos* ('without rights'), himself and the sons born to him and his property shall be confiscated, etc."[283] A third-century inscription from Itanos[284] speaks of an oath not to cause a redistribution of lands, as does the fourth/third-century foundation decree of the colony Black Corcyra in the Adriatic. While we note prescriptive frameworks of comprehensive land allotments based on drawing lots and equal size, uncertainty about whether this would succeed is evident from the start. What is clear, in any case, is that, unlike other ancient societies, Greeks tried and articulated the notion of sharing equal portions by lot, even if it did not always work too well.

Such threats indicate how uncertain people might have been about successfully implementing their ideal division and allotment pronounced in the decree. To discover, centuries on, that material reality on the ground was different from what was envisaged before the foundation should surprise nobody, and the possibility is already implied in the foundation decrees' threats. No archaeological evidence can refute the prescriptions about equality and the lot in a Greek foundation decree, yet the latter is excellent evidence for intention and the makeup of an egalitarian mindset. Both the practice (we do see the implementation of equal plots in some cases) and the explicit values of equality and fairness are historical ("mental") facts, impacting history in their turn.

Herodotus, writing about a century before the fourth-century inscription that quotes the seventh-century Theran foundation decree of Cyrene, said he had his independent sources and even paraphrased the essence of the decree (he uses the form of indirect quotation "accusative and infinitive"):

The Therans decided *to send* [infinitive, "quotation mode"] out men from their seven regions, taking by lot (*palo*[*i*] *lanchano*) one of every pair of brothers,

---

[281] *SEG* 9.3, ll. 45–46.
[282] Graham (1983) 225.
[283] This is a common entrenchment clause. Brea: *IG* I³ 46.
[284] *IC* III iv 8; *SIG*₃ 526, ll. 21–23.

and *to make* [infinitive, "quotation mode"] Battus leader (*hegemon*) and king (*basileus*) of all. Then they *manned* [past tense, narrative mode: Herodotus's voice] two fifty-oared ships and sent them to Platea.[285]

As noted, the fourth-century inscription, so rich in detail, does not follow Herodotus. For our purpose, I shall only point out the issues relevant to this discussion, stressing the points that overlap in Herodotus's text and the inscription. First, let me quote from Graham's translation:[286]

> Decided by the assembly: Since Apollo has given a spontaneous prophecy to Battos and the Therans ordering them to colonize Cyrene, the Therans resolve that Battos be sent to Libya as leader and king (*archegetes, basileus*); that the Therans shall sail as his companions (*hetairoi*); that they shall sail on fair and equal terms (*epi tai isa[I k]ai homoiai plen*), according to family (household); that one son be conscripted from each family; that those who sail be in the prime of life; and that, of the rest of the Therans, any free man who wishes may sail. If the colonists establish the settlement, any of their fellow-citizens who later sails to Libya shall have a share in the citizenship (*politeia*) and honors (*timai*) and shall be allotted a portion of the unoccupied land (*gas tas adespoto apolanchanein*).

Earlier, we noted how, two generations after Cyrene's foundation, another wave of settlers arrived with the encouragement of the Delphic oracle. The foundation decree foresees future colonists from Thera who "shall be allotted a portion of the unoccupied land," whereas Herodotus, as we saw (4.159.2), reports that the "Cyrenaeans invited them (Greek immigrants), promising a *ges anadasmos*," a notion repeated in Apollo's own words and in Herodotus's own words that huge tracts of land were then distributed.

The few relevant points of agreement and overlaps between Herodotus's account and the quoted foundation decree are clear:

- Like Herodotus, the decree is in agreement about the selection of one brother from each household.[287]

---

[285] Hdt. 4.153. Θηραίοισι δὲ ἕαδε ἀδελφεόν τε ἀπ' ἀδελφεοῦ πέμπειν πάλῳ λαγχάνοντα καὶ ἀπὸ τῶν χώρων ἁπάντων ἑπτὰ ἐόντων ἄνδρας, εἶναι δὲ σφέων καὶ ἡγεμόνα καὶ βασιλέα Βάττον. οὕτω δὴ στέλλουσι δύο πεντηκοντέρους ἐς τὴν Πλατέαν.

[286] Graham (1983) 224–226. Graham (1960) for Herodotus's independent sources.

[287] What were these households? "The abundance of multiple-family graves, often used for successive periods, suggests that the *kinship groups*, in terms of an extended *oikos*, played an important role in the socio-political structure...." Yet no "classes" seem to be implied: "finds from all the graves imply no great differences in the wealth exhibited." Kaklamani and Damigos (in print). The lottery would have further "mixed" the population.

- The decree envisages "unoccupied land" to be settled by future Theran colonists, while Herodotus describes the fulfillment of that vision, yet on a much larger scale, comprehending "all Greeks." Much later, in the fourth century, we observe Therans arriving in Cyrene and asking for citizenship on the strength of that clause in the decree.
- In the decree (not in Herodotus), the Theran colonists are called "companions" (*hetairoi*) as if Battos, the prospective founder, and Odysseus, another prospective founder in the ninth book of the *Odyssey*, were both leaders of *hetairoi*—implying, again, the equality of status *among* settlers.
- The "right of return" to Thera (*apimen . . . therande*) is specified in the decree in case Theran colonists fail to settle Cyrene. Its fulfillment took a strange turn and went in both directions. Around 520, the king of Cyrene, Arkesilaos III, dispatched his enemies to be killed in Cyprus; they were rescued by Knidians and sent *to Thera*, Cyrene's mother city, where they were received (Hdt. 4.164.1). Thus there is no *a priori* reason to disbelieve the reverse direction mentioned in the fourth century: Therans arriving and integrating into Cyrene.
- The decree adds the detail of the category of settlers: a *classe d'âge* of young men. This is implied, not stated, by Herodotus, who speaks of brothers.
- What is highly significant in the decree (not mentioned by Herodotus) is the phrase *isai kai homoiai*, "equal and fair terms," probably an archaic formula. It illustrates the consistent theme of "fairness as equality" rather than what one deserves according to status.
- Finally, the lot: Herodotus speaks of the use of the lot (*palo[i] lanchanonta*) at Thera, the mother city, to select settlers; the decree refers to the lot (*apolanchano*) expressly in terms of lands distributed at the destination, Cyrene. A parallel case is that of Theras, the founder of Thera, who had set out from Sparta. The settlers were chosen "from the tribes," which implies in the Spartan mindset using the lot.[288]
- Since the formula "from each household" seems to recur, we note that the term is partitive, implying all households that belong to the community and its "seven regions"; the comprehensive lottery breaks up kinship groupings and local divisions.[289]

In the final analysis, the case for authenticity rests on assessing probability. This is not the place for a detailed analysis, but even if the entire decree is a fourth-century forgery (which I doubt), it seems clear that Herodotus and the "author"

---

[288] Hdt. 4.147–148.1.
[289] The mixture effect of the comprehensive lottery overcame local groupings, as pointed out by Damigos and Kaklamani (in print), who emphasize the existence of two cemeteries and clusters of family groupings of tombs at eighth-century Thera.

of the Cyrenaian inscriptions drew independently from their sources. Hence the points that agree or overlap with Herodotus's account can be trusted as highly probable. He had paid much attention to the various versions of Cyrene's foundation, but none contradicted his report on the decree.

Finally, let us zoom in on some decrees dating within a period of three centuries, indicating, aside from *ad hoc* idiosyncrasies, continuity of values and practices. The texts point to the community as an existing, sovereign collective body that legislates for itself and regards the entire land of the *polis* as under its jurisdiction. They confirm the formula "one *kleros* = one *oikos*" and attest to the practice of allocating plots of land in the city and the country and the reservation of land for future settlers. The use of drawing lots is explicit.

The Lokrian inscription mentioned above is on a bronze plaque dating to the last quarter of the sixth century (525–500).[290] It concerns an already-existing Ozolian Lokrian foundation west of Aetolian Thermos. It sheds light, remarkably, on how the reservation of land for a future *ges anadasmos* might have worked out. It also confirms the community's control over its territory. The text seems to relate to the second phase of activity in its territory. It makes decisions about the plains of Liskara and Hyla when the nonpartitioned land is divided among the citizens. The law expressly recognizes lands reserved by the community, which is about partitioning the plain "as yet not-allocated" (*andaithmon*). It applies to both "public" (*demosion*) land and the free "separate lots," perhaps the steep hill-land (*apotomon*, good for terraces for olive orchards).[291] Once cut up into plots and allocated, each plot of land could be inherited:[292] first by parents; if not by parents, then by a son; if there are no sons, then the daughter inherits, and so on. The land division and distribution are intended to remain fixed, preserving the *oikoi*. As noted, the law adds that anyone proposing a new "division" (*daithmon*)—or, in our words, a "redivision and redistribution" of the land—will be given the same punishment as a murderer. So the *oikoi*, especially the primordial ones, were taken very seriously as a communal concern.

Moreover, under the threat of war (and only under such a constraint), two hundred men of military age may be invited as *new* colonists (*epoikoi*; *epoikos* is a latecomer *apoikos*, colonist). "The land shall belong half to the previous settlers, half to the additional settlers." At some point (line 20), the text seems to say that the "deep portions in the valley" (*koiloi moroi*), probably the most fruitful *kleroi*, may be exchanged (*allaga*), provided the exchange was made before a magistrate.

---

[290] *Nomima* vol. 2, no. 44: 187–192; ML 13 (*IG* IX I² 3.609); cf. Musti (1979).

[291] ML prefer to see sacred precincts here, same root as *temno*. Cf. *Nomima* vol. 2, no. 44: 187–192.

[292] *Epinomia* has been alternatively translated as "pasturage rights," which makes little sense in view of the stipulations that follow that seem to denote specifically demarcated plots of land, inheritable, and bearing fruit ("whatever a man plants he shall be immune from seizure"). See also Maffi (1987).

The statement implies some form of a registry office.[293] The community, it seems, regarded all such *kleroi*, while privately possessed, as only partially *owned* since the state oversees procedures of exchange of lands. The inscription appears to take the mechanism for allocation by drawing lots for granted, yet does not mention the lot explicitly. However, the exchange provision points to the conclusion that people got their "klaroi" (= *kleroi*), or "parts" (*moroi*), not by personal choice but haphazardly, and are now provided with the permission to exchange and rearrange (but not split) those lots.

The relation between *oikos* and *kleros* is clearly shown to be the concern of the entire community, which also had the right to confiscate the lands of transgressors.[294] Legislating about a landed property is a public, sovereign affair. As Emily Mackil says, "In doing so, they created both the state's *territorial jurisdiction* [original emphasis], the geographical boundaries within which its laws were recognized as binding, and its *meta jurisdictional authority* [original emphasis], the exclusive authority of the state to alter its own jurisdiction, by claiming new land as territory whether by settlement, annexation, or war."[295]

This observation is also relevant for the foundation inscription concerning Naupaktos (similarly dated around 500), which we discussed earlier and in the context of inheritance rights: a *kleros* may be inherited on condition the son will live on it (see ch. 4).[296] A settler cannot leave his lot unless he leaves an heir behind, and the number of lots and settlers was to remain constant. Apparently, the authorities in Naupaktos retained the right to assign the lot to another if the need arose. We also mentioned the Athenian foundation decree of Brea, which specifies that "ten distributors of land (*geonomoi*) shall be chosen, one from each tribe these shall allot the land."[297]

At the beginning of the fourth century (ca. 385; some prefer to date it later), probably at a site of a defunct Knidian settlement of the sixth century on the island of Korčula in the Adriatic was founded.[298] An inscription found at Lumbarda, a colony of Issa, is variously interpreted as either a foundation decree or one drafted later to define the privileges of the original settlers.[299] Rarely do we

---

[293] Faraguna (2015).
[294] Mackil (2017) 78.
[295] Mackil (2017) 79. Mackil discusses also Cretan and other laws.
[296] *IG* IX 1² 718; *Syll.* 3.47; ML 20; *Nomima* 1, no. 43; Graham (1983) ch. 4. As emphasized earlier, the Foundation Decree begins and with the foundation as a *cult community*. See Blok (2018) 90. For commentary, Graham (1983) 49–51.
[297] Graham: "chosen"; RO no. 142 "elected."
[298] Pseudo-Scymnus 425; Pliny *N.H.* III. 30. 2; Strabo 7. 5. 5. See Graham (1982) 43; Cabanes (2008).Cf. Cabanes and Drini (1995-2016).
[299] *Syll.*³ 141. A fragment recently discovered sheds further light: Marohnić, J., Potrebica, H., Vuković, M. (2021), "A New Fragment of the Greek Land Division Decree from Lumbarda on the Island of Korčula", *ZPE*. I would like to thank Dan Etches for discussing the inscription and for his observations. See Lombardo (1993a).

find evidence for such a detailed, collective vision of an ancient Greek community. The land kept in reserve (*adiairetos*) and the number of future settlers (*tous epherpontas*) are estimated in advance since the specific size of the plots is also mentioned. Equalization seems to depend also on quality: because the less fertile land was reserved for future settlers, the plots of land would be more extensive as compensation. We noted a similar difference at Himera, although the reasons may have been different. Unlike the eighth-century plots of land we have seen at Megara Hyblaia, it would appear that "equality" became more flexible (equitable rather than strictly equal) when concerning land. Such equality in terms not of size but produce is similarly indicated in an inscription on a bronze tablet from Taras's colony Heraclea in southern Italy (founded 433) about sacred lands where both arable and barren lands are mentioned. A professional *geometres* was invited from Naples; finally, the god Dionysos received more than Athena, apparently because his lands were less fertile.[300] Similarly, Plato says that equality may be ensured "by making those of good land small and those of inferior land larger."[301]

The settlers came from Issa (modern Vis, a major Croatian island), and the remarkable inscription attests to their practices concerning citizenship and land. The critical criteria and terminology conform to what we have seen, dating three centuries earlier. This is a foundation decree by the assembly of the people with a view to the future. The *ad hoc* circumstances reveal a contract between two prominent persons, perhaps local (Illyrian? Liburnian?) chiefs and the Greek settlers. The inscription expressly speaks of a town plot within the city's perimeter and agricultural land outside the walls for each citizen who belongs to the initial foundation, a distinction similar to Plato's and Aristotle's suggestions that each citizen should get two plots of land.[302]

I have chosen the translation by Nicholas Cahill since he further supports the view that one of the means of using the lot for colonial allotment of lands was to establish turns instead of simply pairing lots with settlers. The drawing of lots determined someone's turn to pronounce his choice. We have observed this option in the context of partible inheritance by lot. We may assume that this had sometimes been the case in colonies.[303] In his phantasmagoric image of how the souls get their allotted life, Plato's words may support Cahill's interpretation: "Let him to whom falls the first lot first select a life to which he shall cleave of necessity"

---

[300] Uguzzoni and Ghinatti (1968) 165–218, esp. tables at 180, 200. See also Metraux (1978).
[301] Plato *Laws* 745b–e.
[302] Plato *Laws* 745b–e; Cahill (2002) 59–75. esp. 69–71.
[303] Cf. *sullexis, sullanchano* in the Appendix.

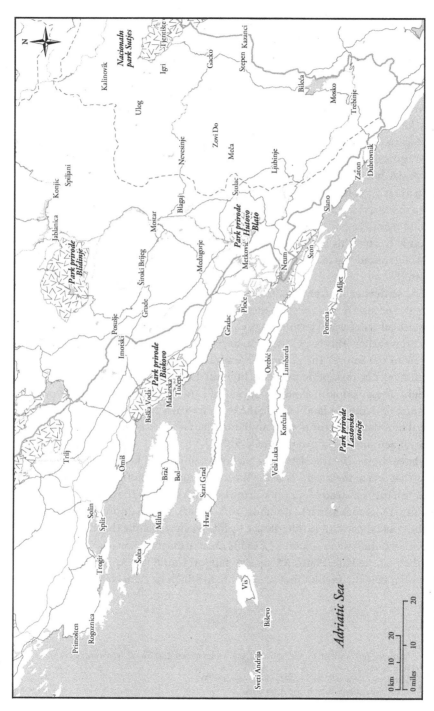

Map 6.3 The Adriatic, Vis and Korčula (Black Corcyra, Lumbarda).

(*Republic* 617b [617e]).³⁰⁴ Specifically for this inscription, Cahill's argument also rests on the word "choice," *exairetos*:

> Goddesses of good fortune! ("*Agathai tychai*") . . . the agreement about the founding of the settlement was drawn up between the people from Issa and Pyllos and his son Dazos (the local chiefs). The founders ["*oikistai*," a plausibly restored word] agreed and the Assembly of the People decided:
> The first (colonists) who [took possession of the la]nd and surrounded the city with a wall (or "fortified") will take the *exairetos* land ("choice," in the sense of better quality, as in "a choice cut of meat"). [Cahill's alternative: "will take by choice," i.e., an act of personal choice and not by drawing lots];³⁰⁵
> —Of the fortified city a *choice* house p[lot, one each,] together with his portion.
> —Of the land outside of (the walled city), the same colonists *will take a choice* "first allotment" (*protos kleros*) of the territory (consisting of):
> —[Of the best land], three plethra.
> —Of the other (types of land), the portions
> —(The magistrates) shall write up [——]s each (colonist)
> received *by lot (elache—lanchano)*. One and a half *plethra* (of land) shall be inalienable, for them and for their offsprings.
> Those who come later shall receive:
> —Of the [city], one house plot, and
> Of the undivided (land), four and one half *plethra*.
> The[e magistrates shall swear neve]r to make a redistribution of the city or of the territory [in any way. If a magistrat]e proposes or a private citizen advocates anything that is contrary to what has been decreed, let him be deprived of civic rights, and his property confiscated, and [whoever kills him will go] unpunished . . . (two lines missing)
> [—if the peop]le dec[ree—]
> These people took possession of the country and fortified the city:
> (A list of names follows, divided into three groupings according to the three Dorian tribes).

---

³⁰⁴ Plato *Rep.* 617b [617e]. This may be Plato's personal vision, however. The expression *klerosin te kai hairesin* (κλήρωσίν τε καὶ αἵρεσιν) appears again in Plato *Phaedros* 249b: "But in the thousandth year both come to draw lots and choose their second life, each choosing whatever it wishes." Cf. Eur. *Androm.* 384 κλήρωσιν αἵρεσίν τέ with Stevens's commentary (1971).

³⁰⁵ For consistency, I proceed with Cahill's translation, p. 220. Following the new fragment, certain elements of the translation would need further adaptation. As in English, "choice," *exairetos*, may mean both a quality and an action of making a choice. Contrary to Cahill's view, in the foundation decree of the Athenian colony to Brea (OR 142; ML 49) that precedes the one to Black Corcyra by half a century, *ta exeiremena* definitely does not refer to any action of choice but to prechosen and predefined "marked out" or "set aside" precincts. The word is used in the context of the action of *geonomoi*, the official land surveyors, not of choice: "The sacred precincts which had been reserved (*exeiremena*) shall be left just as they are and others should not be established." See Malkin (1984) 46.

A comprehensive land division is a "reset," returning the land to a state of virginity when it belongs to no one or a state of "emptiness" (*eremos chora*). Redistribution of lands was always a revolutionary cry, as we noted with the term *ges anadasmos*; no wonder the community insisted that those arrangements remain fixed forever.

The second part of the text enumerates a name by individual name, the ones "who first took and fortified the city." A list of about 200 names is inscribed, of which some 158 are preserved. The men are divided into the three traditional Dorian "tribes" (Dymanes, Hylleis, and Pamphyloi), a conventional means for organizing the citizen body for service in the army and various institutions. It is important to note that the division of the "unselected" land (twice: *andaitos chora, adiairetos*) had been in direct relation to the number of future settlers (*tous epherpontas*).

Whereas First Lots in archaic colonies were supposedly inalienable but probably not consistently so, by the time we reach the foundation of Black Corcyra a further distinction appears. Only half of the *protos klaros*, about one and a half *plethron*, seems inalienable (*katamonon*).[306]

The agreement may have been with local Illyrian chiefs, but the group of settlers was exclusively Greek. This is the clearest illustration of my claim that the group of settlers is predefined, down to their personal names, adhering to the formula "one man–one *oikos*–one *kleros*," indicating at once the exclusiveness of the group of those sharing in the land as well as their equal and fair status, marked by their eligibility to participate in the distributive lottery.

6.3.11 Saving a *polis*: Lottery, mixture, and social engineering

> The lot causes disputes to cease, and decides between the mighty.
> (Proverbs 18:18)

The lottery is an excellent means for equalization, mostly of providing equal chance in distribution to all participants. "Equal and fair" terms for division and distribution appear as a major function of the lottery. We have seen examples of the division of inheritance by lot and of distributing sacrificial meat, booty, land, and the entire cosmos among the gods. We also noted the role of drawing lots for selection, whether of individual heroes (e.g., Aias), special risk (blinding the Cyclops), and even the military draft (choosing a brother to go to war).[307] We remarked that when the Therans set out to settle in Libya they chose the colonists

---

[306] Zurbach (2017) 701 n.90.
[307] Hom. *Il.* 24.399–400.

by lot, one brother from each household to sail on "equal and fair terms," clearly referring to what each colonist could expect once he would have arrived in Libya.

However, the Theran lottery achieved something else at home: it provided a metaphorical and concrete *mixture* of the home community. For example, the Therans could have decided that only men of a certain property class should go, as the Athenians first tried when they intended to settle Brea. An addendum to the decree stipulated that "the colonists to go to Brea shall be from the Thetes and Zeugitai." Or they might have prioritized those Therans hit harder than most by natural disasters.[308] Such a lottery would still be considered "fair" precisely because it would *not* have been equal, a kind of affirmative action in the priorities of colonization. But the Therans did not do this. Instead, as Herodotus says, "The Therans determined to send out men from their seven regions, taking by lot one of every pair of brothers."[309] The action of the lottery implies that the community was perceived as a whole entity, with the lottery expressing a fair mixture of society. Thus while the "equal and fair terms" relate to what colonists would get by lot once they had settled in Libya (equal *kleroi*), the lottery *at home* expresses the unity of the community by its comprehensive mix of households.

Mixture, therefore, constitutes a major social and political aspect of drawing lots. We shall see this on a grand scale (ch. 8) in the reforms of Cleisthenes, who introduced democracy to Athens. Some scholars characterize "citizenship" in a Greek *polis* as being based not on the individual's status vis à vis the state, like a modern citizen holding a passport, but on his "corporate" belonging. One belonged to an *oikos*, to a phratry, to a cult association, to a tribe (usually to all of the above), and *therefore* one was acknowledged as a citizen, and also vice versa; as a member of the corporate group of the *polis*, one also belonged to the *polis*'s subgroups.[310] As Josine Blok rightly emphasizes, for Athens citizenship was perceived in terms of descent, the right to an inherited *kleros*, and sharing (*metecho*) in *hiera* and *hosie* (cult practice and obligations to gods and humans).[311] Holding a political post may be relevant for citizenship, but not *de rigeur*, despite Aristotle's theoretical notions that had perhaps too much impact on modern interpretations of ancient citizenship.

Various circles of solidarity in the ancient city might have worked against the unity or cohesiveness of the state. Among elite groups, this was sometimes expressed in the *symposion*, the reclined banquet, which was exclusive and off-limits to most.[312] The family, too, had its values of solidarity. In short, *polis*-society had plenty of elements that might have fragmented it. A mixture,

---

[308] Hdt. 4.151.
[309] Hdt. 4.153.
[310] Ehrenberg (1969).
[311] See Blok (2017).
[312] Murray (2018); Schmitt-Pantel (2011); Węcowski (2014).

therefore, was of paramount importance, aiming to transcend solidarity groups with their fragmenting "strong ties" and strengthen the political community by turning it into a network of "weak ties" if we follow Mark Granovetter's distinctions (Introduction 3).

Mixture and redistribution could also constitute a rallying cry for reform, a "restart" of the entire state. We noted that at Sparta, the meaning of the term *ges anadasmos* became a rallying cry for the cancellation of debts and *re*distribution of land, tantamount to a re-mix of the *kleros*-based society.[313] There was good reason to be worried: Sparta's citizen body had shrunk to such a degree (ca. one-fifth) that disenfranchised Spartans demanded a reshuffling of the deck.

Civil strife in Greek cities often followed groupings that threatened to break up the *polis*. In contrast, reconciliation aimed to reverse such situations by restoring the primacy of weak ties and (re)introducing social and political mixture by lot. Civil strife was especially acrimonious in small states. The smaller the state, the worse it was, as Aristotle notes, since there was no "middle" (*meson*) to cushion and mitigate issues.[314]

A mixture of the society by lot could be enforced to reconcile civic tensions. Aristotle says that at Heraia, the lottery replaced elections to avoid civil strife.[315] A fourth-century writer on military matters, Aeneas the Tactician, tells the story of Herakleia Pontike (in the Black Sea), where, under the democracy, the rich conspired against the people.[316] That was a struggle for power with an *ad hoc* solution, which had a long-term effect: it was decided to divide the population into sixty units so that the rich would be a minority within each one. We are not told how the division was made, but since the purpose was to dilute and distribute "the rich" *over* social units, wherein each such unit could not have had a majority, the use of the lot seems highly probable.

We are fortunate to have a rare find, an inscription on a bronze plaque that surfaced in the black market of antiquities in the 1980s.[317] It specifies with amazing detail a reconciliation following civil strife at the minuscule Hellenistic *polis* of Nakone in Sicily, which was at least sufficiently large to strike its coinage and suffer an acrimonious civil discord. It is another case of a city too small for the existence of a "middle," in Aristotle's terms, to cushion the shock waves. The date is the middle of the third century, well into the Hellenistic period when three

---

[313] Cartledge and Spawforth (2002) 35–54.
[314] Arist. *Pol.* 4.1296a10; Loraux (2002) 219.
[315] Arist. *Pol.* 1305a.28; 1303a.14–16; cf. Ps. Arist. 1424a12–20.
[316] Aen. Tact. 45; *Poliorcetica*, XI.10 bis.
[317] Loraux (2002) 215–228. A good and thoughtful discussion is Gray (2015) 36–77. See also Ampolo (2001a; 2001b); Asheri (1982); Van Effenterre and Van Effenterre ; (1988); Dubois (1989) no. 206; SEG 30.1119; Lupu (2004) no. 26, 347–358.

arbitrators from the neighboring city of Segesta arrived and resolved the conflict by a fascinating remix of the citizens.[318]

The bronze plaque contains the text of the decision of the council and assembly of the Nakonians. It recognizes that "it is beneficial that they should conduct their lives as citizens in harmony for the future." So it is decided to convene an assembly on a particular day. Each side of the conflict should make a list of thirty names from the opposing faction, which will then be *paired by lot* to create thirty pairs of sixty men: "For those among whom there was conflict ... let them, having been summoned to the assembly, conduct a reconciliation with each other, a list of thirty members having been written in advance for each side. Let those who were previously adversaries draw up the respective lists, each of the other faction" (trans. Gray [2015] 38).[319]

Unlike the personal selection of the names, the lottery is an official process: having paired opponents by lot, three more citizens, unrelated by blood, are to be selected by lot and be joined to each of the pairs to form thirty pentads of citizens. "The magistrates should write the names of each group separately on lots, and put them in two urns, and draw one from each group, and from the rest of the citizens, they should draw lots for three more members, excluding those relatives whom the law requires to be absent from trials in court." So now each of the named opponents not only gets paired with another, but three more citizens are chosen by lot from the entire community, creating a "pentad" of five in which the "majority" of one side or the other is randomly determined. Note the prohibition on the "strong ties" of family members. The list must have undergone scrutiny by the magistrates to avoid having kin in each pentad; that would have introduced an element of family solidarity and loyalty, defeating the purpose of the lottery's randomness.

The apparent paradox is that on condition there should be no consanguinity, those now joined by lot should be recognized as "brothers by choice" to each other.[320] The solidarity of the actual family, which might work against the unity of the society, now becomes metaphoric and all-inclusive: "and those who have

---

[318] For other cases of boards chosen by lot for arbitration and other issues, see sections 7.2.2 and 7.2.4 in this volume.

[319] Lupu's (2004) translation: "Those who have previously been enemies shall write their names each before the other. (14) The archons shall transcribe the names of each faction separately on ballots, put them in two hydrias, and chose by lot one (member) of each faction. They shall then choose by lot three men from the rest of the citizens in addition to the (former) two, avoiding relationships which the law states deviate from the (practice of the) courts. (19) Those united into the same group (shall live) as elective brothers with each other harmoniously in full justice and friendship. (21) When all the sixty ballots have been drawn and those united by lot in addition to them, they (the archons) shall allot all the rest of the citizens into groups of five, avoiding in the allotment the relationships as has been written (above). Those united by lot into the same group (shall) also (live) as brothers like the former ones."

[320] They are not called *phrateres*, a term with a classificatory function, but *adelphoi*; Loraux (2002) 215–228. On *adelphothetia*, Asheri (1982) 1040–1045; (1982) 141–145; Nenci (1990).

been (l. 20) drawn together should be chosen brothers of one another, united in concord with each other with all justice and friendship."

Thus far, the lottery has created thirty pentads, but they constitute only a section of society. However, reconciliation demanded a remix of the entire citizenry: hence, "When the sixty lots have been drawn, and also the others drawn together with them, let them assign the rest of the citizens by lot to groups of five, not drawing (l. 25) relatives together, as has been written, and those drawn together should be *brothers* of one another like those previously drawn together."

The entire procedure is then solemnly sealed by public ritual to Harmony, henceforth an annual public affair: "The *hieromnamones* should sacrifice a white goat for the sacrifice, and the steward should provide whatever is necessary for the sacrifice. And likewise, all (30) the succeeding magistrates should sacrifice on this day each year to the ancestors and to Homonoia (Harmony), a sacrificial animal which they have had tested, one for each, and the citizens should all participate in a festival in groups, in accordance with the creations of brotherhoods. Let the archons inscribe this decree on a bronze plaque and set it up in the entry hall of the temple of Olympian Zeus."

The inscription opens with a conventional invocation to the gods and ends with an oath addressed to them. The entire procedure takes place in one full day, publicly and in front of the temple of Zeus.[321] Yet throughout the various casting of lots, the gods are absent. The sortition is done under their auspices, but that seems to be the extent of any divine intervention.[322] The entire procedure is civic and consensual, with the community as a whole aware that comprehensive mixture by lot is the remedy, the opposite of the dividing lines of entrenched sections that had split up their society.

Endnote 1: The *cui bono* argument and the ancient sources

A conventional point in ancient source criticism is the *cui bono* argument: who would benefit from relying on "ancient" (invented) evidence," and in which historical context? To point out "an invention of the past," one would need to identify the contemporary agents interested in such invention to justify, validate, and legitimate the claims of said agents. One would then need to assess whether to

---

[321] Van Effenterre and Van Effeenterre (1988) 694. At 689 they argue against the interpretation offered by Dubois, relying on the sense of *kleros* as "plot of land" who thinks this has to do with property of exiles. They cite Dubois's translation: "*qu'ils seraient associés comme des frères pour leur lot à eux, c'est-à-dire pour l'exploitation en commun de leur parcelle de terrain.*"

[322] Paul Demont (2010) thinks that the very use of the lot implied divination. See, however, my remarks h. 1

judge the case as an *ad hoc* invention or rather as historical evidence selected explicitly by an interested party, which is a historical fact regardless.

For example, let us observe the term discussed earlier, *ges anadasmos*. As noted, there were revolutionary calls in Sparta to redistribute the land and to *return* to the values and practices of the primordial time when Lycurgus, the quasimythical founder of Sparta's regime, conducted an equal distribution of *kleroi*, the number of which was equal to the number of Spartans. In Greek, this demand was expressed as a cry for *ges anadasmos*, literally, "land for distribution." There are earlier examples of such demands.[323] For Sparta, the *cui bono* argument claims that the primordial allotment never happened and that it was an invention of the past to legitimize contemporary political needs. The claim makes perfect sense and fits a common (modern) historiographical tradition that narrows such issues to a simple, single, often political solution. That is precisely the weakness of the *cui bono* argument about the uses of the past.

It is not enough to discover a convenient context (e.g., granting Cyrenaean citizenship to Therans in the fourth century) that would fit using the past as precedent. That "same past" can be used repeatedly for similar reasons, with no bearing on whether that past is historical. For example, Spartan Agesilaos, Alexander the Great, and Pyrrhus of Epirus explicitly used the *Iliad* to lend authority to their wars. Yet it would be illegitimate to infer that the *Iliad*, the most ancient text of Greek literature, had been composed for the sake of any one of those figures. Or take another example: the Bible had been used already in antiquity to justify conquest, but its most expressive political employment has been in the twentieth century CE in service of modern Jews legitimizing their right to return to their ancient homeland. One can easily imagine a scholar, perhaps some centuries hence, who will expose "interpolations" or inventions of entire biblical books. Based on a compelling *cui bono* argument, she may argue for a twentieth-century composition of the "old" Testament. Since we know that the *Iliad*, the *Odyssey*, and the Old Testament were written long before the events they came to serve politically, such arguments would be absurd. However, they appear absurd just because we happen to know differently. In short, a *cui bono* argument may be valid only when substantiated in a larger context and with more supporting evidence. Otherwise, it is merely a clever scholarly guess.

Endnote 2: *Isomoiria*

Luigi Gallo (2009) argues against the existence of *isomoiria* in the archaic period. He understands *isomoiria* as applying strict equality to portions of land

---

[323] Hdt. 4.159, 163; Thuc. 5.4.2. We noted Solon and Tyrtaios, and Endnote 2 on *isomoiria*.

distributed to colonists. He assumes that archaic Greek society was fundamentally different from classical times when colonization was indeed based on *epi isei kai homoiai* (ἐπὶ τῇ ἴσῃ καὶ ὁμοίᾳ: Thuc. 1.27.1, colony to Epidamnos); *SEG* 1.³.41 (Histiaia, 446/5); Diod. 12.11.2 (Thourioi); Plut. *Tim.* 23.2). He is followed by Andreas Morakis (2015), who admirably provides the fullest bibliography I know on the subject (esp. 2015, 36 n.30). One major problem with the approach is an assumption that there was such a thing as "aristocracy" in archaic Greece, a concept that has undergone severe revision, if not annihilation, in recent scholarship (Ma 2016; Duplouy 2006). Moreover, based on that assumption, like Figueira (2015), he assumes a reduplication of the class situation at home when founding a new colony. I fail to see any support for that proposition which makes little sense *a priori*: the model of a *group* of aristocrats with their "retainers" is imaginary. Whenever we get any evidence, we note a single founder whose descendants never gain any special prominence (Cyrene excluded; Malkin 1987a ch. 7). Sometimes a founder may be joined by other notable leaders such as Dorieus and Philippos of Kroton; neither was accompanied by a class of aristocrats.[324] Morakis, like Gallo, denies *isomoiria* (cf. Bravo 1992). Both employ what seems to me a fallacy: they exaggerate the argument as if by *isomoiria* one also claims "democracy." But that is an anachronistic red herring. There was no democracy in the eighth, the seventh, and much of the sixth centuries: democracy is too easy to refute and hence irrelevant.

Gallo is primarily concerned with the issue of democracy, following Eric Robinson (1997: 71) concerning notions of equality and the early emergence of democracies among colonies, as issuing from *isomoiria* (Robinson does not use the term). He ignores Ian Morris's thesis on the emergence of the "strong principle of equality" (Morris 1996b). However, the issue of democracy is not pertinent to the question of *isomoiria* for most of the period between the late eighth and the late sixth centuries. I see little point in arguing *against* democratic notions that early (Gallo), rightly (and self-evidently) concluding they were absent, and then inferring that *isomoiria*, like "democracy," was absent too. In contrast to egalitarianism, it is a nonissue.

What is the basis, then, for denying *isomoiria*? Gallo does not discuss the term *isomoiria* as such but considers it as precisely equivalent to the formula *isei kai homoiai* in literary texts and the epigraphical evidence. He takes the equivalence as self-evident, although I would prefer to see *isomoiria* as a subset of the general "equal and fair terms" granted to settlers. Unless one accepts as authentic the relevant lines in the fourth-century quotation of the seventh-century foundation decree of Cyrene (*SEG* 9.3.11.27–28: "they shall sail on equal and fair terms"), our first explicit evidence for the expression does not predate the classical period,

---

[324] Hdt. 5.42, 47.

FOUNDING CITIES AND SHARING IN THE *POLIS* 263

which is generally the situation anyway. However, in contrast to what Gallo says, *isomoiria* does predate the classical period and precisely in the context of calls for land distribution.

Gallo neither presents a lexicographic discussion of the term *isomoiria*, nor of its two components. For example, through a related word, *isomoros*, the concept is evident already in the *Iliad* (15.29; Poseidon claims he is *isomoros* with Zeus). Ignored in Gallo's study, *isomoiria* appears explicitly in connection with the land distribution in a fragment attributed to Solon, which attests to contemporary (late seventh, early sixth centuries) demands for *isomoiria*, even if the fragment is not actually by Solon himself.[325] Compared with the call mentioned by an even earlier poet (mid-seventh century), Tyrtaios, for *anadastos poiein*,[326] it appears that calls for equal redistribution of land were very much an issue of both the archaic and the classical periods, and colonies could satisfy them with relative ease.[327]

It is facile to argue backward and claim that since inequality in colonies is evident after about two generations postfoundation, this inequality argues against *isomoiria*. However, there is no contradiction here since Gallo avoids asking *why* there was inequality. I pointed out the answer earlier: personal wealth and no upper limitation on land acquisition quickly contributed to social and economic differentiation in Greek colonies. One settler may have enough money to buy a plow and farm animals on-site, whereas his neighbor, although owning an equal plot, has no money and might develop some dependency rather quickly. We noted that elites of "first settlers" are named after their property or wealth (e.g., Pacheis) acquired at the colony; in some cases, their name may also point to equality with regard to land, such as the Syracusan *Gamoroi* owning "portions" of the land/country.

In short, the emergence of postfoundation elites is irrelevant to the issue of the initial equality of plots of land, the minimum entry ticket for a "share" in the community. That equality was expressed by holding a lottery, by distributing equal plots, and perhaps by sharing in "rights," or *timai*, about which we usually know very little for the early colonies.

As far as archaeological evidence is concerned, the cases of Metaponto and the Chersonese are relatively late, as Gallo says; however, Megara Hyblaia, the strongest and earliest case for equal allotment (end of the eighth century), is glossed over. Gallo mentions Megara Hyblaia but in the context of another argument rather than deal with what seems apparent *isomoiria* on the ground. Gallo infers from the relatively short time between the foundation of a colony

---

[325] Solon fr. 34 West; cf. Lardinois (2006)
[326] Aris. *Pol.* 5.1306b36–1307a2 = Tyrt. Gerber fr. 1.
[327] There is no doubt that this was also a common issue also in the sixth and fifth centuries: Hdt. 4.159, 163; Thuc. 5.4.2.

and a secondary foundation of another colony that there was a shortage of land, which is an argument against *isomoiria*. He speaks of Megara Hyblaia and Selinous, although I cannot see how one hundred years, the interval between the two foundations, might be considered a short time. His stronger example is Herakleia Pontike, which founded Kallatis, on the western side of the Black Sea, shortly after its settlement at the end of the sixth century. But was Kallatis founded because of the need for land? There were other reasons aside from the need for land to found colonies; in this case, Herakleia probably also wanted a colony "on the other side" of the Black Sea, a phenomenon observed already by Georges Vallet for strait colonies.[328]

Herakleia aside, the argument could be turned on its head: because of *isomoiria* and the need to maintain the formula "one *oikos* = one *kleros*," scarcity of available lands became almost automatic since First Lots were supposedly indivisible. There may have been *ad hoc* reasons in certain colonies why the land kept in reserve for distribution was not distributed to sons of colonists. There were perhaps too many sons, and perhaps the land kept for future distribution was gobbled up in some cases; the trouble is that we hear of reserved land only in prescriptive foundations decrees and have no way of knowing to what degree the instruction was universally respected.

In conclusion, Gallo's methodology is wanting, and he is wrong to claim that *isomoiria* did not exist in colonies in the archaic period. He conducts no philological examination of *isomoiria*, neglects to observe the *isomoiria*-fragment attributed to Solon, assumes a precise overlap between *isomoiria* and *isei kai homoiai* (whereas the former is a subset of the latter), avoids the implications of the archaeological evidence from Megara Hyblaia, infers with no basis a lack of *isomoiria* from the practice of secondary foundations, and finally, introduces the issue of democracy, which is irrelevant (too late) to the case. *Isomoiria* (if it had been called that early on) constituted a *minimum* prescription for an entry ticket to share in a new community. It expresses egalitarianism but not absolute equality since settlers were unequal in terms of personal means, and there was no limit on the individual expansion of land holdings except for the First Lots that were ideally inalienable.

Endnote 3: Women and the *kleros*

For women, the *kleros* system held some advantage, especially with regard to inheritance (Ch. 4). In Greek, an heiress was often called an *epikleros* ("attending, responsible for the *kleros*") or *patriouchos* (holder of the ancestral estate). This

---

[328] Vallet (1958; 1996).

probably signified that a husband was expected to come and live in the woman's *oikos* instead of the other way around.[329] A husband could thus perpetuate the *oikos*, and the size of the entire Spartan citizen body and the army would supposedly be kept stable. That is consistent with the Lycurgan ideal of one *oikos* per one *kleros*, supposedly since the time of the foundation of Sparta as a "Dorian colony"[330] (in contrast to the Homeric Sparta of Menelaos).[331] As did most Greek city-states, Sparta told the story of its ancient foundation in terms of migration and colonization, followed by a comprehensive land distribution.

Remarkably, the wish to preserve the *kleros/oikos* seems to have improved the status of women as preservers of the *kleros*.[332] In this respect, there is a point of similarity between ancient Spartans and ancient Hebrews, who similarly had a tradition of wandering, conquest, and assigning lands by lot:[333] Both believed in an ancient exodus that culminated in settlement of their respective, divinely promised lands.[334] In the Old Testament the elders from the "Families of Joseph" (unlike his brothers, Joseph had no tribe named after him) came to Moses with the following complaint and demand:

> The LORD commanded my lord (Moses) to give the land for distribution by lot (*goral !*) as *nachala* (the Hebrew equivalent of *kleros*) to the children of Israel; and my lord was commanded by the LORD to give the inheritance of Zelophehad our brother unto his daughters. And if they be married to any of the sons of the other tribes of the children of Israel, then will their inheritance be taken away from the inheritance of our fathers, and will be added to the inheritance of the tribe whereunto they shall belong; so will it be taken away from the lot of our inheritance (*nachala*). (Numbers 36:2–3, New King James Version 1885, amended)

Then the women also appear before Moses to make the same demand:

> Why should the name of our father be done away from among his family, because he had no son? . . . Give us an *achuza* [equivalent to *nachala*] among our father's brothers. (Numbers 27:4, New King James Version, amended)

---

[329] Polybius (12.6b.8) claims that several men (perhaps brothers?) could marry the same woman at Sparta, supposedly to keep a *kleros* intact. On the Greek *epikleros* (and the Spartan *patroiouchos*), see Cartledge (1981); Finkelberg (1991), especially on royal succession through women; Hodkinson (1986); Patterson (1998); Schaps (1979); Cantarella (2005). See in general Hodkinson (2000).
[330] Pind. *Isthm.* 7.12–15.
[331] Malkin (1994a) ch. 1. Sparta oscillated between stressing links with its Homeric predecessors while recounting how their invading ancestors toppled the Homeric dynasty and took over.
[332] For women in Greek colonization, see Graham (1984); Coldstream (1993); Hodos (1999); Malkin (2020).
[333] Malkin (2015).
[334] Malkin (1994) 22–26.

The wish is granted and God commands it to become a general rule applied to all Israelites:

> And thou shalt speak unto the children of Israel, saying: If a man die, and have no son, then ye shall cause his inheritance (*nachala*) to pass unto his daughter." (Numbers 27:8, King James Version)

The right of a woman to inherit is a property issue: since a *kleros* was not to be transferred to another family, neither through inheritance nor by means of a dowry, we see the same principle in operation: the "First Lots" as initially distributed by lot, were to remain intact and stay "in the family." In reality, this kept failing.

Endnote 4: Archaeology and "text-based information"

The rift between archaeology *tout court* and "text-based information" seems to be growing. The assumption is that archaeological evidence and written sources present very different perspectives on the "ideals, concepts, and practices of occupying territory."[335] Lin Foxhall and David Yoon wish to know about ancient inhabitants whether "their lived experience of the landscape maps on to the boundaries and models of 'territory' presented in the written sources." Their study presents a good methodological test case: it examines a few centuries of settlement and encounters between Lokroi and Rhegion in southern Italy. The authors are particularly troubled by the term "territory" and claim that (unsurprisingly) people living on the land cared more for their property than for notions of "boundaries and territories." These terms are misapplied, claim the authors, quite justly in my view, since they are anachronistic when used in our contemporary sense. Yet the authors do not engage with equivalent Greek terms and similar issues as studied in detail by Giovanna Daverio Rocchi.[336] So we need to examine these terms and why they contradict what Foxhall and Yoon are saying.

Territorial boundaries were less defined than expected with our contemporary connotations of the terms "territory" and "boundary." The question is essential if we are to understand the allotment of land *within* a city's territory. Expansion in colonies differed in its dynamics and direction from the Greek mainland. For example, in the "old country," Megara Nisaia was sandwiched between Athens

---

[335] Foxhall and Yoon (2016) 433.
[336] Daverio Rocchi (1988)—a major study on borders, frontiers, and boundaries—is not cited by Foxhall and Yoon. Cf. Pollini (2012).

and Corinth, with land borders on all sides. In contrast, initially, Greek colonies had border *lines* only on the coasts, whereas the hinterland was a rolling frontier. Syracuse, for example, was established on the islet of Ortygia but, within a single generation, expanded across to the Sicilian "mainland."

The countryside survey between Lokroi and Rhegion, as reported by Foxhall and Yoon (starting around 490), tells us a lot about the nature of rural life and the evident contradiction with the image of perennial hostility between Lokroi and Rhegion. This observation is indeed a significant contribution. But it does not follow that if we deny bounded "territory," we must deny equal allotment of portions of land in the *early* days of settlement. To argue that no equal land allotment took place based on that survey, as do the authors, ignores the distinction between the category of *minimum* allotment of equal portions, sometimes expressed as the *protoi kleroi*, and further expansion and land acquisition that were unrestricted, which is mostly what the survey finds.

The facts of the archaeologists complete the picture I have given; they do not contradict it, nor can they be independent of it.[337] The survey of Foxhall and Yoon begins with the period starting around 490. The authors claim that the literary evidence is too late (e.g., Diodorus, Strabo), full of anachronisms, and therefore unhelpful. However, they ignore texts that are even earlier than 490 or perhaps contemporary. The first (see 6.3.10) concerns other Lokrians: an inscription on a bronze plaque dating around 525–500 that probably originates from Ozolian Lokrian and relates to a foundation (already in existence) west of Aetolian Thermos. Its date is around the last quarter of the sixth century.[338] The inscription deals expressly with land reserved by the community and regulates land allotments. It demonstrates that the contrast between "city" ("urban," sometimes "urban elite") and "country," accepted by Foxhall and Yoon, is a fallacy. Their approach nicely fits Max Weber's claim that city and country were opposites, but Weber was thinking about the late-medieval city with its "market," not the ancient Greek *polis*.[339] Another text (see 6.2.8) is the inscription dating 493 (!) from Himera that specifies measured land plots for new colonists while creating a new tribe for them.[340] I find it difficult to accept such texts as irrelevant.

The distinction between norms and values (present but not consistently implemented) is essential for the relationship between literary and archaeological evidence. The literary and epigraphic sources variously express or imply that the first plots of land in a new colony should be of equal size and distributed by

---

[337] Lin Foxhall speaks of "the conceptualization and reification of a territory through practice, generating a concept of territory based on the aggregate of whatever those households and communities on the ground think it is." How would one know what they "think"?
[338] *Nomima* vol. 1 no. 44: 186–192; ML 13; 13 (*IG* IX I² 3.609); cf. Musti (1979).
[339] Weber (1958).
[340] Lombardo, Aversa, and Frisone (2001) 120–121.

lot. These are "things said," namely the articulation of intention and practice. Yet an examination of the landscape by an archaeologist paints a very different picture: rich and poor burials are observed, and throughout the landscape, there may exist plenty of unequal lots, individual farms, small villages, and so on. What people do and say they do (or will do) belong to two sets of questions. One needs to evaluate both "things said and done," and how they stand in relation to each other, case by case.

The First Lots, as we saw, form a discrete category of equal *kleroi*, apart from other forms of Greek presence and land ownership in colonial areas.[341] The exciting discovery by archaeologists of some mixed communities does not have much bearing on the matter since those were apparently not foundations. A few sites indicate mixed communities with Greeks living among others in various forms, such as the Greek *emporion* with its temples at Etruscan Gravisca, or the apparently mixed settlement at Francavilla Maritima.[342] Not only modern scholars but ancient Greeks too knew of such mixtures, as Herodotus remarks about the Geloni and the *mixhellenes*.[343] But the novelty of the archaeological discoveries must not lead to the supposition that such sites are somehow "representative" of the entire process of founding new cities, stretching from the western Mediterranean to the Black Sea. For example, Taras was a Spartan colony, founded in 706. It had Spartan *nomima* (Tarentines even worshipped Orthia),[344] spoke a Dorian-Spartan language, and its character as a Greek *polis* was never in question. By its third generation after its foundation, we find growing differences in wealth expressed especially in burials. In contrast, L'Amastouola is a small hinterland site not too far from Taras. Its findings indicate a mixture: both Greeks and non-Greeks lived there. The latter were either local or non-Greek immigrants who came from elsewhere in Italy. That l'Amastouola was "hybrid" is a plausible inference; that it may compare with Taras as representative of the mixture and slow processes of Greek colonization is simply wrong.[345]

---

[341] There are various other elements in a territory of which the founders of colonies must have been aware. The terminology varies, including *pedion*, preferably delimited by a river not far from the sea; peripheral zones (*eschatia*); with hills (*perioresia*) and/or forests; Agricultural land, *ge arosimos*, was sometimes called *ariste* or *exairetos chora* ("choice land"); Greeks distinguished between barren land, *ge psile*, from merely uncultivated land (*agroike*). The peripheral lands were not part of the primary division and belonged to the entire community. Asheri (1966) 10–11 discusses further distinctions between the divided-up land (*he ton idioton chora*) and the nondivided, common section (*he koine chora* or *ge adiairetos*)..

[342] See the rewarding discussion of the problem by Demetriou (2012).

[343] Hdt. 4.108; Casevitz (2001); cf. Ustinova (2021) 162.

[344] Abruzzese Calabrese (2009); Nafissi (1999).

[345] Taras: Wuilleumier ([1939] 1968); Malkin (1994a) ch. 4; L'Amastuola: Bergers and Crielaard (2007; 2016).

Josine Blok

PART III
DRAWING LOTS IN POLIS GOVERNANCE

7
Setting the Stage

7.1 Introduction

7.1.1 The lot becomes political

Selecting citizens by lot for political office may well be the most eye-catching application of drawing lots in ancient Greece. Many Greek *poleis* introduced the practice into their systems of government in the classical age, but its wide-ranging use in the democracy of classical Athens (ca. 500–300) has elicited particularly keen interest among observers, both in Antiquity and today. Indeed, the selection by lot for office as it was practiced in Athens has become emblematic for the notion of democracy and equal citizen participation.

In a nutshell, from the 460s down to the late fourth century, most *polis* offices in Athens were distributed by lot among the entire male citizen body. With annually twelve hundred political offices and six thousand functions as *dikastai* (jurors) distributed among around thirty thousand male citizens on average, 4 percent of the males held a *polis* office and 20 percent participated in the jury courts—in total almost a quarter of the male citizens every year. Of the twelve hundred offices, about a hundred were elected, with all others distributed by lot. During his adult life from thirty years of age, a male Athenian would take his turn for one of these offices: for the archonship no more than once, for the council no more than twice, and for the jury courts multiple times. Due to this high rotation, with the lot selecting randomly among the eligible candidates comprising a sizeable part of the male citizen body, the male Athenians took turns in governing and being governed.[1] After 450, new priesthoods were drawn by lot from among all male or female citizens. The introduction of a modest pay for the council and jury courts in the 440s and 430s allowed the poorer sections of the citizen population to stand for allotment to these offices, because now they could afford to dedicate the necessary time. The system described here concerns only the political offices at *polis* level, to which numerous posts at the level of the *demes* (local

---

[1] Aristotle regarded the ideal situation in a *polis* that citizens should rule and be ruled in turn: *Pol.* 1254a14–35; 1277a28–30: the quality of the good citizen is the ability to do both; cf. 1283b42–1284a3. However, the fact that this situation applied to Athens did not detract from his criticism of the radical democracy.

subgroups) and many cultic offices should be added; most of these were likewise drawn by lot. Athens used the lot also for numerous other purposes in the governance of the *polis*—for instance, for taking turns in presiding over the council, in collective duties (guards, military commands), for distribution of sacrificial meat at *polis* festivals, for distributing duties across official boards, and for all steps in the composition of jury courts.

The democracy of Athens, which lasted in this form until 322 and was resumed on a somewhat different footing in 307, became the best-known case of a political system with allotment from all for public (*polis*) office and more broadly speaking in its governance. Its most striking feature was, and still is, the use of lot drawing for the implementation of the equality of its citizens—mostly of male citizens, though in cultic offices also of female citizens. In the fourth century, Athens had become the byword of radical democracy and of its major instrument—the system of sortition. Precisely for this reason we need to apply a degree of caution. It is tempting to regard Athens as representative of all Greek *poleis*, and for many Athenian practices we indeed find parallels in other *poleis*. That said, one of our conclusions will be that no other *polis* seems to equal Athens in the degree to which the city had integrated the use of the lot in its governance, even if we take into account that we know much more about Athens than about any other *polis*. Athens was in many ways exceptional, and also, it appears, in its systematic application of the lot.

Among all the uses of sortition in ancient Greece, drawing lots for political office offers a singular case for study. As the previous chapters show, other applications of drawing lots—notably for divination of the will of the gods, for the distribution of land and inheritance, for selecting groups bound for colonization overseas, for selecting individuals for specific tasks, and for taking turns in competitions—were common in the Greek world from the eighth century and are attested both in literature and on the ground. Compared to these applications, the allotment of political office arrived relatively late on the historical scene. The earliest case known to us was instituted in 594, when in Athens the lawgiver Solon introduced the selection by lot from preselected candidates for two offices, a procedure that also involved a mixture of the highest two classes of citizens (see section 8.1.1 in this volume). Not only did this introduction of the lot into the political sphere take place much later than its use in other domains, but Solon's original innovation was also only partially successful: for one group of offices, namely the Nine Archons, the selection by lot was abandoned after just a few years. It took about a century before the Athenians reinstituted this system, and another twenty years before the use of the lot for political office began increasing to the large-scale allotment for which the city would become famous. Against the background of its common use in other areas, the faltering beginning of drawing lots for public office and the problems specific to that application in the political domain require an explanation.

Drawing lots, when applied in societal contexts, is an instrument applying equality of chance for all participants in specific forms of decision-making. It takes place in definite social settings, but it also creates such a setting itself by the mechanisms of the procedure; it is based on shared values about its use, and it shapes the expectations and conduct of the (section of) society wherever it is applied.

In principle, the social and political significance of drawing lots depends on two crucial factors: one, the choice to apply the lot with its inherent equality of chance for decision-making, instead of any other means; and two, the composition of the group participating in the procedure. Whoever is part of the group has an equal chance to or an equal share in the outcome and shares a belief in the outcome based on equal and fair conditions; all others are excluded. In ancient Greece and also today, the members of the group sharing in an allotment are considered to be largely similar and equivalent (in Greek: *homoios*) regarding the terms relevant to the decision—it is one among several reasons why the lot is chosen as a procedure—but the framework of the sortition itself makes them all truly equal (in Greek: *isos*) in the parity determined by random selection.

Recent socio-psychological research by W. Hofstee shows that in present-day Western societies, people can easily accept the distribution by lot of whatever goods are not seen as rewards for individual qualities—in other words, goods for which recipients are all equally qualified from the outset, without distinction. By contrast, distribution by sortition is considered unfair when it involves desirable goods normally received for merit—in other words, for which the recipients prove themselves better qualified than their competitors.[2] It is essential for the stability and continuity of any state, group, or organization that its members sense that the distribution of privileges and duties is by and large a just and unbiased one.[3] Quite a substantial section of the literature on distribution by lot today is concerned with the issue of justice, notably for the allocation of desirable goods that are too scarce to supply everyone equitably.[4] Political office is a desirable good because it is a privilege: it elevates the holder of the position and gives her or him authority over others; furthermore, in most societies this privilege is conventionally assigned on the basis of perceived excellence. Hence, its

---

[2] Hofstee (1990). This evaluation concerns the distribution of desirable goods; for undesirable goods (e.g., selection for army service), random selection by lot is more often felt to be just than of desirable goods.

[3] Crucial here are the perceptions of the insiders, the members of the society, group, or system; whether outsiders regard the system as just is a different matter.

[4] For a succinct discussion of this debate, see the *Envoi*.

distribution by lot creates tensions both in the evaluation of competence and in the sphere of justice—at least in people's opinion.

Although in ancient Greece, unlike in modern Western societies, distribution by lot was common and entrenched in the socio-cultural mindset, the ideas about justice in the allocation by lot of political office seem to have been quite similar. Political office was considered an honor, an immaterial good of a kind for which traditionally not all members of the group were considered equally qualified. In other words, the values in Greek society regarding those who could hold office revolved around inequality, the opposite of the values conditional to the use of the lot, which revolved around equality. Given this situation, we might wonder how Solon managed to introduce sortition for office in the first place, and how Athens and other *poleis* could ultimately become committed to a wide use of allotment for office in the classical age. Furthermore, over time most of the Greek *poleis* began using lotteries for many other purposes, such as selection for juries in festivals, assigning cases to courts, and more. How and why did these *poleis* come to establish this practice?

These questions take us to the broader inquiry into the history of drawing lots for political office in Greece. We need to examine more precisely how the selection for political office was different from other types of assignment by lot among the citizens, and to investigate in more detail the dynamics of inequality that appointments for office entailed. On the intersection of these two factors we investigate how over time the values of égalitarianism regarding lot casting were negotiated with the values of social distinction attached to political office, and how the results took shape in actual, historical practices.

For this investigation, the net needs casting more widely and to include a survey of the other purposes for which *poleis* employed sortition. Here we draw on the results of the previous chapters, in which the other practices of drawing lots are discussed. Some of them are first attested outside the *polis* in the strict sense; they belonged to Greek community life before it took the more formal shape of a *polis* with its typical institutions. Belonging to this kind are the application of lot drawing for dividing an inheritance, for oracle consultation, for distributing booty and sacrificial meat, for positions in chariot racing, and for the selection of prominent individuals for special or heroic tasks.[5] Other lotteries clearly belonged to the domain of the *polis* as a political, social, and

---

[5] Thomson (1978⁴) 297–331 and after him Borecký (1963) hypothesized a "tribal" prehistory of social equality before the *polis* as the origin of the elementary forms of allotment. I do not concur with this hypothetical prehistory, but I regard the society depicted in the Homeric epics as a semihistorical pre-*polis* stage that in important respects was not (yet) a historical *polis* (e.g., there are no distinct *polis* offices or a stable conception of membership), whereas in other respects it had social practices (people meeting on the *agora*) and values (*time*, see section 7.3.1 in this volume) typical of the historical *polis*. For the historicity of Homeric society, see Raaflaub (1998); Malkin (1998) 259–271 (Appendix).

religious entity: the lot was used for the selection of individuals to found a colony, for the distribution by lot of newly appropriated land among citizens, and for mixing old and new citizens by allotment into new groups for the foundation or refoundation of *poleis*. The evidence so far invites us to regard the first group as the elementary, foundational uses of the lot system on which its uses in *polis* contexts were predicated. In other words, we might construe a "genealogy" of drawing lots whose application in the context of the *polis* was built on the elementary, foundational implementations, and in which the use of the lot for political office appears even later. Of all these applications, the use of lots for assigning political office was the only area in which the system met with the occasional contestation. However, it would be misleading to claim the elementary applications as entirely or essentially "pre-*polis*," for they all remained in use until the end of Greek antiquity. Last but not least, in all these applications of drawing lots—including those in *polis* contexts—we need to take into account the interaction between the human and the divine worlds in order to form a more comprehensive picture.

In this chapter I argue that the introduction and the spread of allotment for *polis* offices and governance can only be understood in the context of the applications of lot drawing in Greece as a whole, both of the elementary kind and those for other purposes in the *polis*. Since in all these practices a far wider societal domain was involved than what is generally understood by the term "government," I prefer to use the term "*polis* governance" for the framework in which the uses of the lot discussed in this chapter took place. Governance includes not only the formal institutions of a distinct social unit—in our case, the *polis* and its administration—but also the norms, values, language, expectations, social conditions, and informal institutions that sustain and connect the formal institutions. Accountability is a crucial feature of governance,[6] as are the ways of decision-making in selection, distribution, and procedure—all of which were central in the ancient Greek practices of drawing lots. Investigating the application of the lot in *polis* governance entails determining how these practices actually unfolded, and how they spread over time across the Greek *poleis*. The results of our inquiry also shed light on the Greek concept of citizenship itself, which meant being a member of a *polis*, and sharing in what the *polis* aimed to be and to accomplish in multiple ways. Drawing lots became one method among many in which this system of sharing was put into practice.

---

[6] Today, accountability and transparency are prominent standards of good governance, against which the quality of governance is measured. Accountability was a strong principle also in the Athenian government, but in other *poleis* not demonstrably to the same degree. I use the term "governance" here also for *poleis* that did not resemble Athens in this respect.

7.1.2 Agents, time frame, and sources

The first of its kind, the present study aims to provide a broad survey and a comparative analysis of the uses of the lot for *polis* governance in ancient Greece. Since by its very nature *polis* governance involves the history of citizenship and politics in ancient Greece, a few introductory remarks on this wider background may be helpful.

First, the protagonists of the political history of Greece need to be briefly introduced, before we encounter them in the intricate struggles for the distribution of offices in the Greek *poleis*. The people of a given *polis* were known as the *demos*, the collective of free inhabitants of the territory; the word refers to the land upon which the people lived, and off which they drew their living. In the Homeric epics, the male section of the people also appears as the *laos*, the collective of warriors under the command of a leader (*hegemon*).[7] From the early archaic age (eighth–seventh centuries) onward, an elite distinguished itself from the *demos* in wealth and power; when contrasted with this elite, the *demos* acquired the meaning "common people." Previous scholarship understood this elite to be an aristocracy, defined by birth from distinguished high-born families. More recently, however, historians agree that the claim to "high birth" was instead a form of self-presentation of an elite group whose main qualification was substantial wealth, allowing a distinctive lifestyle. Anyone who accrued enough personal wealth could be acknowledged as a peer and enter the elite; in this sense, it was a socially more flexible group than a true birth-aristocracy, but its distinction from the common people was no less meaningful.[8] In this chapter, I use the term "elite" in this way, denoting a class of citizen above and distinct from the common folk. It may come as no surprise to learn that among this elite, internal competition and upward and downward social mobility created social tensions that could and did lead occasionally to violence. Yet this same system also prevented power from becoming concentrated in a few hands, thanks to laws restricting the terms of office and fixed terms of iteration, all aimed at nipping such conflicts in the bud.

Due to its economic power and an overwhelming experience in leadership, and not least an increasingly sophisticated education, over time this socially fluid elite managed to consolidate its position within the *polis*, and its members came to be regarded, both by themselves and by others, as the "finest." When the political philosophers of the classical age such as Plato, Isocrates, and Aristotle referred to an "aristocracy" or to "aristocratic" features of a given *polis*, they had in

---

[7] Werlings (2010) 51–107.

[8] For the elite lifestyle based on wealth, with additional claims to (semi-)divine descent, see Duplouy (2006); for lifestyle marked by the *symposion*, see Węcowski (2014) 19–26; for institutionalization of this elite lifestyle, see Ma (2016) and the contributions to Meister and Seelentag (2020).

mind the social and cultural excellence of this elite group. Their wealth meanwhile was taken for granted. In classical political philosophy, however, "aristocratic" merit was distinguished from "oligarchic" wealth: in political thought, oligarchy had no claim to merit but was driven only by (greed for) wealth, a constitutive feature fundamentally distinct from aristocracy—even if the latter presupposed a lifestyle of leisure. This philosophical understanding of "aristocratic" as "distinguished by merit" is relevant to our discussion on methods of selection for office.

Second, a schematic framework of the political history of the Greek *poleis* may be useful, to be further explained and filled in with details later. When the Greek communities coalesced into the entities we now call *poleis*—roughly from the ninth to the early seventh centuries—among their distinctive characteristics were a more or less stable community of citizens on the one hand, and on the other the leadership of the *polis*, represented by *polis* offices and usually a council. Traditionally, the *demos* had the right to assemble in a meeting, to voice its views regarding matters of importance to the community, and to hear out the discussions.[9] In this sense, in formal terms the *demos* was "sovereign" and acted as an egalitarian entity within the *polis*. However, in the archaic age this sovereignty rarely entailed actual power; although communal decisions were made in the name of the *polis*, by and large the *demos* acted as a sounding board to their leaders, because as a body it lacked the position and competences of actual executive and legislative leadership.[10] That prerogative belonged to the elite—as we see in detail later—and *polis* leadership embodied in the various offices reflected the hierarchical values in the *polis*. The elite exercised its leadership over the *demos* in the political and military domains, but also in the realm of justice. Traditionally, while adjudication was a public matter enacted in full sight of the *demos* and with their consent, the actual judging was in the hands of a few accredited individuals. All these roles of political authority, military leadership, and judicial power came to be vested in distinct *polis* offices in the early archaic age, and the distribution of these agencies by lot drawing holds center stage in this chapter.

As regards distinguishing types of political regimes, the leading question remains: who had access to the *polis* offices—the elite or the *demos* as a whole? Aristotle addressed this question extensively at the theoretical level in his *Politics*, written in the second half of the fourth century. In historical realities, the typical situation of the archaic age involved cooperation between the elite holding the actual power of office and the *demos*, which attended deliberations

---

[9] Raaflaub (1997); Hölkeskamp (1997; 2002); Hammer (2005).
[10] For the difference between formal sovereignty and actual sovereign powers, see Waltermann (2019) 31–32.

in its role as a sounding board. After ca. 480 throughout the classical period, the pattern of power distribution varied, and we find on the one hand fully-fledged oligarchies in which a restricted, wealthy elite controlled the body of offices and sidelined the *demos* as much as possible, and on the other democratic systems whereby the *demos* had access to the offices or had the true sovereign voice in decision-making, or both. Further, we find *poleis* with constitutions that cannot be classified as wholly oligarchic or democratic, as they combined features of both systems and should therefore be rated somewhere on a spectrum between oligarchy and democracy. In the Hellenistic age after ca. 320, in the sprawling empires built upon Alexander the Great's conquest of the Greek and west Asian world, the inter-*polis* and international power relations mutated quite drastically. Most historians agree that the constitutions of the Greek *poleis* did not change to the same degree, but that democratic *poleis* veered toward an increasingly stronger elitism.

For our investigation into the use and implementation of drawing lots, an important part is played by the federacies or leagues between *poleis*, a development that increased in the Hellenistic age. These federacies added a new layer of citizenship and governance to the constituent *poleis*, some of which applied lot-casting for offices and other aspects of governance.[11] More fundamental changes ensued after ca. 150, when Roman imperialism created a new supra-*polis* power structure, and weighed upon the established internal configurations of *poleis* and their civic policies.

In sum, this chapter features a time frame from the early archaic age until around 150 BCE. With the parameters of the regime types used in a loose fashion, a simplified political history of the Greek world can be divided into four periods:

Period 1: From the early archaic age until the late sixth century (ca. 750–520): government (office holding) by the elite, with sounding-board support from the *demos*;

Period 2: From the late sixth to the early fifth centuries (ca. 520–480): movements in favor of more democracy, but the elite still powerful;

Period 3: From the early fifth to the late fourth centuries (ca. 480–320): full-blown oligarchies, full-blown democracies (more of the first than the latter), and many *poleis* in between;

Period 4: From the late fourth century to the mid-second century (ca. 320–ca. 150): full-blown oligarchies, full-blown democracies (more of the latter than the former), many *poleis* in between, democracies increasingly inclining toward elite political prerogatives.

---

[11] For the citizenship of federal states, see Lasagni (2017); also see contributions to Beck, Buraselis, and MacAuley (2019).

The evidence on drawing of lots for *polis* governance in the Greek *poleis* is plentiful, but it is very unevenly spread as regards time and place. Classical Athens is exceptionally well documented, and its use of the lot has been intensively studied, but never in a consistent diachronic analysis, nor in a systematic comparison with other *poleis*. Here, Athens will again be a principal focus, for this *polis* provides us with the first attested case of allotment for office, its development toward widespread use, and the debates about its use in detail. For other *poleis*, the relevant evidence is scarce, uneven, or entirely absent. As in any historical investigation, the nature of our sources has a deep impact on the answers we may find to our questions. A short discussion of the potential and limitations of these sources is therefore necessary before embarking on our historical investigation.

Literary texts in the widest sense offer representations of a wide scope of political relations and social values, constrained by the purposes and conventions of the literary genres in which they appear. For the archaic age, we are largely dependent on poetry, both epic and lyric, which offers valuable evidence on the practice of drawing lots and the values attached to it, but which is only indirectly connected to concrete, historical circumstances. The same holds true for classical drama; tragedies and comedies illuminate what was important and familiar to their audience, but most texts refer only rarely or indirectly to the practices of *polis* governance such as drawing lots. Historical and political philosophical prose did not yet exist in the archaic age. All the major historians and other intellectuals writing about *polis* governance lived in the classical age or later. For the archaic age, historians have had to rely on miscellaneous information, either documentary or oral, whose accuracy in relating past events is difficult to establish, as much then as now. Later I address some problems in more detail, when trying to reconstruct whether the lot was used in a particular case, and if so, how and why it was employed. Furthermore, when using the historical, political, and other literary accounts, we need to keep in mind that drawing lots for assigning *polis* office was a contested practice, notably in the intellectual circles to which the authors belonged. Let me give a few examples.

The *Athenaion Politeia* (*The Constitution of the Athenians*; *Ath.Pol.* for short) is an essential late-fourth-century source for Athenian political history, written by an author in the circle of Aristotle. He used various sources, among which were the historical accounts by Herodotus, Thucydides, and Xenophon and by the Atthidographers—historians writing accounts of Athens largely on an annalistic (year-by-year) basis. But the views of the author in question were also demonstrably influenced by Aristotle's *Politics*, a philosophical project in the context of which the text came about. Aristotle's views on allotment for office as such were nuanced, but he was fiercely critical of the Athenian system as a whole. Most philosophers were wary or downright critical of allotment for political office; Plato is a prominent example. By contrast, the classical orators of the fifth and fourth centuries—whether Athenian citizens or immigrants writing for Athenians—were deeply involved in the Athenian political and juridical system and the values on which it rested: for them, drawing lots for *polis* office was the normal—and normative—state of affairs.

In sum, most of these texts were written when drawing lots for offices was well established and widely known, for better or for worse. When writing about earlier history, the authors were often inclined to project their contemporary experiences and worldview onto the past. Similarly, when historians of the classical and Hellenistic ages were writing about the history of other *poleis* and federacies, local traditions with historical information were viewed through the lens of their own interests.[12] Needless to say, such conflicting traditions and views in our sources also affect how modern historians assess the origins, spread, and implications of allotment for office.[13]

Compared to the complexities of time, place and worldview of literary sources, epigraphical material is invaluable for providing straightforward evidence of the use of the lot, whatever the purpose or genre of the text: when the verbs *lanchano* or *kleroo* or *kuameuo* indicate the assignment of a position, we can be sure this involved drawing lots.[14] But epigraphical texts have their own pitfalls, and not merely because many texts are damaged beyond repair.

The extant corpus of these sources is the outcome of two contingent factors. The first is the so-called epigraphical habit of the Greek *poleis*, namely the propensity to inscribe various kinds of texts in durable material, which differed immensely from *polis* to *polis*, and changed substantially over time. There is not simply a steady increase of such texts in number and size everywhere in equal measure from the seventh century—when laws first came to be inscribed—down the ensuing centuries. Instead, the habit of keeping written records developed quite unevenly across Greece, and many such records were made not on durable material but on waxed wood, papyrus, and other perishable supports. To survive for posterity, they also had to be inscribed in stone or bronze, and this habit also spread over Greece somewhat erratically.

For instance, the cities of Crete began inscribing laws in stone and bronze before many other *poleis* did so. The cities in Asia Minor had known law-based governance and had inscribed their religious rules since the archaic age, before they began inscribing public decisions (such as decrees and treaties) in stone on

---

[12] These local histories, written from the late fifth century throughout the Hellenistic era, were highly popular across the Greek world; the Atthidographers can be considered to belong to this genre; cf. Thomas (2019).

[13] For the analysis of drawing lots for political office as both a historical and a historiographical problem, see Demont (2001).

[14] For this terminology, see Appendix.

a regular basis, roughly beginning in the later fifth century. The Spartans hardly took to recording public decisions at all, not being particularly keen on writing anyway. By contrast, Athens produced more inscriptions across its history than any other *polis*. Generally speaking, democracies tend to be overrepresented in our epigraphical corpus because obviously they were more inclined to publicize decrees and other decisions on stone than were oligarchies. Nonetheless, not all democracies did so equally: in Sicily, the epigraphical habit was far more limited than in the eastern Mediterranean, regardless of the political regime. And for the present study of Greek political history, including allotment of office, oligarchies are as significant as democracies.

Second, the extant (and still growing) corpus of epigraphical documents is the outcome of the irregular chances of survival of the stone and bronze objects on which they were inscribed. Many such objects were either lost or destroyed, and although we can estimate the representativeness of our current corpus, it remains an estimation, no more. Enough inscriptions on bronze survive to indicate that this metal was commonly used for recording laws and other public documents, yet there are so few of them that we can be certain the majority were lost to the later recycling of bronze artifacts. Many gaps in our epigraphical records may well be due to the disappearance of bronze originals. In most *poleis* other than classical Athens, inscriptions on stone—whether numerous or few—make an uneven appearance, with the result that many texts remain rather isolated as testimony. If an inscription tells us that at some point in time an office was assigned by lot, we cannot tell how long this practice had existed prior to the appointment, nor if it was continued for some time when such additional information is lacking.

How the epigraphical tradition and chance survival may affect our historical reconstruction is typified by the earliest extant decree in which lots are used to assign a new citizen to a *polis* subgroup upon receiving a grant of citizenship: the decree in question is from Troizen, and probably dates to 369.[15] Yet we cannot deduce from this text that sortition of new citizens for their enrollment began around 370, neither in Greece generally nor even just in Troizen; this is the earliest extant decree of Troizen, from where only one earlier inscription, a dedication, is known.[16] As for the enrollment of new citizens in Troizen before 369, there is nothing to explain how these appointments came about, nor in other *poleis* of which no older decrees are preserved. The discovery of a new text with such an enrollment clause might cause a change of scholarly views about

---

[15] *IG* IV 748.
[16] Dedications: *IG* IV 761 (fifth cent.); 764 (fourth cent.). One more *polis* decree survives, dated to the fourth cent.: *IG* IV 753. Jones (1991) 94 tentatively infers from the verb εἶμεν in the Troizenian decree, which also occurs in seven out of twenty-one "choice" enrollment clauses, that before the sortition perhaps choice was the common practice at Troizen.

the emergence of this practice in ways we cannot foresee. For now, we need to create a framework of the history of granting citizenship and of the distribution of citizens over subgroups, based on other evidence, in which to tentatively fit the decree from Troizen.

As a result, the evidence on the political regimes of the archaic down to the Hellenistic era—and, most pertinently, on the use of the lot in these regimes—is highly uneven. What we know about the classification of regimes as oligarchic, democratic, or other forms, membership of a *koinon* (league) or the countless regime changes derives overwhelmingly from the Greek historians and from political treatises as divergent as Aristotle's *Politics* and *Rhetoric*, Isocrates's political writings, and the *Rhetoric for Alexander* by Anaximenes of Lampsakos. On the actual practices of political governance, these texts rarely inform us in a systematic and detailed way. For day-to-day politics, including the selection for office by vote or by lot, we must rely overwhelmingly on epigraphical evidence, notably inscribed decrees. And here the vast regional differences in epigraphical customs carry weight: for instance, the *poleis* in western Greece published very few decrees—even in democratic periods—whereas Athens, Delphi, and the cities in Asia Minor produced hundreds of documents.

Finally, archaeological evidence occasionally shows the application of lot. The previous chapters show such evidence for the distribution of *kleroi* when new *poleis* were founded in colonies. The lead tokens found in Kamarina and the clay balls found in various places in Sicily, southern Italy, and elsewhere—identical objects inscribed with names—all testify to the drawing of lots, most probably for the distribution of land plots in the refoundation of cities.[17] For other aspects of *polis* governance—material evidence such as the fifth-century clay allotment tokens and the fourth-century bronze allotment plates (nametags) in Athens and elsewhere, and of stone *kleroteria* (lottery machines) in Athens, on Delos, and in other places in eastern Greece—demonstrate the large-scale drawing of lots, notably for the jury courts (*dikasteria*). Especially outside of Athens, such archaeological evidence may be the only indication—albeit eloquent—of the use of the lot in the *polis* in question.[18]

7.2 What did *poleis* use the lot for?

Drawing lots, as set out in this book, is an instrument of decision-making. Depending on the purpose for which it is used, we give it a specific

---

[17] Walthall and Souza (2021); the clay balls may have served participation in *polis* governance (Cordano 2016), but specifics are unclear. See also p. 207, 289.
[18] See Kroll (2015) for examples of allotment tokens.

name: divination, selection, distribution, or procedure, such as taking turns or mixing groups. In the governance of Greek *poleis*, some applications fell neatly into one such category, and a specific Greek vocabulary was current for the procedure and the result.[19] Other applications seem, however, to combine or fall between such categories. Considering the ubiquity of the practice, drawing lots must have been thoroughly familiar to the Greeks, and perhaps more importantly, so were the specific rules of the game in each particular form of application. Among such familiar factors were the degrees to which the gods were supposed to be involved in the process. In divination, discerning the will of the gods was precisely the point. In cases of selection and distribution, the gods were expected to safeguard the procedure and ensure equality of chance for an (equal) share, while not remaining directly responsible for the outcome—barring a few notable exceptions, among which was the assignment of specific priesthoods. In other cases, divine involvement is elusive, and the perception may also have depended on the particular situation and on individual belief.

Many practices of drawing lots for *polis* governance are attested from the early archaic down to the late Hellenistic age, but some appear only in the classical age, and not only due to chance survival of sources. A first example is the enrollment in *polis* subgroups of new citizens by lot, briefly mentioned earlier. Formalizing this procedure became necessary when citizen status had become sufficiently stable, either in law or by custom, as to bring about a closure of the citizen body.[20] By "stable" and "closure" we do not mean forever fixed or rigidly exclusive, but a concept of citizen status that set effective legal and social boundaries between citizens and noncitizens. Varying from *polis* to *polis*, this stabilization of citizen status took shape in the seventh and sixth centuries, was being laid down in written law from ca. 600 onward, and further consolidated by legislation after ca. 500. In the classical age the procedures for transforming outsiders into citizens—and their enrollment in *polis* subgroups—became increasingly formalized, and numerous such honorific grants of citizenship were inscribed. A second example is the judgment of drama contests held in Athens. According to the tradition, the first such event took place around 530, but the form of competition relevant here—with a complicated procedure of judgment that included the use of lots—did not begin until the early fifth century. Both applications of the lot are further discussed later.

An overview of drawing lots in *polis* governance, other than for distribution of office, indicates the range of its applications; the list is not comprehensive but offers instances of each type of application.

---

[19] For this vocabulary, see Appendix.
[20] See Vink (2017) on stability of membership of the citizen body as a condition for the rights and duties attached to citizenship and political self-determination.

7.2.1 *Divination*, or oracular consultation, by lots was a feasible way for *poleis* to decide a challenging issue, especially—though not only—when the cult or the property of the gods was involved.

A colorful case is the public divination by lots in Athens in 352/1 that involved deciding how to deal with the sacred area belonging to Demeter and Kore on the border between Athens and Megara.[21] Since a special committee set up for this question could not find a satisfactory solution, the oracle of Apollo was asked to choose between two options, which were written on tin plates and then sealed in terracotta vessels—a complicated procedure of "long-distance" oracular consultation by lots.[22] The method was entirely public and democratic, with the citizens involved in the sealing of the vessels, and subsequently revealing the selected option in the assembly.

7.2.2 *Selection* of one or more people for a particular task can be distinguished from selection for office by the type and the regularity of the occurrence.

The term *selection* applies when drawing lots took place for a specific moment or duty only, whereas offices were allotted regularly and entailed fixed duties; the latter overlaps with the category of distribution (see section 7.2.3). Selection by lot was used for many and varied purposes, therefore, most of which took place in the regular domains of *polis* governance, such as justice and arbitration, along with war and military matters, and related endeavors such as colonization efforts. Often the people selected were the *polis*'s own citizens, but occasionally citizens of other *poleis* selected by lot were invited for the task. A few examples illustrate these practices.

Selecting citizens by lot to act as judges or arbitrators became increasingly frequent across the classical and Hellenistic ages. Such boards were often asked to judge competitions in festivals—for instance, three men selected from seven by lot for the contests at a festival for Hermes in Beroia (Macedonia).[23] Allotted boards of judges were particularly appreciated for arbitration in difficult issues that lay beyond the powers of the regular courts or threatened to fuel civic

---

[21] On divination by lots, see ch. 2. For an overview of *poleis* seeking cultic advice at oracles, though not necessarily by lots, see Parker (2011) 265–272; Bonnechere (2013). On consultation of the oracle of Delphi by the *polis* Athens, see Bowden (2005).

[22] RO 58; ll. 22, 40–41 indicate the democratic principle in inviting any Athenian who wants to may be involved; ll. 23–38, 42–48 do so by situating the authority over the consultation in the Assembly; ll. 54–57 see to inscribing the result and two copies to be set up. See also p. 124–25.

[23] Beroia: *EKM*, 1 Beroia 1, B ll. 49–54 (early second century).

conflict.[24] We find such boards acting within a single *polis*—for instance, five men selected by lot from thirty elected by the *demos* to oversee the settlement of debts in Ephesos, or three men selected by lot from nine individuals elected by the *demos* to act as public advocates (*synegoros*) in Zeleia, or eleven men from the council in Delphi to arbitrate in disputes about a breach of the law on interest.[25]

For disputes between *poleis* it was not uncommon to create boards composed from a third party to arbitrate, to guarantee impartiality.[26] For example, a *dikasterion* of 301 men was allotted in Eretria when this *polis* was asked to arbitrate in a conflict between Paros and Naxos; the ensuing settlement was determined on Delos.[27] Elsewhere, in the late third century a board of 15 judges decided a dispute over land between Epidauros and Arsinoe.[28] In the second century, recurrent disputes between Eretria and Karystos (on Euboia) were laid before the Amphiktyones of Delphi for arbitration; to reach a decision, first a board of 31 men was selected by lot from all citizens in the *polis* of Hypata, but later a group of *dikastai* elected by the *demos* of Hypata "on their merits" (*aristinden*) was added, apparently to give more weight to the decision.[29] A treaty of *sympoliteia* (bringing two *poleis* together in a common *politeia*) between Myania and Hypnia, signed in Phocis around 190, instructs the archon to select by lot a *dikasterion*, whose duties are unknown due to the damaged text.[30] Just as in the regularly allotted office of *dikastai* in Athens (see section 8.2.2.4 in this volume), the use of the lot for selection of such special boards was probably meant to guarantee impartiality; if the allotment took place immediately before the actual judgment was delivered, then bribery—an omnipresent fear in ancient Greece—was virtually impossible.

Selection by lot for the formation of military units is frequently attested on Crete, where *poleis* formed a common front to deal with military threats by selecting soldiers by lot and unite these forces.[31] Interestingly, the booty captured

---

[24] Walser (2012) 96–107 observes that conferring cases to boards of a few allotted judges, instead of to the regular *dikasteria*, was always a decision of the assembly and that the conflicts for which allotted boards of judges from elsewhere (*xenika dikasteria*) were created often had to do with debts, loans, taxes, and landed property.

[25] Ephesos (ca. 297): *Ephesos* 4, *IEph* 4 + Add. p. 1, A. 8–9; Zeleia (late fourth cent.): *IMT* Aisep/Kad Dere 1135; Delphi: *FD* III 1:294, early fourth cent.; cf. Gortyn (Crete) *IC* IV 162 (ca. 250–200), seven men drawn by lot to assess a financial issue on the *agora*.

[26] Walser (2012) argues that the practice began with extra- or inter-*polis* arbitration, and next was increasingly resorted to for intra-*polis* adjudication.

[27] *IG* XI, 41065, early second cent. Cf. Ager (1996) for such interstate arbitration; this case no. 83; Walser (2012) 103–104.

[28] *IG* IV², 1 72.

[29] Allotment of 31 men, *FD* III 1:578, date 146; *CID* 4:121, date 110; elected *dikastai*, *CID* 4:122, date 110.

[30] *IG* IX, 1² 3: 748; *FD* III 4:352.

[31] For instance, between Malla and Lyttos, *IC* I xix 1, ll. 4–8 (third cent.); cf. Chaniotis (1996) no. 12, 208–23; between Hierapytna and Lyttos (second cent.; *IC* I xvi 5; *SEG* 26.1049), Chaniotis no. 25, 26, 79c.

by allied forces formed in this way was likewise distributed by lot.[32] Since most of these Cretan military arrangements were components of a *sympoliteia* or of an alliance between *poleis*, they constituted a limited instance of mixing disparate groups into new units through use of the lot. A similar agreement to form manpower selected by lot was made for the cavalries of Orchomenos and Chaironeia in ca. 280.[33] Although the text of this accord does not refer to a wider political context, the arrangement undoubtedly belonged to further institutionalization of the Boiotian confederacy during this period, in which territorial units (*tele*) were created for the administrative and military organization of federal Boiotia.[34] Such agreements between *poleis* creating overarching political administrations added to those of the constituent *poleis* offer a form of refoundations lite, whereby diverse groups were conflated into new units among the *poleis* involved by means of sortition.

For the foundation of a colony, besides an invitation to whoever was interested to join, citizens could be selected by lot to do so.[35] When the decision to found a colony and select citizens took place to face a crisis such as a famine, the enterprise could take the shape of a *dekateusis* (sacrifice of a tithe) to achieve a purification of the *polis*.[36] The act of sending away of a tenth of the citizenry resembles the ritual expulsion of scapegoats (*pharmakoi*). Selection by lot of scapegoats, beside their voluntary self-sacrifice, occurs in mythical stories, where the lot might fall on a son or daughter of the ruler; by contrast, in historical scapegoat-rituals the victim was often a single man of low status, who would be selected by various means.[37]

7.2.3 *Poleis* used *distribution* by lot for many purposes.

As noted earlier, since the early archaic age Greek communities used the lot system for the distribution of various kinds of goods, and when the communities solidified into *poleis*, its members—the citizens—typically were the recipients of the allotted goods.

---

[32] Chaniotis (1996) 93–94.
[33] *SEG* 28.461.
[34] Knoepfler (2000); Corsten (1999); Müller (2011).
[35] Hdt. 4.153: among the Therans the lot (*palos*) decides which one among brothers is to sail off to found a colony, implying that in every household at least one son was to maintain the *oikos*; see also ch. 6.3.
[36] *Dekate* underlying colonization was plausible in the case of Rhegion, but overall is a rare phenomenon: Malkin (1987a) 37–41; for the foundation story of Rhegion, see Arist. fr. 611.55 (Rose); Diod. 8.23.2; Str. 6.1.6 (C 257); cf. Knibbeler (2005) 241–279.
[37] Knibbeler (2005) on selection of *pharmakoi*, 48–52; 147–155; 281–299. Mythical selection by lot of *pharmakos*: Diod. 4.42.1–5; Herodotus (4.94) relates how among the Getai in Thrace, a man is selected by lot to contact the realm of the dead and is effectively sacrificed to do so.

Distribution of portions of sacrificial meat at festivals, either to citizens individually or to groups of citizens in communal banquets, was a widespread practice, and partaking in the distribution was a clear marker of citizen identity.[38] Not all portions were always equal; the type, quota, and number of such allotted portions were further markers of status differences among citizens.[39] Indeed, priests and priestesses—who were also citizens—normally received choice parts of animal sacrifices, both edible (meat) and economically valuable (hides, for instance), before the remainder was distributed among the other participants. Citizens in office likewise often received more than the others: even in democratic Athens, at the "Little Panathenaia," ninety-nine officials, probably the *kanephoroi* (girls carrying baskets with cultic materials, in this festival a hundred of them) and "others in the procession" received special quotas, namely multiples of the equal portions of meat received by the other Athenians, in the numbers each deme provided to the procession.[40] In this case, the idea of an equal portion was transformed into a marker of rank of the individual's role in office. The act of including noncitizens in sacrificial distributions was a clear sign of their acceptance in the citizen group as a united cult community, though such guests did not always share with the citizens on an equal basis.[41]

For the distribution by lot of plots of land (*kleroi*) of conquered territory to citizens, classical Athens is particularly notorious, establishing its first *klerouchoi* in 506 after defeating the Chalcidians, and continuing this policy far into the fourth century.[42] Although the allotment procedure of these plots appears to be similar to that in the founding of colonies, the governance involved was quite different, because the *klerouchoi* remained citizens of their original *polis* (Athens in this case), and many did not live on the allotted lands, but operated as absentee landlords.[43] Unlike colonization—often triggered by demographic pressure or

---

[38] For distribution of sacrificial meat by lot, see ch. 3.

[39] For *polis* banquets, see Schmitt-Pantel (1992); status differences in sacrificial portions attested in epigraphical evidence, see Paul (2018), and Tsoukala (2009) for iconographical evidence.

[40] RO 81, the law and decree of ca. 335; on the distribution B 1-26, plus comm.

[41] The first attestation in inscriptions in Athens is *IG* I³ 244 (C 6-9) of ca. 460, when the deme Skambonidai assigned sacrificial meat also to *metoikoi* in the festival of the hero Leos. For the partial inclusion of metics in *polis* festivals, see Wijma (2014).

[42] In 506, the Athenians confiscated the lands of the Euboian *hippobotai* ("horse-rearers") and gave it to four thousand *klerouchoi* (Hdt. 6.100.4); see p. 212. Athens also established klerouchies in Aegina, Amisus, Astacus, Brea, Carystus, Eretria, Histiaia, Imbros, Lemnos, Melos, Naxos, Salamis, Samos, Skyros, and Sinope; see Salomon (1997); Moreno (2007); Igelbrink (2015).

[43] In 446 the Euboians revolted and were suppressed by Pericles, who expelled the inhabitants of Histiaia and gave their land to Athenian *klerouchoi* (Thuc. 1.114; cf. RO 131), some of whom collected great wealth by holding vast property there while living in Athens—for instance, Oionias of Atene, whose property was publicly sold for his involvement in profanation of the Mysteries in 415 (*IG* I³ 422, col. III, ll. 217-219, 375-379; for these wealthy landowners, Moreno [2007] 89-91). In 427, after suppressing the Mytilenean revolt, the Athenians annexed the larger part of Lesbos, dividing it into three thousand *kleroi* of which 10 percent was dedicated to the gods, and the rest allocated by lot to Athenians, who next leased the plots back to Lesbians for 2 *mnai* rent per annum (Thuc. 3.50.2).

internal strife—establishing klerouchies served Athens's hegemonial imprint on the Aegean world, and its need for a secure grain supply.

Not only goods, but duties, too, were distributed among citizens by lot. In Athens, the financial maintenance of the navy was assigned to the wealthiest citizens by lot as a liturgy (honorific tax), the trierarchy; it was primarily a tax on wealth, but it also implied service of the trierarch on the ship, if he was physically able to do so. Due to the high costs of this upkeep, it was not always possible to allot all ships to the wealthy, and such leftover ships are listed as "unallotted" in the records for the year.[44] Guarding the city was another such duty many cities assigned to their citizens; duties as a guard could be assigned by lot, and so were the turns taken in the actual guarding and the sections of the city's defense walls. Assigning quotas of standing guard duties by lot was not just a matter of equal distribution, but also a way to prevent advance knowledge of who was to guard which part of the wall, and thereby reduce the risk of malpractice and possible treason.[45] In Athens, standing guard was a duty for citizens, and in the first half of the fifth century there were fifty such guards.[46] In Miletos, acting as guardians of the city was allotted among the citizens, but newly made citizens were excluded for ten years from this duty, which apparently was only entrusted to fully integrated, long-standing citizens.[47]

Besides assigning goods and duties to their citizens, the *poleis* distributed the citizens themselves by lot over groups and positions. Assigning offices by lot can be understood as the distribution of citizens over the available political and cultic offices, which were formally considered an honor rather than a duty, as we will see in more detail later.

Since by definition a *polis* had the authority over its membership, it was also responsible for citizens joining *polis* subgroups, a crucial feature of citizen status. These subgroups were diverse and served a variety of functions. Some, such as the *phylai* (tribes), acted as military units and as political units to facilitate the distribution of offices and duties. Others, such as the phratries or *patra* (depending on the Greek dialect), supported its member-families in matters of birth and death, and they supervised the legitimacy of their children for their citizen status. Many of these subgroups had very ancient roots; the traditional *phylai* and phratries were fictive kin groups claiming common, mythical descent, whereas others were based on ritualized social practices, such as the men's dining groups in Sparta and on Crete. The subgroups formed the backbone of the *polis*,

---

[44] *IG* II² 1604–1609 (377–370); Gabrielsen ([1994] 2010) 80–82.
[45] Aen.Tact. 18.21, 20.2, with several historical cases of cities taken by treason due to foreknowledge.
[46] *Ath.Pol.* 24.3. Proxenoi, if they were to settle in Athens, could be exempt from this duty; *IG* I³ 159 (ca. 430); *IG* I³ 164 (440–425).
[47] *Miletos* 39 (*Milet* I 3, 150) ll. 50–53.

integrating their members in the various units of the *polis* with common duties, cults, rituals, and other social practices.[48] When in the archaic age citizen status became more clearly defined by convention and law, membership of the *polis* and its subgroups came to be firmly based on descent; in colonies, the starting point of citizen status was new, but often the subgroups of the mother city were reintroduced in the new *polis* and subsequently transmitted by descent. So, normally, a *polis* did not have to distribute its citizens over subgroups, because membership was acquired by hereditary transmission.

Yet occasionally *poleis* moved to actively distribute citizens over subgroups, and they did so in two circumstances: when a *polis* decided to change the existing allocation and redistribute the citizens deliberately to mix them, either over the existing subgroups or creating new ones, or when a *polis* added new citizens to the citizen body and hence had to assign them to subgroups. For both types of distribution, the lot was a feasible instrument.

First, *mixture* of citizens in redistribution over subgroups by drawing lots can be classified as combining the distribution proper and the procedure. The act of assigning citizens to different subgroups than they used to belong to in a *polis* represented a partial or complete refounding of the *polis*, as did changing the *polis*'s subgroups themselves. Doing so also required new cultic foundations of the citizen body. In section 8.2.2.3 of this volume we look into three such cases in more detail: the reorganizations of the *phylai* at Sikyon, Cyrene, and Athens. In the case of Athens, the use of the lot is certain; in the other two cases either not, or less so. In Cyrene and Athens, a crucial motive for the redistribution was to integrate new citizens into the citizen body and mixing old and new citizens in the subgroups; simultaneously, the political constitution was made more democratic. The use of the lot in the refoundation of mid-third century Nakone in Sicily was discussed in the previous chapter.

In the Sicilian *polis* of Kamarina the use of the lot in the refoundation of the city remains unclear. Here, lead tablets were found collected in a sanctuary, each inscribed with a name, a patronymic (father's name), and a number, (probably) of a phratry. It is highly likely that the tablets were used to assign citizens to phratries when Kamarina was refounded after its destruction by war. In 461 the cities of Magna Graecia decided on a Common Agreement to oust the tyrants and their mercenary forces holding power in these cities, and to start anew, with a refoundation of the citizen body and a redistribution of land.[49] The lead tablets

---

[48] In the archaic age, before the contours of the citizen body were firmly consolidated by law, such subgroups were essential in assimilating newcomers into the community of citizens; cf. Walter (1993); Ismard (2010) (Athens); Seelentag (2014) (Crete).

[49] Diod. 11.76.6; Teegarden (2018); for Kamarina, see also ch. 6.2.10.

of Kamarina must belong to this refoundation, but how exactly they were used is unclear.[50]

Second, from the classical age onward, new citizens were formally included in the citizen body and had to be assigned a place in a subgroup using procedures laid down in the so-called enrollment clauses of the inscribed decrees granting the citizenship; earlier we saw the example from Troizen.[51] Some *poleis* enrolled the new citizens by lot, others by giving them a choice in which subgroup they wished to enter. Nicholas Jones has investigated the extant enrollment clauses of fifty-three *poleis*, dating from the fifth to the first centuries.[52] Twenty-four *poleis* practiced distribution by lot, some of which were restricted to a selection of the subgroups to which the new citizen could be admitted. The other *poleis* offered a free choice, albeit sometimes restricted to one or a few subgroups, from which the candidate was persuaded to choose. The preference for either procedure appears to be spread more or less geographically, with the "lot" to the east of an imaginary line in the Aegean running from Thasos to the Cyclades, and "choice" to the west of that line, but with some exceptions, such as Troizen (lot) and Kolophon (choice). Jones also tentatively suggests a historical development from choice to sortition in the Hellenistic era. This change, however, is less clear than the geographical spread, and here we may also recall that assigning citizens to subgroups by lot had a long tradition, stretching back to the late archaic age; if and how this tradition may have affected later practices is difficult to ascertain. The reason why new citizens could occasionally get access only to a restricted choice of subgroups is easier to explain: admittance to particular subgroups could be undesirable—for instance, due to relative overcrowding—so potential friction between the new member and the group was more easily avoided.

In some twenty *poleis* across mainland and eastern Greece we find the clause "[*ep'*] *isei kai homoiai*" (on equal and similar, equitable terms) for the conditions on which new citizens were integrated in the *polis*, and for other arrangements relating to citizenship.[53] On this clause, the new citizens would be equal to the existing citizens in conditions where equality pertained to all citizens, and be treated fairly, just like the others, in other situations. The evidence does not unequivocally show a connection between this clause and the method of distribution

---

[50] Cordano (1992), Cecchet (2017). The soft material (lead) made the tablets unsuitable for use as *pinakia* for *kleroteria*, such as used in fourth century Athens; see Robinson (2002).

[51] The earliest extant decrees conferring privileges belonging to citizenship to outsiders are from Crete (Gortyn honoring Dionysios, *LAC* G64, ca. 525–500); Datala, Spensithios-decree, *LAC* DA1, ca. 500), but these are not yet grants of full-blown citizenship. The first extant inscribed decree of this kind is the citizenship grant of Athens to Thrasyboulos of Kalydon, *IG* I³ 102 (410/09), with the enrollment clause in ll. 16–17.

[52] Jones (1991).

[53] For *isei kai homoiai*, see also ch. 6.3.9.

of new citizens to subgroups, and cities do not seem to use the clause consistently in citizenship grants.[54]

Athens gave new citizens a free though later limited choice for the phratry and deme, which automatically also included a *phyle*, a method the city shared with many other *poleis* west of the imaginary boundary (for deme and *phyle* in Athens, see below).[55] Yet, given the degree to which more than any other *polis* Athens was keen to use the lot for so many purposes in governance, the fact that the city never changed this aspect of the enrollment procedure begs an explanation. The cause of Athens's continuous use of choice may be the long tradition of its procedures for citizenship grants. On our present evidence, the first grants were given to Menon of Pharsalos and possibly to a certain Hegelochos (*polis* of origin unknown) in the mid-470s, both men who had given substantial support to Athens in the wars with the Persians.[56] These grants were made before the *polis* shifted toward broad allotment in the 460s, at a time when election was the prevailing method for selection in Athens. In this climate, choice would probably seem a matter of course in the enrollment procedure inaugurated for these men. Once this procedure was initiated, it became firmly entrenched. A similar path dependency shaped the Athenian formula for the citizenship grant itself: when in the late fifth / early fourth centuries other *poleis* began inscribing citizenship decrees and introduced the expression "to give *politeia*" to accept their new citizens, Athens stuck to its conventional formula "that he be an Athenian" until the year 229, when the city also adopted the *politeia* formula.[57]

7.2.4 The drawing of lots for a variety of rules in *polis* governance may be termed *procedural*: Taking turns, assigning places, and so on.

Using the lot for setting the order of turns had a long tradition in competitions held at funerary rituals and religious festivals.[58] Drawing lots for taking turns

---

[54] The clause figures together with sortition of new citizens on Samos, in Magnesia, Ephesos, Smyrna, Temnos, and Assos, with choice for new citizens in Kolophon and Tralles, and with an unidentified method of enrollment in Thermos, Bargylia, Alabanda, Larbeni, Mylasa, Phalanna and Delphi. The clause is used with other instances of communal and citizenship-related events, such as common oaths and shared settlement, at Cyrene, Athens, Gortyn, and Itanos.

[55] An exception in Athens were mass grants—for instance, for the Plataians who received citizenship in 427 and were not assigned to subgroups (phratries, demes), perhaps to prevent imbalance in the numbers or because their citizenship was expected to be only temporarily implemented.

[56] For the evidence and assessment, see Osborne III-IV T 1 (Menon); Blok (2017) 254–257 (Menon and Hegelochos).

[57] For the first extant decrees, see, e.g., *Ephesos* 80, *IEph* 1417; Andros *IG* XII Suppl. 245; for Athens Osborne I.

[58] Hom. *Il.* 23.288–350: drawing lots for who is first to start in chariot races. See also p. 58–59, 166.

was a convention also in other religious contexts, notably the consultation of oracles. In Delphi, after the cities enjoying *promanteia* (the honor of consulting the oracle first) had their turns, the order of all others who wished to consult the Pythia was established by lot.[59] The sanctuary in Delphi also held a festival in honor of Apollo, and following the example of the festival for the Olympian Zeus in Elis, Delphi refurbished its festival on a grander scale in the early sixth century. For Olympia, the festival with its competitions was crucial to its development into a semi-independent sanctuary within Elis, and a similar process turned Delphi with its oracle and festivals into a *polis*.[60] Other *poleis* followed suit, incorporating festivals already existing in sanctuaries nearby, or setting up new ones, the most prominent being the festivals at Olympia, Delphi, Nemea, and Corinth, together called the Crown Games. Athens elevated its Panathenaia for Pallas Athena with a similar pan-Hellenic ambition. The *poleis* were now responsible for the governance of the competitions, in which lots were drawn to assign turns in chariot races and for pairing competing wrestlers with other athletes, an application combining procedure and mixture.[61]

As a result, when lotteries came to be used to determine turns in *polis* governance itself, the Greeks had been familiar with the practice for centuries. Clearly, the individuals or groups taking turns were considered equal; otherwise the use of lots would not have been feasible. Such was the case in oligarchies as well as in democracies. In the classical and Hellenistic ages, we find examples all over the Greek world of lots used for setting turns. As noted earlier, the drawing of lots was applied for turns standing guard. For some offices, the turns for holding one's term of office was decided by lot. In Priene, for men who were elected by show of hands to be *nomophylax* (guardian of the law) the lot decided in which two months of the year each would exercise this office.[62]

Between *poleis*, too, the lot was used for procedure. When Athens and Sparta concluded a treaty in 421 at the end of the Archidamian War, they drew lots to determine which of the two parties had to take the first steps in making restoration of their positions.[63] In the late fifth or mid-fourth century Mytilene and Phokaia decided to issue coinage in tandem, taking turns to mint the electrum currency, for which Mytilene was first by drawing lots.[64]

In democratic Athens, where from the 460s onward distribution of office was increasingly run by sortition, drawing lots for procedure also increased over the years. The order of the prytanies (the terms of presiding the council and

---

[59] For the evidence and discussion, see ch. 2.4-2.6.
[60] Morgan (1990).
[61] Chariot races in Delphi: Soph. *El.* 709. Athletes: Miller (2004) 49–50, 116, 127.
[62] *Priene* 124, *IK Priene* 51 (second cent.).
[63] Thuc. 5.21.1.
[64] *IG* XII, 2 1; *SEG* 34.849.

assembly) of the ten *phylai* was determined by lot; the chairman was selected by lot from the *phyle* in prytany, and the secretary was selected by lot from the other nine. In the fourth century, a presiding board (the *prohedroi*) of nine was installed, selected by lot every day by the chairman of the *prytaneis* from the nine *phylai* who were not in prytany.[65] In this last instance, procedural use overlaps with selection by lot for a single occasion.

In judicial procedures the lot was used in various ways. For settling a border dispute between the *poleis* Halai and Boumeliteia in Lokris Opuntia in the second century, the judges decided by lot which of the two was to begin the procedure.[66] This case shows the role of the lot in taking turns to settle a dispute. In some *poleis* we find the expression *lanchano diken* (*vel sim.*, depending on the local dialect and vocabulary) for initiating a lawsuit: literally, obtaining justice by lot. In Athens, for instance, the expression occurs frequently.[67] The pithy phrasing makes what exactly lay behind it hard to identify. According to the dictionary of LSJ, the expression means "to obtain leave to bring a suit (esp. a private suit), probably because the presiding magistrates decided the order of hearing by lot."[68] The assumption that the lot decided the order in which the cases would be dealt with is plausible, because the alternative—drawing lots for assigning cases to judges—is not very likely: in Greece, the law usually prescribed to which judicial procedure and to which type of judge or court a particular case was referred. For instance, in ca. 500 in Gortyn on Crete the law distinguished between citizens and others in the kind of trial they would get (*lanchano*).[69] In Athens, this was also the case, both for citizens and others; Robin Osborne argues that Athenians had access to a variety of legal actions, some of which were prescribed by law, others liable to the preference of the plaintiff.[70] In the fourth century, however, the number of cases assigned to a *dikasterion* (jury court of allotted citizens) was so high that here the lot decided to which *particular* court among several courts meeting on the same day the case was referred. By this time, every procedural step in the composition of the *dikasteria* and the assignment of cases to courts was decided by lot; only the judgment itself was carried out by secret ballot.[71]

---

[65] Cf. *Ath.Pol.* 44.7–9; attested in numerous decrees.
[66] *FD* III, 1: 362 + 4: 345, l. A 15.
[67] Antiph. fr. 70; Isoc. 18.7, 11, 23; Pl. *Laws* 762b3; 909c5; frequently in Isaeus, etc. Plausibly restored in two fifth-century honorific decrees granting access to jurisdiction: *IG* I³ 55 (c. 431) on behalf of Aristonon; *IG* I³ 19 (late 420s), a proxeny decree for Acheloion; for the date Mattingly (1996) 363–366: 422/1; Rhodes (2008): late 420s.
[68] LSJ, s.v. λαγχάνω I.3.
[69] *IC* IV 13; *LAC* G13 (600–525): ἀϝτὸς λάϱοι ϝαστίαν δίκαν.
[70] Osborne (2010a), with a response to critical reactions to the original publication (1985).
[71] For the intricate procedures of the *dikasteria*, see *Ath.Pol.* 63–66.

A remarkable case of procedural use of the lot was the judgment of the drama competitions at the Dionysia in Athens, which deserves more discussion here.[72] Nearly a year before the Great Dionysia, the archon (eponymous) decided who among the dramatists who had submitted a proposal was to present a play at the festival. That a single man made such an important decision was a highly unusual procedure, which nonetheless does not seem to have elicited objections or even comments.[73] Next, for selecting the judges of the competition, all ten *phylai* proposed several candidates per *phyle*, whose names were written on tablets and stored in sealed jugs. Whether these men knew they had been named as candidates is not clear, but they certainly had to be proposed by others. Opening the sealed jugs before the right moment was punishable by death. Finally, the order in which the plays were performed was determined by lot.[74]

After the performance of the plays, right before the actual judging was to take place, one name per *phyle* was drawn from the jug. In principle, any male citizen could be entered as candidate and end up selected, so the final choice would come as a surprise to the men involved. This part of the procedure is a *klerosis ek prokriton*, a selection by lot from preselected candidates, a common procedure for the distribution of office (see section 8.1 in this volume).[75] The judges then swore an oath to judge according to their own best judgment (i.e., not following pressure from the audience).

While all of this is still quite straightforward, the puzzling part is the assessment itself. The ten judges each wrote down the name of the chorus or of the playwright they thought best. The ten names were then put into a jug, following which five were drawn—probably by the archon—to establish the winner with the majority of the five selected lots; it was a procedure that amounted again to a *klerosis ek prokriton*.[76] If the selected five did not yield a clear winner, more tablets were drawn until one name had a majority.[77] Due to this procedure,

---

[72] I combine here the reconstructions of the procedure by Marshall and Van Willigenburg (2004) and Hartmann and Schaefer (2006), based on the evidence discussed in Csapo and Slater (1995) and Schuller and Dreher (2000).

[73] Hartmann and Schaefer (2006) observe: "eine eher autokratisch als demokratisch anmutende Entscheidung" (98); cf. Schuller and Dreher (2000) 524–525; criteria for his decision are unknown. At this moment, the archon also appointed the *choregoi* who were to pay for the chorus (*Ath.Pol.* 56.3).

[74] Ar. *Eccl.* 1154–1162; Marshall and Van Willigenburg (2004). In this respect, the dramatic competition was organized in the same way as athletic competitions.

[75] Cf. Hartmann and Schaefer (2006) 100–101.

[76] Whereas dramatic competitions and athletic competitions both took place in a cultic context and in honor of the gods, and both relied on the lot to decide the order of the contest, the assessment undercuts further similarities between them, because in athletic competitions the judgment lay squarely with human judges; see Mann (2017).

[77] Marshall and Van Willigenburg (2004) 97 calculate the necessary number of draws to get a majority: "a winner will be determined after the initial drawing of five votes 42.8% of the time . . . by seven votes 47.1% of the time, eight ballots will need to be counted 2.9% of the time, as will nine. All ten 4.3% of the time."

it was possible to win the competition with only three out of the original ten votes.[78]

What was happening here? W. Schuller and M. Dreher see the drawing of the lots as a divine selection, underlining that the whole enterprise was after all part of the cult of Dionysos.[79] Against this view, E. Hartmann and C. Schaefer contend that if this were the case, the lot drawing of names of the competing choruses or playwrights could have taken place directly, without any role of the judges. To their mind, the risk of bribery was the motive for including the lot as an element of chance.[80] C. Marshall and S. Van Willigenburg show that the odds that the winner indeed had the majority of the votes was 82.6 percent, and that someone with only three votes would win was 8.2 percent. With annual competitions, the off chance that a minority won occurred once in a decade, and such outcomes were recalled precisely because they had upset the audience's expectations.[81] Marshall and Van Willigenburg conclude that in the vast majority of competitions, the winner satisfied the expectations of the audience and hence their sense of fairness, whereas when the audience's expectations were confounded it was deemed that the god Dionysos had brought his own preference into effect.[82] On this conclusion, the procedure would be another interesting example of collaboration between humans and gods, with a large share of human responsibility and a flexible degree of divine involvement.

7.2.5 For regulating elements of military command, the lot could be used in ways one might label either *procedural* or *distributive*

Distribution by lot of areas of command was not uncommon. Assigning the places on the battlefield by lot is attested in Homer's *Iliad*, in which the position of the Trojan allies is determined in this manner.[83] In Aeschylus's tragedy *Seven against Thebes*, the seven besiegers draw lots at which of the seven gates of the city each will take his stand.[84] At the heart of the conflict are two brothers who

---

[78] For instance, if one voted for A, four for B, and five for C, and the draw is one for A, three for B, one for C; Marshall and Van Willigenburg (2004) 100; Hartmann and Schaeffer (2006) 102.
[79] Schuller and Dreher (2000) 534–536.
[80] Hartmann and Schaefer (2006) 104, referring to the ubiquity of sortition in the Athenian democracy.
[81] Marshall and Van Willigenburg (2004) list the relevant cases.
[82] Marshall and Van Willigenburg (2004) 91, 100. They add more profane reasons such as contingent factors in the performance and the chance effect of lotteries for the occurrence of unexpected results.
[83] Hom. *Il*. 10.430.
[84] Aesch. *Sept*. 376. For the lot as crucial, symbolic instrument in the *Septem*, see Berman (2007) and section 5.2 in this volume.

have inherited the kingship of Thebes and partition it by lot: they will take turns in being king. When one brother, Eteokles, refuses to yield his turn, the other, Polyneikes, attacks the city with six helpers. When lots for the gates are drawn, he draws the "seventh" gate, and Eteokles decides to fight his brother in the name of justice. In this way, Apollo, the god of the Seventh, makes them slay each other. In this world of the *imaginaire*, the lot does not work with random chance, but implements divine will.[85]

In real life, too, military command was distributed by lot. On their way to conquer Sicily in 415, for instance, on Corcyra the Athenian *strategoi* divided the navy with its manpower into three parts and distributed the parts by lot among themselves, and when they were in action on Sicily, they did so again.[86] In 412/11, the Athenian generals at Samos drew lots to divide the navy between them and to decide who of them would attack which city.[87] Likewise, troops could be assigned by lot: for instance, the Spartan contingents taking turns in the occupation of Sphakteria in 425 were drawn by lot from all the troops.[88]

In the battle of Marathon (490), where the Athenians and Plataians defeated the invading Persian army, the lot seems to have been used in two different ways: in the formation of the Athenian army on the battlefield and for the appointment of the archon Kallimachos as *Polemarchos*. Both much-discussed cases are relevant to the wider use of the lot in Athens.

According to Herodotus, on the battlefield at Marathon, Kallimachos stood on the right-hand side, following convention (*nomos*), and the *phylai* were stationed "according to their number."[89] The last clause has conventionally been taken to mean that the order of the *phylai* here followed the order of their fixed numbers known from the later fifth century: Erechtheis (I), Aegeis (II), Pandionis (III), Leontis (IV), Akamantis (V), Oeneis (VI), Kekropis (VII), Hippothoontis (VIII), Aiantis (IX), and Antiochis (X). However, this view is unconvincing for several reasons. First, Plutarch offers two traditions about the battlefield of Marathon: that the tribes Antiochis (X) and Leontis (IV) stood together in the

---

[85] Aesch. *Sept.* 799–813. "Things are well for the most part—at six gates; but at the Seventh the victor was the awesome Master of Sevens, Lord Apollo, wreaking the consequences of Laius' old act of unwisdom upon the offspring of Oedipus" (799–802; trans. A. H. Sommerstein, Loeb ed.). The number seven was sacred to Apollo, e.g., the seventh of each month.

[86] Thuc. 6.42.1; 6.62.1. The same manner of distribution of the forces by lot is ordered for the commanders of the fleet "who have legitimate children and are not older than fifty years of age," in the "decree of Themistocles" (ML 23, ll. 21–23) on the eve of the battle of Salamis (480). The decree is extant in a third-century inscription and suspect of being a fabrication of possibly the late fourth century, see the comm. in ML and Davies (1996) and for the context Liddel (2020) 221–223. Despite this possible later fabrication, some elements mentioned in the text are plausible enough, according to van Wees (2004) 307 n.25, among which is the allotment of commanders to ships, because such pairing by lot clearly was a traditional practice. See p. 33, 104, 124.

[87] Thuc. 8.30.1.

[88] Thuc. 4.8.9.

[89] Hdt. 6.111: ὡς ἀριθμέοντο αἱ φυλαί.

center, and that Aiantis (IX) stood on the right. The last point fits the fact that Kallimachos belonged to Aiantis. W. W. How and J. Wells observe in their commentary that the information reported by Plutarch seems quite random and does not square with these fixed numbers, and therefore suggest that the order was determined by lot.[90] Indeed, this system of arranging positions on the battlefield could be traditional, considering the account in the *Iliad* mentioned earlier. Furthermore, the fixed order of the *phylai* did not yet exist in the first decades of the fifth century; a more likely date for this arrangement is the reform associated with Ephialtes of 462 (see below).[91] Lastly, Herodotus's phrasing would mean that the order on the battlefield was fixed, which is implausible given that in hoplite phalanx battles the place of greatest danger—and therefore of the greatest honor—was on the right; and this was the reason the *Polemarchos* was stationed there. If the *phylai* were arranged in the numerical order indicated, they would have had to give precedence to Erechtheis (I) and Aegeis (II) on the field of honor, a practice that would be seen as grossly unfair and contrary to the principle of equality of the *phylai*. In sum, it is highly likely that the order of the *phylai* at Marathon was established by lot, except Aiantis, whose position on the right was due to the office of Kallimachos.

The second, potential use of the lot at Marathon concerns the office of Kallimachos himself. According to Herodotus, Kallimachos held his office "drawn by lot by the bean."[92] Herodotus's statement does not square with the account in the *Ath.Pol.*, that Athens reintroduced the selection of the archons by lot from a preelected group in 487, in the archonship of Telesinos.[93] The reference in *Ath.Pol.* to the archon year shows that the author derived this information from an Atthidographer, based on the events listed per archon year. If we accept this information as more reliable, Herodotus's comment can be explained in two ways. The first possibility is that lots were drawn among the nine elected men to distribute the nine archonships among them, and in this way Kallimachos became the *Polemarchos*.[94] In the late fourth century, such a distribution of the archonships by lot among the ten selected candidates was standard practice, but in the early fifth century there is no corroborating evidence that this was so, only a tentative analogy.[95] Of the ten *strategoi*, who were equals as a board, Herodotus

---

[90] How and Wells (1928) *ad loc.*, adding that if the position of Aiantis was due to the office of Kallimachos, one would expect Herodotus to have written αἱ ἄλλαι φυλαί. This phrasing would certainly be more correct, but the omission is perhaps not decisive for discarding the role of the *nomos* in Herodotus's account.
[91] Raubitschek (1956). How and Wells ascribe the fixed official order to Cleisthenes, who created the tribes (Hdt. 5.66.2), and because Paus i.32.3 mentions arrangement by tribe on the monument at Marathon (cf. the stele of the tribe Erechtheis, *IG* I³ 1147, 460/459). However, Hdt. 5.66.2 mentions only the creation of the tribes, not their order.
[92] Hdt. 6.109: ὁ τῶι κυάμωι λαχών; "in the past, the *Polemarchos* had a vote equal to the *strategoi*."
[93] *Ath.Pol.* 22.5. For a clear discussion of the available evidence, see Rhodes, *CAAP ad loc.*
[94] For a detailed discussion of the selection of archons from Solon's time on, see ch. 8.1.2.
[95] Distribution by lot: *Ath.Pol.* 55.1.

tells us that they took turns each day for the highest command.[96] How this worked is not documented, but the use of lots to determine turns would seem plausible, considering similar practices for taking turns discussed earlier. This reconstruction of both arrangements, for the *strategoi* and the archons, must remain speculative, but at least they match with better-attested cases of taking turns and distribution by lot. The second possibility is that Herodotus is partly mistaken, because he had only oral accounts to rely on. He had correct information on the name of the *Polemarchos* and on the onset and the order of the battle, but no information on the manner of Kallimachos's selection. In this regard, Herodotus was projecting back on the situation at Marathon the system of allotment of the archonships common in his own time.

Clarifying this problem is made even more complicated by the narrative tenor of Herodotus's account. He assigns the decisive role—pressuring the army leaders to attack the Persians—to Miltiades, who is eager to take the initiative, coaxing the other *strategoi* to award their own turns as first commander to him; meanwhile he persuades the hesitating Kallimachos to side with him in the vote, and to change the tie into a majority for the attack. If the *Polemarchos* does so, Miltiades says, he will secure his fame forever, following in the footsteps of the tyrannicides Harmodios and Aristogeiton, to secure the freedom of Athens and its prominence in Greece. It is in the prelude to Miltiades's decisive speech that Herodotus emphatically portrays Kallimachos as owing his office to the lot, rather than by implication to any military excellence of his own.[97] Now, so Herodotus implies, Kallimachos can opt for glory by supporting the man portrayed as outstanding for his courage and his activism. Miltiades's appeal to Kallimachos ends poignantly with the death of the latter at the closure of the battle, while the first survives.[98] Herodotus's account reflects the political salience of Athens and his broader historiographical perspective at the time he was writing (430s), including his view of Athens as a defender of freedom, a role turned into a tyrannical power in the Athenian Empire.[99] While this context tilts the balance in our interpretation toward an anachronistic "back-projection," the fact that Herodotus did most of his research in the 450–440s—when many veterans were still alive to be consulted and who could evidently correct each other's accounts—rather tilts the balance the other way, meaning that the process of assigning the office of *Polemarchos* by drawing lots was well known. Presently, we have insufficient unequivocal evidence to settle the issue.

---

[96] Hdt. 6.110.
[97] Hdt. 6.109–110. On the example of the tyrannicides for Kallimachos, see Azoulay (2014) 115–116, and his honors, 130.
[98] Hdt. 6.114.
[99] Raaflaub (2010).

Distributing turns and areas to be guarded by lot was not merely a matter of equality, but also of rendering the assignment of these duties unpredictable, and therefore less liable to corruption—for instance, collusion with enemies or thieves.[100] In Athens, the turns of a military guard-watch were established by lot; the guard-shift is articulated as *moira*, a "portion" of the overall guard duty, in the expression *klerou kata moiran*, "the shift as determined by the lot."[101] According to Diodorus, in the case of the guards overseeing the topaz mines of Zabargad Island in the Red Sea, the sections of the area each was to patrol were distributed by lot.[102] Presumably, the random distribution was meant to forestall any attempt at collusion among the guards to steal the jewels.

All these examples together provide a representative picture of the applications of lots in *polis* governance. For distribution of goods and duties, for selecting individuals and for taking turns, *poleis* could draw on long-standing traditions familiar from daily life (e.g., distribution of inheritance), from special events (taking turns in competitions), and not least from (epic) poetry. For the Greeks, drawing lots was so common and self-evident a practice that there was no need to explain it. While the reasons for using the lot for guarding cities and treasures or assigning land plots to settlers are reasonably easy to fathom, in other instances the motivation is not immediately clear. A few sources that are discussed later explicitly explain certain motives for drawing lots (along with their purposes), or at least allow clear inferences about the concepts behind the practice. But many texts do not indicate why the lot was used in the case in question. Indeed, drawing lots came to be so much a part of the Greek mindset that the choice of this method may sometimes even have been an unconscious decision.[103] In our historical analysis of such opaque cases, we can only offer explanations of our own, doing our utmost to avoid modern reasoning and to reconstruct the intentions of the ancient Greeks.

For instance, the distribution of new citizens to *polis* subgroups by lot appears as a practical method to parcel out new members of the civic body randomly—and therefore evenly—through the subgroups. But what to make of the distribution of sections of the army to generals by lot? In Athens, the *demos* elected their own generals per *phyle*, because soldiers needed to trust their commanders and preferred to serve under those on whose strategic qualities they could rely. Why break that bond of trust by assigning armies to commanders by lot? As noted above, it is often necessary to rely on contextual or circumstantial evidence to reconstruct the procedure and make sense of what drove the drawing of lots.

---

[100] Aen. Tact. 18.21; 20.2.
[101] Eur. *Rh.* 545.
[102] Diod. 3.39.1.
[103] See the Introduction on "mindset."

Fortunately, the circumstantial evidence sheds some light on the ideas, values, and logic behind the actual cases of drawing lots.

7.3 The political background of office distribution in ancient Greece

The remainder of this part of the book focuses principally on the system of drawing lots for *polis* offices. Earlier we saw briefly that with its essential precondition of equality, the lot hardly suits the principles of officeholding, which usually revolve around merit and status, not parity. Here this conundrum is examined in greater depth. First, we need to know what the societies that instituted these offices understood them to be, and which values were involved in the selection—whatever the means applied—of individuals for office. Subsequently, we investigate more closely how drawing lots for political office compares to other applications of the lot.

7.3.1 *Polis* offices and social value (*time*)

The Greek *poleis* preferred governing the *polis* with a wide variety of distinct offices, namely multiple bodies with several or even numerous members.[104] Notably, in all the public offices in every *polis*, generally speaking there were two kinds. Many offices originated in the archaic age, many more were added and adjusted (and only in exceptional cases abolished) in the classical and Hellenistic ages, but the two main types remained in place.

The offices of the first type were collectively called *archai*, the plural of *arche* (ruling power or principle), usually translated as "political offices." Every *polis* had an array of names for its *archai*, such as *archon*, *kosmos*, or *epistates*, or compounds with the suffix *-archos*, such as *polemarchos* or *gymnasiarchos*. The *archai* wielded authority over other citizens, and the majority were held collectively by boards, rather than by a single man. The offices could be specifically concerned with either the legislative, the judicial, or the executive domains, but some offices combined authority in two or even three of them; the council (*boule*) was a case in point, as in many *poleis* it was endowed with an (advisory) legislative function, executive tasks, and some jurisdiction.[105] As part of their regular assignments, many offices had financial duties, such as keeping budgets and fining offenders, and nearly all of them included substantial religious tasks,

---

[104] Fröhlich (2013).
[105] Wallace (2013).

such as sacrificing, leading, and organizing festivals, and saying prayers for the community. *Archai* were open only to male citizens.

The second group were religious offices, whose titles often included a form of the lexeme *hieros* (belonging to the gods). They included priests and priestesses, who regularly acted alone, and other cult personnel, alone or in small groups, with a large variety of titles. Their duties were to serve the gods on behalf of the community, a task that also entailed responsibility for the finances and oversight of the ritual integrity of the sanctuary, with concomitant duties such as punishing offenders. Religious offices were open to male and female citizens, depending on the rules of the cult.

Both types of offices had essential duties in common, namely responsibility for *polis* religion and accountability to the *polis*, but they differed in other important respects, as the distinct stems of their terminology (*arch-* and *hier-*) imply.[106] The *archai* all held formal authority over the citizens (and occasionally other inhabitants) of the *polis*; in the classical age, each office had a clear responsibility of its own. The overall policies of the *polis*, both internal and external, were the domain of the legislative boards, whether supported by or identical with the sovereign assembly or not. The cultic (*hieros*) offices held ritual authority over a particular cult, sanctuary, or religious event, some of which were of great impact for the entire *polis*, and some priesthoods clearly held a moral authority. Some cultic offices were doubtless regarded as ritual experts, in a way the *archai* were not, even if the latter performed specific ritual duties.[107]

This outline of the *polis* offices and their functions is based on modern observations. Our sources offer no systematic description of them, for very few Greeks were interested in the political or administrative nature of public office.[108] For Plato and Aristotle, religious offices were essential to the *polis* because they created and maintained the connections of the *polis* with the divine world. Plato envisaged political offices of his own making for his ideal *polis* in the *Republic*, and critically reflected on the offices in Athens in the *Laws*, but he did not systematically investigate the nature of *polis* offices.[109]

Aristotle is the only political philosopher who did so.[110] In the first three books of the *Politics*, he defines the state as a community (*koinonia*), and next he

---

[106] For both types of offices, see Blok (2017) 188–198.
[107] Ritual expertise: Chaniotis (2008) and the other contributions to Dignas and Trampedach (2008); prominence and impact, Lambert (2012); of priestesses, Connelly (2007); impact and moral authority, Thonemann (2020).
[108] The criteria Hansen advanced to distinguish legal demarcations between *archai* and other offices in classical Athens, based on Aeschin. *Ctes.* (Hansen [1980]; [1991] 226, are relevant, but not watertight; Blok (2017) 189–197.
[109] I could not consult Lane (2023), which appeared as this book was completed.
[110] And so did, presumably, his student and successor Theophrastos in a work on laws, where he discussed what kind of qualifications were necessary or desirable for which kinds of offices. Of this work, only fragments are extant; see Oliver (1977).

examines the necessary role of *arche* (authority) in every form of community. In the state, this *arche* is divided over the three domains of legislative, judicial, and executive authority, each implemented by particular *archai* with distinct powers and fixed tenure. To get a representative picture of the offices and their distribution in Greece, and the effects of these factors on the *politeia*, he had a collection of descriptions made of 158 *politeiai* and their histories.[111] Of this collection, only the *Athenaion Politeia* (see above) is extant: it consists of a history of the Athenian *politeia* until ca. 400, and a systematic description of the *politeia* of the later fourth century, including a list of offices; their means of selection, payment, and tenure; and an extensive description of the institutions of the jury courts.

Aristotle's interest was not historical, however, but analytical, with the aim of designing the best possible *polis*. In book four of the *Politics*, he argues that for the nature of the *politeia* (constitution of a polity), the distribution of offices over the socioeconomic groups (wealthy elite or *demos*) and the methods of their distribution are crucial. Aristotle's arguments tie in with what mattered most to all Greeks: who among the citizens was entitled to hold office and how they were selected (by vote or by lot), and the rules for tenure, payment (or not), and accountability. Aristotle also elucidates why the offices and their distribution were so significant to Greek society more broadly:

> For we call the offices [*archai*] "honors" [*timai*], and if the same persons always hold the offices, the others are inevitably *atimos* [without honor].[112]

Indeed, the *archai* were considered *timai* ("honors") bestowed on specific citizens.[113]

Timai is the plural of *time*, a key notion in ancient Greek society, which we find in Greek discourse from the Homeric epics down to late antiquity. It occurs often as a noun (*time*) or an adjective (usually the negative, *atimos*), but even more frequently as a verb: to give, grant, or withhold *time*.[114] Classicists conventionally translate *time* as "honor", an adequate rendering when *time* refers to someone's standing in society. But *time* has a much wider range of meanings: aside from immaterial goods such as honor and standing, it can refer to the value of material goods, and can imply both a positive and a negative relation to someone else or to

---

[111] For the relation between the Aristotelian *politeiai* and the local histories, see Thomas (2019) 358–385.

[112] Arist. *Pol.* 1281a31: τιμὰς γὰρ λέγομεν εἶναι τὰς ἀρχάς, ἀρχόντων δ'αἰεὶ τῶν αὐτῶν ἀναγκαῖον εἶναι τοὺς ἄλλους ἀτίμους.

[113] Plato has Socrates remind his fellow citizens (Plato, *Ap.* 35b) that they honor those who excel in virtue with offices (*archai*) and other *timai*.

[114] The centrality of *time* in Greek societies is reflected in the frequency of *tim-* vocabulary: in the *TLG* the verb τιμάω shows nearly twenty-eight thousand occurrences; the noun τίμη, thirty-one thousand (consulted May 13, 2020). For *time* in Homer, see p. 304–5.

society.[115] When used for material goods, *time* means (positive) "price," "worth" (in monetary terms); and (negative) "fine." In social terms, it means (positive) "recognition," "honor," "office," "reward," "compensation," "[domain of] power," "satisfaction"; and (negative) "penalty."[116] Behind this variety we may construe a core meaning of *time*, "value." Value is "the outcome of an exchange between two parties" (= the value of something or someone) and "the way people represent the importance of their own actions to themselves" (= value as an estimation held in society).[117]

In terms of anthropological theory, *time* was a crucial institution of reciprocity in Greek society, more precisely of balanced reciprocity. The concept itself pivots on receiving something equivalent in return for a gift or contribution, and especially on what the expectation of such a reciprocal response means to the relationship between the two parties. The gift and its corresponding response may concern one individual giving something to another, or an individual who contributes something to the group to which she or he belongs, or when a group confers something upon another group.[118] When individuals live at some social distance from each other (no direct kin, for instance) and may expect to receive something in return that matches the value of their own gift (and that the reciprocation happens within a preset or a foreseeable time), this relationship is called "balanced reciprocity."[119] Since no two human beings are identical, the contribution of each individual to the group is as varied as the number of individuals it comprises, and so is the reciprocal value of that contribution. The same complexity applies to reciprocity between subgroups and the community as a whole. Reciprocity of value thus tends to highlight the differences between groups and among individual members of each group. For instance, a strong warrior contributes more physical power to the community than an

---

[115] Graeber (2001) 83–84 for the "positive" and "negative" sides of the same social values. For the application of *time* in various sectors of Greek society, see also http://research.shca.ed.ac.uk/honour-in-greece/.

[116] LSJ, s.v. τιμή. When in Hom. *Il.* XV.183–197 the gods divide the *kosmos* among them, their *timai* are the domains they receive in recognition of their equality as heirs and as victors distributing spoils; see ch. 1; 4.1.

[117] All *tim-* vocabulary relies on recognition of value by others, both within the legal sphere and beyond it, and evaluation and negotiation are also the core elements of the cognate verbs. The verb τιμάω (giving someone his or her due *time*) carries the same meaning as English "to honor" in the sense of "to grant just acclaim" and "to answer according to expectations." See Graeber (2001) 23–47; on transformation of values into social action, see Robbins (2015); for *time* as "value" and further discussion of the evidence, see Blok (2017) 198–204, with references.

[118] The classic conceptualization of models of reciprocity is Sahlins (1965; 1972), building on the foundational work of Mauss ([1925] 1954); the usefulness of these models for understanding ancient Greek societies is explored among others in Gill et al. (1998).

[119] Balanced reciprocity is distinguished on the one hand from general reciprocity, in which no specific counter gifts are expected or any time limit is set to receiving them, a form of reciprocity normal among socially close people such as family members, and on the other hand from negative reciprocity, in which people, who are often at a great social distance from each other, claim or take from others without having offered anything in return.

average woman, whereas a woman may contribute a newborn life to the group in a way no warrior can match. The community assigns to each group a recognition of their contribution—for instance through the assignment of a specific role or honor. Logically, within a given group of warriors, one or two of exceptional strength or leadership may expect to receive extra recognition for their individual achievements.

In Greece, *time* was the outcome of this balanced reciprocity; the noun and its cognates entailed the acknowledgment in the widest sense of a person's actions by another, or by the entire group, and such terms referred to the specific form this acknowledgment could take. *Time* and *tim-* vocabulary also pertained to the exchange between two individuals—for instance, in expected reciprocal benefits, in conduct (cordiality and respect), or in trade negotiations—but the present discussion concerns society at large. In the social dynamics of Greek societies, *time* indicated the value of an individual in the group to which he or she belonged: the army of the Achaeans, a military contingent, a kinship group, the family, the *polis*, and so on. Each individual brought a specific benefit to the group—for instance, military prowess, wealth, wise counsel, childbearing capacities, beauty, labor, or crafts—and the recognition of this contribution entailed his or her value (*time*) to the group.[120] This recognition was declared publicly, for the entire group to witness and acknowledge.[121] A positive account of someone's input was valued as approbation (*time* = acclaim, honor), while a negative account, due to failure or misdemeanor, could be punished (*time* = penalty, fine). Individuals could in principle expect due recognition if they met the conventional standards. But in any event, it was the group as a whole that carried the final say in the matter; although bound by convention or law, ultimately it was up to the group to decide to honor convention, or diverge from it.

The origins of the informal dynamics of *time* presumably lie before recorded history, since in the Homeric epics we find them in the shape of robust norms and expectations, entrenched in oral communication and social practices. In the *Iliad* and *Odyssey*, what is due to the leaders and especially to the best among them—such as the superior fighter Achilles or the ingenious Odysseus, on whom the success of the army depends—is consolidated in the values shared by all: the leaders may speak in the army assembly, and they receive a *geras* from the booty fitting their special contribution. When this norm of due *time* is thwarted, and publicly at that, as happens to Achilles, the result is resentment of the individual and the risk of social fissure. The *laos* (common army) have as their basic *time* that they meet as an army acting collectively as a sounding board, and they

---

[120] The discussion here is restricted to the human level, but the gods were involved in a structurally similar way in the relationships in the *polis* based on *time*; see Blok (2017) 201–202.

[121] For the importance of public visibility for communal recognition of *time*, see van 'tWout (2010).

receive an equal part of the booty by lot.[122] The Homeric epic illuminates how *time* originated and functioned as an informal institution, but the society of Homer was not a historical Greek *polis*.

By the seventh century, Greek settlements were becoming increasingly organized into *poleis* and *ethne* (regional affiliated groups), though at an uneven pace and in different forms. Leadership was getting formalized into political offices, and the community took shape in a more or less stable civic body.[123] In this institutionalization, increasingly anchored in written laws, *poleis* defined distinct groups, each with their own claims to *time*: citizens versus others; free citizens versus unfree and slaves; men, women, and children, each further distinguished into age groups.[124] For access of each group and individual to their *timai*, procedures, qualifications, and other conditions were regulated and laid down in written laws, but the principle that it was up to the community to grant or withhold *time*, and not a fixed "right" of an individual vis-à-vis the *polis*, largely remained in place. However, for acknowledged members of the groups, some entitlements gradually turned into "rights," especially when backed by written law—for instance, to leave one's inheritance to the rightful heirs in the case of a legitimate citizen.[125]

Within each group, egalitarian values prevailed: all acknowledged members could claim a basic form of *time* fitting their group (even slaves had a modest kind of *time*) and were similar or equivalent (*homoios*) in *time*. An adult male citizen of modest wealth could expect to participate in certain religious events for men only (or for men and women together), to serve in the army in some way, and to attend the assembly. An adult female citizen could expect to participate in certain religious events for women only, but also for both sexes. But *between* them, the groups were anything but *homoios*: they were clearly differentiated, as noted earlier, and gender, qualifications, and wealth were defining factors in access to offices and other *timai*.[126]

Individuals who made exceptional contributions to the *polis* and therefore of special worth to the community could expect to receive special *timai*, beyond the basic level of the group. Some were labeled *megalai* or *megistai timai* (great

---

[122] See ch. 1, esp. Endnote 1..
[123] Hall (2013); Giangiulio (2018) 289–293.
[124] For written laws, see Hölkeskamp (1994); the local character of written laws, Hölkeskamp (2000); continuity of unwritten law, Thomas (1995); transformation of traditional norms in writing with emphasis on the written character of laws, Gagarin (2008); basic distinction between citizens and others in early Greek law, Blok (2018).
[125] For a clear example, see the decree at Naupaktos, p. 243–44, 252. For notions of "right" in ancient Greek political and legal thought, see Miller (2009).
[126] Many *poleis*, both colonies and "ancient" ones, held free people of a different ethnic background within their territory—for instance, the Indigenous people living there before the Greeks arrived. Usually, they were subaltern to or even oppressed by the Greek citizens, with a modest *time* of their own but not included in the distribution of *timai* among the Greek citizens (cf. Giangiulio 2017).

or the greatest honors), and they could be awarded to individuals, be they citizens or outsiders. Of these special honors, *sitesis* (dining at public expense in the *prytaneion*) is one of the earliest such privileges attested in Athens; later on, the many special grants included *prohedria* (a front seat in the theater), the right to erect a statue in a public space, and the gift of a golden crown to dedicate to the gods.[127] *Timai* of this kind were never distributed by lot, and are therefore not included in the present discussion, but for our understanding of public offices it is relevant that they belonged to an overarching system of the honors the *polis* could bestow.

In sum, over time the Greek *poleis* created political offices (*archai*) and religious offices, together called *timai*: prominent positions in a system ascribing and distributing differences in value (*time*) to social groups and to the individuals belonging to them. Access to such positions therefore hinged on the intrinsic differences and inequality of the citizens. By contrast, the system of drawing lots for selection and distribution was an institution predicated on baseline equality. The question therefore remains: How does random sortition square with claims to positions of distinction?

7.3.2 Drawing lots for office: A special case

The inherent incompatibility of the equality of the lot system with the inequality of officeholding is not the only riddle in allotment for office, which occupies a special place in drawing lots also for other reasons.

First of all, it is not easy to classify drawing lots for office relative to the other applications of sortition, from which it differs in several aspects. Second, given the basic concept of office as a civic honor, the composition of the group of candidates poses complexities far exceeding the other cases of selection. Both issues deserve a closer look, beginning with the first: how to compare allotment for office with other applications of the lot.

Is drawing lots for office a form of selection or of distribution? Allocation of office is not exactly a form of selection by lot, a formula we apply in this study for the selection of an individual or a limited group of individuals for a specific task, occasionally *ad hoc*. Instead, *polis* office was a regular, recurrent duty of several, even many people, lasting for a fixed term, and then assigned to a new group by lot; unlike the roles assigned by lot as "selection," officeholding was based on rotation. Moreover, this rotation had political and social effects that incidental "selection" had not: over time, when virtually all members had held the office in turn, this rotation generated a certain equality throughout the group.

---

[127] For *sitesis* and other *timai* in classical Athens, see Blok and van 't Wout (2018) with further refs.

Is it a form of distribution? Depending on the *politeia* of the *polis* in question, the number of citizens eligible for office could be large or small, and the lot would distribute them randomly over the available offices. However, it is not a clear case of distribution by lot either. Normally in such cases, everyone in the group was equal in the participation and in the results, all receiving an equal share of land, booty, or sacrificial meat. But *polis* office was an immaterial good that was never itself "equal"; within a single board, all officeholders were equal and held equal "portions" of authority, but not all boards were equal in authority. Equality primarily resided in the equal eligibility for office, either of a particular group or of all citizens, but the office itself elevated the individual—or rather a few of them—temporarily above the others and gave them authority over the community.

This temporary quality is a further complicating factor. All other distributions by lot concerned goods the recipient was to keep, either forever or to enjoy on the spot. By contrast, office was a good that an individual could only hold for a limited amount of time.[128] It was a share in the self-governance of the community, and the principle of rotation was essential: every year (or whatever term applied to the office), others would fill the positions left by their predecessors. While on the one hand the rotation among the group reinforced the sense of equal sharing and coherence, on the other hand the temporal restriction of its enjoyment intensified the competition for the offices, at least for the coveted ones. Distribution by lot would, or could be expected to, reduce this competition. After a year of holding office, a citizen reverted to equal status with the others, a fact that might restrain him while in office or might prompt him to take advantage of it for his own benefit while it lasted (Greek officeholders were invariably suspected of doing the latter).

While this elevation to the honor of office of a single citizen or group of citizens above the others might recall the grant of a *geras*, here too there were essential differences. *Geras* was a gift of honor granted by the community to an outstanding individual, outside and preceding the equal distribution by lot among all.[129] For *polis* office, moreover, the number of candidates was generally much larger than the few entitled to *geras*, and unlike the latter, their role in providing or contributing the goods for the community was (as yet) opaque, or at least open to discussion. One could even say that every magistrate still had to prove what as an individual he would contribute to the community while holding office.

Finally, we might consider allotment for office to be a distribution by lot of turns (hence a form of procedural lottery), but even this solution is not entirely

---

[128] Kingship was an office that one could keep but usually could not be divided by lot, as the conflict between Polyneikes and Eteokles illuminates (see earlier discussion). Sparta had two kings, but they were not assigned to their offices by lot. Kingship was rare in Greece anyway.

[129] See above, ch. 1, esp. Endnote 1.

satisfactory, because some people might never get their turn. In sum, distribution of office is unlike other selections and distributions by lot.

The second issue concerns the composition of the group and the effects of allotment. Because holding office was an honor, an expression of the value that the *polis* assigned to an individual, the means of selection for office had a deep impact on the political climate of the *polis*. Since all eligible candidates vied for honor, election stimulated the competition between them, for votes clearly showed who was favored by the *demos* to hold power and who was not. By contrast, drawing lots would in principle reduce the competition, because this selection method removed all arguments pro and con, all love and hatred, from the selection procedure and its results. This system could only work if all candidates were more or less equal (*homoios*): the inequality that the outcome of the lottery for office would create among them was only temporary, for rotation would bring another group to temporary prominence and ultimately, perhaps, all would have had their turn. Agreement as to who was included in the group of candidates was therefore vital. In other words, when political office was distributed by lot, it rendered the problem of who was to be included in the group of candidates arguably even more pressing than in other distributions by lot, because inclusion provided an equal chance to be elevated—if only for a limited time—to honor and authority over the others.

We have now found that in Greece, by its very name (*time*), *polis* office marked the constantly shifting social distinctions between groups and between individuals in the *polis*, and that political offices literally and in practice were positions of authority (*arche*) over other citizens. Every *polis* had to decide who had access to these *timai*, and on which conditions. With "inequality" writ large over *polis* office itself, its distribution by drawing lots created an equality (*isos*) that required an equivalence (*homoios*) of the citizens participating in the procedure. The equality of chance would reduce the competition for office, but the steps preceding the actual drawing of lots made the tension between (political) equality and (social) inequality manifest. We also found that political office posed complications compared to other practices of drawing lots. In sum, using lots for the assignment of political office, for fixed rotating periods that implied equality of chance for access to some or all *timai* over the long term, was an innovation in both domains—politics and lots, a fact that largely explains why it came about much later than other uses of the lot. At this point, we need to examine how drawing lots came to be introduced in the domain of politics at all, and how this instrument—that would appear essentially unsuitable for the appointment of *polis* office—ultimately became a successful innovation, at least in several *poleis* and in multiple forms.

Later we see that the anchoring of this novel selection system in Greek society followed a trajectory that was anything but linear, nor was it a sudden success.[130]

---

[130] For the concept of anchoring innovation, by attaching what is considered new to what is familiar, see Sluiter (2016).

I argue that acceptance of the lot for the assignment of *polis* office was gradual, and the result of three factors. First, the introduction of the lot system in the political domain was predicated on its regular applications in other contexts. Precisely because drawing lots was an *institution* in Greece, the lot was seen as applicable in other areas—provided the conditions could be made to resemble the other institutional contexts where use of the lot was familiar. Second, the gradual transfer of the lot into the domain of political office was facilitated by, or even depended on, an intermediate form known as *klerosis ek prokriton* (allotment from preselected candidates), which combined selection due to *time* with the equality of the lot. Third, when the use of the lot had been accepted in a high-profile social context, it acquired a legitimacy that apparently made it more readily acceptable elsewhere.

7.3.3 Political inequality and equality in the Greek *poleis*

In the Greek *poleis* of the early archaic age the social landscape was dominated by the wealthy elite. While the composition of this group was always in flux due to social mobility and internal rivalry, as a group they distinguished themselves from the *demos* by a distinctive and costly lifestyle. For the men of this elite, sociability as refined equals in the *symposion*, military prowess, competition in the great pan-Hellenic Games, and display of grandeur in burial rituals were markers of their identity. Membership of the elite was based on household wealth, which lay primarily in landed property. In the western colonies, although founded on an equal distribution of land, over the years differences in wealth between individuals increased, often quite rapidly; here, too, the typical features of the Greek elite are evident from the early archaic age onward.[131] While the *symposion* enhanced egalitarian relations among elite men in a private setting, competition between them for public *time* was strong. Excellence and leadership had to be publicly demonstrated by military valor on the battlefield and wise counsel in the circle of the elite and on the *agora*.[132]

The prominence of this elite distinct from the *demos* and—within this same elite—the tension between equality and coherence on the one hand, and inequality and competition on the other, were reflected in the political structures of most *poleis*.[133] As we saw earlier, the Greeks preferred power to be invested in

---

[131] De Angelis (2016) 136–79 and p. 191–92 and fig. 6.1.

[132] See for instance Hom. *Il.* 9.443, depicting the excellence of Achilles in both domains as an ideal type. On legislation and adjudication based on socially highly stratified societies of early Greece, see Papakonstantinou (2008) 19–46.

[133] See Hall (2013); Ma (2016); Simonton (2017) 7–19, with many refs.; Meister and Seelentag (2020). See also Simonton (2017) 8 n.22 and 10 n.28 on the problem of how to define "elite" and *demos*, the first defined primarily by wealth, the latter all who were not the elite.

several magistrates or in bodies with multiple members, rather than in a single individual; individuals who excelled were counterbalanced, or held in check, by their peers.[134] Due to their wealth and concomitant other assets, the elite as a group could claim far more *time* than the *demos*, and hence the prerogative of political leadership and religious authority in the shape of *polis* offices (*timai*), and likewise judicial authority acting as judges and in courts. Yet, for whatever they wanted to achieve, the elite leaders needed the consent of the *demos* (here: common people) in the assembly to become enacted, since ultimately the *demos* (here: the collective of citizens) was sovereign.[135] For the distribution of offices this consent was also required, because the *timai* were formally granted by the community.[136] This formal sovereignty of the *demos* became an influential factor when from the late sixth century quite a number of *poleis* saw a (temporary) shift to more democratic policies, but until that change the archaic *poleis* cannot be called democratic. In institutional terms, an assembly that acted only as a sounding board and was expected to consent to proposals made by the elite leadership cannot deserve that label. In many archaic *poleis*, furthermore, a sizeable section of the free population was not included in the citizen body at all.[137] MaurizioGiangiulio rightly observes that democracies in any real sense of the word emerged only in the (early) classical age, where and when economic growth and warfare brought about a substantial change in the social expectations and military significance of the *demos*, with ensuing claims to larger and more effective political roles.[138]

In the seventh and sixth centuries, however, Greek *poleis* were divided into two layers, partly in reality and partly in perception: on the one hand the elite called the *agathoi* (good ones) or *gnorimoi* (notables) or similar terms—who manifested themselves as prominent individuals also in *polis* offices—and on the other hand all other citizens, the *demos*—which enacted its sovereign power as a collective.[139] To some degree, this situation persisted through to the Hellenistic

---

[134] See Harris (2006) with a list of all known boards of magistrates in Greek *poleis* down to 400; for the Greek distaste of single rulership, see Luraghi (2013); archaic legislation holding competitive elite in check, Hölkeskamp (1999).

[135] As confirmed in a law from Dreros (*LAC* Dr1, ca. 650) on iteration of the office of *kosmos*, decided by the *polis*; a law from Chios (ML 8, early sixth cent.) with *rhetrai* (A l. 2), binding pronouncements of the *demos* on property of the goddess Hestia, and (on side C) a *demosie bo(u)le* of fifty members per *phyle*; a contract in Datala on Crete with the *hieromnamon* Spensithios confirmed by the *polis* (*LAC* Da1, ca. 500).

[136] For the role of the sovereign *demos* in the development of tyranny in archaic Greece, see Hammer (2005).

[137] Giangiulio (2018) points out that the so-called fixed numbers of some archaic *poleis* were the citizen body meeting as an assembly, not those entitled to political office, and therefore these numbers as such do not indicate oligarchic regimes.

[138] Giangiulio (2015) 10, 45–48.

[139] Hall (2013) 12–13. According to Morris (1987; 2000 155–191; Hanson (1995); Raaflaub (2006; 2007), in the archaic age a "middling group" emerged, which were the *zeugitai* in Solon's system (see ch. 8.1.1), the hoplite forces that also were the core of the upcoming democracy. Against this view,

era. The division into two sociopolitical compartments was embodied in a wide variety of political systems (*politeiai*) and gave rise to political thought about social and political justice and its relation to equality.[140]

Let us first look at the political practice. For *polis* rule by the wealthy elite, Matthew Simonton draws an illuminating distinction between the archaic age, when the elite was firmly in control in an (unequal) cooperation with the *demos*, and the oligarchies of the classical age, where access to *polis* office was formally restricted to the elite, which consistently aimed to sideline the *demos* entirely. Several of these oligarchies came to power in a violent reaction to the democratic tendencies beginning in the late sixth century, while others tightened traditional prerogatives to prevent democratic tendencies from gaining strength.[141] As Simonton argues,

> The typical oligarchies of the Classical period were based overwhelmingly on the leisure class, which provided the backbone of the regime, but . . . they also incorporated several of the richer hoplites from the demos, who might hope to aggrandize themselves via participation in the oligarchy to the point of achieving true elite self-sufficiency. . . . The great majority of oligarchies were significantly narrower than the one-third to one-half of the population that comprised the hoplites.[142]

Such regimes formed the one extreme end of a spectrum of *polis* constitutions running from these full-fledged oligarchies or tyrannies, through *poleis* with a moderate constitution combining oligarchic and democratic features, to radical democracies at the other end of the spectrum. Indeed, the variety in *politeiai* was such that 158 of them were collected to get at a representative picture of Greek political systems for Aristotle's research. In the middle range of this spectrum, the political nature of the constitution might seem ambivalent, but it was usually recognized by insiders and outsiders as leaning more to either an oligarchic or a democratic climate. On Crete, for instance, the archaic model of an elite

---

Foxhall (1997) and van Wees (2006) point to the economic disparity between the elite and the rest; van Wees (2001; 2002; 2004) argues that the hoplite forces did not form a solid and numerous group until the late sixth century. Recently Valdés Guía defends the *zeugitai* anew as a group of "middling" farmers (see below), but Robinson (1997) 66–70; Hall (2013); and Simonton (2017) 41–50 show that in the political structures of the archaic age no such middling group can be identified.

[140] For the balance between justice and equality as the major topic in Greek political thought, see Balot (2006); Cartledge (2009); for its background in the Greek *polis* and wider setting, Raaflaub (2009); for Plato and Aristotle on equality, see section 9.1.1 in this volume.

[141] Simonton (2017) 5–8, 31, 150 and *passim*. Between 520 and 440, an estimated three times as many *poleis* were oligarchies than democracies; between 440 and 360, numbers were much closer, but still oligarchies slightly outnumbered democracies; see Fleck and Hanssen (2018) 225, table 7.6, and 228, table 7.9.

[142] Simonton (2017) 51–52.

government with a complying *demos* persisted in most *poleis* far into the classical age, with an ideology that claimed equality (being *homoios*) of all citizens but masked the real inequality between the two groups.[143] In many *poleis*, finally, the political situation also shifted over time from one prevailing system to another, often with outbreaks of internal conflict.

From the perspective of the elite, both in the archaic model and in the classical oligarchies, the crucial means for maintaining power vis-à-vis the *demos* was keeping an egalitarian consensus within—if not downright control over—their own circle. If one of their group decamped and made common cause with the *demos*, he might trump the others and establish a tyranny.[144] In the archaic age, tyrannies enforced in this way were frequent, but they usually lasted at most three generations. In the classical age, the frequency of tyrannical rule first decreased, only to increase again in the fourth century and the Hellenistic era. The threat of a tyranny was real for the elite, who were to lose the most in such a case. To prevent coups of this nature, the elite enhanced the coherence of their group by the political maxim to bring issues *es (to) meson*, to the center of the group.[145] Just like the political vocabulary of *isos* and *homoios*, the maxim *es (to) meson* was intrinsically neither oligarchic nor democratic, but it began its political career in the archaic elite circles: this political maxim and the *symposion* mirrored each other as forms of egalitarian exchange in a distinct social setting.[146] Political debate *es to meson* suggests discussion in a (limited) circle, in contrast to a speech by a single orator to an assembled mass.[147] In the classical age, the oligarchic elites further enhanced their internal coherence by voting in secret ballot and by distribution of office by lot.[148]

Turning now to political thought, the split between the elite and the *demos* engendered debates about the relationship between justice and equality—more precisely, how the division of society in distinct socioeconomic groups would relate to concepts of justice, which inherently meant a balance of interests between parties, and hence some form of parity.[149]

---

[143] Seelentag (2013).

[144] For the "plebiscitary politics" of cooperation between elite individuals and the *demos* in archaic and classical politics, see Hammer (2005); in the fifth century, Mann (2007).

[145] See also p. 72–74. *Es to meson* meant (a) the space between two warring parties, where the conflict may be decided, for instance, in between two armies (Hom. *Il.* VI.120; XX.159; Hes. *Th.* 709) or the area opened for adjudication (Hom. *Il.* XXIII.574) or both (Hom. *Il.* XXIII.814); (b) the space in the middle of a group assembled to dance or to listen (Hom. *Od.* 8.262; *H.Hymn Pan* 22; Sol. fr. 10; Pind. fr. 42) or to distribute goods. As a political-spatial concept, *es to meson* is not necessarily democratic; the mass of the people may only be onlookers of what the leaders are doing in the middle.

[146] Simonton (2017) 85–86, with refs. among others to Theogn. 493–496, Pl. *Prot.* 338b.

[147] Simonton (2017) 148–149, 239; cf. Hammer (2005); Mann (2007) on the continuity of "tyrannical" speeches by the democratic orators.

[148] Simonton (2017) 88.

[149] Cf. Arist. *Pol.* 1282b17–23: "Justice is a form of equality in relation to other persons."

One possible solution was that justice meant proportional equality: more public *time* and political authority for the "better" citizens, less for the lower orders. Implementation of this concept generated a brand of *politeia* known as *eunomia* (good distribution = good order, good law), a type that was conceived in the archaic age and continued to be valued as a just and sound form of *politeia*.[150] In the classical age political philosophers considered proportional equality to be the best principle for the distribution of duties and rewards.[151] In his *Politics*, Aristotle's "anatomy of the *polis*" encompassed a society divided not in two but three socioeconomic groups, each with their own interests: the wealthy, the *mesoi* (those in the middle), and the *demos*. His concept of a mixed constitution did not entail an amalgam of the three types of constitution (aristocracy, oligarchy, democracy) in the *polis*'s institutions, but a balanced representation of the three interest groups in the constitution.[152] He called such a constitution simply *politeia*, "the" constitution, referring to a political structure that in various forms prevailed in many *poleis*, situating these *poleis* in the middle region of the spectrum between (strict) oligarchy and (radical) democracy. For his part, Plato's *Republic* proposes three groups for the ideal *polis*, based on functional rather than economic distinctions, but with clear distinct socioeconomic and political roles for each group.

A second line of political thought reflected on equality as a political principle, on the question of who could be equal to whom, and on which conditions. We should note here that in the archaic age the ancient tradition of equality (*isotes*) in the distribution of material goods by lot (inheritance, land, and so on) had no effective corollary in political practice or political thought across class divisions. Colonies started on a basis of equality, showing a keen awareness of the connection between inequality in landed property and inequality in political power, a connection that often had been the driving force behind colonization itself: starting anew from zero, as it were. However, there is no sign that the equal land plots assigned to colonizers were also the foundation of political equality (see also below), and after just a few generations differentiation in wealth became prominent and influential. That said, the awareness that fair distribution in the *polis* entailed a proper allocation of wealth fostered wider notions of what constituted "right" shares. As a topic of reflection, egalitarianism germinated

---

[150] *Eunomia*: Hom. *Od.* 17.487; Hes. *Th.* 901–902; Sol. fr. 4, with Ostwald (1969) 62–72; Blaise (2006); to some, Sparta seemed the paragon of *eunomia* (Hdt. 1.65), cf. Raaflaub (2006); for *eunomia* as a positive-sounding equivalent of oligarchy, see Simonton (2017) 59, with many refs. The archaic conception of proportional equality (*eunomia*) was transformed in political philosophy of the classical age into the theory of geometric, as opposed to arithmetic, equality; see Harvey (1965) and below.

[151] Gray (2015) argues that the two kinds of equality represent two distinct views of civic virtue and how it should be made manifest; "proportional" equality had to be supported by a sense of civic unity akin to unspecified "equal" homogeneity among the citizens.

[152] Arist. *Pol.* 1289b27–1290a13; Canevaro and Esu (2018).

among the elite, whose identity revolved around being *homoios* (similar, equivalent) in their *time*, and whose power depended on maintaining this in-group equivalence. It was onto this notion that a more robust idea of equality, cast as being *isos* (equal), was grafted.

This *isos*-vocabulary could apply to any collective, and it spurred related concepts, notably *isonomia* (equal distribution = equal order) that did not designate a concrete type of government but the idea of equal entitlement in a defined group.[153] Probably the earliest attested form of this notion is the adjective *isonomos*, designating Athens in one out of a group of four popular anonymous songs all celebrating the tyrannicides Harmodios and Aristogeiton: "They slew the tyrant and made Athens *isonomos*."[154] The songs are difficult to pin down to a date; some scholars argue for an origin relatively close to the institution of the cult of the tyrannicides in the 470s, others for significantly later in the fifth century.[155]

The first author known to us who applied the abstract noun *isonomia* is Herodotus. He uses the noun for attempts at more democratic government after the demise of tyranny on Samos and in Miletos in the late sixth century, and famously to describe democratic government with allotment of offices in the so-called Constitutional Debates.[156] In this section of his *Histories* (3.80–83), Herodotus presents a small group of Persian nobles engaged, allegedly in 522, in discussing the best *politeia* for Persia after their successful coup against an imposter-king. The first speaker, Otanes, defends a constitution he labels *isonomie*, which he specifies as follows:

> But the rule of the multitude has in the first place the loveliest name of all, *isonomie*, and does in the second place none of the things that a monarch does. It determines offices by lot, and holds power accountable, and conducts all deliberating publicly. Therefore I give my opinion that we make an end of monarchy and exalt the multitude, for all things are possible for the majority.[157]

This passage renders in shorthand the major qualities for which the Athenian democracy valued itself at the time Herodotus was writing: political engagement

---

[153] Robinson (1997) 63–73; Raaflaub (2007); Simonton (2017) 72, 77. Cf. Ostwald (1969) 99–106 on *isonomia*, for instance, used in a medical-philosophical context (Alcmaeon, ed. Most-Laks [Loeb] D30; ca. 500) as "balance between two powers." The root of *isonomia* could either be *nomos* (order, law, tradition; cf. Vlastos [1953] 347–350) or *nemein* (to distribute), cf. Borecký (1963), who argues that *nomos* itself is derived from *nemein*. See also p. 117, 137.

[154] Ath. XV, 695a: 10 (= *PMG*, no. 893); Ath. XV, 695—b:11–13.

[155] Shear (2012) 33 on the debate; she suggests a date before 480 on p. 36; Samons (2020) points to elements suggesting much later developments and emphasizes that the songs could serve different political viewpoints and audiences.

[156] Hdt. 3.142.3; 5.37.2; 3.80.

[157] Hdt. 3.80; trans. A. D. Godley (Loeb-ed. 1920), modified.

of the full citizen body (*plethos*) instead of single-man rule, accountability of officeholders (*archai*), and public debate.[158] The said "Otanes" associates *isonomie* with the rule of the masses, and its first typical feature is that offices are assigned by lot (*palos*).[159] Yet *isonomia* is not by definition a democracy: it could equally refer to an oligarchy, as noted by Thucydides, who has the Thebans call their own oligarchy *isonomia*.[160] Giangiulio regards *isonomia* as akin to *eunomia* in that both refer to a situation of balance and that both evoke the role of norms to safeguard social order.[161] Charles Fornara argues that *isonomia* refers to "equality" primarily as "absence of tyranny," rather than "democracy."[162] Indeed, although the noun *isonomia* cannot be dated with any certitude to the late sixth century, what seems certain is that the concept served as a rallying cry to close ranks against tyrants, present or future.[163] Such thinking paved the way for an acute sense of equality (*isotes*), which could be translated politically into oligarchy, but when it included the *demos* meant democracy. Drawing lots, the instrument of equality, likewise was an appropriate means of selection in both constitutions: in an oligarchy the group of candidates was limited; when all citizens were eligible, the method consolidated a democracy.[164]

As Patrice Hamon has shown, in the Hellenistic age *isotes* came to be recognized as one of the standard virtues of magistrates and judges, who were praised for applying the equality among citizens that the laws expected. Clearly, officials had to be reminded of this duty of their office in a society in which inequality between segments of the *polis* had become more pronounced and institutionalized. At the same pace, however, the norms of who belonged to this society widened to include noncitizens in various ways, marking a significant move away from classical concepts of the *polis* as a unity of citizens.[165]

---

[158] In the classical age, *plethos* refers to the whole mass of citizens; cf. *Ath.Pol.* 26.3. In the Hellenistic age, according to Grieb (2008), *plethos* refers to the whole (free) population of a *polis*, thus including noncitizens, while all citizens are the *demos* or *damos* (depending on the Greek dialect).

[159] Herodotus here associates *isonomia* with the mass of the people; this association is not inherent to the concept *isonomia*, which could also be held among a minority. Later (3.128) he recounts how King Dareios of Persia, when asking for a volunteer among the Persian nobles to catch an enemy and thirty men presented themselves, made the lot decide among them all. His use of the typical democratic vocabulary for this restricted, elite group (Δαρεῖος κατελάμβανε κελεύων πάλλεσθαι· παλλομένων δὲ λαγχάνει ἐκ πάντων Βαγαῖος ὁ Ἀρτόντεω) is surely ironic and may even be an ironic reflection on the outcome of the Constitutional Debates.

[160] Thuc. 3.62.3, with Hornblower (1991) *ad loc.* Cf. Hdt. 5.92a: *isokratia* for a constitution led by a group of equals, here leaning toward oligarchy, in contrast to tyranny.

[161] Giangiulio (2015) 46.

[162] Fornara and Samons (1991) 41–44, 166–167; Vlastos (1953) 354: *isonomia* "a banner."

[163] The spirit of elite mentality is vivid in skolion 907 P. (fr. 24 Fabbro).

[164] Demont (2001); Pope (1988) 290–292.

[165] Hamon (2012) 72–73: "Dass der Gebrauch von Begriffe wie *to koinon* (Gemeinwesen) oder *to ison* (Gleichheit) sich im Laufe der hellenistischen Zeit signifikant verschob. . . . Der ursprünglich demokratisch konnotierte Begriff der Gleichheit wurde nunmehr mit Bezug auf Nicht-Bürger verwandt, also erweitert und ins Feld des Nicht-Politischen verlegt: Man könnte sagen, dass er allmählich entpolitisiert und aufgelöst wurde."

8
Drawing Lots for *Polis* Office

8.1 Introducing the lot for office

8.1.1 The lot in Solon's *politeia*

Based on our present evidence, allotment for *polis* office was introduced for the first time in Greece in the constitution that Solon created for Athens when he was appointed as archon and lawgiver in 594.[1] In this system, the Nine Archons—*archai* that already existed—and the *Tamiai* (treasurers) of the goddess Athena—a body that perhaps existed or may have been instituted by Solon—were to be drawn by lot from a preselected group. Moreover, according to some accounts, Solon instituted a new council consisting of well-to-do citizens, besides the existing council of the Areopagos that consisted of former archons, and a people's court of judicial appeal.

The *Ath.Pol.* gives a rather straightforward account of why a radical revision of Athens's *politeia* and society was necessary.[2] At the time, Athens was embroiled in economic and political conflicts: deep economic inequality between the wealthy landowners and the poor peasants—who had no political influence or any legal recourse for redress—had pushed the *polis* to the brink of *stasis* (violent civic conflict). Elected as archon and entrusted with exceptional authority to reconstitute the *polis*, Solon erased existing agricultural debts, rendered illegal enslavement of Athenians for debt, and issued a set of new laws. Among those that can with some confidence be ascribed to Solon are regulations for membership of the citizen body, a sacrificial calendar, and political measures that for later commentators heralded a new *politeia*.[3]

What exactly Solon changed in the *politeia* has been a topic of intense debate, because Aristotle states in his *Politics* that Solon did not destroy existing institutions, a statement that is at odds with the account in *Ath.Pol.* (8.1) that Solon instituted the selection of the archons and the *Tamiai* by lot. Yet I would argue that the account of the *Ath.Pol.* accords with the principal tenets of the

---

[1] For the historical problems concerning Solon's archonship and laws, see Endnote 1.
[2] *Ath.Pol.* 8.1 (lot); background and further events: 2; 5–9.
[3] For Solon's regulation of family law underpinning citizenship, Lape (2002/3), Blok (2017) 107–15; for Solon's debt cancellation and abolishment of debt slavery, and the example of the Mesopotamian kingdoms for both, Blok and Krul (2017).

Politics and perfectly fits the political climate of the archaic age.[4] In antiquity, *abolishing* institutions was a very rare act; usually, laws and lawgivers changed existing institutions, or added new structures to old ones.[5] Keeping at least some part of the previous institution, or using means that were otherwise familiar, was essential for providing the foundations on which the innovation could be anchored. For Solon, this was particularly important because he wished to make several drastic changes, notably in the selection of the most prestigious offices in Athens, the Nine Archons.[6]

The Nine Archons had probably begun as a board of three, one of which was called *Basileus* (king), one the *Polemarchos* (war-leader) and one called just "the archon," who was the annual eponym (name-giver) since 683/2, when a term of office of one year for the archonships was consolidated.[7] Perhaps the offices of the archons were by then also more clearly differentiated.[8] At some point, six *thesmothetai* (lawgivers) were added to the board.[9] The three main archons held authority in religion, law, and jurisdiction: the *Basileus* and the eponymous archon supervised the major *polis* festivals, and the *Polemarchos*, who was supreme commander when the *polis* as a whole went to war (see section 7.2.5, the battle of Marathon), supervised important sacrifices; all three had procedural authority in jurisdiction, notably assigning cases to courts.[10] After their year in office, ex-archons were co-opted into the Areopagos council, which supervised the laws of the *polis* and held judicial authority as a court.[11] How candidates for the

---

[4] For the debate, see Rhodes *CAAP ad loc.* and Endnote 2 for the relation between the *Ath.Pol.* and *Politics* on this issue.

[5] One of these rare cases of abolished institutions would seem to be the *naukrariai*, sociogeographical fiscal units of Attica each responsible for the equipment of a ship, which Cleisthenes abolished and replaced by the demes, according to *Ath.Pol.* 21.5. However, even here it seems the *naukrariai* only lost some of their functions to the demes and retained others, among which was the financing of ships, according to Cleidemus (*FGrHist* 323 F 8), for which see van Wees (2013) 46–47.

[6] *Ath.Pol.* 2.3; 5.1; the picture in *Ath.Pol.* 2–3 of "the ancient constitution before Draco" is only a rough sketch. According to *Ath.Pol.* 4, the *politeia* immediately before Solon was instituted by Draco, but scholars agree this passage is a later addition; cf. Verlinsky (2017).

[7] *Ath.Pol.*'s (3.1, 3.4) account—that originally the archonships were held for life and next for ten years—probably goes back to Hellanicus of Lesbos, the first Atthidographer, who tried to bridge the gap between the mythical prehistory of Athens and the first known annual archon; cf. Harding (1994) 10 with further references.

[8] Archaic offices were initially not clearly circumscribed but filled in accordance with means and ability; Foxhall (1997) 120. *Ath.Pol.* 3.1–5 thinks that the *Basileus* and *Polemarchos* were older than the eponymous archon, because the religious rites performed by the first two were considered older ("ancestral") than those assigned to the latter. But "ancestral" is a value term as much as an indication of time; many rituals supervised by all three archons had a very ancient core that had been adapted to new circumstances over time, so the *Ath.Pol.*'s statement cannot be corroborated.

[9] *Ath.Pol.* 3.4. It is assumed that this took place in the seventh century; Develin (1989) 2.

[10] *Ath.Pol.* 56–58, with Blok (2017) 212–214.

[11] *Ath.Pol.* 3.6; 8.4; Androtion *FGrHist* 324 F 3 implies a wider judicial authority; cf. Harding (1994) 86–87. Fulfilling both judicial and other roles was common among Greek officials; cf. Papakonstantinou (2008) 83–93. Contra Wallace (1989) that before Solon the Areopagos was primarily a court of homicide, David Lewis *CR* (1990) 40.2, 357 argues that no distinction between the Areopagos council and court existed. Beside the Areopagos, a board of fifty-one *ephetai* probably selected (by voting) from the Areopagos, adjudicated in homicide cases since Draco (*IG* I³ 104 l.17).

archonships were nominated is not exactly clear from the *Ath.Pol.*: one gets the impression of a combination of election by the *demos* under compelling guidance of the Areopagos. Candidates were eligible on "excellence and wealth," the highest claims to *time*.[12] Competition for the offices was fierce, frequently leading to actual violence and to deeper impoverishment of the peasants due to the pressure among the elite to outdo each other in splendor.[13] The Areopagos made the final selection among the most successful competitors, assigning to each man the archonship probably suiting him best.[14] Yet the consent of the *demos* with the choice of the Areopagos was sought in some way. The *Ath.Pol.* tells us that Solon was chosen by both the elite and the poor as archon and arbitrator, and consent by both parties was particularly important in this case because of the tense situation.[15] In sum, in the archonships and the Areopagos, the elite exercised a firm hold on the formal and informal power in the *polis*.

In his new *politeia*, Solon divided the citizen population into four classes, defined by assessment of their agricultural wealth: the *pentakosiomedimnoi* (five-hundred-bushel men), the *hippeis* (horse-men), the *zeugitai* (oxen-men), and the *thetes* (workers).[16] Each household was evaluated as to economic wealth (*timema*) and assigned to one of these four classes (*tele*), each with fiscal duties (*telos*) to which a clear sociopolitical status (*time*) was attached.[17] The *pentakosiomedimnoi*, whose properties yielded at least five hundred *medimnoi* (bushels) grain produce, and *hippeis*, who could raise horses, were the two wealthiest classes, together comprising on a very tentative estimation 5 to 10 percent of the population.[18] But for the *zeugitai* and the *thetes* it is contested which sections of the population were included in these classes. The *Ath.Pol.* 7.3–4 states that

---

[12] *Ath.Pol.* 3.1, 3.6, ἀριστίνδην καὶ πλουτίνδην; cf. Androtion (*FrGrHist* 324 F 4). ἀριστίνδην could mean "on high birth" but also "on excellence."

[13] The "Cylon affair," an attempt by one family and their followers to enforce tyrannical power in Athens in ca. 620, led to wide bloodshed; a mass grave of young men killed by violence found near Phaleron in 2016 seems to confirm these accounts. See ref. in Rönnberg (2021) 361. Only after the laws of Draco regulating retribution on homicide, and a ritual cleansing of the city by an external authority, Epimeneides from Crete, life could be resumed. For the cycles of competition, strife, and extortion in archaic Greece, Link (1991a), esp. 159–170, van Wees (1999), Blok and Krul (2017).

[14] *Ath.Pol.* 8.2. The verbs used here are κρίνω (to assess) and διατάσσω (to distribute).

[15] *Ath.Pol.* 5.1–2. That Solon was chosen or selected (αἱρέω) by both parties is confirmed by Plut. *Sol.* 14.3; *Mor.* 763d–e. Cf. Barucchi (2004/5) 71–73.

[16] Possibly, some names of the classes were traditional and given a new meaning by Solon. Foxhall (1997), van Wees (2006), and Valdés Guía and Gallego (2010) argue convincingly that the functions, criteria, and terminology of the classes were economic-agricultural, not military as contended by Raaflaub (2006) and De Ste. Croix (2004b). Duplouy (2014)'s view that the classes were no formal "classes" but socioeconomic interest groups, cannot account for their role in the selection of the archons.

[17] For their fiscal purpose van Wees (2013) 84-91, Valdés Guía (2022a), Rhodes, *CAAP ad Ath.Pol.* 7.3–4. How the evaluation took place in the sixth century is unclear; Connor (1987) suggests that all well-to-do households presented themselves in a ritual procession.

[18] As Foxhall (1997) 131 observes, "What the formalisation of the *tele* must have achieved was to fix rules for belonging to that elite, perhaps along new lines."

the *zeugitai* had a yield of at least two hundred *medimnoi* from their properties, and the *thetes* comprised everyone from just under this quota, meaning all those on the spectrum from moderate wealth down to those with (next to) nothing.[19] If the two hundred *medimnoi* were agricultural produce in the early sixth century, as Lin Foxhall and Hans van Wees argue, the *zeugitai* were a wealthy, leisured class of landowners, roughly another 10 percent of the population.[20] But if the *zeugitai* comprised all farmers who owned a yoke of oxen, corresponding to a "middling" landholding of around five hectares, while the criterion was formalized in *medimnoi* in the revision of Solon's laws between 410 and 399 to distinguish between the wealthier and less wealthy sections of this large group for fiscal reasons, as Miriam Valdés Guía and Julián Gallego argue, the picture of Solon's society is quite different.[21] Both views on the socioeconomic composition of the *zeugitai* are tightly connected to their military implications: van Wees regards the archaic hoplites as a fairly limited group, but for Valdés Guía they constituted a far more sizeable segment of the citizen population.[22]

What matters here first of all is the purpose of Solon's organization, namely a clear and more equitable distribution of political and judicial powers.[23] For the distribution of offices, it seems that Solon gave to every property class some share in the *politeia*. The highest three classes had access to an office or a set of offices (*timai*); the lowest class had no access to offices, but they had an active vote in the assembly and in the selection procedures, and moreover the possibility of legal redress when acting as a court of appeal (see section 8.1.3).

Solon made the wealthiest men, probably of the first two classes, eligible for the archonships and introduced a new procedure.[24] Candidates were elected by the *demos* in each of the four Ionian *phylai* (subgroups); each *phyle* elected ten candidates, amounting to forty in all.[25] This first stage in the procedure was

---

[19] The *Ath.Pol.* is followed by Poll. *On.* 8.130, which further details the fiscal obligations of each class.

[20] These figures are very rough estimates based on (a) Foxhall (1997), who offers a detailed discussion of the parameters of the classes in the amounts of wheat or barley, resulting in an estimated size of the landholdings in each class; cf. van Wees (2001) for the top three classes as 15 to 20 percent of the population; (b) Bresson (2016) 144–146 who estimates the percentages in the population of landholdings in classical Attica; cf. Foxhall (2002). On the social and legal structure of Solon's Athens, Dmitriev (2017) takes too many fourth-century references to Solon as instances of Solon's own laws, disregarding the fact that the laws had been revised in 410–399 and that quite a number of the laws ascribed to Solon in the fourth century were of a later date.

[21] Valdés Guía and Gallego (2010).

[22] Van Wees (2002); Valdés Guía (2019b; 2022a).

[23] Cf. Solon fr. 4 W 32–39 for his belief in *eunomia* as the righteous principle for society.

[24] *Ath.Pol.* 7.3–4 does not state clearly which classes were eligible for the archonships, but it is doubtful if the first class alone could offer sufficient candidates year after year; that probably the highest two classes were eligible is further implied by the fact that the office was opened also to the third class shortly before 457 (*Ath.Pol.* 26.2) while no earlier change is reported.

[25] For this procedure, *Ath.Pol.* 8.1–2. Cf. Isoc. 7.22 for *prokrisis* before allotment at the time of Solon; Isoc. 12.145 is too imprecise to be pertinent evidence. For the shifting perception of the Ionian roots of Athens and the four *phylai*, see Hall (1997) 40–56. Valdés Guía (2022a) argues that Solon

called *prokrisis* (preassessment of qualification).[26] From among these forty, nine men were selected by lot.[27] Who exactly performed this drawing of lots, and where, remains unclear, along with how the archonships were assigned to each person, but we may assume the selection took place in public.[28]

The political meaning of this type of selection, known as *klerosis ek prokriton*, allotment from preselected candidates, is essentially different from *klerosis ex hapanton*, allotment from all.[29] The *prokrisis* (preassessment) predefines the group among which the lots are drawn either by setting specific criteria or by election from a larger group, at times by combining both methods; the procedure substantially restricts the size of the group of candidates for the lot.[30] "Allotment from all," by contrast, sets no criteria or other restrictions but defines the entire group as eligible; the expression *ex hapanton* or *ek panton* ("from all") later became strongly associated with democracy.[31]

Solon's implementation of the lot was therefore anything but democratic. On Aristotle's classification of selection methods in the *Politics*, the restriction of eligibility of the archons to the highest two property classes, with fixed requirements in wealth for access, would be considered oligarchic. Since the election from these wealthy few of the forty candidates was presumably based on merit, this was "aristocratic."[32] Both steps—first great wealth, then election—made the preassessment of qualification, the *prokrisis*, in Solon's system highly selective. Since the Areopagos, which held the highest authority in the *polis*, consisted of ex-archons, it was therefore solidly elitist. In this respect, Aristotle correctly observed that Solon did not change the existing institutions, since for Aristotle the part held by each socioeconomic group in the *polis* institutions was decisive for the nature of the *politeia*, more so than other elements of the institutions. The fact that the selection procedure now included election by the *demos* of the candidates, and that the final selection was made by the lot, mattered less for Aristotle's assessment of Solon's *politeia* than the fact that the archons still were

---

introduced the four *phylai* for the military organization of Athens, although *Ath.Pol.* 8.3 holds that there were four *phylai* and four *phylobasileis* "as before" (sc. Solon).

[26] LSJ, s.v. προκρίνω. Cf. Abel (1983) 7–13, 68: although it preceded the allotment, in *prokrisis* the pronoun *pro-* has not a temporal meaning but refers to preference or selection.

[27] On this passage, see Endnote 2.

[28] *Ath.Pol.* 55 describes the qualification procedure and the oath of the Nine Archons before entering office, which were clearly long-standing practices, but whether they date back to Solon is unknown.

[29] On *prokrisis*, Abel (1983); for the differences between allotment from few and from all, cf. Demont (2001).

[30] Arist. *Pol.* 1300a38–41: "And for some to appoint from all, to some offices by vote and to others by lot or by both (to some by lot and to others by vote) is oligarchical."

[31] Xen. *Mem.* 4.6.12; Arist. *Pol.* 1300a33–36.

[32] Arist. *Pol.* 1300b4–5: "For some to elect from all and then that all elect from them is aristocratic."

selected "on the basis of wealth and excellence." The account of the *Ath.Pol.* and the *Politics* thus agree on Solon's *politeia*.[33]

Applying the lot to the political sphere was new, however, and so was the composition of the elite. Men from the highest property class, the *pentakosiomedimnoi*, who still could boast more *time* than the *hippeis* just below them, were now classified together with them as *homoios* (equivalent) in the election procedure for the archonships, and the lot made them *isos* (equal). Whatever the results of the election, both groups must have been represented among the forty candidates and next selected by the lot, creating boards of archons of different backgrounds. On a very limited scale, Solon thus brought about a degree of social mixing, and he may have hoped the lot would reduce the conflicts about appointment to the archonships.[34] The *prokrisis*, furthermore, not only formalized the preselection of the candidates and placed the election in the hands of the *demos*, but also distributed eligibility over the four *phylai*; this balanced distribution would reduce the competition, before it was further reduced by the final allotment, thus enhancing the sense of equality among the elite.[35] Election normally took place by show of hands, allotment by drawing dark and light beans.[36]

If the highest "few" were disgruntled about their forced mixing with the second class, they were compensated by an office for which only they were eligible: the *Tamiai* (treasurers) of Athena. Perhaps Solon created this office, or he only changed its means of selection.[37] The archaeological evidence on the cult of Athena on the Acropolis suggests that by the late seventh century officials were needed to guard the valuable bronze tripods and other dedications held in the sanctuary.[38] The *Tamiai*—originally meaning "dispensers of household wealth," later just "treasurers"—guarded the treasures on the Acropolis; a decree of 485 commands them to take full responsibility for the safety of the treasures, in addition to supervising the conduct of cult personnel and worshipers.[39] As

---

[33] See also Endnote 2.
[34] Cf. Rhodes, *CAAP ad Ath.Pol.* 8.1. On the strong social mobility in archaic Greece, and Solon's *politeia* as an attempt to guide this movement in Athens into regulated social sections, see Canevaro (2022); Węcowski (2023).
[35] Cf. Grote (2016) 243–262 for *phylai* as unifying segments of the *polis* and as a framework for even distribution of offices.
[36] *Kuameuo* of the archons in Solon's *politeia*: *Ath.Pol.* 8.1, 22.5.
[37] *Ath.Pol.* 8.1 states that Solon made "the offices" *klerosis ek prokriton* (see also Endnote 3) and next discusses the archons and the *Tamiai*, suggesting that both offices had already existed; the *Tamiai* featured before in "Draco's constitution" (*Ath.Pol.* 4). However, the latter reference is unreliable (see above, note 6). Bubelis (2016) 21–60 argues that Solon created the office of the *Tamiai* as a "trade-off" for the wealthy upper classes, calling it the Law of Solon on the *Tamiai*. Mussa (2019) 252, 262, does not seriously question the "constitution of Draco" (*Ath.Pol.* 4.2) and regards the late seventh century as a possible date of origin of the *Tamiai*.
[38] On the first centuries of the cult of Athena, see van den Eijnde (2010) 96–99; 354; for the stone sanctuary, Hurwit (1999) 95.
[39] In the first extant record of their duties as a board inscribed in bronze (*IG* I³ 510; ca. 550), they pronounce to have collected—and probably made an inventory of—the bronzes of Athena.

a civic board combining cultic duties and financial accountability, the *Tamiai* exemplify a common Greek form of office, but their setup fits the patterns of Solon's *politeia*: the board of eight men, two per *phyle*, was selected by lot from the highest class, the *pentakosiomedimnoi*.[40] In the classical era, they served for four years, from one Greater Panathenaia to the next, although accounting for their work year by year.[41] This pattern of tenure was probably established when the Panathenaia were founded in their new splendid shape in 566/5; the earlier tenure of the *Tamiai* is unknown.

8.1.2 Solon's introduction of the lot: A first anchorage

Since on our current evidence Solon was the first to introduce drawing lots for *polis* office, first we need to discern where he found inspiration for this idea, and then whether it was successful; the two questions may even be connected.

For his other, radically new measure—the cancellation of debts—Solon was probably influenced by the tradition of debt remission of the Ancient Near East.[42] Could he have found the example for his political innovation there, too? Drawing lots was a traditional practice in the Ancient Near East, and the correspondence in meaning and usage of the regular Akkadian word for lot, *isqu*, with the Greek *kleros* and *moira* is striking, as is the application of the lot for division and distribution.[43] Yet there are three important differences between the Eastern and Greek traditions. First, the agency of the gods is overtly present in the Near Eastern material, whereas it is often ambiguous in the Greek case. Second, the frequency of use differs markedly: the term *iqsu* is scarce relative to the numerous extant Akkadian texts, whereas *kleros* and its cognates are attested very frequently all over the Greek world. Third, in the Ancient Near East the connection between drawing lots in a social context and equality gradually disappeared, whereas in Greece it became ever more salient over time. This difference is especially notable in the selection for office.

Supervision on the Acropolis and safeguarding treasures: *IG* I³ 4 with Blok and van Rookhuijzen (2023); the date is ascertained by Stroud (2004).

[40] *Ath.Pol.* 8.1 states, "That Solon stipulated appointment by lot (of the archons) from the property-classes is confirmed by the law on the *Tamiai*, which remains in use even today: it orders the appointment of the treasurers by lot from the five-hundred-bushel class." In the fifth and fourth centuries, they were ten, one from each Cleisthenic tribe. In *IG* I³ 510, five names are legible, but there is space for three more; on the analogy with the classical practice, it is plausible the board began as two per Ionian *phyle*.
[41] For this term of office, Develin (1984). According to Marcaccini (2015), following the decree of Kallias A (probably of 433/2) the annual accounts of the *Tamiai* were aligned to the calendar of the *boule*.
[42] For the debt remission, see Blok and Krul (2017).
[43] See Endnote 4.

Only one official in the Assyrian Empire was drawn by lots, in the shape of dice (*puru*): the eponym (*līmum*).[44] The tradition went back to the Old Assyrian Empire, where the eponym was the highest official after the king and was the head of the city hall; his role may have had a cultic dimension.[45] The office was part of a career path for high-ranking families. However, in the Neo-Assyrian Empire, beginning in the reign of Shalmaneser III (858–824), the candidates consisted only of a few high court officials and the king, and the selection by lot had changed into a largely fixed order for several years of the highest officials in the realm, with the king always in the second place.[46] The allotment was now hardly more than a symbolic, ritual moment.[47] Hence, even if Solon knew of this venerable practice, it would hardly work as a model for him for the selection of the archons.

Moreover, the Assyrian example certainly would not carry sufficient authority to make the lot acceptable among the *time*-driven archaic elite of Athens.[48] For them, the distribution of high-ranking benefits had to fit their *time* as a group and as individuals, and for the gratification of their expectations they drew on the values and practices pictured in Homeric epic. In the area of distribution of goods by lot, *polis* office did not match the epic models, and the elite rather expected to receive a *geras*. When used for selection, in the epics the lot was to select a single hero from a small group of elite peers to perform a singular feat of valor, not for a rotating office. So, if Solon were to make the elite accept using the lot for assigning the highest offices of the *polis*, he could not draw on the epic as a model for distribution by lot, but instead had to find a different model with

---

[44] The lots were dice; the selected lot was placed in front of the deity; cf. Taggar-Cohen (2002) 100-101; the word *puru* is used with the verbs *sialāu* and *kararu*, "to put down," with secondary meaning "to throw, cast"; contrast Hom. *Il.* 6.182 (ἐκ δ ἔθορε κλῆρος κυνέης): the lot springing up from the helmet.

[45] Dercksen (2004) 53–56. This Assyrian practice differed from the Southern Babylonian tradition to name the year after the most important event.

[46] Yamada (2000) 322–333; Dercksen (2004) 58–59. An extant clay die is inscribed with the name of a candidate, prayers for good results, and prayer to the gods (Aššur, Adad) to be selected; it was used in 833 and 825. The word *puru* is used here as synonym of the eponymate (*līmu*); Millard (1994) 8; Dercksen (2004) 57.

[47] Finkel and Reade (1995) argue that selection by lots had in effect ceased in the Neo-Assyrian period, replaced by a fixed order with slight changes due to contingent circumstances. Against this view speaks evidence such as the die.

[48] According to scholars who doubt that Solon introduced the lot as a method for choosing archons, the elite's objections to this method must have been insurmountable; cf. Day and Chambers (1962) 82; Rhodes, *CAAP ad Ath.Pol.* 8.1. Hansen (1990) objects that selecting the *Polemarchos*, the leader of the army in battle, by lot must have been especially unacceptable, in comparison with the classical era, when numerous officials were drawn by lot, but the Athenians still preferred to elect their military leaders. In my view, the two situations are fundamentally different. The classical armies were drawn from across the citizen body, comprising many men inexperienced in military leadership; they wanted to choose a leader whom they trusted to be so qualified (but to whom they could be assigned by lot, nonetheless). The prominent men in the archaic elite, by contrast, were all high-profile, experienced martial men who considered certainly themselves and probably their peers *qualitate qua* capable of military leadership.

an equally authoritative pedigree. Such a model existed, not in the Ancient Near East, but right in his own *polis*.

In Athens, in the archaic age and through until the mid-fifth century, all *polis* priesthoods were selected from the *gene*, fictive kin groups of families who traditionally laid claim to certain priesthoods. Although much of the evidence on the *gene* dates to the classical age and later, it allows the reconstruction of *genos* traditions far back into the archaic age, notably to the seventh century.[49] By Solon's day, the most prominent *gene*, the Kerykes and Eumolpidai who were in charge of the cults at Eleusis, and the Eteoboutadai whose two distinct branches provided the priestess of Athena Polias and the priest of Poseidon Erechtheus on the Acropolis, had been holding sway over their cults and offices for an unknown stretch of time.[50] According to their traditions, the *genos* cults had been established by the ancestor of the *genos* in primeval times, a claim that made eligibility for the priesthood a collective inheritance, transmitted among the families of the *genos* on strict endogamy. Due to their Athenian descent on both sides, the *gene* claimed to be of "pure descent" (*ithageneia*) and a "nobility of birth" (*eugeneia*), which gave the *gene* collectively a unique, high *time*, regardless of wealth (some *genos* families were not wealthy at all).[51] Eligibility for their cultic offices being a hereditary good in these families, the selection among the *gennetai* of the right gender and age for actual officeholding followed the model of distribution of inheritance and took place by drawing lots.[52] Their service of the gods on behalf of the *polis* may have given their selection by lot, the inauguration of their civic function, also an aura of divine approval (for divine selection of priests and priestesses, section 8.2.4).

From the *gene*, then, Solon may have derived the selection for high *timai* by lot, first for the idea itself and next for expecting that the high status of the precedent would persuade the Athenian elite to accept this means of selection.[53] Insofar as this example drew on the distribution of inheritance by lot, the elite was familiar with the model. But were the offices for which Solon introduced this method sufficiently similar to those of the *gene* to make the conditions of their distribution sufficiently similar, too? The *Tamiai*, a civic board serving Athena on behalf of the *polis*, held an institutional position between the cultic priesthoods and the civic board of the archons, and they shared the space and authority with

---

[49] Cf. Blok (2017) 234–239; Blok and Lambert (2009).
[50] It is extremely difficult to reconstruct when and how the more than fifty *gene* had acquired their priesthoods and other cultic *timai*, but their claims that their prerogatives went far back, to the imagined "origins" of the *polis*, seem not entirely fictitious; cf. Lambert (1999). According to the tradition, the Kerykes received the honor of *sitesis* at the Delion in Solon's laws, LR Fr. 88 (Ath. VI 234E–F). For the evidence on virtually all *gene*, Parker (1996) App. 2.
[51] Lambert (2015); for the *gene* as models of citizenship and autochthony, Blok (2009a; 2009b).
[52] Blok and Lambert (2009); Blok (2017) 217–225.
[53] For the view that the elite accepted selection by lot when it carried the values of divine selection, Wade-Gery (1958) 113.

the priesthoods on the Acropolis.[54] While the *gene* enjoyed the highest *time* through birth, the *pentakosiomedimnoi*-class did so in wealth, and for the *Tamiai* to be selected from among their peers in the same manner as priests from the *gene* would be new, but not dishonorable. The archons had major cultic duties as well as the judicial and military authority in the *polis*. If selection by lot was acceptable for the *Tamiai* from the highest class, perhaps it would be thus also for the archons, selected from the top two classes.

Yet the sequel shows that Solon's novel method worked for the *Tamiai* but not for the archons. The (scarce) evidence of the sixth century shows the *Tamiai* performing their duties without apparent problems, and in the fifth century the duties of the board, now ten men strong, were continued and even extended.[55] The law about their selection by lot from the *pentakosiomedimnoi* was in still in force in the fourth century, although by then the property classes had lost their meaning in other respects.[56] For the archons, however, Solon's system worked for four years but then went awry, as *Ath.Pol.* reports, due to political strife (*stasis*); consequently, several years went by without an (eponymous) archon, after which a certain Damasias was archon for more than two years, then ten archons were elected.[57] On this internal strife, in the mid-sixth century Peisistratos managed to trump his peers and establish a tyranny. According to the tradition, he largely maintained Solon's laws, but for the selection of the archons the final allotment was abandoned, only the election remained, either by tribe or in the full assembly.[58] Only in 487/6, twenty years after Cleisthenes had introduced the new *politeia* for Athens, Solon's model for the archons was reinstated, with allotment as the final stage after *prokrisis* by *phyle*, now in the ten new *phylai* of Cleisthenes's system and carried out in the demes.[59]

In sum, distribution of the archonships by lot, even if restricted to the wealthy two classes and preceded by election (*prokrisis*), was a bridge too far for the elite of archaic Athens. The contest for the highest *timai* in the *polis*, the offices with the highest authority and military leadership, was too fierce to make subjection to equal chance acceptable. In the uppermost class, this resistance to lot-drawing

---

[54] Confirmed and enhanced in *IG* I³ 4.
[55] *IG* I³ 510, ca. 550; for inventories made by the *Tamiai* in the fifth and fourth c., Harris (1995).
[56] *Ath.Pol.* 47.1: "the ten treasurers of Athena, one appointed by lot from each tribe, from the *pentakosiomedimnoi* in accordance with Solon's law (this law is still in force): the men who are appointed hold office even if they are quite poor."
[57] *Ath.Pol.* 13.1–3; for the selection of archons from the time of Solon to the archon Telesinos (487/6), see Develin (1979); Barucchi (2004); and Endnote 3.
[58] *Ath.Pol.* 16.1–2: he ruled more *politikos* than *tyrannikos*; 16.8–9: he was occasionally removed from office (= *archon*), but later appointed again.
[59] *Ath.Pol.* 22.5: "In the archonship of Telesinos [487/6], for the first time since the tyranny, the nine archons were appointed by lot on a tribal basis, from a short list of hundred [or: five-hundred] elected by the members of the demes: all the archons before this were elected (*hairesthai*)" (trans. P. J. Rhodes, slightly modified).

was perhaps exacerbated by having to share their chances with those they held to be inferior to their exclusive circle of the wealthiest *homoioi*. The competitive attitude of the elite led first to conflict and ultimately to the loss of their collective power to the tyrants. Only in the selection of the *Tamiai* by *klerosis ek prokriton* (selection by lot of preselected candidates) of which the *prokrisis* (preselection) consisted of the wealth criterion of the first class, the Athenian elite abided by Solon's regulation, probably because it concerned an office that invoked less competition due to its more restricted powers.

8.1.3 Solon's *politeia*: The council and the court

What about the two further novel institutions of Solon's *politeia*, a new council and the people's court? In the classical age, the council and the jury courts came to be drawn by lot—was this practice also originally Solonian?

According to *Ath.Pol.* (8.4), Solon created the council of four hundred, composed of one hundred per *phyle*, but whether it really came into existence is disputed; on balance, the council most likely did exist.[60] On the logic apparent in Solon's *politeia*, giving each fiscal class access to specified political bodies with competences of their own, a council also open to the third class, the *zeugitai*, would make sense. If Valdés Guía's reading of the zeugite class is correct, they made up a substantial part of the population, providing a solid base for Solon's *politeia*. Furthermore, in an admittedly circular argument, the council established by Cleisthenes in 508/7 makes more sense as a revision of an existing council than as a completely new institution. Like its successor, the function of the Solonian council was likely probouleutic, namely to prepare the agenda of the assembly, a role in which the council mediated between the archons and the assembly.[61] The means of selection for the council are unknown. An analogy with the election of the archons would point to election by the *demos* of one hundred men per *phyle*, but this is no more than a conjecture.

Beside the council of four hundred, Solon also accorded the *zeugitai* access to the other offices, the *poletai* (who made all contracts on behalf of the *polis*), the *kolakretai* (who handled financial transactions on behalf of the *polis*), and the Eleven (in charge of offenders and enforcing penalties, notably executions). In the classical age, these offices were drawn by lot, but there is no indication that this was also the case in the sixth century.[62]

---

[60] *Ath.Pol.* 8.4; see Endnote 5.
[61] Rhodes (1972) 208–210. Valdés Guía (2022b) assigns also a judicial function to the council of four hundred and regards it as identical with the *heliaia*. Combining a deliberative with a judicial function was common for archaic councils, but *Ath.Pol.* 8.4 states explicitly that the council of the Areopagos retained the primary judicial role in the *polis* (and see below on the *heliaia*).
[62] *Ath.Pol.* 47.2; 52.1; the *kolakretai* were abolished in the late fifth century.

Regarding the people's court, the evidence is likewise far from consistent, but there is no reason to doubt its existence in one shape or another. For the *demos* to act as a court of appeal to decisions of the other courts and magistrates, Solon could build on the traditional entitlement of the *demos* to hear public adjudication. Furthermore, Solon's aim, according to the *Ath.Pol.*, was to give the *demos* a representation in the *politeia*, and while the lowest fiscal class had no access to any office, they needed means to defend themselves against the overpowering elite; this judicial entitlement was precisely its innovative feature, again according to *Ath.Pol.*[63] Were the members of this public court drawn by lot, as Aristotle contends in the *Politics*?[64] This seems unlikely. When meeting for judicial cases, the *demos* was called the *heliaia*, a term used also in other Greek dialects for "assembly," meaning the undivided *demos*, sometimes further explicated with the adjective *teleia* (full).[65] Selection was therefore out of place in a *heliaia*. In Athens, its division into *dikasteria* (jury courts) probably began in the late 460s, but the *heliaia* was never abolished.[66] For the selection by lot in the Solonian court, then, it seems that Aristotle projected a fourth-century practice back on the sixth century.[67]

In conclusion, our current evidence indicates that Solon introduced the use of the lot for political office in Athens in 594, for two offices: the *Tamiai* (treasurers) of Athena and the Nine Archons. In both cases, criteria of considerable affluence applied. The *Tamiai* were selected by lot from the wealthiest class, a very small group. For the archons, *prokrisis* (election) took place among the top two classes, followed by allotment to select from among those who had been elected (*klerosis ek prokriton*). Possibly, Solon derived the use of sortition as a means of selection for *polis* office from the traditional appointment by lot for priesthood from among the *gene*. Such an origin would have been familiar and come with an aura of legitimacy and high standing, making this method acceptable to the elite. Solon formalized the structural division of the *polis* on the one hand into a small wealthy elite with access to the highest *polis* offices, and on the other into a large *demos* without access to these leading political and military positions. But to strengthen the position of the *demos* in the *politeia* (constitution of the *polis*), Solon gave the *zeugitai* class access to minor offices and to a council with an advisory role (probouleutic) in between the archons and the *demos*. He also gave

---

[63] *Ath.Pol.* 9.1: Solon's judicial innovations were the procedure of *ephesis* (to ask redress on behalf of other persons) and the people's court; cf. Gagarin (2006).

[64] Arist. *Pol.* 1273b38–1274 a6; see also Endnote 2.

[65] Cf. *heliaia* on Delos (*IG* XI 2 199) juxtaposed with *dikasteria*; *haliaia*: *IG* IV 497 (Mykenai); IV 557 (Argos), IV 479 (Kleonaia), *IG* IV² 1 69 (Epidauros).

[66] The *demos* met for special occasions as a *heliaia*, for instance, in the fourth cent. for a case involving the *gene* of Eleusis (*Ag.* XVI 56[1]), and for a special honorific meeting (*IG* II³ 1 911) in 270.

[67] Arist. *Pol.* 1274a2–6; his inference was probably induced by the terms *dikasterion* and *ek panton* (from all) combined with the allegedly democratic effect of the Solonian court, for which *Ath.Pol.* 9.1 uses the classical word δικαστήριον.

judicial powers to the people's court, which over a century later were to turn into an institution of political power as well, thanks to its jurisdiction in the accountability of officeholders. Solon's institution of the *Tamiai*, including their selection by lot, worked well over the following centuries, but for the archons it was short-lived. For his method to be acceptable, more structural revisions of the *polis* and its governance were necessary.

8.2 Political divergence and patterns of allotment

In Aristotle's *Politics*, written in the later fourth century, selection for *polis* office by lot is typical of two types of *politeia*, oligarchies and democracies.[68] One would expect the reason for this to be that the lot disregards differences in qualifications and applies rigorous equality, in a limited group for oligarchies and among all citizens for democracies, whereas election values differences among the candidates. But Aristotle is hardly interested in how these methods work and why one should prefer one or the other simply as a system. Rather, he evaluates all selection methods for their political effect in combination with other factors: who is to carry out the selection, and from among whom? In line with Aristotle's principles previously discussed, the share of the distinct socioeconomic groups in the procedures matters most for the political effect of the selection methods. Instead of the previous three groups, in this context he distinguishes two: "the few," defined by "property assessment or birth or virtue or some other such qualification, for instance at Megara only those were eligible (for office) who returned in a body from exile and fought together against the *demos*," or "the many" (the *demos*, no qualifications). In an oligarchy the few determine access to office, be it by lot or by vote; in a democracy the many do so. Among fourteen possible combinations of groups and procedures, Aristotle favored those that would create a balance between the two groups.[69]

What is striking in this section of Aristotle's treatise and the collection of *politeiai* on which it drew is how self-evident the lot had become as a method for selection for political office, next to election. Clearly, much had changed in the 250 years since Solon. For understanding how this change came about, we need to look briefly at the political changes of the late archaic and classical periods, especially the divergence of *poleis* into predominantly democratic and

---

[68] Arist. *Pol.* 1300a13–1300b5; among preselected few, election is "aristocratic" (sc. by deliberate, qualitative selection). Cf. 1273a26–27: election by wealth is oligarchic; election by merit (*arete*) is aristocratic.

[69] Arist. *Pol.* 1300a16–19. He refers here to the oligarchic party in Megara, which after returning from exile imposed by the democrats established an oligarchy in 424 that was to last long (Thuc. 4.66–74).

overall oligarchic polities. The differences between Greek *poleis* became more pronounced from the archaic age on, due to contingent factors such as location, economic potential, and social composition. By the classical age, this diversity had crystallized into a diverse political landscape, with each *polis* having its own political structure, habitus, culture, and social climate—in other words, its own *politeia*. Depending on the grain of the picture we make or on the distance from which we look at this political landscape, we see notable similarities between the *politeiai*, such as the preference for republican government in multiple bodies, and between clusters, such as of largely democratic or oligarchic *politeiai*. By contrast, when zooming in, the differences between the *poleis* come more sharply into view, and here the use of the lot for *polis* office comes into play.

The two labels "oligarchy" and "democracy" thus reduce the more diverse realities of Greek political regimes discussed here to two basic types.[70] However, this reduction is justified by the perception, attested across our evidence, of *polis* regimes as leaning or belonging to either one or the other side. The duality between democracy and oligarchy is a corollary to the partly real and partly perceived split between the elite and the *demos*, whereas the political divergence into two main types of regime was the outcome of the political shifts of the late archaic, early classical period.[71]

The structure of the archaic *polis* described earlier—divided into a wealthy elite in control of the *polis* but competing among its members for social and political prominence, and a large *demos* that could be asked to support contenders for power—was a volatile situation, conducive to violent upheavals. In the late seventh and sixth centuries, in many *poleis* charismatic elite leaders trumped their peers by drawing on the *demos* to support them as tyrants.[72] In this process, the *demos* itself grew into a political power to be reckoned with, especially under the strong leadership by a member of the elite. In the decades between ca. 520 and 480, several *poleis* saw the establishment of political constellations in which the *demos* held, at least for a while, a more powerful political position than earlier, following on the fall of local tyrants or a restricted elite rule. This trend drew on the traditional sovereignty of the *demos*, both in the colonies and in the "old" *poleis*, and prominent cases include Athens, Argos, Cyrene, Megara, Miletos, Naxos, Samos, Kroton, Syracuse, and the Tauric Chersonesos, some of which also applied various forms of ostracism.[73]

---

[70] For the variety existing at the time in Greece reflected in descriptions of 158 *politeiai*, see the earlier discussion.

[71] Cf. Ober (1989) for the partly real and partly perceived distinction between "mass" and "elite," balanced by an ideology of "equality," as the formative factors in classical Athenian politics.

[72] See esp. Hammer (2005).

[73] Robinson (1997) optimistically labels these *poleis* "democracies"; for a more nuanced view, Robinson (2011) 217–247. Forsdyke (2005) 283–288; Robinson (2011) 198; and Giangiulio (2015) 86 deny that the other cases of ostracisms depended on Athens's example; contra Berger (1989). Węcowski (2022) 17–37 finds that all reliable evidence beyond Athens (Argos, Miletos, Megara,

Whether these *politeiai* can be classified as democracies depends on how democracy is defined. Labels like *isonomia* (equal distribution = equal order) and *demokratia*, circulating half a century after these events, indicate egalitarian values rather than clear-cut types of democratic governance.[74] In the eyes of the Greeks, notes Eric Robinson, the following features were typical for democracy:

> the primacy of the *demos*, freedom and equality as guiding principles of the [political] order, low property qualifications, use of the lot for some offices, and on occasion public pay for participation of the commons. Ostracism and accountability of magistrates ... were also associated with *demokratia*.[75]

Yet democracies, just like oligarchies, came in many kinds, with a huge variety in constitutional details, and full-blown democracies emerged only in the classical age. As we have seen, they were the expression of social shifts brought on by incisive military, economic, or demographic events, and were not merely the outcome of a gradual extension of the political franchise of a previously more restricted political system. As Giangiulio observes, *demokratia* by its very term entailed the manifestation of the social power (*kratos*) of the mass of the people (*demos*) rather than an institutional order.[76] In this sense, Greek *demokratia* can be compared to universal suffrage in western Europe in the nineteenth and twentieth centuries CE. In liberal democracies such as France, the United Kingdom, Belgium, the Netherlands, or Denmark, political rights had always been dependent on specific qualifications, and even when after a while all qualifications (wealth, education, etc.) together added up to including virtually all adult citizens, this situation was still considered essentially different from the kind of universal suffrage which by definition belonged to every citizen, without any qualification. In ancient Greece, the radical form of democracy with allotment involving the entire populace was, likewise, perceived as a phenomenon on an essentially different scale than just an enlargement of the group entitled to political agency.

Cyrene, Tauric Chersonesos, Naxos on Sicily, Syracuse [*petalismos*; Diod. 11.86.4–87.6] etc.) is later than the introduction of the practice in Athens; in some cases, Athenian influence is very likely, but independent origins cannot always be ruled out.

[74] Hdt. 5.37–38: in 499 the tyrant Aristagoras of Miletos gives up his position and installs *isonomia* for his own city and next in other Ionian cities, as the starting point of the revolt; 6.131: Cleisthenes creates the new *phylai* and the democracy (Κλεισθένης τε ὁ τὰς φυλὰς καὶ τὴν δημοκρατίην Ἀθηναίοισι καταστήσας); 6.43.3: the Persian commander Mardonios installed *demokratiai* in various Greek cities in Ionia, which apparently had returned to tyrannies after Aristagoras's attempts at *isonomia*. In all these cases, Herodotus applies mid-fifth-century labels for much earlier *politeiai*, which were not necessarily real democracies.
[75] Robinson (2011) 4.
[76] Giangiulio (2015) 10, 45–48.

Even if the political movements of the later sixth and early fifth centuries did not yet establish full democracies, the growing political salience of the *demos* in some *poleis* was unmistakable. Reflections of this shift appear in the political vocabulary of the time, as summarized by Daniela Cammack: "*demos* indicated all those who participated in politics through a collective agent" and more poignantly "the (common) people in assembly... in contradistinction from those who had personal political significance.... *Demokratia* was born when the balance of power tipped towards the assembly, away from those who (among other things) addressed it."[77]

In reaction to this democratizing trend, in many *poleis* the elite solidified itself into an oligarchy.[78] The empowerment of the *demos* increased the danger to their own ranks: if one of them made common cause with the *demos*, he might establish a tyranny or a democracy. To counter this threat, the oligarchic elites reacted with a dual policy: first, they set policies in motion to render the *demos* powerless, either by keeping them out of the political way entirely, or by manipulating the proceedings of the scarce assembly meetings. Second, in contrast to the archaic age when they had preferred the competition among themselves to prevail, now the elites deliberately closed ranks and kept a balance of power by policies reinforcing equality within their own group.

Oligarchic power-sharing became based on strict control of conduct, consensus-building by bringing issues *es to meson* ("to the middle"), secret ballots, and use of the lot for rotating the offices among the restricted group.[79] Oligarchic political discourse around an ideology of equality was cast in terms of *isos* and cognates—just as in democracies—but it applied only to their own confined group.[80] Simonton argues that the idea of equality among oligarchs also differed from that in democracies, in that "oligarchic equality is fiercely individualistic, with each oligarch viewing himself as indispensable *qua* concrete personality."[81] Among such individuals, drawing lots could be an effective means to reduce power display and overt competitiveness, and over time the rotation of office would implement the *isotes* among them, in the same way as among all citizens in democracies.

In the classical age many *poleis* unraveled, spawning oligarchic and democratic factions openly opposed to each other, which led to recurring regime changes from democracy to oligarchy, sometimes alternating with tyrannies and

---

[77] Cammack (2019) 53, 60.
[78] Simonton (2017).
[79] Simonton (2017) 75–106. On the "middle" see p. 312.
[80] *Isos/isotes* recognized as the leading principle in oligarchies: Isoc. 3.15; Dem. 20.108; Plut. *Mor.* 827b, with Simonton (2017) 76–79. Simonton (2017) 77, 81 notes that Thucydides is the main source for *isonomia* vocabulary in the Boiotian *koinon* after the battle of Coronea in 447, notably Thebes.
[81] Simonton (2017) 79. Cf. Cammack's description earlier: the *demos* in contradistinction from those who had individual political significance.

back again.[82] Against this convulsive backdrop, Athens proved to be an exceptionally stable *polis*: in two hundred years of democracy, it knew one internal oligarchic coup (in 411) and one oligarchic regime imposed from outside (in 404, but wholeheartedly embraced by the oligarchic faction). Over time, not only the number of democratic regimes in Greece increased, but also their duration.[83] But in the Hellenistic era few *poleis* and other political constellations that were called or called themselves a democracy resembled the political system of classical Athens. After the fourth century, most democracies came in various forms of elite prominence supported by the *demos*. Christian Mann observes that from the fourth century on, *demokratia* became a positive value term, as the only legitimate *politeia*, regardless of the real political structure of a constitution.[84] *Demokratia* referred to a republican *politeia*, free from a single ruler, and this use of *demokratia* applied not only to *poleis*.[85] The Achaean League, of an undoubted aristocratic-oligarchic nature, was called "democratic" by Polybius, because the Achaeans had created their federation of their own free will, not forced by a tyrant or Hellenistic monarch, according to Peter Scholz.[86]

Returning now from these political developments to drawing lots for office, it becomes clear that the picture Aristotle provides in the *Politics* of the lot as a self-evident method, just as "normal" as election, reflects the situation in the classical age, hence roughly from 480 to the late fourth century, when drawing lots had become apparently quite common both in oligarchies and in democracies. But as we saw earlier, in the archaic age until the late sixth century, whereas the use of the lot in other domains was widespread, allotment for office was extremely rare—the only certain case being the *Tamiai* (treasurers) at Athens. So what happened in the interim decades? When, where, and how was allotment for office adopted? Was just one *polis*, notably Athens, the example for others, or did the practice emerge more or less spontaneously everywhere? And on what scale?

The historical spread of drawing lots for office has hardly been investigated, if at all, perhaps because historians by and large assumed that the practice followed the spread of democracy. Scholars searching for the origins of democracy in the sixth century have proposed two major candidates: Athens with the Cleisthenic

---

[82] A good impression of the volatility of Greek political regimes in the classical age results from comparing the list of oligarchic regimes in Simonton (2017) 287–290, with the list of democracies in Robinson (2011) 248–250, and the overall pattern of transitions and regimes in Fleck and Hanssen (2018). For an analysis of the political processes and the violence of these transitions, see Gehrke (1985); Gray (2015).

[83] Simonton (2017) 287–290: from the sixth to the fourth centuries, oligarchies slightly decreased in number and lasted ever shorter periods. For Hellenistic Athens and other democratic *politeiai*, see Ma (2018).

[84] Mann (2012) 21–22.
[85] Giangiulio (2015) 77.
[86] Scholz (2012) 35–36.

politeia, and the western colonies. With Athens to be discussed later, we begin with the other candidate.

Since the *poleis* of Magna Graecia were founded on the basis of equal First Lots (*protoi kleroi*) distributed by lot, some scholars have argued that they were also the birthplace of democracy, with *isonomia* and *isegoria* (equal opportunity to speak publicly) already in place in the early archaic age.[87] Attractive as this idea might be, the evidence nonetheless points in a different direction. Soon after the egalitarian land distribution, social and economic inequality and competitive behavior among the elite were as pronounced in the *poleis* of Sicily and southern Italy as in mainland and eastern Greece.[88] The vast meeting places of the *demos*, such as at Metapontum for eight thousand people, do not imply the access of the *demos* to political offices or other essential criteria of democracy, but they could rather serve as the stage where the elite could address the *demos* and solicit their consent.[89] Greek tyrannies of single elite men and their families, with support by a strong *demos*, dominated the political landscape in the western Mediterranean for longer stretches of time than in mainland Greece, and persisted even far into the classical era. Oligarchies emerged in the archaic age in Syracuse, Kroton, Lokroi, and Rhegion, and seem to have existed in Megara Hyblaia, Selinous, and Gela before turning into tyrannies in the late sixth century.[90]

While there is therefore no ground for assuming political equality in the *poleis* of western Greece before the late sixth century, in the decades around 500 several *poleis* in the region partook in the wave of democratization visible across the Greek world. Vestiges of the egalitarian ideology typical of the foundation of the colonies probably supported this trend and seem to have been a particularly strong influence when subaltern groups raised their voice for the redistribution of land and inclusion in the citizen body. In the wake of the recurrent violence, *poleis* had to refound themselves or change their political regime. In his perceptive study of Greek democracies, Maurizio Giangiulio emphasizes that the process of *polis* consolidation—by integrating citizens and other inhabitants, by the formation of political coherence, and by reducing the internal conflicts—was a long, difficult, and often violent path. Democracy was anything but an automatic outcome: it came about in some *poleis* where incisive military events and rapid socioeconomic growth together profoundly reshaped the traditional structures of society. Establishing democracy marked not just an institutional change, but first and foremost a societal makeover of the kind that emerged

---

[87] For this debate, De Angelis (2016) 173–79. For the distribution of the first *kleroi* by lot, see ch. 6.2.2-3; 6.3.1-4..

[88] For the socioeconomic conditions and distribution of wealth in the *poleis* of Sicily, see De Angelis (2016) 147–193. See also ch. 6.3.4. The elites were, however, open to accepting some non-Greeks among themselves as citizens; ibid., 178.

[89] For the meeting places as signs of democracy, cf. McInerney (2004) 25–26.

[90] Simonton (2017) 287; De Angelis (2016) 174–177.

only in the fifth century. The most prominent examples are on the mainland of Greece Athens and Argos, and in western Greece Kroton, Taras, Syracuse, and Thourioi.[91]

In sum, based on our current evidence, western Greece cannot be regarded as the "origin" of democracy, and even less so the source of drawing lots for office in the archaic age. For the picture of how allotment for office became widespread in ancient Greece in the classical age, we need to compare the situation in Athens and in other democracies. So before turning to the extensive evidence from Athens, to complete our overview we should first examine how the lot worked in oligarchies.

8.2.1 Allotment for *polis* office in oligarchies

Overall, oligarchic regimes produced notably fewer inscribed documents than democracies, for the obvious reason that informing anyone beyond their own narrow circle was rarely in their interest.[92] As a result, there is no epigraphical evidence for allotment in oligarchies; hence, we must make do with other sources, which are few, both in absolute terms and in proportion to the number and variety of oligarchic regimes.

The most outspoken viewpoint is presented in the *Rhetoric to Alexander*, traditionally ascribed to Aristotle but more recently attributed to Anaximenes of Lampsakos (second half of the fourth century). In Book Two, the following passage about distribution of offices deserves to be quoted nearly in full. First the author tackles the question of democracies:

> [II.14] In democracies the legislation must be done so as to allot the minor offices, that is, the majority of them—since this is least likely to cause strife [*stasis*]—and to elect the most important ones from the common people [from all, *plethos*]. In this way the people are sovereign in giving honors [*timai*] to whomever they may wish and will not envy those who receive them, and the more prominent people will exercise more respectability in the knowledge that having a good reputation among the citizens will not lack rewards [*telos*] for them. [15] . . . We must guard that the laws deter the populace from plotting against those who have property and arouse in the wealthy an ambition to take on the costs of public services willingly. [16] One might organize this in this way if some offices were actually reserved by law for those with wealth in return

---

[91] Giangiulio (2015).
[92] Simonton (2017) 145 n.138 lists a total of twelve decrees by oligarchic regimes across the classical age, with further references. None of these indicates anything about allotment.

for their taking on costs for the public and, of the poor, if farmers and shippers were privileged over those who hang about in the marketplace. In this way the wealthy will willingly do services for the city, and the common people will have an appetite for hard work and not malicious litigation. [17] In addition, there must be strong laws—and great penalties against those transgressing them—that there be no land redistribution and no confiscation of the property of those who have done public services.[93]

Next, the author deals with distribution of offices in oligarchies:

[18] In oligarchies, however, the laws must distribute the offices equally [*ex isou*] among those who share [*metecho*] in government [*politeia*], to allot most of them, and to vote on the most important, with a secret ballot, with oaths and the greatest accuracy. [19] In oligarchies the penalties must be very great for those attempting to abuse any of the citizens. The common people are not as annoyed at being deprived of public offices as they are at being grievously abused. It is necessary to resolve differences among citizens as quickly as possible and not to delay or to have a mob from the countryside collect in the city. The common people gain strength from such meetings and overturn oligarchies. [20] One must say in general that in democracies the laws prevent the many from conspiring against the property of the wealthy, and in oligarchies they discourage those who share in the government from abusing the weaker and persecuting the citizens.[94]

The text is prescriptive rather than descriptive, but the methods the author recommends are attested in historical oligarchic policies.[95] All measures are geared to keeping the ruling elite together, such as imposing equality by lot, and coherence by secret ballot: no open disagreement should split the ruling group. Especially interesting is the advice not to antagonize the *demos* by abusing them; the *demos* will not mind being excluded from office, but if they are maltreated, they will turn their mass against the wealthy few and topple the oligarchy.

Aristotle observes that quite a number of oligarchies were indeed overturned from within, notably due to the system of elections for office: some of the ruling oligarchs canvassed the electorate for their favors like demagogues so as to effectively eject their peers from power.[96] This strategy was an oligarchic variation on

---

[93] [Arist.] *Rhet.Al.* 1424a10–35; 2.13–17, trans. R. Mayhew, D. C. Mirhady, Loeb-ed.
[94] [Arist.] *Rhet.Al.* 1424a10–35; 2.18–20, trans. Loeb-ed. 18: ἀπονέμειν ἐξ ἴσου πᾶσι τοῖς τῆς πολιτείας μετέχουσι.
[95] See further for this Simonton (2017).
[96] Arist. *Pol.* 1305b23–1306b16; he mentions historical examples from Athens (404), Larisa, Abydos, Herkleia Pontica, Syracuse, Amphipolis, and many more.

the model of decampment-for-tyranny, and drawing lots for the offices prevented this kind of internal competition. For actual uses of the lot in oligarchies, however, the evidence remains very scarce. Apparently, in Thebes—an oligarchy from 446 until 382—some offices were appointed by allotment.[97] Meanwhile, Heraia in Arcadia maintained long-standing ties to oligarchic Sparta. Although the city's constitution is not altogether clear, it seems to have been only moderately oligarchic. Offices were elected, but at some point—according to Aristotle—the *demos* became so fed up with being solicited for votes that they opted for an allotment system for office appointments; this switch has been dated to around 370.[98]

After several decades of democracy with drawing of lots (see section 8.2.2.4), in the year 411 Athens was abruptly taken over by an oligarchy-leaning group. The new regime is relatively well covered in the *Ath.Pol.*, and both Thucydides and the actual deeds and plans for the future provide considerable insights into oligarchic policies brought into play, including the use of the lot.[99] The oligarchs created a council by election, now of four hundred instead of the previous democratic five hundred, which began by selecting *prytaneis* (chairmen) among themselves by lot, and by offering sacrifices—both of which pertain to procedures established in the democratic constitution.[100] Soon afterward, the new regime applied indirect elections to a select five thousand wealthy citizens who would henceforth be the politically active citizen body (the *politeuma*). These five thousand elected a hundred from among themselves to draw up a new constitution. As they saw it, the oligarchs were reestablishing the ancient constitution of Solon, a more robust form of democracy than the radical one that had prevailed until then.[101] However, by reducing the *politeuma* to about a fifth of the previous male citizen body on a substantial wealth criterion, the ruling group was decidedly oligarchic, albeit perhaps only moderately so.

The oligarchic constitution-for-the future provided for around fifty offices, among which the Nine Archons, the main military commanders, and the *Tamiai* of Athena and the *Tamiai* of the Other Gods (a financial board instituted in the late 430s) were to be elected by the council from a list of *prokritoi* (preselected candidates) and all other offices to be selected by lot, probably from the five thousand. Of the five thousand, those persons over age thirty were to divide themselves into four subgroups, which clearly were not

---

[97] Plut. *De gen. Socr.* 597a (ὁ κυαμευτὸς ἄρχων).
[98] Arist. *Pol.* 1303a14–17. Date: Hansen and Nielsen (2004) 514.
[99] Thuc. 8.67–70; *Ath.Pol.* 29–31. The accounts differ in details, but the overall picture is the same.
[100] Thuc. 8.70.
[101] *Ath.Pol.* 29.3; 31.1: a council of four hundred *kata ta patria* (as was ancestral). See also Endnote 5.

the old Ionian *phylai* but probably derived from the Boiotian *koinon*, likewise an oligarchic regime with a property qualification for the *politeuma*.[102] The four groups were each to draw lots to form a council—without payment for office—and the lot was again to decide which of these four councils was to be in power for a year.[103] Furthermore, five men were drawn by lot from the council to decide the outcome of voting, and one of them drawn (again by lot) to put motions to the vote. The five also drew lots among those wanting to bring something before the council as to who should speak first. The leading oligarchs brought this plan to the assembly, meeting in an exceptional place outside the city, who accepted the proposal, but Thucydides recounts in his inimitable manner how the assembly was won over by intimidation, violence, manipulation, and discord.[104] The planned *politeia* never became operational, for after increasing violence and dissension, the oligarchy was dissolved under pressure from its democratic opponents. In many respects, the oligarchic "*politeia* for the future" resembled the Athenian democratic *politeia* but with a restricted *politeuma* instead of the entire male citizen body, and with all *misthos* (payment) for office canceled.

Whereas this oligarchic *politeia* remained only a plan, a similar type of oligarchy was imposed on Athens in reality when, after the Lamian War (323–322), Athens had to accept incisive changes to its *politeia* from its Macedonian overlord Antipater. Inscriptions show that the main institutions were still in place, but the *politeuma* (active citizenship) was based on a census of two thousand drachmai, removing twenty-two thousand citizens from active participation in the offices.[105] In 317 Kassander appointed Demetrius of Phaleron to regulate the city, who extended the census to include those holding one thousand drachmai property—wider than the previous regime, but still oligarchic compared to the full democracy.[106] After Demetrius's removal in 307 by Demetrius Poliorketes, Athens retained its main institutions but was, time and again, the target of military interventions by the various imperial powers, who would on occasion also interfere with the city's governance. The defeat of Athens and its allies in the

---

[102] Rhodes (2006) 162, 245; Hansen and Nielsen (2004) 432–458. Boiotia, in the late sixth century loosely connected, consolidated into a coherent federation that existed from 446 to 171, interrupted for short intervals. For the constitution of the federation in 395, see *Hell. Ox*. 19. Some offices in the Boiotian confederacy were elected (boiotarchs; Plut. *Pel*. 13.1); the members of the federal council may have been drawn by lot (Beck and Ganter [2015] 143).

[103] *Ath.Pol*. 30; the text is corrupt here in several places and not altogether clear; see Rhodes, *CAAP* ad loc.

[104] Thuc. 8.65–66.

[105] Diod. 18.18.4–5.

[106] Diod. 18.74.3. Demetrius's regime, characterized at the time as oligarchic, was more in accordance with the democratic constitution than either its predecessor or its successor; cf. Tracy (2003) 11–13; full discussion O'Sullivan (2009) 105–163.

Chremonidean War (267–261) brought a period of strong Macedonian domination in the city (262–229); while some of the *polis*'s institutions continued to function, how the *politeuma* was defined and how citizens were selected for office is unclear, but a full democracy it certainly was not.

Founded in the seventh century, Cyrene had a rather extraordinary constitution compared to other Greek *poleis*, with the presence of a king or queen (the descendants of the first founder Battos), besides the regular *polis* institutions of council and assembly. In the mid-sixth century, Demonax of Mantineia refounded the regime and transferred most of the offices from the king to "the middle" (*meson*) of the people, either a limited circle of citizens or a wider group.[107] In this case, the resulting constitution was a moderate oligarchy, which after a violent upheaval was replaced by a democracy of sorts in 440, lasting until 401.[108] Ptolemy I provided a constitution for Cyrene in a decree (*diagramma*); it has often featured in debates about *politeiai* because it allegedly provided for sortition among a moderate oligarchy, but in fact the text does not offer any reliable evidence.[109]

In sum, there can be little doubt that drawing lots for office was a regular practice in the oligarchic regimes of the fifth and fourth centuries, but direct evidence of the practice in such regimes is extremely scarce. Moderate oligarchies could consist of a restricted but still sizeable *politeuma* with voting rights, or hold strictly limited access to the *polis* offices for only a small elite to be elected by a larger citizen body. Besides such elections, oligarchic groups could rotate offices among themselves by drawing lots, and one would expect such a practice as prevailing in more radical oligarchies whose policies were sidelining the *demos*. Drawing lots in the *politeia*-for-the-future of the oligarchs at Athens in 411 in some respects was a continuation of the democracy on a restricted scale, but the combination of a restricted census of the *politeuma*, elections for particular offices, and drawing lots for others may be quite like other oligarchies in the Greek world. Neither the *Ath.Pol.* nor Thucydides says explicitly that the oligarchs abolished the allotted *dikasteria*, but the course of events implies that they did so: the *dikasteria*, drawn by lot from all male citizens over thirty years of age and receiving payment for their sessions, embodied the core democratic control over magistrates in the democracy. So it is high time to examine when and how these and similar practices were established in the democracy itself.

---

[107] See section 8.2.2.3. For the "middle," see Introduction 7.
[108] Diod. 14.34.3–6, with Robertson (2010) 372–373; in ML 5. l.11, the fourth-century decree on *politeia* for the Thereans holding the foundation story of Cyrene, the *demos* made the decision.
[109] See Endnote 6.

8.2.2 Democratic Athens

8.2.2.1 Cleisthenes's constitution

Classical Athens has become exemplary for the wide-ranging use of the lot for *polis* office and for governance more widely. Athens, the comprehensive name of the city of Athens and its surrounding territory Attica, was an exceptional *polis* because it had one of the largest territories and the largest population of all *poleis*. In the fifth and fourth centuries, Athens became very wealthy, but it faced high costs for its public life and its recurrent warfare. It is also by far the best documented of all Greek *poleis* from the classical age onward. Due to its democratic constitution and a concomitant, relatively high literacy rate, Athens developed an unparalleled epigraphical habit, producing an incomparable amount of inscribed public documents from the fifth century far into the Imperial Roman period.[110] Furthermore, owing to its leading position as a cultural center and its climate of political debate, the city hosted an intellectual elite who created a wealth of literary, philosophical, and scholarly texts illuminating, directly or indirectly, the *polis* where they were written.

Many scholars regard Athens as the place of origin of democracy and Cleisthenes's reform of the political structure in 508/7 as the starting point of democratic selection for office by lot.[111] However, I argue that the full democracy with "allotment from all" came about more gradually than is usually thought, and that in that respect the notion of the "Cleisthenic" revolution in Athens might be misleading. The view that the shift to allotment of office was an innovation introduced by Cleisthenes deserves closer scrutiny, too: allotment as a means of selection for office was first introduced in the Solonian constitution, and we need to determine when and where it demonstrably came into use in Athens again, and on a wider scale.

For a historical account of Cleisthenes's reforms, we depend on two sources, Herodotus and the *Ath.Pol.*; close reading of both texts reveals that the latter made use of the first, but also of other sources.[112] Both authors relate how, after the fall of the dynasty of the tyrants (the Peisistratidai), the prominent men in Athens became embroiled in a struggle for power, in which Cleisthenes trumped his rival Isagoras by drawing the *demos* into his camp.[113] His strategy was a common one in archaic regime changes, as we saw earlier, and the increased political salience of the Athenian *demos* fits the broader trend of these years toward more

---

[110] Although oral and visual forms of communication remained influential far into the fourth century, Missiou (2011) convincingly shows the necessity of (low) literacy of the citizens for the democracy to function at all, at all levels of the *polis*.
[111] Hansen (1990; 1991); Kosmetatou (2013) 235–236.
[112] *Ath.Pol.* 19–22; Hdt. 5.66–69, 72–73. All details of how the system was implemented are known from epigraphical evidence.
[113] Hdt. 5.66: τὸν δῆμον προσεταιρίζεται. *Ath.Pol.* 20.1: προσηγάγετο τὸν δῆμον.

power for the *demos*.[114] Both authors tell that Cleisthenes reorganized the *demos* into ten new *phylai*.[115] But they diverge on his reasons for doing so. Herodotus claims that Cleisthenes acted on a combination of arrogance and opportunism in a bid to change the identity of the Athenians.[116] According to the *Ath.Pol.*, he wanted to mix all the citizens to give them a larger share in the *politeia*.[117] The facts about the new *politeia* reveal that the *Ath.Pol.* was much better informed than Herodotus and apparently drew on different sources for its account: the principal feature of Cleisthenes's intervention was the refoundation of the *polis* by the creation of ten new *phylai* to support a new *politeia*. The four Ionian *phylai* were not abolished, keeping their traditional functions for some cultic and judicial institutions, but they lost their roles as military and political units to the ten new *phylai*. The composition of the new *phylai* was highly complicated, in order to bring about a thorough mix of the citizen body, while simultaneously keeping anchorage in the traditional settlements of Attica.[118]

The basis of the new system was the deme (in Greek also *demos*): as a subunit of the Attic people (*demos*) it was first a social entity, but it was also attached to a geographical location, be it a village, small town, or part of the city of Athens. The association of the *demos* (people) with their *demos* (territory) was confirmed by the boundary markers of the deme's property.[119] Most of the 139 demes were traditional settlements or neighborhoods, though not all of them; in the creation of each deme, the size of its population was a factor.[120] The demes were spread over Attica, which Cleisthenes divided into three main regions: the City, the Inland,

---

[114] Hdt. 5.72 and *Ath.Pol.* 20.3-4 report that the *demos* took the initiative to oust Isagoras and his allies the Spartans with their king Kleomenes, and to recall Cleisthenes and others who had been exiled. Ober (1993) compares the agency of the *demos* and their reinvention of themselves as sovereign body to the French Revolution in 1789, whereas Grote (2016) 206 claims (without clear arguments) that the *demos*'s role was passive. Ismard (2010) 87-90, 117-121 deemphasizes Cleisthenes as the decisive agent and regards the reform as a redistribution of rights and duties in the frame of *isonomia*, comparable to the democratization in other *poleis* in the late sixth century. For a valuable analysis of the debate on Cleisthenes, Węcowski (2022) 189-195.

[115] *Ath.Pol.* 21; Hdt. 5.69.

[116] Hdt. 5.69 says that Cleisthenes despised the Athenian people, whose help he enlisted only to win his political struggle, and since he despised the Ionians even more, he abolished the Ionian *phylai* and gave the Athenians a new identity (see section 8.2.2.3, on predecessors). This erroneous and incredible story reveals that for accounts about Cleisthenes, Herodotus drew not only on (pro-)Alkmaionid sources, but also on traditions hostile to the "accursed" family; cf. Thomas (1989) 238-282.

[117] *Ath.Pol.* 20.1: ἀποδιδοὺς τῶι πλήθει τὴν πολιτείαν; handing over the *politeia* to the mass of the people; 22.2: πρῶτον μὲν συνένειμε πάντας εἰς δέκα φυλὰς ἀντὶ τῶν τεττάρων, ἀναμεῖξαι βοθλόμενος, ὅπως μετάσχωσι πλείους τῆς πολιτείας. He first distributed all (citizens) over ten *phylai* instead of four, because he wanted to mix them thoroughly, so that more (citizens) would share in the *politeia*. Arist. *Pol.* 1319b20 follows *Ath.Pol.*'s account.

[118] For this mixing, cf. Cecchet (2017) 54-61, and earlier, Introduction 8 and 9, and section 6.2 of this volume.

[119] Deme-property: Papazarkadas (2011) 128-129. On the recurrence of the term *demos*, reinforcing the solidarity within the *demos*, Osborne ([1990] 2010) esp. 40-42.

[120] *Ath.Pol.* 21.5: "[Cleisthenes] gave some of the demes their name after their localities, but others from their founders, because not all demes corresponded to the places."

and the Coast. Each of these three regions was subdivided into ten parts, forming thirty parts-of-thirds (*trittyes*) in all.[121] While in most of these *trittyes* the demes lay close to each other and formed local units of sorts, in a few *trittyes* the demes lay at a considerable distance from each other—a fact indicating that, like the demes, the *trittyes* were subgroups of the citizen body in the first place and that the geographical location was secondary.[122] Coherence in the *trittyes* came about through meetings held in a theater situated in the *trittys*, and they assembled in the city at so-called markers, probably for military purposes and grain distribution.[123] The ten new *phylai* were composed by combining one *trittys* from the City, one from the Inland, and one from the Coast in each *phyle*. Each *phyle* contributed fifty men to a new council, now of five hundred members. Assuming that Solon had indeed created a council of four hundred consisting of one hundred members from the four Ionian *phylai*, Cleisthenes adapted the Solonian model to the new structure, with the new council of five hundred members, namely fifty members from ten *phylai*.[124] The number 10 now became a regular number in Athenian governance representing the ten *phylai*, until the introduction of two extra *phylai* in the Hellenistic era.[125]

The members of the council (*bouleutai*) were selected in the demes, in numbers proportionate to the size of the deme's population. For instance, the small City deme Plotheia sent only one man to the council; the mid-sized Coastal deme Thorikos sent five; and the large Inland deme Acharnai fifteen. With fifty *bouleutai* per *phyle* from across the demes, the population size of a deme must have played a role in its allocation to a *trittys*. Some scholars think that this number was estimated and that the Cleisthenic construction meant the beginning of citizen registers, while others argue that the system depended on an already existing citizen registration.[126] In any case, John Traill's reconstruction reveals the intricate balance of the distribution of demes over *trittyes* and of the latter over *phylai*.[127]

---

[121] Traill (1986). If the large deme of Acharnai is treated as a split deme, the total number is 140 demes; see Traill (1986) 133–134.

[122] That membership of the group prevailed over geographical location in deme-membership is borne out by the fact that if an Athenian moved to another part of Attica, he kept his original deme-affiliation (demotic).

[123] Theater in each *trittys* as locus of *trittys* coherence, Paga (2010); markers in the city, Raubitschek (1956); Traill (1986) 112–113.

[124] This is confirmed by *Ath.Pol.* 21.3.

[125] The decimal system itself was not new, nor its use for *polis* government: Greek numerals have a base of ten, and Solon had applied the decimal system to the election of four times ten candidates for the allotment of the archons.

[126] Faraguna (2015) for the debate, arguing in favor of existing registers.

[127] Traill (1986). Over time, the size of the demes changed, and the bouleutic quota were adjusted in the constitutional revisions of 403 and 307/6; see Rhodes (1972) 8–12; Hansen (1986) 51–69. For Traill's map of the Cleisthenic structure, see http://www.agathe.gr/democracy/political_organizatio n_of_attica.html.

The new *phylai* were composed in a very different way from the old four Ionian ones. In each *phyle*, citizens from the three regions of Attica that previously formed the home base of competing political factions of the elite were now mixed. Beside this geographical mixture, Cleisthenes also brought a social mixture about in the citizen body itself. By the end of the sixth century, the inhabitants of Attica held a variety of claims to citizenship. Most of them were citizens based on descent according to the laws of Solon; numerous immigrants had been accepted as citizens due to their craftsmanship or other assets; an unknown number of Athenians who had returned to Attica after Solon's termination of debt slavery but had not recovered their lands; various citizens who returned to Attica after exile and had to find their place again; and many others, who had settled in Attica, for instance, as mercenaries.[128] Although the details of the process are unclear, Cleisthenes apparently enrolled as "citizens" all free people living in a deme who wished to be included, regardless of their background.[129] It was a true refoundation of the citizen body, in a new system that was to last for centuries. Both in the *phylai* and in the demes, the old and the new citizens were all expected to cooperate in religion, in the army, and in the political system. Implementing the new system took a few years: the Cleisthenic council met for the first time, swearing the bouleutic oath, in 501/0.[130]

8.2.2.2 Did Cleisthenes reintroduce allotment for political office?

According to the *Ath.Pol.*, Cleisthenes aimed at a "larger share in the *politeia*" for the *demos*. What exactly did this "larger share" in access to political power entail? The new political structure, cutting through traditional allegiances and dependencies, clearly undermined the established power relations and weakened the grip of the elite on the institutions.[131] If Cleisthenes also introduced allotment for the main offices "from all," as is usually supposed, this would certainly mean a real empowerment of the *demos*. That said, there are quite compelling reasons to doubt this was the case.

In Cleisthenes's *politeia*, the political power of the *demos* was embodied first of all in the legislative sovereignty of its assembly, explicitly attested in the "enactment clause" of *polis* decrees, namely the formula stating which sovereign body made the decision. Some early decrees feature only the *demos* as the legislative

---

[128] For the debate about this part of the reform, see Endnote 7.
[129] *Ath.Pol.* 21 states that "καὶ δημότας ἐποίησεν ἀλλήλων τοὺς οἰκοῦντας ἐν ἑκάστῳ τῶν δήμων, ἵνα μὴ πατρόθεν προσαγορεύοντες ἐξελέγχωσιν τοὺς νεοπολίτας, ἀλλὰ τῶν δήμων ἀναγορεύωσιν" ("and he made all those living in each deme fellow-demesmen of each other, and to avoid drawing attention to the new-made citizens let them address them not by their fathers' names, but officially by their demes"). This can only partly be correct, because the common use of demotics only began in the later fifth century (except on *ostraka*) and became normal in the fourth century.
[130] *Ath.Pol.* 22.2; cf. Rhodes (1972) 210.
[131] See Valdés Guía (2019a) for the grip of the elite on military and political institutions in sixth-century Athens.

authority; others mention both the council, as probouleutic body, and the *demos*; later in the fifth century, both the council and the *demos* normally appear in the enactment clause.[132] The sovereignty of the *demos* was also expressed in their right to hold an ostracism, that is, sending an individual citizen into exile for ten years if they feared he aspired to too much power. Ostracism is a form of "negative election," in this case a secret ballot with *ostraka* (sherds) inscribed with the name of the candidate.[133] With this instrument, clearly meant to reduce inter-elite conflict and prevent attempts at tyranny, it was the *demos* who decided who was to leave the *polis* for a fixed period, instead of the feuding elite parties who exiled each other for an uncertain amount of time, as had previously been the case. Once a year it was up to the assembly to decide whether to hold an ostracism, and for an affirmative answer a quorum of six thousand citizens was required to be legitimate; in the second stage, when the actual *ostraka* were cast, the people were to assemble en masse (*plethos*) in the agora.[134]

What about the major *polis* offices? For the Nine Archons, Cleisthenes reinstituted the means of selection that had come about a few years after Solon but had been abandoned by the tyrants: election from the top two classes through a show of hands (*cheirotonia*) by the *phylai* in assembly. Since there were now ten *phylai*, a secretary (*grammateus*) was added to make up a body of ten, each *phyle* providing an archon. In 487 the Athenians changed the procedure: a group of five hundred candidates was elected from the upper two classes—still per *phyle*, but now in the demes—and from this group the archons were selected by lot.[135] With this procedure, the Athenians reinstituted Solon's *klerosis ek prokriton*.

A new office was the *strategos*, a military leadership that remained an elected office with unlimited possibility of reelection until the end of the democracy.[136] In 501/0, when the Cleisthenic council of five hundred met for the first time, the Athenians also began electing the *strategoi*. Although the *Ath.Pol.* does not say so explicitly, the *strategoi* were also probably already part of Cleisthenes's system, considering the crucial military functions of the *phylai* right from the

---

[132] *IG* I³ 1, on *klerouchoi* on Salamis, ca. 510–500, and *IG* I³ 4 (485) on the conduct on the Acropolis, feature the *demos*; in the damaged first line of *IG* I³ 2 the council seems to be included in the enactment clause.

[133] Whether the law on ostracism was part of Cleisthenes's system or was introduced in 488/7 when the first ostracism took place—namely of Hipparchos, a relative of Peisistratos—is deeply debated. Harding (1994) 94–97, Forsdyke (2005) 281–284, and Węcowski (2022) 40–64 offer clear analyses of the problem, on textual and historical grounds, respectively, all arguing for a Cleisthenic date.

[134] Węcowski (2022) 124–176.

[135] *Ath.Pol.* 22.5; the ms. of *Ath.Pol.* has "five hundred elected," which some take to be a scribal error for "a hundred" (see Rhodes *CAAP ad loc.*), but yet seems correct, both compared to other bodies of five hundred elected in the demes (cf. Kroll [1972] 85–86) and because five hundred is the more plausible number for candidates elected in the 139 demes (cf. De Ste. Croix [2004a] 218).

[136] *Ath.Pol.* 22.2. In *Ath.Pol.* 4, the *strategoi* already figure in the "constitution of Draco," but this can be discarded as erroneous (see note 6). *Contra* Develin (1989) 3.

beginning.[137] Each *phyle* elected its own *strategos*; over time, the system became more flexible, probably because military leadership weighed heavier than any other criterion, but the number of *strategoi* remained ten.[138] Certainly in the beginning, but still throughout the classical age, *strategoi* tended to be drawn from the elite. Claire Taylor has shown that in democratic Athens, elections were biased toward candidates from the City demes, where the most affluent and best-educated citizens were living right in the public eye, many with a famous pedigree, and were the most experienced in military and political matters; allotted offices, by contrast, were filled by Athenians from all across Attica.[139] In Cleisthenes's *politeia*, in sum, the leading offices—namely the archonships and *strategia*—were still in the hands of the elite. Archons were selected first by election and after 487 by a combined system of election and the drawing of lots, whereas the *strategoi* were elected directly.

Did the council provide a "larger share" for the *demos* through its method of selection, or in terms of social class? In the second half of the fifth and in the fourth century this was definitely the case, when the members of the council (*bouleutai*) were selected by lot from all male citizens, organized per deme.[140] But what was the situation like in the first half of the fifth century? For the answer we have only circumstantial evidence. The *Ath.Pol.* does not reveal anything about the selection of the *bouleutai* for the new Cleisthenic council. Silence in our sources can never be decisive, but since the *Ath.Pol.* is always keen to mention the means of selection of political bodies—and especially any significant changes—this silence about the council seems to imply that the means of selection did not change from the previous practice, namely that the *bouleutai* were still elected. Only the place where the election was held shifted from the *phylai* in assembly, to the demes, fitting the new distribution of *bouleutai* per deme. The probouleutic function of the council did not change either.[141] As to social class, from our reconstruction it emerges that access to the Solonian council had been limited to the top three classes. If Cleisthenes wanted to enlarge the share of the *demos* in the council, he had to remove this restriction, extending eligibility

---

[137] Van Wees (2004) 99–101; Valdés Guía (2019a). At Marathon (490), Miltiades was one of the ten *strategoi*.

[138] Two *strategoi* from the same tribe are attested in several years beginning in 441/0 with Pericles of Cholargos and Glaukon of Kerameis; see Taylor (2007), esp. table 1. According to L. Mitchell (2000), the election of generals, including such doubles, remained *phyle*-based until at least 357/6, and the election may have included a preselection (*prokrisis*).

[139] Taylor (2007), esp. Table 2. Kierstead and Klapaukh (2018) did not find a statistically significant correlation between attested wealth and regions of demes, but they did find an overrepresentation of wealth in the intramural City deme of Kydathenaion and in the area between the mountains of Aigaleos, Pentele, and Hymettos, around the city.

[140] Thuc. 8.69.4: the allotted *bouleutai* are removed from office by the oligarchs. For the fourth c., *Ath.Pol.* 43.2; 62.1.

[141] Rhodes (1972) 208–210.

also to the thetic class, which included, as explained earlier, everyone below the *zeugitai*, and therefore not only the poor but also some reasonably well-off citizens. According to Valdés Guía, the *zeugitai* were a substantial group. On this circumstantial evidence, the assertion that Cleisthenes removed the formal restrictions for access to the council is plausible.[142]

If in the new *politeia* the participation of all citizens in the council was indeed possible in principle, in practice it was impossible for the lower classes, simply because they lacked the means or the time to do so. P. J. Rhodes observes that no evidence states explicitly that only the upper three classes were eligible for the new council, but that the practical and financial constraints tended to restrict attendance to the more affluent.[143] Such hindrances still applied in the second half of the fifth century. By then, the *polis* remunerated offices with *misthos* (payment), and for *bouleutai* this remuneration probably began in the 430s.[144] The *misthos* itself was very modest, considering that by then the duties of the council had increased into a time-consuming office. In the fourth century, when certainly no formal restrictions applied, wealthy citizens were still overrepresented among the *bouleutai*.[145] Basically, only the more affluent citizens could afford to take the necessary time off to attend council proceedings. If the conclusions reached so far are tenable—that in the Cleisthenic *politeia* there were no formal restrictions for access to the council and that in the first decades of the fifth century the councilors who could afford to hold office were elected in the demes—when did allotment begin?

The most plausible moment that selection by lot of the *bouleutai* was introduced can only be reconstructed by combining, on the one hand, a series of inscribed decrees with regulations concerning Erythrai (a city on the coast of Asia Minor), and on the other hand, the political reform of Athens associated with Ephialtes in the late 460s.

An Athenian ally, Erythrai defected in the late 450s and again in the 430s, but in both cases it eventually returned into the Athenian orbit.[146] It would seem that

---

[142] *Contra* Blösel (2014), who argues that until the very end of the democracy (322), *thetes* could not stand for selection for office, including the council, because formally the Solonian property-classes and the exclusion of the *thetes* from office had never been abolished. However, institutions were allowed to lapse or change, rather than be formally terminated; without at least a substantial, and probably the more affluent, part of the *thetes*, the democratic *boule* could not function.

[143] Rhodes (1972) 2–5.

[144] The earliest evidence dates to the 420s (*IG* I³ 82); Pericles instituted *misthos* for the *dikastêria* in the 440s or perhaps 430s, rather than in the 450s; *Ath.Pol.* 27; Plut. *Per.* 9.4; with Blok (2009b) 148 n.23; for a list of other payments from the 430s, see Blok (2015) 93–94. In the 320s, *bouleutai* received 5 obols a day, less than attendance of the assembly remunerated with 1 or 1½ drachma (= 6–9 obols) and less than a day's wage of an unskilled laborer, who received 1 to 1½ drachma; a skilled man, 2 to 2½ (= 12–15 obols).

[145] For overrepresentation among *bouleutai* of families able to pay for a triere as a liturgy (public financial service), costing at least a talent a year, Rhodes (1972) 5–6.

[146] The series consist of *Erythrae* 33 (*IEryth.* 2; OR 122); *IG* I³ 14 (OR 121), *IG* I³ 15, and *IG* I³ 16; see also *AIUK* 4.2 no. 2. Originally, all were dated to the late 450s, but for *IG* I³ 14, 15, and 16, Moroo

the Athenians obliged Erythrai to apply reforms that were based on institutional systems existing in Athens. In what is possibly the earliest decree—of Erythrai itself—the extant text mentions offices allotted "by the bean" as well as (elected) *timai*, together meaning "all offices."[147] Exactly which allotted offices are intended here cannot be retrieved from the damaged text, but the decree covers jurisdiction and requires the judges to take the same oath as the council. In a separate decree—probably of a later date and issued by Athens—the council at Erythrai is (re)instituted, consisting of 120 allotted men no younger than thirty years of age and a *dokimasia* (scrutiny of qualifications) to be held before entering office.[148] All decrees together suggest that the constitution in the later decrees is the same as or highly similar to that in the earlier decree. This would mean that in the late 450s Erythrai had a council of allotted male citizens of at least thirty years of age, who took the oath upon entering office. All of this is so similar to the setup in Athens that we may assume Erythrai followed the Athenian example—whether of its own free will or not. This reconstruction provides a *terminus ante* for the allotment of the *bouleutai* in Athens before the 450s. Below we shall see why the reforms of the late 460s are the most plausible candidate for this change.

The foregoing overview allows us to roughly estimate what effectively made Cleisthenes's system democratic or *isonomos* and what did not. On the *isonomia* side, the major change was the creation of the said ten new *phylai* based on a geographical and social mixture, integrating the Attic countryside and the city on a basis of equality. In the demes, the new system made the socioeconomic classes—along with the old and the new citizens—cooperate in political and religious activities close to home. This liaison was particularly relevant for the elections of candidates for the archonships and of members of the new *boule* that took place in the demes. Furthermore, the *demos* acquired full sovereignty in matters of legislation: for any new law to be enacted, the assembly had to be consulted and its approval ascertained through vote. Lastly, while eligibility for the *boule* was probably no longer formally restricted to the three uppermost classes, in practical terms it was feasible only for those with the time and financial means to attend the council. Conversely, all major offices remained formally in the hands of the elite. The archons and *strategoi* were elected offices; only the *tamiai* (treasurers) were still drawn by lot from the wealthiest class, as instituted by Solon. As far as we know, the courts were still those of the Areopagos and the

---

(2014) recently argued persuasively for a date in 435/4. The four texts do not necessarily all belong to the same events. I regard *Erythrae* 33 (*IEryth.* 2; OR 122) as belonging to the late 450s and the other three to the 430s. The latter are clearly imposed by Athens; the first one seems to be a decision of Erythrai itself, but the terminology of the jury court resembles that of Athens.

[147] *Erythrae* 33 (*IEryth.* 2 [OR 122], A 1); the same combination occurs in B 25–31.
[148] *IG* I³ 14 (OR 121) 8–12. In this decree, as in *Erythrae* 33, drawing lots is rendered by the verb κυαμεύω.

heliaia, as before. To summarize, no initiative for selection for office by lot can ascribed with any confidence to Cleisthenes.

However, among the traditions collected in the *Ath.Pol.* ascribed to Cleisthenes, two instances of using the lot appear. The first took place when Cleisthenes, having divided (*dianemo*) the land of Attica among the thirty *trittyes*, assigned the latter by lot to the ten *phylai*, in such a way that each *phyle* shared in all the regions. Is this a feasible account? In a foundational article on the Cleisthenic organization, David Lewis showed that Cleisthenes created the *trittyes* in such a way that many were quite distinct from traditional regional units, and that some of the clustering cut directly through the cultic hubs that held together the power base of the elite families—notably of families aligned to the tyrants.[149] Lewis remarked that once Cleisthenes had determined these politically expedient *trittyes*, "it could be left to Apollo to create the tribes."[150] Since the *trittyes* were *homoios* in size, each providing around seventeen *bouleutai*, allotting these subsections to the *phylai* was a plausible procedure, on the familiar practice of distribution of equal portions to equal recipients (*dianemo*) by lot.[151]

With his remark about Apollo, Lewis hinted at the second instance. The *Ath. Pol.* (21.6) recounted that Cleisthenes "instituted ten eponymous (name-giving) founding heroes (*archegetai*) for the *phylai* which the Pythia picked from a preselection (*prokrisis*) of a hundred."[152] Once again, we are left wondering if this is plausible. The *Ath.Pol.* reports the episode as a part of Cleisthenes's constitutional reforms, without attaching it to his long-standing connection with Delphi.[153] By contrast, while Herodotus has much to tell about Cleisthenes in Delphi, he does not mention this event, and instead reports that the Alkmaionidai—the family to which Cleisthenes belonged—had good relations with Delphi, especially since they resided there in exile during the tyranny.[154] Furthermore, Herodotus heard rumors that the Alkmaionidai (and Cleisthenes in particular) had bribed the Pythia to tell every Spartan turning up at the oracle that it was their duty to liberate Athens from the tyrants; however, when the Spartan king Kleomenes discovered

---

[149] Lewis (1963). Walters (1982) criticized some of Lewis's inferences, but I find Lewis's overall argument still convincing because it explains the "outliers" in Cleisthenes's system, such as the separation of Probalinthos from the other *poleis* of the Tetrapoleis into a different *trittys*, and the remarkable inclusion of Probalinthos and Rhamnous into the "City" category.

[150] Lewis (1963) 36.

[151] See ch. 1 and section 5.1 in this volume.

[152] *Ath.Pol.* 21.6: ταῖς δὲ φυλαῖς ἐποίησεν ἐπωνύμους ἐκ τῶν προκριθέντων ἑκατὸν ἀρχηγετῶν, οὓς ἀνεῖλεν ἡ Πυθία δέκα.

[153] *Ath.Pol.* 19 recounts the activities of "the exiles headed by the Alkmaionidai," elaborating on several enterprises that failed, but also mentions their building of the new temple at Delphi, suggesting that they earned much money from this activity that they used to persuade the Spartans.

[154] According to Hdt. 5.62 they contributed lavishly to the reconstruction of the temple.

the deceit, he abandoned his intentions to do so.[155] Cast in the political gossip of fifth-century Athens, these accounts confirm the long-standing connection between the Alkmaionidai and Delphi. Hostile voices would inevitably depict their lavish funding of the temple repairs in Delphi as a "bribe" of sorts. Yet, as Lewis points out, unlike most elite families in Attica, the Alkmaionidai had no major traditional cult center in their territories, and as an "accursed" family they needed ostensible divine support more than most.[156] Moreover, as the father of their eponymous hero, early king Ion, and patron of the Athenian phratries, Apollo was the "ancestral god" of the Athenians—his sanction was indispensable for any change to the citizen body.[157] Lastly, like most Greeks, Cleisthenes would duly ask the gods for the proper course of action, especially if he needed advice on cultic matters or on possible cultic innovations. Apollo in Delphi was the most prominent deity to convey such messages, and he did so via the Pythia. The verb in the *Ath.Pol.* passage translated here as "picked" is *anhaireo*, meaning to take up something, but it is also a common expression for a deity giving an oracular response or selecting the appropriate cultic personnel.[158]

Asking the god about the right cults for the new *phylai* is what Cleisthenes certainly must have done. In ancient Greece, every institution and sociopolitical unit, such as a *polis* or subgroup, was founded on or around a core of cult. The act of performing sacrifices to a tutelary deity or to a hero anchored the community (*koinonia*), be it large or small, in the divine and human world, and forged the ties between the human faithful and the divine.[159] Gods or heroes from the mythical past usually appeared as the metaphorical founder-ancestor (*archegetai*) of such social entities.[160] For consultations on religious matters—and therefore for the foundation of new cities—Apollo was the god par excellence. Indeed, *archegetes* was a crucial epithet of the Pythian Apollo, who for cultic purposes nominated both historical *archegetai* (notably *oikistai*), and heroes-*archegetai*.[161]

---

[155] Hdt. 5.63, 66, 90. For Herodotus's trust in oracles and response to the stories about bribes, Harrison (2000) 140–142.

[156] Lewis (1963). The Alkmaionidai were accursed since they were involved in putting to death the coup-faction of Cylon when they had sought refuge at an altar on the *Acropolis*.

[157] *Ath.Pol.* fr. 1; for Apollo as patron of the phratries (metaphorical descent groups), Lambert (1998²) 209–218. I prefer "metaphorical" to "fictive" descent; see Blok (2017) 138–139.

[158] LSJ, s.v. ἀναιρέω III. And see p. 30.

[159] For the role of cult in creating and maintaining social structures, Blok (2017) 58–63 with further refs.

[160] For the role of the *archegetes* as legatee of material and immaterial goods (such as membership of the group) to the metaphorical "descendants" as heirs of equal parts, Blok (2017) 138–146. Anderson (2003) 127 renders the institution of the eponymous heroes "as *Stammvater*" of the *phylai* a "conceit," as he takes such fictive ancestors (the choice of German is inappropriate if not tendentious) to have been the prerogative of phratries and *gene*, whom he implicitly designates as of high status. For the phratries, this supposition of high status is unwarranted, and taking fictive kinship to be a conceit essentially misunderstands such cultural forms of kinship.

[161] Plut. *De Pythiae oraculis* 407f–408a; *archegetai* in the foundation of colonies, Malkin (1987a) 241–250; Malkin (1989), esp. 141–142.

Cleisthenes in effect refounded the city and needed heroes as founders to anchor the new *phylai* in cult practices. The question was, which gods or heroes to choose?

Delphi was the place for guidance in this choice, but how was the selection made? Consulting the oracle could take various forms, such as choosing between two options—an open question—or selecting one or more persons from a group by means of beans, or putting oracular lots in a *phiale* (bowl) for the Pythia to select.[162] According to the *Ath.Pol.*, Cleisthenes used this last method: he wrote a hundred names on tokens, put them into a container, and the Pythia drew ten of them—a procedure akin to *klerosis ek prokriton*. Of those hundred, however, some heroes were more desirable than others. Erechtheus had been growing in prominence throughout the sixth century, and represented the power of the ancient Athenian kings on the Acropolis under the divine protection of Athena.[163] Similarly, Kekrops had grown into a pivotal figure in the cult of Athena on the Acropolis. The inclusion as *phyle*-hero of Hippothon, son of Poseidon and mythical king of Eleusis, further consolidated Eleusis, which had been merging with Attica since the seventh century, into the *polis* Athens.[164] Meanwhile, Aias represented his home, Salamis, conquered during the conflict with Megara in the sixth century, and now incorporated in Attica, albeit on a distinct footing.[165] Interestingly, the first three are also proclaimed heroes who already enjoyed an established *polis* cult; in the case of Aias, it was rather his father (or son) Eurysakes who had an established *genos*-cult.[166] Asking the god to select randomly from the hundred heroes, however, could result in founders who were less conducive to Cleisthenes's plans.[167] For this reason, Cleisthenes may therefore have made the *prokrisis* more precise, asking the Pythia to draw one from a number of Eleusinian heroes, plus one from a number of heroes associated with Salamis, and so on, in series. Irrespective of these details, the account that Cleisthenes asked Apollo to select the ten eponymous heroes is convincing, since it fits traditional patterns of action and legitimacy.

---

[162] See also ch. 2. A choice between two alternatives, Bowden (2005) 88–95; Eidinow (2007); selection of one or more from a group—for instance, a king among the Thessalians (Plut. *Mor.* 492A–B) or for a colony, cf. Lopez-Rabatel (2020); open question: to which god should I sacrifice? (Xen. *Anab.* 3.1.5–8); lots in a *phiale*, Egleston Robbins (1916). For the prominence of cultic matters in oracular consultation, Nissinen (2017) 237–241.

[163] Hom. *Il.* 2.547–548; for Erechtheus and Kekrops in the sixth and fifth centuries, Shapiro (1998).

[164] De Polignac (2011).

[165] De Polignac (2007).

[166] Aias had a cult of his own on Salamis (Taylor [1997] 177, 183–184), but the cultic focus of the *phyle* Aiantis was the sanctuary of Aias's father (or son) Eurysakes in the deme Melite, close to the agora (*Ag.* XVI 86, of 327/6; Kron [1976] 172–174; Kearns [1989] 82; Taylor [1997] 49), served by a priest of the *genos* Salaminioi (RO 37; Parker [1996]).

[167] By contrast, Humphreys (2018) 666 thinks that the tradition that the ten heroes were drawn by lot "tells us that neither selection seemed obvious to the Athenians." The other selection she has in mind here is the assignment of the demes to the *trittyes*.

Apollo's consent was also required for the new cults of the eponymous heroes, served by a special priest. Providing priests for *polis* cults was the prerogative of the *gene* until 450, so for new cults, too, priests were drawn from these groups. With their traditional cults and their priests, the heroes Erechtheus, Kekrops, and Hippothon were now assigned as eponyms to three *phylai* of Cleisthenes's system. For the seven others, new priests were provided from a *genos* belonging to the *phyle*, confirming that these cults were instituted when the *phylai* were created.[168]

We may conclude that Cleisthenes did not introduce the selection for office by lot in Athens, but that he used the lot for two crucial steps in the creation of the new constitution and the refoundation of the *polis*.[169] First, as subsections of the *polis*, he allocated the new *trittyes* by lot to the ten new *phylai*. Although the demes belonging to the *trittyes* were attached to geographical locations with their own cultic programs, the demes were in the first and last resort a *polis* subgroup, namely a social rather than geographical unit. In this way the *trittyes* were even more removed from any defined geographical region, and thus Cleisthenes applied a method typical to the parceling of land for the allocation of subsections of the citizen body, heralding a new sociopolitical framework devised to mix the citizens. The second step involved selecting the founding heroes of the new *phylai* by drawing oracular lots, thereby securing the authority and sanction of Apollo—through the Pythia—of the entire reform that hinged on those heroes, and on what they implied in terms of regional and cultic-mythical allegiances. Apollo's role as Archegetes—the god of new foundations—is consistent here. By this means, all ten heroes played a role in the mythical past of Athens and would henceforth serve as the founder-protectors of the ten new *phylai*.

8.2.2.3 Forerunners of Cleisthenes's innovations

At this point it is expedient to ask if there were any precursors to Cleisthenes's revision of the *polis*. The answer is made no easier by the weaknesses of our sources, starting with Herodotus, whose lapses are partly due to the gap in time between the events and his writing.

Herodotus explicitly compares Cleisthenes's handling of the Athenian *phylai* with how his grandfather Cleisthenes of Sikyon treated the Sikyonian *phylai*. The author suggests that the Athenian followed in the footsteps of his forebear. According to Herodotus, both men renamed the existing *phylai* of their fellow citizens, and both acted out of disdain.[170] What precisely happened at Sikyon is

---

[168] Schlaifer (1940); Blok and Lambert (2009); Lambert (2010) 150.
[169] Cleisthenes's system was a superstructure overlaying the foundations of citizenship by descent, as laid down by Solon (cf. Lape [2002/3]), and based on cultic associations, for which further Ismard (2007; 2010); for an analysis of what changed and what remained the same, Blok (2017) 116–126.
[170] Hdt. 4.69: ὑπεριδών.

virtually impossible to retrieve from Herodotus or any other source.[171] The historian ascribes to grandfather Cleisthenes the wish to eradicate any influence of the powerful neighbor Argos.[172] Modern attempts to make sense of this motive suppose that Cleisthenes senior aimed at a new *polis* identity and a strong internal cohesion of Sikyon.[173] If this was indeed what Cleisthenes of Sikyon was after, the key strands of Herodotus's account are ill conceived: in particular, the other motive he ascribes—primarily the disdain for the Dorian element of his people, exemplified in the derogatory names he allegedly assigned to three of the Sikyonian *phylai* (the one he supposedly gave to his own tribe, the *Archelaoi*, means "masters of the people"). Such an approach would be counterproductive to his aim of unifying and strengthening the *polis*.

Herodotus also ascribes "disdain" to Cleisthenes for his fellow citizens of Athens—a notion that surely must be an anachronistic projection.[174] More importantly, Herodotus holds that Cleisthenes junior replaced the previous four *phylai* with the ten new ones, an error repeated in the *Ath.Pol.*[175] Even more remarkable is that Herodotus does not seem to know what was really essential in this case, that Cleisthenes mixed the citizens—a fact that *Ath.Pol.* was instead aware of, apparently from another source. So Herodotus is wide of the mark, not only on Cleisthenes of Sikyon but also on the Athenian Cleisthenes: although the historian knew that the latter created the ten *phylai*, he seems not to know what had really been going on, and even less what was at stake.

This seems also to be the case in Herodotus's confusing and brief account of Demonax of Mantineia's reorganization of Cyrene, some forty years before Cleisthenes of Athens; Aristotle already drew a comparison between the two *polis* reorganizations.[176] Civic strife arose in Cyrene due to incremental settlement by groups of colonists from different origins, vying for land both among themselves and with the neighboring Libyans. When Demonax was asked to restore order,

---

[171] Hdt. 4.68 situates four *phylai* at Sikyon: the regular three Dorian *phylai* and the Archelaoi, to which Cleisthenes senior belonged.

[172] Hdt. 5.66–69: Cleisthenes of Sikyon, obsessed by a rivalry with Argos and its mythological hero Adrastos, wanted to segregate the citizens of Sikyon forcefully from any ties with Argos, consisting of the three Dorian *phylai* Dymanes, Hyllees, and Pamphyloi. Renaming the *phylai* of the Sikyonians, he deliberately degraded them with names derived from "pig" and "ass."

[173] Grote (2016) 3–64, esp. 57–58, with references to earlier lit.

[174] Cecchet (2017) 57 tries to make sense of Herodotus's account by supposing that by "the Ionians" the historian meant the Eupatrid elite with their luxurious Ionian lifestyle. This solution is unconvincing: *all* Athenians belonged to the Ionians, and there is no sign of disdain in Athens for the Ionian lifestyle (rather the contrary) and certainly not by the Eupatrid Cleisthenes for his fellow elite. Herodotus's explanation is simply incorrect; see also above, note 116.

[175] Hdt. 5.66–69; *Ath.Pol.* 21.2. Not only was abolishing institutions against the grain of ancient attitudes, dispensing with the Ionian *phylai* and their *phylobasileis* was inconceivable due to their religious and judicial functions (sacrifices listed in the Sacrificial Calendar, cf. Lambert [2002]; special cases of homicide, *Ath.Pol.* 57.4).

[176] Arist. *Pol.* 1319b19–27.

he made them [the Cyrenaians] into three *phylai*, arranging them in the following manner: he made one part (*moira*) of the Theraeans and the *perioikoi* [noncitizens living close by], another of the Peloponnesians and Cretans, and the third of all the islanders. After selecting special domains and priestly functions for the king Battos, he put the other prerogatives, which formerly the kings held, into the middle of the *demos*.[177]

When combined with other evidence on Cyrene, scholarly readings of Herodotus's account have been varied. Karl-Joachim Hölkeskamp argues that Demonax retained the traditional structure of the three Dorian *phylai* and their subdivisions that the original settlers had brought from their homeland to Cyrene, but he redistributed the citizens over these divisions, mixing the three subgroups (*moirai*) he identified in the population (Therans, both first settlers and later colonists; Spartans and Cretans; and Dorians and Ionians from the islands) across the three *phylai* and their subdivisions (*hetaireiai*).[178] In order to reduce the tensions between them, the trio of "ethnic" groups had to be distributed evenly over the three *phylai* and work together within them, according to Hölkeskamp.[179] However, Lucia Cecchet arrives at a different conclusion[180] and argues that each of the *moirai* was already a blend of various groups, which, moreover, had settled in consecutive waves of migration on ever-wider areas of land. By her reasoning, mixing the three groups equally over the three *phylai* would not have diminished the danger of conflict over the land; instead, by arranging the three groups each in a *phyle*, "the separation of the three groups of the colonists was a way to regulate land-ownership and prevent the risk of redistribution."[181] In this way, Demonax integrated the later colonists into the citizen body, but he left the specific rights of the first settlers (the Therans) intact, first of all the rights to the land they had acquired, but probably also to the civic offices that had meanwhile been handed over to the *polis*.[182] While each of these

---

[177] Hdt. 4.161. Herodotus's account that Demonax made the other prerogatives of the king into *archai* accessible to the whole *demos* (τὰ ἄλλα πάντα, τὰ πρότερον εἶχον οἱ βασιλέες, ἐς μέσον τῶι δήμωι ἔθηκε) might be an anachronism, reflecting the Cyrenaian democracy of ca. 440–401, so partly Herodotus's own time, for which Robinson (2011) 129–136 (and *pace* Robinson [1997] 105–108, who takes Herodotus at his word for Demonax).
[178] Hölkeskamp (1993), elaborating on a proposal by Jeffery (1961).
[179] Hölkeskamp (1993) 409.
[180] Cecchet (2017).
[181] Cecchet (2017) 66.
[182] Cecchet (2017) 68–69, with ref. to Arist. *Pol.* 1290b12–15, stating that in many colonies, among which was Thera (a Spartan colony) only the first settlers had access to public offices. Such a division into an "aristocratic" group holding the offices and the others would also feel familiar to settlers from Crete (cf. Seelentag [2013]) but could be brought into effect in Hölkeskamp's model as well as in Cecchet's model. Cecchet's view finds some confirmation in the even more lacunose account of Diod. 8.30.2, stating that Demonax resolved the conflict "between the *poleis*," a term suggestive of (ethnic) peoples with their territories.

readings of the events at Cyrene has much to commend it, their common point is clear: Demonax integrated old and new settlers into the citizen body of Cyrene and reassigned subgroups of these citizens and the land on which they lived to the three *phylai*.

How did he go about in this? Herodotus is silent on this issue, but it is plausible that Demonax used lot-drawing to achieve the desired outcome. Although conjecture, it is logical that the lot was the default method for guaranteeing even distribution, as noted throughout the present study, and that was surely the case here. According to Hölkeskamp's "mixed" model, Demonax may have used the lot to assign subgroups of the *moirai* to each of the *phylai* and their subdivisions—in Cecchet's "*moira* into *phyle*" model, to assign subgroups of the *moirai* to the subdivisions (*hetaireiai*) within *phylai*. Either way, Demonax may have served as an example for Cleisthenes, both for the integration of old and new citizens and for the concomitant refounding of the *polis*'s subdivisions; for the final step, we know that he applied the lot system to bring about the mix of citizens-by-subdivisions he desired. Both Demonax and Cleisthenes used the instance of refoundation to allocate a degree of political power to a wider group of citizens. In sum, the novelty of Cleisthenes's system is the creation of ten new *phylai*; depending on how we understand Demonax's model, we should (or should not) add the root purpose of mixing the citizens in the intricate system of subdivisions underlying the *phylai*. With Cleisthenes of Sikyon, finally, both rulers shared the understanding that for terminating inner conflict and creating new cohesion in the *polis*, resetting the subdivisions such as the *phylai* was a major instrument. It is highly plausible that for the idea to create a new *polis* using the lot to distribute and mix people and land, the colonies served as a model, also for the refoundation of existing *poleis*.[183]

8.2.2.4 Reforms in the mid-fifth century: Toward full allotment

After Cleisthenes's reform, Athens achieved a fully fledged democracy in two stages: first with reforms of the late 460s, associated with Ephialtes, and then with Pericles's Citizenship Law of 451/0.[184] Both steps were crucial in the turn to widespread use of the lot for office and for other elements of *polis* governance.

After the framework created by Cleisthenes was formally put in place in 501/0, the *polis* began to grow accustomed to this elementary form of democracy. The new *politeia* did not put an end to the split between elite and *demos*, neither formally nor informally, and throughout the fifth century the political arena

---

[183] Cf. Malkin (2023).
[184] Of course, after 450 the democracy continued to evolve, not least following the loss of the empire in 404, the revision of the laws in 403, and the restructuring of the fiscal system in the fourth century. My point here is that the structure of citizenship underlying the democracy came about in the stages discussed here.

was divided into one faction defending the interests of the elite and one favoring the *demos*.[185] Although both factions were in fact led by members of the upper classes, elite leaders cooperating with the *demos* had been an ingredient of Greek politics since the archaic age.[186] Yet owing both to such strong leadership and to the increasing experience in politics of a sizeable number of citizens serving in the council of five hundred, in the first half of the fifth century the *demos* gained in confidence to curb the hold of the elite on *polis* governance, and to rise to governing the *polis* themselves.

As we saw above, in Cleisthenes's *politeia* the *demos* was sovereign in legislation, but the executive power was firmly in the hands of the elite. After their term of office, the archons, who belonged to the top two classes, became members of the Areopagos-council. It was the most powerful body of the *polis*, combining great wealth with vast experience in governance and military matters. The Areopagos held the authority to control magistrates and oversee the laws (guardians of the *nomoi*). It was also the primary judicial court.[187] With the archonships still assigned by elections, competition among the leading men of the elite was as fierce as before. But enforcement of exile was now in the hands of the *demos*, and beginning in 488/7 they began carrying out ostracisms, ejecting a major leader almost every year throughout the 480s.[188] This policy began just three years after the victory in the battle of Marathon (490) had made the people more confident, while rumors held that the Peisistratidai tried to return to Athens. Yet for the *demos*, the rivalry among the elite remained the major motive for ostracism. In 487/6, the *polis* brought the Solonian system for the selection of the archons by *klerosis ek prokriton* back into force.[189] Allotment was therefore returned to the selection process for office in Athens, albeit on a very limited scale. While both measures clearly aimed at reducing the inter-elite antagonism, the selection of the archons did not bring more power to the *demos*.

In the late 460s, important changes were made to the democratic institutions, which the *Ath.Pol.* dates to 462/1 and ascribes to a certain Ephialtes as the main agent behind the reforms.[190] Matteo Zaccarini has recently questioned the

---

[185] *Ath.Pol.* 23, 28.
[186] For the continuity of interplay between leaders and the *demos* in the fifth century, Mann (2007).
[187] *Ath.Pol.* 23.1–2; 25.1–2.
[188] In 487 Hipparchos son of Charmos, a relative of the tyrant Peisistratos; 486 Megakles son of Hippocrates, Cleisthenes's nephew; 485 an unknown individual; 484 Xanthippus son of Ariphron, Pericles's father; 482 Aristeides son of Lysimachus; 471 Megakles again; 470 Themistocles son of Neokles; 461 Cimon, son of Miltiades. Cf. Forsdyke (2005) 149–178, for ostracism not as an instrument against tyranny but to dampen elite conflict, in which the *demos* in fact carried out a political judgment of its leaders. Węcowski (2022) argues that Cleisthenes's intention, with a matching procedure, was to compel the competitive leaders to some form of cooperation.
[189] De Ste. Croix (2004a) 216–217 supposes that the law reinstating Solon's method, to be brought into effect in 487/6, was enacted in 488/7. The decision on this law and the first ostracism thus took place in the same year.
[190] Nothing more is known about the background of Ephialtes or his motives for empowering the *demos* at the cost of the Areopagos. *Ath.Pol.* 25.3–4 offers an account full of intrigue, with

solidity of the historical tradition about Ephialtes, rightly pointing out that the connection between the institutional changes and the rather vague figure of Ephialtes is both tenuous and ambiguous.[191] Yet even if we cannot attach a prominent individual nor a single year to the reforms, institutional changes did take place in this period, and far-reaching ones at that.[192]

Behind these shifts in favor of the *demos* lay a tremendous societal change, brought about by the creation of the Athenian navy, paid by the revenue of the rich silver mines found near Laurion in 483. After the victory in the sea battle at Salamis in 480 against the Persians and the ensuing institution of the Delian League, the Piraeus harbor engendered an economic transformation that radiated far beyond the Piraeus area and into Athens on a broader scale. Moreover, the Athenian navy made the lower-class citizens manning the oars of the fleet a crucial military power. Evidence of the 430s shows that for special tasks, some two thousand men were distributed per *phyle* by lot among the ships; the practice may have helped to forge stronger links between the power of the navy, of the *demos*, and the drawing of lots.[193] In any case, this combined social, military, and economic change transformed the Athenian *demos* itself in political terms. Giangiulio emphasizes that in the political movements after 479 the *demos* was no longer just a majority in terms of number, but became the critical mass holding the power of the *polis* implied in the noun *demokratia*.[194] The *Ath.Pol.* mentions the major features of the reform, and further details can be inferred from its effects, attested in a variety of documents and archaeological evidence. The reforms increased the powers of the *demos*, and effectively became the launch pad for large-scale allotment practice in Athens.

Key executive and judicial powers were transferred from the Areopagos to the council of five hundred and to the people's court, with radical democratic implications. The council of five hundred saw its powers increased considerably. To its probouleutic function, a range of responsibilities were added for the day-to-day affairs of the *polis* and for executive duties, notably for financial and religious

---

Themistocles in the main role, which cannot be correct because in 462 Themistocles had long left Greece, whereas Arist. *Pol.* 1274a8–10 presents Pericles as Ephialtes's associate (for the complexities of the political situation, Rhodes, *CAAP*, ad *Ath.Pol.* 25.3–4). The attack on the Areopagos began with charges against individual members, but details are lacking. According to the *Ath.Pol.*, Ephialtes was murdered a few years later.

[191] Zaccarini (2018). Although I agree with his main arguments, his portrayal of the *Ath.Pol.* as merely as a mirror of fourth-century debates and almost devoid of reliable information on the fifth century is demonstrably unjustified.

[192] Zaccarini (2018) 511 does not "deny altogether that Athens underwent some process of institutional reform in the late 460s, or that a (minor?) politician named Ephialtes was active in the same period."

[193] Evidence of the 430s, when they were tasked with collecting the tribute: *Ath.Pol.* 24.3; IG I³ 60, ll. 12–14 (date uncertain, between 430 and 425?).

[194] Giangiulio (2015) 49–53, 61–64.

matters. Scrutinies of all officeholders, both before entering office (*dokimasia*) and by the end of their term (*euthynai*) now also fell under its authority, as well as other assessments of citizens and their conduct for praise, honors, or penalties (*time*). In effect, the reform made the council the main standing committee for *polis* governance, a task for which a collective of five hundred was too large.

To meet this need in the council for a leaner executive board, several key features of its governance were now established, in which the lot played an essential role.[195] Each of the ten *phylai* was to preside over the council for one-tenth of the year, acting as the executive board of the council and the assembly. The turns of the *phylai* in holding this presidency—called the prytany—were established by lot. The fifty *prytaneis* were assisted by a secretary from one of the other nine *phylai*, again drawn by lot, while a chairman for the day of both the council and the assembly was drawn by lot from among the *prytaneis*. Based on the twelve lunar months—each named after its most prominent festival—for an equal division into ten units the calendar of Athens was unsuited, so beside the existing lunar calendar a specific "bouleutic" year was created, divided into ten virtually equal parts indicated by the *phyle* in prytany.

With this new setup, the *bouleutai* became far more actively involved in running the *polis* than they had been. Their active share in the governance was also represented in a visible, tangible location: a new, round meetinghouse (*tholos*) was built between 460 and 450, where the *prytaneis* met and dined together in an equal setting, all using the same black-glazed simple service and receiving fixed, equal amounts of wine.[196] Clearly, sharing actively (*metecho*) in the council in large numbers on an equal footing, supported by recurrent uses of the lot, was one major aim of the reforms. It is therefore also the most probable context for the switch from the election of the *bouleutai*, implied in Cleisthenes's *politeia*, to selection by lot, for which we found earlier a plausible date *ante quem* in the late 450s. Only more well-to-do citizens did in fact present themselves, but everyone who did so was eligible for the allotment—that is, within the numerical distributive framework of the demes, of course. The allotment was carried out with beans, the traditional method introduced by Solon for the *Tamiai* and the archons, and continued for the major offices down to the fourth century.[197]

Around the same time, the so-called minor offices, namely all executive offices other than the archons, were drawn by lot from the demes in the same proportions as the distribution of the councilors. Four clay tokens have come to

---

[195] Rhodes (1972) 16–20.
[196] Steiner (2018). The date of the pottery in the Tholos (Steiner [2018] 216) is established independently from the date of Ephialtes.
[197] Fifth century: in the council of the democracy Athens imposed on Erythrai (*IG* I³ 14); in the regulations for Histiaia (*IG* I³ 41); the *Tamiai* of the Other Gods (*IG* I³ 52); archons in the deme Plotheia (*IG* I³ 258); the *bouleutai* in 412 (Thuc. 8.69.4); fourth century: the archons (Dem. 24.150).

light, three of which, from excavations of the *agora*, dated to the mid-fifth century.[198] Before firing, on one side of each token was painted with the name of a *phyle*, on the other with the name of a deme or an office; for instance, on two tokens the letters ΠΟΛ indicate *poletes*. According to *Ath.Pol.* 62.1, in the fifth century the minor offices were drawn by lot from the demes, until the Athenians changed the system to allotment from the whole *phyle*, because demes were selling their offices. The tokens provide a *terminus ante quem* for the drawing of lots for the minor offices, and it is attractive to suppose that the switch from election to drawing lots was made as part of the same reforms of the late 460s.

In the fourth century, the allotment of the offices took place in the Theseion.[199] In his sanctuary Theseus received godlike honors; runaway slaves and refugees could find asylum here.[200] Several mythical accounts came to be attached to the place: Diodorus tells that the Athenians made it an asylum because Theseus himself had been a fugitive, and Plutarchus notes that it was also called Place of the Oaths, because here the war with the Amazons was terminated and a sacrifice was made to the Amazons before the Theseia.[201] As befits a hero and deified human, Theseus's sanctuary would be an ideal place for the selection of *polis* offices by humans under divine supervision; and as a place for asylum, the sanctuary had a fairly large *temenos*. Last but not least, Theseus represented Attica in its entirety. As Christiane Sourvinou-Inwood observes, "Kekrops and Erechtheus were eponymous tribal heroes; Theseus was not, for he was the greatest Athenian king, refounder of the *polis*, and represented the whole of Athens, and could not be associated with only one tribe."[202] When and where the Theseion was built is difficult to ascertain, but it certainly existed in the later fifth century.[203] It is highly plausible that the fourth-century practice of allotting offices here was a continuation of the fifth-century custom.

For jurisdiction, most procedures were now moved away from the Areopagos, leaving this body only with specific cases of homicide; cases falling under the archons remained as before. Procedures of control and assessment of officials

---

[198] See Endnote 8.
[199] *Ath.Pol.* 62.1; Aeschin. 3.13. Voting for the elected offices took place in the assembly or *phyle* assembly.
[200] Philochoros, *FrGrHist* 328 F 177; Diod. 4.62–63: οἱ δ' Ἀθηναῖοι μεταμεληθέντες τά τε ὀστᾶ μετήνεγκαν καὶ τιμαῖς ἰσοθέοις ἐτίμησαν αὐτόν.
[201] Diod. 4.62–63; Plut. *Thes.* 27.7–8.
[202] Sourvinou-Inwood (2011) 61. Zaccarini (2015) rightly questions the story that Cimon brought Theseus's bones to Athens in the late 470s, but too easily dismisses the evidence of a possible cult of Theseus in the late sixth and early fifth centuries. The Theseion already functioned as an asylum in 424 (Ar. *Eq.* 1311–1312; cf. Ar. fr. 577, Loeb-ed.), and such institutions did not come about overnight. Nor did the perception of Theseus as the founder of Athens, as recounted by Thuc. 2.15.
[203] The location of the Theseion is still unidentified; see Endnote 8. According to *Ath.Pol.* 15.4, the sanctuary already existed in the mid-sixth century, as it features in the account on Peisistratos's seizure of power; its fifth-century existence is undisputed (Thuc. 6.61.2; Ar. *Eq.* 1311–1312). My argument here pushes the construction of the Theseion back to the 460s at the latest.

were moved to the council and all major judicial procedures to the people's court. This was, since Solon, the full assembly acting as a court (*heliaia*), to hear cases of appeal and charges on acts against the welfare of the *polis*.[204] With these reforms, the new duties of the people's court went far beyond its previous tasks, both in number and in political impact. Cases concerning the control of magistrates and cases with severe penalties such as high fines and the death penalty had deep political influence, turning the people's court over time into one of the central institutions of the *polis*.[205] To address these increased duties, the *heliaia* was divided into several smaller courts, the *dikasteria*, each consisting of five hundred citizens over thirty years of age.[206] If the gravity of a case required a *heliaia*, two or three such courts were combined.[207] John Kroll points out that the number of five hundred suggests a selection in the demes proportionate to the size of the deme, analogous to the *bouleutai* and the preselected candidates for the archonships, and, we may add, the minor offices. For a total pool of six thousand *dikastai*, twelve such groups of five hundred were selected.[208]

Were the *dikastai* also drawn by lot? In Pericles's time they certainly were, and all evidence combined suggests that the system was a part of the reforms of the late 460s. If Kroll's suggestion is correct, a fixed number from each deme was allotted from those who presented themselves.[209] No property requirement applied for admission to the courts, following the regulations of Solon; notably, once payment for the sessions began in the 440s, poorer citizens presented themselves more readily for selection.[210] In the early fourth century, the citizens selected as *dikastai* were assigned en bloc to specific courts in sections per *phyle* indicated by letters (*grammata*) by means of a device called a *kleroterion*, a "ballot box," situated on the agora.[211] Later, a new device was introduced, likewise called

---

[204] Among such charges were those of *eisangelia* for treason, deceit of the people, and other misdemeanors; see Carawan (1987); Hansen (1989). I am not convinced by Valdés Guía (2022b) that the Solonian council of four hundred acted as *heliaia*.

[205] Further illuminated by Hansen (1991) 178–180.

[206] At least for important public cases; at some point, the number of *dikastai* per court was set at 501, to prevent a tie (Dem. 24.9: 1001 *dikastai*; *Ath.Pol.* 68.1 [ed. Chambers] 501 *dikastai*). For (private) cases with claims up to one thousand drachma, the court held 201; for higher amounts, 401 *dikastai* (*Ath.Pol.* 53.3).

[207] Harp., s.v. Ἡλιαία καὶ ἡλίασις; Poll. *On.* 8.123.

[208] Kroll (1972) 86, elaborating on a suggestion by U. v. Wilamowitz-Moellendorff, on *Ath.Pol.* 22.5; 62.1; And. 1.82–84. Kroll argued from a more limited number of minor offices than was to be the case after Hansen (1980) convincingly defended the number given in *Ath.Pol.* 24.3 of ca. 700. See Endnote 8.

[209] Selection by lot: *Ath.Pol.* 27.4–5. *Ath.Pol.* 26 recounts that on the initiative of Aristeides the Athenians set up a food supply for their officials, including six thousand *dikastai*, but the figures mentioned do not reflect the time of Aristeides but the entire period before Pericles introduced payment for the jury courts; within this time span, no element of this account can be firmly dated.

[210] *Ath.Pol.* 27.4–5; Ar. *Wasps* (of 422); *Ath.Pol.* contends that the influx of poor citizens made the courts liable to bribery. However, for the entire court of five hundred to be bribed, the allocation of citizens to courts would need to take place quite a while before the actual sessions, and no evidence suggests that this was the case.

[211] Ar. *Eccl.* 681–688 (of ca. 391); for the letters, Ar. *Plut.* 1166–1167 (of 388); Kroll (1972) 5–6.

a *kleroterion*, a marble lottery machine that could be used for selecting individual *dikastai*, still per *phyle* but no more en bloc.[212] Every male citizen over age thirty had an individual allotment plate (*pinakion*) first made of bronze, later of wood, carrying his name, his patronymic, and his demotic. The plate was inserted into the lottery machine for a selection by means of black and white cubes running through a tube alongside the inserted plates. The *Ath.Pol.* describes the main features of the complex system of selection and assignment to courts, a procedure with several instances of drawing lots, presumably to prevent malpractice.[213] This new *kleroterion* was probably introduced to serve a changed system instituted in 378/7, when the Second Athenian League and a threatening war with Sparta required greater flexibility of the Athenian manpower, and hence led to reforms of the offices.[214] Lastly, in the late 370s or 360 the *kleroteria* came to be used for selection of all allotted offices, now drawn by *phyle*; only the *bouleutai* and the guards remained selected by the demes to keep the proportional numbers in the representation of the demes.[215]

The reforms of the late 460s shifted the power in the *polis* into the hands of the *demos*, involving a wider section of the citizen body in the council and the courts on the principle of equality with large-scale allotments. Shortly after 460, the Athenians also extended eligibility for the archonships to include the *zeugitai*, the third class; the first eponymous archon from this class was selected in 457/6.[216] Democratization was now well under way.

The second and final move toward democratization was due to Pericles. In 451/0, when the "First Peloponnesian War" with Sparta and the disastrous war with Persia in Egypt were coming to a close, Pericles introduced a law that required having two parents of citizen descent for legitimate citizen status.[217] Until then, one Athenian parent formally sufficed for citizen status, but descent from a non-Athenian mother (*metroxenos*) was not really appreciated. Pericles'

---

[212] *Ath.Pol.* 63–69. Fifteen Athenian *kleroteria* all from the Hellenistic age are extant in fragments; Alfieri Tonini (2001); Kosmetatou (2013) nos. 1–14; Lopez-Rabatel (2020), plus a new find, Papazarkadas (2019), who persuasively dates the four items with the name of Habron of Bate to the 160s. Although framed at the front as a grave stele or *naiskos*, at the back the *kleroterion* resembled a stele and it was used as such for two decrees honoring the prytany of Erechtheis in 164/3 (*Ag.* XV 220 and 221; the provision that the stone is to be dedicated in a *temenos* "which the lot decides" is both unique and restored, so unreliable as evidence for drawing lots).

[213] Although with the new system citizens were selected by lot individually, this allotment still took place per *phyle*, overseen by the archons and their secretary from the same *phyle* (*Ath.Pol.* 59.7; 63.1). In *Ag.* XVI 86 (Schwenk no. 61) of 327, the *phyle* Aiantis honors its *thesmothetes* for his conscientious handling of the *klerosis* of the archons and of the *dikastai* of the *phyle*.

[214] Ath. X.450b; XIV.640b-c (riddles by Euboulos); for the date, first argued by G. M. Calhoun, Kroll (1972) 5–7.

[215] *Ath.Pol.* 62.1; Kroll (1972) 93–94.

[216] *Ath.Pol.* 26.3: archon Mnesitheides.

[217] Pericles's Law did not forbid marriages with non-Athenians, but rendered them highly unattractive because children from such unions would not be legitimate citizens. Prohibition by law of marriage with non-Athenians dates to the early fourth century.

Citizenship Law enhanced equality by creating homogeneity among the citizens, who henceforth could all claim the same *time* in terms of descent, namely from Athenian citizens on both sides.[218] More specifically, all citizens were now raised to the same quality of pure descent (*ithageneia*) like the *gene*, who descended from two Athenians on both sides.[219]

On this new sense of equality, new prospects for distribution of *polis* offices arose. First, all citizens were now equally qualified for *polis* priesthoods: for new priesthoods, all citizens of the right gender and age were eligible.[220] Selection was made by drawing lots, now "from all" (*klerosis ex hapanton*) because all citizens were now qualified. Based on current evidence, the very first allotment for office from all in Athens—not by subgroup and without any formal restriction or preselection—was not the political office of a man, but the cultic office of a woman, the priestess of Athena Nike, instituted probably between 438 and 435.[221] Whether this case is also the first "allotment from all" in ancient Greece as a whole is difficult to ascertain; for example, we do not know if the council at Erythrai established in the late 450s was based on *klerosis ek prokriton* or *ex hapanton*, the fully democratic selection that the grave monument of Myrrhine, the first priestess of Athena Nike, proudly shows. Her epigram tells that "by divine fortune [*Tyche*] her name was Myrrhine [myrtle]," and next calls her selection "good fortune [*Tyche*]," suggesting that her name made her fitting for divine selection for priesthood as the first from all.[222] After this priestess, quite a number of new priesthoods were instituted over time, for women and for men; some of the male priesthoods allotted from all came to rotate by *phyle* in the fourth century at the latest.[223]

Beside these new priesthoods, for men the political offices likewise became more and more allotted "from all," meaning "without property requirements." By the fourth century, explicit reference to "all" as candidates for drawing lots

---

[218] *Ath.Pol.* 26.3 ascribes the motive behind Pericles's Law to be "the large number of citizens," a concern typical of Greek political theory but implausible as a real issue at this point in time, considering the huge losses in manpower of the preceding years. For the Law, its background, and its aims, Blok (2009b); for non-Athenians Blok (2017) 249–275, with further refs.

[219] For the "aristocracy of birth" of the *gene*, Lambert (2015); significance for Pericles's Citizenship Law, Blok (2009b).

[220] Priesthoods existing before Pericles's Law, all filled by the *gene*, remained the same; for priesthoods before and after the Law, Lambert (2010).

[221] *IG* I³ 35 ll. 4–5 (ἐχς Ἀθεναίον hαπα[σō]/[ν]); OR 137, opting for the date 438–435 or 450–445, and Blok (2014a) arguing for a decision probably before 437, but slightly later also possible. An interval between the decree and its implementation is very likely. In 435, a girl born in 450 would be around fifteen years of age, presumably able to serve as a priestess. However, not birth after Pericles's Law would be decisive, but a double Athenian descent demonstrated at her *dokimasia*.

[222] *IG* I³ 1330 ll. 7–17: ὡς ἀπὸ θείας / Μυρρίν<η ἐ>κλήθη συντυχίας· ἐτύμως ⁚ / πρώτε Ἀθηναίας Νίκες ἕδος ἀμφεπόλευσεν / ἐκ πάντων κλήρωι, Μυρρίνη εὐτυχίαι. Ar. *Lys.* 207–208 also refers to Myrrhine as the one who was allotted first.

[223] Lambert (2010) for all the evidence.

disappears from the (epigraphic) evidence—it went without saying.[224] In practice, the drawing of lots among all male citizens was probably based on distribution by demes, until the *kleroteria* were used to draw, beside *dikastai*, also offices per *phyle* (see earlier). For every office, besides the relevant number of citizens to be drawn by lot (the *lachon*), an equal number of substitutes (the *epilachon*) had to present themselves, in case the first allotted candidate did not pass his *dokimasia* after selection and could not take up his post, or fell ill or died during his term.[225] As a result, even if demes occasionally struggled to find the required number of candidates, over time the entire male citizen body participated in selection by lot. Drawing lots by various means (clay tokens, *pinakia*, etc.) and holding offices assigned by lot became a part of everyday life for the Athenians, as casual references to the practice in Old Comedy from the mid-420s down to the fourth century confirm.[226]

For the later fourth century, the *Ath.Pol.* describes in a large section (42–69) the main offices at Athens except the priesthoods, detailing the method of their selection, and some of their main tasks. While the list is not exhaustive, it is instructive.[227] For instance, the author mentions occasionally that an office used to be elected but was allotted by the time of writing.[228] Above all, the *Ath. Pol.* confirms the general picture derived both from the epigraphical evidence and from literary sources, namely that from the mid-fifth century onward the Athenians increasingly made allotment the default method of selection, while filling by election offices that required experience or capabilities beyond those of the average citizen.[229] These positions included the chief military offices, specific functions—such as the reader of documents at the assembly and the council who

---

[224] From the fourth century onward, inscribed references to selection "from all Athenians" only concern elections for specific tasks, notably embassies and similar assignments: *IG* II² 31, ll. 17–18; 116, ll. 22–23; 128, l. 17; *IG* II³, 1 292, l. 6; 412, ll. 13–14.

[225] Harp. E (102) Ἐπιλαχών. Cf. Plato Com. Fr. 182 K-A: the *epilachon* for Hyperbolos, *lachon* for the council; Aeschin. 3.62: Demosthenes being a *bouleutês* neither as *lachon* nor as *epilachon*, but through bribery; [Dem.] 58.29: the defendant Theokrines took over the office of *hieropoios* from his deceased brother, although Theokrines was neither *lachon* nor *epilachon*. Cf. Laffon (2016).

[226] Ar. *Ach.* 724: an "*agoranomos*"; *Eq.* 258: Cleon; *Nub.* 623: Hyperbolos as *hieromnemon* on behalf of Athens in Delphi; *Av.* 1022: an "*episkopos*" of Cloudcuckooland drawn by the bean, who also receives *misthos*; *Av.* 1111: anyone allotted to an office will use it for his own gain. Ar. *Eccl.* is all about distribution of benefits by lot, although the protagonist Praxagora is elected as *stratege* (*Eccl.* 714–715). Ar. *Pl.* 277, 972 pokes fun at drawing lots for the courts.

[227] Hansen (1980) provides an essential supplement to the list in *Ath.Pol.*

[228] *Ath.Pol.* 54.3: the secretary of the *prytaneis*; 56.4: the *epimeletai* of the procession at the Great Dionysia, who also paid the expenses themselves when elected, but now, as allotted officials, received public means for the procession.

[229] [Xen.] *Ath.Pol.* 1.3 sneers that people who do not wish to share in offices that must be done well to bring safety to the *polis*, but that are dangerous when ill-performed—namely the *strategia* and the cavalry command—still want a share in offices that bring revenues and benefits to one's *oikos* (sc. in the shape of *misthos* or other revenues); see also section 9.1.1. Arist. *Pol.* 1317b19–22 gives a more balanced rendition of this view, calling democratic a *politeia* where all offices are selected by all from all, either by election or by lot, the latter all those offices that require no experience or special skills.

presumably needed to have a clear voice beside high reading skills—and a few major financial offices that required insight in budgeting, in contrast to holding and accounting for existing budgets, skills that every citizen was expected to master.[230] The financial offices requiring budget know-how were instituted in the fourth century, indicating how the Athenians deliberately distinguished between the by-then default method of lot drawing and offices they preferred to remain elective.[231] The system of *prokrisis* (election before allotment) was abandoned by the fourth century: for the archonships the first stage of selection in the *phylai* was maintained, but switched from election to drawing lots, and the archonships were at this point filled by double allotment.

An interesting example of how the Athenians adjusted the organization of their offices to new needs or new considerations are the *metronomoi* (guardians of weights and measures). In the late fourth century (*Ath.Pol.* 51.2) five *metronomoi* for the city and five for Piraeus, one per *phyle*, were drawn by lot; but on a decree of 222/1 they became seven, including one elected and one allotted secretary, and in the second century this became eight, with an additional under-secretary.[232] In this way, the board was large enough to cover all its duties, and also mixed personal expertise with equal representation.

All in all, by the fourth century Athens had developed a dense structure of offices and duties in legislation, administration, jurisdiction, and cult, in which all citizens—fitting their gender and age—participated on a regular basis, and the majority of these functions was distributed by lot. For specific duties, the council or the assembly selected committees of a few men, either by election or by lot. In 403/2 a new important body was instituted in the *politeia*, to be composed by sortition, and with this new *politeia*, the *polis* distinguished decrees (*psephismata*), decided by the council and assembly for particular cases, from laws (*nomoi*) for general and enduring legislation. For such *nomoi* to be enacted, the assembly appointed a large board of legislators (*nomothetai*) with authority for one day only; they were either selected by lot from the six thousand *dikastai* or, perhaps more plausibly, a special meeting of the assembly.[233] In ca. 380 a new

---

[230] Elected military offices (*Ath.Pol.* 61.1): the ten *stratêgoi*, first one per *phyle*, later from all; ten *taxiarchoi*, one per *phyle*; two *hipparchoi* from all, and ten *phylarchoi*, one per *phyle*. Reader: *Ath.Pol.* 54.4. Other elected offices (*Ath.Pol.* 57.1): the *epimeletai* of the Mysteries: two from all citizens, one from the Eumolpidai, one from the Kerykes, two *gene* in charge of Eleusis.

[231] *Ath.Pol.* 43: election by show of hands of the *tamias stratiotikou* (treasurer of the army funds, including the grain supply), the *tamias ton theorikon* (treasurer of the theatre funds), and the *epimeletes ton krenon* (inspector of the water supply), all with a term of office from (Greater) Panathenaia to Panathenaia. For details on the financial offices, Rhodes (2007).

[232] *SEG* 24.157. Eight: *IG* II² 1710 (early second c.) with a clerk (*hyperetes*) and *IG* II² 1711 (mid-second c.) with a *hypogrammateus*. An honorific decree of 334–314 (*IG* II³, 1 458) shows a group of six officials (not *metronomoi*, who were still five at the time) plus an allotted *grammateus*; the space left on the damaged stone would leave room for an elected *grammateus* next to him. The *agoranomoi* of Athens on Delos in the second c. were four, including one allotted *grammateus* (*ID* 1500; 1833).

[233] Dem. 24.20–38; Aeschin. 3.38–40. Cf. Canevaro and Esu (2018; 2023).

board (the *prohedroi*) was instituted for chairing the council and, if it convened, the assembly; they were drawn by lot every day from the *phylai* who were not in prytany, a use of the lot combining sortition and procedure.[234] Besides selection for office, Athens also increasingly applied the lot for distribution—for instance, for shares in the maintenance of warships, and for order, such as the procedures in the jury courts mentioned earlier.

However, following this rich evidence for the Athenian democracy, should one conclude that wide allotment was typical of *all* democracies? We need to investigate what the situation was like in the other *poleis* of Greece.

8.2.3 Selection for office by lot elsewhere in ancient Greece

For the governance of the *polis*, "political" offices (*archai*) were not only essential, they were also the most powerful and hence the object of the fierce competitions manifest throughout Greek political history. Nonetheless, priests, priestesses, and other cult personnel were indispensable for the *polis*'s well-being too, because the *polis*'s cults ensured the support of the gods and *agatha tyche* (good fortune) for the *polis* in both its internal and external relations.[235] Due to the important cultic duties of "political" offices on the one hand, and conversely, the administrative duties of many "cultic" offices on the other, the two types of office were anything but fundamentally distinct.[236] This is also apparent in some of the criteria: in many *poleis*, priests and priestesses were expected to be *holoklaros* (with all limbs), and in some *poleis* this condition was also required of some major *archai*.

Concerning the selection methods, some scholars have hypothesized that within a *polis* the methods for "political" office and "cultic" office were generally congruent and that the second was based on the first.[237] Indeed, while some such congruence is apparent, the primacy in derivation does not lie with the political offices alone, but might also work the other way around—as I argued earlier for the likely precedent of the *gene* for the introduction of drawing lots for office at Athens. Nonetheless, the selection methods of political and cultic offices also had dynamics of their own. Beside lots and election, sale of priesthoods became common in eastern Greece from the fourth century on, incidentally just like the sale of citizenship; no straightforward sale of *archai* existed, but *euergetism*

---

[234] After 380, countless decrees refer to "the *prohedroi* drawn by lot by then" for actions to be taken in the future. The *prohedroi* were added to the system of prytanies and their order by lot and did not replace it.
[235] For discussion of "*polis* cult," Lambert (2010).
[236] For full discussion and evidence in Athens, Blok (2017) 187–217.
[237] E.g., for Athens, Aleshire (1994); on priesthoods across Greece, Dignas and Trampedach (2008).

(donating large amounts of money to the city, in exchange for honors) brought most *archai* within the circle of the wealthy elites. Criteria for eligibility for priesthoods appear to have been stricter and more exclusive than for many other offices: as a rule, newly made citizens were entitled to share in public offices, but in many *poleis* priesthoods were open only to descendants of citizens on both sides, in some *poleis* even of three generations, meaning that only the next generations after the citizenship grant were eligible.[238] All officeholders were subjected to scrutiny (*dokimasia*) on their legitimacy as citizens, and in some *poleis* evaluated for their political viewpoints; in Athens any hint of oligarchic leanings could cause problems. This scrutiny took place after the individual citizen had been selected.

Among all these regulations, the means of selection are the leading topic for our inquiry, first of the political offices, next of the cultic ones. Since the distribution of office by lot in oligarchies was discussed earlier, we now turn to the political offices in democracies. Where and when were officials drawn by lot outside of Athens?

8.2.3.1 Drawing lots for political office outside Athens

In the fifth and fourth centuries, democracy in its various constitutional forms gained in strength and number across the Greek world; oligarchies seem to have slightly outnumbered democracies, but their duration tended to decrease.[239] This is the picture we get from Eric Robinson's helpful list of democracies across the Greek world in the fifth and fourth centuries, arriving at forty-five polities for which democracy is attested with a high degree of certainty, and another six for which the evidence is more ambiguous.[240] But not all democracies were democratic to the same degree, and after the fourth century the tendency to use *demokratia* and its main features as a banner of legitimacy rather than as an accurate description of a constitution makes a historical assessment even more difficult. The Hellenistic era saw a growth in allegedly democratic regimes, where on closer inspection the elite prevailed in political offices and legislation, even in decrees enacted by council and *demos*.[241] What was the role of drawing lots in

---

[238] Exceptions to sharing in public office were the guardians at Miletos, only open to new citizens after ten years (see section 7.2.3), and the archonship at Athens, open only to second-generation citizens.

[239] For the estimated figures of oligarchies, democracies, and tyrannies, Fleck and Hanssen (2018); for the decreasing length of oligarchies, Simonton (2017) 287–290, estimating that the length of oligarchies decreased to almost half that of earlier regimes.

[240] Robinson (2011) 248–250. M. H. Hansen, in his *BMCR* review of Robinson's book (https://bmcr.brynmawr.edu/2013/2013.01.17/).

[241] On the democratic degree of Hellenistic democracies, Carlsson (2010) is optimistic, and so is Grieb (2008) but with more reservations; Dmitriev (2005) shows the strong elite presence. Serious doubts are voiced in the contributions to Mann and Scholz (2012), among which is Fabiani (2012), who shows that in Iasos elite officeholders dominated the decrees of council and assembly.

this context? Can it be regarded as an index of the democratic nature of the *poleis* in question? And was it widely practiced, considering that Aristotle in the late fourth century in *Politics* treats the lot as a common means of selection for office, next to the traditional election?

Pace Aristotle, direct evidence for the allotment of offices beyond Athens is anything but plentiful. Descriptive historical information on the constitutions of *poleis*; epigraphic evidence on allotted bodies, magistrates, and cult personnel; and material evidence such as allotment tokens and (parts of) *kleroteria* are scattered unevenly as to time and place. It is certainly unjustified to assume that in democratic regimes by definition all or most offices were allotted: election by all, and especially also from all, was democratic, too.[242] Most *politeiai* considered "democratic" in fact were of a mixed kind, where drawing lots took place, if at all, alongside elections. In Hellenistic democracies, notably in the east where the evidence is relatively rich, cases of the same person repeatedly holding a particular office increased markedly over time, as did the recurrence of a limited group of names in office.[243] Such instances seem to rule out the drawing of lots, unless it took place among a very limited group of candidates—a situation that would effectively be oligarchic. The evidence rather points to election, with the successful candidates apparently belonging to a smallish elite group. Again, democracy in these Hellenistic cities was quite different from its classical Athenian counterpart.[244]

Although relatively scarce, the available evidence on allotment does allow us to at least attempt to map its spread—and question how this spread can be explained and what role may be assigned to allotment in these democratic *poleis*. Did Athens play a leading role by enforcing a radical democracy, or just by setting an example? Or was selection for office by lot a practice that emerged throughout the Greek world independently from Athens?

Across the Aegean, Athens dominated its "allies" in the heyday of its empire from the 450s to 404, imposing a democratic regime on some of them, and backing local regime change toward democracy in others.[245] As discussed earlier, Erythrai was an early case in point in the late 450s, where besides elective processes the evidence reveals the allotment of magistrates and of the council, apparently after the Athenian example. Ephesos was probably a democracy for

---

[242] Cf. Arist. *Pol.* 1317b19–22.
[243] Dmitriev (2005) 217–228, with the epigraphic evidence.
[244] Reelection for some elected offices, notably the *strategia*, was possible in classical Athens, with Pericles famously holding the office for twenty-nine years, and elected officials tended also to belong to the elite, too, but the size of the group was not as limited nor the recurrence of the same families in office as prominent, as in the Hellenistic eastern cities. Most importantly, in Athens the high level of allotted offices involving all citizens counterbalanced the election of the elite; see Taylor (2007) and above p. 344.
[245] In the Athenian klerouchies on Imbros and Lemnos, the resident Athenian citizens upheld the same political institutions as in Athens itself, including allotted offices; see e.g., *IG* XII 8 46.

a large part of the fifth century, with support from Athens.[246] Both Erythrai and Ephesos were believed to have been settled originally from Athens, their ties to Athens dating back to before the Athenian *arche* (empire).[247] On Paros, the Athenians helped remove an oligarchy and restored the democracy that had been in place there before oligarchs had taken over, in 410; parts of a *kleroterion* found here dating to the second century show allotment of office, presumably jury courts.[248] On Thasos, which saw several constitutional changes, democracy was imposed by Athens more than once.[249]

For a large part of the fifth century, Miletos was ruled by an oligarchy, but after a revolt from the Delian League, Athens intervened and established a democracy, probably in 426/5, which lasted until 405 and was resumed in the fourth century.[250] Some of the prominent offices in Miletos were created through election, among which were the executive *synhedroi* and a board of magistrates comparable to the Athenian *strategoi*.[251] Other offices were allotted, among which (probably) were the *bouleutai* and *prytaneis*. The most interesting application of lottery, briefly mentioned earlier, concerns the guardians of the city and their commander: they were drawn by lot from among the citizens, but newly made citizens were excluded for ten years from taking part in this, since apparently these offices were only entrusted to fully integrated, long-standing citizens.[252]

Athens enforced a democracy on Samos that was probably short-lived (441–440); when the Samian oligarchs faced a democratic revolt in 411, the Athenian oligarchs supported them, while the Athenian fleet backed the efforts of local democrats to retain their democratic regime (411–404).[253] Samos's ties to Athens—where democracy was restored in 411—remained close until the end of the Peloponnesian War. After another oligarchic period (404–394), democracy was probably reestablished once more on Samos.[254] The direct evidence

---

[246] Robinson (2011) 172–173.
[247] Osborne (2009) 119–126.
[248] Diod. 13.47.8. Kosmetatou (2013) 249, nos. 20 and 21.
[249] Robinson (2011) 180–181.
[250] Robinson (2011) 176–178. The date of the revolt and institution of a democracy is debated: [Xen.] *Ath.Pol.* 3.11 gives no indication of the chronology, and for *IG* I³ 21, the Athenian decree on the arrangements with Miletos, formerly dated to the 440s, the date of 426/5 (archon Euthynos) that H. B. Mattingly proposed is now largely accepted; cf. Papazarkadas (2009) esp. 71.
[251] Grieb (2008) 212–213: the ᾑρημένοι ἐπὶ τῇ φυλακῇ. Of the third century *epistatai* the means of selection is not attested but election seems the most likely (Grieb [2008] 218). Epigraphic evidence on the *prophetes* (priest of Apollo) at Didyma dates to late Hellenistic and Roman times and shows a combination of election and lot (*Didyma* 344).
[252] *Miletos* 39 (*Milet* I 3 150) ll. 50–53, an *isopoliteia*-agreement (giving the citizens of one *polis* the right to acquire citizenship in the other; Saba [2020] 1–19) in a treaty of Miletos and Herakleia of 180; Grieb (2008) 211–212 relates this restriction to the allotment of new citizens over *phylai* in Miletos. *Miletos* 61 (*Milet* I 3 149), a *sympoliteia* treaty between Miletos and Pidasa of 183, ll. 15–16 features the allotted *phrouarchos* and the guards sent to Pidasa.
[253] Thuc. 1.115.3; 8.63–76.
[254] Simonton (2017) 289; Robinson (2011) 179–180.

for allotted offices on Samos is very thin, however: a dedication of the first century shows that the *neopoiai* (temple officials) of the sanctuary of Hera were allotted.[255] On the other hand, over fifty extant inscriptions from the late fourth century down to Roman times prove the use of the lot for the assignment of new citizens to *polis* subgroups, a practice showing that in this respect Samos was more in line with many other *poleis* in eastern Greece (such as Ephesos) than with Athens.[256] So even within the Athenian orbit, democratic institutions show features significantly different from the Athenian model, and they did so even more clearly when Athens was no longer a major influence.

As for Delos, Athens maintained a firm hold on the sanctuary and the island from 478, when it became the headquarters of the Delian League, until 315, when Antigonos Monophthalmos declared the Greek cities independent, with an interval lasting from 404, owing to Athens's defeat in the Peloponnesian War and the ensuing collapse of the Delian League, until 394. In 167 the Roman Senate awarded Delos to Athens once more. Although Delos boasted a democracy during its period of independence, there is no evidence that its magistrates were allotted; as we shall see in section 8.2.4, the priesthoods were elected, and the evidence provides only one instance of a cult official appointed by lot.[257] To judge from remains of *kleroteria* found on the island dated to this period, it seems that only jury courts were allotted.[258]

The three Rhodian *poleis* of Lindos, Kamiros, and Ialysos joined the Delian League voluntarily, and at some point in the fifth century Athens supported the democrats on the island in overturning the traditional oligarchic regime.[259] After conflicts with Athens in the final decade of the Peloponnesian War, with support from Sparta in 408/7 the Rhodian elite regained the upper hand and brought about a *synoikismos*, forging the three existing Rhodian *poleis* into one political entity titled "Rhodes." This Rhodes joined the Second Athenian League in 378/7, but evidence shows that politically the *polis* switched back and forth between oligarchy and democracy. In the Hellenistic era, however, the democracy was firmly established. Although all its major magistracies were elected, the jury courts were selected by lot.[260]

Meanwhile in Byzantion, a democratic constitution was established in 390 by the Athenian general Thrasyboulos on the invitation of the local democratic

---

[255] *IG* XII 6 1:187.
[256] Samos: *IG* XII 6 1:17–79; Ephesos, the first case dating to c. 400 (?), *Ephesos* 82; *IEph* 1418 Ib; cf. above, section 7.2.3.
[257] *IG* XI 4 1032 (early second cent.): a *neokoros* of the Serapeion.
[258] Kosmetatou (2013) 248–249, nos. 17, 18, 19.
[259] The exact dates of these events cannot be ascertained, Berthold (1980) 32 n.3.
[260] Grieb (2008) 292–300: elected bodies: the *prytaneis*, who were not just the chair of the council but an independent executive body; the *nauarchos*, holding the military command; and other officials. Grieb (2008) 316–320 denies that the political emphasis on election of capable magistrates created again an "aristocracy" on Rhodes. Allotment of *dikastai*, see Grieb (2008) 301–302.

faction; at least some of its offices might have been drawn by lot, but no direct evidence is available. Calchedon, the city opposite the Bosporus, was enveloped by Byzantion and its democratic constitution in the mid-fourth century, and here the board of *aisymnetai* was selected by lot, at least in the early Hellenistic period.[261]

A special case was Thourioi, a colony founded in what is now Calabria, Italy, in 444/3 by Sybaris and Athens, with an invitation to other Greeks to join. Equality was a leading principle in the construction of the city, designed by Hippodamos of Miletos, who had designed the grid structure of Piraeus.[262] The political setup was created by the philosopher-intellectual Protagoras, who drew on the legal traditions of the ancient lawgivers Zaleukos and Charondas for the new *politeia*. In some respects, the *politeia* resembled that of Athens, such as the creation of ten *phylai*, in this case based on ethnic origins—and in the office of the *symboloi*, resembling the Athenian *thesmothetai*. But there were also notable differences. For example, the *strategoi* were elected for one year, and then had to wait four years until they could stand for election again. Giangiulio regards the *politeia* in Thourioi as a democracy with a strong emphasis on balance of powers—that is, until around twenty-five years later when the city fell into a *stasis* and shifted toward an oligarchy.[263] The absence of any evidence of drawing lots in Thourioi may be coincidence, but also suggests a deliberate differentiation from the Athenian system, owing to Protagoras's view of a balanced democracy based on "ancient" models.

Eretria, which just like Chalcis had been subjected to Athens in the fifth century and probably compelled to a similar form of democracy, turned oligarchic in 411 and remained so until ca. 395 when the city renewed its contacts with Athens on its own accord. A Law against Tyranny of ca. 340 stated that the *politeia* had to consist of a council and a prytany drawn from all citizens by lot.[264] This type of government obviously resembled that of Athens, which previously had imposed this type of *politeia* on Eretria, but now the city reintroduced it on a voluntary basis.

While Athens thus clearly urged its subject *poleis* toward democracies during its *arche* of the Delian League, notably in its last twenty years, in the fourth century it stimulated democracy elsewhere and supported existing democracies, while diverse democracies also developed independently from Athens.

---

[261] *IK Calchedon* 6. For the *aisymnetai* both in Megara and its colonies and in Miletos and its colonies, Barrio Vega (2011); for the politics in Byzantion and Calchedon, Robinson (2011) 146–149.
[262] See also above, section 6.3.3.
[263] Giangiulio (2015) 115–128.
[264] *SEG* 51.1105, ll. 17–20: "If anyone puts to the vote or writes or supports, either as official or as private citizen, the proposal to institute any other politeia of Eretria than a council and prytany drawn by lot from all Eretrians as is written"; for the text and historical context, Knoepfler (2002) 150–161.

Argos had grown into a *polis* thanks to a steady integration of its hinterland into an overarching framework in the archaic age. After a terrible defeat and the massacre of most Argive men at the hands of the Spartans in the Battle of Sepeia in the 490s, the *polis* had to be refounded. A democratic movement emerged after the Persian wars, and by the 460s a democracy was firmly established—even before the reforms in Athens—and Argos became an ally of Athens for many years.[265] However, the methods of selection of its offices are unknown. Other democracies, however, had nothing to do with Athens, and certainly not in terms of cooperation; this fact is particularly clear on Sicily.

On Sicily, after the democratizing moments of the late sixth–early fifth centuries, in many cities tyrants came and went, or returned to power. Between 472 and 461, however, they were ousted and expelled in a wave of popular resistance. In 461 a large number of cities on Sicily and in southern Italy decided in the Common Agreement to eject their tyrants, along with their mercenary forces, and to start anew with a refoundation of the citizen body and a redistribution of land (see section 7.2.3).[266] A period of new violence and political unrest ensued, exacerbated by the influx of former exiles who demanded to be reincluded, along with outsiders who likewise insisted to be accepted; this turmoil led to the redistributions of land and the refoundation of various *poleis*—frequently through sortition—as exemplified in Kamarina. Only some of these *poleis* became democratic, and even fewer remained so. That said, regimes with some measure of democracy were established in several cities, among which were Gela, Himera, Leontini, Syracuse, Selinous, Akragas, Kamarina, Messana/Zankle, and Rhegion.[267] Once again, we can note how the label "democracy" covers a great variety of *politeiai*, and the western cities—with civic bodies split into an elite and a *demos* as elsewhere in Greece—were certainly not radical democracies like Athens, but rather, according to David Teegarden, "at the very least broad oligarchies."[268]

In Syracuse, a colony of oligarchic Corinth, the defeat of the military, landholding upper class of *Gamoroi* by the forces of Gela in the 490s led to a social upheaval, when free noncitizens claimed a share in the land and the body politic.[269] But this "democratic" wave was short-lived: in 485/4 the city's tyrant Gelon restored the remaining *Gamoroi*, restructured the entire citizen population, and established a tyranny of his family, the Deinomenids.[270] After the fall of the dynasty in 466, unrest ensued between the "original" citizens and free

---

[265] Hansen and Nielsen (2004) 604; Giangiulio (2015) 30–31.
[266] Walthall and Souza (2021) 371–372.
[267] Robinson (2011) 67–106; 248–249; Teegarden (2018) 455–456.
[268] Teegarden (2018) 456 n.3.
[269] On the *Gamoroi*, see section 6.3.3.
[270] Giangiulio (2015) 78–79.

inhabitants—as yet excluded from citizenship and land holding—with attempts at a refoundation of citizenship of Syracuse. In 461 or shortly thereafter, some balance and a democracy of sorts were established, which lasted until 406. In this moderate democracy the assembly played a powerful role, but the offices were largely assigned, perhaps by election, to the members of the elite; notably, no offices were distributed by lot.[271] Again, this democracy had nothing to do and little in common with that of Athens. Syracuse was allied to Sparta and famously defeated the Athenians on their attempt to conquer Sicily in 413. In 412 an influential leader, Diokles, introduced a new democratic constitution including allotment of magistrates; the fact that Diokles's proposal was regarded as an innovation confirms that until then all offices were elected.[272] In 405, however, the democracy was overturned and replaced by the tyranny of the Dionysii, who remained in power until the mid-fourth century. By and large, Syracuse continued alternating between democracy and tyranny.

Taras, a Spartan colony in southern Italy, was ruled in the sixth century by a wealthy elite proud of its horsemanship. In the recurrent warfare with the local population, this cavalry was crucially defeated and massacred in ca. 470.[273] The social upheaval following this military defeat and demographic disaster led to the institution of a moderate democracy. Gradually, from ca. 450 on, Taras became more fully democratic, probably also due to pressure from the poorer sections of the population. Here, too, the establishment of a radical democracy was tightly connected to a deep social, economic, and military reconfiguration of the *polis*.[274] According to Aristotle, in the Tarentine democracy half of the *polis* offices were elected, half of them allotted, the first to have a better government, the second to give the *demos* a share, an approval of a well-ordered democracy that seems to have been more common among political thinkers.[275] Giangiulio regards this distribution of offices as fitting the *politeia* of Taras under the leadership of the philosopher-statesman Archytas in the first half of the fourth century, highly admired by both Plato and Aristotle.[276] Details on the allotment for

---

[271] Giangiulio (2015) 89–94; cf. Rutter (2002).

[272] Diod. 13.34.6. *Strategoi* were still elected in Diokles's constitution; Berger (1989) 307. Berger's suggestion that Diokles followed the Athenian example is implausible, considering that in 413 this man was deeply hostile to the Athenians, persuading the Syracusans to kill the captive Athenian generals and to consign the other Athenians to the quarries for labor under starvation (Diod. 13.19.3–4; 13.33.1), an event Berger does not discuss.

[273] Arist. *Pol.* 1303a4-7; Berger (1989) 308–309.

[274] Giangiulio (2015) 134–138.

[275] Arist. *Pol.* 1320b10–16 and the views of the *Rhetoric to Alexander* on the distribution of offices in democracies. Robinson (2011) 115–119 underlines that the offices in Taras were quite different from those in Athens, and that also otherwise the Tarantine democracy had nothing to do with Athens.

[276] Giangiulio (2015) 142. Harvey (1965) 104–107 argues attractively that Archytas was the first to develop the theory of arithmetical and geometrical equality for application to politics.

office in Taras are unfortunately lacking. The democracy in Taras was remarkably stable, lasting from ca. 450 to 272.

In archaic Kroton, the one thousand citizens of the original colony formed an oligarchic bastion, in which Pythagoras and his followers exercised long-lasting influence from the sixth century on. After defeating Sybaris in 510, the city traversed a period of deep tensions and upheavals. Public pressure that free inhabitants should be included in the citizen body and other sociopolitical forces led to a regime change toward a full democracy in the mid-fifth century, probably the early 440s, which lasted until ca. 410. Later sources claim that in democratic Kroton, magistrates were scrutinized by the people and selection took place by lot *ex hapanton* (from all).[277]

Elsewhere in the Greek world, notably in the east and south, the evidence shows glimpses of allotment application too incidental to allow for a wider picture. In Hellenistic Smyrna, new citizens who were allotted to *phylai* were inscribed on *kleroteria*; it is possible that the *phylai* used such lottery machines for selection for jury courts.[278] In Magnesia on the Maeander, in the second century some offices were drawn by lot while others were elected; a decree of the council and the *demos* of 197/6 for the arrangement of the festival for Zeus Sosipolis determined the place of both groups of officials in the procession.[279] Vincent Grieb shows that drawing lots for a few offices—and especially for the jury courts, combined with election of all other offices—was a quite common political model in the Hellenistic eastern Aegean.[280] In this type of elite-oriented *poleis*, Andreas Walser argues, jurisdiction by the people in the shape of allotment to jury courts was pivotal to the very notion of "democracy." When over time more and more complex cases were assigned to experienced, semiprofessional judges instead of to the jury courts, this was always decided by the people in the assembly—in other words a democratic decision for a less democratic influence on jurisdiction.[281]

In the federations, flourishing especially on the Greek mainland, drawing lots was applied to several aspects of governance. Some of these practices might have had a traditional background, others were probably established in the institutionalization of these confederacies to ensure some mixing of and a balance of power between the member *poleis*.

---

[277] Iambl. *VP*, 248–250, projecting the classical democracy of Kroton back onto to the late sixth century. On the political vicissitudes of Kroton, Giangiulio (2015) 97–114; Hansen and Nielsen (2004) 268; Robinson (1997) 76–77; (2011) 107–109.

[278] A *sympoliteia*-decree between Smyrna and Magnesia of 245 (?); *Smyrna* 14, l. 53. For *kleroteria* also used as *stelai* to list citizens, see above, note XX.

[279] *Magnesia* 2; *IMagn.* 98 + p. 295, ll. 37–38.

[280] Grieb (2008).

[281] Walser (2012).

The confederacy the leading citizens of the *poleis* of Boiotia created in the course of the fifth century consisted of a division of Boiotia into units of a roughly equal number of citizens plus their territory/*polis*, each represented by a *boiotarchos* and a fixed number of councilors in the federal council, which consisted of 660 *bouleutai* subdivided into four subcouncils. The selection of the *bouleutai* and their distribution into the subcouncils was probably by drawing lots, because the aim was clearly to mix the members from various *poleis*.[282] This combination of local basis, representation by numbers, and mixing in the central governance body resembles the Cleisthenic system, but unlike Athens after 462, the Boiotian league was not geared to equality: access to office was patently oligarchic, and in the fifth and early fourth centuries Thebes held unmistakable pride of place within the league. In the Hellenistic era, the hierarchical differences between the members were reduced.[283] In the grand Great Daidala-ritual, held every sixty years, the wagons of the league's member *poleis* on which wooden statues (*xoana*) were carried in procession across Boiotia were set in order by lot. As Emily Mackil observes, "The random order of the wagons prevented any attempt to impose a hierarchy within the framework of the *koinon*, a feature of Hellenistic but not of classical Boiotia."[284] Common military contingents of the league were also created by drawing lots to mix soldiers from various *poleis*.[285] After the battle of Leuktra in 371, one of the boiotarchs, Xenokrates, was selected by lot to offer the trophy to Zeus commemorating the victory over the Spartans.[286]

The Aitolian league came into existence in the first decades of the fourth century to bring the incidental collaboration of the Aitolian communities together in a stronger institution. Every member *polis* was headed by a college of archons, and the same model applied to the confederacy. The federal boards of the league all seem to have been elected, and reelection was possible and frequent.[287] However, in a lost play, *Meleager*, Sophocles pictured an Aitolia where the offices were distributed by lot (with beans), and the man who drew a white bean was selected.[288] Was this a real contemporary phenomenon in Aitolia, or did Sophocles project the Athenian practices of the later fifth century onto the Aitolian scene? The fact that Sophocles's lost play *Inachos* set in Argos provided

---

[282] For the system in more detail, Beck and Ganter (2015); for the Boiotian system as a model for the *politeia* of the future in Athens in 411, see earlier discussion.
[283] Cf. Müller (2011) on the revised system.
[284] Mackil (2013) 255.
[285] See above, p. 285–86.
[286] *IG* VII 2462, the epigram of the boiotarchs; cf. Mackil (2013) 470–471.
[287] On the Aitolian league Funke (2015). In *Milet* VI 3 1031 (*Miletos* 35), a treaty of *asylia* of the Aitolian league with Miletos, 250–200, some aspect of the arrangements is based on drawing lots (l. 15) but the context is illegible.
[288] Hesych. k 4343 Latte; the fragment of *Meleager* (fr. 404 Radt) is not included in the recent Loeb-ed.

dikastai with voting beans, just as in Athens, suggests the latter possibility, but some historical background of both the Argive and the Aitolian scenes cannot be ruled out.[289]

The value of drawing lots for creating a political balance was presumably well known by the late fourth century. In the pan-Hellenic league set up by Demetrius Poliorketes in 302, a revival of Philip of Macedon's Corinthian League, an executive board of five was to be drawn by lot from the confederate board in such a manner that no *ethnos* or *polis* had more than one representative.[290] Likewise, in the board of the Thessalian league (196–146), the *grammateis* (secretaries) were drawn by lot.[291] In this way, drawing lots secured random and even distribution of office.

8.2.4 Drawing lots for cultic offices, in Athens and beyond

As argued above, all forms of drawing lots in Greece were based on cooperation between humans and the gods, in which divine guidance could be effective to varying degrees. At one end of the spectrum, divine intentions were central: through divination, the gods were asked to express their views. At the other end of the spectrum, humans decided to apply the lot and expected the gods to safeguard the justness of the procedure, but not to determine the outcome. In all forms of distribution, including drawing lots for office, the composition of the group of candidates who would have an equal chance of being selected was an essential component of the procedure, and in all respects a human responsibility. For some priesthoods, however, the selection by lot of the priest or priestess was regarded as the choice the god(ess) had made. Other priests and priestesses, however, were elected, an entirely human decision, which occasionally was supported by arguments about the qualifications candidates ought to possess.[292] For instance, in Elis, a board of sixteen holy women had a range of sacred duties: at the sanctuary of Olympia, they organized the games of women and girls for Hera and wove a peplos for Hera; they organized choral dances for Dionysos, Hippodameia, and a local heroine; they were in charge of cults of the

---

[289] Hesych. k 4343 Latte; Soph. *Fragments* (Loeb-ed.) no. 288. For voting with pebbles or beans, see the cup by Douris (Vienna 3695) with the judgment by the Greeks in the dispute over the arms of Achilles. In the fourth century, voting in the Athenian jury courts was done by bronze tokens (*psephoi*, literally: pebbles). For representation of drawing lots in drama, see ch. 5.

[290] *IG* IV² 1 68 (the treaty dedicated at Epidauros with the constitution of the League) A ll. 76–78.

[291] Moretti, *ISE* II:103.

[292] Election: beside the priesthoods in Epidauros, the one in Priene and the one-to-be in Herakleia Latmia, in Amblada in Lykaonia a priestess who was "first elected according to a decree" dedicated to Aphrodite (*Anatolian Studies* 18 [1968]: 80, no. 30). I thank Vinciane Pirenne-Delforge for her advice.

dead; and more. The sixteen women, who were all married, were "outstanding in age, esteem, and understanding," so clearly elected.[293]

Whatever the means of selection, holding a priesthood was an attractive *time* for the sake of its function—the public performance of exchange with the gods on behalf of the community—but also because priesthoods usually came with perquisites in the form of special portions of sacrificial meat, the proceeds of the sale of the hides or the bones of the animal, remuneration in money, or all of these. Priests and priestesses rarely performed the sacrifices themselves, but they oversaw the actual slaughter performed by a *mageiros* (slaughterer) and the distribution of the meat, and they were responsible, often together with *polis* officials, for organization of the festivals. High city officers, such as the archons in Athens, were likewise the leading officials of sacrifices and other *polis* rituals and festivals.

In several *poleis* in eastern Greece, priesthoods came to be sold—a practice without parallel for political office, but comparable to the sale of citizenship; both types of sale begin in the fourth century.[294] Selection by sale and by election obviously was an entirely human affair, but even in these cases divine sanction of the procedure or the result would be desirable. The city of Herakleia Latmia, for instance, asked Apollo in his oracle at Didyma whether they should select the priestess of Athena Latmia by sale of the office for life, or have her elected by the *polis* for a year; the god preferred the latter option.[295] Sale of the office did not detract from the requirements for eligibility for the priesthood: in Kos, descent from citizens on two sides was taken for granted, and when in the third century Halikarnassos decided to institute a priestess of Artemis Pergaia, a priesthood to be sold and held for life, she had to be a woman of citizen descent on both sides for three generations.[296]

Athens is the most conspicuous case for selection by lot of priests and priestesses of *polis* cults, also long before the democracy. Traditionally, as we saw earlier, priests and priestesses were drawn from the *gene* on the basis of their purity of birth, that is, of Athenian descent on both sides.[297] Once Pericles's Citizenship Law had raised all Athenians to the same level of purity of birth, new priestesses and priests were drawn by lot from all citizens, and, in the case

---

[293] Paus. 5.16.2–9; 6.24.10, 26.1. According to the tradition, one woman was elected in each of the sixteen most prominent cities of Elis and Pisatis, but from the fourth cent. on, two women were elected from each of the eight *phylai*. Cf. Mitsopoulos-Leon (1984).

[294] Sales of priesthoods: Kos, Chios, Priene, Halikarnassos, Erythrai (*Erythrae* 60), Miletos (*Milet* VI.3; *CGRN* 39, *CGRN* 100), and in many other cities in Asia Minor; see Parker and Obbink (2000) 421–422 n 16. Sale of citizenship, as e.g., in Dyme (Rizakis, *Achaie* III 3, third cent.) is not to be confused with a formal sale of offices within the citizen body.

[295] *Herakleia Latmia* 27, ca. 100.

[296] *Halikarnassos* 3, *LSA* 73, ll. 4–8.

[297] For all evidence on the selection in the *gene*, Blok and Lambert (2009).

of male priests by rotation, per *phyle*.²⁹⁸ For the archonships, just as for the priesthoods, only Athenians born from two Athenian parents were eligible, because they had extensive cultic roles. Of newly made citizens, when they married Athenian women, the next descendants would have two Athenian parents and hence could partake in the drawing of lots for these offices.²⁹⁹ Besides the numerous priesthoods held by the *gene*, another ancient office was the "child of the hearth," a boy or a girl drawn by lot by the *basileus* to be initiated in the Mysteries of Eleusis on behalf of the city. The child was selected from candidates registered by their parents; in the fourth century all children were eligible, but in late Hellenistic times they appear to have been preselected from prominent families.³⁰⁰ While in Athens virtually all priesthoods were selected by lot, some cult personnel in Athens were elected—for instance, the *epimeletai* (overseers) of the procession to Eleusis (later they were drawn by lot) and the four *epimeletai* of the Mysteries: two elected from all citizens, one from the *genos* Eumolpidai and one from the Kerykes.³⁰¹

In Athens, the proliferation of cultic, political, and administrative offices distributed by lot among citizens was a direct result of the democratic ideology and constitution. "Democratic" male priests served in office for one year, just as the "political" offices, whereas *genos* priests served for a lifetime, as did priestesses, including the "democratic" ones in the fifth and fourth centuries. Yet the selection by lot among the *gene* long preceded the democratic spread of allotment, based on the model of distribution by lot of the inheritance, but also with a hint of divine selection, which carried over in the selection of the first priestess from all the Athenian women, Myrrhine. Plato expresses a similar view of the principles underlying the selection when in the *Laws* he states that the gods use the divine chance (*tyche*) of the lot to make their own choice of priests and priestesses.³⁰²

---

²⁹⁸ E.g. "democratic" priestesses: Athene Nike, Aphrodite Pandemos; priests: Asklepios and Hygieia, Dionysos, Poseidon Pelagios, Zeus Soter, Meter. Priest and priestess of Bendis: *IG* II² 1361 (330-324/3), with comm. on AIO. Priests and priestesses of various hero-cults (not always identifiable) served by *orgeones* and *thiasotai* were drawn by lot from the worshipping group; in some of them citizens and noncitizens worshiped together, but priest(esse)s were normally citizens (Parker [1996] 333-342; Wijma [2014] 139-155, 169-171 lists eighteen attested *orgeones*-groups in Attica). *Hieropoioi* (a civic office serving a cult) are first attested in the mid-sixth century (*IG* I³ 507, 508); they were a small group serving the cult of Athena, and how they were selected is unclear. In the classical age, *hieropoioi* were numerous and involved in many cults, selected by lot from all male citizens. *Zakoroi* (male or female cult personnel) were selected in varying ways, not always clearly attested.

²⁹⁹ Blok (2017) 257-265.

³⁰⁰ *Ag.* XVI 56(1) = 56(3); Clinton (1974) 98-114. Likewise, the *Pythaistai*, an Athenian delegation occasionally sent to Delphi, were drawn by lot but from prominent families only in the late Hellenistic and Roman ages (*FD* III 2:14, Parker [2005] 83-86) and the prominent roles in the group were elected by show of hands (*FD* III 2:6, 54, 63). I have not been able to ascertain how the young *arrhephoroi* (serving Athena) and *kanephoroi* (heading religious processions) were selected, but it would seem plausible that the procedure for them followed patterns similar to that of the "child of the hearth."

³⁰¹ *Ath.Pol.* 56.4; 57.1.

³⁰² Plato, *Laws*, 759b-c. For this passage, see also ch. 2.

Earlier I argued that the venerable practice of the *gene* may have served as an anchoring device, a framework serving as a precedent for the allotment of the *Tamiai* and the archons in Solon's *politeia*. The fact that in Athens since early times the *genos* priests and priestesses were selected by lot raises the question to what extent this tradition eased the exceptionally wide use of the lot for all offices in democratic Athens. To answer this question, a detailed comparison with other *poleis* is necessary, and here again the scarce and unevenly distributed evidence is not as helpful as we might wish. Evidence of priests and priestesses drawn by lot is slightly richer than that of election, but the coincidence of survival precludes firm conclusions about which method prevailed in the Greek world and why.

Of some priesthoods in several *poleis* the evidence is explicit that the selection by lot of cult personnel was a form of divine selection. In Astypalaia, in the Dodecanese, the cult group of the "ancestral gods" saw the selection of the priest Ophelion by the lot as a choice of the goddess Atargatis herself; the decree to honor him was decided by the goddess and the cult group together.[303] In the oracle sanctuary of Didyma, the *prophetes* was selected by Apollo himself by lot, as shown in an honorific decree for one of them, who was three times drawn by "pious lots" and garlanded by "immortal crowns."[304] Likewise, in Didyma the priest of Artemis Pytheia was drawn by lot; in his dedication to the goddess, one of these priests described his selection as "a *geras* among mortals ... owing to divine grace."[305]

For the Pythia in Delphi, no evidence relates explicitly that her selection by lot from among all Delphic women was a divine selection, but the parallels just mentioned render this highly likely.[306] Drawn from all the city's women, the Pythia would represent the entire community by choice of the god, whereas the two priests serving the cult of Apollo were recruited from select families, as were the five *hosioi* (holy, pious men) selected from families claiming descent from the first man Deukalion.[307] Whether the priests and *hosioi* were selected by lot or election is not recorded, but considering the similarity of the entitlements of the *hosioi* to those of the Athenian *gene*—namely mythical genealogy underpinning eligibility for cultic office as an inheritance—selection by lot of the *hosioi* would be plausible.[308]

---

[303] *IG* XII 3 178, end third–early second cent.
[304] *Miletos* 455; *IDidyma* 282; classical or Hellenistic.
[305] *Didyma* 550; *IDidyma* 118, ll. 10–11.
[306] Eur. *Ion*, 1322–1323: 'Φοίβου προφῆτις, τρίποδος ἀρχαῖον νόμον/ σῴζουσα, πασῶν Δελφίδων ἐξαίρετος. "Prophet of Phoebus, preserving the ancient law of the tripod, selected from all Delphic women"; αἱρέω/αἱρεῖσθαι can mean "to select" regardless of the method, cf. Abel (1983) 18–19; Plut. *Mor.* 405c-d (*De Pyth.* 22) implies that the selection was unpredictable, hence by lot, because he seems to think she was a poor peasant girl, whereas election might have favored the rich and educated women. For life: Aesch. *Eum.* 38; *FD* III 1 553 (Rom. era); Diod. 16.26.6; Plut. 405c-d.
[307] Select families: Eur. *Ion*, 416; Plut. *Mor.* 292d; Fontenrose (1978) 218–219.
[308] See also ch. 2.6.

In other *poleis* where priests were drawn by lot, it is unclear if the selection was considered a divine choice or not, such as in Lindos the priest of Helios, in Pergamon a priest of an unknown cult for a term of a year, and in Andania all priests and priestesses.[309] In Epidauros, the priest of Asklepios was presumably drawn by lot since the cult was founded in the late sixth century; the election of additional priests was probably a later development.[310] On Delos, the numerous inscriptions do not specify the method of selection, while in Hellenistic-Roman times, when the island was again under Athenian rule, the priest of Hestia, Demos, and Rome was elected by show of hands, and the treasurers of the Delian sanctuaries were likewise elected.[311]

Particularly interesting are the arrangements for the sale of priesthoods, which occasionally provide insights into the practices prior to the change to sale of *timai*, which became a rather common practice across the *poleis* in the east from the fourth century on. One such *polis* was Chios, where a contract of ca. 400–350 for a priesthood of Herakles allows the tentative reconstruction of the cult's organization before the office came to be sold. This local cult belonged to a *genos*:

> To the priest of Herakles is to be given, whenever the *genos* sacrifices: tongues, the entrails which [are placed] in the hands [of the statue], a double portion of meat, and the skins. If an individual sacrifices, to the priest of Herakles is to be given: tongues, the entrails which [are placed] in the hands [of the statue] and a double portion of meat. The one sacrificing is to call out to the priest, and if the priest is not present, one of those assigned by lot is to act as deputy-priest. But the one sacrificing should [nevertheless] give the proceeds [i.e., the perquisites] to the priest. All of the same things are to apply to the other priests who purchase a priesthood.[312]

The text states that this priesthood had been or was to be sold, but that the claims of the *genos* to the cult and its proceeds were maintained. Hence it would seem that the priesthood was sold to a member of the *genos*, rather than to just a random citizen. If the priest was absent, one from a group of people would act as deputy-priest; these individuals had been drawn by lot, presumably from all members of the right age and gender of the *genos*, to whom the cult belonged. Who from this group was to act as deputy is not stated; perhaps once again lots

---

[309] Lindos: *IG* XII 1 833 (1st c.); Pergamon: *IPergamon* I 40; *CGRN* 124, second half of the third century; Andania: *IG* V 1 1390 (92/1).
[310] Lot: *IG* IV² 1 235, dedicating to Asklepios and Apollo (fourth–third cent.); election: *IG* IV² 1 89, second–third cent. AD.
[311] Priest: *ID* 1877, ll. 2–3 (129/8). Treasurers: *ID* 1417, 1421, etc.
[312] *CGRN* 50, text and translation. See also ch. 3.5.

were drawn for this role, but it also could be any one of them who happened to be around. The potential deputy-priests had been drawn by lot in advance, perhaps selected once a year, or even longer ago. Apparently, this priesthood of the cult was previously filled by drawing lots among the *genos* to whom it belonged, and when the procedure was turned into a sale the proceeds of which were for the *polis*, the members of the *genos* were the only ones who could make a bid; the other *gennetai* still drew lots to choose a deputy.

On Kos, a *synoikismos* in 366 set a reorganization of most priesthoods and a substantial number of cultic regulations in motion. Of the contracts for the sale of priesthoods, both of male and female priests, quite a number are extant dating to the late fourth and early third centuries.[313] From one such document, concerning the priestesshood of Demeter, we may infer that, before the office came to be sold, women were drawn by lot to serve the goddess, and that those who had been thus selected retained this religious status after the introduction of the sale system.[314] The priesthoods of Zeus Polieus and Demeter Olympia were filled from subdivisions of the *polis* to be sold, again pointing to an older system of distribution to which sale had been added.[315] For other priesthoods, combinations of sale and lot were in place, which may point to drawing lots between those willing to pay the asking price. Many but not all of these priesthoods were for life.[316] In their edition of the documents, Robert Parker and Dirk Obbink suspect that the shift to the sale system was driven by lack of public funds in Kos, and presumably this condition also obtained in the other *poleis* where the sale of offices was introduced.[317]

With the introduction of sale, in some *poleis* all three modes of selection for office were practiced, providing distinct degrees on the spectrum of human and divine collaboration in the governance of the *polis* and its cults. One such *polis* was Priene, where in the second century a certain Anaxidemos son of Apollonios became priest of an unknown cult by drawing lots, the priest of King Nikomedes II Epiphanes was elected, and several other priesthoods were sold.[318] These arrangements show a combination of venerable procedures, political versatility, and economic pragmatism, an arrangement that kept Greek *poleis* afloat in turbulent circumstances without losing their anchorage in *polis* traditions.

---

[313] *CGRN* 85, 147, 163, 164, 167, 208, 220, 221. Cf. Parker and Obbink (2000; 2001).
[314] *IG* XII 4 1:356; *LSCG* no. 175; Parker and Obbink (2000) 420.
[315] *LSCG* no. 156 A; 154 A. Parker and Obbink (2000) 420.
[316] Parker and Obbink (2000) 420, 424.
[317] Parker and Obbink (2000) 420.
[318] Lot: *Priene* 212, *IPriene* 205; election: *Priene* 12, *IPriene* 43 (128/7) ll. 10–11. Sale: *Priene* 210, *IPriene* 174 (130), *Priene* 211, *Priene* 213, etc.

Endnote 1: The historicity of Solon and his laws

For over a century, every aspect of the life, background, and work of Solon of Athens has been the subject of intense scholarly debate. Various approaches to the intrinsic difficulties of the written sources—which all were recorded or written long after Solon's ascribed lifetime—and to potential historical reconstructions of Attica in the archaic age based on archaeological research have generated a broad spectrum of disparate positions. At the one end of the spectrum, reasonable doubts about the nature of the evidence do not essentially undermine the trust in the historical veracity of Solon's reported lifetime, his archonship, the authorship of his poetry and laws, and his role as statesman and founder of the democracy of Athens. At the other end, the problematics of the written tradition mean that every statement about Solon must remain hypothetical, and that the only "facts" we have are the imagined, idealized reconstructions of him dating to the fourth century and later, plus abundant archaeological evidence that is nigh impossible to match with the textual tradition. Each of these positions (and all shades in between) are represented through a plethora of scholarly publications.[319] This is not the place to review all this literature, nor to enter a full-length debate of the sources, but given the role the present study assigns to Solon, I need to clarify my own position on this issue.

In my view, it is certain that the re-edition of the laws of Athens between 410 and 399 meant a codification of laws dating from the late seventh to the early fifth centuries, many of which were henceforth canonized as issued by Solon. In the fourth century, with his reconfiguration as the founding father of the democracy and of the "ancient *politeia*," claiming Solon as its originator gave any law an appealing aura of quality and antiquity; that numerous laws of the period cannot realistically be attributed to Solon has now been established beyond doubt. Regarding the perception of Solon as the ideal statesman of old, the *Athenaion Politeia* offers a telltale testimony.[320] A similar process of hypothetical attribution is likewise detectable in the poetry ascribed to Solon: by the fourth century, all oral elegiac poetry of the archaic age—and with an implied provenance in Attica—boasted Solon as its author and original performer, and was canonized into collections of his poetry.[321] Of the complex chronology of Solon's lifetime, the year 594 for his archonship seems the most plausible,[322] but hardly rock solid. I regard all these incontrovertible observations as strong warnings not to take the traditional evidence at face value, and to be wary of possible anachronisms

---

[319] For a recent representative of the skeptical position, see Rönnberg (2021) 40–56, with extensive bibliography.
[320] Gehrke (2006).
[321] Lardinois (2006).
[322] Wallace (1983).

and later projections onto the archaic age; however, they should not be taken as signs that Solon and all his laws are largely, let alone entirely, figments of later imaginations.

In the present study, I use the year 594 as a chronological peg; whether his archonship was exactly in this year or a few years later, or even earlier, is immaterial to the argument put forward here. Even if we accept 594 as the year of his archonship, it would be impossible for Solon to achieve all his measures in a single year, so the laws ascribed to him and accepted as authentic must be dated to sometime after his archonship. Together with Julia Krul I have presented evidence supporting our contention that Solon abolished debt slavery, canceled existing debts, and forbade debts on the person—which means that these measures, along with fragments 4 and 36 of the poems, are effectively Solon's.[323] Although there is no definitive evidence, it seems to me that trying to solve the debt problem was Solon's uppermost priority, and that he therefore enacted these measures first.

Solon also took other measures, and though he enacted numerous new laws, they should not be taken to form a law code as such, certainly not in the present-day sense.[324] Yet I think there are valid reasons for acknowledging that Solon issued several coherent statutes with the aim of reducing the tensions in Athenian society. Among those reasons is the wider context of attested social conflict and comparable legislation in other archaic-era *poleis*, clearly meant to address conflicts of this nature and various other underlying issues—notably property, inheritance, and conditions for belonging to the citizen body *in nascente*. Laws of this kind are, for instance, the earliest parts of the Gortyn laws; early legislation hailing from elsewhere in Crete, Asia Minor, and mainland Greece; and likewise in some colonies (Cyrene, Naupaktos).[325] Of specific laws in the Solonian corpus, it is difficult to ascertain with confidence that they are indeed Solon's, rather than stemming from (early) sixth-century Athens, without an identifiable agent behind them. While I am hesitant to ascribe the archaic Athenian funerary laws to Solon himself, legislation on legitimacy and inheritance rights seems more plausible to be his own, considering the significance of such rules for ownership of property and for citizenship, both of which were demonstrably core issues in the developing *poleis* of the archaic age.[326]

On Solon's *politeia* and the property classes, opinions diverge as strongly as on anything regarding Solon, ranging from scholars who follow the *Athenaion Politeia* to the letter, to those who contest the very existence of the

---

[323] Blok and Krul (2017). Interestingly, Rönnberg (2021) quotes from our article only what supports his skeptical view, not the core argument running counter to it.
[324] For this argument convincing Hölkeskamp (1999).
[325] Important collections are *inter alia Nomima* (1994–1995); Koerner (1993); and for Crete, *LAC*.
[326] Funerary laws, see Blok (2006); legitimacy, see Lape (2002/3); Blok (2017) 107–116.

property classes. As I explain in chapter 8, in my view Solon created—or perhaps reshuffled—a grouping of the population of Athens according to their agricultural wealth and their concomitant obligations for contributions in kind to the community (taxes and perhaps military power). His purpose must have been the same as in everything else he is credited with: attempts at reducing rivalries and competition among the elite for political power by structuring the access to governmental offices, restoring and grounding the free status of all citizens, and offering some say in the *polis* to all compartments of the free population, in proportion to their social status. All of this squares well with the current perception of what was unfolding in archaic *poleis*, diverse though they were.

The concept of *politeia*—a noun that only appeared over a century later—perhaps suggests a strong legal system for the entire *polis*, either by tradition or in the form of a theoretical scheme, not properly applicable to early sixth-century reality. Regarding Solon's endeavors, I use *politeia* in a looser way, indicating the social and political results he envisaged to bring about in the society to which he belonged. In his understanding of this social environment, and how the relations between the various groups should be, Solon was not a revolutionary at all. On the contrary, he reduced the extreme effects of wealth and its concomitant element of competition by regulating access to power, mixing social groups and implementing measures constraining accumulation of wealth. He created a foundation supporting the *demos*, notably in the judicial domain. In this way, Solon sought a balance among the distinct groups of the *polis*, in accordance with the political ideas, socioeconomic realities, and legislative interventions of the time.

Endnote 2: The *Ath.Pol.* and the *Politics* on Solon's constitution

On the selection of the *archai*, *Ath.Pol.* 8.1 states the following:

> The *archai* he instituted to be selected by lot from preselected candidates [*klerotas ek prokriton*], which each of the *phylai* elected by preliminary vote [*prokrino*]. For the Nine Archons each made a preliminary election of ten, and from them they were drawn by lot; hence it is still the tradition in the *phylai* that each draws ten by lot [*klero*] and then from these they draw [the archons] by the bean [*kuameuo*]. The proof that he instituted the selection by lot according to the property assessments [*timema*] is the law about the *Tamiai*, that is followed and still in force even today; for it orders the *Tamiai* to be drawn by lot from the *pentakosiomedimnoi*.

In his final evaluation of Solon's *politeia, Ath.Pol.* 9.1 says,

> The three features in Solon's *politeia* that were most to the benefit of the *demos* [*demotikos*] seem to be these, first and most important, the prohibition of loans secured on the person, second, to allow to anyone who wished to seek redress on behalf of people who had been treated unjustly, and third, what some say has been foremost the source of power of the multitude [*plethos*], is the right of redress (*ephesis*) to the jury court [*dikasterion*]; for the demos having power over [*kurios*] the vote in court [*psephos*] has power over the *politeia*.

In the *Politics*, Aristotle states,

> [Solon] established our traditional [*patrios*] democracy with a skillful blending of the constitution: the Council on the Areopagus being an oligarchic element, the elective magistracies aristocratic and the law-courts representing the interests of the *demos* [*demotikos*]. And although really in regard to certain of these features, the Council and the selection [*hairesis*] of magistrates, Solon seems merely to have abstained from abolishing [*katalusai*] institutions that existed already, he does appear to have founded the democracy [*demos*] by constituting the jury-court [*diskasterion*] from all the citizens [*ek panton*]. For this he is actually blamed by some persons, as having dissolved the power of the other parts [*thatera*] of the community by making the law-court [*diskasterion*], which was elected by lot [*kleroton*], all-powerful.[327]

Combined, these passages in the *Ath.Pol.* and the *Politics* have raised questions and notably doubts about the selection of the archons.[328] Some scholars hold that Aristotle's statement in *Politics*—namely, that Solon did not destroy existing institutions—is at odds with the account in *Ath.Pol.* 8.1 that Solon instituted the selection of archons and the *Tamiai* by lot. For those scholars who regard Aristotle as the author of the *Ath.Pol.*, this would also mean that the philosopher changed his mind on Solon's laws. The perceived discrepancy between the two texts reinforces the conviction of those scholars who regard the equality of the lot for political office as typical of the democracy, and as being incompatible with the elite values of the archaic age. For them, it must have been Cleisthenes who introduced drawing lots for political office, and the *Ath.Pol.* is therefore mistaken, projecting the fourth-century law on the *Tamiai* back onto the sixth

---

[327] Arist. *Pol.* 1273b38–1274a6. Cf. 1274a16–17, 1281b25–34 (trans. H. Rackham [Loeb ed.], slightly modified).

[328] For the best overviews of the debate, see Develin (1979); Rhodes, *CAAP ad loc.*; Hansen (1990); Barucchi (2004/5). See also Endnote 3 for details.

century.³²⁹ The discussion is further complicated by the fact that the verb *haireo* (figuring in *Politics*) can mean "to elect," but also simply "to appoint" or "to select," notably if the method of selection is not decisive or specified.³³⁰

Nonetheless, I would argue that the texts are not really at odds, but instead agree on the main elements of Solon's institutional measures concerning the archons and the courts, on the outcomes of which they also take a fourth-century viewpoint. They do so in different ways: *Ath.Pol.* gives an account of the various procedures to the best of his abilities, while Aristotle evaluates the results of the whole *politeia* in the framework of his political theory.

Both authors regard Solon's *politeia* as the foundation of the fourth-century democracy because it made the first step in the power of the people's court. Beginning in Solon's *politeia* with the right of redress (*ephesis*), in the fourth century the power of the *dikasteria* had developed into the full control of the magistrates. Both authors refer to critics, who later, in their own time, held Solon responsible for initiating what they felt had grown into a democratic excess of power (Aristotle reports this in a way in which he seems to distance himself from such criticism). Looking back, this viewpoint is reflected in the fourth-century vocabulary (*demotikos, dikasterion, ek panton*) with which they describe Solon's institutions for the people's court. In Aristotle's account, the critics even ascribe the fourth-century selection procedure for the courts by lot to Solon; I explain in chapter 8 why this assumption cannot be correct.

Ath.Pol. gives a matter-of-fact account of the selection of the archons (*klerosis ek prokriton*) and of the *Tamiai* (*klerosis* from the *pentakosiomedimnoi*) instituted by Solon and the shape these procedures had acquired in his own time. The fact that by the fourth century the political meaning of the *pentakosiomedimnoi* as a class was obsolete in other respects, and that even as a wealth criterion it was no longer functional, indicates that *Ath.Pol.*'s account of Solon's institution is the more reliable.³³¹ For Aristotle, the nature of the *politeia* depended not on the method of selection *per se* but on the share—created by whatever means—that the various socioeconomic groups held in the *polis*'s institutions.³³² Solon firmly secured the hold on the *archai* by the elite, first defined in terms of wealth (oligarchic) and next by merit (aristocratic). Compared to what went on before, namely selection of the archons "by excellence and wealth" (*Ath.Pol.* 3.1), Solon indeed did not change anything; the changes that he did make to the procedure did not alter what, in Aristotle's view, really mattered for the *archai*. What mattered for

---

³²⁹ For example, De Ste. Croix (2004b); Hansen (1990); see the main text for further explanation and my refutation of this position.
³³⁰ See, for instance, the crucial passage on selection in Arist. *Pol.* 1300a8–1300b5, further discussed below. Cf. Abel (1983) 18–19, 41; Rhodes, *CAAP* 182; contra Bubelis (2016) 36 n.26.
³³¹ Cf. *Ath.Pol.* 47.1.
³³² Canevaro and Esu (2018); see further the main text.

the *politeia*, however, was Solon's institution of the power of the people in the court: Aristotle duly notes that this was the change that in one particular point redressed the share of each socioeconomic group in the *politeia*, which would ultimately lead to the democracy of the fourth century.

Endnote 3: *Ath.Pol.* 8.1 on the procedure in Solon's *klerosis ek prokriton*

The *Ath.Pol.* is preserved in several papyri, of which parts are lost or damaged and other parts seem to be a bit confused. The passage 8.1 on Solon's procedure has this partly illegible sentence:

προὔκρινειν δ' εἰς τοὺς ἐννέα ἄρχοντας ἑκάστη δέκα, καὶ του ... ληρουν
Each (*phyle*) made a preliminary election of ten for the nine archonships, and ... by lot.

F. Kenyon, in the first edition of the text (1891), restored here καὶ τού[τους ἐκ]λήρουν; in his fourth edition (Berlin 1903) he amended the text into καὶ <ἐκ> τού[των ἐκ]λήρουν. Chambers (1965) 35 supports Kenyon's first restoration, translated as "they used to assign these men to the offices by lot." Rhodes, *CAAP* 148–149, follows Kenyon's later emendation, because it better expresses what the text clearly means to say, not that the elected men were assigned by lot to the archonships, but that the archons were selected by lot from the *prokritoi*. Barucchi (2004/5) 74–75 follows Chambers's choice, and she takes this to imply that the *phyle* was involved in the whole procedure of *prokrisis* and allotment, whereas in Rhodes's version the final allotment would have been handled by others, possibly the Areopagos (Barucchi does not mention this). I agree with Barucchi that Chambers's restoration better fits the extant MS, but I do not agree with her inference. In neither version does the text indicate who actually made or oversaw the allotment, be it the *phyle* or another body. That from the forty *prokritoi*, nine were selected by lot to be archons is unmistakable. Whether they were each allotted to specific archonships, the text does not specify: κληρόω just means "to draw lots"; for assigning specific items to each by lot, one would rather expect ἐπικληρόω. How the nine archonships were distributed over the nine men selected by lot therefore remains unclear.

Endnote 4: The vocabulary of the lot in the Ancient Near East

The Assyrian Dictionary of the Oriental Institute of the University of Chicago (*CAD*) vol. I, ed. M. T. Roth (Chicago: Oriental Institute, University of Chicago) offers *s.v. isqu*: 1. lot (as a device to determine a selection; 2. share (a portion of land, inheritance, property or booty, income from a secular or a temple office, assigned by lot); 3. lot, fortune, fate, destiny (assigned by the gods); 4. nature, power, special qualification, emblem. The word appears from Old Babylonian onward. The semantic range of the term *isqu* is conditioned by the Akkadian as well as by the Sumerian background. The Akkadian refers to the aspect of "assigned object," while the Sumerian giš.šub.ba "cast lot" (lit. wood) indicates the way in which these assignments were made, either in fact or in theory. The nuance "fate" is already in evidence in the Sumerian proverb giš.šub ús.sa.ab, "accept your lot." In inheritance cases, the "lot" vocabulary refers to an assignment of portions to which all agree; this usage is particularly attested in Sumerian and Old Babylonian, where it referred to an "egalitarian criterion," but later it meant any portion (cf. Milano [2020] 41). In the meaning "prebend," *isqu* (giš.šub.ba) corresponds to Old Babylonian mar.za. The use of *iqsu* for the distribution of temple perquisites and as an emblem of the king distinguishes this usage in the Ancient Near East from uses of the lot in ancient Greece, with its quite different organization of state and society, but in other respects the meaning and uses of lot-vocabulary in both civilizations show striking similarities.

Endnote 5: Solon's council of four hundred

According to *Ath.Pol.* 8.4, Solon created a council of four hundred, with one hundred men elected per *phyle*. The main reason why some scholars doubt the accuracy of this statement is the contention that such a council would fit the *politeia* of Solon neither in functional terms nor as an archaic institution, a view raising the suspicion that the *Ath.Pol.* may have projected later institutions back in time. *Ath.Pol.* 31.1 states that the oligarchs of 411 wanted a council of four hundred *kata ta patria* (as was ancestral). Was this claim of an ancestral council an invention of tradition, or did the oligarchs draw on a real precedent? Following on these questions, can we regard the passage in 8.4 as an independent reference to a historical council, or did the author believe the oligarchs' claim and project their planned council back in time? The debate also has implications for the interpretation of Herodotus's account that "the council" resisted the attempted coup by Kleomenes and Isagoras (Hdt. 5.72.1) when the latter had lost the primacy in the *polis* to Cleisthenes shortly before 508/7. If this account is correct, was Herodotus referring to the Areopagos or the council of four hundred? Finally, how to read Plutarch's *Life of Solon*, considering that Plutarch, although writing over seven hundred years after Solon, had far more sources at his disposal than we have today? When Plutarch states that Solon wanted "the ship of state resting on two anchors" (Plut. *Sol.* 19.1), was this Solon's own simile or Plutarch's? And do the anchors refer to the two councils or something else? Is Plutarch's account (*Sol.* 19.3) a summary of the *Ath.Pol.* in which he projects the probouleutic role of the council of five hundred back in time onto Solon's of four hundred, or did he use independent evidence on the council of four hundred?[333] In short, had there actually been a council of four hundred under Solon, or did our late sources project a democratic institution known to them back to 594, because in the fourth century Solon was regarded as the founder of the democracy?

My views on these questions, further reflected in the main text, are, first, that if the council existed on the terms listed by *Ath.Pol.*, it would fit the logic underlying Solon's *politeia*: a clearly defined role in the *polis*'s institutions for each of the property classes. Furthermore, the probouleutic function of the council, as an intermediary between the top-class archons and the people, would diminish the frictions between the classes and reduce the risk of strife or tyranny. Second, there were councils in other *poleis* in this period, such as on Chios (ML 8). Third, unless there are clear and solid reasons to do so, I see no reason to doubt the accuracy of the *Ath.Pol.*, which demonstrably had access to a range of independent sources. An example of such solid reasons to reject the reliability of the *Ath.Pol.* is Draco's constitution in *Ath.Pol.* 4, but on (aspects of) Solon's measures, *Ath.Pol.* was better informed. In sum, personally I am convinced that Solon instituted a council of four hundred.

Herodotus also reports (5.72) that Kleomenes banished seven hundred families that Isagoras had listed for him, and then tried to dissolve the council by granting the *archai* to three hundred of Isagoras's followers, but that the council resisted him. Whether Herodotus refers to the Areopagos or the council of four hundred is hard to determine, because both had good reasons to resist the coup; the story therefore offers neither proof of the existence of the council of four hundred, nor of the opposite. It is highly unlikely that the court in this account was the new council of five hundred, because it took several years for Cleisthenes's new scheme to be implemented; the first meeting of the new council is commonly dated to 501/0.

Endnote 6: The *diagramma* for Cyrene

An inscription, dated to 321 in present scholarship, holds a decree of Ptolemy I establishing a new constitution for Cyrene and its surrounding area. Since its *editio princeps* of 1925 and an emended edition of 1928, this decree, called a

---

[333] For the main arguments in the debate, see Rhodes, *CAAP ad Ath.Pol.* 8.4, and more recently Tsigarida (2006) 101–106 and Valdés Guía (2022b), who all believe this council existed, and Bartzoka (2012), who doubts it.

diagramma, has evoked ample scholarly debate among epigraphists and (political) historians. The constitution provided for a *politeuma* (active citizenship) on a census of twenty *mnai* (two thousand drachma), the same property threshold as Antipater instituted at Athens in 322/1, and a minimum age of thirty years. From this *politeuma*, called the "Ten Thousand," a jury court of fifteen hundred to deal with homicide cases was to be selected by lot, and a council of five hundred to be selected by lot from those over fifty years of age. In his detailed analysis of the constitution, J. O. Larsen labeled it "moderately oligarchic."[334] Due to its informative details, the *diagramma* has become a foundational document for historians of Greek political history of the Hellenistic era, of the reign of the Ptolemies, and of Cyrene.[335]

Considering this wealth of scholarship generated by the *diagramma*, the article by P. M. Fraser in *Berytus* (1958) makes for sobering reading. On his account, both the *editio princeps* of 1925 and the emended edition of 1928 stated that the damaged condition of the stone made reading extremely difficult, and clearly indicated the tentative nature of the abundant restorations. However, in the text published as *SEG* 9.1 in 1944, nearly all these critical signs were omitted; only an endnote warns about the difficulties. On autopsy and comparison with a squeeze, Fraser found lines 1 to 46 to be largely illegible, except for a few letters that certainly cannot support the extensive restorations. Of lines 47 to 73, fewer than half of the letters on the margins were more or less legible, while the middle section of the stone was impossible to make out. Lines 73 to 90 carry a list of names, for which Fraser indicates whether he can confirm earlier readings or not.

In sum, by Fraser's reckoning, the text of *SEG* 9.1 underlying the scholarship on the constitution of Cyrene is a figment of overzealous restoration, and the publication in *SEG* incorrect. Publications such as Larsen's were based on the first editions of the *diagramma*, but these readings likewise left entirely out of account the marks of uncertain readings. Most publications of the last fifty years duly refer to Fraser's article, but nonetheless they use the "constitution" in full, without any reservations, raising the question of whether or how the authors digested Fraser's article. The current reproduction of Fraser's work in *PHI*, with reference to its inclusion in *SEG* 18.726, shows what Fraser could decipher in lines 2 to 73, and for lines 73 to 90 only his results for conflicting readings in the first two editions.[336] The extant text does not allow a substantial reconstruction of Cyrene's constitution in general, nor for the use of the lot in particular.

---

[334] Larsen (1929).
[335] See for example Bagnall (1976) 28–29; B. Mitchell (2000).
[336] https://inscriptions.packhum.org/text/324430?&bookid=172&location=1695 (accessed 2 November 2023).

Endnote 7: The new body politic in Cleisthenes's system

The refoundation of the citizen body by Cleisthenes raises some much-debated questions. What precisely did Cleisthenes do? Who were the people who were now included as citizens? And what was the procedure by which the new citizen body was established?

One such question focuses on *Ath.Pol.* 20.1, stating that Cleisthenes made the *demos* switch to his side ἀποδιδοὺς τῶι πλήθει τὴν πολιτείαν (giving the *politeia* to the mass of the people). This clause can be taken to mean that he gave citizenship (in the sense of citizen status) to everyone, or that he handed over the constitution (i.e., power over the state) to the *demos*.

The reading "citizenship" is favored by scholars who argue that, after the expulsion of the tyrants, a *diapsephismos* (scrutiny of the citizen body by voting on legal status) took place, as reported in *Ath.Pol.* 13.5.[337] Yet it is unlikely that this is what *Ath.Pol.* means to say here. First of all, considering the legal arrangements of citizenship in the late sixth century, it is highly doubtful that the *diapsephismos* was about legal status and pure birth; more likely it was a scrutiny regarding political allegiance to the supporters of the tyrants who just had been expelled, or to their opponents.[338] The vocabulary is also at odds with the reading "citizenship." In the fourth century, the meaning "citizenship" for *politeia* became common and would be fitting for the *Ath.Pol.* to describe "citizenship."[339] However, "giving citizenship" was regarded as a gift, indicated by the verb δίδωμι without ἀπό, which means "handing over." "Citizenship" for *politeia* also sits uneasily with the object *plethos*, which means the *demos* in its totality, whereas among those who—according to the scholars just mentioned—had been robbed of their citizenship, many members of the elite were included. For giving citizenship (back) to them all, one would rather expect πᾶσι than πλήθει, and πολιτείαν without the article (cf. Dem. 23.127, 151, 199, 200, but 23.89 τὴν πολιτείαν). The passage seems to have more in common with and prepare for *Ath.Pol.* 27.2, telling that Pericles's policies further encouraged "τοὺς πολλοὺς ἅπασαν τὴν πολιτείαν μᾶλλον ἄγειν εἰς αὑτούς" (the masses to take the whole *politeia* more into their own hands). In sum, in 20.1 *Ath.Pol.* relates that Cleisthenes "handed over the *politeia*" to the *demos*, in other words, gave them full sovereignty over the *polis*.

Nonetheless, Cleisthenes's refoundation unmistakably gave citizen status to many who either had lost it in some way or had never possessed it. The reports about this measure are rather muddled, however, and clearly influenced by later political misgivings. One such is Arist. *Pol.* 1275b36–37, which states,

---

[337] The reports about this post-tyranny *diapsephismos* are riddled with contradictions. Recent defenders include Manville (1990) 173–185; Walter (1993) 203–205; Grote (2016) 205–208.
[338] Cf. Poddighe (2010); Blok (2017) 118.
[339] Blok (2017) 53–57.

"Κλεισθένης μετὰ τὴν τῶν τυράννων ἐκβολήν· πολλοὺς γὰρ ἐφυλέτευσε ξένους καὶ δούλους μετοίκους" ("After the expulsion of the tyrants . . . Cleisthenes enrolled in his *phylai* many foreigners and slaves living in the territory"). This statement is partly erroneous: in Athens slaves were never granted citizenship straightaway; they had to be freed before such a step was feasible and grants of citizenship to them were scarce. Possibly some who received citizenship in 508 were *former* slaves, notably (descendants of) Athenians who after being enslaved had been freed by Solon. Quite a few outsiders were probably around, settled in Attica on the immigration policy ascribed to Solon,[340] and they presumably included mercenaries (cf. Bicknell [1969]). One such was Anaxilas from Naxos, buried in the Kerameikos, who lived among the Athenians (*metaoikos*) and was deplored after his death for his prudence and courage (*IG* I³ 1357). Such events appear to lie behind the reports, such as in *Ath.Pol.* 21.4 about the introduction of the demotic (see above, note 129). In effect, Cleisthenes implemented a "one-off" *ius soli* to all free inhabitants of Attica who wanted to become citizens. Yet the expression in the *Politics* "foreigners and slaves" sounds first and foremost like an invective, a slander about illegal descent prohibited for citizen status of the kind leveled in the classical political arena against any citizen standing in the way of the speaker (e.g., that of Lys. 31 against Nikomachos; Demosthenes against Aeschines, etc.).

Endnote 8: Allotment tokens from Athens

In the excavations of the southeast corner of the agora, three terracotta tokens came to light and were published by Homer Thompson in *Hesperia* (1951), now listed as *Agora* nos. MC 820 (no. 1), 821 (no. 2), and 822 (no. 3).[341] One more token of this type had been found close to the Dipylon in 1878 (no. 4; *IG* I² 916).[342] The tokens are around three centimeters long and wide, and roughly one centimeter thick, straight on three sides and cut in varying shapes on the fourth side. Clearly, they are the halves of a companion piece with a matching serrated shape; combined, they were rectangular tokens of about six by three centimeters. Letters were painted on the tokens before firing. No. 1 has ΗΑΛΙΜ/ΟΣ on one side and ΛΕΟ on the other, no. 2 has ΠΟΛ on one side and ΛΕΟ on the other, no. 3 has ΠΟΛ on one side and probably ΕΡΕ on the other, and no. 4

---

[340] Papachrysostomou (2019).
[341] Thompson (1951); I am grateful to James Kierstead for sharing his unpublished work on these tokens with me. For the tokens, see https://agora.ascsa.net/id/agora/object/mc%20820,
https://agora.ascsa.net/id/agora/object/mc%20821,
https://agora.ascsa.net/id/agora/object/mc%20822.
[342] Koumanoudes (1879) no. 6.

ΧΣΥΠΕΤ/ΑΙΩΝ on one side, and possibly ΚΕΚ on the other. The letters ΛΕΟ, ΕΡΕ, and ΚΕΚ were written in the middle of the tokens before they were cut in two (only one half of the letters is visible), and must be abbreviations of the *phylai* (ΛΕΟ = Leontis, etc.). The archaeological context and the shape of the letters date the tokens to the mid-fifth century. The tokens looked fresh, as if rarely used.[343] No. 4 has also a small round hole in the middle; most scholars assume that this allowed the token to be worn on a string.

For the use of these tokens, Mabel Lang proposed an ingenious solution.[344] She argued that they served as tools for allotment in the historical context described by *Ath.Pol.* 62.1:

> The allotted offices were formerly of two sorts: those allotted with the nine archons from the whole *phyle*, and those allotted in the Theseion which used to be distributed over the demes. But since the demes were selling [the offices], they now allot these offices also from the whole *phyle*, except members of the council and guards; these they refer to the demes.

In all likelihood, "formerly" means before 403. Given that the tokens were organized by *phyle* and involved the demes, the offices were not the archons drawn from the *phylai* (so ΠΟΛ ≠ Polemarchos), but the numerous other offices (hence ΠΟΛ = *poletes*). Getting an even distribution of available offices over the demes, also considering other rules such as prohibition of iteration, allotting these other offices by drawing beans was a complex matter. And with demes selling offices to other demes, a system was needed to curb malpractice of this kind. The distribution could build on the proportional distribution between demes for members of the council, and the procedure was possibly as follows. For each *phyle*, a thin clay strip was cut into fifty rectangular pieces of about six by three centimeters. On one side of each piece, the abbreviated name of the *phyle* was painted in the middle, and through this name the piece was cut in two with an irregular cut, making each set a unique combination of an upper and lower half. After the pieces had dried, all the upper halves and the lower halves were collected separately. On the upper halves, the names of the demes of this *phyle* were painted in the same numbers as for the council—for example, for Halimous (in Leontis) three pieces, for Xypete (in Kekropis) seven. Randomly picked from the total of fifty, the lower halves were inscribed with the offices available for the *phyle*. Then, each batch of the resulting halves was fired, *phyle* by *phyle*. On the allotment day, Halimous (to continue this example) sent six men over thirty years of age, namely three primary candidates and three reserve, to the Theseion along

---

[343] Thompson (1951).
[344] Lang (1959).

with their demarch. He received the three upper halves with the deme name, and next took them to the *thesmotetes*, who had all the lower halves of Leontis-tokens laid out on a table. Fitting the upper halves to the corresponding lower halves would reveal which offices the random distribution had assigned to Halimous. Wherever a Halimousian had held this office before, he would withdraw, and the office would be allotted among the other Halimousians by beans.[345]

Lang's solution was accepted with some modifications by E. S. Staveley and D. Whitehead.[346] The latter rightly pointed out that since the publications of Lang and Staveley, the estimation of the total number of offices had changed drastically from ca. 150 to the ca. 700 mentioned by the *Ath.Pol.* 24.3, a number convincingly demonstrated by M. H. Hansen in 1980;[347] probably, therefore, all five hundred citizens sent by the demes received an office on the allotment day.

Some scholars, however, rejected Lang's theory entirely or in part. For instance, S. C. Humphreys agrees that the tokens had to do with the distribution of offices, but suggests they were used for identification when a citizen claimed his office.[348] She also supposes that the system concerned the office of *poletes* in particular, which appeared on two tokens; this was a coveted office because the ten *poletai* were in charge of all financial contracts on behalf of the *polis*.[349] Furthermore, if the tokens were used for allotment, every year there must have been ca. five hundred of such clay tokens, a number that contrasts sharply with the mere four tokens found. Due to this discrepancy, allotment is not a likely purpose of the tokens, and it was anyway probably a short-lived experiment of no more than a few years.[350]

Lang's approach is supported and brought up to date by J. C. Kierstead, who fittingly calls the tokens "jigsaw" tokens. He situates their use in the wider context of the social and economic profile of the demes and their access to office, and addresses other pertinent questions such as the comparison with other allotment systems. He explains the low number of tokens found so far by the fact that the Theseion has not yet been convincingly identified, but that it probably must be located at quite some distance from the agora. In other words, numerous tokens may be found on a spot still lying unexcavated under modern Athens.[351]

---

[345] Lang (1959). An alternative would be that only the primary candidates went up to the Theseion, and a substitute only joined them in case one of the first group had to step back. See Staveley (1972) 70–72.
[346] Staveley (1972) 70–72; Whitehead (1986) 286–287.
[347] Hansen (1980).
[348] Humphreys (2018) 745 n.64, objecting that "[s]ince the names of demes and offices were painted on the tokens before firing, the assignation of offices to demes was known in advance. It would not be Athenian practice to have a secret list of assignations known only to tribal officials and potters" apparently overlooked that the half tokens were separated before they were painted and fired.
[349] *Ath.Pol.* 47.2-3.
[350] Humphreys (2018) 744–745.
[351] Kierstead (forthcoming).

I think that Lang was basically correct about the purpose of the tokens and how they were used, with Whitehead's modification of the numbers of offices involved. Yet, since according to the *Ath.Pol.* 62.1, even though the distribution of these offices was changed to selection from the whole *phyle* once the demes were found to be selling offices, the malpractice apparently continued, revealing that the system with the jigsaw tokens was not watertight. After they were cut, the tokens were left to dry for one to three days before being separated, turned, painted with deme names and offices, and fired. Therefore they were produced well in advance before the allotment day, allowing time for certain people to take a sneak preview. Given that of all these tokens that must have existed for this system to operate, the fact that two of the only four tokens so far found were of *poletai* may be explained by their particular findspot on the agora, where the *poletai* conducted a sizeable part of their tasks and set up their accounts.[352] With these tokens, when questioned by others the officiating citizens could prove they were truly the selected *poletai*. In this sense, the tokens may also have served for identification purposes.

---

[352] *Ag.* XIX: 57–58.

9
Drawing Lots for Governance: A Political Innovation

9.1 Drawing lots for *polis* governance: An evaluation

9.1.1 Ancient Greeks on selection for office by lot

What did the Greeks think about drawing lots for *polis* governance? Regarding the application of the lot for distributing inheritances, sacrificial meat, booty, and plots of land for settlement, no explicit reflection is extant, and the same holds true for its use in divination, procedure, and sortition. That drawing lots was highly valued for these purposes speaks first of all to its widespread use, reflecting the Greek mindset as analyzed in the first parts of this book. The use of the adjective *isos* and other indications point to the fact that in such contexts equality was the driving principle. As an informal institution across Greece, drawing lots was a familiar practice that was based on shared values and needed no explicit articulation. In the course of time, when communities solidified into structured polities with formal institutions, and when rules and laws were increasingly committed to written forms, drawing lots was gradually integrated into these formal structures and became a formal institution itself.

The allotment for *polis* office, notably for political offices, was the only application of the system that became the object of explicit reflection, most of it critical. Yet even those reflections are strikingly scarce. Individual citizens, leaders, or governing boards must, at some point, have proposed to draw lots for a certain office, and then introduced this method, either in an oligarchic or in a democratic setting. Although a few such individuals are known to us (Solon, perhaps Archytas), we know nothing of their actual arguments.[1] Numerous political discourses by politicians and orators have survived, either directly in their own words—such as the Attic orators—or as reported by others, such as through speeches rendered by Thucydides or Xenophon. The speakers in these texts refer abundantly to the citizens' equality in the law and in active participation

---

[1] Insofar as political thought in the fragments of Solon—for instance, aiming at a balance and temperance between the elite and the *demos* in fr. 5—can be ascribed to Solon himself, here, too, no reference is made to drawing lots as an instrument to realize this ideal.

Drawing Lots. Irad Malkin and Josine Blok, Oxford University Press. © Oxford University Press 2024.
DOI: 10.1093/oso/9780197753477.003.0010

(*metecho*) in the *polis*, but arguments why this equality had best be implemented by allotment for office from all are, to my knowledge, lacking. The evidence, much of it epigraphical, shows the citizens of classical Athens and of other *poleis* doing so, neither explaining nor defending it. Probably the use of the noun *kleros* and its cognates—vocabulary deeply familiar from a range of practices, including the division of inheritances that every household had to engage with—would have eased introducing the practice in a domain where, at least initially, it had no accepted pedigree. Such a common ground in language might have created a bridge between the old and the new.[2] But we can only hypothesize such discursive effects; the evidence provides no cases where drawing lots is persuasively introduced or explicitly evaluated in these terms by those wishing to use it or who already did so.

Evaluative comments were made by observers judging the state of affairs from outside, either because they were citizens living in another *polis* or they belonged to the *polis* in question but looked at the situation from a critical distance. For oligarchies, it was Anaximenes of Lampsakos who pointed out the expediency of distributing offices by lot within the restricted circle of the oligarchs to keep their ranks closed. He did not do so as a member of an oligarchy himself, but as the author of a broader textbook on effective political reasoning. For democracies, it was Herodotus, the so-called Old Oligarch, Plato, and Aristotle who observed that the lot was used in this type of constitution to implement the equality of all citizens. They did so as observers of the system, and perhaps with the exception of Herodotus, they were critical of what they saw happening, especially in Athens.

Around 420 an anonymous Athenian author, nicknamed in Anglophone scholarship the "Old Oligarch," wrote a pamphlet on the Athenian constitution, in which he—not a supporter of the democracy—grudgingly admitted that the system worked well for the *demos*, and was moreover tolerable for people like himself. The text has nothing of the analytical sophistication typical of philosophical treatises, and even lacks the elementary systematic reasoning of the *Dissoi Logoi* we discuss later.. But the author clearly knew the Athenian system from the inside. Concerning the distribution of offices, it is not the lot itself he objects to, but the kind of offices the *demos* wants and distributes by lot.

> [Since the common people row the ships and thus make the city powerful] it seems fair that they should all share in the offices of state by the processes of lot and election, and that any one of the citizens who wishes should have the right to speak. . . . [But] all those offices that bring safety to the state as a whole

---

[2] For this function of "common ground" discourse, see https://anchoringinnovation.nl/domains/discourse-and-rhetoric.

when they are well performed, danger when they are not, in these offices the common people do not require any share. They do not think they should share in the generalship by having it allotted, nor in the cavalry command. For the common people recognize that they derive greater benefit by not holding these offices themselves but allowing the most capable men to hold office. But all those offices which involve the receipt of money and benefit for one's household, these the common people seek to hold.[3]

With the sneering view that the *demos* is only after immediate gain and avoids difficult offices involving serious responsibilities, the author also suggests that truly demanding offices requiring special capacities and skills had better be in the hands of capable people, and that only minor tasks of the kind anybody can perform should be distributed by lot. According to the author, the common citizens themselves held these differences between offices and their distribution to be to their own benefit. His view is the mirror image of the objection that the lot is inappropriate for selection for office because it does not take the abilities of the selected person into account.

This objection is one of two arguments against using the lot for office presented in the *Dissoi Logoi*, a sophistic treatise on various topics of debate, written by an author of a Doric linguistic background between 355 and 338.[4] For good government one needs people who are good politicians, and the lot may draw someone who has no competence for governing whatsoever, maintains the author. He compares this with professional competence in other areas: a good harpist is not a good flutist, and so on. In the introduction to this section, the author states, "Some of the public speakers say that offices should be assigned by lot; but this opinion of theirs is not a very good one."[5] His remark confirms what we supposed earlier, that political leaders must have defended allotment in public, otherwise the method would not have been introduced in so many places.

The second objection against drawing lots for office in the *Dissoi Logoi* is more surprising. The lot is supposed to be democratic, states the author, but this is not the case: the lot may select men who hate the *demos* and will try to destroy them—it is therefore better for the *demos* to elect people whom they know are well disposed toward them. Isocrates voiced the same view. It is a curious argument, because the randomness of the lot and the size of allotted boards would render such a coup against the *demos* highly unlikely, and no historical instance of an oligarchic coup occurring in this way is known. Rather, the argument seems

---

[3] [Xen.] *Ath.Pol.* 1.2–3, trans. R. Osborne (*Lactor* 2).
[4] Molinelli (2018) 48.
[5] *DissLog.* 7.1, ed. and trans. Molinelli (2018).

an objection against allotment from all, framed as a hypothesis and disguised as a pro-democratic position.

A similar argument appears in Isocrates's *Areopagiticus*, a eulogy of what he held the ancient constitution of Athens led by the Areopagos to have been. In this treatise, Isocrates addressed the question: what did equality and difference mean for entitlement to government in the ideal(ized) setting of the early democracy? The Athenians of old recognized the difference between the two types of equality: dispensing the same to all who are alike and giving to those who are different, each to his due. Since they knew that giving the same *time* to both the commendable and the disgraceful was unjust, they did not fill the offices by lot from all citizens, but they first elected (*prokrino*) from the best and ablest for handling the state's affairs. This was also more democratic: the lot would often by chance (*tyche*) fall on citizens favoring oligarchy, whereas election guaranteed that the *demos* could choose leaders favoring the democratic constitution.[6] In the ancient constitution, the *demos* was sovereign by appointing the magistrates and holding them to account, and by judging disputes; those citizens held the offices who had the time and the means to do so, and who considered their service of the state a *time* (sc.: did not receive payment).[7]

Beside raising the imaginary specter of drawing a latent oligarch by lot—an objection to full political equality disguised as a pro-democratic argument also advanced in the *Dissoi Logoi*—Isocrates shifted almost imperceptibly from a just choice of the best and ablest to the just selection of those with sufficient wealth, a position reflecting the political realities of ancient Greece. Although it was widely recognized that excellence (*arete*) in conduct, courage, and judgment was not the same as having great wealth, the average Greek believed that excellent individuals could be found most of all among the wealthy, or rather, among the elite who used their wealth to develop and display their excellence. Value terms expressing admiration for excellence in action, looks, and success—*kalos kâgathos* (splendid and successful), *andragathia* (manly courage and achievement), *arete* (excellence)—were used almost synonymously for individuals of the wealthy elite.[8] As Aristotle notes, "The rich are regarded practically everywhere as holding the position of those who are *kalos kâgathos*."[9] He himself observed

---

[6] Isoc. 7.22–23; the best and ablest: τοὺς βελτίστους καὶ τοὺς ἱκανωτάτους. Isocrates's claim that the lot gave oligarchs the opportunity to grasp power is not founded on historical evidence. For the lack of discernment of most citizens, who manned the jury courts drawn by lot, Isoc. 7.54.

[7] Isoc. 7.26; those in office "τοὺς δὲ σχολὴν δυναμένους καὶ βίον ἱκανὸν κεκτημένους."

[8] See Adkins (1972), who evaluates such value terms on their effect for competition versus cooperation. Dover (1974) 37–45 shows the qualification of social class in these values terms. Whitehead (1993) examines this vocabulary applied in honorific decrees in Athens, where democratic ideology led to a gradual shift from *arete* (excellence due to what one *is*) to *andragathia* (excellence due to what one *does*).

[9] Arist. *Pol.* 1294a18, who himself distinguishes having wealth from the virtues of *kalokâgathia*; see Dover (1974) 44 n.22.

that the mass of the citizens could arrive at a sensible judgment because *as a collective* they brought the qualities scattered among them together, but the *demos* was not the group in which to look for sufficiently qualified *individual* political leadership.[10] We saw the effects of this belief on the political history of Greece in the divergence between oligarchy and democracy.

Against this common view, Socrates defended a different principle, portrayed by Xenophon in the *Memorabilia*: the capacity for good government resides neither with kings, nor with demagogues, nor with the citizens who happen to be elected or allotted, but with those who know how to rule.[11] This principle, that the ability for good government is based on wisdom and virtue, was developed by Socrates's student Plato in an incomparably profound and sophisticated way.

In several dialogues, among them the *Protagoras* and the *Republic*, Plato argues that political excellence cannot be taught because it rests on the virtue of wisdom—a quality given by the gods that needs to be fostered with care. The government of the city should be entrusted to those who possess this quality; this principle is incompatible with drawing lots, with its equal chance for all. In the *Laws*, Plato developed a conception of an ideal *polis*, in which he responded critically to the practices of Athens in his own time. In this ideal *polis*, human policy is made under the guidance of the gods.[12] Here, the virtue of wisdom is leading, and political office is in principle not to be distributed by lot. The equality involved in drawing lots is an absolute equality, cast in measure, weight, and number; with this system, every state or lawgiver can assign fitting honors (*timai*) to citizens and then have the lot decide between the equals, and thus create a simple kind of justice. But true justice is the judgment of Zeus that applies a different kind of equality, giving "more to the greater and less to the smaller, giving due measure to each according to nature."[13] When a state applies this proportional equality, it achieves "political justice" and well-being. Plato distinguishes here between a straightforward kind of equality dispensed easily by grading individuals according to set standards, and a proportional equality, based on qualities only the gods can apportion.[14] For the first, merely man-made type of equality, the lot is an appropriate instrument of selection. But a just state follows the second type, knowing that god-given, natural (*kata physin*) equality is to be recognized in inequality.[15] Nonetheless, every state needs to apply a bit of each type of justice,

---

[10] Arist. *Pol.* 1281a38–b37. Thucydides puts a similar viewpoint on the competence of the *demos* as a collective in the mouth of Athenagoras, a democratic leader in Syracuse in 415 (Thuc. 6.39), reflecting a democratic style of demagogy; cf. Mader (2013).

[11] Xen. *Mem.* 3.9.10.

[12] Plato, *Laws*, 767c.

[13] Plato, *Laws*, 757c–758a; 757b, trans. R.G. Bury (Loeb-ed.).

[14] "The truest and best form of equality is not an easy thing for everyone to discern. It is the judgment of Zeus, and men it never assists save in small measure, but in so far as it does assist either States or individuals, it produces all things good." Plato, *Laws*, 757b, trans. R. G. Bury (Loeb-ed.).

[15] Plato, *Laws*, 757d.

otherwise it cannot survive. Even for lawgivers who aim at true justice, it is prudent to employ the imperfect kind of equality and the drawing of lots, too, to prevent the discontent of the mass of the citizens (*hoi polloi*). When we (the speaker and other imaginary lawgivers) do so, we must pray to the god and *agathe tyche* that the outcome coincides with true justice (= expressed in the second type of equality)—but we should do so as little as possible.[16]

When would this be necessary? For several offices, Plato allowed a restricted use of the lot on specific conditions.[17] In the ideal city of the *Laws*, the ultimate authority was to be held by the three best citizens, chosen by a multilayered election procedure and therefore recognized by all citizens as truly the very best; these three would be dedicated as priests to Apollo and Helios. Only when in the final election two or all three would end with the same number of votes, the lot would decide who was to be first, second, and third.[18] In other words, only when in a *prokrisis* by thorough evaluation of merit some would end in an absolute equality (*isos*), the use of *klerosis* would be appropriate. Arnaud Macé rightly regards the use of the lot in this case as meant to break the tie, as one of order, rather than of selection.[19] The 360 councilors, too, were to be selected by a multilayered election procedure, in which the obligation to vote was more compelling for the higher, propertied classes than for the lower. When from each of the four propertied classes 180 candidates had been elected, the lot was used to select half their number, and these were submitted to *dokimasia* before entering office.[20]

Traditional priesthoods holding ancestral religious offices would remain as they had always been. For new cults, officials should be instituted selected partly by election, partly by lot, mixing methods that please the *demos* and methods that do not, to create friendliness in every district of the city and the countryside. The priests and priestesses were always to be drawn by lot, since the gods would use the divine chance (*tyche*) of the lot to make their own choice.[21] Once selected by lot, each priest would be subjected to a *dokimasia*, to assess whether, first, he was physically unblemished and of legitimate birth, and next whether he came from households as pure as possible, being clean from murder and from all offenses against the divine himself, and likewise his father and his mother. They were to receive from Delphi all *nomoi* on religion and appoint interpreters of these laws. The term of office for these priests was to be no more than one year,

---

[16] Plato, *Laws*, 757e–758a.

[17] For an overview of all offices and their manner of selection in the *Laws*, Reid (2020); on election and sortition in Plato and Aristotle, see also Piérart (1993).

[18] Plato, *Laws*, 946a–c: "they shall commit the matter to good luck and chance (ἀγαθῆι μοίραι καὶ τύχηι)."

[19] Macé (2020) 104.

[20] Plato, *Laws*, 756b–e.

[21] Plato, *Laws*, 759b–c. For the selection of priests by lot, see section 8.2.4, and for this passage, see also p. 105, 375.

and an age threshold of sixty years. All these rules also applied to priestesses. The interpreters were to be elected: the three *phylai* each elected four men, the man from each *phyle* with most votes was selected anyway and submitted to *dokimasia*; the other nine were sent to Delphi, where one man from each triad was selected by the oracle. The interpreters held their office for life; the rules for *dokimasia* and age were the same as for priests.[22]

Plato's conception in the *Laws* shows how he understood and wanted to revise Athenian practices. The *demos* saw the lot as the instrument of equality and therefore of their claim to power; a good *politeia* would need to take their wishes into some account. Doing so in the best possible way should be in accordance with the true nature of the lot: an instrument of good fortune and chance in the hands of the gods. When applied to political offices, the lot should only be used to decide when a thorough *prokrisis* as to merit resulted in an absolute equality of numbers or an equivocal assessment of merit. For religious offices, those belonging to (in Athenian terms) the *gene* should be left as they were. New offices supporting cults were to be selected by both election and lot, to please the divergent political preferences among the population; in Athens, all *hieropoioi* were selected by lot, and certain other officials by election (see earlier discussion, personnel for the Mysteries). All new priesthoods were to be selected by the gods through the lot, from among all, and for one year (just as in Athens) but with a high age threshold (unlike Athens); just as in Athens for all offices, a strict *dokimasia* took place once selection was complete. Throughout, Plato's envisaged system is a collaboration between humans and gods—as everywhere in Greece—but reconfigured in accordance with his own principle that divine justice be normative in the *politeia*.

Although Plato's student Aristotle also saw election as a method of selection based on merit, whereas the lot was not, his main concern was not with methods but with the balance between the socioeconomic groups from whom and by whom the selection was made. People who were truly excellent in virtue and birth were anyway rare.[23] Both the wealthy and the poor were driven by their own interests, and supreme power by either group would lead to injustice. An oligarchy would lead to oppression of the poor. A democracy with allotment from all, combined with supreme authority of popular jury courts over magistrates, was of the worst type of constitution because there was no room for any consideration of distinctive qualities.

Aristotle's approach to the best possible *polis* differed radically from Plato's, but like him he held justice to be based on equality and sought ways to understand and define it.[24] Plato differentiated, as we just saw, between absolute, man-made

---

[22] Plato, *Laws*, 759c–e.
[23] Arist. *Pol.* 1302a1–3.
[24] Pl. *Laws*, 757a; Arist. *Pol.* 1282b17–26.

equality measured in numbers, and proportional equality, according to the innate human qualities only the divine could dispense and measure. The second kind is by far the best, but every state needs to have a bit of both. The same argument appears in book 5 of the *Politics*, in which Aristotle discusses the causes of political discontent and ensuing regime change. He also distinguishes between numerical equality, which is *isos* and the same in number or dimension, and proportional equality, which measures equality as to worth (*kata axian*). He explains both kinds in figures: in numerical equality, 3 is more than 2, and 2 more than 1, with the same amount of difference; in proportional equality, 4 is more than 2, and 2 more than 1 in the same manner, because both 2 and 1 are the halves of 4 and 2, respectively. According to Aristotle, everyone agrees that proportional equality represents the absolutely just, but people disagree on what this means in terms of numerical equality, namely whether being "more" than others in one sense implies that also one may have or be more than others in other senses. In other words, both Plato and Aristotle regarded equality as the crucial element of justice, but they also saw that the meaning of equality for the framework of *polis* offices (*timai*) was a topic of philosophical disagreement as well as a source of social conflict.[25] Drawing office by the lot, requiring equal candidates and giving an even more equal result, placed this problem center-stage and in a sharp light.

9.1.2 What does selection for office by lot mean for *polis* governance? Some modern views

Modern scholars have examined what the use of the lot for *polis* office meant for *polis* governance. Until now, the debate has focused on Athens as the best-documented *polis*, and also, to go by the current evidence, the one with the widest application of the lot for both selection and procedure. At the center of this debate are the political offices at *polis* level, while the offices at deme level and cultic offices are largely omitted from the discussion. Some modern opinions mirror ancient concerns, but others take a fully etic perspective. I select here for discussion two influential interpretations.

In a set of essays on the political history of Athens in the sixth and fifth centuries, written in the 1960s but published nearly twenty years ago, G. E. M. de Ste. Croix gave new vigor to a long-standing viewpoint.[26] Since the nineteenth

---

[25] Harvey (1965) 118 points out that *isos* means—besides "equal"—"fair." Or perhaps, it rather *implies* fairness, thus giving room for different conceptions of equality to achieve that fairness. The core of Harvey's argument is that understanding *isos* as "of fair proportion" or "balance," supported the principle of proportional (geometrical) equality that was developed as a better alternative to the democratic policy of radical (arithmetical) equality. This line of argument was philosophically "a complete failure"; so Harvey (1965) 129.

[26] De Ste. Croix (2004b; 2004a).

century, ancient historians had argued that filling important offices by lot is irrational, since no state should want to entrust its leading positions to just anybody regardless of their capacities.[27] Hence, important offices in Athens were filled by election, while those of minor importance were distributed by lot. Vice versa, if just any individual was suited to fill a post, then that post was deemed not demanding or valuable; and when in Athens an office changed from being filled by election to being filled by lot, loss of the post's standing either prepared or followed this change. When the *Ath.Pol.* was published in 1891, this judgment was advanced in particular against the *klerosis ek prokriton* of the archons in Solon's *politeia*. The *Ath.Pol.*'s report was considered implausible, indeed erroneous, because in the archaic age the archons, and most prominently the *Polemarchos*, were eminently important and therefore could not have been selected by lot.[28] According to De Ste. Croix, only two points of evidence could support the possibility of the *klerosis ek prokriton* in Solon's *politeia*: the contenders for the archonship in the turbulent years after Solon were apparently distributed randomly as to social and geographical background, and in antiquity everyone was aware that the lot prevented the rivalry fueled by elections. But these points did not weigh up against the principal objections against the *klerosis ek prokriton* of the archons in the archaic age.[29]

De Ste. Croix revived this venerable viewpoint to explain the remaining problematic case that was beyond any doubt: the adoption of *klerosis ek prokriton* for the archons in 487 reported in the *Ath.Pol.* 22.5. Distinguishing between important offices and all others, De Ste. Croix defined important offices as "*those who exercised major political powers or held high military commands.*"[30] Regarding the principles mentioned earlier, the archons' selection by drawing lots indicated that by 487 their offices *must* have lost their importance. And this fact revealed the true reason behind the change. "What really mattered . . . was not the demotion of the archons but the promotion of the Strategoi, who, unlike the archons, could be *re-elected year after year, so that the best men would always be available.*"[31] Although the *Ath.Pol.* fails to mention it, the real point of the change was to assign the highest command to the *strategoi*; and since with this move the archons, notably the *Polemarchos*, were no longer important, their offices might as well be drawn by lot. The only archon who was still significant was the eponymous archon, and he could not be reelected anyway.[32]

---

[27] De Ste. Croix (2004b) 91–92. Note the difference with the opinion of the "Old Oligarch" that the Athenian *demos* left the difficult offices to their betters and distributed the easy, lucrative ones among themselves ([Xen.] *Ath.Pol.* 1.2–3).

[28] For this debate, in which *Ath.Pol.* is supposed to be at odds with Arist. *Pol.*, see ch. 8.1.2 and Endnote 2.

[29] De Ste. Croix (2004b) 101.

[30] De Ste. Croix (2004b) 93; emphasis in original.

[31] De Ste. Croix (2004a) 221–222, emphasis in original.

[32] De Ste. Croix (2004a) 220–223.

De Ste. Croix's argument was driven by two strong and connected points of disagreement. The first was with H. Wade-Gery, who had defended the *klerosis ek prokriton* in Solon's *politeia* by pointing to the possible factor of divine selection, while in De Ste. Croix's view, religion played no role in political history and priesthoods were not "important offices," because they did not require any competence.[33] This view resulted in the second point: De Ste. Croix wanted "to demonstrate that the Athenians were not the quaint and rather silly people so often pictured in modern books, who devised eccentric political institutions: census classes fixed on a highly unsuitable basis, ostracism as a device for getting rid of potential tyrants (a purpose for which it was quite unsuited) and election partly by lot of their principal magistrates."[34]

Regardless of his polemics, De Ste. Croix's contention on the *strategoi* is interesting, but his view is unconvincing, both with regard to the historical events and in the general tenet of his argument. Concerning the highest military command, it is certain that at some point it shifted from the *Polemarchos*, who held it at Marathon, to the board of *strategoi*, who were Athens's military commanders in the Peloponnesian War. De Ste. Croix may well be right that this shift had to do with the possibility of reelection of the *strategoi*, with the best men building up experience over the years. But his contention that this shift lay behind the change to *klerosis* of the archons in 487, who henceforth would lag far behind the *strategoi* in competence, is not borne out by the evidence. The *Ath.Pol.* recounts how after the Persian Wars the Areopagos enjoyed immense esteem at the expense of the *strategoi*, because at the battle of Salamis the latter had given up, not knowing what to do, whereas the Areopagos took effective steps to man the ships; also, under the leadership of the Areopagos, Athens was governed well in those years—that is, from the 480s until the late 460s.[35] One might object, as did James Headlam, that this strong Areopagos consisted of ex-archons who all had been elected without drawing lots before 487, but that is not very plausible; in the twenty-five years about which the *Ath.Pol.* reports here, quite a few archons must have been selected after 487, by lot from *prokritoi*.[36]

A more plausible motive for the reintroduction of Solon's system than the demotion of the archons was reducing the competition for the archonships, a motive that further evidence supports. Presumably, the reelection of men of the caliber of Cimon and Pericles as *strategoi* led to the shift in the military command. When the Athenians chose between selection by election or drawing lots, it seems they did not classify offices as "important" or not, but they distinguished

---

[33] Wade-Gery (1958); De Ste. Croix (2004b) 94–95.
[34] De Ste. Croix (2004b) 104.
[35] *Ath.Pol.* 23.
[36] Headlam (1891) 185.

for elections those offices that required special experience or competences from the other offices that were to be assigned by lot.

This observation affects De Ste. Croix's ideas on the importance of offices. He assumes "importance" in modern terms that privilege politics and the military over religion. But to the self-understanding of the *polis* and its confidence about its well-being, the religious domain was essential, as the three major archons illustrate who held their religious duties from Athens's early days until the Roman era, regardless of the ways in which they were selected. Nor did the shift of the military command to the *strategoi* and consequent loss of military authority of the *Polemarchos* affect the religious authority of the three archons in any way. Furthermore, De Ste. Croix's view of which offices were "important" and why is too limited. After the late 460s, political power in Athens was formally divided between the assembly, the council, and the courts. With the council leading the governance of the *polis* and the courts holding the ultimate control of the officeholders, in De Ste. Croix's terms these offices also *"exercised major political powers,"* and yet they were all allotted. The *strategoi* held the highest military commands, but their political power was largely informal and personal.[37]

In political scientist Bernard Manin's analysis of the selection by lot in Athens, the distinction of offices as "important" or not does not play any role, nor does he think selection by lot is a sign of lack of seriousness on the part of the Athenians.[38] On the contrary, elaborating the pioneering insights of James Headlam, Manin argues that the combination of large-scale allotment and rotation of office was essential for the democracy of Athens.[39] Since the Athenians were convinced that for the majority of the offices no special qualifications were required, no distinction applied between those who held the offices and those who did not. As they all swapped positions in the following years, this rotation prevented a professional class of politicians to emerge, meaning that the distance between the government in office and the citizens without offices remained minimal, securing the sovereignty of the *demos*.[40] Election, by contrast, is always based on differences in qualifications between the voters and those who are elected to represent them, creating a representative government that is both in principle and in practice at a (large) distance from the citizens. This type of republican government, in which political authority is in the hands of an elite—perhaps a

---

[37] Pope (1988) 291–292 decisively refutes the contention that the *strategoi* were "important" and the archons, being allotted, were not: "for those who believe in the political importance of the generalship in Athens to minimize the importance of sortition on the grounds that Thucydides says to [*sic*, JB] little about it is to use a self-defeating argument.... If Thucydides' silence is to be taken as a measure of unimportance, then sixty or seventy percent of the Athenian *strategoi* will have been as unimportant as it is possible to be."

[38] Manin (1997).

[39] Headlam (1891; 1933²) and see Endnote.

[40] Manin (1997) 32; cf. Staveley (1972) 55.

social elite but in any case an administrative elite—is essentially different from the direct democracy of Athens. Built on the example of the Roman Republic, this elective, representative model has prevailed in Western democracies since the late eighteenth century.

Using the figures on democratic Athens developed by Mogens Hansen, Manin observes that in Athens the rotation of offices among the male citizens was exceptionally high.[41] Of all offices—not counting the *dikastai*—only one in eight was elected, the majority of which were the military officers and commanders; in the legislative and judicial domains, no offices were elected, and in the executive domain only very few. This distribution was how most Athenians of the fifth and fourth centuries wanted their *politeia* to be: their city was the paragon of civic equality, expressed in the drawing of lots from all. The evidence, disparate though it is, suggests that no other democratic *polis* in Greece had an equally high level of drawing lots for office, nor for other aspects of governance. Athens was and has remained a unique case in its extent of the use of the lot for ensuring civic equality.

Today in many Western democracies, initiatives are being taken to institute forms of civic government based on or inspired by the Athenian example. Dissatisfaction with the conventional representative government, with its distance between government and citizens, and with the party politics concomitant with universal suffrage creates a new urge for more democratic power. In states around the globe, enthusiastic plans are proposed and implemented for drawing lots among the citizens for new democratic bodies, beside the elected representation. Such systems do not resemble the Athenian direct democracy in all its facets, but at least they guarantee a strong voice from a wider section of the population than is usually involved in elected bodies. And, in contrast to the referendum, in the meetings of citizen bodies drawn by lot, deliberation is firmly maintained as a central principle of democracy.[42]

9.2 Conclusions: Drawing lots for *polis* governance in ancient Greece

In ancient Greece, drawing lots was a traditional institution widely applied for distribution and selection long before the consolidation of the *polis* as a sociopolitical system; subsequently, when the *poleis* acquired stable, formalized institutions, lot-drawing became an institutionalized feature of *polis* governance. The system was considered a just method of distribution or selection, on two

---

[41] Hansen (1980; 1991).
[42] See Envoi in this volume.

conditions: first, the group of people involved in the procedure had to be similar (*homoios*), namely, more or less equal in social standing (*time*); only among them the absolute equality (*isos*) created by the chance of the lot could decide. And second, while the decision to implement the lot and who was to participate as a member of the group was a human affair, the procedure itself was safeguarded by the gods: divine oversight of the process vouchsafed that the outcome was just and right. The ancient practice of divination by lots supported this sense of divine approval and involvement, the degree of which would depend on the situation and on individual belief. For the traditional applications of the lot for distribution of goods and sortition, the first condition of being more or less equal was not difficult to meet, or rather, was a prerequisite for drawing lots at all. But for the distribution of *polis* offices (*timai*), this condition did not apply. Public roles were traditionally assigned according to distinctions, to inequality in *time*, and *polis* office was also a type of "goods" different from other goods distributed by lot.

Drawing lots for *polis* office, then, meant that this method had to be transposed from domains where it was considered the just method for distribution, selection, or order, to a domain where its application might be perceived as unjust. The evidence shows that this tension between what was considered just or unjust in terms of equality and competence never fully disappeared, even when the practice had become widespread. The justice of using the lot for distribution was never in doubt, but its use to appoint anyone "from all" to the highest *timai* of the city remained by and large controversial. Only in a few so-called radical democracies—first and foremost, classical Athens—drawing lots was applied to *polis* offices on this scale and appreciated by the majority of its citizens.

Introducing the lot into this domain of *polis* offices and then getting it accepted were innovative moves that needed to be grounded in familiar practices and values. How exactly this happened, why drawing lots was persuasively introduced for *polis* office, and how the practice spread over the Greek world—none of the existing evidence provides any explicit detail. Consequently, the process must be reconstructed from the disparate, contingent reports on events and allotted offices, supported by circumstantial evidence and arguments of plausibility. In this way, it appears that the traditional, other applications of drawing lots served as the bridge between the old and the new, the familiar and innovative.

The extant evidence indicates one traditional application of drawing lots for office, namely for priesthoods and other functions in the cultic domain. The most conspicuous case is Athens, where the priests and priestesses of *polis* cults were selected from the *gene* by drawing lots among the members of the *genos* of the right gender and age, a practice that can be reconstructed as dating to at least the seventh century. Their privilege to be eligible for priesthood was their inheritance as the pure descendants of the original "founders" of the cult. The drawing of lots to select one of them to be priest(ess) combined two types of application of the lot: the assignment of a "share" of an inheritance, and divination, because the lot showed the will of the gods in the selection of their servants. In other *poleis*, the evidence for the allotment of priests is scarcer and of a much later date, so whether that tradition also went back to the archaic age cannot be ascertained. Yet, it is very plausible that also these practices were quite ancient, because the consent of the gods required for the selection of these priests was structurally similar to that in the *gene*, and the strict rules of descent applied to all of these priesthoods.

A second, familiar pattern of drawing lots was the selection among outstanding individuals for particular tasks. Famous scenes in Homer's *Iliad* show that sortition could offer public honor (*time*) for one individual among his high-standing peers. This kind of procedure was strictly guarded by the gods, and Zeus in particular vouchsafed the rightness of the selection by lot. This application of drawing lots was essentially different from that for the allocation of office, because the selection was for one, unique moment only and did not imply sharing or rotation, but it made drawing lots familiar among the elite.

Against this traditional background of drawing lots for priestly office and for special selection, we might hypothesize that drawing lots for political office, at least among the elite, emerged across the Greek *poleis* in the archaic age. However, the scarce evidence does not support such a hypothesis, but rather speaks against it. Unless new evidence turns up, or radically different viewpoints are convincingly developed, a wide emergence of selection for political office by lot in the archaic age cannot be more than a speculation that must, after consideration, be discarded. The evidence we do have points to Athens for the first allotment for political office in Greece, in Solon's new *politeia* of 594, and also reveals the limits of the practice.

When he introduced the new procedure of *klerosis ek prokriton*, Solon probably drew on the two ancient practices, both for the idea of drawing lots and for the anchorage among the elite. The selection for office in the *gene*, an elite of birth, and the selection of individual heroes in the *Iliad* together provided drawing lots for office with the high standing and familiarity Solon needed for this novel application. The aim of his innovation was to reduce the competition among the Athenian elite who enjoyed great wealth and vied for political office to the point of violence. While its pedigree in the *gene* and in Homer might have made the lot a feasible instrument for this group, to getting it accepted for distributing office among them was a formidable task. To this end, Solon recognized the elite publicly, in law, as the group with the highest *time* and restricted the eligibility for high office to them, signifying the replacement of individual *time* with that of a class: in each class everyone now had equal *time*, which made them interchangeable in principle. For the office of the *Tamiai*, only the wealthiest class could stand for drawing lots. For the archons, the procedure probably mixed into one group two formally distinct classes of the wealthiest and the slightly less wealthy citizens, probably holding both established and new wealth among its ranks. The election of candidates from among this group by the *demos* secured public recognition of their excellence as individuals beyond their wealth and class-based *time* alone. Next, among this elected group, lots were drawn for the high offices. After a few years, however, this policy failed for the archons, perhaps because the highest class resented the mixture as well as the final sortition. As far as we know, the *Tamiai* thus remained the only allotted *polis* office in Greece until the early fifth century, perhaps because the office of *Tamias* was perceived as a largely cultic one and restricted to the uppermost class.

From the late sixth to the early fifth centuries (ca. 520–480), democratizing upheavals and initiatives appeared in *poleis* across the Greek world, from Asia Minor to the west. For their political legitimacy, these movements built on the traditional sovereignty of the *demos*, which under the elite leadership of the preceding centuries had been hardly more than a formality, even if in some *poleis* (Athens, Chios) a council existed with a somewhat broader recruitment base. In the cities of western Greece and in other colonies, the equal allotment of land upon which they had been founded long ago probably supported ideas of more civic equality, and pressed for greater influence of the *demos*. Reacting to these pressures, in some *poleis* a tendency toward democracy gained strength; in others the elite consolidated their position into firm oligarchies. *Isonomia* was a rallying cry serving either political program, proclaiming equality in law for either the few or the many, but in the first decades it did not demonstrably lead to allotment of *polis* office.

Yet these developments were not a matter of political power alone. Eligibility for political office is one of the benefits of citizenship, and for any state to attain political self-determination, it needs a stable conception of the citizen body to whom these benefits are to be allocated. In other words, for entitlement to participation it must be clearly established who belongs to this group and who does not. Drawing lots makes this principle even more visible: all who share in drawing lots are in, and all others are out. When the Greek *poleis* were consolidating into states with circumscribed territories and evolving political structures, they also took measures to define their citizen bodies. Of course, not all *poleis* developed in the same manner and at the same pace, but generally speaking this process of determining citizen bodies began in the (late) seventh century and continued throughout the later archaic and classical ages. Political expediency was not always the intended purpose of such citizenship policies, but over time, implementing citizens' rights and duties went hand in hand with formally regulating the citizen body. Since democracies gave active political rights to a far larger section of the population than oligarchies, they were also more inclined to regulate citizen status more stringently. For the equality conditional to drawing lots, such policies were indispensable.

Beginning in the early archaic period—but more consistently from the late sixth century on—the Greek *poleis* formally consolidated their citizen bodies by descent, as the defining condition for citizen status. Traditionally one citizen parent, usually the father, sufficed for citizen status; for priests, double citizen descent was often required. Overall, endogamy, marrying within one's own *polis*, was highly valued. Even if in the archaic age marriages across *poleis* were not uncommon, especially among the elite, such unions were probably the exception rather than the rule.[43] For the inclusion of outsiders as new citizens, this criterion of descent created problems of law, kinship, and property that were not always smoothly solved. In colonies, a new citizen body was created once the *polis* was more firmly settled and the descent principle was reinstituted, often by continuing kin groups of the mother city.

If the situation in a *polis* led to a political crisis, after a military disaster or other incisive events, the citizen body could be refounded. At such a moment, old and new citizens were mixed in the *polis* subgroups by drawing lots, a practice with a long pedigree in the composition of groups of colonists, and in the distribution of plots of land in the foundation of colonies. Solon applied mixture to the elite for a broader political equilibrium. In Cyrene in the mid-sixth century, Demonax refounded the city by mixing old and new citizens and attached to this change a new constitution, presumably a moderate oligarchy. In Athens in 508/7, after a period of political turmoil, Cleisthenes did the same, using the lot for the distribution of sections of the citizen population over new *phylai* and as divination to select the eponymous heroes for their cults. He created a moderately democratic constitution, but no selection for office by lot can be securely ascribed to him. Refoundations of the citizen body by mixing citizens by lot continued to take place in the classical and Hellenistic ages, just as before to incorporate new citizens or to resolve inner *polis* conflicts; interesting examples are Kamarina and Nakone.[44] After such (re)foundations, descent as criterion for citizen status was (re)established.

Athens is a clear example of the firm connection between the legal framework of citizenship and political entitlement. After Solon laid down the rules for hereditary citizen status, Cleisthenes redefined and reorganized the citizen body, giving the new administrative unit of the deme a key role in checking legitimacy

---

[43] For full discussion, Vérilhac and Vial (1998); Patterson (1998).
[44] In Nakone, the mixing went so far as to cut through ties of blood-kinship, to establish harmony (*homonoia* and *philia*) between the citizens in new fictive kin groups (*adelphothetia*) to "reconfigure basic social relationships and habits through a complex and ambitious process of social engineering" supporting very high standards of civic virtue; Gray (2015) 40. See also section 6.3.11 in this volume.

of male citizens.[45] For all of them, the political revisions of the late 460s associated with Ephialtes brought a stronger sense of equality and wider active participation. With his Citizenship Law of 451/0, Pericles made having two citizen parents conditional for citizen status, raising the status of all citizens to full equality in law, and in effect closing off the citizen body. Embedded in the dense structure of *polis* subgroups with membership based on heredity, citizenship—namely, sharing in the *polis*—now more than ever meant having a share of the *polis* as a common inheritance. This conception of citizenship, which was further justified by the rapidly spreading myth that all Athenians were autochthonous—first meaning the "original inhabitants" and later "born from the land," hence "born equally"—facilitated wide allotment from all for both priesthoods and political offices.

But not only Athens turned to a closed system of dual parents for citizen status. Among the Spartans, endogamy must have been part of the system from an early stage, long before Athens made it the legal condition of citizenship. Laws on the composition of citizen bodies and procedures for including new citizens were established across the Greek world from the fifth century on. In the classical and Hellenistic eras, many *poleis*—among which Byzantion, Kos, Miletos, Rhodes, Tenos, and Delos—established dual descent for citizenship, and *poleis* with double affiliation were inclined to give more civic rights to female citizens.[46] According to A. M. Vérilhac and C. Vial, the move toward double affiliation for citizenship was an expression of pride in the *polis*'s self-sufficiency and independence.[47] Moreover, all these *poleis* were more or less democratic at the time, requiring clear boundaries for their citizen bodies in order to make their political system work.[48] Grants of citizenship created new citizens-by-decree; with one exception, such grants are attested only in democracies.[49] New citizens were distributed to *polis* subgroups either by lot or by choice. The preference for one or the other method seems largely a matter of regional custom and has no

---

[45] Cf. Kierstead (2019).
[46] Vérilhac and Vial (1998), on women 53; Grieb (2008).
[47] Vérilhac and Vial (1998) 79–81. For the changing constitution at Tenos from democracy to oligarchy and back again, Hansen and Nielsen (2004) 777.
[48] Arist. *Pol.* 1280b32–39 observes that for the self-sufficiency and cohesion of the *polis*, endogamy is a necessary condition, and in 1275b22–24 he regards double citizen parentage as a condition of citizen status as normal. In 1278a27–35 Aristotle states that democracies relax their rules due to demographic scarcity, a point which is true for Athens in the Peloponnesian War (cf. Carawan [2008]), but not for the institution of Pericles's Citizenship Law, either in 451/0 or 403/2 (Blok [2009b]). Nor does it apply generally: overall, democracies sought to replenish their numbers in case of scarcity by immigration (for Miletos, Köcke [2012]), with treaties of *epigamia* and *sympoliteia* and similar means to introduce new male and female citizens into the citizen body.
[49] The exception is telling: the oligarchic regime of Erythrai awarded citizenship to Mausolos, "citizen of Mylasa" but in fact the king of Caria and satrap of the Persian king, in the mid-350s (RO 56) and to his brother Idrieus (*SEG* 31.969) between 351/0 and 344/3. In both cases, citizenship was meant as an honor to someone more powerful than the oligarchs of Erythrai.

demonstrable connection with the lot or election as the prevailing manner of selection for office in the *polis*.

In the governance of the *polis*, the lot was used for a variety of public responsibilities. Sortition became common for special tasks in the judicial sphere, notably for arbitration of debt issues and for judging in festival competitions. The lot generated mixed groups for military service, distributed military commands and other duties, and was applied for a variety of procedural matters, notably for establishing the order of chairing meetings. But the most conspicuous application was in the selection for political office.

Beginning in the early fifth century and especially for the fourth century and the early Hellenistic period, *poleis* diverged into fully or largely oligarchic and predominantly democratic, or switched back and forth between the two regimes; on Sicily and in Magna Graecia, tyrannies remained a powerful part of the political scenario. The two labels "oligarchy" and "democracy" cover a variety of constitutions, in which the selection of *polis* offices could be effected by lot or by election. As Aristotle rightly noted, it was not each instrument per se, but its combination with other factors that determined the political color of the *polis*. Democracies could be of a more radical type, exemplified above all by Athens, where all citizens became eligible for allotment to a great many offices, or of a moderate type, with most offices filled by election "by all." Most democracies seem to have been of this moderate kind. In some democracies, especially in the Hellenistic east, election was in principle from all, but in practice from a wealthier group, whereas the jury courts and some offices were filled by lot. Oligarchies applied allotment as well as election among the restricted power group, and probably also co-optation. Using the lot for political office clearly spread quite rapidly, albeit unevenly, in the Greek world from the early fifth century on. How did this happen?

Athens's early democracy belonged to democratic movements emerging all over the Greek world from the late sixth century down to the Hellenistic era, but democracy did not necessarily mean the use of the lot for office. Since Solon, the political agency of the *demos* was formalized in their right to elect candidates for office, and to form the court of appeal. Eligibility for the offices was restricted to the well-to-do layers of society, and by the time of Cleisthenes only the *Tamiai* were selected by lot. With the reintroduction of *klerosis ek prokriton* for the selection of archons in 487, the lot was back on the political stage, with the venerable name of Solon attached to it; just as in Solon's time, the method was not meant to bring equality as a political principle into effect, but to reduce inter-elite competition. With the political reforms of the late 460s, drawing lots had become a familiar custom associated with the highest offices, and carrying the hallmark both of Solon and the archonships. Acting on the force of the democratic ideology fostered by Themistocles and Aristeides, and sensing the deep social changes that the Delian League and the navy effected in Athenian society, the *polis* aimed for more equality for the *demos* with the wealthier sections of society who had held the offices until then, and to this end selection by lot was widely applied. The election for the council changed to selection by lot, and so were the "minor" offices; for both, the distribution followed the representation in the demes. The *heliaia* was divided into several jury courts drawn by lot from the *phylai*. In this way, a far larger section of the male citizen body than before acquired the experience of selection by lot and of involvement in the government. Applied as well to the meeting procedures of the council, drawing lots became a central feature of Athenian governance.

Seen from this outcome, drawing lots for political office became accepted in several stages in Athens from Solon's time up until the mid-fifth century. In each stage, the high standing of the context where it was previously used facilitated introducing the method into new contexts. For the method to be acceptable in that new context, on the one hand it had to draw on the familiarity with the institution of drawing lots in other domains of life—and on the other, on its accommodation in societal values more broadly: the willingness to reduce competition as a root cause of civic strife, and on an ideology that increasingly combined recognition of differences in *time* with the principle of political equality.

Based on our present evidence, then, Athens was using the lot for *polis* offices in the first half of the fifth century: on a restricted scale from 487, and on a larger scale from ca. 460. Athens exerted strong influence on Erythrai in the late 450s to institute an allotted council, and likewise probably on Eretria. In Miletos, allotment for some offices was adopted under Athenian influence after 426. Argos became democratic in ca. 460 on its own accord, but it is unknown whether they used allotment. Taras became democratic from ca. 450 on, and in the early fourth century began allotting half of its offices. Oligarchic Thebes began using allotment for some of its offices at some point after 446. The short period of allotment of all offices at Syracuse after 412 was not plausibly induced by Athens, its defeated foe. In Hellenistic Delos, Rhodes, and Smyrna, the jury courts were allotted with *kleroteria* in a manner developed in Athens in the fourth century. Jury courts drawn by lot represented the strongest democratic element in the cities of the Hellenistic east, whose democracies in other respects were very different from classical Athens.[50] In other words, Athens was the source of selection by lot in some cities certainly, in others possibly, and in yet others certainly not. By the mid-fifth century, allotment for office was clearly well known everywhere, and it did not need Athens to be introduced or not. Some signs that from the fifth century onward the practice was far more widespread than the extant evidence shows directly are the matter-of-course references in Aristotle's *Politics*

---

[50] Walser (2012).

to allotment on *polis* level, and its use in the boards of leagues of *poleis* from the fourth century on.[51]

Two interlocking processes seem to have been involved. Throughout Greek history, persons, knowledge, laws, practices, skills, and cultural features traveled across the Greek world through the intensive networks and peer-polity interaction between *poleis*.[52] Traders, proxeny-relations, mercenaries, skilled workmen and intellectuals seeking new opportunities, traveling arbitrators, contenders and judges in competitions and festivals—all this intensive travel brought ideas and practices into wide circulation. Using the lot for distribution of *polis* offices was such an idea that appears to have been carried from one place to another: we cannot see how exactly it happened, only the results. If this wide connectivity was indeed the way, the *idea* of selection by lot was spreading: for its actual application another process was necessary. First, someone had to propose using it in the governance of his *polis*. This initiative was only the first step, because, just as in Athens, more was needed to get this new application of the lot accepted: a familiar ground and a political climate conducive to a method of allocation based on cohesion among equals. Again, this familiar ground probably consisted of the traditional applications of the lot for other purposes, such as the distribution of plots of land. In this way, drawing lots for *polis* office was adopted in many *poleis*, but nowhere does allotment for office seem to have been so widely applied as in classical Athens.

Endnote: James W. Headlam, *Election by Lot at Athens* (Prince Consort dissertation 1890; London 1891; 2nd. ed. rev. D. C. MacGregor, Cambridge 1933[2])

Election by Lot at Athens is one of the essential studies of drawing lots for *polis* office in classical Athens, and for the understanding of political allotment more widely. Prominent scholars such as Mogens H. Hansen and Bernard Manin used this brilliant and lucid exposition for their own systematic analysis of the Athenian system. Headlam wrote the work as his dissertation in 1890 for Cambridge University, and it won him the Prince Consort Prize (named in honor of Queen Victoria's late consort Prince Albert) for the best dissertation in its field. The prize money provided for the publication of the work, and the book was due to go to press, just before the widely publicized discovery of the *Athenaion Politeia*, which was about to go into print (1891). Given such short

---

[51] In the future, new epigraphical evidence may expand the dossier.
[52] Networks and peer-polity interaction: Ma (2003); Malkin (2011); Robinson (2011); Taylor and Vlassopoulos (2015).

notice, Headlam did not have the time revise his entire text (it had already been typeset), but he managed to add various comments to the introduction, and an extensive Appendix, where he systematically discussed which of his original views were confirmed, which had to be adjusted and how, and which had to be discarded in light of this authoritative new source.

Headlam's work is fundamental for two major aspects of drawing lots in Athens: the principle of rotation of office and its effects for democracy, and the question of divine guidance in selection by the lot. *Election by Lot at Athens* is famous, but not easily available. A summary of the book is in place here, followed by some comments.

With this study, Headlam aimed primarily to correct the contemporary view that in Athens the lot was an instrument in the hands of leaders of political factions or parties to manipulate the selection for office and with it the entire political arena (19–26). Instead, Headlam argues, no political parties in the late-nineteenth-century sense existed in Athens, and the lot worked in a different way and with an entirely different purpose: (a) all important offices were in principle subject to distribution by lot, not just the executive offices as had been assumed; (b) drawing lots was typical of the democracy, as its purpose was to diminish the distance between legislation, the executive, and the *demos*; if, as a side-effect of sortition, the status of offices decreased, that was not a problem, but something intended; (c) drawing lots reduced strife between political leaders and factions, and prevented fraud. A group in which every man is drawn by lot to sit together for no longer than a year—men who do not know each other beforehand and finally are scrutinized—cannot conspire to embezzle money or grab power. Drawing lots prevents reelection of the same people for office.

Athens did not seek a representative democracy of the modern type, in which elections always bring competition and strife between parties. In a state resorting to allotment, the competition between rivals and the will of the people take place in the law courts. Hence, the intermittent litigation so prominent in Athens is typical of this kind of *politeia*. All power remained vested in the *demos*, and the allotment of the offices supported this ongoing situation. The application of lot-drawing reined in the power of the Areopagos while strengthening that of the *demos*. Due to the intense rotation, the council of five hundred was unable to develop an independent position vis-à-vis the *demos*, but as an executive board it provided the necessary support (26–51). Rotation was not a principle only of democracy; oligarchies, too, used the lot for a limited rotation. In Athens, the vast number of offices—many of which were collegiate bodies consisting of several members—ensured that rotation included the entire *demos*. There is no sign in Athens of the suspicion Headlam noticed among his contemporaries that the lot could be used as a means to distribute power in a devious way, or to select particular individuals. The *dokimasia* (check as to citizen status and other criteria) was applied to make sure only those who were entitled to hold office would effectively do so. All offices were allotted, except military leaders and special assignments such as public works; these tasks required men with experience and connections, qualifications that some democrats would regard as typically oligarchic and therefore not above suspicion. The lot made sense as a means of selection when Athens had by and large a homogeneous population; when at the end of the fourth century the city became divided into a section for the wealthy and another for the poor, and disintegrated into two cities within one, the lot became an anachronism (88–121).

A second popular viewpoint that Headlam addressed concerns the lot as an expression of divine will. The French historian Numa Denis Fustel de Coulanges (1830–1889) had advanced a far-reaching and influential thesis on the religious foundations of ancient societies in his *La cité antique* ([1864] 1984), and, specifically, that in the early stages of antiquity, selection by lot was understood as divine selection. For Fustel, the ancient belief in the lot as a sign of a decision made by the gods was the only way to explain why an intelligent people such as the Athenians could resort to a bizarre system that was so contrary to rational political thinking.[53]

Headlam appreciated Fustel's work in principle but thought the French scholar had overstated his case, at least for Athens. For Headlam, belief in the lot as a form of divination belonged to an early stage of deep religiosity; if selection by lot was still regarded as divine selection in Athens in the classical age,

> then we should have to consider it as we do omens and oracles; it would be another case of an old superstition interfering with the political life of the people; its preservation would be another instance of that deep-rooted conservatism in all that concerned their worship which often reminds us that the Athenians were not all philosophers or sceptics. (4–5)

That selection by lot could be seen as guided by the gods was demonstrated by the fact that almost everywhere in Greece priests were chosen by lot, so one could argue that the gods chose their own servants, so Headlam. However, in classical Athens, there was no clear proof that selection by lot was generally regarded by the population as a practice led by divine guidance. After reviewing several cases in which such signs might have been relevant (but are not attested in the sources), Headlam concluded, "Soon amidst all the busy political and legal life at Athens what there was of religious feeling about it [the lot] died out" (12).

---

[53] Fustel de Coulanges's view on the lot as divine selection was adopted by Gustave Glotz in his influential lemma "Sortitio" in the encyclopedia known as Daremberg-Saglio (1907); for Fustel's primary response to allotment, compare G. E. M. De Ste. Croix, above, on drawing lots as "eccentric political institutions" ascribed to the Athenians as "quaint and rather silly people."

Instead, besides explaining the lot for distributing office as a democratic instrument, Headlam held that for understanding the cultural-political background to selection by lot, one should distinguish between the archons—for whom selection by the lot probably had been used of old to prevent strife—and all other offices, which were instituted later (80–86). That selection by lot had once also been an aristocratic method of governance was unmistakable—even if Fustel went too far by declaring that therefore drawing lots could never be truly democratic (Fustel de Coulanges ([1864] 1984) 390). For all other offices that were later instituted, the manner of selection had to be instituted, at which point the lot was introduced once more, but on a new footing. The problem was that it was unknown when this had happened. All scholars agreed that the lot could not have been used before Cleisthenes, but clearly it had been established before 450.

Such had been his original viewpoint, but after reading the just published *Ath.Pol.*, Headlam returned to this issue in the Appendix to his own publication. Although he recognized at once that the section in the *Ath.Pol.* on Draco's constitution (*Ath.Pol.* 4) could not be authentic, in the section on Solon (8.1) he found proof that the archons had been selected by the lot, and that this method preceded Solon, which was precisely why Solon could bring it to apply; this was an important new confirmation of Fustel's method (183–184), because it showed that selection of *polis* offices by lot was more ancient, and long predated Cleisthenes. But the section in *Ath.Pol.* 8.1 also had new information on the other offices, so Headlam (185):

> The statement of chapter 18 [*sic*, read: 8.1] "he [Solon] made the offices selected by lot from preselected candidates" seems to apply not only to the Archonship. The other offices which had existed at that time must also have been filled in the same way.

According to *Ath.Pol.* 7, these included the *Tamiai*, the *poletai* (vendors of contracts), the Eleven (a body for enforcement of judicial sentences), and the *kolakretai* (paymasters). Headlam concludes that not only those offices were much older than had previously been thought, but that the fact that Solon had them all drawn by lot from preselected candidates reinforced the importance of Fustel's ideas, because here too the *Ath.Pol.* confirmed the antiquity of selection by lot for office, and even on a large scale (185–186).

Headlam's study is a groundbreaking contribution toward a systematic understanding of allotment for political office, notably for the connective logic determining rotation, equality, and democracy. His work continues to impress today with its originality, clarity, and open-mindedness. I wish here to add two comments.

1. Hansen and Manin both underline that Headlam was right in showing that for the Classical age "not a single good source ... straightforwardly testifies to the selection of magistrates by lot as having a religious character in origin."[54] Headlam's argument in the first version of his text to distinguish the Archaic selection of the archons from the offices instituted later (sc. by Cleisthenes), has been given even more force by Hansen, who argues that selection by lot only began with Cleisthenes.[55] However, Headlam's position on Fustel's reading of divine selection in the Archaic-era use of the lot was far more nuanced—both in the original text and even more in the Appendix—than we might gather from the later uses of his work.

2. I cannot agree with Headlam's reading of the first sentence of *Ath.Pol.* 8.1, that Solon instituted *klerosis ek prokriton* for *all* the offices, including the council. Although the text does not preclude his reading, it does not make it necessary either, because here as elsewhere the *Ath.Pol.* continues its account with simple δέ (... and ... and). In historical terms, it would mean that Solon effected a revolution in the selection for *polis* office on an unprecedented, and in my view unthinkable, scale. No other evidence suggests that besides the archons and the *Tamiai*, the other offices were also drawn by lot; the manner of their selection is simply not discussed until the Classical age. One case, the contention in Arist. *Pol.* 1274a2–6 that the Solonian court was drawn by lot, is explained in the main text as a projection of the fourth century back in time; an example of "all offices" in this case certainly cannot be either. So, until new evidence comes to light, or existing evidence is convincingly reexamined, I take the first sentence of 8.1 to refer to the two *archai* discussed in that section, the archons, and the *Tamiai*, and I have used this conclusion as the point of departure for my analysis.

---

[54] Hansen (1991) 49–52, quote on 51; Manin (1997) 26–27.
[55] Hansen (1990).

PART IV
CONCLUSIONS AND ENVOI

Irad Malkin
Conclusions and Implications

1 The Mindset: Antiquity, Ubiquity, and Religion

During some three centuries before the rise of democracy and its extensive employment of lots, the drawing of lots had been used, far and wide, in a broad spectrum of applications, revealing a mindset and an outlook.[1] Whether *selective*, *distributive*, or *procedural*, the lottery is always a lottery: it discloses a rational decision to employ a random device to get a reasonable (not irrational) result that is fair and equal, with no *ad hominem* resentment at the outcome. Instead of a top-down hierarchy, it expressed an egalitarian, horizontal mindset while indicating the group's sovereignty or the community's decision to draw lots for selection, distribution, procedure, or social mixture. By the late sixth century, Greeks were used to expressing their communities' contours by identifying who had access to the lottery and who did not. Moreover, they seem to have believed such lotteries best expressed their ideas of equality, fairness, and justice. A direct line leads from *isomoiria* to *isonomia*: from "equal portions" to "equal portions of law" (in modern parlance, "equality before the law") and even to democracy.

We have yet to learn why and how it all started. The trouble is that we already find a full spectrum of practices and consistent vocabulary in Homer, our earliest source. One possible candidate for the practice's origins is the inheritance rules of partible inheritance by lot (ch. 4). Another venue would be to investigate state formation and nucleated sites in the Iron Age that may indicate the emergence of self-aware communities. Finally, perhaps an egalitarian pirate codes, with a unique portion to a leader and equal sharing from the middle among the rest, is responsible for the mindset and its expression in the drawing of lots. We can only speculate, and perhaps others may pick up the challenge. I commented earlier that the question "What came first: was it the egalitarian mindset or the practice?" is faulty. Again, we cannot know but may assume with a high degree of probability that one kept impacting the other. It was a reciprocal relationship between "that is how we do things" (practice) and "that is why we do them that way" (mindset).

---

[1] The conclusions were written by Irad Malkin. I summarize conclusions and implications deriving from each of the chapters (with a special emphasis on the first six) and how, in my view, they reflect on each other. For contemporary and future implications, see the Envoi, written by Josine Blok.

Drawing Lots. Irad Malkin and Josine Blok, Oxford University Press. © Oxford University Press 2024.
DOI: 10.1093/oso/9780197753477.003.0011

During the archaic period (the eighth through the early fifth centuries), we note several concurrent phenomena: the rise and crystallization of political communities and their institutions through local developments, deliberate *synoikismoi* ("coalescence," discrete units joining in a single political community), or the founding of new settlements abroad. The latter category is responsible for nearly 30 percent of all Greek city-states in the archaic period.[2] We noted a constant tension between the elitist and egalitarian vectors—between, on the one hand, egalitarianism, and on the other, material and social differentiation. Colonization perhaps best illustrates this: following conditions of inequality at home, young men set out to acquire a *kleros* (landed property) abroad, sailing on "equal and fair terms" and eventually getting, by lot, equal portions of plots of land as First Lots. However, the checkerboard equality of First Lots constituted only the minimum possession, expressing one's share in the new political community. There was no cap on personal wealth, and within a generation or two after foundation, the elitist vector would dominate yet again. A common reaction would be either to set out and found a new settlement on equal and fair terms or attempt a revolution, calling for a return to the primordial state of equality via land redistribution.

Compromise reforms sometimes attempted to return power to the middle (*es to meson*), a key term in lotteries, politically expressing some form of power to the people. The reason is sometimes explicit: to make everyone "equal" in civic status or *homoioi*. As I claim at the end of the conclusions, the institution of drawing lots constituted a significant aspect of the makeup of the *polis*, whether employed as a democratic instrument or not. Let us first summarize our findings in a way that ought to present a complete picture of the history and the uses of drawing lots.

The Homeric version of the myth about the division and distribution of the portions of the world among Zeus, Hades, and Poseidon remarkably contains most of the vocabulary relevant to lotteries. It expresses a horizontal vision of participants as "sharers" receiving "portions" while exclusively defining the "group" with the right to access the lot. The divine lottery is, after all, a human projection; these features have been consistent throughout the archaic period. Authority rests with the participants; the group members are the ones who decide to conduct a lottery and abide by its outcome; their authority is their own. In the same way that the Olympian gods did not ask a higher divinity whether to conduct a lottery, nor did those gods ask another deity for its preferred outcome. Greek communities also derived their authority from within themselves, feeling sufficiently sovereign to conduct the drawing of lots and to abide by the result.

---

[2] Hansen (1999) 84.

They were not conducting lotteries for divination, a specific, discrete function (on lot oracles, see ch. 2).

The fundamental values expressed by the lot are apparent in Homer, Hesiod, and the *Homeric Hymns*: a claim to be (or to have) *isomoros* (obtaining an equal portion and, hence, supposedly equal status); a horizontal vision of the society of the gods where *timai* and *gera* are drawn by lot. The myth alludes to practices of partible inheritance by lot (chs. 4, 5) with no primogeniture; however, because the three brothers (Zeus, Poseidon, and Hades) had just been victorious over the Titans, their division of the world is also equivalent to the division and distribution by drawing lots of war booty, the practice we examined among Homeric soldiers and leaders.

The certain, the probable, and the possible are three categories into which historians of antiquity attempt to classify their reconstructions of the past, often trying to upgrade the "possible" to the "probable," the "likely" to "highly likely," and, rare as it is, to that about which we can be certain. The "uncertain, improbable, and impossible" play a counterpart role. Our knowledge is too scanty, and the bricks to build an argument's wall are scarce. Nevertheless, when reconstructing the modes of distribution of Homeric booty and the values they express, we find them remarkably consistent with other practices and values of distribution by lot, as we shall see, for example, with the distribution of portions of meat for the feast and the sacrifice.

The cosmic distributive lottery persisted in holding an essential place in the frame of reference of all ancient Greeks, being referred to and alluded to time and again, as we have also seen with Pindar and Plato. Greece was not unique in its use of the lot, and we noted that the Hittites, ancient Israel, and Rome, among others, also employed the drawing of lots. However, its centrality among Greeks and the broad spectrum of use are incomparable. The degree to which we find concrete expressions of the values implied in drawing lots makes ancient Greece distinctive. Was the cosmic lottery a "Greek myth"? Its divine distributive lottery framework also existed in the Ancient Near East. However, if the myth originated there, it acquired distinct Greek aspects, such as "Olympus and Gaia" as a "common ground." Another difference with the ancient Near Eastern myth is that the latter assumes various dimensions since the world is not perceived as a single entity, a "universe." By contrast, Greeks perceived the gods as distributing portions (*moira, aisa*) of some whole. Those portions were perceived either as grand categories (Heaven, the Depths and the Sea, Hades) or in terms of a specific province or domain, *time* or *geras* (e.g., Aphrodite, Hestia, and Helios). The expression *emmore times* illustrates well that a specific *time* is but a portion of some general one. The vision of portions of some whole may also afford an exciting insight into the nature of polytheism, a much-discussed term. It may also be a telling antecedent to Greek philosophical monism.

Most allocations resulting from drawing lots are accompanied in archaic poetry not by a verb of giving (*didomi*) but of distributing (*dateomai*; cf. *dasmos*). *Dasmos*, the term for the divine distribution, and *dateomai*, the common verb form expressing it, refer to distribution by group members to themselves (*dateomai* often appears in the plural and the middle voice), or by someone presiding over the process and conducting it on their behalf.[3] Sometimes, we are not told how the *dasmos* was conducted, especially with Hesiod. When we get a description, it involves drawing lots.

The word *kleros* illustrates the overlapping, integrated meanings of the lottery and its results, sometimes confusing the cause-and-effect order. As we have seen, especially with partible inheritance by lot, *kleros* indicates both the instrument (e.g., a piece of wood), the link to the act of casting lots, and the result of the lottery—all may be called *kleros* or *klerosis*. Semantically, one may point out parallels in Latin (*sors*), Celtic *Clar*, and Biblical Hebrew (*goral*); all can mean the material "lot," and all are linked both with the act of drawing lots and its result (e.g., a portion of inherited land). Such parallelism with *sors* and *goral* may need further study. The surrounding vocabulary is often semantically similar (e.g., להפיל גורל to "drop a *goral*").[4] Already in Homer, a *kleros* may mean "an estate," with no reference to its origins. What matters for our sake is that, although it could signify a concrete result (e.g., *kleros* = inheritance), *kleros* did not become a dead metaphor but retained its strong actual and semantic associations with lotteries, down to and including the days of the Athenian democracy. Its association with the lot could never have been far off a Greek's mind.

For example, when associated with land, *kleros* came to signify "an inheritance." In colonies, it meant a plot of land (the result of allotment). The overlap between inheritance conventions and colonial practices is striking. In both, we find interchangeable participants and drawing of lots for equal portions determined in advance of the drawing of lots. The "community" (as small as three brothers or as large as a colony) is sovereign to decide on the procedure (agreeing on predetermined equal or equitable portions and drawing lots for them) and validate results. In that respect, the sovereignty of the community is evident in the archaic period. As we have seen with the Homeric *temenos* (estate, precinct), the community grants the *temenos*, which then becomes "private." By contrast, no special land grants were allocated to founders of historical colonies, nor did their posterity enjoy distinct privileges. The *kleros* consistently retained its association with its primary meaning sense of the lottery and its outcomes.

The verb most associated with the lot is *lanchano* (and its derivatives, e.g., *lachos*). It usually signifies "getting by lot." Down to the late fifth century, *lanchano*

---

[3] See ch. 1, Endnote 3.
[4] Cf. Bar On (2020); Létoublon (2014).

mostly retained its lot associations, as the studies of B. Borecký, supplemented by our own, strongly suggest. Since *lanchano* could sometimes mean "to get" (not necessarily by lot), we needed to determine in context whether the lot was indeed meant. In most cases we have examined, the lot was implied (see the tables in the Appendix, and *kleros.org.il*).

Achilles and Odysseus distinguish between two types of "getting": the *geras* as a ritualized public gift from the people and, on the other hand, what the hero gets *by lot* with everyone else (*lanchano; lachos*). We noted, for example, that Achilles explicitly contrasts between what he was publicly given (*didomi*) and "all that fell to me by lot (*lanchano*)." We distinguished between three Homeric types of "getting": a public gift, private capture (*enara*), and getting by lot through sharing in a distributive lottery with others. Generally, in the *Iliad* and the *Odyssey*, *lanchano* is explicitly associated with the vocabulary of drawing lots. The egalitarian aspect of booty distributed by lot contrasts with a top-down vision of the trickling-down gifts.

The general Homeric scheme seems straightforward: booty is brought to the middle, whence it is distributed by lot to all participants, including the leaders. Aside from that, a leader gets a special honorary prize (*geras*) as a gift *from* the army that recognizes status and honor. Scholars arguing for inequality and a top-down approach relegate to the sidelines the relevant terminology of drawing lots and equality. Homer speaks of riches and booty far exceeding the relatively equal portions implied by the comprehensive, distributive lottery. However, what seems to have confused the issue is the neglect of ample evidence that heroes could amass wealth in the field "privately," since there existed a third category of getting: warriors could grab *enara*, booty consisting of personal enslavement and ransom, stripping the armor off the slain, and capturing horses. Such personally acquired loot could make a hero rich but not famous. *Kleos* (renown, reputation) depended on the middle and the recognition attached to the public distribution. The *enara*, equivalent to the biblical *bizzah* (as distinguished from *šelal*), resolves the apparent contradictions between equal distribution and private wealth. *Enara*, in short, are not "portions" but property. By contrast, the concept of "portions of booty" (*moirai*) presupposes some whole from which booty is distributed *equally* (i.e., to *all* and by lot).

2 Equality and fairness

Distribution of booty by lot implies precise notions of fairness. However, what was considered fair? In contrast to Henry Morgan's pirate code, in which fairness consisted in what was proper to one's status, fairness in the Homeric distribution of booty by lot was much closer to ideas of equality: equal chances before the lot.

We encountered, for example, the formula for fair distribution: "so that nobody will be defrauded of his *equal* share" (some would translate "fair"). The point becomes more apparent in the formula *isei* (*isai*) *kai homoiai*, "equal and like/fair terms," in the context of what Greek settlers could expect when founding a new city. We have also observed such notions expressed on the ground as exact, equal-sized land plots (*kleroi*) distributed by lot to new settlers. In other words, the yardstick of Greek fairness was to be as close as possible to equality, a consistent feature of Greek distributions by lot throughout the archaic and classical periods.

3 Group definition

Whether selective or distributive, lots are drawn within a predefined group. The group might consist of gods conducting a distributive lottery, sons sharing in partible inheritance, companions (*hetairoi*) sharing booty, or colonists selected by lot to leave their mother city—and once having arrived at the new settlement site, drawing lots for individual, equal plots of land. Greek settlers also kept land in reserve for distribution to future Greek colonists. There must have been an inherent interest in such a group not to let outsiders share in whatever distribution (I also examine the implication of excluding non-Greek locals). The lottery, therefore, presupposes the contours of the group of sharers and, depending on the context, probably enhanced group identity. The drawing of lots is conducted within a recognized, predefined group whose members are all interchangeable (hence equal) and have equal status before the lot.

4 The will of the gods

What did Greeks expect of their gods in the context of drawing lots? Did they expect the gods to reveal their intention or express wishes through the lots? Greeks did expect that when the lot was used for divination (ch. 2), but distributive, selective, mixing, and procedural lotteries were conducted for a different purpose. The very existence of the category of lot oracles and the explicit purpose of using the lots mark this category apart. It is the only framework in which lots are explicitly used for divination and only in a context of sanctuaries dedicated to divination, thus sharpening their distinction.

That is not to say that the gods were absent. They were invoked, and lotteries were conducted under their auspices, like any public affair. But on the spectrum between lots as divination and lots as a rational and practical mechanism, such lotteries were mainly on the latter's side. They concerned political and social matters, while the decision to hold a lottery was also human. Eligible participants were predefined by other humans and were equal before the chance. Nowhere do we hear of an oracle ordering humans to conduct a drawing of lots, nor are there complaints against any god because of unsuccessful results in a lottery.

The lottery existed on a spectrum of associations, enhancing our understanding of the lots in their overlapping, broad applicability, revealing both mental attitudes and attesting to practices and institutions. Lotteries' salient features are randomness and unpredictability, ensuring equality before the chance. In distributive, selective, mixing, and procedural lotteries, that is also their justification and purpose; it is not to reveal something divinely predetermined. In any case, the question, current among modern scholars, does not seem to have been a major concern for ancient Greeks (although views may have varied among individuals). By the late fifth century, when the lot was used thousands of times in any given year in the framework of the Athenian democracy, the rational and practical side of the spectrum was the clearest. The gods did not select Athens's magistrates and judges; the Athenians did. In drawing lots, the gods mostly preside but do not decide.

5 Lot oracles

Delphi provides an excellent illustration for the distinction between the oracular and the "civic" use of the lot: whereas all oracular inquiries employing drawing of lots seek a divine response, we also noted other types of drawing lots at Delphi itself: the turns for inquiry with the Pythia were established by lot (procedural), and the Delphic personnel were selected by lot (selective). Apollo and the oracle do not seem to have been involved in either. Finally, Delphi's constitutive myths (in Aeschylus's version) explicitly speak of the rotation of the owners of the Delphic Oracle by drawing lots (e.g., Themis), until finally Apollo became its possessor.

Lot oracles existed at Delphi. There were probably at least two modes of divination by lot that must not be confused:[5] first, "picking up" (*anaireo*) by the Pythia one lot from among several presubmitted lots for a selective lottery. To this category belong a Thessalian inquiry, submitting several names from which to select a single king, and probably Cleisthenes's submission of one hundred names of Attic heroes for the Pythia to pick out the ten eponymous ones for the new Athenian tribes (see also section 8.2.2.2 in this volume). In addition, for the yes/no types of inquiries (selection between

---

[5] Maurizio (2019) treats the two as the same, and since selective lotteries are indeed different from a yes/no type of lot oracles, she then denies the existence of the latter as contradicting the former.

only two possibilities), an oracle by "the two beans" was probably used, perhaps even aside from the very few (nine!) annual working days of the Pythia during the archaic period. One might suspect, for example, that that is how "Delphi" answered the famous question of whether anyone was wiser than Socrates. The Athenian inquiry about whether to work sacred lands was also a yes/no inquiry, albeit executed in a roundabout way (blindly placing the alternatives in gold and silver water jugs that remained at Athens and asking Apollo to choose between the water jugs). In short, there was a lot-oracle at Delphi worthy of costly state inquiries (e.g., Skiathos's inquiry), but it is difficult to determine its workings. There may have been several lot-oracles, perhaps one at Mount Parnassos. At Dodona, the existence of thousands of personal inquiries submitted for a drawing of lots in personal handwritings and dialects clarifies the mostly yes/no aspect of such inquiries and how they were made among surprisingly literate people.

Plato, the only source close to associating the *kleros* with the divine, also provides an explicit, if phantasmagoric, vision of pairing lots, combining lots, and personal choice. Cases where lotteries sometimes determined one's turn to make a choice may have also existed in the world of Greek colonies for the distribution of *protoi kleroi*, or First Lots (see ch. 6). Plato also refers to a common Greek notion that such *kleroi* ought to be kept intact and inalienable.

Whereas lot-oracles are based on binary answers (yes/no), *inspired* prophecies in response to open-ended questions ("*Where* should I colonize?") were regarded on a higher level. However, lot oracles and verbal prophecies both were viewed as if coming from the god. Apollo and especially Hermes are associated with lots and prophecies, although inspired prophecies, supposedly of a higher order, are Apollo's as the divine Expounder (*exegetes*). Nevertheless, both myths (*moirai/semnai*) and known practices associate Delphi too with drawing lots for prophecies. Hermes's own primordial actions concern a distributive lottery of cutting up and dividing equal portions of sacrificial meat to be distributed by lot (ch. 3).

6 Frequency, ubiquity, and sacrifice

Modes of distribution by lot appear remarkably consistent with other practices and values of distribution by lot, as we see with the distribution of portions of meat for the feast and the sacrifice. This consistency is prominently expressed in the ubiquitous feasting and sacrificing, unlike the rare and singular occasions of distribution of booty, inheritance, and portions of land in colonization. The practice of such distribution by lot also implies a mindset and associated values that were concretely expressed in the relatively more recurrent distribution and consumption of meat. Meat distribution can be occasional (as any feast would be) and ritualized on fixed days and in unforeseen circumstances, such as funeral games. The difference between the distribution of booty and the distribution of meat by lot is in how frequent and present they were in the community's life: sacrifice was a common occurrence, whereas the distribution of booty was rare. There is no contrast here, but complementary and mutually reinforcing values and practices.

Booty and sacrifice do not form a contrast (especially in Homer), as some think: both are ritualized and publicly visible, regulated according to public conventions, and fair or equal shares are apparent in both.[6] The distribution of booty overlaps with the distribution of the sacrifice not only in the vocabulary but also in expressing the contours of the group: those who participate in the drawing of lots "belong," and those who do not are excluded. To a significant extent, a Greek community is defined by those who sacrifice together,[7] namely, those entitled to *share* in the sacrifice ritual and, "man to man," receive equal portions by lot.

Scholars often discuss the distribution of colonial plots of land, inheritance, portions of sacrificial meat, and so on, in discrete categories of scholarly expertise such as "land and property," "sacrifice and religion," "inheritance and Greek laws," and so on. Instead, I suggest that all those are subsets of "distribution": how did Greeks distribute stuff? Answer: by lot. Some salient features seem common to the distribution by lot of portions of sacrificial meat (all meat was consumed as a sacrifice) and to other prominent distribution contexts such as inheritance, land, and booty. The distributive values of drawing lots indicate a common mindset in which some salient features are apparent:

- Equality before the chance.
- Equality of resulting portions (sometimes called *iso-moiria*).
- Fairness, but not in the sense of "proper to one's status" but as *homoios*, "equal/like."
- Defining, exclusively, the contours of the group whose members have access to the lot.
- The distribution of "portions" is relational and horizontal, the opposite of the hierarchical "top-down" distribution.
- Interchangeability of recipients among specific group members: they all have the same status before the lot.
- No resentment following "unfair" distribution (except for "bad luck").

---

[6] See ch. 1, Endnote 1.
[7] Parker (1998; 2005); Blok (2017).

7 Partible inheritance by lot

The mindset, conventions, vocabulary, and practice consistently converge when we observe what every Greek household must have experienced at some point: death and the need to distribute the inheritance (ch. 4). From Homer to Isaeus (eighth–fourth centuries), and, spatially, from Crete to the Black Sea and the western Mediterranean, conventions of partible inheritance by lot, while varying in detail, were ubiquitous in Greek, often bypassing local and subethnic differences. Conventions and patterns were formed through network dynamics and reciprocal recognition of values.

All brothers were *interchangeable* before the lot; there was no primogeniture in such cases. That is yet another aspect of the horizontal vision of equality with significant implications for when such a vision was extended beyond the family to the sharers in the *polis*.[8] Moreover, it was not the gods who decided the outcome: the inheritor got a *moira* (portion) of the inheritance, but he was not destined ("it was not his *moira*") to choose it.

We observed instances where the purpose of the lottery was not pairing the name of a brother with a specific portion (both assigned by lot), but establishing turns: the first brother whose lot comes up then makes a personal choice between the predetermined, equal (or equitable) portions. I further suggest that is how First Lots were sometimes allotted in new foundations (colonies). We thus get a combination of chance and free choice.

Partible inheritance encouraged colonization: instead of two brothers dividing up a *kleros* at home, each brother now got a whole *kleros*, one at home, the other in a colony. When colonies kept the First Lots (*protoi kleroi*) intact, they would run out of reserve land for future migrants (*epoikoi*). Along with the material differentiation that would become prominent in the second and third generations postfoundation, the partible inheritance would also create similar problems among relatives born in the colony, hence the impetus to establish more settlements and colonies of colonies.

The distribution of land by lot in partible inheritance and the allotment of First Lots in a colony indicates a remarkable overlap of values and practices: first, equal allocation (i.e., same chance for all participants), and second, equally sized portions of land, distributed to members of the group (brothers, colonists), a group that is predefined and composed of those eligible to participate in the lottery. Partible inheritance, with its lack of primogeniture and the use of the lot, appears like a fractal of the entire *polis*: the group is predefined; all of its members

---

[8] Cf. Blok (2018) 97: "I suggest that partible inheritance and its concomitant system of allotment have played a crucial role in the conception of equality that became so important in Greek political life."

have "shares"; the authority stems from within the group; an arbitrator may help resolve a dispute about family inheritance or resolve civil strife, like Demonax of Mantineia at Cyrene.[9] We observe no recognized innate hierarchy; all "group" members are interchangeable.

In general, distributive and lottery-associated vocabulary is ubiquitous and consistent. The verb most often used for the distribution of inheritance is again *dateomai*, which we observed with other kinds of distribution and refers early on to distribution *among* a known group in contexts associated with a lottery.[10] There is a significant link between the lot vocabulary (*kleros, apo-lanchano, pallo, diapallo, klerosis, diakleroö, kuameuo, epiballo, lachos, lexis, palos*) and associated practices of colonization and inheritance. The closeness of the semantic fields and the resonance of such terminology, all linked with practices of lotteries, point to a horizontal, nonhierarchical mental filter through which archaic Greeks could observe their society. In Greek drama (ch. 5), the theme of drawing lots, taken from a common store of Greek myths, appears traditional and well-known while also reflecting contemporary issues. The vocabulary is yet again consistent, and the language of drawing lots moves between the concrete and the metaphoric, playing with the overlapping meanings of *lanchano, kleros, epiballo, palos,* and some *moira*-related words. It also ranges beyond the plain meaning: the word *daimones*, for example, is rooted in allocation (*dateomai*).

Inheritance and fairness in distribution by lot are significant issues in Greek drama (ch. 5), where the lot is a narrative device, an idiom, and a poetic metaphor. Despite the idiosyncrasies of this or that playwright, the argument that what appears on the Athenian stage must have been familiar to thousands of Athenians is valid. We can safely assume a shared mental frame of reference that viewed lotteries as ubiquitous. The entire spectrum of the use of the lot is present on stage: selective lotteries (e.g., Iphigeneia), distributive lotteries (e.g., captives to captors in the *Trojan Women*), procedure and allocation (e.g., paring heroes and city gates in Aeschylus's *Seven*), and most significantly, inheritance. While Homer avoided matters of inheritance in the "real" stories (unlike Odysseus the Bastard of the lying tales, both Odysseus and Telemachos were conveniently only sons), the "Curse of Oedipus" on his two sons, Eteokles and Polyneikes, lies at the heart of the conflict about inheritance. The *Seven* is rich with lottery associations and implications. Paul Demont rightly observes that the allocation of gates by lot is the opposite of tyranny (or "horizontal," in my terms), whereas assigning them by the ruler (in Thebes) was a mark of precisely that.[11] This corresponds to our general distinction between a top-down and a horizontal authority that depends

---

[9] Malkin (2023).
[10] E.g., Hes. *WD* 37–39; Hes. *Th.* 605–607; Hom. *Il.* 5.155–159; *Od.* 2.335–336, 2.367–368; 3.313–316; 15.10–13; 16.383–386; 17.79–81; 20.213–216.
[11] Demont (2000).

on the group (whatever its size or composition) and draws its legitimacy from the mutually recognized, relational context. Aeschylus's *Seven* further clarifies the nature of the use of the lot and the role of free will: brothers are supposed to agree in advance on what is equitable and then let the lot decide which brother will make the first choice. As noted, such a combination of chance and choice is also apparent in Greek colonies.

8 New foundations

It is hard to overstate the historical significance of new Greek foundations during the Archaic period. Hundreds of new *poleis* were established within huge geographical horizons within two and a half centuries. Thousands of Greeks of varying origins needed to adapt to new situations while applying similar conventions for planning their foundations' physical and social makeup. For their part, such conventions became integrated into the horizons of expectation of new settlers and a yardstick by which to judge what was wrong "at home." All the elements discussed in the chapter on colonial *kleroi* (ch. 6) appear consistent, whether expressed in myth, quasihistorical myths, historical accounts, or inscriptions, or are apparent, archaeologically, on the ground.

Aside from treating land for settlement as "empty" (*eremos chora*), splitting it into equal *kleroi*, and then distributing those by lot, we do not hear of any other way of doing things in factual descriptions or imaginary scenarios. No alternative (e.g., a leader giving extra portions to his followers and grabbing the lion's share) is ever mentioned, invented, or even imagined in any available source (except for tyrants). I cannot exaggerate the importance of this methodological point. What lies beyond the frame of reference of our sources and is never mentioned, even in pure inventions, is no less a historical fact than what lies within it. Romans had no problem inventing stories about prominent men, such as Claudius, who got far more than their followers. However, the Greeks never invented such stories about their founders. The scheme is consistent: a founder with temporary full powers (*autokrator*) oversees the distribution of equal plots by drawing lots.

The egalitarian values apparent in the distribution of equal *kleroi* by lot are also consistent with other distributive and selective lotteries' contexts, which we observe in the different domains studied in this book. The equal "portion" (*moira, meros, isomoiria*) granted by lot to each individual at once defines him as a discrete citizen with a household (*oikos, kleros*), a part of a whole. The colonial First Lot (*protos kleros*) is the concrete expression of equal community sharing and an egalitarian ethos. Its formation and distribution by lot existed in the archaic Greek mindset as "directions for use" for how to (re)found a community.

CONCLUSIONS AND IMPLICATIONS 431

Historians find it challenging to assess intentions when they only see results. However, we can observe explicitly articulated intentions in this case: the best source for Greek expectations is the small corpus of decrees concerning land and foundation. These are prescriptive texts pointing to what *should* be done; they do not testify to their implementation. However, they set the standard and reflect values and expected practices. However, as often with such directions, full implementation on the ground often depended on *ad hoc* circumstances. To summarize, these are the main elements in colonial traditions with different models for founders and settlers.

1. Nausithoos (Phaiakia), like Neileos (Miletos), a leader of an exodus-type migration (evacuation of the homeland), and a founder.
2. No exodus, no clear mother city: a leader and a group of followers or "companions" (we observed Odysseus, Thoukles, and Philippos of Kroton); the leader is distinguished by a *geras* (Odysseus), and presumably Thoukles got a heroic cult after his death.
3. Organized by a *metropolis*: Selection of settlers by lot at the home community, like the conscription of soldiers by lot in the *Iliad*, or the prospective colonists to Cyrene. The *oikistes* (founder) is identified with the mother city.
4. No "aristocracy" from a homeland joins a foundation in any of the models; elites develop locally.
5. Founders and religion: the founder is the personal choice by Apollo at Delphi, a sanction that ritually formalizes the status of the "elevated leader and equal followers"; the foundation itself was a sacred act.
6. Recognizing the "tent generation" (*campement*) under the leadership of the *oikistes*: temporary habitations on a settlement site while organizing the space (public areas, sacred areas, roads, house-blocks, etc.) and starting house construction. The tent generation is an essential consideration for archaeologists wondering about the relative paucity of built houses in the first generation of founding a new settlement.
7. The lottery implies a double action at both the mother city and the colony: ensuring the continuing existence of *oikoi/kleroi* in the home community and providing a brother with an overseas *kleros* (instead of just a smaller portion through partible inheritance at home).
8. Equality and the implication of personal means: plots were allotted ([*dia-*]*nemein*), and the privileged status of the *protoi/palaioi kleroi* or *archaia moira*—the "first lots"—was established as a discrete category.

Further territorial expansion and land acquisition usually went beyond the marking of the First Lots, and the community did not restrict the increase of personal property. There was no limit on personal means: settlers were *unequal* regarding moveable wealth (*chremata*). Social and economic differentiation is often marked not before the second or third generation. This may explain why the political terminology characterizing colonial elites is not "blood-aristocratic" but relies on material features, such as "those wearing purple" at Akragas or "those in possession of the portions of land" at Syracuse, the Gamoroi. Archaeological evidence pointing to inequality in land possession over several centuries is therefore irrelevant to the question of the equality of the First Lots.

Egalitarianism in the foundation of new settlements was expressed in the *protoi kleroi*, the First Lots. Their equality consisted of the same size and distribution by chance. Equality was therefore expressed arithmetically, cutting up the "empty land" (*eremos chora*) into precisely measured, equal (*isos*) portions. However, in terms of location and perhaps soil quality, lots were unequal but merely "like" each other (*homoios*).

Pairing settlers with *kleroi* by sortition is rarely stated explicitly but seems probable as one of the means for distribution by lot, as we see in other distributive lotteries. Alternatively, or in some specific cases, it is also probable that the lottery established *turns* (as it probably did in partible inheritance) to declare for specific, predefined lots, thus combining the arbitrariness of the lot with free choice and preference.

Land and redistribution were a general Greek concern, explicitly attested since the seventh century when the vision of a society composed of "units" of "one man, one *oikos*, one *kleros*" became conventional.[12] Once that vision became a practical option, Greeks suffered an automatic overpopulation or, in Greek terms, *stenochoria*, "the place/space is too narrow,"[13] and colonization was a solution. The colonial category of reserved land for future settlers was probably a measure to avoid that problem in "old Greece." Land distribution and the reservation of land imply a sovereign control of territory by the community and a comprehensive vision that society has of itself.

The earliest equal *kleroi* are evident on the ground during the last quarter of the eighth century (Megara Hyblaia) in a secure context of a comprehensive settlement plan formed as a kind of grid. In and of themselves, grids do not necessarily imply egalitarianism and a horizontal society. In medieval towns, the grid rather expressed centralized "power"; in the modern United States, it expresses public authority and central planning; however, combined with all the evidence accumulated and reviewed in chapter 6, it appears that, among archaic Greeks, the grid did express an egalitarian outlook. Our earliest evidence at Megara Hyblaia (ca. 730–700) indicates that what lies beside the grid points to

---

[12] Cf. Pl. *Laws* 737e: ἀνὴρ καὶ κλῆρος συννομή.
[13] Pl. *Laws* 708b.

a community, with its public spaces, the common temples, and sacred precincts that were carved out at the same time as the private *protoi kleroi*.

What we note on the ground is an expression of the values and "directions for use" implied in the formula "on equal and fair" ("like") terms (*isei* [or *isai* in Dorian] *kai homoiai*): equality was perceived in terms of reciprocal relations, whose source of authority is the community itself. The implied terms of equality in *isei kai homoiai*, first attested in the early classical period, find their equivalence on the ground already in the last quarter of the eighth century, as colonial archaeology illustrates. Equal is not identical. Equality rather consists in "likeness" in specific respects and, as such, is considered "fair," instead of the idea of fairness as what is "proper" to one's status (cf. the Caribbean pirate codes). The *homoios* clarifies what is meant by *isos*, that is, in what respect people should be equal to each other.

The gods intervene in colonization by granting a general, *a priori* religious sanction to the founders (usually by Apollo at Delphi) to establish a new city. Let us recall that founding a city was also a sacred act, and gods were "settlers" as well.[14] The gods were not involved in the distribution by lot as they might be in cases of divination. Their sacred precincts were defined and set aside from the general distribution of *kleroi*,[15] parallel to a *geras* set aside from the general distribution of Homeric booty. When a *mantis* accompanied a founder, he may have conducted rituals at the time of the initial lottery and when the sacred precincts were carved out, a ritual that was obviously under the auspices—but not the direction—of the gods.[16]

Whenever our sources are explicit, the foundation of colonies was limited to "Greeks,"[17] thus enhancing the Small-World effect of sharing commonalities of mindset and practice. For example, Delphi addressed a second migration oracle to Cyrene *eis Hellenas pantas*, "to all the Greeks." We noted how Archilochos complained that "all the misery of the *panhellenes*" converged on Thasos. In general, it seems that colonization was effected through an organized nucleus, and any Greek who wished (*ho boulomenos*) could join, sometimes under subethnic restrictions (e.g., "no Ionians," in the foundation of Herakleia Trachinia).[18] With its one thousand city-states spread along coasts as distant from each other as the Sea of Azov is from the French Riviera, Greeks shared similar values and practices concerning the selection of participants and the collective distribution of that most important of resources: land. Concepts, practices, and underlying assumptions remained more or less constant throughout centuries and were

---

[14] Scully (1990); Malkin (1987a).
[15] Malkin (1987a) ch. 4.
[16] Malkin (1987a) ch. 2. Cf. Foster (2018).
[17] Malkin (2017a).
[18] Malkin (2009).

shared over vast spaces. This adherence to norms, expressed primarily in terms of fairness and equality, is remarkable since there was no "Greece" in antiquity, no Greek central authority, and no contiguous territory connecting the disparate *poleis*. There were no Romans around to spread their norms in "their sea" from a center of an empire. In contrast, as I have claimed in *A Small Greek World* (2011), Greek civilization functioned as a decentralized "Small World Network," with mutually copied and mutually evolving standards over huge physical distances.

The norms and standards were mainly concerned with defining and belonging to the entire "community of sharers": portions of the spoils of war and land (often *conquered* land). Circumstances permitting, sharing in the community (or "citizenship"), and *equal* land holdings came to be regarded as equivalent and best observed at foundational moments when the First Lots were defined and distributed by lot. A schematic image of what was a desired community in the archaic period, based on the ideal of "one man–one *oikos*–one *kleros*," seems to emerge through colonization practices, partible inheritance by lot, and, especially, revolutionary calls for redistribution of land. For example, by 356, revolutionary Syracusans explicitly demanded houses in addition to land: they passed a bill for the "redistribution of *kleroi* and houses" (*ges kai oikon anadasmos*). Equality (*isotes*) was the explicit purpose at Syracuse, expressing the convergence of equality's political and economic aspects in terms of *isomoiria*.[19] As at Sparta, the calls for revolution were based, so it seems, on the dissonance between that ideal (equal portions by lot) and the reality of social and economic differentiation. In modern terms, the desired imagined community was like a checkerboard, finite in its limits and consisting of equal units. Calls for a restart of society were articulated as a return to a "colonial" status of *homoioi*, based on the image of *ges anadasmos* in the sense of *redistribution* and a return to the primordial state of equality expressed in political and economic equal "portions." Sparta is best known for calls for redistribution, but the issue was universal and perennial, attested consistently, as we saw, since the seventh century.[20]

When we turn from revolutions in existing cities to the foundation of new ones, the equality could be articulated in terms of the equal chance of being selected at the home city to participate in colonization and an equal chance of getting equally sized portions of land as a First Lot (which might not have been equal in quality or location). This is the vision for the future in prescriptive foundation decrees drafted at a mother city. Upon arrival and settlement, the comprehensive, distributive lottery implies well-defined boundaries for the self-aware "community of sharers." There would have been a self-interest to limit allotment

---

[19] See Fuks (1968) on the episode in Plutarch's *Dion*.
[20] I discuss Tyrtaios's *anadaston poiein*, Solon confronting demands for *isomoiria*, the complaints of Theognis, the Lokrian inscription, and demands for *ges anadasmos* at Leontinoi and Herakleia Pontike.

CONCLUSIONS AND IMPLICATIONS 435

to group members and an *a priori* boundary that nonparticipants (e.g., local, non-Greek populations) would not cross, with some exceptions depending on local variants.

We noted that Greeks, "anyone who wished" (*ho boulomenos*), from all over the place, could join organized nuclei of colonization. The distributive lottery of initial *kleroi* was, therefore, also a *mixture* lottery, erasing distinctions of origins among settlers from the mother city and those Greeks who joined (we never hear of non-Greeks in that context). Thus all participants in the distribution were "sharers," getting their (equal) "portions," probably anticipating the perception in the classical period of the "citizen" as the one "who has a share" (*metechein*) in the *polis*.[21] We also note that when the lottery is comprehensive, as in Thera's case and the colonists' conscription to Cyrene, it transcends class, clan, and descent categories. It "mixes up" an entire society, both the one at the mother city and among the settlers of the new settlement, and unifies them both in the process.

While the lot implies egalitarianism, it did not emerge as a "democratic" institution (see also chs. 7 and 8).[22] Aristotle says that there was something akin to a descent-base "aristocracy" (*eugeneia*) of first settlers at Thera and Apollonia.[23] Curiously, the blood-criterion of ancestry is replaced by ancestry from a "Mayflower generation." We noted the *Gamoroi* (sharers in the land in Syracuse), perhaps the Hundred Houses at Lokroi, the (Adriatic) Apollonians, the Therans, and the Spartans who exemplify how equality among first settlers (or those believed to be so) could create a ruling class made up of *homoioi* ("equals, peers") who are equal among themselves yet superior to others. In the fifth century, such notions of "equality within" were typical of more formal oligarchies. Nevertheless, the *homoios* mindset, once in place, was capable of being extended comprehensively to the entire *demos*. The *isomoiria*, the equal "distribution/allotment" of "portions" of law (note also [*dia-*]*nemein, dateomai, dasmos*) anticipated democracy, or, more precisely, the *isonomia* at Athens.

One might ask: if most Greeks of the archaic period shared the egalitarian mindset and its expression in drawing lots, why did it not result in a more significant number of democracies? It is almost impossible to answer a "why not" question in history beyond speculation. Specifically, some oligarchies employed drawing lots (egalitarianism within a narrower circle), while some democracies did not. However, the main point is that there is no necessary, inevitable link between drawing lots, egalitarianism, and its transformation into the political

---

[21] Note the analysis of *ison echein, ison nemein,* and *ison didonai* in Borecký (1963; 1965). Cf. Blok (2018; 2017) and ch. 8 here.

[22] Cf. Fustel de Coulanges: "*Le tirage au sort n'était ni un procédé égalitaire, ni un procédé essentiellement oligarchique. Il a pris l'un ou l'autre caractère suivant les temps et suivant la façon dont il a été appliqué. Il a été aristocratique quand la société athénienne l'était; il est devenu relativement démocratique lorsque la société l'est devenue.*" Fustel de Coulanges (1891) 157, 166.

[23] Arist. *Pol.* 4.1290b13–14.

arena of governance. As I tried to demonstrate, egalitarianism expressed itself in a broad spectrum of social and religious interactions. Perhaps the transition to the political realm was exceptional. As we see in part III, even among democracies, Athens had been exceptional in the extent to which it applied the drawing of lots.

We keep noticing how overlapping meanings shift between notions of equality (*isotes*), expressed in material portions (e.g., booty, meat, inheritance, colonial *kleroi*), and the more abstract idea of political portions. Both physical *isonomia* (assigning equal portions of land in klerouchies) and political ones, expressed in the establishment of *isonomia* (assigned "equal portions of law" to each citizen), later called "democracy," appear at Athens. It is probably significant that Athens's political *isonomia* and its first *klerouchia* (with its concrete distribution of equal portions of land) were almost precisely contemporary.[24]

Greeks seem to have trusted supreme arbitrators. Following some two hundred years of founding new cities, the overlap between founders (*oikistai*), tyrants, and comprehensive reformers became very close by the end of the sixth century. All enjoyed plenipotentiary powers (*autokratores*), and, except for tyrants, their role was limited in time. As with an early Roman dictator, authority was *ad hoc*, and reformers functioned as supreme arbitrators, limited in the term of autocratic office. Pittakos, for example, was *aisymnetes* for ten years; Solon a *diallaktes* for one; Demonax came to Cyrene as a *katartister*, implemented a comprehensive reform, and happily returned home to Mantineia. Similarly, the autocratic status of an *oikistes* would vanish with his death, and his descendants had no special privileges. Tyrants often modeled themselves on *oikistai*, and all three categories—*oikistai*, reformers, and tyrants—turned to Delphi for legitimation.[25] We know too little about Cleisthenes's term at Athens. Still, he too turned to Delphi, probably employing some form of an oracular drawing of lots, to sanction his comprehensive reform of Athenian citizenry.

Those supreme arbitrators started or restarted the *polis*, establishing a new *polis* or "returning" an established one to some primordial condition of *isotes*, equality. *Oikistai* founded cities in an "empty country" (*eremos chora*), regardless of the local precedent, as Archias, for example, had done at Syracuse, throwing out the natives, destroying their oval houses, having Greek houses with right angles built on top, and implementing a new settlement plan based on an axis joining the newly established sacred precincts of Athena and Apollo. A restart of an existing state was sometimes perceived (e.g., at Sparta) as equivalent to a return to a primordial situation when society was more horizontal than

---

[24] Cf. McInerney (2004) 21: "Accordingly, long before abstractions such as *isonomia* (political equality) existed in Athens, an *isonomia* of a more literal sort had already been achieved in the colonies, the *isonomia* of equal plots of land."

[25] Malkin (1989).

vertical, and each "sharer," whether a settler in a colony or a citizen of an existing *polis* was a *homoios*. In a sense, Greeks were always either founding new cities, "refounding" their existing ones, or just articulating revolutionary calls in terms of "back to square one," or, in Greek terms, "back to equal squares" for each "sharer in the *polis*."

9 Cleisthenes and the constitutive lottery

The Athenian Cleisthenes revolutionized Athens toward a democracy, expressed in terms of *isonomia*. As an egalitarian value, that was not new since *isonomia* had been a rallying cry for members of the Athenian elite against tyranny before democracy. Cleisthenes expanded the circle of *isonomia* to include the *demos*: the critical mass mattered, and *isonomia*, with the sense of equal portions of law for each citizen sharing in the *polis*, developed into democracy. However, as I have tried to show, the "horizontal values" and the distribution of equal portions were no novelty and had been around for centuries.

Three years after the Athenian victory at the battle of Marathon (490), right after the eighteen-year-old democracy had gained confidence, its archons were first drawn by lot (section 8.2.2.4 in this volume). Within the next two centuries, the circle of offices and office holders became more and more democratic: lots were first drawn from lists of candidates chosen from the upper economic classes, and in time the circles were enlarged until finally every citizen, regardless of the economic census, was eligible to be drawn by lot for office. However, the constitutive years during which Cleisthenes refounded Athens in terms of *isonomia* (ca. 508–500) were not occupied with reforming the selection of archons. Instead, we noted a remarkably comprehensive "mixture lottery" of the entire community of Athenians. Like a colony founder, Cleisthenes laid down new, unprecedented *nomima* that were based on a decimal system newly applied to the political sphere. There were to be ten new tribes whose eponymous heroes were probably drawn by lot by the Pythia from a list of one hundred names.

Aside from that divinatory, *selective* lottery, what Cleisthenes accomplished by dividing Athenian citizenry into ten tribes was a *mixture-and-distribution* lottery on a vast scale. In one fell swoop, he reshuffled the deck, distributing by lot citizens of different localities over the tribes, thus bypassing entrenched local interests and power bases, foci of patronage, and traditional allegiances. He achieved what the other mixture-lotteries we examined were designed to accomplish: coalescence and cohesiveness of the overarching political identity of all citizens (including those who had just become that). When Athenians began drawing lots for office, first from preselected lists and then "from all" (*ex hapanton*), their notion of "all" had already been in place due to that constitutive mixing by lot by Cleisthenes. Historically and more generally, the drawing of lots had, since Homer, implied the contours of the legitimate group or community. Each *polis* had its discrete history, and egalitarianism did not necessarily result in democracy. However, what made the foundation of democracy in Athens possible was also due to the previous centuries of Greek history when the egalitarian mindset and its concomitant historical vector were expressed in drawing lots while recognizing equality and fairness as the measuring rods by which to assess the place of the individual in society.

10 Our modern democracies

> Many forms of Government have been tried, and will be tried in this world of sin and woe. No one pretends that democracy is perfect or all-wise. Indeed, it has been said that democracy is the worst form of Government except for all those other forms that have been tried from time to time. (Winston S. Churchill at the House of Commons, November 11, 1947)

Churchill (apparently referring to an earlier quote) is misleading: not because there are preferable regimes, but because the democracy he is speaking about relied solely on elections of representatives, a *politeia* that Aristotle might have considered an "oligarchy." Our democracies suffer precisely from features opposite to those we have observed in a democracy based on the drawing of lots: a general sense of alienation and unfairness seems prevalent, combined with a sense that "there is nothing one can do about it": after all, we have already achieved a democracy (see the *Envoi* following these conclusions). The trouble is the fallacy of regarding a democracy strictly as a "regime of representatives." It ought not to be so, at least in ancient Greek terms.

While the ancient drawing of lots constantly engaged citizens who very frequently rotated both posts and functions, thus also becoming knowledgeable about their country, a modern citizen is often ignorant and has become distasteful of both politicians and politics, no matter how much passive knowledge one gets from a supposedly free media.[26] Compare, for instance, a knowledgeable Athenian citizen who knew a lot about the working of his state because, on a probable minimal list, he may have served several times on the board of judges, perhaps once in a body that oversees the market, and then, possibly even twice in his lifetime, as a member of the *boule*, Athens's supreme council. He would have been drawn up by lot to all the posts just listed. By contrast, modern democracies

---

[26] The process has been going on for decades. See Crick ([1962] 2000).

suffer from alienation and ignorance, distancing between rulers and ruled, often with an occasional manipulative hype around election time. Ancient criticism of democracy warned against the danger that the *demos* would act like an *ochlos*, a rabble easily led by demagogues, a threat of *demokratia* becoming an *ochlokratia*. The "Laws" (*nomoi*) were supposedly a guarantee against that: they were supposedly greater than the citizens who enacted them. Sometimes it failed in Athens, but only for brief periods. By contrast, modern "ochlocracy," led by populist leaders and dictators who win their initial position by elections, is far more detrimental.

In sum, drawing lots expressed fundamental values but was never a value in its own right. When precise equivalence was possible (e.g., gold discovered and distributed at Siphnos), no drawing of lots was necessary. The lottery as such was not a value, but the means to achieve a fair and equal outcome, not "from above" as a pharaoh's favor, but horizontally, following a decision by the community, and for its sake, while recognizing the individuality of each participant. Specifically, at Athens, in the Athenian proposal to distribute ten drachmas for each citizen from the revenues of the mines of Laurion, no lottery was considered since the equality was precisely measurable: one batch of ten drachmas was just like another (*isos = homoios*). However, as we have seen, most distributive lotteries did not involve precisely quantifiable figures. Hence the relation between *isos* and *homoios* was usually just approximate, with the latter qualifying the former as "equal, *namely*, like (fair)." With procedural and selective lotteries in the Athenian democracy, constant rotation of officeholders was considered a salient feature of the regime; randomness and the drawing of lots were the means to effect that.

In Euripides's *Suppliant Maidens*, the Theban herald, arriving in Athens, asks, "Who is the ruler of this land?" Theseus provides a democratic answer, emphasizing the values of equality and mixture (rotation):

> You have made a false beginning to your speech, stranger, in seeking a despot here. For this city is not ruled [405] by one man, but is free. The people rule in succession year by year, allowing no preference to wealth, but the poor man shares equally with the rich. (Euripides, *Supplices* 404–406, trans. E. P. Coleridge)

The guiding lines for selection and distribution were (a) the values of equality and fairness (*isotes, isos kai homoios*); (b) the interchangeability and equality of participants for selective, procedural, distributive, and mixture lotteries; (c) reciprocal and reversible political relations among citizens; (d) the horizontal perspective of society in which each participant is counted as equal; (e) citizens deserving an equal portion (*moira*) of whatever gets selected or distributed: from the concrete to the abstract, from the portions of land, booty, or meat to the equal portion (share) in the *politeia* and its laws. In the Funeral Oration that celebrates Athenian democracy and the merit of the citizens, the drawing of lots is not mentioned as it is not a "value" as such. On the other hand, Thucydides has Pericles describe Athens's road to greatness: "I shall portray the way of life that brought us to our present position and the institutions and habits of mind behind our rise to greatness" (trans. Jeremy Mynott).[27] The drawing of lots and its implied values was such an institution, ubiquitous throughout and familiar to the Greek world. In Athens, it was a significant factor in the revolution that made it democratic.

So far, from the emic Greek perspective. However, from the modern historian's perspective, the picture becomes multidirectional: the common practice and the convention for drawing lots also shaped Greek values—not merely expressed them. Behaviorally, Greeks have been drawing lots in all walks of life and death for several centuries, as shown in this book. Drawing lots became, therefore, integral to their worldview. It was always a viable option on the horizon of Greek expectations. It constituted a convention of "how to do things" and why: to adhere to notions of equality and fairness, with the latter as close as possible to the former. Drawing lots was not just a practice; it both emerged from and shaped the ancient Greek mindset. We had better rediscover some of its salient features.

---

[27] Hornblower (1991): "I should like to describe the principles (*epitedeusis*) underlying our actions in our rise to power, and the institutions (*politeia*) and the way of life (*tropos*) through which our empire became great" (Thuc. 2.36.4). Pericles never mentions the drawing of lots (nor any other specific institution, such as the *boule*); he is delivering a funeral oration that highlights private and public virtues, not specific instruments of democracy.

Josine Blok
Envoi
Drawing Lots Today: Fair Distribution and a Stronger Democracy

In this Envoi, I explore briefly how our study of drawing lots in ancient Greece may reflect on discussions about the use of the lot in present-day Western liberal states. Drawing lots is central in policy debates on two main topics: fair distribution and a stronger democracy. Taking off more than fifty years ago, these debates are intensifying today because the issues they deal with are increasingly urgent.[1]

Until the mid-twentieth century, drawing lots among citizens was by and large unknown in Western nation-states, except for the selection for military service and jury service. But in the 1960s and 1970s, social scientists became interested in the lot as a potential method for allocation among citizens. Their interest was both practical and theoretical—practical because it was becoming clear that, in due course, the growth of populations would set limits to the capacities of welfare states to distribute benefits among the citizens. It would become necessary to create methods that would still suit both the principles of equal entitlement of the citizens and their differences in need—theoretical because balancing such divergent purposes raises fundamental questions about fairness, efficiency, and ethics in allocation.[2]

In modern Western, liberal states, citizens have equal access to essential benefits in education, health care, and legal rights, but in some countries, what is considered "basic" is minimal (e.g., ensuring subsistence). Beyond that level, the public distribution of cultural and social goods is primarily based on individual merit (e.g., exceptional education grades), capability (e.g., athletes, musicians), or personal need (e.g., physical challenges).[3] At any level, the scarcity of certain indivisible goods raises huge problems of distribution and, therefore, of decision-making beyond a certain point of evaluating arguments. Allocation by lot would

---

[1] In some domains of today's world, the use of lots is common and not contested at all—for instance, in sports (who is on the field, who is on the bench; which teams will play against each other in the first rounds of a world cup match); more generally, applying lots for taking turns seems to be a relatively uncontested application, for instance taking turns in cleaning duties (in a student dorm, in a school camp, etc.) Here we focus on the areas where allotment is complicated and often contested.

[2] A useful selection from the immense debates since the 1960s is Stone (2011b).

[3] Depending on the state's governance, private wealth is usually the main resource for access to goods beyond the public basic or average level.

therefore seem a fair and efficient solution. However, the equal chance offered by the lot is perceived as just only when all candidates are equally qualified. That said, people are always different in some way. Bypassing arguments about individual merit or need could create challenging ethical problems, as well as social tensions.[4] A crucial case is the distribution of scarce health care, such as donor organs, for instance. The distribution problem became exceptionally urgent in the years of the Covid-19 pandemic when there were not enough vaccines or intensive care beds in some countries.[5] Another case regards access to coveted schools and higher education with restricted admission numbers. This case also elicits questions about the justice of reallocation by lot of benefits that traditionally were an elite privilege—if not by wealth alone, then at least by transmitted habitus.[6]

Although triggered by actual problems of fair distribution in contemporary welfare states, the discussions always include a theoretical element involving arguments about the use of lots for decision-making in general, that is, in terms of ethics, justice, and social impact. The question is whether and how a balance is possible between efficiency and justice, equality and competence or necessity.[7] In using lots for distribution, arguments of rationality (efficiency, transparency) may support arguments of justice and fairness, but can also clash with them. Which principles are at stake, and how can they be evaluated when drawing lots is chosen to solve a problem of allocation? Where and why does one reach a point in which arguments and assessments yield no ground for decisions anymore, and the lot is the most sensible solution? In this line of inquiry, the perspective is on drawing lots as a method for policymakers, or more widely, for those who apply drawing lots to decision-making.

By contrast, the perspective of the recipients/candidates/society is the topic of dedicated questioning in the inquiry by Hofstee introduced earlier. For his respondents, allocation by lot is more acceptable when it concerns exemption from "negative goods"—for instance, unpleasant duties—than for assignment of "positive goods," notably the goods one typically acquires due to merit or special qualifications (jobs, education). That said, for the allocation of positive

---

[4] On allocation of welfare goods by lot, see Elster (1992); on health care, see Saunders (2009).

[5] On allocation of coronavirus vaccines by lot, see pro Tavares da Silva (2021), contra Fumagalli (2021).

[6] On allocation of education, see Stone (2008). In the densely populated western parts of the Netherlands, access to coveted secondary schools is regulated by drawing lots, and so is access to closed-number studies in higher education, among which is medical school, by a combination of grades and weighed sortition. Salvatori (2001) and Ten Cate (2021) defend drawing lots for medical school on the impossibility of predicting the competence of eighteen-year-olds for the medical profession.

[7] See, for instance, Greely (1977), Goodwin ([1992] 2005), Buchstein (2009), Buchstein and Hein (2009), Stone (2011a), and Nissan-Rozen (2012).

goods, the respondents preferred to see a variety of decision-making methods combined, instead of just one single method.[8]

In the debate on the allocation of goods by lot, scholars occasionally draw on the example of ancient Greece, more precisely, classical Athens. In this comparison, the selection for office by lot in Athens serves as an essential case to show that a quite complex society used the lot to allocate political power and considered the method valuable and just. However, it is questionable if the selection for office is the best example from ancient Greece for the present-day distribution of benefits and goods (for political office, see later in this Envoi). Comparison with the distribution of goods—rather than offices—by lot in ancient Greece reveals significant differences. In Greece, the system of distribution by lot covered goods (land, property, booty, meat) that were divisible into parts that were not identical but as equal as possible, and sufficient in quantity to provide every member of the community or group with a part.[9] One could even propose a more radical conjecture: Greek communities decided to distribute goods by lot, provided that these goods were such in quantity and quality that they could be equally divided. The concept of community came first, and distribution second. Today, distribution concerns goods, some of which are not divisible, and which are in total too few to provide the entire community with in equal measure. When a recipient is provided with a particular good (i.e., a job, intensive care bed, organ transplants), someone else gets a smaller or less valuable one, at times nothing at all. With this outcome, the present-day distribution of goods by lot instead recalls selection in ancient Greece of individuals for *ad hoc* tasks—usually honorific. The moment the lot selects one Achaean hero to fight Hector, for example, all others are excluded. Perhaps later one of the others gets a chance to shine. For present-day applications, that is only sometimes the case: the debate concerns the allocation of potentially life-changing or even lifesaving goods.

The second topic of debate about the lot today, even more complex but certainly as exciting, is its use for political office selection. For this application, classical Athens is an eloquent example. Yet even here, this example is not straightforward and needs to be more fully understood. Above, we explained why the use of the lot for office was different from its use for other purposes in ancient Greece, in a society that in many relevant respects was essentially different from present-day Western states. *Mutatis mutandis*, in modern societies drawing lots for political office likewise is separate from other applications of the lot, since it requires taking into account such critical factors as democracy and representation, along with justice, ethics, and efficiency. Moreover, ideas of what

---

[8] Hofstee (1990).
[9] From the classical age on, booty was no longer distributed by lot among all army members in the "Homeric" way. Still, at least the bulk of it came to the benefit of the *polis* in its entirety by dedicating a part to the gods of the *polis*, and depositing the remainder in the public treasury.

democracy is—or should be—diverge strongly, as do views on the meaning of representation.

Interest in the random selection for political office arose in tandem with the debate over distribution by lot, spurred along by the democratic waves of the 1960s and 1970s.[10] The idea was raised first in analogy with a system of jurisdiction by jury courts: it is based on the principle that a randomly selected board of citizens will represent a common notion of social justice.[11] The question is whether this notion of representation in justice also applies to the domain of political office, with its different rules of authority and accountability.[12]

The groundbreaking study by Bernard Manin (1997) has brought a substantial reorientation about in the understanding of political representation.[13] He shows that the present-day type of representation by election to parliament is not (only) the result of practical considerations of how to accommodate the political views of large numbers of citizens, but first and foremost a deliberate choice made in the late eighteenth century to create an institution of decision-making in the hands of a governmental elite, above and detached from the *vox populi*. The present-day liberal democracies are the heirs of these principles of representation. In his argument, the democracy of classical Athens is the touchstone and prime case of an essentially different type of representation, in which a high rotation of a relatively large section of the citizenry drawn by lot results in a minimal disconnect between government and the governed.

The direct democracy of classical Athens—primarily as understood in the terms proposed by Manin—is the primary source of inspiration in the current debates about present-day liberal democracies. The growing political dissatisfaction among a sizeable segment of the population and the volatility of voters in the past twenty years merely add to the sense of urgency. Political parties have become part of the problem, rather than the solution. In principle, they are necessary intermediaries between the mass of the electorate, with its divergent views and interests, and the representative government, with its duty to see to the common good. In practice, many parties cannot live up to what they promise their voters, and some turn to malpractice to further their own advantage. As a result, the prevailing system of representation by election creates a distance between voters and actual policy-making, a distance many citizens regard as

---

[10] See, for example, Greely (1977) and Engelstad (1989).

[11] By the Norwegian sociologist Vilhelm Aubert in an article "Chance in Social Affairs" (1959); see Stone (2011b) 23–44. Today, a minority of citizens in the United States regards jury service as an unpleasant duty, but a sizeable majority values it as a civic responsibility; https://www.pewresearch.org/fact-tank/2017/08/24/jury-duty-is-rare-but-most-americans-see-it-as-part-of-good-citizenship/.

[12] An interesting comparison is that many Hellenistic cities claimed to be democratic, with jury courts selected by lot, and offices elected by all from an elite; see section 8.2.3.1.

[13] Manin made ample use of the work of Headlam (see Endnote to ch. 9) and that of Mogens Hansen, who himself advocated introducing forms of direct democracy (not necessarily through drawing lots) in the 1980s.

unsatisfactory. In extreme cases, the system is damaging to the very notion of liberal democracy and the rule of law.

Aware of these problems, scholars and political activists are searching for means to bridge the gap between voters and government. Crucially, the advantage of randomly selected boards of citizens compared to other means of direct democracy, notably the referendum, is that decisions in such boards are made by citizens equipped with adequate information, and after ample deliberation.[14] But even with such clear advantages, drawing lots for political office or policy-making raises legal and practical questions. Among the many issues that need to be addressed in each state and anchored in its constitution are where and when allotted boards are to be entrusted with decision-making or advice, how the selection by lot must be conducted to get a representative sample of citizens, and how the accountability of such boards is to be implemented. Locally, nationally, and in international forums, selecting boards of citizens by lot to obtain a more even representation of the population to involve in policy-making is gaining currency as a solution to improve and enhance the quality of deliberative democracy.

The potential of drawing lots as a method of implementing political responsibilities more widely is spreading rapidly as a theoretical debate topic, a discourse propagated by international organizations, and occasionally put into practice.[15] For over two decades, political scientist James Fishkin has organized polls in states around the globe of randomly selected citizens who deliberate on a political problem for a few days, and then propose a solution.[16] In Belgium, publicist David Van Reybrouck, originally a classical archaeologist, wrote a well-received book in 2013 on the necessity of more direct democracy in the shape of allotted boards, and he played a crucial role in the democratic "G1000" project, whereby a body of allotted citizens "steered" the country in 2011 in response to the failure of elected representatives to create a proper government.[17] Elsewhere, boards of citizens selected by lot prepared the revision of the constitution in Iceland in 2016, and in Ireland in 2018. In France, a citizen assembly selected by

---

[14] On the distrust and the role of political parties in today's democracies and on the advantage of allotment to a referendum, see Blok (2023). In many states, the elected government consists of one or a few parties, and the referendum can be used by the "outsiders" merely to thwart the government; in Switzerland, the government holds a representation of all parties, and the referendum, which rests on a long tradition, operates within this political structure. As an alternative to the referendum with a simple "yes" or "no," some political thinkers advocate a "preferendum," with several options on a scale of preference.

[15] The debates are booming; a few examples are Dowlen (2009), Farrar (2010), Landemore (2013), Blok (2014b), Owen and Smith (2018), Gastil and Wright (2018), Landemore (2020), and Pope (2023). International organizations: https://www.sortitionfoundation.org/; https://equalitybylot.com/.

[16] See for example Fishkin (2009).

[17] Van Reybrouck (2016; 2013).

lot was convened by President Macron in 2019 to propose ways to deal with the climate crisis.

For such initiatives, it is worth recalling that the democracy of classical Athens—which now so often (and for good reasons) serves as a model—did not arise out of the blue. As we argue in this book, the radical democracy of Athens was not only unique in its wide-ranging application of the lot, but it was also possible because it was embedded in a long tradition of drawing lots in many other domains of daily life. Drawing lots was not just a method of selection; it was the expression of a distinct concept of citizenship, in which the good of the community came before that of the individual.[18] Today, in meritocratic societies with citizenship embodied in individual rights, the relationship between the individual, society, and state is essentially different in spirit and in practice. Given such conditions, introducing the drawing of lots for political office and policy-making is a steep challenge, though far from impossible and definitely worth attempting.

---

[18] For a good discussion of this issue, see Miller (2022).

APPENDIX

A Lexicographical Survey of Lottery Practices in the Archaic and Classical Periods

Elena Iaffe

The aim of this lexicographic survey is to identify all possible literary and epigraphic evidence for lottery practices in archaic and classical Greece. I performed a lemmatized search of the corpus of Greek literary texts, using the *TLG* search engine, up to the end of the classical period.[1] I have also conducted a lemmatized search of the corpus of Hesychius for the same lemmas. The initial search was based on earlier lexicographers, and all lemmas mentioned in Hesychius with a connection to lottery were examined as well. For epigraphic evidence, I searched the *PHI* engine for parts of any possible forms of the key terms (e.g., "λαχ," "ληξ," "λαγχ," "λογχ" for lanchano).

I collected all the literary and epigraphic evidence for the practices of the lottery in political, religious, legal, military, and civil contexts. I also provide an overview of each of the forty lemmas explored. This overview presents evidence for different areas of the use of lotteries and different modes of the practice itself.

- At the first stage of the research, I collected all the instances of the lemmas listed below in literary and epigraphic texts up to the beginning of the Hellenistic period.
- In the second stage, I classified the texts by genre, examined each instance in context, and identified the various meanings in cases of polysemy and the degree of the relation to lottery practices and the type of lottery, wherever applicable.
- In the third stage, I performed a quantitative analysis of the distribution of meanings, the correlation between the use of the word and the literary genre, as well as the correlation between the meaning and the context.[2]

This lexicographic study is based on a usage-based corpus analysis of literary and epigraphic data, enabling description of each word in the most precise way, applicable to a specific time frame of archaic and classical Greek. The corpus of literary texts is limited to the authors dated up to the second third of the fourth century. The corpus of the epigraphic evidence includes all the inscriptions up to the end of the classical period, as well as inscriptions up to the end of the fourth century, and inscriptions dating to a large span of time (e.g., 500–300 BCE) in order to include all the possible evidence.

---

[1] Lemmatized search of the *TLG*, ordered by date, up and including Theophrastus, according to the *TLG* chronology.

[2] In the following passages, references appear for the purpose of illustration of specific meanings. For the full list of references, see below.

448 APPENDIX

Lexicographic overview of the key terms of lottery

Below are words used to indicate lottery practices, grouped by their function:

1. Instruments used in lottery practices (pieces of wood, stones, or beans).
2. Words indicating a participant in the lottery.
3. Words for the procedure of lottery.
4. Words indicating the outcome of the lottery.
5. Verbs used in lottery practices, classified by function.

*A few lemmas, marked by an asterisk, are excluded from the database. The reasons are given for each lemma.

**The verbs used in different types of lotteries will appear in several categories.

1. Instruments used in lottery practices

κλῆρος—A *kleros* is an object, such as a piece of wood or stone, that is distinctively marked with each participant's name, used in many forms of lotteries. It is our corpus's second most represented lemma, comprising 501 attestations. *Kleros* has three main distinct meanings: (1) the instrument of lottery, usually employed in *dat. instr.* (2) object of lottery, e.g., portion of land. (3) rarely (0.5 percent), in the metaphoric sense of one's lot in life, Fate, attested only in poetry. For a detailed overview of the semantic field, see p. 456.

κληρωτήριον—A tool used for the drawing of lots at the selection to offices. Only four Hellenistic and Roman inscriptions contain this lemma, which is absent from the classical epigraphic material. In literary texts, however, the word appears in *Ecclesiazousai*, Euboulus. *Olbia.* fr. 74.5 (Kock), in fr. 146 (Kock) of Aristophanes (the context is unknown), and in five passages of the *Athenaion Politeia*. Our knowledge of this tool mostly relies on the information given by lexicographers—Pollux, Hesychius, the Suda, and the scholia to Aristophanes.

πάλος—An instrument of lottery, a synonym of *kleros* in instrumental usage. Literally, anything that is being shaken in order to mix the lots. This lemma has 22 instances in our corpus. *Palos* may represent a piece of wood or a stone thrown for a lottery. Similarly, as well as other synonyms of *kleros*, it may indicate a voting ballot (Aesch. *Eum.* 753). However, in all other instances in our corpus, the meaning clearly points to a lottery.

κύαμος—A bean used as an instrument for selective/procedural lotteries or for voting. Out of 114 instances of the lemma in our corpus, only 17 are in the context of the lottery. The participants would draw from a pile of mixed white and dark beans. The ones who had drawn a white bean were chosen ("[Pericles] separated his whole force into eight divisions, had them draw lots, and allowed the division which got the white bean to feast and take their ease, while the others did the fighting"—Plut. *Pericles* 27.2, trans. Bernadotte Perrin).

καυνός—A bean used for voting and drawing lots. This lemma is attested in one fragment of Cratinus and one fragment of Aristophanes. Hesychius and all later lexicographers (Photius, the Suda, Pseudo-Zonaras) list this word as a synonym of *kleros*. Notwithstanding that the meaning in both fragments is clear—beans being counted, that is, used for voting—we cannot disregard the meaning of the verb *diakauniazo*: to cast beans for a lottery and the possibility that there were more texts available to Hesychius with *kaunos* in the meaning of a lottery-bean. It is highly probable that beans were used both for lotteries and for voting, just as other instruments of a lottery have overlapping meanings.

2. Words indicating a participant in a lottery

ἔγκληρος—A person possessing something acquired by lot. This lemma has five instances in our corpus, all in tragedy (Eur. *Hipp.* 1011, Eur. *Her.* 468, Eur. *IT.* 682, Soph. *Ant.* 814, Soph. *Ant.* 837).

ἀπόκληρος—A participant in a lottery who had not drawn the winning lot, apparently in a selective or distributive lottery. This lemma has three instances in Classical Greek (Pindar *Pythian* 5.54, Empedocles fr. 147.7, Aristot. *Topica* 112b19) and has no attestations in the epigraphic record.

σύγκληρος—A person sharing his allotted portion with another participant in a lottery. There is only one attestation of this lemma in Classical Greek, in Euripides, *Heraclidae* 32, and no attestations in pre-Hellenistic epigraphic material.

κληροπαληδός—A person is chosen by lot. This is a *hapax legomenon* from the Lille's Stesichorus (l. 224). This lemma has not yet entered any of the modern lexicons but is expected to appear in *DGE*.

κυαμόβολος—A participant in a lottery who throws the bean. The lemma appears in Classical Greek only once in Sophocles fr. 288 (Radt): "κυαμοβόλον δικαστήν." Hesychius's mention and interpretation of the fragment attests the context of the lottery. He strengthens his interpretation of "κυάμῳ πατρίῳ" with fragment 377 of Sophocles's *Meleager*, where the meaning is clearly that of a lottery.

κυαμευτός—A person is chosen by lot in a selective lottery. Usually, the one who has drawn a white bean from a mix of dark and white beans (Plut. *Pericles* 27.2). There is only one instance of this lemma in Classical Greek (Xen. *Mem.* 1.2.9) which records the use of a bean as a lottery instrument rather than for voting purposes.

κληρωτός—A public official, chosen by lot. This lemma has 56 instances in our corpus. The largest number of instances, 41, appears in Aristotle. However, the lemma is well represented in legal and forensic texts: Aeschines, Isocrates, and Demosthenes. In inscriptions, the lemma is most frequently used together with a scribe (*grammateus*) and a messenger (*kerux*)—evidently, offices assigned by lot.

ἄκληρος—A person who did not receive his lot, e.g., inheritance, or his share in a distributive lottery. This lemma has 14 instances in our corpus, half of them in forensic speeches.

3. Words for the procedure of drawing lots

κλήρωσις—The process of conducting a lottery. Notwithstanding the conceptual centrality of the term in the vocabulary of lottery, it has only four instances in Classical

Greek literary texts. The epigraphic evidence also has a few attestations, dated to the late fourth century.

Words for the outcome of lottery

λῆξις/λᾶξις—The outcome of what is obtained by lot, such as a "good" or an office. As a legal term, it is a written complaint or an application to the Archo, regarding inheritance (*kleros*). The lemma has 75 instances in Classical Greek and is mainly represented in forensic speeches.

σύλληξις—Pairing by lot. This lemma is attested in Classical Greek only twice, in Plato *Tim.* 18e, Plato *Leg.* 819b.

λάχος/λόγχη (Ion.)—One's fate, with neutral connotation. In prose, it also appears as the object of drawing lots, such as a portion of land or a portion of sacrificial meat. The lemma has 16 instances in Archaic and Classical Greek (including one instance of the Ionian form λόγχη in Ion of Chios (*BNJ* 392 F3). The lemma is mostly represented in poetry and metrical inscriptions in the meaning of one's Fate (ca. 80 percent).

κλῆρος—Kleros has three main distinct meanings. Initially signifying an instrument used for drawing lots, it also signifies an object of a lottery, e.g., a portion of land or a good, traditionally or initially assigned by lot, as an inheritance. In this meaning, the explicit mention of the practice of drawing lots is sometimes absent. In forensic speeches, it often appears as the object of contention, e.g., a portion of land. As evident from the diachronic analysis of the meaning, we may see a sharp rise in the fourth century in its use as "inheritance," probably as a result of the flourishing of a new genre of forensic speeches at that period.

ἀνεπικλήρωτος—An adjective qualifying a ship, not assigned by lot, as an exception to the regular practice of liturgy. It is used in 5 Attic inscriptions dated to 377–369, with a total of 59 instances referring to military ships (IG II^2 1604, 1606–1609). This lemma is absent from the literary evidence, except for lexicography (Photius).

κληροπαλής—A part assigned by lot. This is a *hapax legomenon* (*H.H.Hermes.* 4.129), an adjective describing *moirai* assigned by lot.

πότμος*—One's lot; the major part of the semantic field of this lemma is Fate, specifically at death. The lemma is most frequent in poetry and in metrical funeral inscriptions. This lemma has 117 instances in Archaic and Classical Greek, 108 of which are in poetry. The instances are not included in the database, as they point mostly to the metaphoric sense.

4. Verbs of lottery practices

(a) Verbs related to the participants of a lottery

Two verbs refer to the participants of a lottery and, accordingly, to the two phases of the practice. *Kleroo*—to cast lots, and *lanchano*—to receive by lot.

κληρόω—To cast lots: 119 attestations in our corpus, with more than 50 percent of the attestations in Aristotle (63). In classical inscriptions, as a rule, prefixed forms are used, e.g., *epikleroo*. All the instances of the verb indicate a lottery taking place. Unlike the noun *kleros*, the verb is never used in a metaphoric sense, except for one instance in Pindar with *potmos*, in a figurative phrase: "You have been allotted to

Zeus Genethlios" (*Ol.* 8.15–16), denoting the Fate at the birth of the hero. This verb is exceedingly rare in poetry in general (8 instances of 119). *Kleroo* is also used for divination by lot.

λαγχάνω—This verb is attested already in Linear B[3] and was probably also used during the early Iron Age before it appears in Greek alphabetic writing. The semantic field of the verb is complex and should be analyzed as a potentially polysemic verb rather than trying to define a single "correct" meaning. The verb has two core meanings: (1) to obtain by lot or to obtain a "good" traditionally distributed by lot (73 percent in our corpus); (2) in a metaphorical sense, mainly in poetry and metrical inscriptions—to obtain one's Fate (15 percent in our corpus). However, in technical treatises dating to the fourth century (medicine, cosmology) the verb is disconnected from its lottery associations. See also ch. 1, Endnote 2.

προλαγχάνω—To get by lot, first in line before other participants. The lemma has one instance in Classical Greek (Ar. *Eccl.* 1159).

ἐκλαγχάνω—"To get one's Fate." The preposition "ἐκ" here expresses completion, with the combination of Fate, denoting a fatal turn in one's life. This lemma has four instances in our corpus (Soph. *Elec.* 760, Soph. *OC.* 1337, Ar. *Thesm.* 1071, 1071 bis).

All other prepositional derivatives of both verbs also refer to the participants of a lottery. However, they are classified below by the type of lottery (distributive, selective, etc.).

(b) Verbs indicating the type of lottery

Distributive

διαλαγχάνω—To distribute by lot. The lemma has 9 instances in our corpus. The prefix δια- signifies distribution and diffusion.

διακληρόω—To distribute by lot, but also to be chosen by lot. This verb is used both for distributive lotteries (of lands: Plato *Laws* 760c2; Arist. *Ath.Pol.* 30.4), and for procedural lotteries in military contexts (Xen. *Cyr.* 6.3.34; Thuc. 8.30.1). This lemma has 12 instances in our corpus, the earliest in Aeschylus, with the remaining 11 in prose, mainly historiography.

Selective

ἀποκληρόω—To choose by lot from a number of participants, used in selective lotteries. This lemma has 15 attestations in our corpus and is absent from pre-Hellenistic epigraphic material, with the earliest attestation in 302. In literary texts, it is equally represented in the genres of rhetoric (6), philosophy (5), and, to a lesser extent, in historiography (4).

ἀποκυαμεύω (epigraphy only)—To be chosen by lot using white and dark beans, a verb of a selective/procedural lottery. This lemma is attested once in the epigraphic evidence, in *IG* I[3] 52.13, dated to ca. 433/2.

ἀπολαγχάνω—To get a part of something by lot. The lemma has 9 instances in literary evidence and 1 instance in a Lokrian inscription dated to the first half of the fifth c. (*IG* IX, 1[2] 3:718). It is also partially restored in the Cyrene foundation decree (*SEG* 9:3, l. 33; ML 5). The prefix απο- means "out of a whole".

---

[3] Bartonek (2003) 319.

Procedural

ἐπικληρόω—To succeed someone in a public office assigned by lot. This lemma has 14 occurrences in literary texts and 2 instances in classical inscriptions (SEG 26:72; 35:62). In the Hellenistic period, the word is widely used in honorary decrees with citizenship grants, mainly from Ionia, for distributing new citizens to *polis* subgroups.

ἐπιλαγχάνω—To inherit or to succeed someone in an office assigned by lot. This lemma has 3 instances in our corpus (Soph. *OC*. 1235; Dem. 58.29, Aeschin. 3.62). The prefix ἐπι- signifies succession, being next in line. In instances of the verb related to inheritance, the practice of lottery is implicit.

διακληρόω—To distribute by lot, but also to be chosen by lot. This verb is used both for distributive lotteries (e.g., land: Pl. *Laws* 760c2), and for procedural lotteries in military contexts (Xen. *Cyr*. 6.3.34; Thuc. 8.30.1). This lemma has 12 instances in our corpus, the earliest in Aeschylus, while the remaining 11 are in prose, mainly historiography. The lemma is absent from pre-Hellenistic inscriptions.

ἀποκυαμεύω (epigraphy only)—To be chosen by lot using white and dark beans, a verb of selective/procedural lotteries. This lemma is attested in one inscription, *IG* I^3 52.13, dated ca. 433/2.

Mixture

συγκληρόω—To obtain a shared good by lot, metaphorically—to share a common fate. This lemma is attested 3 times in our corpus in Plato, Demosthenes, and Aeschines and is absent from pre-Hellenistic epigraphic material.

μεταλαγχάνω—To participate, to take part in something, traditionally assigned by lot or by Fate, both metaphorically and, specifically, to share one's Fate, to participate in a battle. The lemma has 4 instances in Classical Greek: in Euripides and in Plato. Each instance is in a different context and has a different meaning. The preposition μετά signifies participation.

συλλαγχάνω—To be paired by lot. The lemma has 5 instances in Classical Greek prose, four of them in *participia*. In *part.pf.* the verb is used in philosophy and medicine in the meaning of sharing the same qualities or destiny. The only instance as an inflected verb, in Plato *Tim*. 18e2, mentions an actual lottery taking place, but it is related to marriage by lottery, namely the pairing of men and women by lot.

(c) Verbs related to the procedure itself, e.g., the action "of" or "upon" the instrument of drawing lots

διαπάλλω—To shake the lots so that one jumps out. The prefix δια- signifies the movement of the lots in different directions. This lemma has 2 instances in Classical Greek: Aesch. *Sept*. 732 and another instance in a dubious fragment attested in Arist. *An. Hist*. 633a22, attributed to Aeschylus *Tetralogy* 44a fr. 609a l. 4 or Sophocles fr. 581 l. 4.

κληρόω—To cast lots, this lemma has 119 attestations in our corpus, with more than 50 percent of the attestations in Aristotle (63). The verb has derived from the noun *kleros* and signifies an action upon *kleros* as an instrument of the lottery. See above 5(a).

κυαμεύω—To choose by lot, using a bean. This lemma has 3 instances in Classical Greek (Dem. 24.150.1; *Ath.Pol*. 8.1; 22.5) and 6 attestations in epigraphic material—all in classical inscriptions. This word was not in use during the Hellenistic and Roman periods, which suggests that the practice is characteristic of classical Greece only.

διακαυνιάζω—To cast beans (dark and white) for a selective lottery. The one who draws the white bean wins in a dispute / obtains the office. This lemma is attested only once in Classical Greek, in Ar. *Peace* 1081. Hesychius is our only source that connects the meaning of *kaunos* and *kleros*. All the later lexicographers—Photius, the Suda, Pseudo-Zonaras, Symeon—have adopted Hesychius's interpretation. However, the context in *Peace* 1081 rules out the possibility of voting and suggests drawing lots.

ἐπιβάλλω*—To throw, to cast. Although this verb is not traditionally associated with lotteries, the textual and epigraphic evidence indicates that some of the semantic fields of this verb are connected to lottery practices. This verb is related to lottery under the following conditions: (1) as *part.masc.act.*: in inscriptions related to inheritance, the verb refers to the relatives splitting up the inheritance (*IC* IV 72); (2) as a verb, only in the active voice, usually with an additional word related to the lottery (*apolanchano*, Hdt. 7.23.3); or (3) with a word related to division (*meros, moira*), in a metaphoric sense of one's Fate (Theogn. 1.355, Arist. *Pol.* 3.1278b22).

πίπτω*—To fall. It is metaphorically used in connection with lotteries, only in perfect tense—"the lot has fallen." The use of the verb πίπτω in the context of a lottery is always accompanied by at least one key term—an instrument of a lottery or a verb associated with a lottery. The verb reflects an important moment of the lottery process—when the lot falls and dictates the outcome.

5. The semantic fields of the disputed key terms of lottery: *lanchano* and *kleros*

λαγχάνω[4]—The verb has two core meanings: (1) to obtain by lot, or to obtain a good traditionally distributed by lot; (2) in a metaphorical sense, mainly in poetry and metrical inscriptions, to obtain one's Fate, or to have an innate quality as one's Fate. The verb is attested already in linear B, which testifies to a long history of use and therefore implies a high probability of many semantic changes along the periods it was in use. We find also idiomatic use of the verb, which may be classified into two groups: context-dependent and object-dependent. The lemma has 699 instances in our corpus. The most represented genre is rhetoric, comprising 36 percent of all evidence from the archaic and classical periods. ref

Over 73 percent of the instances are lottery-associated (see Chart 1). However, it is important to underline that part of the semantic field of this verb has only an allusive connection to lotteries.[5] The charts here show the distribution of the core meanings of the verb in different genres. Aside from evidence for historical uses of lotteries, much of the evidence is poetic, hence a looser connection with historical reality. Note the apparent difference in meaning in prose and poetry (Charts 2 and 3), and the similarity in two different types of evidence—historiographic (literary) texts (88 percent lottery-associated) and epigraphic evidence (81 percent lottery-associated) (Charts 4 and 5). These charts illustrate the verb's meaning in texts, most relevant for historical inquiry.

---

[4] See ch. 1, Endnote 2.
[5] See also 5(a) above.

454 APPENDIX

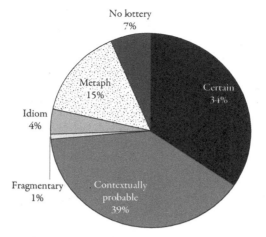

Chart 1 *Lanchano* indicating distribution by lot in the literary corpus.

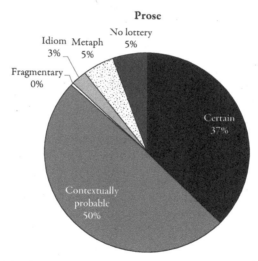

Chart 2 *Lanchano* indicating distribution by lot in prose (excluding epigraphical evidence).

APPENDIX 455

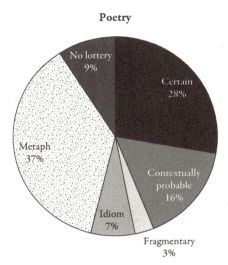

Chart 3 *Lanchano* indicating distribution by lot in poetry (excluding epigraphical evidence).

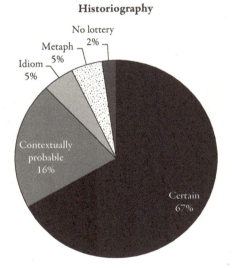

Chart 4 *Lanchano* indicating distribution by lot in historiography.

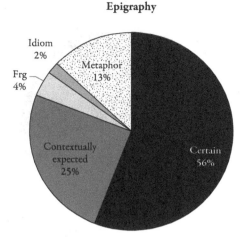

Chart 5 *Lanchano* indicating distribution by lot in the epigraphic evidence.

κλῆρος—The second-largest lemma in our corpus, comprising 501 attestations. *Kleros* has two main distinct meanings, described earlier: (1) the instrument of lottery, usually employed in *dat.instr*; (2) object of lottery, e.g., piece of land. In addition, (3) the word is used in Classical Greek in the metaphoric sense of one's lot in life, Fate (as a rule in poetry). However, this sense is extremely rare (fewer than 1 percent of instances in our corpus).

The diachronic distribution of the three distinct meanings of the word is demonstrated in Chart 6. There is a debate about whether the instrumental meaning of the word was still in use after the archaic period. Our conclusion is that it was. The instrumental meaning of the word *kleros*, with direct reference to drawing lots, has been in use since Homer right to the end of the classical period.[6] In the archaic and early classical periods (up to ca. 450), as may be induced from the chart, the instrumental meaning prevails. The word is almost absent from poetry; hence, the metaphoric meaning is extremely rare (0.5 percent). In oratory, 98 percent of the instances refer to a piece of land. Given that the instances in this genre comprise over 60 percent of the word's attestations, this meaning seems to prevail. However, being aware of the genre differences, and specific technical use of the word in the forensic language (often dealing with inheritance), we may observe that in other genres, when we exclude forensic speeches, the instrumental use is equally frequent (Chart 8). Chart 9 shows a similar distribution of meaning, representing only evidence most relevant for historical research—prose, excluding a repetitive formula for bringing a lawsuit for inheritance.

---

[6] Cf. Zurbach (2017) 1:224–231 claims that by the classical period *klēros* might have lost its original sense of an instrument used in lottery, retaining only the sense of a plot of land. His conclusion is indeed compatible with the evidence from forensic speeches, but it appears to be incorrect in view of the corpus-based analysis and the evidence shown in our study that attests the continuous instrumental use of the word up to the end of the classical period.

APPENDIX 457

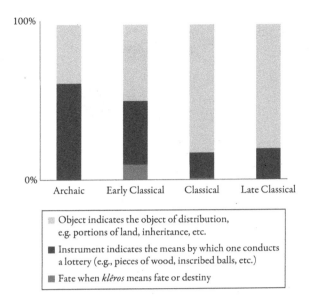

Chart 6 A diachronic distribution of the meaning of *kleros* in the literary evidence.

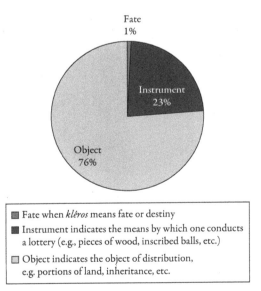

Chart 7 A synchronic distribution by genre of the meaning of *kleros* in the literary evidence.

458 APPENDIX

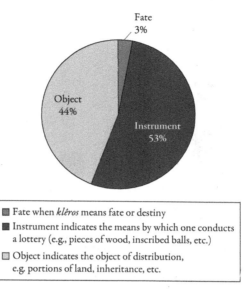

Chart 8 The meaning of *kleros* in all literary evidence, excluding oratory (where it is often used as a technical term).

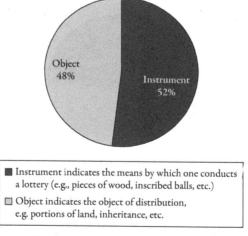

Chart 9 The meaning of *kleros* in prose, excluding oratory (where it is often used as a technical term).

6. List of references for key lottery terms in archaic and classical Greek literature and inscriptions

The following list provides all the references to sources mentioning the lottery, excluding instances of key terms unrelated to lottery practice, that is, metaphoric sense, voting, and so on. This list was created by manually examining all the texts containing instances of lemmas associated with lottery described here. Texts containing more than one key term are cited once by the first line of the relevant passage.

Key lottery terms, excluding metaphoric usages

Acusilaus: Acusilaus 2; *FGrHist* 40; **Aeneas Tacticus:** *Poliorc.* 3.1, 16.20, 18.21, 20.2; **Aeschines:** 1.19, 1.21, 1.33, 1.62, 1.63, 1.106, 1.113, 1.188, 2.82, 2.99, 3.3, 3.13, 3.15, 3.28, 3.29, 3.30, 3.62, *epist.* 10.10; **Aeschylus:** *Ag.* 333; *Choeph.* 361, *Eum.* 5, 32, 310, 334, 349, 385, 400, 715, 931; *Pers.* 187, 779; *Sept.* 55, 126, 376, 423, 451, 457, 727, 789, 818, 907; *Supp.* 978; **Alcman:** fr. 65 (Page); **Amphis:** *Dith.* fr. 1.7 (Meineke); **Anaximenes:** *Rhet.Alex.* 2.14.3, 2.18.4; **Andocides:** 1.82, 1.96, 1.120, 1.121, 4.4; **Andron:** fr. 12.6 (Müller FHG); **Antimachus:** *Theb.* fr. 53.2 (Wyss); **Antiphon Rhet.:** *Chor.* 6.11, fr. 64.1, fr. 70.3 (Thalheim); **Antiphon Soph.:** *test.* 7.3 (D-K); **Antisthenes:** fr. 117.14 (Caizzi); **Aristophanes:** *Acharn.* 724; *Aves.* 1022, 1111; *Eccl.* 683, 836, 1159; *Equit.* 258; *Lys.* 208; *Nub.* 623; *Pax.* 364, 1081; *Plut.* 277, 972, frs. 146, 660 (Edmonds); **[Aristotle]:** *Ath.Pol.* 47.2, 48.1, 48.3, 48.4, 49.3, 49.4, 50.1, 50.2, 51.1, 51.2, 51.3, 51.4, 52.1, 52.2, 53.1, 53.5, 54.1, 54.3, 54.4, 54.6, 54.7, 54.8, 55.1, 55.2, 56.4, 56.6, 57.2, 57.4, 58.2, 59.5, 59.7, 60.1, 62.1, 63.1, 63.2, 63.5, 64.2, 64.3, 64.4, 65.1, 65.2, 65.3, 65.4, 66.1, 66.2, 67.3, 68.2, 69.1, 69.2; **Aristotle:** *De Mund.* 397b, 400a, 401b; *Divis.Arist.* 3.1.5; *Eth.Nic.* 1160b; *Pol.* 1265b, 1266a, 1266b, 1273a, 1274a, 1294b, 1298a, 1298b, 1293a, 1300a, 1300b, 1301a, 1317b, 1318a, 1319a, 1320b, 1335b; *Rhet.* 1365b, 1393b, fr. *var.* 40, 195, 385, 412, 414, 417, 418, 420, 421, 422, 424, 426, 427, 433, 434, 436, 437, 438, 439, 440, 442, 444, 443, 445, 446, 447, 449, 450, 451, 453, 454, 460, 464, 469, 498, 641 (Rose); **Astrampsychus:** *Sortes.* 1.1.15-82, 1.2.10-58, 1.3.1-3 (Stewart 2001); *Sortes.* 1.11.74 (Hercher 1863); **Bacchylides:** 11.70; **Callisthenes:** *test.* 7.28 (D-K); **Corinna:** frs. 1a, 654, 677 (Page); **Cratinus:** *Pyt.* 20 (Meineke), fr. 194 (Kock); **Demades:** fr. 23.5 (de Falco); **Democritus:** fr. 159.4 (D-K); **Demosthenes:** 4.35, 14.18, 14.19, 14.21, 14.22, 14.23, 19.1, 20.90, 21.13, 21.25, 21.78, 21.81, 21.82, 21.87, 21.93, 21.111, 21.120, 21.133, 21.227, 22.8, 22.48, 23.6, 24.83, 24.87, 24.89, 24.112, 24.150, 24.160, 25.11, 25.23, 25.26, 25.27, 25.30, 25.50, 25.54, 25.55, 25.58, 25.67, 25.79, 25.80, 25.83, 29.2, 29.6, 29.16, 29.30, 29.58, 30.15, 30.17, 30.34, 32.10, 32.26, 33.4, 33.23, 33.35, 34.2, 34.16, 35.3, 36.3, 36.17, 36.20, 36.21, 36.22, 36.23, 37.3, 37.9, 37.16, 37.18, 37.20, 37.34, 37.39, 37.50, 37.51, 37.57, 38.1, 38.2, 38.4, 38.6, 38.8, 38.11, 38.13, 38.15, 38.16, 38.19, 38.20, 38.27, 39.1, 39.2, 39.6, 39.10, 39.11, 39.12, 39.15, 39.16, 39.17, 39.21, 39.25, 39.37, 40.16, 40.17, 40.18, 40.28, 40.31, 40.35, 41.4, 41.12, 43.1, 43.3, 43.5, 43.6, 43.7, 43.15, 43.16, 43.20, 43.27, 43.28, 43.30, 43.31, 43.32, 43.33, 43.34, 43.40, 43.43, 43.44, 43.45, 43.48, 43.49, 43.51, 43.56, 43.63, 43.65, 43.69, 43.70, 43.76, 43.77, 44.2, 44.7, 44.8, 44.11, 44.13, 44.15, 44.21, 44.27, 44.29, 44.31, 44.34, 44.38, 44.40, 44.42, 44.45, 44.46, 44.50, 44.52, 44.53, 44.54, 44.61, 44.64, 45.4, 45.5, 45.47, 45.50, 46.22, 46.23, 47.17, 47.21, 47.45, 47.69, 48.20, 48.22, 48.26, 48.29, 48.43, 48.45, 49.20, 52.14, 52.30, 53.14, 54.1, 54.6, 54.13,

54.28, 55.20, 55.23, 55.34, 57.25, 57.28, 57.46, 57.47, 57.48, 57.49, 57.62, 58.29, 58.32; [**Demosthenes**]: 59.3, 59.45, 59.52, 59.54, 59.60, 59.72, 59.98, 59.103, 59.106; **Dialexeis**: fr. 7 (Diels Kranz); **Dinarchus**: 2.10, 16.2, frs. 1.1, 6.6, 9.5, 18.2, 57a.1, 60.3, 62.1, 63.1, 69.3, 80.1, 94.1 (Conomis); **Empedocles**: frs. 46.8, 127.2, 147.7, 154.7, test. fr. 97.2 (Diels Kranz); **Ephorus**: Ephor. 70; *FGrHist*. 29.3, 96.17, 115.30; **Eubulus**: *Olbia*. fr. 74.5 (Kock); **Eudoxus of Knidos**: fr. 292.20 (Lasserre); **Euripides**: *Andr*. 384, 385, 386; *Bacch*. 1291; *Elec*. 668; *Hec*. 100; *Her*. 331, 468; *Heraclid*. 32–36, 545–547, 876; *Hipp*. 1011, 1057, 1136; *Ion*. 416, 609, 908; *IA*. 1151, 1198; *IT*. 682; *Orest*. 963; *Phoen*. 68, 838; *Rhes*. 545, 564, 874; *Supp*. 1078; *Troi*. 31, 186, 240–277, 282–291, 296, 1271, frs. 723, 989, 1132.4 (Nauck); **Hellanicus**: Hellan. 4; *FGrHist*. 14.2, 18.11, 36a.4, 36b.2, 37.2, 133.6, 164.1, 168a.10; **Herodotus**: 1.167.1, 1.76.1, 1.94.5, 1.94.6, 2.109.1, 2.109.2, 2.32.3, 3.25.6, 3.80.6, 3.83.2, 3.25.6, 3.80.6, 3.83.2, 3.128.1, 3.128.2, 4.21, 4.68.3, 4.94.2, 4.114.4, 4.115.1, 4.145.4, 4.153, 5.57.1, 6.109.2, 7.23.3, 8.117, 9.43.2, 9.94.2; **Hesiod**: *WD*. 37, 341; *Th*. 203, 422–424, fr. 37.12 (Merkelbach-West); **Hipassus**: fr. 5.6 (Diels Kranz); **Hippocrates**: *Epist*. 20.6 (Littré); **Hipponax**: fr. 26.4 (West); **Homer**: *Il*. 3.316, 3.328, 4.49, 7.171–179, 9.367, 10.430, 15.190–192, 15.498, 18.327, 23.352–357, 24.70, 24.400; *Od*. 5.40, 9.160, 9.331–334, 10.207, 11.490, 13.138, 14.64, 14.209, 14.233, 20.282; **Homeric Hymns**: *Demeter* 2.86–87; *Hermes*. 4.129, 4.428–430; *Aphrodite* 6.2; *Pan*. 19.6; *Hestia* 29.3; **Hyperides**: *Eux*. fr. 29.12 (Jensen), frs. 66.3, 108.3, 160.3 (Jensen); **Ion of Chios**: Ion Ch 392; *FGrHist*. 3b.329.3; **Isaeus**: 1.17.1, 1.20.6, 1.28.6, 1.38.6, 2.2.3, 2.29.5, 2.46.2, 3.1.5, 3.2.5, 3.3.6, 3.9.3, 3.30.4, 3.32.6, 3.33.2, 3.41.6, 3.43.2, 3.44.2, 3.46.3, 3.50.5, 3.51.6, 3.52.4, 3.53.2, 3.57.4, 3.58.2, 3.59.2, 3.60.5, 3.61.5, 3.62.4, 3.67.2, 3.69.6, 3.73.2, 3.75.4, 3.78.8, 4.2.4, 4.3.4, 4.4.3, 4.5.6, 4.12.2, 4.15.8, 4.24.4, 4.25.2, 5.1.4, 5.2.6, 5.3.7, 5.5.4, 5.6.6, 5.7.1, 5.8.4, 5.12.9, 5.13.5, 5.14.6, 5.15.4, 5.16.3, 5.17.2, 5.18.4, 5.19.7, 5.20.5, 5.21.4, 5.24.4, 5.26.8, 5.27.2, 5.29.7, 5.35.8, 5.40.6, 6.3.3, 6.4, 6.46.2, 6.52.4, 6.56.4, 6.57, 6.59.2, 6.61.4, 7.3.4, 7.4.7, 7.6.3, 7.20.8, 7.21.3, 7.23.2, 7.24.4, 7.26.6, 7.29.6, 7.31.2, 7.35.5, 7.37.2, 7.42.7, 7.44.3, 7.45.4, 8.1.8, 8.2.6, 8.3.3, 8.25.2, 9.1.2, 9.3.2, 9.24.1, 10.1.5, 10.3.3, 10.4.5, 10.5.6, 10.7.4, 10.8.2, 10.14.4, 10.15.1, 10.16.3, 10.17.7, 10.19.2, 10.21.2, 10.23.10, 10.26.5, 11.3.8, 11.5.6, 11.7.4, 11.9.3, 11.10.3, 11.13.7, 11.15.6, 11.17.3, 11.18.4, 11.19.7, 11.20.5, 11.21.7, 11.22.3, 11.23.4, 11.24.4, 11.25.4, 11.26.6, 11.27.3, 11.28.6, 11.31.2, 11.33.3, 11.44.5, 11.45.6, 11.46.2, 11.47.7, 12.11.4, frs. 3.1.1.3, 13.2.1.5 (Roussel); **Isocrates**: 7.22.3, 7.23.2, 7.54.4, 12.153.6, 12.177.4, 15.150.5, 16.2.1, 17.21.3, 17.31.4, 18.7.3, 18.11.4, 18.23.5, 18.52.7, 19.16.3, 19.43.2, 19.47.1, 19.50.4; **Lycurgus**: 1.26, 1.54, 1.103; **Lysias**: 6.4.3, 6.11.4, 17.3.8, 17.5.9, 17.8.5, 22.16.8, 23.1.4, 23.3.6, 23.4.2, 23.5.3, 23.13.5, 26.6.2, 31.2.2, 31.33; *Adunaton*. 13.4, 13.8, fr. 5.1.1.1 (Albini), frs. 336.7, 340.16 (Thalheim), frgs. 5.10, 12.29.col 2.4, 12.50.4, 13.30.2, 14.31.4, 33.71.2, 33.73.2, 38.86.5, 38.87.1, 38.88a.7, 39.91, 63.125–127, 68.155, 98.217, 101.226.2, 135,286, 138.297, 308.col 1.5, 308.col 1.42, 317a.487–491, 482.4 (Carey); **Matron**: fr. 6 (Brandt); **Panyassis**: fr. 13.3 (Matthews); **Pherecydes**: fr. 106a (Müller FHG); **Pindar**: *Nemean*. 6.3, 7.4, 9.45, 10.85, 11.1; *Olympian*. 6.34, 7.58, 8.15, 13.62, 14.2, *Pythian*. 4.190, 5.54, fr. *Paian* 52d.48 (Maehler); **Plato Comicus**: *Hyp*. frs. 3–4 (Meineke); **Plato**: *Critias*. 109b, 109c, 113b, 113c, 114a, 114b, 116c, 119a; *Euthydemus* 5b; *Gorgias* 447a, 473e; *Laws* 1.630e, 3.690c, 3.692a, 5.737e, 5.740a, 5.740b, 5.741b, 5.741c, 5.744a, 5.744e, 5.745a, 5.745c, 5.745d, 5.745e, 5.747e, 6.755a, 6.756e, 6.757b, 6.757e, 6.759b, 6.760b, 6.760c, 6.762b, 6.763e, 6.765b, 6.765c, 6.765d, 6.768b, 6.775e, 6.776a, 8.835b, 8.846b, 9.855a, 9.855b, 9.856d, 9.857a, 9.873c, 10.909c, 11.923d, 11.923e, 11.924d, 11.924e, 11.925b, 11.925c, 11.928c, 11.937a, 11.938b, 12.945b, 12.946b, 12.948d, 12.949c, 12.956e; *Philebus* 61c; *Pol*. 266c, 290e, 291a, 298e, 299a, 300a, 307c; *Rep*. 386c, 414a, 425d, 429a, 460a, 461e, 516d, 557a, 561b, 617d, 617e, 618a, 619b, 619d, 619e, 620b–e; *Symp*. 180e; *Theataeus*

149b; *Timaeus* 18e; **Sappho**: fr. 33.2 (Campbell); **Sophocles**: Ajax. 1185, 1284–1285; Antigone 275, 396, 814, Electra 379, 710, 760; OC. 1235, 1337, frs. 24.7, 288, 659.1 (Radt); **Stesichorus**: *PLille* 76.224 (Parson); **Theocritus**: 4.20, 8.30, 24.130, epigr. 11.5; **Thucydides**: 3.50.2, 4.8.9, 5.21.1, 5.35.3, 6.42.1, 6.62.1, 8.30, 8.66.1, 8.69.4, 8.70.1; **Tyrtaeus**: fr. 23.5 (West); **Xenocrates**: frs. 213.5, 225.8 (Parente); **[Xenophon]**: *Ath.Rep.* 2.9; **Xenophon**: *Anab.* 4.5.23–24; *Cyr.* 1.6.46, 4.5.55, 6.3.34, 6.3.36, 7.1.16, 7.3.1, 7.2.2; *Mem.* 1.2.9, 3.9.10, 4.35.5.

Metaphoric and idiomatic usages of lottery terms

Aeschylus: Aesch. *Ag.* 380, 557; *Prom.* 48; *Sept.* 690, 947; *Supp.* 692; *Tetr.* 34a.355.11 (Mette); **Aeschines**: 1.149.5; **Aesop**: *Proverbs* 13, 53, 56, 63, 121; **Alcaeus**: frs. 41.17, 309.1 (Campbell); **Andocides**: 1.124.1; **Antimachus**: *epigram* 321.1; **Aristophanes**: *Eccl.* 999; *Pax.* 309; *Thesm.* 1071; *IFF.* fr. 62 (Meineke); **Aristotle**: *De Anima* 410a; *De Mund.* 391b.13; *Pol.* 7.1323b; *Topica* 112b, fr. *var.* 12, 20, 98, 326, 624 (Rose); **Bacchylides**: 1.151, 1.166, 1.180, 3.11, 4.20, 6.2, 10.39, 13.187, 19.3, 19.14, *encomia*. fr. 8.6 (Irigoin), fr. 20e.6 (Maehler); **Calliphon and Democedes**: fr. 1.9 (Diels Kranz); **Chaeremon**: fr. 36.4 (Snell); **Cratinus**: *Pyt.* fr..12.1; *Troi.* fr. 2.1 (Kock); **Democritus**: frs. 5.94, 21.2, 135.134 (Diels Kranz); **Dinarchus**: 1.64; **Diocles**: fr. 182.127 (van der Eijk 2000;; **Empedocles**: *phys.* fr. 20.6 (Diels Kranz); *test.* 96.18, 102.2, 115.51, 154.6 (Diels Kranz); **Eubulus**: fr. 107.26 (Kock); **Euripides**: *Elec.* 1193; *Hel.* 214, 377; *Hipp.* 80; *IT.* 863, 914, 1009; *Phoen.* 1484, 1576; *Supp.* 309, 539, 1086; *Troi.* 644, 1192, fr. 50.33 (Austin 1968); *Hyps.* fr. 1.iv.5 (Bond) fr. *Antiop*.9.2 (Kambitsis), fr. 360.33, 403.3, 446.1, 641.3 (Nauck), ftrs. 12.94, 15a.15 (Page); **Herodotus**: 2.62.2, 3.106.1, 3.130.3, 6.23.5, 7.53.2; **Heraclitus**: fr. 25.2 (Diels Kranz); **Hippocrates**: *Sept.part.* 9.57 (Littré); **Hipponax**: 40.2; **Homer**: *Il.* 7.80, 15.350, 22.343, 23.76, 23.79, 24.76; *Od.* 5.311, 11.304; **Lycurgus**: 1.100; **Lysias**: *Epitaph*.79.1 (Carey 2007); **Mimnermus**: fr. 12.1 (West); **Phocylides**: fr. 2.8 (Gerber); **Pindar**: *Olympian* 1.53, 9.15, 10.61, 10.88; *Isthmian* 4.49, 8.64; *Nemean*. 1.24, 1.70, 7.4, 7.54, 9.45, 10.27; *Pythian* 2.27, 2.74, 5.96, 8.88, frs. 35a.1, 52d.53, 70b.27, 75.6, 140a.76, 165.1 (Maehler); **Plato**: *Epinom* 988c7, 992d3; *Leg.* 2.669d, 3.696e, 4.704c, 5.738a, 6.782a, 7.791a, 8.838d, 10.903e; *Phaedr.* 107d; *Philebus* 37b, 49c, 55b; *Pol.* 269d, 269e, 289a; *Soph.* 227c; *Theaet.* 210c; *Tim.* 23d, 38d, 41b, 46e, 52a, 54a, 63b, 92c; **Sappho**: fr. 58.26 (Campbell); **Simonides**: fr. 15.1.5 (Page); **Sophocles**: *Ajax* 1058; *Antigone* 580, 699, 820, 837, 918, 1241; *Electra* 364, 751; *OC* 450, 790, 1746; *OT* 1366; *Philoctetes* 1115, fr. 278.2 (Radt); **Stesichorus**: fr. 55.3 (Page); **Theocritus**: 4.40, 7.103, 16.46, 16.84; **Theognis**: 1.453, 1.592, 1.666, 1.729, 1.934, 1.1111; **Theophrastus**: *De sens.* 22.5, 66.5; **Thucydides**: 2.44.1, **Xenophanes**: fr. 2.10, 6.2 (West); **Xenophon**: *Anab.* 3.1.11; *Cyr.* 3.1.24; *Hiero.* 6.9.

Epigraphic evidence for lottery, excluding metaphorical usages (a selection up to the end of the fourth cent.)

Agora XVI 20[1]; *Agora* XVI 41[1]; *Agora* XIX, Leases L 4a = SEG 21.527; *Ephesos* 19, *Ephesos* 21, *Ephesos* 22 = IEph 1421, *Ephesos* 23, *Ephesos* 25, *Ephesos* 26, *Ephesos* 37, *Ephesos* 53, *Ephesos* 54, *Ephesos* 61; *ID* 36 Delos, *IG* I³ 19, *IG* I³ 244, C1, *IG* I³ 254, *IG* I³ 49, *IG* I³ 52, *IG* I³ 55, *IG* I³ 71L, *IG* I³ 82, *IG* I³ 91, *IG* II² 514, *IG* II² 136, *IG* II² 248, *IG* II² 354, *IG* II² 4841, *IG* IV 748, *IG* IX 1² 3:718, *IG* V² 39, *IG* V² 40, *IG* V² 41; *Miletos* 10, SEG 33:147,

Miletos 455, *IPArk* 15, *IG* IV² 1 68, face A, fr. III = Peek, *Asklepieion* 23, *Samos* 20 = *IG* XII⁶ 1:18, *Samos* 54 = *IG* XII⁶ 1:44, Schwenk, *Athens* 18 fr. b, 19 = *IG* II² 330, Schwenk, *Athens* 54 = *IG* II² 354, *SEG* 39:1014[1], *SEG* 47:1427, *IG* II² 1232, *IG* II² 1263, *IG* II² 136, *IG* II² 248, *IG* II² 30, *FD* III 1:294, *HGK* 17, *Agora* XIX, Leases L 3, *CGRN* 88 = *Chios* 6 (McCabe), *IC* IV 13, *IG* V² 343, *IG* XII² 1 = *SEG* 34:849, 18, *SEG* 25:140 = *IG* II² 1146, *SEG* 32:86 = *IG* II³,1 449, ll.4, 12, *SEG* 31:745.

Bibliography

Aaronson, Scott (2014). "Quantum Randomness." *American Scientist* 102 (4): 266ff. https://www.americanscientist.org/article/quantum-randomness

Abel, V. Lynne Snyder (1983). *Prokrisis*. Ann Arbor, MI: U Microfilms International

Abruzzese Calabrese, G. (2009). "Una dedica ad Orthia: appunti per una ricerca." In D'Angela, C. and Ricci, F. (eds.), *Il Castello aragonese di Taranto: Studi e ricerche 2004-2006. Atti del II Seminario, Taranto, Castello aragonese, 6-7 giugno 2007.* Taranto, 209-14

Adkins, A.W.H. (1972). *Moral Values and Political Behaviour in Ancient Greece. From Homer to the End of the Fifth Century.* London: Routledge

Ager, Sheila L. (1996). *Interstate Arbitrations in the Greek World, 337-90 B.C.* Berkeley: University of California Press

Ajootian, A. (2007). "Heroic and Athletic Sortition at Ancient Olympia." In Schaus, G., Wenn, S. (eds.). *Onward to the Olympics: Historical Perspectives on the Olympic Games.* Waterloo, ON: Wilfrid Laurier University Press, 115-129

Aleshire, Sara B. (1994). "Towards a Definition of 'State Cult' for Ancient Athens." In Hägg, Robin (ed.) *Ancient Greek Cult Practice from the Epigraphical Evidence. Proceedings of the Second International Seminar on Ancient Greek Cult, Swedish Institute at Athens, 22-24 November 1991.* Stockholm: Paul Åströms Förlag, 9-16 (Acta Instituti Atheniensis Regni Sueciae, 13)

Alfieri Tonini, Teresa (2001). "La documentazione epigrafica del sorteggio ad Atene ed in altre città greche." In Cordano, Grottanelli, 107-118

Algavish, David (2002). "The Division of the Spoils of War in the Bible and in the Ancient Near East." *Zeitschrift für Altorientalische und Biblische Rechtsgeschichte* 8: 242-273

Algazi, Gadi (2005). "Between the Desert and the Forest: Reading a Foundation Story." *Zmanim: A Historical Quarterly* 89: 50-59 [in Hebrew]

Amandry, Pierre (1939). "Convention religieuse entre Delphes et Skiathos." *BCH* 63: 183-219

Amandry, Pierre (1950). *La mantique Apollinienne à Delphes: Essai sur le fonctionnement de l'oracle.* Paris: De Boccard

Amandry, Pierre (1984). "Le culte de Nymphes et de Pan à l'Antre Corycien." *BCH Suppl.* 9: 395-425

Amandry, Pierre, Jacquemin, Anne (eds.) (1984). *L'antre corycien 2.* École française d'Athènes. Paris: Éditions de Boccard

Ampolo, Carmine (1999). "La frontiera dei Greci come luogo del rapporto e dello scambio: I mercati di frontiera fino al V secolo A.C." In Stazio, A. et al. (eds.). *Confini e frontiera nella Grecità d'Occidente. Atti del 37o convegno di studi sulla Magna Grecia.* Taranto: Istituto per la storia e l'archeologia della Magna Greca, 451-463

Ampolo, Carmine (ed.) (2001a). *Da un'antica città di Sicilia: i decreti di Entella e Nakone. Catalogo della mostra.* Pisa: Scuola Normale Superiore di Pisa

Ampolo, Carmine (2001b). "Nakone: Come fu risolta una lotta civile." In Ampolo, *Da un'antica città di Sicilia: I decreti di Entella e Nakone. Catalogo della mostra,* 203-205

Anderson, Greg (2003). *The Athenian Experiment: Building an Imagined Political Community in Ancient Attica, 508-490.* Ann Arbor: University of Michigan Press
Angelis, F. De (ed.) (2020). *A Companion to Greeks Across to the Ancient World*, Malden, Wiley-Blackwell
Antonaccio, Carla M. (1995). *An Archaeology of Ancestors: Tomb Cult and Hero Cult in Early Greece.* Lanham, MD: Rowman & Littlefield
Antonaccio, C. (2007). Colonization: Greece on the Move 900–480, in H.A. Shapiro (ed.), *The Cambridge Companion to Archaic Greece.* Cambridge: Cambridge University Press, pp. 201–224.
Antonetti, Claudia (1997). "Megara e le sue colonie: Un'unità storico-culturale?" in Antonetti, Claudia (ed.). *Il dinamismo della colonizzazione greca-Atti della tavola rotonda Espansione e colonizzazione greca d'età arcaica: Metodologie e problemi a confronto (Venezia, 10-11 November 1995).* Napoli: Loffredo, 83–94
Appert, Nicolas (1810). *L'art de conserver.* Paris: Patris et Cie Imprimeurs
Aquinas, Thomas (1963). *Liber de sortibus ad dominum Iacobum de Tonengo (1270-1271).* Carey, P.B. (trans.). Dover: Dominican House of Philosophy
Aquinas, Thomas (2007). *Summa Theologica* [1269–1272]. Fathers of the English Dominican Province (trans.). New York: Cosmo Classics
Asheri, David (1963). "Laws of Inheritance, Distribution of Land and Political Constitutions in Ancient Greece." *Historia* 12 (1): 1–21
Asheri, David (1965). "*Distribuzione di terre e legislazione agraria nella Locride occidental.*" *JJP* 15: 313–328
Asheri, David (1966). *Distribuzione di terre nell'antica Grecia.* Turin: Memorie dell'Accademia delle Scienze di Torino, classe di scienze morali, storiche e filologiche, Serie 4a X
Asheri, David (1974). *Il caso di Aithiops, regola o eccezione?*, in Parola de Passato 29: pp. 232–236.
Asheri, David (1982). "Osservazioni storiche sul decreto di Nakone." *ASNP* III.12 (3): 1033–1045
Aubert, Vilhelm (1959). "Chance in Social Affairs." *Inquiry* 2: 1–24
Aubriot-Sevin, Danielle (1992). *Prière et conceptions religieuses en Grèce ancienne jusqu'à la fin du Ve siècle av. J.-C.* Lyon: Maison De L'Orient
Aune, David Edward (1983). *Prophecy in Early Christianity and the Ancient Mediterranean World.* Grand Rapids, MI: Eerdmans
Azoulay, Vincent (2014). *Les tyrannicides d'Athènes. Vie et mort de deux statues.* Paris: Seuil
Babbit, Frank (1936). Plutarch, *Moralia.* Loeb Classical Library Cambridge Mass: Harvard University Press
Bagnall, Roger S. (1976). *The Administration of the Ptolemaic Possessions outside Egypt.* Columbia Studies in the Classical Tradition vol. 4. Leiden: Brill
Bagnasco, Gianni (2001). "Le *sortes* etrusche." In Cordano, Grottanelli (2001), 197–220
Bailly, Anatole (2000) Dictionnaire Grec- Français. Paris: Hachette
Balot, Ryan K. (2006). *Greek Political Thought.* Oxford: Oxford University Press
Bar-On, Shraga (2020). *Lot Casting, God, and Man in Jewish Literature: From the Bible to the Renaissance.* Ramat Gan: Bar Ilan University Press [in Hebrew]
Barrett, W.S. (1964). *Euripides Hippolytus.* Edited with introduction and commentary. Oxford: Clarendon Press
Barrio Vega, M.L. de (2011). "The *Aisimnatai* at Megara." In Luján, E.R., Alonso, García, Luis, Juan (eds.). *A Greek Man in the Iberian Street. Papers in Linguistics and*

Epigraphy in Honor of Javier de Hoz. Innsbrucker Beiträge zur Sprachwissenschaft. Innsbruck: Universität Innsbruck, 17–24

Bartoněk, Antonîn. (2003). *Handbuch des mykenischen Griechischen*. Heidelberg: Universitatsverlag C. Winter

Bartzoka, A. (2012). "Solon fondateur de la *Boulê* des Quatre Cent?" *Historiká* 11: 127–156

Barucchi, L. (2004/5). "Il metodo di selezione degli arconti in Atene arcaica." *MEP* 9/10: 69–85

Beauchet, L. (1897). *Histoire du droit privé de la République athénienne*, vol. 3. Paris: Chevalier-Marescq et Co.

Beck, Hans (ed.) (2013). *A Companion to Ancient Greek Government*. Malden, MA: Wiley Blackwell

Beck, Hans, Buraselis, Kostas, McAuley, Alex (eds.) (2019). *Ethnos and Koinon: Studies in Ancient Greek Ethnicity and Federalism*. Heidelberger Althistorische Beiträge und Epigraphische Studien; Bd. 61. Stuttgart: Franz Steiner Verlag

Beck, Hans, Ganter, Angela (2015). "Boiotia and the Boiotian Leagues." In Beck, Hans, Funke, Peter (eds.). *Federalism in Greek Antiquity*. Cambridge: Cambridge University Press, 132–157

Beekes, Robert S.P. (2010). *Etymological Dictionary of Greek*. Leiden: Brill

Beekes, Robert S.P., Beek, Lucien van (2010). "μείρομαι." In Beekes (2010), 922–923

Beerden, Kim (2013). *Worlds Full of Signs: Ancient Greek Divination in Context*. Leiden: Brill

Belvedere, O. (1987). "Himera, Naxos, Camarina, tre casi di urbanistica coloniale." *Xenia* 14: 5–20

Belvedere, O. (1988). "Topografia storica." In Belvedere, O., et al., *Himera iii.1: Prospezione archeologica nel territorio*. Rome: L'Erma di Bretschneider, 189–225

Bennett, Deborah J. (1998). *Randomness*. Cambridge, MA: Harvard University Press

Bérard, R.-M. (2017). *Mégara Hyblaea 6: La nécropole méridionale de la cité archaïque. 2: Les données funéraires.* .Rome: Ecole française de Rome

Berger, Sh. (1989). "Democracy in the Greek West and the Athenian Example." *Hermes* 117 (3): 303–314

Berman, Daniel W. (2007). *Myth and Culture in Aeschylus' Seven against Thebes*. Filologia e Critica 95. Roma: Edizioni dell'Ateneo

Bernabé, Alberto (1996). *Poetae Epici Graeci Testimonia e fragmenta*. Pars I. Berlin: De Gruyter

Bernstein, Frank (2004). *Konflikt und Migration. Studien zu griechischen Fluchtbewegungen im Zeitalter der sogenannten Großen Kolonisation*. St. Katharinen: Scripta Mercaturae

Berthiaume, G. (1982). *Les rôles du mágeiros: études sur la boucherie, la cuisine et le sacrifice dans la Grèce ancienne*. Leiden: Brill

Berthold, R.M. (1980). "Fourth-Century Rhodes." *Historia* 29 (1): 32–49

Bianchi, U. (1953). *DIOS AISA: Destino, uomini e divinità nel Epos, nelle Teogonie e nel culto dei Greci*. Rome: Angelo Signorelli

Bicknell, P.J. (1969). "Whom Did Kleisthenes Enfranchise?" *PP* 24: 34–37

Bintliff, John (2006). "City-Country Relationships in the 'Normal Polis.'" In Rosen, Ralph, Sluiter, Ineke (eds.). *City, Countryside, and the Spatial Organization of Value in Classical Antiquity*. Mnem. Suppl. 279. Leiden: Brill, 13–32

Blaise, Fabienne (2006). "Poetics and Politics: Tradition Reworked in Solon's 'Eunomia' (Poem 4)." In Blok, Lardinois (eds.), 114–133

Blok, Josine (2006). "Solon's Funerary Laws: Questions of Authenticity and Function." In Blok, Lardinois (eds.), 197–247
Blok, Josine (2009a). "Gentrifying Genealogy: On the Genesis of the Athenian Autochthony Myth." In Walde, C., Dill, U. (eds.). *Antike Mythen. Medien, Transformationen, Konstruktionen. Fritz Graf zum 65. Geburtstag*. Berlin: De Gruyter, 251–275
Blok, Josine (2009b). "Perikles' Citizenship Law: A New Perspective." *Historia* 58: 141–170
Blok, Josine (2011). "*Hosiê* and Athenian Law from Solon to Lykourgos." In Azoulay, Vincent, Ismard, Paulin (eds.). *Clisthène et Lycurgue d'Athènes—Autour du politique dans la cité classique*. Paris: Editions de la Sorbonne, 233–254
Blok, Josine (2014a). "The Priestess of Athena Nikê: A New Reading of *IG* I³ 35 and 36." *Kernos* 27: 99–126
Blok, Josine (2014b). "Participatory Governance: The Case for Allotment." *Etnofoor* (Theme issue: *Participation*) 26 (2): 73–80
Blok, Josine (2015). "The *Diôbelia*: On the Political Economy of an Athenian State Fund." *ZPE* 193: 87–102
Blok, Josine (2017). *Citizenship in Classical Athens*. Cambridge: Cambridge University Press
Blok, Josine (2018). "Retracing Steps. Finding Ways into Archaic Greek Citizenship." In Duplouy, Brock (eds.), 79–101
Blok, Josine (2023). "Sortition and Democracy." In Pirenne-Delforge, Vinciane, Wecowski, Marek (eds.). *Politeia and Koinonia*. Leiden: Brill, 289–309
Blok, Josine, Krul, Julia (2017). "Debt and Its Aftermath: The Near Eastern Background to Solon's *Seisachtheia*." *Hesperia* 86: 607–643
Blok, Josine, Lambert, Stephen D. (2009). "The Appointment of Priests in Attic *Gene*." *ZPE* 169: 95–121
Blok, Josine H., Lardinois, André P.M.H. (eds.) (2006). *Solon of Athens: New Historical and Philological Approaches*. Mnem. Suppl. 272. Leiden: Brill
Blok, Josine, Rookhuijzen, Janric van (2023). "Priestesses in the Sacred Space of the Acropolis: A Close Reading of the Hekatompedon Inscriptions." In Dirven, Lucinda, Icks, Martijn, Remijsen, Sofie (eds.). *The Public Lives of Ancient Women (500 BCE–650 CE)*. Leiden: Brill, 107–126
Blok, Josine, Wout, Evelyn van 't (2018). "Table Arrangements: *Sitêsis* as a Polis Institution (*IG* I³ 131)." In Eijnde, van den, Blok, Strootman (eds.), 181–204
Blösel, Wolfgang (2014). "Zensusgrenzen für die Ämterbekleidung im klassischen Griechenland. Wie gross war der verfassungsrechtliche Abstand gemässigter Oligarchien von der athenischen Demokratie?" In Blösel, Wolfgang, Schmitz, Winfried, Seelentag, Gunnar, Timmer, Jan (eds.). *Grenzen politischer Partizipation im klassischen Griechenland*. Stuttgart: Franz Steiner, 71–93
Boedeker, Deborah (1983). "Hecate, a Transfunctional Goddess in the Theogony." *TAPA* 113: 79–93
Bonnechaire, Pierre (2007). "Divination." In Ogden, Daniel (ed.). *A Companion to Greek Religion*. Malden, MA: Blackwell, 145–160
Bonnechere, Pierre (2013). "The Religious Management of the Polis: Oracles and Political Decision-Making." In Beck (ed.), 366–381
Bonnet, Corinne (2017). "Les dieux en assemblée." In Pironti, Gabriella, Bonnet (eds.). *Les dieux d'Homère: polythéisme et poésie en Grèce ancienne*. Kernos Suppl. 31. Liège: Presses universitaires de Liège, 87–112

Borecký, Bořivoj (1963). "The Primitive Origin of the Greek Conception of Equality." In Varcl, L., Willets, R.F., Borecký, B. (eds.). *Geras, Studies Presented to George Thomson on the Occasion of His 60th Birthday*. Prague: Charles University, 41–60

Borecký, Bořivoj (1965). *Survivals of Some Tribal Ideas in Classical Greek: The Use and the Meaning of lagchanō, dateomai, and the Origin of ison echein, ison nemein, and Related Idioms*. Acta Universitatis Carolinae, Philosophica et historica. Prague: Univerzita Karlova

Borecký, Bořivoj (1983). "Der Sinn der Sieben gegen Theben." *Folia philologica* 106 (3): 151–154

Borges, Jorge Louis ([1941] 2015). *The Lottery at Babylon*. Hurley, Andrew (trans.). Harmondsworth: Penguin Audiobooks. Orig. *La lotería en Babilonia* [in Spanish]

Boisacq, Emile 1916 Dictionnaire étymologique de la langue grecque, étudiée dans ses rapports avec les autres langues indo-européennes.Heidelberg: C. Winter

Bouché-Leclercq, Auguste (1879–1880) *Histoire de la divination dans l'antiquité*. Vol. 1. repr. 1963. Bruxelles: Culture et civilisation

Bowden, Hugh (2005). *Classical Athens and the Delphic Oracle: Divination and Democracy* Cambridge: Cambridge University Press

Bowra, C. M. (1958). "A Prayer to the Fates." *CQ* 8: 231–240

Boyd, Th.D., Jameson, M.H. (1981). "Urban and Rural Land Division in Ancient Greece." *Hesperia* (Special issue: *Greek Towns and Cities: A Symposium*) 50 (4) (October–December 1981): 327–342

Bravo, Benedetto (1992). "Citoyens et libres non-citoyens dans les cités coloniales à l'époque archaïque. Le cas de Syracuse." In Lonis, R. (ed.). *L'Étranger dans le monde grec II (Actes du Deuxième Colloque sur l'Étranger. Nancy, 19–21 septembre 1991)*. Nancy: Presses Universitaires de Nancy, 43–85

Bravo, Benedetto (1984). "Commerce et noblesse en Grèce archaïque." *DHA* 10: 99–160

Bremmer, Jan N. (2007). "Greek Normative Sacrifice." In Ogden, Daniel (ed.). *A Companion to Greek Religion*. Malden, MA: Wiley-Blackwell, 132–144

Bresson, Alain ([2007–2008] 2016). *The Making of the Ancient Greek Economy: Institutions, Markets, and Growth in the City-States*. Princeton: Princeton University Press

Brixhe, C., Hodot, R. (1988). *L'Asie Mineure du nord au sud*. Nancy: Presses Universitaires de Nancy

Brock, Roger, Hodkinson, Stephen (eds.) (2002). *Alternatives to Athens: Varieties of Political Organization and Community in Ancient Greece*. Oxford: Oxford University Press

Brugnone, A. (1997). "Le legge di Himera sulla distribuzione della terra." *PP* 52: 262–305

Brugnone, A. (2011a). "Considerazioni sulla legge arcaica di Himera." *Rivista di Diritto Ellenico* 1: 3–17

Brugnone, A. (2011b). "Le sferette bronzee iscritte da Himera." *Kernos* 24: 77–94

Bubelis, William S. (2016). *Hallowed Stewards: Solon and the Sacred Treasurers of Ancient Athens*. Ann Arbor: University of Michigan Press

Buchstein, Hubertus (2009). *Demokratie und Lotterie. Das Los als politisches Entscheidungsinstrument von der Antike bis zu EU*. Frankfurt: Campus

Buchstein, Hubertus (2015). "Countering the 'Democracy Thesis': Sortition in Ancient Greek Political Theory." *Redescriptions: Political Thought, Conceptual History and Feminist Theory* 18 (2): 126–157. DOI: http://doi.org/10.7227/R.18.2.2

Buchstein, Hubertus, Hein, Michael (2009). "Randomizing Europe: The Lottery as a Decision-Making Procedure for Policy Creation in the EU." *Critical Policy Studies* 3: 29–57

Buck, R.J. (1959). "Communism on the Lipari Islands (Diod. 5.9.4)." *CPh* 54: 35–39

Burgers, Gert-Jan, Crielaard, Jan Paul (2007). "Greek Colonists and Indigenous Populations at L'Amastuola, Southern Italy." *BABesch* 82: 77–114

Burgers, Gert-Jan, Crielaard, Jan Paul)2016). "The Migrant's Identity: 'Greeks' and 'Natives' at L'Amastuola, Southern Italy." In Donnellan, Nizzo, Burgers (eds.), 225–238

Burke, Peter (1997a). "Strengths and Weaknesses in the History of Mentalities," in Burke (1997b) 162–182; revision of *History of European Ideas* 7 (1986): 439–451

Burke, Peter (1997b). *Varieties of Cultural History*. Cambridge: Polity Press

Burkert, Walter (1985). *Greek Religion*. Raffan, J. (trans.). Cambridge, MA: Harvard University Press

Burkert, Walter (1992). *The Orientalizing Revolution*. Cambridge, MA: Harvard University Press

Cabanes, Pierre (2008). "Greek Colonisation in the Adriatic." In Tsetskhladze (ed.), Vol. 2, 155–186

Cabanes, Pierre, Drini, C. (1995-2016). *Corpus des Inscriptions Grecques d'Illyrie Méridionale et d'Epire. Études épigraphiques* 2. Rome: Collection de l'École française de Rome no. 188

Cahill, Nicholas (2002). *Household and City Organization at Olynthos*. New Haven, CT: Yale University Press

Cameron, H.D. (1970). "The Power of Words in the Seven against Thebes." *TAPA* 101: 95–118

Cammack, Daniela (2019). "The *Dêmos* in *Demokratia*." *CQ* 69 (1): 42–61

Canevaro, M. (2022). "Social Mobility vs. Societal Stability: Once Again on the Aims and Meaning of Solon's Reforms." In Bernhardt, Johannes C., Canevaro, Mirko (eds.). *From Homer to Solon: Continuity and Change in Archaic Greece*. Mnem. Suppl. 454. Leiden: Brill, 363–413.

Canevaro, Mirko, Erskine, Andrew, Gray, Benjamin, Ober, Josiah (eds.) (2018). *Ancient Greek History and Contemporary Social Science*. Edinburgh Leventis Studies 9. Edinburgh: Edinburgh University Press

Canevaro, Mirko, Esu, Alberto (2018). "Extreme Democracy and Mixed Constitution in Theory and Practice: *Nomophylakia* and Fourth-Century *Nomothesia* in the Aristotelian *Athenaion Politeia*." In Bearzot, C., Canevaro, M., Gargiulo, T., Poddighe, E. (eds.). *Athenaion Politeiai tra storia, politica e sociologia: Aristotele e Pseudo-Senofonte*. Milan: LED; Quaderni di Erga-Logoi, 105–145

Canevaro, Mirko, Esu, Alberto (2023). "Once Again on Aristotle and the Identity of the Athenian *Nomothetai*: A Response to Gertrud Dietze-Mager." *Erga-Logoi* 11: 7–28

Cantarella, Eva (2005). "Gender, Sexuality, and Law." In Gagarin, Cohen (eds.), 236–253

Capdetrey, Laurent, Zurbach, Julien (eds.) (2012). *Mobilités Grecques: Mouvements, Réseaux, Contacts en Méditerranée de l'époque Archaïque à l'époque Hellénistique*. Scripta Antiqua 46. Bordeaux: Ausonius

Carawan, Edwin M. (1987). "*Eisangelia* and *Euthyna*: The Trials of Miltiades, Themistocles, and Cimon." *GRBS* 28: 167–208

Carawan, Edwin M. (1998). *Rhetoric and the Law of Draco*. Oxford: Clarendon Press

Carawan, Edwin M. (2008). "Pericles the Younger and the Citizenship Law." *CJ* 103: 383–406

Carbon, Jan-Mathieu (2015). "Five Answers Prescribing Rituals in the Oracular Tablets from Dodona." *Grammateion* 4: 73–87

Carbon, Jan-Mathieu (2018). "A Network of Hearths: Honors, Sacrificial Shares, and 'Traveling Meat." In Eijnde, van den, Blok, Strootman (eds.), 340–375
Cargill, J. (1995). *Athenian Settlements in the fourth century BC*. Leiden: Brill
Carlier, Pierre (1984). *La Royauté en Grèce avant Alexandre*. Strasbourg: AECR
Carlier, Pierre (2006). Ἄναξ and βασιλεύς in the Homeric Poems." In Deger-Jalkotzy, I.S. Lemos, I. (eds.). *Ancient Greece. From the Mycenaean Palaces to the Age of Homer*. Edinburgh: Edinburgh University Press, 101–110
Carlsson, Susanne (2010). *Hellenistic Democracies: Freedom, Independence and Political Procedure in Some East Greek City States*. Stuttgart: Franz Steiner
Carter, E., Donald, J., Squires, J. (eds.) (1993). *Space and Place: Theories of Identity and Location*. London: Lawrence and Wishart
Carter, J.C. (1990). "Metapontum—Land, Wealth, and Population." In Descoeudres, J.-P. (ed.). *Greek Colonists and Native Populations*. Oxford: Oxford University Press, 405–441
Carter, J.C. (1994). "Sanctuaries in the *chora* of Metaponto." In Alcock, Susan E., Osborne, Robin (eds.). *Placing the Gods: Sanctuaries and Sacred Space in Ancient Greece*. Oxford: Oxford University Press, 161–198
Carter, J.C. (2000). "The *chôra* and Polis of Metaponto." In Krinzinger, Gassner, Kerschner, Muss (eds.)., 81–94
Carter, J.C. (2003). *Crimean Chersonesos: City, Chora, Museum and Environs*. Austin: Institute of Classical Archeology
Carter J.C. (2006). *Discovering the Greek Countryside at Metaponto*. Ann Arbor: University of Michigan Press
Carter, J.C., Crawford, M., Lehman, P., Nikolaenko, G., Trelogan, J. (2000). "The Chora of Chersonesos in Crimea, Ukraine." *AJA* 104 (4): 707–741
Cartledge, Paul (1981). "Spartan Wives: Liberation or Licence?" *CQ* 31: 84–105
Cartledge, Paul (1996). "Comparatively Equal." In Ober, Hedrick (eds.)., 174–185
Cartledge, Paul., and Antony. Spawforth (2002). *Hellenistic and Roman Sparta : a Tale of Two Cities*. 2nd ed. London: Routledge
Cartledge, Paul (2004). *The Spartans: The World of the Warrior-Heroes of Ancient Greece, from Utopia to Crisis and Collapse*. New York: Vintage Books
Cartledge, Paul (2009). *Ancient Greek Political Thought*. Cambridge: Cambridge University Press
Cartledge, Paul, Spawforth, Antony (2001). *Hellenistic and Roman Sparta: A Tale of Two Cities*. London: Routledge
Casevitz, Michel (1984). "Temples et sanctuaires: ce qu'apprend l'étude lexicographique." In Roux, G. (ed.). Travaux de la Maison de l'Orient 7. *Temples et sanctuaires*. Lyon: Maison de l'Orient et de la Méditerranée Jean Pouilloux, 81–95
Casevitz, Michel (1985). *Le vocabulaire de la colonisation en grec ancien: Étude lexicologique. Les familles de ktizō et de oikeō-oikizō*. Études et commentaires 97. Paris: Klincksieck
Cassirer, Ernst (1953). *Language and Myth*. Langer, Suzanne K. (trans.). New York: Dover Publications
Cate, T.J. ten (2021). "Rationales for a Lottery among the Qualified to Select Medical Trainees: Decades of Dutch Experience." *Journal of Graduate Medical Education*: 612–15; DOI: http://dx.doi.org/10.4300/JGME-D-21-00789.1
Cazzato, V., Murray, O. (eds.) (2018). *The Symposion: Drinking Greek Style: Essays on Pleasure 1983–2017*. Oxford: Oxford University Press

Cecchet, Lucia (2009). "Γῆς ἀναδασμός: A Real Issue in the Archaic and Classical Poleis?" *Biblioteca di Athenaeum* 55: 185-198

Cecchet, Lucia (2017). "Re-shaping and Re-founding Citizen Bodies: The Case of Athens, Cyrene and Camarina." In Cecchet, Busetto (eds.)., 50-77

Cecchet, Lucia, Busetto, Anna (eds.) (2017). *Citizens in the Graeco-Roman World. Aspects of Citizenship from the Archaic Period to AD 212*. Leiden: Brill

Cerri, G. (1969). "'*isos dasmos*' come equivalente di '*isonomia*' nelle sylloge teognidea." *QUCC* 8: 97-104

Chadwick, John (1967). *The Decipherment of Linear B*. 2nd ed. Cambridge: Cambridge University Press

Chambers, Mortimer (1962). "The Authenticity of the Themistocles Decree." *AHR* 67 (2): 306-316

Chambers, Mortimer (1965). "Notes on the Text of the *Ath.Pol.*" *TAPA* 96: 31-39

Champeaux, J. (1990). "*Sors oraculi: les oracles en Italie sous la république et l'empire*." *MEFRA* 102: 271-302

Chaniotis, Angelos (1996). *Die Verträge zwischen kretischen Poleis in der hellenistischen Zeit*. Stuttgart: Franz Steiner

Chaniotis, Angelos (2008). "Priests as Ritual Experts in the Greek World." In Dignas, Trampedach (eds.)., 17-34

Chaniotis, Angelos (2010). "The Molpoi Inscription: Ritual Prescription or Riddle?" *Kernos* 23: 375-379

Chantraine, P. (1968-1980). *Dictionnaire étymologique de la langue grecque. Histoire des mots*. Paris: Klinksieck

Chartier, Roger (2015). "Cultural History." In Wright, James D. (Ed.). *International Encyclopedia of the Social & Behavioral Sciences*. 2nd ed. Elsevier: 420-425

Ciaceri, Emanuele (1911). *Culti e miti nella storia dell' antica Sicilia*. Catania: F. Battiato

Cingano, Ettore (2000). "Tradizioni su Tebe nell'epica e nella lirica greca arcaica." In Bernardini, Paola (ed.). *Presenza e funzione della città di Tebe nella cultura greca: atti del convegno internazionale, Urbino, 7-9 luglio 1997. Quaderni urbinati di cultura classica. Atti di convegni*, 7. Pisa: Istituti editoriali e poligrafici internazionali, 127-161

Cingano, Ettore (2004). "The Sacrificial Cut and the Sense of Honour Wronged in Greek Epic Poetry: *Thebais*, Frgs. 2-3 D." In Grottanelli, C., Milano, Lucio (eds.). *Food and Identity in the Ancient World*. Padova: S.A.R.G.O.N., 269-280

Clinton, Kevin (1974). *The Sacred Officials of the Eleusinian Mysteries*. TAPhS n.s. 64 (3). Philadelphia: American Philosophical Society

Cohen, Getzel M. (1995). *The Hellenistic Settlements in Europe, the Islands, and Asia Minor*. Berkeley: University of California Press

Cohen, Getzel M. (2006). *The Hellenistic Settlements in Syria, the Red Sea Basin, and North Africa*. Berkeley: University of California Press

Cohen, Getzel M. (2013). *The Hellenistic Settlements in the East from Armenia and Mesopotamia to Bactria and India*. Berkeley: University of California Press

Coldstream, J.N. (1979). *Geometric Greece*. London: Methuen

Coldstream, J.N. (1993). "Mixed Marriages at the Frontiers of the Early Greek World." *OJA* 12 (1): 89-107

Connelly, Joan B. (2007). *Portrait of a Priestess: Women and Ritual in Ancient Greece*. Princeton: Oxford University Press

Connor, W.R. (1987). "Tribes, Festivals, Processions: Civic Ceremonial and Political Manipulation in Archaic Greece." *JHS* 101: 40-50

Consolo, Langher, S. (2005). "Democrazia e antidemocrazia a Siracusa: *isotes e ges anadasmos* nelle lotte sociali del IV secolos." In Bultrighini, U. (ed.). *Democrazia e antidemocrazia nel mondo Greco. Atti del convegno internazionale di studi, Chieti 9-11 aprile 2003.* Alessandria: Edizioni dell'Orso, 235-250

Cook, Arthur B. ([1903] 1964). *Zeus: A Study in Ancient Religion.* New York: Biblo and Tannen

Cordano, Federica (1986). *Antiche fondazioni greche: Sicilia e Italia meridionale.* Palermo: Sellerio

Cordano, Federica (1988). "*Gruppi gentilizi presso i Nassii di Sicilia.*" BA 48: 18-22

Cordano, Federica (1992). *Le tesserae di tempio di Atena a Camarina.* Studi pubblicati dall'Istituto italiano per la storia antica 50. Rome: Istituto italiano per la storia antica.

Cordano, Federica (2001). "Strumenti di sorteggio e schedatura dei cittadini nella Sicilia greca." In Cordano, Grottanelli (eds.)., 83-93

Cordano, Federica (2016). "I Theodoridai della città greca di Megara Iblea (Sicilia)." *MEFRA* 128: 163-167

Cordano, Federica, Grottanelli, Cristiano (eds.) (2001). *Sorteggio Publico e Cleromanzia dall' Antichità all' Età moderna.* Milano: Edizioni Et

Cornford, Francis M. (1991). *From Religion to Philosophy: A Study in the Origins of Western Speculation.* Princeton, NJ: Princeton University Press

Corsten, T. (1999). *Vom Stamm zum Bund. Gründung und territoriale Organization griechischer Bundesstaaten.* Munich: Oberhummer Gesellschaft

Costanzi, Michela (2010). "Les colonies de deuxième degré de l'Italie du Sud et de la Sicile: une analyse lexicologique." *Ancient West and East* 9: 87-107

Costanzi, Michela (2013). "Invitation à une nouvelle réflexion sur les fondations grecques en Libye." *REG* 126 (2): 345-370

Costanzi, Michela (2020). "Mobility in the Ancient Greek World: Diversity of Causes, Variety of Vocabularies." In De Angelis, F. (ed.). *A Companion to Greeks across to the Ancient World.* Malden, MA: Wiley-Blackwell, 18-60

Cox, Cheryl Anne (1998). *Household Interests: Property, Marriage Strategies, and Family Dynamics in Ancient Athens.* Princeton, NJ: Princeton University Press

Crick, Bernard ([1962] 2000). *In Defence of Politics.* London: Continuum

Crielaard, Jan Paul (2000). "Honour and Valour as Discourse for Early Greek Colonialism." In Krinzinger, Gassner, Kerschner, Muss (eds.), 499-506

Crudden, Michael (2001). *The Homeric Hymns.* Oxford: Oxford University Press

Csapo, Eric, Slater, William J. (1995). *The Context of Athenian Drama.* Ann Arbor: Michigan University Press

Currie, Bruno (2006). "Homer and the Early Epic Tradition." In Clarke, M.J., Currie, B.G.F., Lyne, R.O.A.M. (eds.). *Epic Interactions: Perspectives on Homer, Virgil, and the Epic Tradition, Presented to Jasper Griffin by Former Pupils.* Oxford: Oxford University Press, 1-45

D'Agostino, Bruno (2006). "The First Greeks in Italy." In Tsetskhladze (ed.)., 1:201-237

D'Agostino, Bruno, Bats, M. (eds.) (1998). *Euboica: L'Eubea e la presenza euboica in Calcidica e in Occidente.* AION ArchStAnt 12. Naples: Publications du Centre Jean Bérard ; Collection Centre Jean Bérard 16

D'Agostino, Bruno., Soteriou, A. (1998). "Campania in the Framework of the Earliest Greek Colonization in the West." In D'Agostino, Bats (eds.). (1998), 355-368

Dakaris, S. (1996). *Dodona.* 2nd ed. Athens: Archaeological Receipts Fund

Dakaris, S., Vokotopoulou, J., Christidis, A.P. (eds.) (2013). *Τα Χρηστήρια Ελάσματα της Δωδώνης των ανασκαφών Δ. Ευαγγελίδη*, 2 vols. Athens, Athènes, Bibliothèque de la Société Archéologique d'Athènes Nos 285 et 286

Dalby, Andrew (1992). "Greeks Abroad: Social Organisation and Food among the Ten Thousand." *JHS* 112: 16–30

Damigos, S., Kaklamani, O. (in print). "From Thera to Cyrene: Early Society and Complex Networking in rhe Age of Colonization." In Roncaglia, A., Ranieri, S. (eds.). *Ricerche a Confronto. Dialoghi di Antichità Classiche e del Vicino Oriente.* Zermeghedo: Edizioni Saecula

D'Asaro, Leonardo (1991). *Minosse e Cocalo: Mito e storia nella Sicilia occidentale*. Khora 1. Palermo: Augustinus

Daverio Rocchi, Giovanna (1988). *Frontiera e confini nella Grecia antica*. Rome: L'Erma di Bretschneider

David, E. (1981). *Sparta between Empire and Revolution 404–243 B.C.* New York: Arno Press

David, F.N. (1962). *Games, Gods and Gambling: The Origins and History of Probability and Statistical Ideas from the Earliest Times to the Newtonian Era*. London: Charles and Griffin

Davies, John K. (1996). "Documents and 'Documents' in Fourth-Century Historiography." In Carlier, Pierre (ed.). *Le IVe siècle av. J.-C. Approches historiographiques*. Études anciennes 15. Nancy: de Boccard, 29–39

Dawdy, Shannon Lee (2008). *Building the Devil's Empire : French Colonial New Orleans*. Chicago: University of Chicago Press.

Day, John, Mortimer Chambers (1962). *Aristotle's History of Athenian Democracy*. Berkeley: University of California Press

De Angelis, Franco (2003). *The Development of Two Greek City-States in Archaic Sicily*. Oxford: Oxford University School of Archaeology

De Angelis, Franco (ed.) (2013). *Regionalism and Globalism in Antiquity: Exploring Their Limits*. Colloquia Antiqua 7. Leuven: Peeters

De Angelis, Franco (2016). *Archaic and Classical Greek Sicily: A Social and Economic History*. Oxford: Oxford University Press

Delamard, Julie (2014). "Le pot commun ? Céramiques et identités collectives dans quelques apoikiai de Sicile archaïque." *Dialogues d'Histoire Ancienne* Suppl. 10. *Identité ethnique et culture matérielle dans le monde grec*, 83–114

De Mauro, Battilana (1985). *Moira e aisa in Omero: Una richerca semantica e socio-culturale*. Rome: Edizioni dell' Ateneo

Demetriou, Denise. (2012). *Negotiating Identity in the Ancient Mediterranean : the Archaic and Classical Greek Multiethnic Emporia*. Cambridge: Cambridge University Press

Demont, Paul (2000). "Lots héroïques: Remarques sur le tirage au sort de l'*Iliade* aux *Sept contre Thèbes* d'Eschyle." *REG* 133: 299–325

Demont, Paul (2001). "Le tirage au sort des magistrats à Athènes: un problème historique et historiographique." In Cordano, Grottanelli (eds.) (2001), 63–82

Demont, Paul (2010). "Allotment and Democracy in Ancient Greece." *Books and Ideas*. Collège de France, 13 December 2010, https://booksandideas.net/Allotment-and-Democracy-in-Ancient.html

Demont, Paul (2014). "Platon et le tirage au sort." In Fumaroli, M., Jouanna, J., Trédé-Boulmer, M., et al. (eds.). *Hommage à Jacqueline de Romilly: l'empreinte de son œuvre*. Paris: Académie des Inscriptions et Belles-Lettres, 141–159

Demont, Paul (2020). "Selection by Lot in Ancient Athens: From Religion to Politics." In Lopez-Rabatel, Sintomer (eds.)., 112–129
Dercksen, J.G. (2004). *Old Assyrian Institutions.* Leiden: NINO
D'Ercole, Maria Cecilia (2012). *Histoires méditeranéennes.* Arles: Éditions Errance
De Siena, A. (2001). "Il territorio del Metaponto." *Problemi della chora coloniale dall' Occidente al Mar Nero. Atti del quarantesimo convegno di studi sulla Magna Grecia, Taranto, 29 settembre–3 ottobre 2000.* Taranto: Istituto per la storia e l'archeologia della Magna Grecia, 757–769
De Ste. Croix, G.E.M. (2004a). "Archons and Strategoi." In id., *Athenian Democratic Origins and Other Essays.* Harvey, D., Parker, R. (eds.) with assistance of P. Thonemann. Oxford: Oxford University Press, 215–228
De Ste. Croix, G.E.M. (2004b). "Five Notes on Solon's Constitution." In id., *Athenian Democratic Origins and Other Essays.* Harvey, D., Parker, R. (eds.) with assistance of P. Thonemann. Oxford: Oxford University Press, 73–106
Detienne, Marcel (1965). "En Grèce archaique: géometrie, politique et société." *Annales ESC* 20 (3): 425–441
Detienne, Marcel (2007). *The Greeks and Us: A Comparative Anthropology of Ancient Greece.* Cambridge: Polity Press
Detienne, Marcel, Svenbro, Jasper (1979). "Les loups au festin ou la cité impossible." In Detienne, Marcel, Vernant, Jean-Pierre (eds.). *La cuisine du sacrifice en pays grec.* Paris: Gallimard, 215–237
Detienne, Marcel, Vernant, Jean-Pierre (eds.) ([1981] 1989). *The Cuisine of Sacrifice among the Greeks.* Wissing, Paula (trans.). Chicago: University of Chicago Press
Develin, Robert (1979). "The Election of Archons from Solon to Telesinos." *AC* 48: 455–468
Develin, Robert (1984). "From Panathenaia to Panathenaia." *ZPE* 57: 133–138
Develin, Robert (1989). *Athenian Officials 684–321 BC.* Cambridge: Cambridge University Press
Diels, Hermann, and Walther Kranz (1956). *Die Fragmente der Vorsokratiker.* Berlin: Weidmannsche Verlagsbuchhandlung
Dieterle, Martina (2007). *Dodona: religionsgeschichtliche und historische Untersuchungen zur Entstehung und Entwicklung des Zeus-Heiligtums.* Hildesheim: G. Olms
Dietrich, Bernard C. (1962). "The Spinning Fate of Homer." *Phoenix* 16 (2): 86–101
Dietrich, Bernard C. (1965). *Death, Fate, and the Gods: The Development of a Religious Idea in Greek Popular Belief and in Homer.* London: University of London, Athlone
Dignas, Beate (2002). *Economy of the Sacred in Hellenistic and Roman Asia Minor.* Oxford: Oxford University Press
Dignas, Beate, Trampedach, Kai (eds.) (2008). *Practitioners of the Divine: Greek Priests and Religious Officials from Homer to Heliodorus.* Cambridge, MA: Harvard University Press
Dillon, Matthew, Eidinow, Esther, Maurizio, Lisa (eds.) (2017). *Women's Ritual Competence in the Greco-Roman Mediterranean.* London: Routledge, Taylor & Francis
Dilts, M.R. (1971). *Heraclidis Lembi excerpta politiarum.* Greek, Roman and Byzantine Monographs 5. Durham, NC: Duke University Press
Di Salvatore, Massimo (2001). "Il sorteggio tra politica e religione: un caso tesalico." In Cordano, Grottanelli (eds.), 119–130
Dmitriev, Sviatoslav (2005). *City Government in Hellenistic and Roman Asia Minor.* Oxford: Oxford University Press

Dmitriev, Sviatoslav (2017). *The Birth of the Athenian Community*. London: Routledge
Donlan, Walter (1975). "Changes and Shifts in the Meaning of *demos* in the Literature of the Archaic Period." *PP* 25: 381–395
Donlan, Walter (1989). "Homeric *temenos* and the Land Economy of the Dark Age." *MH* 46 (3): 129–145
Donlan, Walter (1999). *The Aristocratic Ideal and Selected Papers*. Wauconda, IL: Bolchazy-Carducci Publishers
Donlan, Walter (1998). "Odysseus and the *hetairoi*." In Gill, C., Postlethwaite, N., Seaford, R. (eds.). *Reciprocity in Ancient Greece*. Oxford: Oxford University Press, 51–71
Donnay, G. (1984). "Instrument divinatoire d'époque romaine." In Balty, Janine (ed.). *Apamée de Syrie: Bilan des recherches archéologiques, 1973–1979*. Brussels: Centre belge de recherches archéologiques à Apamée de Syrie, 203–210
Donnellan, Lieve, Nizzo, Valentino, Burgers, Gert-Jan (eds.) (2016). *Conceptualizing Early Colonisation*. Rome: Academia Belgica
Dover, K.J. (1974). *Greek Popular Morality in the Time of Plato and Aristotle*. Oxford: Blackwell
Dowlen, Oliver (2008). *The Political Potential of Sortition: A Study of the Random Selection of Citizens for Public Office*. Exeter: Imprint Academic
Dowlen, Oliver (2009). "Sorting Out Sortition: A Perspective on the Random Selection of Political Officers." *Political Studies* 57: 298–315; doi: 10.1111/j.1467-9248.2008.00746.x
Dowlen, Oliver, Delannoi, Gil (eds.) (2010). *Sortition: Theory and Practice*. Exeter: Imprint Academic
Dreher, M. (2013). "Die Herausbildung eines politischen Instruments: die Amnestie bis zum Ende der klassischen Zeit." In Harter-Uibopuu, K., Mitthof, F. (eds.). *Vergeben und Vergessen? Amnestie in der Antike. Beiträge zum ersten Wiener Kolloquium zur antiken Rechtsgeschichte*. Vienna: Holzhausen, 71–94
Drews, Robert (1983). *Basileus: The Evidence for Kingship in Geometric Greece*. New Haven, CT: Yale University Press
Dubois, L. (1989). *Inscriptions grecques dialectales de Sicile*. Vol. 1. Geneva: Droz
Dubois, L. (2008). *Inscriptions grecques dialectales de Sicile*. Vol. 2. Geneva: Droz
Dunbabin, T. J. (1948). *The Western Greeks: the History of Sicily and South Italy from the Foundation of the Greek Colonies to 480 B.C.* Oxford: Clarendon Press
Duplouy, Alain (2006). *Le prestige des élites: recherches sur les modes de reconnaissance sociale en Grèce entre les Xe et Ve siècles avant J.-C*. Paris: Les Belles Lettres
Duplouy, Alain (2014). "Les prétendues classes censitaires soloniennes ; à propos de la citoyenneté athénienne archaïque." *Annales HSS* 69: 629–658
Duplouy, Alain (2019). *Construire la cité: essai de sociologie historique sur les communautés de l'archaïsme grec*. Paris: Les Belles Lettres
Duplouy, Alain, Brock, Roger (eds.) (2018). *Defining Citizenship in Archaic Greece*. Oxford: Oxford University Press
Dušanić, S. (1978). "The *horkion tōn oikistērōn* and Fourth-Century Cyrene." *Chiron* 8: 55–76
Duval, Nancy (2016). *La divination par les sorts dans le monde oriental méditerranéen du IIe au VIe siècle après J.-C.: Étude comparative des sortes Homericae, sortes Astrampsychi et tables d'astragalomancie en Asie mineure*. Thesis, Université de Montréal
Duxbury, Neil (1999). *Random Justice: On Lotteries and Legal Decision-Making*. Oxford: Oxford University Press

Edwards, Mark W. (2011).g "Moira." In Finkelberg, Margalit (ed.). *The Homer Encyclopedia*. 3 vols. Chichester: Wiley-Blackwell, 526–527
Egleston Robbins, F. (1916). "The Lot Oracle at Delphi." *ClPh* 11 (3): 278–92
Eherenberg, Victor (1948). "The Foundation of Thurii." *AJPh* 69: 149–170
Ehrenberg, Victor (1927). "Losung." *RE* XIII, 2: col. 1451–1504
Ehrenberg, Victor (1969). *The Greek State*. 2nd ed. London: Methuen
Eidinow, Esther (2007). *Oracles, Curses, and Risk among the Ancient Greeks*. Oxford: Oxford University Press
Eidinow, Esther (2011). *Fate, Luck and Fortune: Antiquity and Its Legacy*. London: I.B. Tauris
Eidinow, Esther (2013). "Oracular Consulting, Fate and the Concept of the Individual." In Rosenberger, Veit (ed.). *Divination in the Ancient World: Religious Options and the Individual*. Potsdamer Altertumswissenschaftliche Beiträge 46. Stuttgart: Franz Steiner, 21–39
Eijnde, Floris van den (2010). *Cult and Society in Early Athens, 1000-600 BCE. Archaeological and Anthropological Approaches to State Formation and Group Participation in Attica*. PhD thesis, Utrecht
Eijnde, Floris van den, Josine Blok, Rolf Strootman (eds.) (2018). *Feasting and Polis Institutions*. Mnemosyne Suppl. 414 Leiden: Brill
Ekroth, Gunnel (2008a). "Burnt, Cooked or Raw? Divine and Human Culinary Desires at Greek Animal Sacrifice." In Stavrianopoulou, Eftychia (ed.). *Transformations in Sacrificial Practices: From Antiquity to Modern Times*. Berlin: Lit Verlag, 87–111
Ekroth, Gunnel (2008b). "Meat, Man and God: On the Division of the Animal Victim at Greek Sacrifices." In Matthaiou, Angelos, Polinskaya, Irene (eds.). Μικρός Ιερομνήμων. Μελέτες εις μνήμην *Michael H. Jameson*. Athens: Greek Epigraphical Society, 259–290
Ekroth, Gunnel (2011). "Meat for the Gods." In Pirenne-Delforge, Vinciane, Prescendi, Francesca (eds.). *Nourrir les Dieux? Sacrifice et représentation du divin*. Liège: Centre international d'etude de la religion grecque antique, 15–41
Ekroth, Gunnel (2020). "*École de Paris*: Praising or Debasing an Approach to the Study of Greek Sacrifice." *Cahiers des Mondes Anciens* 13: 1ff.; https://doi.org/10.4000/mondes anciens.2764
Elgavish, David (2002). "The Division of the Spoils of War in the Bible and in the Ancient Near East." *Zeitschrift für altorientalische und Biblische Rechtsgeschichte* 8: 242–273
Elster, Jon (1992). *Local Justice: How Institutions Allocate Scarce Goods and Necessary Burdens*. New York: Russell Sage Foundation
Engelstad, F. (1989). "The Assignment of Political Office by Lot." *Social Science Information* 28: 23–50
Exquemelin, Alexander O. ([1678; 1969] 2000). *The Buccaneers of America*. Brown, Alexis (trans.). Mineola, NY: Dover Publications. Orig. *De Americaensche Zee-rovers* [in Dutch]. Amsterdam: Jan ten Hoorn
Fabiani, Roberta (2012). "*Dedochthai tei boulei kai toi demoi*: protagonisti e prassi della procedura deliberativa a Iasos." In Mann, Scholz (eds.), 109–65
Faraguna, Michele (2015). "Citizen Registers in Archaic Greece: The Evidence Reconsidered." In Matthaiou, Papazarkadas (eds.), 649–667
Faraguna, Michele (2017). "Documents, Public Information and the Historian: Perspectives on Fifth-Century Athens." *Historiká* (Torino.) 7: p. 23–52.
Farnell, Lewis Richard ([1921] 1971). *The Cults of the Greek States*. Chicago: Aegean Press

Farrar, Cynthia (2010). "Taking Our Chances with the Ancient Athenians." In Pasquino, Pasquale, Hansen, Mogens Herman, Hernández, Alain-Christian (eds.). *Démocratie Athénienne, Démocratie Moderne: Tradition et influences: neuf exposés suivis de discussions. Vandœuvres, 2009.* Vandoevres: Fondation Hardt; Entretiens sur l'Antiquité Classique, 56, 167–217, 217–234

Ferrara, Silvia, Valério, Miguel (2017). "Contexts and Repetitions of Cypro-Minoan Inscriptions: Function and Subject-Matter of the Clay Balls." *BASO* 378: 71–94

Figueira, Thomas (1984). "The Lipari Islanders and Their System of Communal Property." *ClAnt* 3 (2): 179–206

Figueira, Thomas (1985). "Theognidea and the Megarian Society." In Figueira, Thomas J., Nagy, Gregory (eds.). *Theognis of Megara: Poetry and the Polis.* Baltimore: Johns Hopkins University Press, 112–158

Figueira, Thomas (1991). *Athens and Aigina at the Age of Imperial Colonization.* Baltimore: Johns Hopkins University Press

Figueira, Thomas (2008). "Classical Greek Colonization." In Tsetskhladze, G.R. (ed.). *A History of Greek Colonisation and Settlement Overseas.* Leiden: Brill, 427–523

Figueira, Thomas (2015). "Modes of Colonization and Elite Integration in Archaic Greece." In Fisher, van Wees (eds.), 313–347

Finkel, I.L., Reade, J.E. (1995). "Lots of Eponyms." *Iraq* 57: 167–172

Finkelberg, Margalit (1991). "Royal Succession in Heroic Greece." *CQ* 41: 303–316

Finkelberg, Margalit (1998). "*Timē* and *aretē* in Homer." *CQ* 48: 14–28

Finley, Moses I. (1978). *The World of Odysseus.* New York: Viking Press

Finley, Moses I. ([1979] 1987). *A History of Sicily.* New York: E. Sifton Books/Viking

Finley, Moses I., et al. (eds.) (1973). *Problèmes de la terre en Grèce Ancienne.* Centre de Recherches Comparées sur les Sociétés Anciennes. Paris: Mouton Civilisations et Sociétés

Fischer-Hansen, Tobias. (1996). "The Earliest Town-Planning of the Western Greek Colonies, with Special Regard to Sicily." In Hansen, Mogens Herman (ed.). *Introduction to an Inventory of Poleis: Copenhagen Polis Centre 3.* Copenhagen: Royal Danish Academy of Sciences and Letters, 317–373

Fischer-Hansen, Tobias, Nielsen, Thomas Heine, Ampolo, Carmine (2004). "Sikelia." In Hansen, Mogens Herman, Nielsen, Thomas Heine (eds.). *An Inventory of Archaic and Classical Poleis.* Oxford: Oxford University Press, no. 34

Fisher, Nick, Wees, Hans van (2015a). "The Trouble with 'Aristocracy.'" In Fisher, van Wees (eds.), 1–57

Fisher, Nick, Wees, Hans van (eds.) (2015). *Aristocracy in Antiquity: Redefining Greek and Roman Elites.* Swansea: Classical Press of Wales

Fishkin, James S. (2009). *When the People Speak: Deliberative Democracy and Public Consultation,* New York: Oxford University Press

Fishkin, James S. (2018). *Democracy When the People Are Thinking: Revitalizing Our Politics through Public Deliberation.* Oxford: Oxford University Press

Fitzjohn, Matthew (2007). "Equality in the Colonies: Concepts of Equality in Sicily during the Eighth to Sixth Centuries BC." *World Archaeology* (Theme issue: *The Archaeology of Equality*) 39 (2): 215–228.

Flacelière, R. (1950). "Le délire de la Pythie est-il une légende?" *REA* 52: 306–324

Fleck, Robert K., Hanssen, F. Andrew (2018). "What Can Data Drawn from the Hansen-Nielsen *Inventory* Tell Us about Political Transitions in Ancient Greece?" In Canevaro, Erskine, Gray, Ober (eds.), 213–238

Fontenrose, J. (1978). *The Delphic Oracle: Its Responses and Operations with a Catalogue of Responses*. Berkeley: University of California Press

Fornara, Charles W., Samons, Loren J., II (1991). *Athens from Cleisthenes to Pericles*. Berkeley: University of California Press

Forsdyke, Sara (2005). *Exile, Ostracism, and Democracy. The Politics of Expulsion in Ancient Greece*. Princeton, NJ: Princeton University Press

Foster, Margaret (2018). *The Seer and the City: Religion, Politics, and Colonial Ideology in Ancient Greece*. Oakland: University of California Press

Foxhall, Lin (1997). "A View from the Top: Evaluating the Solonian Property Classes." In Mitchell, L.G., Rhodes P.J. (eds.). *The Development of the Polis in Archaic Greece*. London: Routledge, 113–136

Foxhall, Lin (2002). "Access to Resources in Classical Greece: The Egalitarianism of the Polis in Practice." In Cartledge, Paul, Cohen, Edward, Foxhall, Lin (eds.). *Money, Labour and Land: Approaches to the Economics of Ancient Greece*. London: Routledge, 209–220

Foxhall, Lin, Yoon, D. (2016). "Carving Out a Territory: Rhegion, Locri and the Households and Communities of the Classical Countryside." *World Archaeology* 48 (3): 431–448

Franklin, John C. (2006). "Lyre Gods of the Bronze Age Musical Koine." *JANER* 6: 39–70

Franklin, John C. (2007). "The Global Economy of Music in the Ancient Near East." In Westenholz, J.G. (ed.). *The Sounds of Ancient Music: Instruments from the Ancient World*. Jerusalem: Keter Press, 27–37

Frasca, M. (2009). *Leontinoi: Archeologia di una colonia greca*. Rome: G. Bretschneider

Fraser, P.M. (1958). "Inscriptions from Cyrene." *Berytus* 12: 101–128

Frazer, James George (1898). *Pausanias's Description of Greece*. London: Macmillan

Frederiksen, R. (2011). *Greek City Walls of the Archaic Period 900–480 BC*. Oxford: Oxford University Press

French, Robert P., II (2016). "The Fuzziness of Mindsets: Divergent Conceptualizations and Characterizations of Mindset Theory and Praxis." *International Journal of Organizational Analysis* 24 (4): 673–691; https://doi.org/10.1108/IJOA-09-2014-0797

Friedl, Ernestine (1963). *Vasilika: A Village in Modern Greece*. Case Studies in Cultural Anthropology. New York: Holt, Rinehart and Winston

Frisk, H. (1960). *Griechisches Etymologisches Wörterbuch*. Heidelberg: Winter Verlag

Fröhlich, Pierre (2013). "Governmental Checks and Balances." In Beck (ed.), 252–266

Fuks, A. (1968). "Redistribution of Land and Houses in Syracuse in 356 B.C. and Its Ideological Aspects." *CQ* 18 (2): 207–223

Fumagalli, Roberto (2021). "We Should Not Use Randomization Procedures to Allocate Scarce Life-Saving Resources." *Public Health Ethics*, 1–17, https://academic.oup.com/phe/advance-article/doi/10.1093/phe/phab025/6444252

Funke, Peter (2015). "Aitolia and the Aitolian League." In Beck, Hans, Funke, Peter (eds.). *Federalism in Greek Antiquity*. Cambridge: Cambridge University Press, 86–117

Fustel de Coulanges, N.D. ([1864] 1984). *La cité antique*. Paris: Librairie Hachette. Rev. ed. Paris: Flammarion

Fustel de Coulanges, N.D. (1891). "Recherches sur le tirage au sort appliqué à la nomination des archontes athéniens." *Nouvelle revue historique de droit français et étranger* 2: 613–643. Reprinted from Jullian, Camille (ed.) ([1891] 1979). *Nouvelles recherches sur quelques problemes d'histoire*. Paris: Hachette; New York: Arno Press

Gabba, E. (1981). "True History and False History in Classical Antiquity." *JRS* 71: 50–62

Gabrielsen, Vincent ([1994] 2010). *Financing the Athenian Fleet: Public Taxation and Social Relations*. Baltimore. Johns Hopkins University Press, e-book

Gagarin, Michael (1986). *Early Greek Law*. Berkeley: University of California Press

Gagarin, Michael (2006). "Legal Procedure in Solon's Laws." In Blok, Lardinois (eds.), 261–275

Gagarin, Michael (2008). *Writing Greek Law*. Cambridge: Cambridge University Press

Gagarin, Michael, Cohen, David (eds.) (2005). *The Cambridge Companion to Ancient Greek Law*. Cambridge Companions to the Ancient World. Cambridge: Cambridge University Press

Gaifman, M. (2018). *The Art of Libation in Classical Athens*. New Haven, CT: Yale University Press

Gaisford, T. (ed.) ([1848]. *Etymologicon magnum seu Verius lexicon saepissime vocabulorum origines indagans ex pluribus lexicis scholiastis et grammaticis anonymi cuiusdam opera concinnatum*. Edited by Thomas Gaisford. Oxonii: E. Typographeo academico, 1848

Gallo, L. (2009). "L'isomoiria: Realtà o mito? In Antonetti, Claudia, Di Vido, S. (eds.). *Temi selinuntini*. Pisa: Edizioni ETS, 129–136

Gantz, Timothy (1993). *Early Greek Myth: a Guide to Literary and Artistic Sources*. Baltimore: Johns Hopkins University Press

Garlan, Y. (1989). *Le partage entre alliés des dépenses et des profits de guerre*. In id., Guerre et économie en Grèce ancienne, Paris: La Decouverte, 41–55

Gastil, J., Wright, E.O. (2018). "Legislature by Lot: Envisioning Sortition within a Bicameral System." *Politics & Society* 46 (Theme issue: *Legislature by Lot: Transformative Designs for Deliberative Governance*): 303–330

Gataker, Thomas ([1627, 2008] 2013). *On the Nature and Uses of Lotteries: A Historical and Theological Treatise*, Boyle, C. (ed.). Exeter: Imprint Academic

Gauthier, Philippe (1966). "Les clérouques de Lesbos et la colonisation athénienne au Ve siècle." *REG* 79: 64–88; DOI: 10.3406/reg.1966.3859

Gauthier, Philippe (1973). "À propos des clérouquies athéniennes du Ve siècle." In Finley et al. (eds.), 163–178

Gavrilov, A.V. (2006). "Theodosia and Its Chora in Antiquity." In Guldager Bilde, Pia, Stolba, Vladimir F. (eds.). *Surveying the Greek Chora: The Black Sea Region in a Comparative Perspective*. BSS 4. Aarhus: University of Aarhus Press, 249–272

Gehrke, Hans-Joachim (1985). *Stasis: Untersuchungen zu den inneren Kriegen in den griechischen Staaten des 5. und 4. Jahrhunderts v. Chr.* Munich: Beck Verlag

Gehrke, Hans-Joachim (2006). "The Figure of Solon in the *Athēnaiōn Politeia*." In Blok, Lardinois (eds.), 276–289

Georgoudi, Stella, Koch Piettre, Renée, Schmidt, Francis (eds.) (2012). *La raison des signes: présages, rites, destin dans les sociétés de la méditerranée ancienne*. Leiden: Brill

Gerber, Douglas E. (1999). *Greek iambic poetry from the seventh to the fifth centuries BC*. Cambridge, Mass.: Harvard University Press

Giangiulio, Maurizio (2015). *Democrazie greche: Atene, Sicilia, Magna Grecia*, Rome: Carocci

Giangiulio, Maurizio (2016). "Aristokrazie in discussione. Verso un nuovo modello per la società greca arcaica?" *Incidenza del antico* 14: 305–317

Giangiulio, Maurizio (2017). "Looking for Citizenship in Archaic Greece. Methodological and Historical Problems." In Cecchet and Busetto, 33–49

Giangiulio, Maurizio (2018). "Oligarchies of 'Fixed Number' or Citizen Bodies in the Making?" In Duplouy, Brock (eds.), 275–294
Gill, D., Postlethwaite, N., Seaford, R. (eds.) (1998). *Reciprocity in Ancient Greece*. Oxford: Oxford University Press
Glotz, G. (1907). "Sortitio." In Daremberg, C., Saglio, E., Pottiers, E. (eds.). *Dictionnaire des antiquités grecques et romaines*. Paris: Hachette, 4:1401–1417
Glotz, G. ([1928] 1988). *La Cité grecque*. Paris: Albin Michel
Goodwin, Barbara ([1992] 2005). *Justice by Lottery*. Exeter: Imprint Academic
Gordon, Aaron (2014). "Does Randomness Actually Exist?" *Pacific Standard* (August 2014; updated June 2017), https://psmag.com/social-justice/free-will-enigma-machine-code-randomness-actually-exist-89285
Gordon, Richard L. (2012). "*Molpoi*." In *BNP* Online https://referenceworks-brillonline-com.ezproxy-prd.bodleian.ox.ac.uk/search?s.f.s2_parent=s.f.cluster.New+Pauly+Online&search-go=&s.q=Molpoi
Graeber, David (2001). *Toward an Anthropological Theory of Value: The False Coin of Our Dreams*. New York: Palgrave
Graf, Fritz (1974). "Das Kollegium der Molpoi von Olbia." *MH* 31: 209–215
Graf, Fritz (2002). "*Aisa*." In *BNP* Online https://referenceworks-brillonline-com.ezproxy-prd.bodleian.ox.ac.uk/search?s.f.s2_parent=s.f.cluster.New+Pauly+Online&search-go=&s.q=Aisa
Graf, Fritz (2005). "Rolling the Dice for an Answer." In Johnston, Struck (eds.), 51–99
Graham, A.J. (1960). "The Authenticity of the *horkiōn tōn oikisterōn* of Cyrene." *JHS* 80: 94–111
Graham, A. J. (1978). The Foundation of Thasos. *The Annual of the British School at Athens* 73: 61–98.
Graham, A.J. (1982). "The Colonial Expansion of Greece;" "The Western Greeks." *Cambridge Ancient History* Vol. III pt.3 chs. 37, 38
Graham, A.J. (1983). *Colony and Mother City in Ancient Greece*. 2nd ed. Chicago: Ares
Graham, A.J. (1984): "Religion, Women, and Greek Colonization." In A.J. Graham, *Collected Papers on Greek Colonization* [Leiden: Brill 2001], 327–48
Graham, A.J. ([1988] 2001). "Megara Hyblaia and the Sicels." In id., *Collected Papers on Greek Colonization*. Leiden: Brill, 150–164
Granovetter, Mark (1973). "The Strength of Weak Ties." *American Journal of Sociology* 78 (6): 1360–1380
Granovetter, Mark (1983). "The Strength of Weak Ties: A Network Theory Revisited." *Sociological Theory* 1: 201–233
Grant, Jill (2001). "The Dark Side of the Grid: Power and Urban Design." *Planning Perspectives* 16: 219–241
Gras, Michel (2019/2021). "De Cumes à Rome. *Kleroi* et *Bina Jugera*." *Parola del Passato* 74: 5–26
Gras, Michel, Tréziny, Henri (2017). "Groupements civiques et organisation urbaine à Mégara Hyblaea." *Aristonothos* 13 (2): 145–170
Gras, Michel, Tréziny, Henri, Broise, Henri (2004). *Mégara Hyblaea*. Vol. 5: *La ville archaïque*. Paris: École française de Rome
Gray, Benjamin (2015). *Stasis and Stability: Exile, the Polis, and Political Thought, c. 404–146 BC*. Oxford: Oxford University Press
Greaves, A.M. (2012). "Divination at Archaic Branchidai-Didyma: A Critical Review." *Hesperia* 81 (2): 177–206

Greco, Emanuele, Lombardo, Mario (2012). "La colonizzazione greca: modelli interpretativi nel dibattito attuale." In *Alle origini della Magna Grecia. Mobilità, migrazioni, fondazioni. Atti del L Convegno di Studi sulla Magna Grecia, Taranto 1–4 ottobre 2010*. Taranto: Istituto per la storia e l'archeologia della Magna Grecia, 37–60

Greely, H. (1977). "The Equality of Allocation by Lot." *Harvard Civil Rights–Civil Liberties Law Review* 12: 113–141

Green, A. (2008). *Cultural History*. New York: Palgrave Macmillan

Greene, W. Ch. (1944). *Moira: Fate, Good, and Evil in Ancient Greek Thought*. Cambridge, MA: Harvard University Press

Grieb, Volker (2008). *Hellenistische Demokratie. Politische Organisation und Struktur in freien griechischen Poleis nach Alexander dem Grossen*. Stuttgart: Franz Steiner

Grote, Oliver (2016). *Die griechischen Phylen. Funktion–Entstehung–Leistungen*. Stuttgart: Franz Steiner

Grottanelli, Cristiano (2001). "La cléromancie ancienne et le dieu Hermès." In Cordano, Grottanelli (eds.), 155–196

Grottanelli, C. (2005). "*Sorte unica pro casibuc pluribus enotata*: Literary Texts and Lot Inscriptions as Sources for Ancient Kleromancy." In Johnston, Struck (eds.), 129–146

Guarducci, Margherita (1967). *Epigrafia greca*. Rome: Istituto Poligrafico dello Stato, Libreria dello Stato

Guidorizzi, Giulio (2001). "Aspetti miti del sorteggio." In Cordano, Grottanelli (eds.), 41–54

Guldager Bilde, Pia, Stolba, Vladimir F. (2006). *Surveying the Greek Chora: Black Sea Region in a Comparative Perspective*. Aarhus: Aarhus University Press

Guzzo, P.G. (2013). "Caronda e coloro che si nutrono dalo stesso granario. Ipotesi sulle strutture circolari di Megara Hyblea, Selinunte e Himera." *MDAI (Rom.)* 119: 33–42

Gysembergh, Victor (2013). "Le tirage au sort des provinces divines chez Homère (*Iliade* 15, 185–199) et ses antécédents mésopotamiens: un état de la question." *REG* 126 (1): 49–64

Hadzis, C. (1995). "Fêtes et cultes à Corcyre et à Corinthe: calendrier d'Epire, calendriers des cités coloniales de l'Ouest et calendrier de Corinthe." In *Corinto e l'Occidente. Atti del trentaquattresimo convegno di studi sulla Magna Grecia, Taranto, 7–11 ottobre 1994*. Taranto: Istituto per la storia e l'archeologia della Magna Greca, 445–452

Hahn, I. (1977). "*Temenos* and Service Land in the Homeric Epics." *AAntHung* 25: 299–316

Hall, Jonathan M. (1997). *Ethnic Identity in Greek Antiquity*. Cambridge: Cambridge University Press

Hall, Jonathan M. (2004). "How 'Greek' Were the Early Western Greeks?" In Lomas, Kathryn (ed.). *Greek Identity in the Western Mediterranean*. Leiden: Brill, 35–54

Hall, Jonathan M. ([2007] 2014). *A History of the Archaic Greek World, ca. 1200–479 BCE*. 2nd ed. Hoboken, NJ: Wiley-Blackwell

Hall, Jonathan M. (2013). "The Rise of State Action in the Archaic Age." In Beck (ed.), 9–21

Hall, Jonathan M. (2014). *Artifact & Artifice: Classical Archaeology and the Ancient Historian*. Chicago: University of Chicago Press

Halliday, William Reginald (1913). *Greek Divination: A Study of Its Methods and Principles*. London: Macmillan

Hammer, D. (2005). "Plebiscitary Politics in Archaic Greece." *Historia* 54 (2): 107–131

Hamon, P. (2012). "Gleichheit, Ungleichheit und Euergetismus: die *isotes* in den kleinasiatischen Poleis der hellenistischen Zeit." In Mann, Scholz (eds.) 56–73

Hanell, Krister (1934). *Megarische Studien*. Lund: Lindstedts Universitetsbokhandel

Hansen, Mogens H. (1980). "Seven Hundred *archai* in Classical Athens." *GRBS* 21: 151–173
Hansen, Mogens H. (1986). *Demography and Democracy: The Number of Athenian Citizens in the Fourth Century BC*. Herning, Denmark: Systime
Hansen, Mogens H. (1989). *The Athenian Ecclesia II: A Collection of Articles 1983–89* Copenhagen: Museum Tusculanum Press
Hansen, Mogens H. (1990). "When Was Selection by Lots of Magistrates Introduced in Athens?" *C&M* 41: 55–61
Hansen, Mogens H. (1991). *The Athenian Democracy in the Age of Demosthenes*. 2nd ed. London: Duckworth / Bristol Classical Press
Hansen, Mogens H. (2006). *Polis: An Introduction to the Greek City-State*. Oxford: Oxford University Press
Hansen, Mogens H., Nielsen, Thomas Heine (eds.) (2004). *An Inventory of Archaic and Classical Poleis: An Investigation Conducted by the Copenhagen Polis Centre for the Danish National Research Foundation*. Oxford: Oxford University Press
Hanson, Victor D. (1995). *The Other Greeks: The Family Farm and the Agrarian Roots of Western Civilization*. Berkeley: University of California Press
Harding, Philip E. (1994). *Androtion and the Atthis*. Oxford: Oxford University Press
Harris, Diane (1995). *The Treasures of the Parthenon and the Erechtheion*. Oxford: Clarendon Press
Harris, Edward M. (2006). "Solon and the Spirit of the Laws in Archaic and Classical Greece." In id., *Democracy and the Rule of Law in Classical Athens: Essays on Law, Society, and Politics*. Cambridge: Cambridge University Press, 3–28
Harrison, Thomas (2000). *Divinity and History: The Religion of Herodotus*. Oxford: Oxford University Press
Hartmann, E., Schaeffer, C. (2006). "Preisrichter oder Publikum? Zur Urteilsfindung in den dramatischen Wettkämpfen des klassischen Athen." *Klio* 88: 96–116
Harvey, F.D. (1965). "Two Kinds of Equality." *C&M* 26: 101–146
Havelock, Eric A. (1978). *The Greek Concept of Justice: From Its Shadow in Homer to Its Substance in Plato*. Cambridge, MA: Harvard University Press
Headlam, James W. ([1891] 1933²). *Elections by Lot at Athens*. Cambridge: Cambridge University Press
Helly, B. (1995). *L'état thessalien: Aleuas le Rouge, les tétrades et les tagoi*. Lyon: Maison de l'Orient et de la Méditerranée
Hennig, D. (1980). "Grundbesitz bei Homer und Hesiod." *Chiron* 10: 35–52
Herda, Alexander (2006). *Der Apollon-Delphinios-Kult in Milet und die Neujahrsprozession nach Didyma. Ein neuer Kommentar der sog. Molpoi-Satzung* (*Milesische Forschungen* 4). Mainz: Von Zabern
Hermary, Antoine, Hesnard, Antoinette, Tréziny, Henri (1999). *Marseille grecque: La cité phocéenne (600–49 av. J.-C.)*. Collection Hauts lieux de l'histoire. Paris: Errance
Herzfeld, Michael (1980). "Social Tension and Inheritance by Lot in Three Greek Villages." *Anthropological Quarterly* 53 (2): 91–100
Hitch, Sarah (2009). *King of Sacrifice: Ritual and Royal Authority in the Iliad*. Washington, DC: Center for Hellenic Studies, Trustees for Harvard University, Harvard University Press
Hodkinson, Stephen (1986). "Land Tenure and Inheritance in Classical Sparta." *CQ* 36 (2): 378–406

Hodkinson, Stephen (2000). *Property and Wealth in Classical Sparta.* London: Duckworth; Classical Press of Wales
Hodos, Tamar (1999). "Intermarriage in Western Greek Colonies." *OJA* 18 (1): 61–78
Hodos, Tamar (2006). *Local Responses to Colonization in the Iron Age Mediterranean.* London: Routledge
Hoepfner, Wolfram, Schwandner, Ernst-Ludwig, Dakaris, Sotiris, Boessneck, Joachim (1994). *Haus und Stadt im klassischen Griechenland. Wohnen in der klassischen Polis;* Bd. 1. Munich: Deutscher Kunstverlag
Hofstee, Willem K.B. (1990). "Allocation by Lot: A Conceptual and Empirical Analysis." *Social Science Information* 29 (4): 745–763. Repr. in Stone (2011b), 201-218
Hölkeskamp, Karl-Joachim (1993). "Demonax und die Neuordnung der Bürgerschaft von Kyrene." *Hermes* 121 (4): 404–421
Hölkeskamp, Karl-Joachim (1994). "Tempel, Agora und Alphabet. Die Entstehungsbedingungen von Gesetzgebung in der archaischen Polis." In Gehrke, H.-J., Wirbelauer, E. (eds.), *Rechtskodifizierung und soziale Normen im interkulturellen Vergleich.* Tübingen: Gunter Narr Verlag, 135–164
Hölkeskamp, Karl-Joachim (1997). "*Agorai* bei Homer." In Eder, W., Hölkeskamp, K.-J. (eds.). *Volk und Verfassung im vorhellenistischen Griechenland. Beiträge auf dem Symposium zu Ehren von Karl-Wilhelm Welwei in Bochum, 1–2 März 1996.* Stuttgart: Franz Steiner, 1–19
Hölkeskamp, Karl-Joachim (1999). *Schiedsrichter, Gesetzgeber und Gesetzgebung im archaischen Griechenland.* Stuttgart: Franz Steiner
Hölkeskamp, Karl-Joachim (2000). "(In-)schrift und Monument. Zum Begriff des Gesetzes im archaischen und klassischen Griechenland." *ZPE* 132: 73–96
Hölkeskamp, Karl-Joachim (2002). "Ptolis and Agore: Homer and the Archaeology of the City-State." In Montanari, F., Ascheri, P. (eds.). *Omero tremilia anni dopo.* Rome: Bretschneider, 297–342
Hölkeskamp, Karl-Joachim (2015). "Pheidon." In *BNP* https://referenceworks-brillonline-com.ezproxy-prd.bodleian.ox.ac.uk/search?s.f.s2_parent=s.f.cluster.New+Pauly+Online&search-go=&s.q=pheidon
Holland, L.B. (1933). "The Mantic Mechanism at Delphi." *AJA* 37: 201–214
Hornblower, Simon (1991). *A Commentary on Thucydides. Vol. 1: Books 1–3.* Oxford: Clarendon Press
Hornblower, Simon (2008). *A Commentary on Thucydides: Vol. 3: Books 5.25–8.109.* Oxford: Oxford University Press
How, W.W., Wells, J. (1928). *A Commentary on Herodotus, with Introduction and Appendixes.* 2 vols. 2nd ed. Oxford: Oxford University Press
Humphreys, Sally C. (1978). *Anthropology and the Greeks.* London: Routledge & K. Paul
Humphreys, Sally C. (2018). *Kinship in Ancient Athens: An Anthropological Analysis.* 2 vols. Oxford: Oxford University Press
Hurlet, Frédéric (2019). "Le tirage au sort dans les cités de l'Occident romain." In Borlenghi, Aldo, et al. (eds.). *Voter en Grèce, à Rome et en Gaule. Pratiques, lieux et finalités.* Lyon: Maison de l'Orient et de la Méditerranée—Jean Pouilloux, 185–202
Hurt, S. (1992). "The American Continental Grid: Form and Meaning." *Threshold* 2: 32–40
Hurwit, Jeffrey M. (1999). *The Athenian Acropolis: History, Mythology, and Archaeology from the Neolithic Era to the Present.* Cambridge: Cambridge University Press
Hutton, Patrick (1981). "The History of Mentalities: The New Map of Cultural History." *History and Theory.* 20 (3): 239; doi:10.2307/2504556

Igelbrink, Christian (2015). *Die Kleruchien und Apoikien Athens im 6. und 5. Jahrhundert v. Chr.: Rechtsformen und politische Funktionen der athenischen Gründungen.* Berlin: De Gruyter
Ismard, Paulin (2007). "Les associations en Attique de Solon à Clisthène." In Couvenhes, J.-C., Milanezi, S. (eds.). *Individus, groupes et politique à Athènes de Solon à Mithridate.* Tours: Presses universitaires François-Rabelais, 17–33
Ismard, Paulin (2010). *La cité des réseaux: Athènes et ses associations, Vie–Ier siècle av. J-C.* Paris: Publications de la Sorbonne
Ivanov, V. (1999). "An Ancient Name of the Lyre." In Ivanov, V.V., Vine, B. (eds.). *UCLA Indo-European Studies.* Vol. 1. Los Angeles: University of California Press, 265–287
Jackman, Trinity (2005). *Political Communities in the Greek Colonies of Archaic and Classical Sicily and Southern Italy.* PhD Phil, Stanford University
Jackson, M. (1978). "Ambivalence and the Last-Born: Birth-Order Position in Convention and Myth." *Man*, n.s. 13 (3): 341–361
Jacquemin, Anne (1993). "Oikiste et tyran: fondateur-monarque et monarque-fondateur dans l'Occident grec." *Ktema* 18: 19–27
Jaillard, Dominique (2012). "Hermès et la mantique grecque." In Georgoudi et al. (eds.), 91–107
James, G.M.G. ([1954] 1992). *Stolen Legacy: Greek Philosophy Is Stolen Egyptian Philosophy.* Trenton, NJ: Africa World Press
Jameson, Michael H., David R. Jordan, and Roy D. Kotansky (1993). *A Lex Sacra from Selinous.* Durham: Duke University
Jeffery, Lilian H. (1961). "The Pact of the First Settlers at Cyrene." *Historia* 10: 139–147
Jim, Theodora Suk Fong (2014). *Sharing with the Gods. Aparchai and Dekatai in Ancient Greece.* Oxford: Oxford University Press
Johansson, Mikael (2001). "The Inscription from Troizen: A Decree of Themistocles?" *ZPE* 137: 69–92
Johnston, Sarah Iles (2008). *Ancient Greek Divination.* Malden, MA: Wiley-Blackwell
Johnston, Sarah Iles, Struck, Peter T. (eds.) (2005). *Mantikē: Studies in Ancient Divination.* Leiden: Brill
Jones, Nicholas F. (1975). *Tribal Organization in Dorian Greece.* Ann Arbor, MI: University Microfilms International
Jones, Nicholas F. (1987). *Public Organization in Ancient Greece: A Documentary Study.* Memoirs of the American Philosophical Society 176. Philadelphia: American Philosophical Society
Jones, Nicholas F. (1991). "Enrollment Clauses in Greek Citizenship Decrees" *ZPE* 87: 79–102
Kahneman, Daniel (2011). *Thinking, Fast and Slow.* New York: Farrar, Straus and Giroux
Kaklamani, Olga (with S. Damigos) (in print). "From Thera to Cyrene: Early Society and Complex Networking in the Age of Colonization." In Roncaglia, A, Ranieri, S. (eds.). *Richerce a confront. Dialoghi di antichità classiche e del Vicino Oriente.* Zermeghedo: Edizioni Saecula
Kearns, Emily (1989). *The Heroes of Attica.* London: Institute of Classical Studies, University of London
Kells, J.H. (1973). *Sophocles Electra.* Cambridge: Cambridge University Press.
Kelly, Afrian (2008). "The Babylonian Captivity of Homer: The Case of the Dios Apate." *RhM* 151 (3/4): 259–304

Kidd, Stephan H. (2017). "Greek Dicing, Astragaloi, and the 'Euripides' Throw." *JHS* 137: 112–118
Kierstead, James (2019). "Incentives and Information in Athenian Citizenship Procedures." *Historia* 68 (1): 26–49
Kierstead, James (forthcoming). "The Athenian Jigsaw Tokens." In Gkikaki, M. (ed.). *Tokens in Classical Athens: Politics, Communities and Contexts*. Liverpool: Liverpool University Press
Kierstead, James, Klapaukh, Roman (2018). "The Distribution of Wealthy Athenians in the Attic Demes." In Canevaro, Erskine, Gray, Ober (eds.), 376–401
Kirk, G. S. (Geoffrey Stephen) et al. *The Iliad: a Commentary*. Cambridge: Cambridge University Press, 1985
Kistler, E., et al. (2015). *Sanctuaries and the Power of Consumption: Networking and the Formation of Elites in the Archaic Western Mediterranean World. Proceedings of the International Conference in Innsbruck, 20-23 March 2012*. Wiesbaden: Harrassowitz Verlag
Kitts, M. (2002). "Sacrificial Violence in the Iliad." *Journal of Ritual Studies* 16 (1): 19–39
Knibbeler, E.J.B. (2005). *Saving the City: Ambiguities in Ancient Greek Crisis Management*. PhD thesis, Leiden
Knoepfler, Denis (1989). "Le calendrier des Chalcidiens et de Thrace. Essai de mise au point sur la liste et l'ordre des mois eubéens." *Journal des Savants*, 23–59
Knoepfler, Denis (2000). "La loi de Daitôndas, les femmes de Thèbes et le collège des béotarques au IVe siècle av. J-C." In Bernardini, P. Angeli (ed.), *Presenza e funzione della città di Tebe nella cultura greca. Atti del convegno internazionale di Urbino, 7-9 luglio 1997*. Pisa: Ist. Editoriali e Poligrafici, 345–366
Knoepfler, Denis (2002). "Loi d'Érétrie contre la tyrannie et l'oligarchie (deuxième partie)." *BCH* 126 (1): 149–204
Knoepfler, Denis (2007). "Was There an Anthroponomy of Euboian Origin in the Chalkido-Eretrian Colonies of the West and of Thrace?" *PBA* 148: 87–119
Köcke, L.S. (2012). "Milet stirbt aus?!—Demographische Überlegungen zu Neubürgern in einer hellenistischen Großstadt." In Günther, L.M. (ed.), *Migration und Bürgerrecht in der hellenistischen Welt*. Wiesbaden: Harrassowitz, 41–49
Koerner, R. (1993). *Inschriftliche Gesetzestexte der frühen griechischen Polis. Aus dem Nachlass von Reinhard Koerner*. Hallof, K. (ed.). Cologne: Bohlau
Kolodny, Emile Y. (1974). *La population des îles de la Grèce: essai de géographie insulaire en Méditerranée orientale*. Aix-en-Provence: Édisud
Kosmetatou, E. (2013). "Tyche's Force: Lottery and Chance in Greek Government." In Beck (ed.), 235–251
Koumanoudes, S.A. (1879). "Ἐπιγραφαὶ Ἀττικῆς Ἀνέκδοτοι." *Ἀθήναιον* 8: 231–238
Kovacs, David (1999). *Euripides*. Vol. 4. Loeb Classical Library 10. Cambridge, MA: Harvard University Press
Krinzinger, F. Gassner, V., Kerschner, M., Muss, U. (eds.) (2000). *Die Ägäis und das westliche Mittelmeer: Beziehungen und Wechselwirkungen 8. bis 5. Jh. v. Chr. Akten des Symposions*. Vol. 4. Verlag der Österreichischen Akademie der Wissenschaften
Kristensen, K.R. (1994). "Men, Women and Property in Gortyn: The *Karteros* of the Law Code." *Studia Classica et Mediaevalia* 45: 5–26
Kroll, J.H. (1972). *Athenian Bronze Allotment Plates*. Cambridge, MA: Harvard University Press

Kroll, J.H. (2015). "A Bronze Allotment Plate from Central Greece." In Matthaiou, Papazarkadas (eds.), 595–598
Kron, Uta (1976). *Die zehn attischen Phylenheroen: Geschichte, Mythos, Kult und Darstellungen*. Berlin: Gebr. Mann
Kurke, Leslie (1999). *Coins, Bodies, Games, and Gold: The Politics of Meaning in Archaic Greece*. Princeton, NJ: Princeton University Press
Laffon, Amarande (2016). "La désignation de suppléants par tirage au sort (ἐπιλαχών) dans l'Athènes classique." *REG* 129 (1): 17–37; doi:10.3406/reg.2016.8397
Lambert, Stephen D. (1998²). *The Phratries of Attica*. Ann Arbor: University of Michigan Press
Lambert, Stephen D. (1999). "The Attic *genos*." *CQ*, n.s. 49: 484–489
Lambert, Stephen D. (2002). "The Sacrificial Calendar of Athens." *BSA* 97: 353–399
Lambert, Stephen D. (2010). "A Polis and Its Priests: Athenian Priesthoods before and after Pericles' Citizenship Law." *Historia* 59: 143–175
Lambert, Stephen D. (2012). "The Social Construction of Priests and Priestesses in Athenian Honorific Decrees from the Fourth Century BC to the Augustan Period." In Horster, M., Klöckner, A. (eds.). *Civic Priests. Cult Personnel in Athens from the Hellenistic Period to Late Antiquity*. Berlin: De Gruyter, 67–133
Lambert, Stephen D. (2015). "Aristocracy and the Attic Genos: A Mythological Perspective." In Fisher, van Wees (eds.), 169–202
Landemore, Hélène (2013). "Deliberation, Cognitive Diversity, and Democratic Inclusiveness: An Epistemic Argument for the Random Selection of Representatives." *Synthese* 190 (Theme issue: *The Epistemology of Inclusiveness*): 1209–1231
Landemore, Hélène (2020). *Open Democracy: Reinventing Popular Rule for the Twenty-First Century*. Princeton, NJ: Princeton University Press
Lane, Christine (2009). *Archegetes, Oikistes, and New-Oikistes: The Cults of Founders in Greek Southern Italy and Sicily*. Vancouver: PhD thesis, UBC Vancouver
Lane, Christine (2012). "Sicilian Tyrants and the Cult of the Oikistes." In Bergemann, Johannes (ed.). *Griechen in Übersee und der historische Raum: internationales Kolloquium Universität Göttingen, Archäologisches Institut, 13–16 Oktober 2010*. Rahden: Verlag Marie Leidorf, 231–236
Lane, Melissa (2023). *Of Rule and Office: Plato's Ideas of the Political*. Princeton, NJ: Princeton University Press
Lane Fox, R. (1985). "Aspects of Inheritance in the Greek World." In Cartledge, Paul, Harvey, David (eds.). *Crux: Essays Presented to G.E.M. de Ste Croix on His 75th Birthday*. Exeter: Imprint Academic. Originally in *History of Political Thought* 6 (1/2): 208–232
Lang, Mabel (1959). "Allotment by Tokens." *Historia* 8 (1): 80–99
Langdon, Merle (2015). "Herders' Graffiti." In Matthaiou, Papazarkadas (eds.), 49–58
Lape, Susan (2002/3). "Solon and the Institution of the 'Democratic' Family Form." *CJ* 98: 117–139
Lardinois, André P.M.H. (2006). "Have We Solon's Verses ?" In Blok, Lardinois (eds.), 15–35
Laroche, E. (1949). *Histoire de la racine nem- en grec ancien*. Paris: Kleincksiek
Larsen, J.A.O. (1929). "Notes on the Constitutional Inscription from Cyrene." *CPh* 24: 351–368
Larson, Jennifer (1995). "The Corycian Maidens and the Bee Maidens of the Homeric Hymn to Hermes." *GRBS* 36: 341–357

Larson, Jennifer (2016). *Understanding Greek Religion (Understanding the Ancient World)*. London: Routledge
Lasagni, Chiara (2017). "*Politeia* in Greek Federal States." In Cecchet, Busetto (eds.) 78–109
Lasserre, François (1968). *Fragments [par] Archiloque. Texte établi par François Lasserre* (Collection des universités de France). Paris: Les Belles Lettres
Lattimore, Richmond (1967). *The Odyssey of Homer*. New York: Harper Torch Books
Lazenby, J.F. (1995). "The *archaía moíra*." *CQ* 89: 87–91
Lebeck, Anne (1971). *The Oresteia: A Study in Language and Structure*. Cambridge, MA: Harvard University Press
Leclerc, Marie-Christine (1998). "Le partage des lots. Récit et paradigme dans la Théogonie d'Hésiode." *Pallas* 48: 89–104
Le Goff, Jacques (1974). "Les mentalités. Une histoire ambiguë." In Le Goff, Jacques, Nora, Pierre (eds.). *Faire de l'histoire*, vol. 3. Paris: Gallimard, 76–94
Le Goff, Jacques (1988). "The Wilderness in the Medieval Imagination." In id., *The Medieval Imagination*. Arthur Goldhammer (trans.). Chicago: University of Chicago Press
Leighton, R. (1999). *Sicily before History*. London: Bloomsbury
Lenz, J. R. (1993). *Kingship and the Ideology of Kingship in Early Greece (c. 1200–700 BC): Epic, Archeology and History*. PhD thesis, Columbia University
Lepore, E. (1968). "Per una fenomenologia storica del rapporto città-territorio in Magna Grecia." In *La città e il suo territorio: Atti del settimo convegno di studi sulla Magna Grecia, Taranto 8–12 ottobre 1967* ed. P. Romanelli, 29–66. Naples
Leschorn, Wolfgang (1984). *Gründer der Stadt: Studien zu einem politisch-religiösen Phänomen der griechischen Geschichte*. Palingensia 20. Stuttgart: Franz Steiner
Lesher, J.H. (1992). *Xenophanes of Colophon: Fragments: A Text and Translation with Commentary*. Toronto: University of Toronto Press
Létoublon, Francoise (2014). "Vote et tirage au sort: deux cailloux qui ont changé le monde.""Επεα Πτερόεντα. *Bulletin du Centre d'études homériques* 22: 35–43
Levy, Harry L. (1956). "Property Distribution by Lot in Present-Day Greece." *TAPA* 87: 42–46
Levy-Bruhl, L. (1910). *Fonctions mentales dans les sociétés inférieures*. Paris: F. Alcan
Lewis, David M. (1963). "Cleisthenes and Attica." *Historia* 12: 23–40
Lewis, David M. (2018). *Greek Slave Systems in their Eastern Mediterranean Context, c. 800–146 BC*. Oxford: Oxford University Press
Lhôte, Éric (2006). *Les lamelles oraculaires de Dodone*. Geneva: Droz
Liapēs, Vayos (2012). *A Commentary on the Rhesus Attributed to Euripides*. Oxford: Oxford University Press
Liddel, Peter (2020). *Decrees of Fourth-Century Athens (403/2–322/1)*. Vol. 2. *Political and Cultural Perspectives*. Cambridge: Cambridge University Press
Lilley, Keith D. (2011). *City and Cosmos: The Medieval World in Urban Form*. London: Reaktion Books
Link, Stefan (1991a). *Landverteilung und sozialer Frieden im archaischen Griechenland*. Historia ES 69. Stuttgart: Franz Steiner Verlag
Link, Stefan (1991b). "*Das Siedlungsgesetz aus Westlokris (Bronze Pappadakis; I.G. IX 1, fasc. 3, Nr. 609 = Meiggs-Lewis 13*." *ZPE* 87: 65–77
Link, Stefan (1994a). *Das griechische Kreta*. Stuttgart: Franz Steiner Verlag
Link, Stefan (1994b). "Temenos und ager publicus bei Homer." *Historia* 43: 241–245

Lloyd, G.E.R. (1999). *Demystifying Mentalities*. Cambridge: Cambridge University Press
Lomas, Kathryn (2000). "The Polis in Italy: Ethnicity, Colonization, and Citizenship in the Western Mediterranean." In Brock, Hodkinson (eds.), 167–185
Lombardo, Mario (1993a). "Lo psephisma di Lumbarda: note critiche e questioni esegetiche." In *Hesperìa. Studi sulla grecità di Occidente* 3: 161–188
Lombardo, Mario (1993b). "Da Sibari a Thurii." In Stazio, A., Ceccoli, S. (eds.). *Sibari e la Siritide*. Taranto: Istituto per la storia e l'archeologia della Magna Grecia, 238–255
Lombardo, Mario (2012). "Greek Colonization: Small and Large Islands." *MHR* 27: 73–85
Lombardo, Mario, Aversa, F., Frisone, Flavia (2001). "La documentazione epigrafica." In Stazio, Attilio, Ceccoli, Stefania (eds.). *Problemi della "chora" olonial dall'occidente al Mar Nero: Atti del Quarantesimo Convegno di Studi sulla Magna Grecia, Taranto, 29 Settembre-3 Ottobre 2000*. Taranto: Istituto per la storia e l'archeologia della Magna Grecia, 73–152
Londblom, J. (1962). "Lot Casting in the Old Testament." *VT* 12: 164–178
Lopez-Rabatel, Liliane (2019). "Mots et utils du tirage au sort en Grece ancienne." *Participations*, 2019, Vol.Hors Série (HS): 35–80
Lopez-Rabatel, Liliane (2020). "Drawing Lots in Ancient Greece: Vocabulary and Tools." In Lopez-Rabatel, Sintomer (eds.), 53–94
Lopez-Rabatel, Liliane, Sintomer, Yves (eds.). (2020). *Sortition and Democracy: History, Tools, Theories*. Exeter: Imprint Academic
López-Ruiz, C. (2010). *When the Gods Were Born: Greek Cosmogonies and the Near East*. Cambridge, MA: Harvard University Press
López-Ruiz, C. (2014). "Greek and Near Eastern Mythologies: A Study of Mediterranean Encounters." In Edmunds, L. (ed.). *Approaches to Greek Myth*. 2nd.ed. Baltimore: Johns Hopkins University Press, 152–199
Loraux, Nicole (1981). "La cité comme cuisine et comme partage." *Annales ESC* 36 (4): 614–622 (Review of Detienne and Vernant ([1981] 1989)
Loraux, Nicole ([1984] 1993). *The Children of Athena: Athenian Ideas about Citizenship and the Division between the Sexes*. Levine, C. (trans). Princeton, NJ: Princeton University Press
Loraux, Nicole. (2002). *The Divided City: On Memory and Forgetting in Ancient Greece*. New York: Zone Books
Luijendijk, AnneMarie, Klingshirn, William E. (eds.) (2018). *My Lots Are in Thy Hands: Sortilege and Its Practitioners in Late Antiquity*. Religions in the Graeco-Roman World 188. Leiden: Brill
Lupu, Eran (2005). *Greek Sacred Law: A Collection of New Documents*. Leiden: Brill
Luraghi, Nino (1994). *Tirranidi archaice in Sicilia e Magna Grecia*. Florence: L.S. Olschki
Luraghi, Nino (1996). "Partage du sol et occupation du territoire dans les colonies grecques d'Occident au VIIIe siècle." In Broze, M. (ed.). *Les moyens d'expression du pouvoir dans les sociétés anciennes*. Leuven: Peeters, 213–219
Luraghi, Nino (2006). "Traders, Pirates, Warriors: The Protohistory of Greek Mercenary Soldiers in the Eastern Mediterranean." *Phoenix* 60: 21–47
Luraghi, Nino (2013). "One-Man Government: The Greeks and Monarchy." In Beck (ed.), 131–145
Ma, John (2003). "Peer-Polity Interaction in the Hellenistic Age." *P&P* 180: 9–39
Ma, John (2016). "Élites, élitisme et communauté dans la polis archaïque." *Annales HSS* 71 (3): 631–658 (trans. Antoine Heudre)

Ma, John (2018). "Whatever Happened to Athens? Thoughts on the Great Convergence and Beyond." In Canevaro, Mirko, Gray, Benjamin (eds.). *The Hellenistic Reception of Classical Athenian Democracy and Political Thought*. Oxford: Oxford University Press, 277-298

Macé, Arnaud (2014). "Deux formes de commun en Grèce ancienne, in Politique en Grèce ancienne." *Annales. Histoire, Sciences Sociales*, 69.3, Paris 2014, 659-89; English version: "Two Forms of the Common in Ancient Greece." *Annales HSS*, 69, no. 3 (July-September 2014): 441-469.

Macé, Arnaud (2016). "La circulation cosmique des âmes. Platon, le mythe d'Er." In Ducoeur, G., Muckensturm-Poulle, C. (eds.). *La Transmigration des Âmes en Grèce et en Inde anciennes*, Besançon: Presses Universitaires de Franche-Comté, 63-80

Macé, Arnaud (2020). "Plato on Drawing Lots: The Foundation of the Political Community." In Lopez-Rabatel, Liliane, Sintomer, Yves (eds.). *Sortition and Democracy: History, Tools, Theories*. Exeter: Imprint Academic, 95-111

Mack, William J.B.G. (2015). *Proxeny and Polis: Institutional Networks in the Ancient Greek World*. Oxford: Oxford University Press

Mackil, Emily (2013). *Creating a Common Polity: Religion, Economy, and Politics in the Making of the Greek Koinon*. Los Angeles: University of California Press

Mackil, Emily (2017). "Property Claims and State Formation in the Archaic Greek World." In Ando, C., Richardson, S. (eds.). *Ancient States and Infrastructural Power*. Philadelphia: University of Pennsylvania Press, 63-90

MacSweeney, Naoíse (2009). "Beyond Ethnicity: The Overlooked Diversity of Group Identities." *JMA* 22 (1): 101-126

MacSweeney, Naoíse (2013). *Foundation Myths and Politics in Ancient Ionia*. New York: Cambridge University Press

Mader, G. (2013). "Fear, Faction, Fractious Rhetoric: Audience and Argument in Thucydides' Syracusan Antilogy (6.33-40)" *Phoenix* 67 (3): 3-4

Maffi, Alberto (1987). "*La legge agraria locrese ('Bronzo Pappadakis'): diritto di pascolo o redistribuzione di terre?*" Biscardi, Arnaldo., and Franco. Pastori. *Studi in onore di Arnaldo Biscardi*. Vol. 6. Milan: Istituto ditorial cisalpino: La Goliardica, 1982, 365-425

Maffi, Alberto (2001). "Nomina per sorteggio degli ambasciatori nel mondo romano." In Cordano, Grottanelli (eds.), 137-138

Maffi, Alberto (2005). "Family and Property Law." In Gagarin, Michael, Cohen, David (eds.). *The Cambridge Companion to Ancient Greek Law*. Cambridge: Cambridge University Press, 254-266

Malkin, Irad (1984). "What Were the Sacred Precincts of Brea? (IG^3 46)." *Chiron* 14: 44-48

Malkin, Irad (1987a). *Religion and Colonization in Ancient Greece*. Leiden: Brill

Malkin, Irad (1987b). "La place des dieux dans la cité des hommes." *Revue de l'histoire des religions* 204 (4): 331-352

Malkin, Irad (1989). "Delphoi and the Founding of Social Order in Archaic Greece." *Metis* 4 (1): 129-153

Malkin, Irad (1994a). *Myth and Territory in the Spartan Mediterranean*. Cambridge: Cambridge University Press. Second edition with a new Introduction and Preface by Nicholas Purcell (2024).

Malkin, Irad (1994b). "Inside and Outside: Colonization and the Formation of the Mother City." *Apoikia. Studi in onore di G. Buchner. AION Archeol* 16: 1-9

Malkin, Irad (1998). *The Returns of Odysseus: Colonization and Ethnicity*. Berkeley: University of California Press

Malkin, Irad (2002). "Exploring the Validity of the Concept of 'Foundation': A Visit to Megara Hyblaia." In Gorman, V.B., Robinson, E.W. (eds.). *Oikistes: Studies in Constitutions, Colonies, and Military Power in the Ancient World. Offered in Honor of A.J. Graham*. Leiden: Brill, 195–224

Malkin, Irad (2003). "'Tradition' in Herodotus: The Foundation of Cyrene." In Derow, Peter, Parker, Robert (eds.). *Herodotus and His World: Essays from a Conference in Memory of George Forrest*. Oxford: Oxford University Press, 153–170

Malkin, Irad (2009). "Foundations." In Raaflaub, Kurt, Wees, Hans van (eds.). *A Companion to Archaic Greece*. Malden, MA: Wiley-Blackwell, 373–394

Malkin, Irad (2011). *A Small Greek World: Networks in the Ancient Mediterranean*. Oxford: Oxford University Press

Malkin, Irad (2015). "Foreign Founders: Greeks and Hebrews." In MacSweeny, Naoíse (ed.), *Foundation Myths in Dialogue*. Philadelphia: University of Pennsylvania Press, 2–40

Malkin, Irad (2016). "Greek Colonization: The Right to Return." In Donnellan, Nizzo, Burgers (eds.), 27–50

Malkin, Irad (2017a). "Vers une conception élargie des cercles de l'identité collective: la fondation des cités-états dans la Méditerranée antique." In Gervais-Lambony, Ph., Hurlet, Fr., Rivoal, I. (eds.). *(Re)Fonder. Les modalités du (re)commencement dans le temps et dans l'espace*. Colloques de la MAE, René-Ginouvès 14. Paris: De Boccard, 63–78

Malkin, Irad (2017b). "Hybridity and Mixture." In *Ibridazione e integrazione in Magna Grecia. Atti del LIV Convegno Internazionale di Studi sulla Magna Grecia*. Istituto per la Storia e l'Archeologia della Magna Grecia, Taranto 2017, 11–22

Malkin, Irad (2020). "Women and the Foundation of Greek Colonies." In Costanzi, M., Dana, M. (eds.). *Une autre façon d'être Grec: interactions et productions des Grecs en milieu colo nial. Actes du colloque international organisé à Amiens (UJVP) et Paris (ANHIMA), 18–19 novembre 2016*. Colloquia Antiqua. Leuven: Peeters, 235–255

Malkin, Irad (2023). "The Supreme Arbitrator and the Demos: City-Founders and Reformers." In Filonik, Jakub, Plastow, Christine, Zelnick-Abramovitz, Rachel (eds.). *Citizenship in Antiquity: civic communities in the ancient Mediterranean*, London, and New York: Routledge 147-165.

Manin, Bernard (1997). *The Principles of Representative Government*. Cambridge: Cambridge University Press

Mann, Christian (2007). *Die Demagogen und das Volk. Zur politischen Kommunikation im Athen des 5. Jahrhunderts v. Chr*. Klio Beiheft 13. Berlin: Akademie Verlag

Mann, Christian (2012). "Gleichheiten und Ungleichheiten in der hellenistischen Polis: Überlegungen zum Stand der Forschung." In Mann, Scholz (eds.), 11–27

Mann, Christian (2017). "Losverfahren in der antiken Agonistik: Überlegungen zum Verhältnis von Religion und Sport." *Gymnasium* 124: 429–448

Mann, Christian, Scholz, Peter (eds.) (2012). *"Demokratie" im Hellenismus: Von der Herrschaft des Volkes zur Herrschaft der Honoratioren?* Berlin: Verlag Antike

Manni Piraino, M.T. (1974). "Alcune iscrizioni inedite dall'area sacra dall'abitato di Himera." *Kokalos* 20: 265–271

Manville, Philip B. (1990). *The Origins of Citizenship in Ancient Athens*. Princeton, NJ: Princeton University Press

Marcaccini, Carlo (2015). "The Treasurers of Athena in the Late 5th Century B.C.: When Did They Take Office?" *Hesperia* 84 (3): 515–532

Marcotte, D. (1994). "Géomore. Histoire d'un mot." In G. Argoud (ed.). *Sciences et vie intellectuelle à Alexandrie (Ier–IIIe siècle après J.C.)*. Saint-Etienne: Publications de l'université, 147–161

Mari, Manuela (2010). "Atene, l'impero e le apoikiai. Riflessioni sulla breve vita di Anfipoli 'ateniese.'" *ASAA* 88, s. 3, 10 : 391–413

Mariaud, Olivier (2015). "A Samian Leopard? Megas, His Ancestors and Strategies of Social Differentiation in Archaic Samos." In Fisher, van Wees (eds.), 259–286

Marshall, C.W., Willigenburg, S. van (2004). "Judging Athenian Dramatic Competitions." *JHS* 124: 90–107

Martin, Roland (1974). *L'urbanisme dans la Grèce antique*. Paris: A. & J. Picard

Martin, Roland (1987). "Relations entre métropole et colonies: aspects institutionnels." *MEFRA* 99: 439–448

Mastronarde, Donald S. (1941). "The Delphian Succession in the Opening of the Eumenides." *CR* 55: 69–70

Matthaiou, Angelos P., Papazarkadas, Nikolaos (eds.). (2015) *Axon: Studies in Honor of Ronald S. Stroud*. 2 vols. Athens: Helleniki Epigrafiki Hetaireia

Mattingly, H.B. (1996). *The Athenian Empire Restored: Epigraphic and Historical Studies*. Ann Arbor: University of Michigan Press

Mauersberg, Martin (2019). *Die »griechische Kolonisation«: Ihr Bild in der Antike und der modernen altertumswissenschaftlichen Forschung*. Bielefeld: transcript-Verlag

Mauss, M. ([1925] 1954). *The Gift: Forms and Functions of Exchange in Archaic Societies*. (Trans. I. Cunnison). Glencoe, IL: Free Press; Orig. "Essai sur le don: forme et raison de l'échange dans les sociétés archaïques." *L'Année Sociologique* n.s. 1 (1923-1924), p. 30–180

Maurizio, Lisa (2019). "A Reconsideration of the Pythia's Use of the Lots: Constraints and Chance in Delphic Divination." In Driediger, Lindsay G., Esther Eidinow (eds.). (2019). *Ancient Divination and Experience*. Oxford: Oxford University Press, 111–133

McInerney, Jeremy (1997). "Parnassos, Delphi and the Thyades." *GRBS* 38: 263–283

McInerney, Jeremy (2004). "Nereids, Colonies and the Origins of *Isegoria*." In Rosen, Ralph M., Sluiter, Ineke (eds.). *Free Speech in Classical Antiquity*. Leiden: Brill, 21–40

Meister, J.B., Gunnar Seelentag (eds.) (2020). *Konkurrenz und Institutionalisierung in der griechischen Archaik*. Stuttgart: Franz Steiner

Ménager, L. (1987). "Les plus anciens témoignages d'appropriation foncière en Grèce." *Droits et Cultures* 14: 105–128

Mertens, Dieter, et al. (eds.) (2003). *Selinus I: Die Stadt und ihre Mauern*. 2 vols. Mainz: Von Zabern

Mertens, Dieter (2006). *Città e monumenti dei greci d'occidente: dalla colonizzazione alla crisi del V secolo a.C.* Rome: L'Erma di Bretschneider

Mertens, Dieter (2010). "Von Megara nach Selinunt. Raumordnung und Baukunst als Mittel zur Identitätsbildung griechischer Poleis während der großen Kolonisation." *MDAI(R)* 116: 55–103

Mertens, Dieter (2012). "Die Agora von Selinunt: Der Platz und die Hallen." *MDAI(R)* 118: 51–178

Mertens, Dieter, et al. (eds.) (2003). *Selinus I: Die Stadt und ihre Mauern*. 2 vols. Mainz: Von Zabern

Mertens, Dieter, Greco, Emanuele (1996). "Urban Planning in Magna Graecia." In Pugliesi-Carratelli, G. (ed.). *The Western Greeks*. Milan: Bompiani, 243–262

Metraux, Guy P.R. (1978). *Western Greek Land-Use and City-Planning in the Archaic Period*. Outstanding Dissertations in Fine Arts. New York: Garland
Milano, Lucio (2020). "Destiny, the Drawing of Lots, and Divine Will in Ancient Near Eastern Societies," in Lopez-Rabatel, Sintomer (eds.), 29–52
Millard, A. (1994). *The Eponyms of the Assyrian Empire, 910–612 BC. With a Contribution by Robert Withing*. Helsinki: Helsinki University Press
Miller, F.D.J. (2009). "Origins of Rights in Ancient Political Thought." In Salkever, S. (ed.). *The Cambridge Companion to Ancient Greek Political Thought*. Cambridge: Cambridge University Press, 301–330
Miller, Jeff (2022). *Democracy in Crisis. Lessons from Ancient Athens*. UK: Imprint Academic; USA: Ingram Book Company
Miller, S.G. (2004). *Ancient Greek Athletics*. New Haven, CT: Yale University Press
Missiou, Anna (2011). *Literacy and Democracy in Fifth-Century Athens*. Cambridge: Cambridge University Press
Mitchell, B. (2000). "Cyrene: Typical or Atypical?" In Brock, Hodkinson (eds.), 82–102
Mitchell, L.G. (2000). "A New Look at the Election of Generals at Athens." *Klio* 82 (2): 344–360
Mitsopoulos-Leon, V. (1984). "Zur Verehrung des Dionysos in Elis. Nochmals: ΑΞΙΕ ΤΑΥΡΕ und die sechzehn heiligen Frauen." *AM* 99: 275–290
Moggi, Mauro (1976). *I sinecismi interstatali creci. Relazioni interstatali nel mondo antico*. Fonti e Studi 2. Pisa: Marlin
Moggi, Mauro (1983). "L'elemento indigeno nella tradizione letteraria sulle ktiseis." *MCPT* 1983: 979–1004
Molinelli, S. (2018). *Dissoi Logoi: A New Commented Edition*. PhD Classics Durham University, http://etheses.dur.ac.uk/12451/
Mondi, R. (1990). "Greek and Near Eastern Mythology: Greek Mythic Thought in the Light of the Near East." In Edmunds, L. (ed.). *Approaches to Greek Myth*. Baltimore: Johns Hopkins University Press, 141–198
Montanari, Franco, Goh, Madeleine, Schroeder, Chad (2015). *The Brill Dictionary of Ancient Greek*. Leiden: Brill
Morakis, Andreas (2015). "The Gamoroi and the History of Archaic Syracuse: A New Examination." *StAnt* 13: 33–50
Morel, Jean-Paul (1983). "Greek Colonization in Italy and the West." In Hackens, T., Holloway, N.D., Holloway, R.R. *The Crossroads of the Mediterranean. Papers Delivered at the International Conference on the Archaeology of Early Italy, Haffenreffer Museum, Brown University, 8–10 May 1981*. Louvain-la-Neuve / Providence, RI: Université de Louvain / Brown University, 123–161
Moreno, Alfonso (2007). *Feeding the Democracy. The Athenian Grain Supply in the Fifth and Fourth Centuries*. Oxford: Oxford University Press
Moreschini, Donatella (1992) *Kasmenai. Bibliografia topografica della colonizzazione greca in Italia e nelle isole Tirreniche* 10: 289–296
Morgan, Catherine (1990). *Athletes and Oracles: The Transformation of Olympia and Delphi in the Eighth Century BC*. Cambridge: Cambridge University Press
Morgan, Catherine (2003). *Early Greek States beyond the Polis*. London: Routledge
Moroo, Akiko (2014). "The Erythrai Decrees Reconsidered: *IG* I³ 14, 15 & 16." In Matthaiou, A.P., Pitt, R.K. (eds.). *Athenaion episkopos. Studies in Honor of Harold B. Mattingly*. Athens: Ellikini Epigrafiki Etaireia, 97–120

Morris, Ian (1987). *Burial and Ancient Greek Society: The Rise of the Greek City-State*. Cambridge: Cambridge University Press

Morris, Ian (1990). "The Gortyn Code and Greek Kinship." *GRBS* 31 (3): 233–254

Morris, Ian (1996). "The Strong Principle of Equality and the Archaic Origins of Greek Democracy." In Ober, Hedrick (eds.), 19–48

Morris, Ian (1997). "An Archaeology of Equalities? The Greek City-States." In Nichols, Deborah L., Charlton, Thomas H. (eds.). *The Archaeology of City-States: Cross-Cultural Approaches*. Washington, DC: Smithsonian Institution Press, 91–105

Morris, Ian (2000). *Archaeology as Cultural History. Words and Things in Iron Age Greece*. Oxford: Blackwell

Morrow, G.R. ([1960] 1993). *Plato's Cretan City*. Princeton, NJ: Princeton University Press

Most, Glenn (2006). *Hesiod: Theogony, Works and Days, Testimonia*. Loeb Classical Library. Cambridge, MA: Harvard University Press

Müller, Christel (2010). *D'Olbia à Tanaïs: Territoires et réseaux d'échanges dans la mer Noire septentrionale aux époques classique et hellénistique*. Scripta antiqua 28. Paris: Ausonius

Müller, Christel (2011). "ΠΕΡΙ ΤΕΛΩΝ. Quelques réflexions autour des districts de la confédération béotienne à l'époque hellénistique." In Badoud, N. (ed.). *Philologos Dionysios: mélanges offerts au professeur Denis Knoepfler*. Geneva: Université de Neuchatel, 261–282

Müller, Christel, Prost, Francis (eds.) (2002). *Identités et cultures dans le monde mediterranéen antique*. Paris: Publications de la Sorbonne

Murray, A.T. (1917). "On the Disposition of Spoil in the Homeric Poems." *AJPh* 38 (2): 186–193

Murray, Oswyn (1990). "Cities of Reason." In Murray, Oswyn, Price, Simon (eds.). *The Greek City: From Homer to Alexander*. Oxford: Clarendon Press, 1–25

Murray, Oswyn (1993). *Early Greece*. 2nd ed. London: Fontana Press

Murray, O. (1996). "Rationality and the Greek City: The Evidence from Kamarina." In Hansen, Mogens H. (ed.). *The Polis as an Urban Centre and as a Political Community*. Historiskfilosofiske Meddelelser 75. Copenhagen: Munksgaard, 493–504

Murray, Oswyn (2018). *The Symposion: Drinking Greek Style: Essays on Greek Pleasure, 1983-2017*. Ed. Vanessa Cazzato. Oxford: Oxford University Press

Mussa, Valentina (2019). "The College of Treasurers of Athena on the Acropolis during the Archaic Period." In Graml, C., Doronzio, A., Capozzoli, V. (eds.). *Rethinking Athens before the Persian Wars*. München: UTZ Verlag, 251–254

Musti, Domenico (ed.) (1979). *Le tavole di Locri*. Napoli: Edizioni dell'Ateneo & Bizzarri

Nafissi, Massimo (1999). "From Sparta to Taras: *Nomima*, *Ktiseis*, and Relationships between Colony and Mother City." In Hodkinson, Stephen, Powell, Anton (eds.). *Sparta: New Perspectives*. London: Duckworth, 245–272

Nagy, G. (1985). "Theognis and Megara: A Poet's Vision of His City." In Figueira, Thomas J., Nagy, Gregory (eds.). *Theognis of Megara: Poetry and the Polis*. Baltimore: Johns Hopkins University Press, 22–81

Nahmer, von Dieter (1972). "Klostergründung 'in solitudine'—ein unbrauchbarer hagiographischer Topos?" *Hessisches Jahrbuch für Landesgeschichte* 22: 90–111

Naiden, Fred S. (2013). *Smoke Signals for the Gods: Ancient Greek Sacrifice from the Archaic through Roman Periods*. Oxford: Oxford University Press

Neils, Jenifer (1992). "The Morgantina Phormiskos." *AJA* 96: 225–235

Nenci, G. (1990). "*Klarographia* e *adelphothesia*: Osservazioni sul decreto di Nacona." In Nenci, G., Thür, G. (eds.). *Symposion 1988: Vorträge zur griechischen und hellenistischen Rechtsgeschichte (Siena–Pisa, 6–8 Juni 1988)*. Cologne: Böhlau, 173–177

Netz, Reviel (2002). "Counter Culture: Towards a History of Greek Numeracy." *Hist. Sci.* 40: 321–352

Nissan-Rozen, I. (2012). "Doing the Best One Can: A New Justification for the Use of Lotteries." *Erasmus Journal for Philosophy and Economics* 5: 45–72

Nissinen, M. (2017). *Ancient Prophecy: Near Eastern, Biblical and Greek Perspectives*. Oxford: Oxford University Press

Nollé, Johannes (2007). *Kleinasiatische Losorakel. Astragal-und Alphabetchresmologien der hochkaiserzeitlichen Orakelrenaissance*. Munich: C.H. Beck

Nowag, Werner (1983). *Raub und Beute in der archaischen Zeit der Griechen*. Frankfurt am Main: Haag Gerchen Verlag

Ober, Josiah (1989). *Mass and Elite in Democratic Athens: Rhetoric, Ideology and the Power of the People*. Princeton, NJ: Princeton University Press

Ober, Josiah (1993). "The Athenian Revolution of 508/7 BCE: Violence, Authority, and the Origins of Democracy." In Dougherty, C., Kurke, L. (eds.). *Cultural Poetics in Archaic Greece: Cult, Performance, Politics*. Cambridge: Cambridge University Press, 215–232

Ober, Josiah, Hedrick, Charles (eds.). (1996). *Demokratia: A Conversation on Democracies, Ancient and Modern*. Princeton, NJ: Princeton University Press

Oliver, James H. (1977). "The Vatican Fragments of Greek Political Theory." *GRBS* 18 (4): 321–339

Onians, Richard Broxton ([1951] 1988). *The Origins of European Thought about the Body, the Mind, the Soul, the World, Time and Fate: New Interpretations of Greek, Roman and Kindred Evidence, Also of Some Basic Jewish and Christian Beliefs*. Cambridge: Cambridge University Press

Orsi, Paolo (1900). "L'Heroon di Antifemo." Notizie degli scavi di antichità, Roma: R. Accademia dei Lincei, 1876, 272–277

Osborne, Robin ([1990] 2010). "The *Dēmos* and Its Divisions in Classical Athens." In id., *Athens and Athenian Democracy*. Cambridge: Cambridge University Press, 39–63

Osborne, Robin (1998). "Early Greek Colonization." In Fisher, Nick, Wees, Hans van (eds.). *Archaic Greece: New Approaches and New Evidence*. London: Duckworth and Classical Press of Wales, 251–269

Osborne, Robin (2009). *Greece in the Making, 1200–479*. 2nd ed. London: Routledge

Osborne, Robin ([1985] 2010). "Law in Action in Classical Athens." In id., *Athens and Athenian Democracy*. Cambridge: Cambridge University Press, 171–204

Ostwald, Martin (1969). *Nomos and the Beginnings of the Athenian Democracy*. Oxford: Clarendon Press

Ostwald, Martin (1996). "Shares and Rights: 'Citizenship' Greek Style and the American Style." In Ober, Hedrick (eds.), 49–61

Ostwald, Martin (2000). *Oligarchia: The Development of a Constitutional Form in Ancient Greece*. Stuttgart: Franz Steiner

O'Sullivan, L. (2009). *The Regime of Demetrius of Phalerum in Athens, 317–307: A Philosopher in Politics*. Leiden: Brill

Owen, A.S. (1939). *Euripides Ion*. Oxford: Clarendon Press

Owen, Sara (2003). "Of dogs and men: Archilochos, archaeology and the Greek settlement of Thasos." *The Cambridge Classical Journal* 49: 1–18

Owen, D., G. Smith (2018). "Sortition, Rotation, and Mandate: Conditions for Political Equality and Deliberative Reasoning." *Politics & Society* 46 (Special issue: *Legislature by Lot: Transformative Designs for Deliberative Governance*): 419–434

Paga, Jessica (2010). "Deme Theaters in Attica and the Trittys System." *Hesperia* 79: 351–384

Papachrysostomou, A. (2019). "Solon's Citizenship Law (Plu. Sol. 24.4)." *Historia* 68 (1): 2–10

Papadodima, E. (2014). "Sortition and Heroic/Moral Values in Greek Tragedy: The Case of Sophocles' *Ajax* and Euripides' *Children of Heracles*." *Athenaeum* 101/2: 388–401

Papakonstantinou, Z. (2008). *Lawmaking and Adjudication in Archaic Greece*. London: Duckworth

Papazarkadas, Nikolaos (2009). "Epigraphy and the Athenian Empire: Reshuffling the Chronological Cards." In Ma, John, Papazarkadas, Nikolaos, Parker, Robert (eds.). *Interpreting the Athenian Empire*. London: Duckworth, 67–88

Papazarkadas, Nikolaos (2011). *Sacred and Public Land in Ancient Athens*. Oxford: Oxford University Press

Papazarkadas, Nikolaos (2019). "Courts, Magistrates and Allotment Procedures: A New Inscribed *kleroterion* from Hellenistic Athens." In Harter-Uibopuu, Kaja, Riess, Werner (eds.). *Symposion 2019. Vorträge zur griechischen und hellenistischen Rechtsgeschichte (Hamburg, 26–28 August 2019)*. Akten der Gesellschaft für Griechische und Hellenistische Rechtsgeschichte 28. Vienna: Verlag der Österreichischen Akademie der Wissenschaften, 105–123

Parke, Herbert William (1940). "A Note on the Delphic Priesthood." *CQ* 34: 85–89

Parke, Herbert William (1943). "The Days for Consulting the Delphic Oracle." *CQ* 37: 19–22

Parke, Herbert William (1967). *The Oracles of Zeus: Dodona, Olympia, Ammon*. Oxford: Blackwell

Parke, H.W., Wormell, D.E.W. (1956). *The Delphic Oracle*. 2 vols. Oxford: Blackwell

Parker, Robert (1991). "The 'Hymn to Demeter' and the 'Homeric Hymns.'" *G&R* 38 (1): 1–17

Parker, Robert (1996). *Athenian Religion: A History*. Oxford: Clarendon Press; New York: Oxford University Press

Parker, Robert (1998). *Cleomenes on the Acropolis: Inaugural Lecture, University of Oxford, 12 May 1997*. Oxford: Clarendon Press

Parker, Robert (2005). *Polytheism and Society at Athens*. Oxford: Oxford University Press

Parker, Robert (2011). *On Greek Religion*. Ithaca, NY: Cornell University Press

Parker, Robert (2015). "The Lot Oracle at Dodona." *ZPE* 194: 111–114

Parker, Robert, Obbink, Dirk (2000). "Sales of Priesthoods on Cos I." *Chiron* 30: 415–449

Parker, Robert, Obbink, Dirk (2001). "Sales of Priesthoods on Cos II." *Chiron* 31: 229–252

Patterson, Cynthia B. (1998). *The Family in Greek History*. Cambridge, MA: Harvard University Press

Paul, Stephanie (2018). "Sharing the Civic Sacrifice: Civic Feast, Procession, and Sacrificial Division in the Hellenistic Period." In Eijnde, van den, Blok, Strootman (eds.), 315–339

Peels, Saskia (2015). *Hosios: A Semantic Study of Greek Piety*. Leiden: Brill

Pelagatti, Paola. et al (2006). *Camarina : 2600 anni dopo la fondazione : nuovi studi sulla città e sul territorio : atti del convegno internazionale, Ragusa, 7 dicembre 2002 - 7-9 aprile 2003*. Ragusa: Centro studi Feliciano Rossitto

Pepe, Laura (Milan) (2015). "Some Remarks on Equality in Homer and in the First Written Laws. Response to Robert W. Wallace." In Leão, Delfim, Thür, Gerhard (eds.). *Conferências sobre a História do Direito grego e helenístico (Coimbra, 1–4 Setembro 2015)*. Symposion 15. Vienna: Österreichische Akademie der Wissenschaften, 15–27

Perpillou, J.-L. (1996). *Recherches lexicales en grec ancien, étymologie, analogie, représentations*. Louvain: Peeters

Piccirilli, Luigi, Magnetto, Anna (eds.) (1973). *Gli Arbitrati interstatali Greci*. Fonti e Studi 7. Pisa: Marlin. *Relazioni interstatali nel mondo antico*.

Piérart, M. (1993). "*Hairesis* et *klerosis* chez Platon et Aristote." In Piérart, Marcel (ed.). *Aristote et Athènes: actes de la table ronde "Centenaire de l'Athenaion Politeia." Fribourg (Suisse) 23–25 mai 1991*. Paris: de Boccard, 119–137

Pierrot, A. (2015). "Who Were the Eupatrids in Archaic Athens?" In Fisher, van Wees (eds.), 147–168

Pironti, Gabriella (2009). "Dans l'entourage de Thémis: les Moires et les 'normes' panthéoniques." In Brulé, Pierre (ed.). *La norme en matière religieuse en Grèce ancienne. Actes du XIe colloque international du CIERGA (Rennes, septembre 2007). Kernos supplément* 21: 13–27

Pironti, Gabriella (2011). "Les moires entre la naissance et la mort: de la représentation au culte." In Hennard Dutheil de la Rochère, M., Dasen, V. (eds.). (2011). *Études de Lettres. Des Fata aux fées: Regards croisés de l'Antiquité à nos jours*. Lausanne: Université de Lausanne, 15–34

Poddighe, Elisabetta (2010). "Mescolanza o purezza? Il diapsephismos tra i Pisistratidi e la riforma di Clistene." *Klio* 92 (2): 285–304

Polignac, François de (1995a). *Cults, Territory, and the Origins of the Greek City-State*. Lloyd, Janet (trans.). Chicago: University of Chicago Press

Polignac, François de (1995b). "Repenser la cité? Rituels et société en Grèce archaïque." In Hansen, Mogens H., Raaflaub, Kurt (eds.). *Studies in the Ancient Greek Polis*. Stuttgart: Franz Steiner, 7–19

Polignac, François de (2007). "Ajax l'Athénien. Communautés cultuelles, représentations de l'espace et logique institutionnelle dans un tribu clisthénienne." In Schmitt-Pantel, Pauline, de Polignac, François (eds.). *Athènes et le politique. Dans le sillage de Claude Mossé*. Paris: Bibliothèque Albin Michel Histoire, 110–132

Polignac, François de (2011). "D'Ajax à Hippothon. Héros "marginaux" et cohérence des tribus clisthéniennes." In Azoulay, Vincent, Ismard, Paulin (eds.). *Clisthène et Lycurgue d'Athènes. Autour du politique dans la cité classique*. Paris: Publication de la Sorbonne, 107–117

Pollini, Airton (2012). "Limits and Occupation of Space in the Greek Colonies in Southern Italy." *Pallas* 89: 123–142; https://doi.org/10.4000/pallas.779

Pope, Maurice (1988). "Thucydides and Democracy." *Historia* 37 (3): 276–296

Pope, Maurice (2023). *The Keys to Democracy: Sortition as a New Model for Citizen Power*. Pope, Hugh (ed.), with introductions by Hélène Landemore and Paul Cartledge. Exeter: Imprint Academic

Porciani, Leone (2009). "L'insediamento degli Cnidî a Lipari nell'ambito della colonizzazione arcaica." In Ampolo, Carmine (ed.). *Immagine e immagini della Sicilia e di altre isole del Mediterraneo antico (atti VI giornate sull'area elima), Pisa 2006*. Pisa: Edizioni della Normale, 315–321

Pouilloux, J. (1952). "Promanties collectives et protocole delphique." *BCH* 76: 484–513

Powell, Anton (ed.) (2018). *A Companion to Sparta*. Vol. 1. Hoboken, NJ: John Wiley & Sons
Pritchett, W.K. (1991). *The Greek State at War*. Berkeley: University of California Press
Pugliese Carratelli, G. (ed.) (1996). *The Western Greeks*. Milan: Bompiani
Purcell, Nicholas (1990). "Mobility and the Polis." In Murray, Oswyn, Price, Simon (eds.). *The Greek City: From Homer to Alexander*. Oxford: Oxford University Press, 29–58
Purcell, Nicholas (2005). "Colonization and Mediterranean History." In Hurst, H.R., Owen, Sara (eds.). *Ancient Colonizations: Analogy, Similarity, and Difference*. London: Duckworth, 115–140
Quantin, F. (2011). "Contribution à l'histoire religieuse des colonies corinthiennes occidentales. Le problème du transfert des cultes métropolitains vers les cités coloniales." In De Sensi Sestito, Giovanna, Intrieri, Maria (eds.). *Sulla rotta par la Sicilia: l'Epiro, Corcira e l'Occidente. Actes du colloque international de Cosenza*. Pisa: Edizioni ETS, 209–232
Raaflaub, Kurt A. (1993). "Homer to Solon: The Rise of the Polis." In Hansen, Mogens Herman (ed.). *The Ancient Greek City-State: Symposium on the Occasion of the 250th Anniversary of the Royal Danish Academy of Sciences and Letters, 1–4 July 1992*. Copenhagen: Munksgaard, 41–85
Raaflaub, Kurt A. (1997). "Soldiers, Citizens and the Evolution of the Early Greek *Polis*." In Mitchell, L., Rhodes, P.J. (eds.). *The Development of the Polis in Archaic Greece*. London: Routledge, 49–59
Raaflaub, Kurt A. (1998). "A Historian's Headache: How to 'Read' Homeric Society?" In Fisher, Nick, Wees, Hans van (eds.). *Archaic Greece: New Approaches and New Evidence*. London: Classical Press of Wales, 169–194
Raaflaub, Kurt A. (2006). "Athenian and Spartan *eunomia*, or: What to Do with Solon's Timocracy?" In Blok, Lardinois (eds.), 390–428
Raaflaub, Kurt A. (2007). "The Breakthrough of *dēmokratia* in Mid-Fifth-Century Athens." In Raaflaub, Ober, Wallace (eds.), 105–54
Raaflaub, Kurt A. (2009). "Early Greek Political Thought in Its Mediterranean Context." In Balot, Ryan K. (ed.). *A Companion to Greek and Roman Political Thought*. Malden, MA: Wiley-Blackwell, 37–56
Raaflaub, Kurt A. (2010). "Herodotus, Marathon, and the Historian's Choice." In Buraselis, K., Meidani, K. (eds.). *Marathon: The Battle and the Ancient Deme*. Athens: Institut du livre, 221–235
Raaflaub, Kurt A., Ober, Josiah, Wallace, Robert W. (eds.) (2007). *Origins of Democracy in Ancient Greece*. Berkeley: University of California Press
Raaflaub, Kurt A., Wallace, Robert W. (2007). "'People's Power' and Egalitarian Trends in Archaic Greece." In Raaflaub, Ober, Wallace (eds.), 22–48
Randolph, A. (1995). "The Bastides of South-West France." *Art Bulletin* 77: 290–307
Raubitschek, A.E. (1956). "The Gates in the Agora." *AJA* 60 (3): 279–282
Rausch, Mario (1999). *Isonomia in Athen: Veränderungen des öffentlichen Lebens vom Sturz der Tyrannis bis zur zweiten Perserabwehr*. Frankfurt am Main: H. Lang
Rawls, John (1985). "Justice as Fairness: Political not Metaphysical." *Philosophy and Public Affairs* 14: 223–251
Ready, Jonathan L. (2007). "Toil and Trouble: The Acquisition of Spoils in the *Iliad*." *TAPA* 137: 3–43
Redfield, James M. (1975). *Nature and Culture in the Iliad: The Tragedy of Hector*. Chicago: University of Chicago Press

Reinhart, Luke (George Cockroft) (1971). *The Dice Man*. London: Talmy, Franklin
Reid, J. (2020). "The Offices of Magnesia." *Polis* 37: 567–589
Rhodes, P.J. (1972). *The Athenian Boulē*. Oxford: Oxford University Press
Rhodes, P.J. (2006). *A History of the Classical Greek World, 478–323 BC*. Malden, MA: Wiley-Blackwell
Rhodes, P.J. (2007). "*Dioikēsis*." *Chiron* 37: 349–362
Rhodes, P.J. (2008). "After the Three-Bar Sigma Controversy: The History of Athenian Imperialism Reassessed." *CQ* 58: 500–506
Richards, N. (2001). "Framing the Gift: The Politics of the Siphnian Treasury at Delphi." *CA* 23: 63–94
Richter, Gisela ([1942] 1970). *Kouroi: Archaic Greek Youths*. London: Phaidon
Rihll, T. (1992). "The Power of the Homeric Basileus." In Pinsent, J., Hurt, H.V (eds.). *Homer 1987: Papers of the Third Greenbank Colloquium, April 1987*. Liverpool: Liverpool Classical Papers, 39–50
Robbins, Frank Egelston (1916). "The Lot Oracle at Delphi." *CPh* 11: 278–292
Robbins, J. (2015). "Ritual, Value, and Example: On the Perfection of Cultural Representations." *Journal of the Royal Anthropological Institute* 21 n.s. (1): 18–29
Robert, F. (1953). "Le sanctuaire de l'archegète Anios à Delos." *RA* 41: 8–40
Robertson, D.S. (1941). "The Delphian Succession in the Opening of the Eumenides." *CR* 55: 69–70
Robertson, Martin (1975). *A History of Greek Art*. Cambridge: Cambridge University Press
Robertson, N. (2010). *Religion and Reconciliation in Greek Cities: The Sacred Laws of Selinus and Cyrene*. Oxford: Oxford University Press
Robinson, Eric W. (1997). *The First Democracies: Early Popular Government outside Athens*. Historia ES 107. Stuttgart: Steiner Verlag
Robinson, Eric W. (2002). "Lead Plates and the Case for Democracy in Fifth-Century BC Camarina." In Gorman, V.B., Robinson, E.W. (eds.). *Oikistes: Studies in Constitutions, Colonies, and Military Power in the Ancient World: Offered in Honor of A.J. Graham*. Leiden: Brill, 61–78
Robinson, Eric W. (2011). *Democracy beyond Athens: Popular Government in the Greek Classical Age*. Cambridge: Cambridge University Press
Robinson (2011) 248–250. M. H. Hansen, in his *BMCR* review of Robinson's book (https://bmcr.brynmawr.edu/2013/2013.01.17/)
Robu, Adrian (2014). *Mégara et les établissements mégariens de Sicile, de la Propontide et du Pont-Euxin: Histoire et institutions*. Bern: Peter Lang
Rollinger, Robert (2015). "Old Battles, New Horizons: The Ancient Near East and the Homeric Epics." In Rollinger, R., van Dongen, E. (eds.). *Mesopotamia in the Ancient World: Impact, Continuities Parallels. Proceedings of the Seventh Symposium of the Melammu Project*. Münster: Ugarit Verlag, 5–32
Rönnberg, M. (2021). *Athen und Attika vom 11. bis zum frühen 6. Jh. v. Chr.: Siedlungsgeschichte, politische Institutionalisierungs- und Gesellschaftliche Formierungsprozesse*. Rahden: Verlag Marie Leidorf
Rose-Redwood, Reuben, Bigon, Liora (eds.) (2018). *Gridded Worlds: An Urban Anthology*. New York: Springer
Rotstein, Andrea (2016). *Literary History in the Parian Marble*. Hellenic Studies Series 68. Washington, DC: Center for Hellenic Studies
Roussel, Denis (1976). *Tribu et cité. Études sur les groupes sociaux dans les cités grecques aux époques archaïque et classique*. Paris: Les Belles Lettres

Rundin, John (1996). "A Politics of Eating: Feasting in Early Greek Society." *AJPh* 117: 179–215
Rutter, N.K. (1973). "Diodorus and the Foundation of Thurii." *Historia* 22: 155–176
Rutter, N.K. (2002). "Syracusan Democracy: 'Most Like the Athenian'?" In Brock, Roger, Hodkinson, Stephen (eds.). *Alternatives to Athens: Varieties of Political Organization and Community in Ancient Greece*. Oxford: Oxford University Press, 137–151
Ruzé, Françoise (1997). *Délibération et pouvoir dans la cité grecque: de Nestor à Socrate*. Paris: Éditions de la Sorbonne
Ruzé, Françoise (1998). "La cité, les particuliers et les terres: installations ou retour des citoyens en Grèce archaïque." *Ktema* 23: 181–190
Saba, Sara (2020). *Isopoliteia in Hellenistic Times*. Leiden: Brill
Sachs, C. (1943). *The Rise of Music in the Ancient World, East and West*. New York: W.W. Norton
Sahlins, Marshall D. (1965). "On the Sociology of Primitive Exchange." In Banton, M. (ed.). *The Relevance of Models for Social Anthropology*. London: Tavistock, 139–236
Sahlins, Marshall D. (1972). *Stone Age Economics*. New York: Routledge
Salomon, N. (1997). *Le cleruchie di Atene: caratteri e funzione*. Pisa: ETS
Salvatori, P. (2001). "Reliability and Validity of Admissions Tools Used to Select Students for the Health Professions." *Advances in Health Sciences Education* 6: 159–175
Samons, Loren J., II (2020). "Who Sang 'the Harmodios'?" *Historia* 69: 2–16
Saprykin, S.J. (1994). *Ancient Farms and Land-Plots on the Khora of Khersonesos Taurike: Research in the Herakleian Peninsula, 1974–1990*. McGill University Monographs in Classical Archaeology and History 16. Amsterdam: J.C. Gieben
Sartori, F. (1996). "The Constitutions of the Western Greek States: Cyrenaica, Magna Graecia, Greek Sicily, and the Poleis of the Massiliot Area." In Pugliese, Carratelli (ed.), 215–222
Saunders, Ben (2009). "A Defence of Weighted Lotteries in Life Saving Cases." *Ethical Theory and Moral Practice* 12: 279–290
Schaps, David (1979). *Economic Rights of Women in Ancient Greece*. Edinburgh: Edinburgh University Press
Scheid-Tissinier, Evelyne (1994). *Les usages du don chez Homère: vocabulaire et pratiques*. Nancy: Presses universitaires de Nancy
Schirripa, Paula (2001). "Il sorteggio di Ecuba. Ultima infamia per le donne di Troia." In Cordano, Grottanelli (eds.), 55–62
Schlaifer, R. (1940). "Notes on Athenian Public Cults." *HSCP* 51: 241–260
Schmitt-Pantel, Pauline (1990). "Sacrificial Meal and *Symposion*: Two Models of Civic Institutions in the Archaic City?" In Murray, Oswyn (ed.). *Sympotica: A Symposium on the Symposion*. Oxford: Clarendon Press, 14–33
Schmitt-Pantel, Pauline (1992). *La cité au banquet: histoire des repas publics dans les cités grecques*. Collection de l'École Française de Rome 157. Rome: École Française de Rome
Schmitt Pantel, Pauline (2011). *La cité au banquet : histoire des repas publics dans les cités grecques*. Paris: Publications de la Sorbonne
Scholz, Peter (2012). "'Demokratie in hellenistischer Zeit' im Licht der literarischen Überlieferung." In Mann, Scholz (eds.), 28–55
Schuller, W., Dreher, M. (2000). "Auswahl und Bewertung von dramatischen Aufführungen in der athenischen Demokratie." In Flensted-Jensen, P., Heine Nielsen, T. (eds.). *Polis & Politics. Studies in Ancient Greek History in Honour of Mogens Herman Hansen*. Copenhagen: Museum Tusculanums Forlag, 523–539

Sclafani, M. (2007). "Zeus Soter, Eracle, Leukathea e tre *sortes* dell'antica Himera." *MDAI(R)* 113: 247–265
Scullion, Scott (2009). "Sacrificial Norms, Greek and Semitic: Holocausts and Hides in a Sacred Law of Aixone." In Brulé, Pierre (ed.). *La norme en matière religieuse en Grèce ancienne. Actes du XIIe colloque du CIERGA, Rennes, septembre 2007* (*Kernos* suppl. 21), Liège: 153–169
Scully, Stephen (1990). *Homer and the Sacred City*. Ithaca, NY: Cornell University Press
Seaford, Richard (1994). *Reciprocity and Ritual: Homer and Tragedy in the Developing City-State*. Oxford: Clarendon Press
Seaford, Richard (2004). *Money and the Early Greek Mind: Homer, Philosophy, Tragedy*. Cambridge: Cambridge University Press
Seelentag, Gunnar (2013). "Die Ungleichheit der Homoioi. Bedingungen politischer Partizipation im archaisch-klassischen Kreta." *HZ* 297: 320–353
Seelentag, Gunnar (2014). "Bürger sein im Bürgerstaat. Soziopolitische Integration im klassischen Kreta." In Blösel, Wolfgang, Schmitz, Winfried, Seelentag, Gunnar, Timmer, Jan (eds.). *Grenzen politischer Partizipation im klassischen Griechenland*. Stuttgart: Franz Steiner, 13–46
Shapiro, H.A. (1998). "Autochthony and the Visual Arts in Fifth-Century Athens." In Boedeker, Deborah, Raaflaub, Kurt A. (eds.). *Democracy, Empire, and the Arts in Fifth-Century Athens*. Cambridge, MA: Harvard University Press, 127–151
Shear, Julia L. (2012). "Religion and the Polis: The Cult of the Tyrannicides at Athens." *Kernos* 25: 27–55
Shepherd, Gillian (2015). "Display and the Emergence of Elites in Archaic Sicily." In Fisher, van Wees (eds.), 349–379
Shipley, Graham (1987). *A History of Samos, 800-188 B.C.* Oxford: Clarendon Press
Shipley, G. (2005). "Little Boxes on the Hillside: Greek Town Planning, Hippodamos and Polis Ideology." In Hansen, Mogens H. (ed.). *The Imaginary Polis: Symposium, January 7–10, 2004*. Copenhagen: Det Kongelige Danske Videnskabernes Selskab, 335–403
Simonton, Matthew (2017). *Classical Greek Oligarchy: A Political History*. Princeton, NJ: Princeton University Press
Sintomer, Yves (2007). *Le pouvoir au peuple. Jurys citoyens, tirage au sort et démocratie participative*. Paris: Cahiers libres. (English edition: *The Power to the People: Citizen Juries, Random Selection and Participative Democracy*. Exeter: Imprint Academic, 2010)
Sintomer, Yves (2011). *Petite histoire de l'expérimentation démocratique. Tirage au sort et politique d'Athènes à nos jours*. Paris: La Découverte
Sintomer, Yves (2020). *Between Radical and Deliberative Democracy: Random Selection in Politics from Athens to Contemporary Experiments*. Cambridge: Cambridge University Press
Sluiter, Ineke (2016). "Anchoring Innovation: A Classical Research Agenda." *European Review* 25 (1): 20–38
Smith, David G. (2013). "A Regional Performance Culture? The Case of Syracuse." In de Angelis (ed.), 127–142
Smith, Jonathan Z. (1982). *Imagining Religion: From Babylon to Jonestown*. Chicago: University of Chicago Press
Snell, Bruno, Meier-Brügger, Michael (1991). *Lexikon des frühgriechischen Epos* Bd.2, Lief.14

Snodgrass, A.M. (1994). "The Growth and Standing of the Early Western Colonies." In Tsetskhladze, G.R., de Angelis, F. (eds.). *The Archaeology of Greek Colonization: Essays Dedicated to Sir John Boardman*. Oxford: Oxbow, 1–10
Sommerstein, Alan H. (1989). *Aeschylus. Eumenides*. Cambridge: Cambridge University Press
Sourvinou-Inwood, Christiane, and Robert Parker (2011). *Athenian Myths and Festivals Aglauros, Erechtheus, Plynteria, Panathenaia, Dionysia*. Oxford: Oxford University Press
Staveley, E.S. (1972). *Greek and Roman Voting*. Ithaca, NY: Cornell University Press
Stazio, Attilio, Ceccoli, Stefania (eds.) (2001). *Problemi della "chora" coloniale dall'occidente al Mar Nero. Atti del Quarantesimo Convegno di Studi sulla Magna Grecia, Taranto, 29 Settembre–3 Ottobre 2000*. Taranto: Istituto per la storia e l'archeologia della Magna Grecia
Steiner, Ann (2018). "Measure for Measure: Fifth-Century Public Dining at the Tholos in Athens." In Eijnde, van den, Blok, Strootman (eds.), 205–232
Stevens, P.T. (1971). *Euripides. Andromache*. Edited with introduction and commentary. Oxford: Clarendon Press
Stone, Peter (2007). "Why Lotteries Are Just." *Journal of Political Philosophy* 15: 276–295
Stone, Peter (2008). "What Can Lotteries Do for Education?" *Theory and Research in Education* 6: 267–282
Stone, Peter (2011a). *The Luck of the Draw: The Role of Lotteries in Decision Making*. Oxford: Oxford University Press
Stone, Peter (ed.) (2011b). *Lotteries in Public Life: A Reader*. Exeter: Imprint Academic
Stroud, Ron S. (2004). "Adolf Wilhelm and the Date of the Hekatompedon Decrees." In Matthaiou, A.P. (ed.). *Attikai Epigraphai: Proceedings of 2000 Symposium in Memory of Adolf Wilhelm*. Athens: Helleniki Epigrafiki Hetaireia, 85–97
Svenbro, Jesper (1982). "À Mégara Hyblaea: le corps géomètre." *Annales ESC* 37: 953–964
Taggar-Cohen, Ada (2002). "The Casting of Lots among the Hittites in Light of Ancient Near Eastern Parallels." *JANES* 29: 97–103
Tamir, Yael (2019). *Why Nationalism*. Princeton, NJ: Princeton University Press
Tavares da Silva, R. (2021). "Theories of Justice Applied to the Pandemic: The Case of Vaccine Distribution." *Revista Portuguesa de Filosofia* 77 (2/3) *Pensando a Pandemia: Perspetivas Filosóficas / Thinking the Pandemic: Philosophical Perspectives*: 643–656
Taylor, Claire (2007). "From the Whole Citizen Body? The Sociology of Election and Lot in the Athenian Democracy." *Hesperia* 76 (2): 323–345
Taylor, Claire, Vlassopoulos, Kostas (eds.) (2015). *Communities and Networks in the Ancient Greek World*. Oxford: Oxford University Press
Taylor, M.C. (1997). *Salamis and the Salaminioi: The History of an Unofficial Athenian Dēmos*. Amsterdam: Gieben
Teegarden, D.A. (2018). "The *koinon dogma*, the Mercenary Threat and the Consolidation of the Democratic Revolutions in Mid-Fifth-Century Sicily." In Canevaro, Erskine, Gray, Ober (eds.), 455–481
Thalmann, William G. (1978). *Dramatic Art in Aeschylus' Seven against Thebes*. New Haven, CT: Yale University Press
Thomas, Rosalind (1989). *Oral Tradition and Written Record in Classical Athens*. Cambridge: Cambridge University Press
Thomas, Rosalind (1995). "Written in Stone? Liberty, Equality, Orality and the Codification of Law." *BICS* 40: 59–74

Thomas, Rosalind (2019). *Polis Histories, Collective Memories and the Greek World.* Cambridge: Cambridge University Press
Thompson, H.A. (1951). "Excavations in the Athenian Agora: 1950." *Hesperia* 20: 45–60
Thomson, George (1972). *Aeschylus and Athens: A Study in the Social Origins of Drama.* London: Haskell House
Thomson, George (1978). *The Prehistoric Aegean: Studies in Ancient Greek Society.* 4th ed. London: Lawrence and Wishart
Thonemann, Peter (2020). "Lysimache and *Lysistrata*." *JHS* 140: 128–142
Tigano, T. (2018). "Zancle-Messana. Nuovi dati e problemi aperti sull'impianto urbano tardo arcaico e classico." In Bernabò Brea, M., et al. (eds.). *A Madeleine Cavalier.* Collection du Centre Jean Bérard 49. Naples: Centre Jean Bérard, 233–246
Todd, Stephen C. (1993). *The Shape of Athenian Law.* Oxford: Oxford University Press
Tracy, Stephen V. (2003). *Athens and Macedon: Attic Letter-Cutters of 300 to 229 B.C.* Berkeley: University of California Press
Traill, John S. (1986). *Dēmos and Trittys: Epigraphical and Topographical Studies in the Organization of Attica.* Toronto: Victoria College
Tréziny, Henri (1999). "Lots et îlots à Mégara Hyblaea. Questions de métrologie." *La colonisation grecque en Méditerranée occidentale. Actes de la rencontre scientifique en hommage à Georges Vallet organisée par le Centre Jean-Bérard. L'École française de Rome, l' Istituto universitario orientale et l'Università degli studi di Napoli Federico II (Rome-Naples, 15–18 novembre 1995). Publications de l'École française de Rome 251.* Rome: École Française de Rome, 141–183
Tréziny, Henri (2002). "Urbanism et voirie dans les colonies grecques archaïques de Sicile Orientale." *Pallas* 58: 267–282
Tréziny, Henri (2016). "Archeological Data on the Foundation of Megara Hyblaea: Certainties and Hypotheses." In Donnellan, Nizzo, Burgers (eds.), 167–178
Trümpy, Catherine (1997). *Untersuchungen zu den altgriechischen Monatsnamen und Monatsfolgen.* Heidelberg: Winter
Tsetskhladze G.R. (ed.) (2006–2008). *Greek Colonisation: An Account of Greek Colonies and Other Settlements Overseas.* 2 vols. Leiden: Brill
Tsoukala, Victoria (2009). "Honorary Shares of Sacrificial Meat in Attic Vase Painting: Visual Signs of Distinction and Civic Identity." *Hesperia* 78: 1–40
Turner, Frederick Jackson ([1921] 1962). *The Frontier in American History.* New York: Holt
Uguzzoni, A., Ghinatti, F. (1968). *La tavole greche di Eraclea.* Rome: Bretschneider
Ustinova, Yulia (2009). *Caves and the Ancient Greek Mind: Descending Underground in the Search for Ultimate Truth.* Oxford: Oxford University Press.
Ustinova, Yulia (2021). "The Story of a New Name": Cultic innovation in Greek cities of the Black Sea and the northern Aegean area." *Kernos* 34: 159–186
Valdés Guía, Miriam A. (2019a). "War in Archaic Athens: Polis, Elites and Military Power." *Historia* 68 (2): 126–149
Valdés Guía, Miriam A. (2019b). "The Social and Cultural Background of Hoplite Development in Archaic Athens: Peasants, Debts, *zeugitai* and *Hoplethes*." *Historia* 68 (4): 388–412
Valdés Guía, Miriam A. (2022a). "Zeugitai in Fifth-Century Athens: Social and Economic Qualification from Cleisthenes to the End of the Peloponnesian War." *Pnyx* 1: 45–78
Valdés Guía, Miriam A. (2022b). "The Solonian Council of 400 and the *Heliaea* in Light of *IG* I³ 105." ὅρμος 14: 293–313

Valdés Guía, Miriam, Gallego, Julian (2010). "Athenian *zeugitai* and the Solonian Census Classes: New Reflections and Perspectives." *Historia* 59 (3): 257–281

Vallet, Georges (1958). *Rhégion et Zancle: Histoire, commerce, et civilisation des cités chalcidiennes du détroit de Messine*. Bibliothèque des Écoles françaises d'Athènes et de Rome 189. Paris: De Boccard

Vallet, Georges (1968). "La cité et son territoire dans les colonies grecques d'occident." In *La città e il suo territorio: Atti del Settimo Convegno di studi sulla Magna Grecia, Taranto, 1967*. Naples: L'Arte Tipografica, 67–142

Vallet, Georges (1996). "Les cités chalcidiennes du Détroit de Sicile." In Vallet, Georges (ed.). *Le monde grec colonial d'Italie du sud et de Sicile*. Collection de l'École française de Rome 218. Rome: École française de Rome, 115–162

Van Effenterre, Henri, Van Effenterre, Micheline (1988). "L'acte de fraternisation de Nakone." *MEFRA* 100 (2): 687–700

Van Reybrouck, David (2016). *Against Elections: The Case for Democracy*. New York: Penguin Random House (orig. Dutch, 2013)

Vergados, Athanassios (2013). *The Homeric Hymn to Hermes: Introduction, Text, and Commentary*. Berlin: De Gruyter

Vérilhac, A.-M., Vial, C. (1998). *Le mariage grec du VIe siècle av. J.-C. à l'époque d'Auguste*. Paris: École française d'Athènes

Verlinsky, A. (2017). "Draco's Constitution in the *Athenaion Politeia* 4: Is It an Interpolation or an Author's Later Addition?" *Hyperboreus* 23(1): 142–173

Vernant, J.-P. ([1963] 1983). "Geometry and Spherical Astronomy in Early Greek Cosmology." In id., *Myth and Thought among the Greeks*. Lloyd, Janet, with Fort, Jeff (trans.). New York: Zone Books

Vernant, Jean-Pierre (1965a). "Geometric Structure and Political Ideas in the Cosmology of Anaximander." In Vernant (1965b), 213–234

Vernant, Jean-Pierre (1965b). *Mythe et pensée chez les Grecs. Étude de psychologie historique*. Paris: Maspero

Vernant, Jean-Pierre ([1974] 1991). "Speech and Mute Signs." In id., *Mortals and Immortals: Collected Essays*. Zeitlin, Froma (ed.). Princeton NJ: Princeton University Press, 303–317

Versnel, H.S. (2011). *Coping with the Gods: Wayward Readings in Greek Theology*. Leiden: Brill

Vidal-Naquet, Pierre ([1970] 1986). "Land and Sacrifice in the *Odyssey*: A Study in Religious and Mythical Meanings." In id., *The Black Hunter: Forms of Thought and Forms of Society in the Greek World*. Baltimore: Johns Hopkins University Press, 15–38

Vink, Maarten (2017). "Comparing Citizenship Regimes." In Shachar, A., Bauböck, Rainer, Bloemraad, Irene, Vink, Maarten (eds.). *The Oxford Handbook of Citizenship*. Oxford: Oxford University Press, 221–241

Vlastos, G. (1953). "Isonomia." *AJPh* 74: 337–366

van de Moortel A. and Langdon M. K. 2017, "Archaic ship graffiti from southern Attica, Greece: Typology and preliminary contextual analysis", *The International Journal of Nautical Archaeology* 46, 382-405

Von Gaertringen, H. (1899, 2014) *Die Insel Thera: in Altertum und Gegenwart*. Vero Verlag GmbH & Co.KG

Vovelle, M. (1990). *Ideologies and Mentalities*. O'Flaherty, Eamon (trans.). Chicago: University of Chicago Press

Voza, G. (1999). *Nel segno dell'antico: Archeologia nel territorio di Siracusa*. Palermo: A. Lombardi

Wade-Gery, H.T. (1958). "Eupatridai, Archons, and Areopagus." In id., *Essays in Greek History*. Oxford: Oxford University Press, 86–115
Walker, Keith G. (2004). *Archaic Eretria: A Political and Social History from the Earliest Times to 490 BC*. London: Routledge
Wallace, Robert W. (1983). "The Date of Solon's Reforms." *AJAH* 8: 81–95
Wallace, Robert W. (1989). *The Areopagos Council to 307 BC*. Baltimore: Johns Hopkins University Press
Wallace, Robert W. (2013). "Councils in Greek Oligarchies and Democracies." In Beck (ed.), 191–204
Wallace, Robert W. (2015). "Equality, The *Dēmos*, and Law in Archaic Greece." In Leão, Delfim, Thür, Gerhard (eds.). *Conferências sobre a História do Direito grego e helenístico (Coimbra, 1–4 Setembro 2015). Symposion 15*. Vienna: Österreichische Akademie der Wissenschaften, 1–14
Walser, A.V. (2012). "DIKASTERIA. Rechtsprechung und Demokratie in den hellenistischen Poleis." In Mann, Scholz (ed.), 74–108
Walter, Uwe (1993). *An der Polis teilhaben. Bürgerstaat und Zugehörigkeit im archaischen Griechenland*. Stuttgart: Franz Steiner
Waltermann, A.M. (2019). *Reconstructing Sovereignty*. Cham, Switzerland: Springer
Walters, K.R. (1982). "Geography and Kinship as Political Infrastructures in Archaic Athens." *Florilegium* 4: 1–31
Walthall, D. Alex, Souza, Randall (2021). "Sortition in Hellenistic Sicily: New Archaeological Evidence from Morgantina." *AJA* 125 (3): 361–390
Warden, J.R. (1971). "The Mind of Zeus." *Journal of the History of Ideas* 32 (1): 3–14
Weber, Max (1958). *The City*. Martindale, Don, Neuwirth, Gertrud (eds., trans.). Glencoe, IL: Free Press
Węcowski, Marek (2014). *The Rise of the Greek Aristocratic Banquet*. Oxford: Oxford University Press
Węcowski, Marek (2022). *Athenian Ostracism and Its Original Purpose: A Prisoner's Dilemma*. Ozarowska, Lydia (trans.). Oxford: Oxford University Press
Węcowski, Marek (2023). "Early Greek Poetry, Social Mobility, and Solon's Reforms." In Pirenne-Delforge, Vinciane, Węcowski, Marek (eds.). *Politeia and Koinōnia: Studies in Ancient Greek History in Honour of Josine Blok*. Mnem. Suppl. 471. Leiden: Brill, 29–45
Wees, Hans van (1992). *Status Warriors: War, Violence and Society in Homer and History*. Amsterdam: Gieben
Wees, Hans van (1998). "The Law of Gratitude: Reciprocity in Anthropological theory." In Gill, C., Postlethwaite, N., Seaford, R. (eds.). *Reciprocity in Ancient Greece*. Oxford: Oxford University Press, 13–49
Wees, Hans van (1999). "The Mafia of Early Greece: Violent Exploitation in the Seventh and Sixth Centuries BC." In Hopwood, K. (ed.). *Organised Crime in Antiquity*. London: Classical Press of Wales, 1–51
Wees, Hans van (2001). "The Myth of the Middle-Class Army: Military and Social Status in Ancient Athens." In Bekker-Nielsen, Tønnes, Hannesta, Lise (eds.). *War as a Cultural and Social Force: Essays on Warfare in Antiquity*. Copenhagen: Det kongelige Danske Videnskabernes Selskab, 45–71
Wees, Hans van (2002). "Tyrants, Oligarchs, and Citizen Militias." In Chaniotis, Angelos, Ducrey, Pierre (eds.). *Army and Power in the Ancient World*. Stuttgart: Franz Steiner, 61–82
Wees, Hans van (2004). *Greek Warfare: Myths and Realities*. London: Duckworth

Wees, Hans van (2006). "Mass and Elite in Solon's Athens: The Property Classes Revisited." In Blok, Lardinois (eds.), 351–389

Wees, Hans van (2013). *Ships and Silver, Taxes and Tribute: A Fiscal History of Athens.* London: I.B. Tauris

Werlings, Marie-Joséphine (2010). *Le dèmos avant la démocratie: mots, concepts, réalités historiques.* Paris: Presses Universitaires de Paris Nanterre

West, M.L. (1966). *Hesiod: Theogony.* Oxford: Clarendon Press

West, M.L. (1997). *The East Face of Helicon: West Asiatic Elements in Greek Poetry and Myth.* Oxford: Clarendon Press

Westbrook, Raymond, Beckman, Gary M. (2003). *A History of Ancient Near Eastern Law.* Leiden: Brill

Whitehead, David (1986). *The Demes of Attica.* Princeton, NJ: Princeton University Press

Whitehead, David (1993). "Cardinal Virtues: The Language of Public Approbation in Democratic Athens." *C&M* 44: 37–74

Wijma, Sara M. (2014). *Embracing the Immigrant: The Participation of Metics in Athenian Polis Religion (5th–4th century BC).* Stuttgart: Franz Steiner

WinterFick, August. 1890 Vergleichendes wörterbuch der indogermanischen sprachen. Göttingen, Vandenhoeck & Rupprecht

Wilkins, J. (1993). *Euripides Heraclidae, with Introduction and Commentary.* Oxford: Clarendon Press

Wilson, D.F. (2002). *Ransom, Revenge and Heroic Identity in the Iliad.* Cambridge: Cambridge University Press

Wout, P.E. van 't (2010). "Visibility and Social Evaluation in Athenian Litigation." In Sluiter, Ineke, Rosen, Ralph M. (eds.). *Valuing Others in Classical Antiquity.* Leiden: Brill, 179–203

Wuilleumier, Pierre ([1939] 1968). *Tarente: des origines à la conquête romaine.* Paris: De Boccard

Yamada, S. (2000). *The Construction of the Assyrian Empire: A Historical Study of the Inscriptions of Shalmanesar III (859–824 B.C.) Relating to His Campaigns to the West.* Leiden: Brill

Yerucham, Amir (2015). *Music, Society and Religion in Archaic Greece.* PhD thesis, Tel-Aviv University

Zaccarini, M. (2015). "The Return of Theseus to Athens: A Case Study in Layered Tradition and Reception." *Histos* 9: 174–198

Zaccarini, M. (2018). "The Fate of the Lawgiver: The Invention of the Reforms of Ephialtes and the *Patrios Politeia.*" *Historia* 67 (4): 495–512

Zelnick-Abramovitz, Rachel (2012). "Slaves and Role Reversal in Ancient Greek Cults." In Hodkinson, Stephen, Geary, Dick (eds.). *Slaves and Religion in Graeco-Roman Antiquity and Modern Brazil.* Newcastle-Upon-Tyne: Cambridge Scholars Publishing, 96–132

Zuchtriegel, Gabriel (2018). *Colonization and Subalternity in Classical Greece: Experience of the Nonelite Population.* New York: Cambridge University Press

Zurbach, Julien (2008). "Question foncière et départs coloniaux. À propos des *apoikiai* archaïques." *ASAA* 86 : 87–103

Zurbach, Julien (2015). "Confiscation, conquête et colonisation dans les cités grecques." *MEFRA* 127 (2): 313–326

Zurbach, Julien (2017). *Les hommes, la terre et la dette en Grèce c.1400–c.500 A.C.* Bordeaux: Ausonius

Index of Names and Places

For the benefit of digital users, indexed terms that span two pages (e.g., 52–53) may, on occasion, appear on only one of those pages.

Achilles 45, 49, 52–54, 57–58, 62–68, 73–76, 79–96, 126, 184–85, 233, 304–5, 423
Aeschylus 51, 101–2, 120–21, 136, 234
  Seven 166–70, 174, 296, 429–30
Agamemnon 48, 54, 57–60, 62–68, 70–96, 101, 106–7, 140, 165, 296
  and Cassandra 166
Aitolia 372–73
Akragas 190, 206–7, 224–25, 230–31, 369, 431–32
Aleuas (Thessaly) 119
Alkman 44–45, 51, 72n.89, 101–2
Anaximenes of Lampsakos 282, 334, 394
Aphrodite 45, 375n.298, 421
Apollo
  and colonization 223, 240, 247–48
  Cleisthenes's reforms 298–99, 347–350, 388–390
  divination 25, 57, 99, 105–10, 114–17, 120–25, 167–68, 284, 374–78, 425–26, 431, 433
  festival of 292
  in Aesch. *Seven* 296
  inheritance 154–55
  priest of 366n.251, 398
  temple of 204–5, 398, 436–37
Ares 170, 174
Argos 51, 55–56, 79–80, 113, 223, 236–39, 329, 351n.172, 369, 372–73, 411–12
Aristotle 4, 9, 18, 27–28, 91–92, 126, 182, 382–84
  democracy 41–42, 220–21, 232–33, 253, 320–21, 327–29, 351, 394, 410, 435, 438
  land allotments 36–37, 203, 215–24, 226, 230–31
  selection for offices 276–77, 279, 282, 301–2, 311–13, 316–17, 332, 334–36, 365, 370–71, 396–400
  social mixture 257–59
Arkadia 51
Arsinoe 285
Artemis 77, 154–55, 374, 376
Asklepios 128, 377
Assyria 42, 47n.21, 322–23, 384–85

Astypalaia 42, 47n.21, 322–23, 376, 384–85
Athena 121
  and colonization 184–85
  cult 204–5, 208–9, 321–22, 349, 360, 374, 436–37
  dedication of spoils 84–85, 168, 212
  land allotment 46, 252–53
  Panathenaia 143, 287, 322, 362n.231
  selection for offices 3, 5–6, 316, 324–25, 327–28, 336–37
Athens 2, 5–6, 14, 17, 19–22, 32, 81–82, 110, 120, 124–25, 134–35, 195–97, 209–10, 236, 266–67, 279–84, 287–89, 291, 296–300, 316–19, 321–22, 331–34, 343–45, 347–49, 353–57, 361–63, 386–89, 391, 393–94, 396–98, 400–2, 405–10, 425–26
  Cleisthenes's reforms 2, 27, 28, 119, 338–51, 388–89, 435–38
  contests 283, 294
  democracy 212, 226, 257, 271–72, 329, 338–41, 365–71, 411–15, 438–40, 443–46
  inheritance 152–53
  isonomia 139, 314
  Panathenaia 143, 287, 291, 322, 362n.231
  priesthood 324, 374–76, 399, 405–6
  selection for offices 25, 118, 146, 167, 173, 271–74, 285, 292–93, 301, 305–6, 324–28, 336, 345–46, 360, 363–64, 403–4, 412–16
  Solon 379–81

Bacchylides 92, 93
Battos 61–62, 80, 225, 249, 250, 338, 352
Beroia (Macedonia) 284–85
Black Corcyra 37, 180, 202, 220, 248, 256
Boiotia 285–86, 372
Boura (Achaea) 110, 115
Byzantion 367–68, 409–10

Callimachus 224–25
Callisthenes 126
Chaironeia 285–86
Chalcis 368

INDEX OF NAMES AND PLACES

Chersonesos/Chersonese (Tauric)   187, 206, 208, 263–64, 329
Chios   145–46, 377, 386, 407
Cicero   126, 131–32
Cleisthenes of Athens   4–6, 17–20, 117–20, 257, 325–26, 339–54, 382–83, 388–89, 408–16, 437–38
Cleisthenes of Sikyon   18n.34, 350–51, 353
Corcyra   223, 296
Corinth   36, 266–67, 291–92, 369–70
Crete (for Gortyn see Gortyn)   146–47, 162, 190, 192–93, 213, 235–36, 242, 280–81, 285–86, 288–89, 311–12, 428
Cyprus   190, 250
Cyrene   232, 408
  constitution   386–87
  democracy   289, 329, 338, 351–52, 380
  equality   16, 18, 61–62, 80
  foundation   14–15, 37, 177n.2, 224–25, 227, 240–41, 245–51, 262–63, 428–29, 431, 433–36
  inheritance   157, 159

Damascus   84
Delos   121, 154–55, 187, 209, 282, 285, 367, 377, 409–12
Delphi   2, 17, 25, 30, 37, 81–82, 104–5, 107, 109–26, 139–40, 154–55, 167–68, 177, 184–85, 236, 240, 282, 284–86, 291–92, 347–49, 376, 398–99, 425–26, 431, 433–34, 436
Demeter   44, 284, 378
Demonax of Mantineia   16–17, 338, 351–353, 408, 428–29
Demosthenes   174–75, 351–53, 361n.225, 389, 409
Didyma   123, 374, 376
Diodorus   18, 182, 225, 242
Dionysos   121, 252–53, 295, 373–74
Dodona   2, 30, 104, 113, 115, 125–29, 160, 425–26

Elis   68–69, 220, 291–92, 373–74
Epidauros   285, 377
Ephialtes   297, 345, 353–56, 409
Eretria   212, 227, 285, 368, 409n.49, 411–12
Erythrai   345–46, 360, 365–66, 411–12
Eteokles and Polyneikes   151, 169–71, 295–96, 409n.49, 429–30
Euripides   32–33, 122, 163–66, 171, 439

Gaia   50, 115, 121, 167–68, 421
Gela   190, 192–93, 197, 206–9, 224–25, 228, 333, 369–70

Gortyn   91–92, 152–53, 290n.51, 293, 380

Hades   23–24, 43–44, 101–2, 138–39, 420–21
Harmodios and Aristogeiton   21, 298, 314
Hekate   56–57, 168
Helios   50, 54–56, 58, 63–64, 72, 103–4, 134, 161, 185, 377, 398, 421
Hellanikos   151, 170–71
Hephaistos   46, 77, 111, 145, 168
Hera   55–56, 113, 176–77, 366–67, 373–74
Heraia   258, 335–36
Herakleia Latmia   374
Herakleia Lucania/Lucana   186–87, 209
Herakleia Pontike   4, 258, 263–64
Herakleia Trachinia   182–84, 186, 209, 433–34
Herakles   51–52, 126, 128, 145–46, 237–38, 377
Hermes   29–30, 48–49, 108–15, 131, 140, 172, 284–85, 426
Herodotus   16, 18, 37, 61–62, 91–92, 166–67, 176–77, 202, 230–31, 240–41, 257, 268, 279–80, 386, 394
  democracy   9, 26, 41–42, 73
  isonomia   314–15
  land division   218, 225, 248–51
  on Cleisthenes   339–40, 347–48, 350–51, 353
  selection for offices   296–98
Hesiod   24, 41, 43–45, 50, 55–57, 92, 95–97, 101–2, 134–35, 154–55, 168, 233–34, 421–22
Hestia   53–54, 377, 421
Hesychius   118
Himera   128, 190, 203, 205–6, 219, 252–53, 267, 369
Hypata   285
Hypnia   285

Isaeus   174–75, 428
Ismaros   58, 68, 83
Isocrates   276–77, 282, 395–97

Kamarina   187, 192–93, 204–5, 206–9, 282, 289–90, 369, 408–9
Katane   187, 190, 203, 206, 228, 231
Kolophon   290
Kore   284
Korope (Thessaly)   124n.99
Kos   231, 374, 378, 409–10
Kronos   42, 43–44, 57, 67, 151–52
Kroton   80, 160, 225, 228, 261–62, 329, 333–34, 371

Lachesis   25–26, 30, 52, 93, 103–4, 108, 131, 134–35, 139–40, 172
Laurion   7–8, 90–91, 177, 355, 439

INDEX OF NAMES AND PLACES 507

Lesbos 62–63, 170–71, 212–13, 242–43
Leukas 220–21
Lindos (Rhodes) 367, 377
Lokroi 221, 243–44, 266–67, 333, 435
Lycurgus 16, 217–18, 237–38, 239–40, 261
Lyrnessos 85–86

Magnesia 371
Marathon 166–67, 296–98, 317–18, 344n.137, 354, 402, 437
Megara 284, 328, 349
Megara Hyblaia 162, 180, 190–92, 195–203, 206–8, 219, 222, 229, 230–31, 247, 252–53, 263–64, 333, 432–33
Megara Nisaia 266–67
Messenia 152, 225, 237–39, 241
Metapontum 333
Miletos 135, 143, 146, 225–25, 232, 288, 314, 329, 364n.238, 366, 368, 372n.287, 374n.294, 409, 411, 432
Mimnermos of Kolophon 36, 222, 461
Moses 265
Myania 285
Mytilene 292

Nakone 20, 258–59, 289, 408
Naupaktos 37, 141, 156–60, 243–44, 252, 380
Naxos 135–36, 188, 190, 206–7, 209–10, 231, 285, 287–88, 329, 388–89

Olbia 146
Olympia 59, 115, 118, 121, 291–92, 373–74
Olynthos 193–95, 208
Orchomenos 285–86

Paros 160, 285, 365–66
Pausanias 51–52, 60, 152
Peloponnese 51–52, 68–69, 152, 163–64, 178, 181, 195–97, 237–38, 239
Pericles 188, 225, 287n.43, 343n.138, 345n.144, 353–54, 358–60, 365n.244, 374, 388, 402, 409, 440
Phocis 285
Pindar 44, 54, 56, 92–93, 136, 162, 421
Plato 46, 103–6, 182–85, 191, 221–22, 279–80, 301, 421, 426
  democracy 41–42, 276–77, 394
  inheritance 153, 155–57, 159–60, 173, 221
  land division 231, 232–33
  on oracles 120
  selection for offices 370–71, 375–76, 397–400
Plutarch 16, 119, 123–24, 139–40, 154, 155, 173, 215, 226, 239, 296–97, 385–86

Polybius 239–40, 331–32
Polyneikes see Eteokles and Polyneikes
Poseidon 3, 23–4, 43–4, 47–50, 58, 101–2, 138–41, 263, 324, 349, 420–21
Priene 146–47, 292, 373n.292, 374n.294, 378
Pylos 68–70, 89, 140–41
Pythia 17, 25, 30, 98–137, 291–92, 347–50, 376, 425–26, 437

Rhegion 266–67, 286n.36, 333, 369
Rhodes 54–56, 58, 134, 161, 234, 367, 409–12

Salamis 167, 212, 227, 349, 355, 402
Samaria 84
Samos 16, 55–56, 73, 176–77, 224–25, 236, 243, 291n.54, 296, 314, 329, 366–67
Selinous 190–91, 197, 198–99, 203–6, 207, 221–22, 263–64, 333, 369
Sikyon 289, 350–51, see also Cleisthenes of Sikyon
Simonides 134–35
Sinope 188
Siphnos 90–91, 177, 236, 439
Smyrna 371, 411–12
Solon 5–6, 20, 36, 379–81, 393–94, 400–1, 406–11, 415–16
  democracy 336
  distribution of land 216, 221, 263–64
  in Aristotle 382–84
  inheritance law 156–57
  selections for offices 272–74, 340–43, 346–47, 356–59
  social reorganization 316–29, 340–41, 385–86, 388–89
Sophocles 164–66, 372–73
Sparta 36, 81–82, 140, 142–43, 288–89, 292, 335–36, 358–60, 367, 369–70, 434, 436–37
  colonization 186–87, 203, 209–10, 216–18, 232, 233, 235, 237–41, 250, 258, 261, 264–65
  egalitarianism 4, 31
Stesichoros 33, 151, 171
Sybaris 225, 226, 368, 371
Syracuse 4, 160, 197–98, 230–31, 266–67, 435
  democracy 224–25, 329, 333–34, 369–70, 434
  foundation 36, 160, 181–82, 195–97, 223, 436–37
  land division 187, 190, 192–93, 204–5, 213, 224–25, 226–27, 236–37, 431–32
  ostracism 205
  selection for offices 411–12

Taras 154–55, 160, 186–87, 209, 241, 268, 333–34, 370–71, 411–12

Tegea 51, 162
Tenedos 62, 71, 242, 243
Thasos 35, 182–84, 290, 365–66, 433–34
Thebes (For *Seven against Thebes* see Aeschylus (*Seven*))
  history 33, 217, 295–96, 335–36, 372, 411–12
Themis 55, 114–17, 120–21, 134–35, 167–68, 425
Theocritus 144
Theognis 15–16, 73, 89–90, 216
Thera 19, 61, 157, 181, 188–89, 211–12, 223–24, 237–41, 246–47, 249, 250, 435
Thersites 62–63, 65, 75, 83–84, 87
Thetis 66
Thourioi 187, 193–95, 225, 226, 261–62, 334, 368
Thucydides 36, 63, 166–67, 205, 212, 223, 279–80, 314–15, 331n.80, 336–38, 393–94, 439–40
Troizen 167, 281–82, 290

Troy 20, 43, 48–49, 60–63, 68, 75–76, 79, 86–87, 126

Xanthos 79, 113, 242–43
Xenophanes 42–43
Xenophon 63, 85, 91–92, 202–3, 218, 279–80, 393–94, 397

Zankle 190, 205–6, 219, 231, 369
Zeleia 284–85
Zeus 23–24, 29, 30, 108–13, 131, 138–39, 140, 238, 242, 260, 263, 291–92, 372, 406, 420–21
  Dodona 126–29
  festival of 371
  in Homer 41–97
  judgement of 397–98
  Klarios 51, 101–2
  prayer 101–2
  priest of 142–43, 378